Adoption and Special Guardianship: A Permanency Handbook

Adoption and Special Guardianship: A Permanency Handbook

His Honour Judge John Mitchell

Family Law

Published by Family Law
a publishing imprint of
Jordan Publishing Limited
21 St Thomas Street
Bristol BS1 6JS

British Library Cataloguing-in-Publication Data

A catalogue record for this book is available from the British Library.

ISBN 978 1 84661 114 8

Typeset by Letterpart Ltd, Reigate, Surrey

Printed in Great Britain by CPI Antony Rowe, Chippenham, Wiltshire

FOREWORD

This government has now been in power for well over a decade during which its approach to family law reform has been ambivalent. It can claim credit for significant reforms in the field of civil partnership and gender recognition. However, those achievements were compelled by human rights considerations and the repeated criticism of the Strasbourg Court.

Thus the statutory reform for which I would give this government greatest credit is the Adoption and Children Act 2002, the creation of which resulted in part from the intervention of the Prime Minister. It is perhaps, not unduly cynical to observe that the evolution of our family law is particularly dependent on political considerations and political judgement. Certainly political advantage motivated the reforms but that does not detract from the outcome, a modernised code that was designed to achieve and which is already achieving better outcomes for children.

John Mitchell has already established a high reputation as a shrewd guide and commentator in the field of child law. It is natural that he should extend his range into adoption and special guardianship. There is a wide potential readership awaiting his guidance. His readers will not be disappointed. He has produced a comprehensive and clear survey of this exceptionally important topic. The opening chapter sets the scene admirably and promises the reader not just a recitation of the statutory provisions but a broader socio-legal understanding of the origins and objectives of the legislation.

In the relatively brief period since its commencement the construction and application of the statute has frequently troubled the Court of Appeal. Aspects of the accompanying regulations have given rise to practical difficulties which we have sought to resolve without the need for rule change. All this and so much more, John Mitchell cogently explains.

I accepted John Mitchell's invitation to write this foreword with enthusiasm. I am in no doubt that this is an essential addition to every family lawyer's library. Its publication is perfectly timed. Early experience of the operation of the statute is essential for any assessment of its strengths and possible shortcomings. The balanced text offers valuable insights and I am in no doubt that the author's views will be regularly cited on the hearing of future appeals.

The Rt Hon Lord Justice Thorpe

PREFACE

With the enactment of the Children Act 1989 the two streams of the law applying to the private care of children and to their protection and care by the state in the form of local authority social services departments came together. The law relating to the adoption of children had flowed as a separate stream but after the Adoption Act 1976 it had edged nearer to that of state care and in some places it was difficult to tell where one ended and the other began. Now, with the advent of the Adoption and Children Act 2002, there is a unified river contained within a strong statutory structure.

The simplicity of the old law has been lost and necessarily so. Children in need of a permanent home to replace that which they had with their birth family often have complex needs which require careful assessment and support. Not least of these may be a need to maintain links with their birth family, perhaps their parents, brothers and sisters or other family members. Sometimes such a home can be within the extended family and the creation of special guardianship has enabled it to be given a legal status which avoids the disadvantages of adoption with its exclusive nature and residence orders which may be too prone to allowing further litigation by parents.

I hope that the Handbook will provide practitioners with a model of the law and practice of all areas of the law concerned with securing permanency for children who are unable to live with their parents.

The law is stated as at 6 July 2009.

I am very grateful to Lord Justice Thorpe for agreeing to write a Foreword to the Handbook and taking time from his duties both in the Court of Appeal and as the Head of International Family Justice to do so.

Greg Woodgate and Gillian Wright at Jordans and my wife, Marlene, did not think that writing the Handbook would take me so long. I thank them for their encouragement, support and patience.

During the years I have worked in family law, I have been fortunate to be helped by the experience, wisdom, courage and humanity shown by many social workers. They seldom receive the acknowledgement they deserve. So, representing them all, Gail, Laura, Patricia, Peter, Jeffrey, Liz, Dewi, Ann, David, Tudor, Maria and Derys, thank you very much.

His Honour Judge John Mitchell
July 2009

TABLE OF ABBREVIATIONS

AAR 2005	Adoption Agencies Regulations 2005
ACA 2002	Adoption and Children Act 2002
ACCR 2005	Adopted Children and Adoption Contact Registry Regulations 2005
ADR	alternative dispute resolution
AFER 2005	Adoptions with a Foreign Element Regulations 2005
AIR 2005	Disclosure of Adoption Information (Post-Commencement Adoptions) Regulations 2005
APC(G)R 1991	Arrangement for Placement of Children (General) Regulations 1991
ASSR 2005	Adoption Support Services Regulations 2005
ATPO 2008	Allocation and Transfer of Proceedings Order 2008
BAAF	British Association for Adoption and Fostering
CA 1989	Children Act 1989
CAFCASS	Children and Family Court Advisory Support Service
CPR	Civil Procedure Rules 1998
ECHR	European Convention on Human Rights 1950
ECtHR	European Court of Human Rights
FGC	Family Group Conference
FHDRA	First Hearing Dispute Resolution Appointment
FP(A)R 2005	Family Procedure (Adoption) Rules 2005
FPC	Family Proceedings Court
FPC(CA)R 1991	Family Proceedings Court (Children Act 1989) Rules 1991
FPR 1991	Family Proceedings Rules 1991
IRM	Independent Review Mechanism
ISR 2005	Adoption Information and Intermediary Services (Pre-Commencement Adoptions) Regulations 2005
NACC	National Association of Child Contact Centres
NYAS	National Youth Advocacy Service
PIU	Policy and Innovation Unit
PSG	prospective special guardian
RCCR 1991	Review of Children's Cases Regulations 1991
RPARR	Restriction on the Preparation of Adoption Reports Regulations 2005
SAR 2005	Suitability of Adopters Regulations 2005
SG	special guardian

SGO   special guardianship order
SGR 2005   Special Guardianship Regulations 2005

CONTENTS

TABLE OF CASES

References are to paragraph numbers.

TABLE OF STATUTES

TABLE OF STATUTORY INSTRUMENTS

References are to paragraph numbers.

Chapter 1

A NEW APPROACH TO ADOPTION: ADOPTION AND CHILDREN ACT 2002

PROPOSALS FOR A NEW ADOPTION ACT

1.1 Until the Adoption Act 1976, local authority care of children under the child protection acts and adoption ran as completely separate streams. It was only in the 1970s that adoption came to be seen as a viable option for planning the future of children who needed a new home, notwithstanding that their parents did not consent to their being adopted. It was a desire to strengthen this option which lay behind the enactment of the Adoption and Children Act 2002 (ACA 2002).

1.2 The annual number of adoptions in England fell from around 20,000 in 1970 to 4,100 in 1992. The main cause was a sharp reduction in the number of babies of unmarried mothers given up for adoption, driven by a decrease in stigma associated with illegitimacy and single motherhood, and the increased access to contraception and abortion.[1]

1.3 However, during the latter part of this period, the number of children 'looked after'[2] by local authorities rose. Following a fall from almost 100,000 in the early 1980s to 49,100 in 1994, it increased by 13% between 1994 and 1999, to reach 55,300.[3]

1.4 Nearly two-thirds of the 'looked after' children (65%) were in foster placements, with less than 10% in local authority community homes.

1.5 According to the *Prime Minister's Review: Adoption*[4] in 2002, 'looked after children' were becoming younger and more challenging. The care population was divided into those experiencing a few weeks of care and those staying for much longer. Two-fifths of those leaving care in 1998/99 had been looked after less than 9 weeks. In contrast, a child who had been in care for 6 months or more had a 60% chance of remaining in care for 4 years or more (and most likely until 16). After 15–18 months, children's chances of remaining in care had stabilised at around 80%.

---

[1] *Prime Minister's Review: Adoption* (Policy and Innovation Unit, 2000) (PIU) para 2.2.
[2] That is, accommodated under s 20 of the CA 1989 or in care under a care order – CA 1989, s 22(1).
[3] *Prime Minister's Review* op cit para 2.6.
[4] Ibid, at para 2.9.

1.6   Adoption was investigated as a possible route out of care as early as the Houghton Committee Report in 1972.[5] The Committee noted the growing belief that adoption could provide a secure permanent future for a sizeable number of children who were in care either of local authorities or voluntary agencies for whom no such future could currently be arranged because parents could not bring themselves to make a plan or refused to consent to adoption even though they were unable to look after the child.[6] Research, for example, by Rowe and Lambert[7] and Tizard[8] drew attention to the urgent need of children in long term care for a permanent home, the misplaced optimism that this would be provided by birth parents if one waited long enough, the detrimental effects of early institutional care and the appropriateness of adoption for some older children albeit that they might have physical, emotional or behavioural problems.

1.7   Following the passing of the Children Act 1975 and, its successor, the Adoption Act 1976, local authorities began to use their new powers to obtain orders 'freeing' children for adoption, in an attempt to resolve the issue of obtaining parental consent or dispensing with it on the ground that it was being unreasonably withheld before the child was placed with prospective adopters. The process of adoption was changing. It was ceasing to be a consensual arrangement between a parent (usually the mother) who was unwilling or unable to look after her baby and adopters, probably unable to conceive themselves, which was monitored by the adopter's local authority or an adoption agency. Instead, it became a non-consensual process instigated by an authority charged with the responsibility of protecting children from parental neglect or harm.

1.8   By 1999, 2,900 children a year were placed with carers with a view to adoption, 5% of the total of looked after children. Although viewed in an international context England already achieved relatively high rates of adoptions for looked after children,[9] the Prime Minister's Review in the following year thought they were too low. The outcomes for children who grew up in the care system were poor. For example, compared to the general population, children who grew up in care were four times more likely to be unemployed; were 60 times more likely to be homeless and constituted a quarter of the adult prison population.[10]

> 'The current system is too often not meeting the needs of looked after children. Too few are enjoying the benefits of adoption and real permanence. This shortfall

---

5   *Report of the Departmental Committee on the Adoption of Children* Cmd 5107 (1972) at para 26.

6   Ibid, at para 221.

7   *Children Who Wait* (ABAA, 1973).

8   *Adoption: A Second* Chance (Open Books, 1977).

9   *Prime Minister's Review* op cit at para 2.5.

10   Ibid, at para 2.14.

in performance is the result of a large number of problems and barriers across the system as it currently operates. Current policy initiatives will not address all of these problems.'[11]

1.9 Agency failure to place children for adoption was, it was suggested, caused by problems of philosophy aggravated by inexperience.

'Some commentators have suggested that these problems are the result of social workers' hostility to adoption. While there can be issues at an individual level, the study found little evidence of an institutional anti-adoption culture in social services departments. The more likely explanation for the limited use of adoption, on the basis of our visits and consultations, is that both social workers and their direct managers are (properly) highly committed to working to reunite children with their birth parents and the structures and procedures are not in place to ensure they think more widely than that. Social workers are also relatively untrained and inexperienced in adoption work.[12]

1.10 There were also problems in delivery which was marked by inconsistency of practice between different authorities and agencies and 'a lack of grip on progress leading to delay and drift'.[13]

1.11 The Report recommended that the Government should:

• set out a new approach to adoption and permanence that puts the needs of the child at the centre of the process;

• set itself a challenging target for increasing adoption; and

• achieve change by reforming, resourcing and driving the whole system to deliver improved performance.[14]

1.12 The Report was followed by the White Paper, *Adoption: A New Approach*.[15] In the Foreword the Prime Minster wrote:

'When children cannot live with their birth parents, for whatever reason, we all share a responsibility to make sure that they have a chance of a fresh start, and an opportunity to enjoy the kind of loving family life which most of us take for granted ... While there are many options suitable to children's needs, adoption can work well. There is scope to increase the use of adoption. But there are clear problems with the way the system of adoption now operates. Poor performance, widespread variations, unacceptable delays, agonisingly high hurdles for adopters to surmount – in far too many parts of the system, there is a lack of clarity, of consistency and of fairness. Most pressingly, children in an already vulnerable position are being badly let down. We have to change this. We have to have a new approach to adoption.'

---

[11] *Prime Minister's Review* op cit, Summary, chapter 4.
[12] Ibid, at para 3.43.
[13] Ibid, at para 3.51.
[14] Ibid, Summary, chapter 4.
[15] Cm 5017 (2000).

1.13 The Adoption and Children Bill, which became the Adoption and Children Act 2002, met a cautious response. Some commentators took issue with the 'article of faith'[16] that not enough children were being adopted from care.

> 'Superficially, this aims seems laudable ... But where is the evidence for the ... flat assertion ... that "We know that adoption works for children?"'[17]

1.14 After all, 6 months earlier, the authors of *Adoption Now: Messages from Research*,[18] sponsored by the Department of Health, had concluded that:

> 'The differences between adoption, long-term fostering and residence order status needs to be clarified both to assist in practice decisions and in considerations of policy. We need to know much more about the processes that determine which options for long-term care are chosen and about the respective strengths and weaknesses of them for children with different needs.'[19]

1.15 There was also concern that the new proposals which would enable an authority to obtain orders, albeit after obtaining a care order, empowering them to place children for adoption who had previously been accommodated at the request of their parents could fundamentally undermine the 'partnership' ethos of Part III of the Children Act 1989 (which is headed 'Local authority support for children and families').[20]

> 'Concerns as to the speed at which the parents could find themselves not only facing the removal of their child but also the irrevocable termination of "their very parenthood"[21] are further exacerbated by the fact that the placement order is of unlimited duration and the grounds upon which it can be revoked are extremely limited.'[22]

FINDING MORE ADOPTERS: REMOVING DELAY

1.16 The Act, its supporting secondary legislation, primarily the Adoption Agencies Regulations 2005, and the Family Procedure (Adoption) Rules 2005,[23] statutory guidance – *Adoption Guidance*,[24] and *Adoption* –

---

[16] Barton 'Adoption: The Prime Minister's Review' (2000) Fam Law 731 at p 733.

[17] Ibid, at p 732.

[18] (Department of Health, 2000).

[19] Ibid, at p 126.

[20] 'The Act gives a positive emphasis to identifying and providing for the child's needs rather than focussing on parental shortcomings in a negative manner ... [It] also emphasises that partnership with parents should not become weaker if it becomes necessary to provide the child with accommodation.' *The Children Act 1989: Guidance and Regulations Volume 2* (Department of Health, 1991) at para 2.15. See also paras 2.28–2.29.

[21] *M v C and Calderdale MBC* [1993] 1 FLR 505 per Butler-Sloss LJ at 512.

[22] Harris-Short 'The Adoption and Children Bill – a fast track to failure?' (2001) CFLQ 405 at p 422.

[23] Based on the CPR, the Rules provided, for the first time, a unified set of rules for the High Court, County Court and Family Proceedings Court.

Achieving the Right Balance[25] non-statutory guidance – *Preparing and Assessing Prospective Adopters*[26] – and benchmark standards – the *National Adoption Standards for England*[27] – attempt to tackle the problems of finding suitable adoptive parents and removing undue delay both from the process within the adoption agency (whether a local authority or registered adoption society) and from the court procedure.

1.17 For the first time, an adopting couple do not have to be married. A couple can now adopt if they are married to each other or in a civil partnership or are two people '(whether of different sexes or the same sex) living in an enduring family relationship'.[28] Prospective adopters now have the right to address the agency's adoption panel[29] and those who are not approved by the agency have the right to have the decision reviewed either by the panel or by an independent panel under the Independent Review Mechanism (IRM) operated by the Secretary of State.[30]

CHANGES TO THE SUBSTANTIVE LAW

1.18 The legislature also took the opportunity to introduce four important innovations to the framework of adoption law which had been established by the Children Act 1975. In doing so, it built not only on the structure of the private and public law applying to children created by the Children Act 1989 (most importantly, the concept of parental responsibility[31]) but on the 1989 Act itself.

The welfare test and checklist

1.19 For the former welfare test which governed decisions taken by the court and the agency (*'first* consideration being given to the need to safeguard and promote the welfare of the child *throughout his childhood'*[32]), the Act substituted a new test.

---

[24] (Department for Education and Skills, 2002).
[25] Local Authority Circular LAC(98)20; see **Appendix 3**.
[26] (Department for Education and Skills, 2006).
[27] (Department of Health, 2001).
[28] ACA 2002, ss 50(2), 144(4). See **2.51** and **2.55**. Nevertheless it has been argued that despite this reform, brought about in the face of strong opposition, 'the adoption process remains discriminatory and generally problematic for same sex couples' – Hitchings and Sagar 'The Adoption and Children Act 2002: a level playing field for same-sex adopters?' (2007) CFLQ 60.
[29] Adoption Agencies Regulations 2005, SI 2005/389, reg 26(4), see **7.124.**
[30] Ibid, reg 27.
[31] 'A golden thread, [running through the Act] knotting together parental status and the effect of orders about a child's upbringing whether in private family proceedings or in care proceedings ...': Lord Mackay of Clashfern LC *Perceptions of the Children Bill and Beyond. The Joseph Jackson Memorial Lecture* NLJ Ap 14 (1989) 505.
[32] Adoption Act 1976, s 6 – see Appendix 5.

'The *paramount* consideration of the court or adoption agency must be the child's welfare, *throughout his life*.'[33]

The child's welfare was no longer the most important of any consideration: it outweighed all other considerations taken together.[34]

1.20 In addition, the Act inserted a 'welfare checklist' into adoption legislation for the first time. It was based on if not entirely identical to the Children Act 1989 checklist, the additional elements emphasising that adoption removes a child in law from his family of birth and places him in a new family. For example, the court and the agency must have regard to 'the likely effect on the child (throughout his life) of having ceased to be a member of the original family and become an adopted person'.[35]

1.21 For some academic writers, these changes were not enough. They argued that there was a need to review the operation of the welfare principle in order to create an approach which was 'more respectful' of the rights of others, notably parents and to achieve, like, Art 8 of the European Convention of Human Rights, 'an equal balancing process prior to the elevation of any one interest'.[36]

Placement orders

1.22 The third innovation was to replace the process of freeing a child for adoption by a placement order. Under the Act a child can be placed for adoption only if there is a placement order or if all those with parental responsibility agree to the child being placed for adoption.[37] A placement order thereby enables the issues of consent and dispensing with consent to be satisfied prior to any placement. In addition, it provides a framework for the care of the child. Parental responsibility is vested in the agency until the child is adopted. After placement, it also vests in the prospective adopters.[38] Unlike freeing orders, the order does not remove parental responsibility from parents.

1.23 Superficially the framework is similar to that provided by the 1989 Act for a child in care[39] but most importantly it does not provide for parental responsibility being exercised in partnership with the parents.

---

[33] ACA 2002, s 1(2). See **6.7**.
[34] *J v C* [1970] AC 668 per Lord MacDermott at 710.
[35] ACA 2002, s 1(4(c).
[36] Choudry 'The Adoption and Children Act 2002, the welfare principle and the Human Rights Act 1998 – a missed opportunity?' (2003) CFLQ 119 at p 136 and see also, for example, Herring 'The HRA and the Welfare Principle in family law' [1999] CFLQ 223.
[37] ACA 2002, ss 18(1), 19(1), see Chapter 3.
[38] Ibid, s 25(2), (3).
[39] *Adoption Guidance* op cit Annex A para 61.

'Where the child is placed with prospective adopters, the sharing of parental responsibility should help make it clear that the agency and the prospective adopters have responsibility for the child and can make day to day decisions.'[40]

In addition, there is no provision such as contained in s 34(1) of the 1989 Act that, unless the court orders otherwise, the authority shall allow the child reasonable contact with his parents. Contact is solely at the discretion of the agency unless the court makes an order under s 26 of the 2002 Act.[41]

Dispensing with consent

1.24 Another important – and contentious – change was to replace one of the old tests for dispensing with parental consent – that the parent 'was withholding his agreement unreasonably'[42] – with one that the court is satisfied that 'the welfare of the child requires the consent to be dispensed with'.[43] The disquiet was not one of nostalgia for the old test – after all, no practitioner enjoyed grappling with what Wall LJ called 'the intellectual complexities imposed by the test'[44] and Steyn and Hoffman LJJ, 'the embarrassment at having to consult the views of so improbable a legal fiction' as the reasonable hypothetical parent.[45] Rather, there was the concern that it removed what Professor Barton called 'one of the two bulwarks which prevent adoption being used against one of the most fundamental of societal principles: that the claims of the birth family ... have priority in the absence of proven unsuitability'.[46] Admittedly this specific criticism was made at the stage of the Bill before the requirement[47] that the child had to be the subject of a care order or that the conditions for making a care order were met was inserted but the general criticism continued after then.

'As critics point out, the new law theoretically enables the judiciary to dispense with parental consent, having interpreted what is in the child's best interests in such a subjective way that adoption will be a foregone conclusion. They also argue that the new formula does not reflect the complexities of adoption. Although an adoption order often ostensibly benefits the child, it deprives the child and his or her birth parents of a unique relationship in a family which can never be retrieved ... Whether when using the new criterion the courts will promote children's rights better, in so far as the child's welfare is unequivocally centre stage, remains to be seen'.[48]

---

[40] *Adoption Guidance* op cit Annex A, para 41.
[41] See **13.112**.
[42] Adoption Act 1976, s 16; see Appendix 5.
[43] ACA 2002, s 52(1)(b).
[44] *SB v County Council: P (A Child)*[2008] EWCA Civ 535 at [76].
[45] *Re C (A Minor)* [1993] 2 FLR 260 at 272.
[46] Barton 'Adoption and Children Bill 2001 – Don't Let Them Out of Your Sight' (2001) Fam 431 at p 432.
[47] ACA 2002, s 21(2).
[48] Fortin *Children's Rights and the Developing Law* (Cambridge University Press, 2nd edn, 2003) at p 436.

1.25 In *SB v County Council: P (A Child)*[49] the Court of Appeal retreated from its earlier provisional view stated in *Re S (Special Guardianship)*[50] that:

> 'At first blush it would appear likely to be the case that once the court has reached the conclusion that adoption is in the best interests of the child, it will follow that his or her welfare will require the court to dispense with parental consent to adoption.'

1.26 Instead, Wall LJ emphasised that 'requires' was a word 'which was plainly chosen as best conveying, as in our judgment it does, the essence of the Strasbourg jurisprudence'.

> '... Viewed from that perspective "requires" does indeed have the connotation of the imperative, what is demanded rather than what is merely optional or reasonable or desirable ... [It] will take its colour from the particular context. Section 52(1) is concerned with adoption – the making of either a placement order or an adoption order – and what therefore has to be shown is that the child's welfare "requires" *adoption* as opposed to something short of adoption. A child's circumstances may "require" statutory intervention, perhaps may even "require" the indefinite or long-term removal of the child from the family and his or her placement with strangers, but that is not to say that the same circumstances will necessarily "require" that the child be adopted. They may or they may not. The question, at the end of the day, is whether what is "required" is adoption.'[51]

Whether this will assuage all the criticism remains to be seen.

OLDER CHILDREN; KINSHIP CARE

1.27 The Act also attempts to deal with two features of permanency which had come forward in recent years. As discussed above, adoption has moved away from a process involving healthy babies to one concerned not just with older children but older, vulnerable children with either physical or emotional special needs arising from inherent medical problems or poor parenting. In one study,[52] for example, 4% of children being adopted had physical special needs, 6%, health special needs, a quarter, emotional special needs and behavioural problems and nearly one-third, learning difficulties. Some had multiple special needs.

1.28 Furthermore, as Baroness Hale of Richmond pointed out in *Down Lisburn Health and Social Services Trust v H*[53] older children have experienced family life and have relationships not only with their parents but also their siblings and other members of the extended family.

---

[49] [2008] EWCA Civ 535, *sub nom Re P (Placement Orders: Parental Consent)* [2008] 2 FLR 625.
[50] [2007] EWCA Civ 54, [2007] 1 FLR 819 per Wall LJ at [69]–[72].
[51] Per Wall LJ at [126].
[52] Lowe, Murch et al *Supporting Adoption: Reframing the Approach* (BAAF, 1999) at p 74.
[53] [2006] UKHL 36, [2007] 1 FLR 121 at [6]–[7].

'They had a history. This might well include damaging experiences from their past. But it might also include significant relationships with members of their birth family. The use of compulsory adoption, dispensing with the need for parental agreement, was increasing. But the fact that these children had a history also meant that their best interests might require that any significant links with the birth family be preserved in a more 'open' form of adoption. It was increasingly recognised that there could be more ways than one of achieving the desired permanency for the child ... Interest began to develop in preserving some limited contact between an adopted child and her birth family. This might serve two rather different functions. One, which can often be accomplished by life story books and occasional letters and cards, is to help the adopted child develop her sense of identity and self as she grows up. Another, which may indicate the occasional face to face meeting, is to preserve significant attachments, prevent the feelings of loss and rejection which the child who remembers her birth family may feel if she is completely cut off from her past and help her not to worry about the family she has left behind, including siblings (see Department of Health, *Adoption Now. Messages from Research,* 1999). This form of contact requires the birth parents to be able to put their own feelings of grief and anger aside so that they do not use their contact to undermine the adoptive placement. But if they can do this it can be a great help to the child in making the transition to her new 'family for life'.

1.29   The second development in providing permanency was the increasing importance placed on children being looked after within their extended family – 'kinship care'. As Hunt has pointed out[54] the Children Act 1989 prioritised the placement of children needing substitute care with relatives or other members of their social network and marked the rediscovery of the extended family after a lengthy period in which such placements had tended to be regarded with suspicion and had come to constitute a decreasing proportion of foster care placements.

'The changed attitude to the extended family as potential providers of care was, like much of the Children Act 1989, based on research evidence. The specific knowledge base at the time, however, was not substantial – there was not a single major study which focused specifically on the value of relative care, and only a few which included relative placements at all. All these studies, it is true, did suggest similar conclusions – that relative care worked and had been unjustly relegated to the doldrums.'

1.30   There are those, with years of experience of the problems faced by local authorities, who think that an interest in kinship care is not wholly driven by a belief in the importance of the family.

'[Kinship care] can often mean placing children with relatives, not necessarily assessed as to their competence as well as they might be. Proposals for Family Group Conferences[55] prior to proceedings will enhance this approach. It is likely

---

[54]   *Family and Friends Carers Scoping Paper* (Department of Health, 2001) at p 1.
[55]   See **18.7**.

to be a cheaper option than foster care. And the fees regime[56] will certainly encourage local authorities to press relatives into service without going through legal proceedings as has historically been the case. If they can persuade (or delude) relatives into caring without the child entering the care system, they might even avoid the payment of allowances entirely.'[57]

1.31 Many of the children placed with family carers have special needs. Hunt,[58] for example, found that a high proportion of children in kinship care outside the foster care system were likely to have needs very similar to those within it. 'Probably, the majority of children in kinship care will have needs greater than children in the general population.' In addition, kinship carers are likely to be significantly more disadvantaged than unrelated foster carers, being more likely to be lone carers, living at least initially in overcrowded conditions, being nearly twice as likely to have a disability or a chronic illness and six times more likely to experience financial hardship.[59] Farmer has commented that 'Many kin carers struggled valiantly to bring order to these children's fragmented lives.'[60] Moreover, it cannot be assumed that carers, because they are family, do not encounter problems with the child's parents which they are able to resolve themselves.[61]

Special Guardianship Orders

1.32 The Act introduced Special Guardianship Orders[62] into the Children Act 1989. The order vests parental responsibility in the carer. It does not operate to remove parental responsibility held by parents but the special guardian is able to exercise it to the exclusion of any other person with parental responsibility apart from another special guardian,[63] unless any enactment or rule of law requires the consent of more than one person with parental responsibility.[64] In addition, some security is provided for the special guardian by the provision that parents are not able to apply for the discharge of the order without first obtaining leave.[65]

1.33 The White Paper, *Adoption – A new approach*,[66] suggested that the order could be an alternative to adoption.

---

[56]   See *R (Hillingdon LBC and Others) v Lord Chancellor and Secretary of State for Communities and Local Government* [2008] EWHC 2683 (QB), [2009] 1 FLR 39.
[57]   White 'The Future of Welfare Law for Children' in Douglas and Lowe (eds) *The Continuing Evolution of Family Law* (Family Law, 2009) at p 255.
[58]   *Family and Friends Carers* op cit at p 44.
[59]   Farmer and Moyes *Children Placed with Family and Friends: Placement Patterns and Outcomes: Executive Summary* (DES, 2005).
[60]   op cit at p 5.
[61]   See **11.11**.
[62]   CA 1989, s 14A.
[63]   Ibid, s 14C(1).
[64]   Ibid, s 14C(2)(a).
[65]   Ibid, s 14D(3).
[66]   op cit at para 5.8.

'Adoption is not always appropriate for children who cannot return to their birth parents. Some older children may not wish to be legally separated from their birth families. Adoption may not be best for some children being cared for on a permanent basis by members of their wider birth family. Some minority ethnic communities have religious and cultural difficulties with adoption as it is set out in law. Unaccompanied asylum-seeking children may also need secure, permanent homes, but have strong attachments to their families abroad. All these children deserve the same chance as any other to enjoy the benefits of a legally secure, stable permanent placement that promotes a supportive, lifelong relationship with their carers, where the court decides that is in their best interests. In order to meet the needs of these children where adoption is not appropriate, [Special Guardianship will] provide permanence short of the legal separation involved in adoption ...'

1.34 There was a cautious welcome for the new order. For example, Deborah Cullen[67] wrote that:

'Those who remember the "custodianship order" introduced in the Children Act 1975 (but only brought into force in 1988, pretty much dead on arrival[68]) will naturally have some scepticism about the likely effect of special guardianship but the legal framework does on the face of it address many of the efficiencies of custodianship (not least the name) and, if properly publicised, and supported by local authorities, it could be a really important option for some children.'

However, she detected some ambivalence in the government, 'perhaps a fear that special guardianship will too readily be seen by the courts as a less controversial option than adoption.'

1.35 Research[69] into the first year in which special guardianship was available found that nearly three-quarters of the orders were made in care proceedings and a quarter in private law proceedings. Kinship carers were by far the most common special guardians (nearly nine out of ten) compared to local authority foster parents (just over 10%). Of the kinship carers, just over two-thirds were of the 'grandparent' generation, with the remainder divided more or less equally between aunts/uncles and cousins, step-parents or siblings. These findings are reflected in reported cases.[70]

Support

1.36 Schemes of local support services for both adoption[71] and special guardianship[72] have been established under the two Acts. Similar in nature and buttressed by statutory guidance, they enable children, and actual or

---

[67] *Adoption – a (fairly new) approach* [2005] CFLQ 475 at p 478.
[68] See **5.6**.
[69] *Special Guardianship: A Missed Opportunity – Findings From Research* [2008] Fam Law 148 and *Special guardianship and permanency planning: unforeseen circumstances and missed opportunities* [2008] CFLQ 359.
[70] See **16.121**.
[71] See Chapter 9.
[72] See Chapter 11.

prospective adopters and special guardians (and in some cases, parents) to apply to be assessed for support. The nature of the support includes counselling, mediation and in some instances, financial support, for example in relation to legal fees, expenses relating to contact and, for former foster carers of the child, maintenance.

1.37 Provision is made in the Acts and secondary legislation for the needs for support to be assessed prior to the making of any order.

1.38 One shortcoming is that although it is widely recognised that any kinship carers require support regardless of the nature of the order (if any) under which they are looking after children,[73] there is no similar scheme for family members who look after a child under a residence order rather than a special guardianship order. They have to rely on the services available to the general population under Part III of the 1989 Act.[74]

1.39 Adoption support had been available for some years but its provision had been uncertain and had varied geographically. The new schemes are intended to be applied uniformly. It is too soon to know how this important change will operate.

'[The] provision is ... in the hands of local authorities and while the legislation, regulations and guidance can demand that all authorities have support provision in place, the consistency of their application cannot really be achieved while they retain discretion over the expenditure of their own resources.'[75]

1.40 A study of a sample of cases where special guardianship orders had been granted in the first year the provision was in force[76] found that 70% of special guardians had been granted financial support. However the chance of obtaining support was greater for former foster parents who were also considered to be 'much more difficult', engaging in lengthy negotiations for acceptable financial packages.

Contact

1.41 The concept of 'open' adoption in which the child has some post-adoption contact – either direct or indirect – with his birth family has become familiar in recent years.[77] Whether or not it brings benefits to most adopted children is a question to be approached with caution. As Lowe and Murch concluded:

---

[73] See, for example, *The role of the state in supporting relatives raising children who cannot live with their parents* (2007), a policy response to the Care Matters Green Paper by Addaction, Barnados, British Association for Adoption and Fostering and eleven other charities.
[74] See **16.57**.
[75] *Adoption – a (fairly new) approach* op cit at p 479.
[76] *Special Guardianship: A Missed Opportunity – Findings From Research* op cit.
[77] See **13.53**.

'Contact can be threatening in situations where there are any insecurities about the adoption but it can work well in cases where the birth parent consents to the adoption, believing it to be in the best interests of the child.'[78]

1.42   Before the 2002 Act came into force, the legal approach to post-adoption contact could be summarised in three propositions.

- Courts are more willing than hitherto to consider post-adoption contact and there are cases where some continuing face-to-face contact is clearly desirable.[79]

- If contact is to take place, it should normally be by way of agreement.

- Only in the most exceptional cases will a contact order be made without the agreement of the adopters.[80]

1.43   For the first time in adoption legislation, the 2002 Act expressly mentions adoption. Under the Adoption Agency Regulations 2005, the issues of whether or not there is a need for the child to have contact are considered at every stage within the internal local authority or agency procedure[81] and during court proceedings.[82] Within the Act itself, the court and the agency are directed to have regard to the relationship which the child has with relatives, and with any other person in relation to whom the court or agency considers the relationship to be relevant including the likelihood of any such relationship continuing and the value to the child of its doing so.[83] Before making an adoption order, the court must consider whether there should be arrangements for allowing any person contact with the child; and for that purpose the court must consider any existing or proposed arrangements and obtain any views of the parties to the proceedings.[84]

1.44   It is too soon to say whether the Act has caused a move in the previous cautious judicial approach to post-adoption contact but in *SB and County Council: P (a child)*[85] Wall LJ expressed the view that, at least in some cases, the court should comply with its duty to consider contact by taking a more active role than hitherto.

---

[78]   *Supporting Adoption: Reframing the Approach* op cit at p 324.

[79]   *Re E (A Minor)(Care Order: Contact)* [1994] 1 FLR 146.

[80]   *Re C (A Minor) (Adoption Order: Conditions)* [1989] AC 1 and *Re T (Adoption Contact)* [1995] 2 FLR 251.

[81]   For example, reg 13(1)(c)(iii) – the child's wishes; reg 14(1)(c)(iii) – the parents' wishes; reg 18(3)(a) – advice to the agency from the adoption panel; reg 24(2)(c) – information to prospective adopters about contact between a child and his parents; Sch 4, Part 1, para 28(h) – information to the Panel about the prospective adopters' views about contact.

[82]   For example, Family Procedure (Adoption) Rules 2005 Practice Direction 5C Annex A Part 2 – report by the local authority on contact arrangements and views of the child, the parents and others.

[83]   ACA 2002, s 1(4)(f).

[84]   Ibid, s 46(6).

[85]   [2008] EWCA Civ 535; sub nom *P (a child)* [2008] 2 FCR 185 at [153]–[154].

'The 2002 Act envisages the court exercising its powers to make contact orders post adoption, where such orders are in the interests of the child concerned.'

1.45 Likewise, in *Down Lisburn Health and Social Services Trust v H*[86] Baroness Hale of Richmond said that:

'The court has to take into account the child's need for contact with the birth parents in deciding whether adoption is in the best interests of the child. These days, as already indicated, adoption can take many different forms. In many cases, particularly those where the child has a significant history, it is not enough for the court to decide in a vacuum whether 'adoption' is in the best interests of the child. It must decide what sort of adoption will best serve her interests. If the court takes the view that some form of open adoption will be best, then it will have to take that into account in deciding whether it will accord with its most important consideration, the welfare of the child ...'

STEP-PARENTS

1.46 The legislature took the opportunity afforded by the Bill to introduce two changes to the substantive law concerning step-parents.

Parental responsibility

1.47 Section 4A was introduced into the Children Act 1989 to allow the married partner or civil partner of one parent with parental responsibility to acquire revocable parental responsibility either with the consent of that and the other parent (if the other parent has parental responsibility) or by court order.

Adoption

1.48 Hitherto, if the spouse of one of the child's parents wanted to adopt the child, the adoption would revoke the status of the parents. Now, the step-parent – who no longer has to be the spouse of the parent but can be his or her civil partner or someone who is in an enduring relationship with the parent[87] – can make a sole application for an adoption order. If granted, the status of the adopter's partner in relation to the child is not changed and he or she retains any parental responsibility he or she has.[88]

1.49 Whether or not these innovations will achieve anything in practice is unclear. Professor Judith Mason,[89] for example, has expressed the opinion that very few step-parents are likely to obtain a formally recognised relationship with their stepchildren.

---

[86]　[2006] UKHL 36, [2007] 1 FLR 121 at [27].
[87]　ACA 2002, ss 51(2), 144(7), 144(4).
[88]　Ibid, s 67(2), (3).
[89]　'Caring for our Future Generations' in Douglas and Lowe *The Continuing Evolution of Family Law* op cit at p 230.

'Despite the growth in numbers of step-families and their recognition in social law, family law remains unsure whether and how to recognise them ... [The restrictions on the grant of parental responsibility] reflects uncertainty about whether parental responsibility for step-parents really matters at all.'

INTERNATIONAL ADOPTION

1.50 Adoptions with an international aspect are increasing. The limited number of babies available for adoption in the UK means that some prospective adopters seek to adopt children who are living abroad. In addition the awareness of the importance of considering whether children who cannot remain with their families should live with members of their extended family may mean the local authority or agency considering families who live abroad as potential carers.

1.51 The Act and secondary legislation contain detailed provisions, based on the requirements of The Hague Convention on Protection of Children and Co-operation in Respect of Intercountry Adoption 1993, to regulate the entry of children into the UK for the purpose of being adopted here and their subsequent adoption and the removal of children from the jurisdiction with the intention that they should be adopted abroad.

THE CURRENT POSITION

1.52 The passing of the Adoption and Children Act 2002 completes the creation of a unified structure for resolving legal problems relating to the care of children who are unable to live with both their parents. The two Acts are based on the concept of parental responsibility and together deal with its grant, revocation and sharing with others as well as conflicts concerning its exercise. In addition, the court has the jurisdiction in a wide variety of circumstances to order contact between the child, his birth parents and anyone else with whom he has a significant relationship. As the 2002 Act states in its opening section: 'The court ... must always consider the whole range of powers available to it in the child's case (whether under this Act or the Children Act 1989)'.[90]

1.53 This is a considerable achievement.

1.54 Deborah Cullen who has many years of experience of the process of adoption[91] commented in 2003:[92]

---

[90] ACA 2002, s 1(6) and see CA 1989, s 1(3)(g).
[91] As the former secretary to the Legal Group of the British Association for Adoption and Fostering (BAAF).
[92] *Adoption – a (fairly new) approach* op cit at p 486.

'Whether these [changes] will amount to a significantly "new approach" remains to be seen. As Wall LJ pointed out in *Re F and J*,[93] there will remain after the implementation of the Act children whose needs require that they should be adopted. Nevertheless the statutory recognition that the making of an adoption order does not automatically involve severance of all emotional ties, and the provision of a new order [special guardianship] which will allow some degree of stability for a child in a family without severing the legal relationship with the birth family may well succeed in helping to produce a more unbroken continuum between the options for permanence.'

1.55   However, significant difficulties relating to the application of the law remain. There is a deep chasm between the legal nature of adoption – the permanent and irrevocable severing of all legal ties with the birth family and the substitution of similar ties with the adopters and their family – and that of the other orders which last only until the child is 16 or attains his majority, are capable of being discharged and involve multiple holdings and exercise of parental responsibility. Although adults on both sides of the divide are subject to the same powers relating to the grant of contact orders, the boundary is marked by the different ways in which, at least currently, those powers are exercised.

1.56   During the Bill stage, Caroline Bridge,[94] pointing to the difference between the adoption of babies and older children,[95] commented that 'conceptual and philosophical tensions within the framework of adoption law and practice abound'. Dilemmas as to whether contact should continue and whether the welfare of the child required a permanent severance of ties with the birth family 'demand a revisiting of the problems inherent in striking a balance between the interests of the three sets of participants in the adoption triangle – those of the child, birth parents and adoptive parents'.

1.57   Professor Lowe had also suggested that a reappraisal was necessary.

'The "mind set" which is, rightly or wrongly, associated with the adoption of babies, still permeates thinking not only behind the law and, possibly to a lesser extent, practice, but also the attitudes of the adopters themselves. Under this "mind set" ... [the "gift/donation" model], adoption is seen very much as the last and irrevocable act in a process in which the birth parent ... has "given away" her baby ... to the adopters who are left to their own devices and resources to bring up the child as their own ... This model however sits uneasily with the adoption of older children and ... in these instances, at least, a different model is needed in which it is recognized that adoption is not the end of the process but merely part of an ongoing and often complex process of family development.'[96]

---

93   [2005] EWCA Civ 349 (unreported).
94   'Adoption law: a balance of interests' in Herring (ed) *Family Law: Issues, Debates and Policy* (Willan Publishing, 2001) at p 200.
95   See **1.28**.
96   Lowe 'The changing face of adoption – the gift/donation model versus the contract/services model' [1997] CFLQ 371. See also Lowe 'English Adoption Law: Past, Present and Future' in Katz, Eekelar and Maclean (eds) *Cross Currents: Family Law and Policy in the US and England*

1.58　These tensions still remain despite the 2002 Act. It has been made clear by the Court of Appeal in *Re S (Adoption Order or Special Guardianship Order)*[97] that:

> 'There is nothing in the statutory provisions themselves which limits the making of a special guardianship order or an adoption order to any given set of circumstances. The statute itself is silent on the circumstances in which a special guardianship order is likely to be appropriate, and there is no presumption contained within the statute that a special guardianship order is preferable to an adoption order in any particular category of case. Each case must be decided on its particular facts; and each case will involve the careful application of a judicial discretion to those facts. The key question which the court will be obliged to ask itself in every case in which the question of adoption as opposed to special guardianship arises will be: which order will better serve the welfare of this particular child?'

1.59　But this does not completely resolve the question to be asked in each case: what is the most appropriate order for *this* child in the circumstances of *this* case? Chapter 16 suggests a process of examining the wishes and needs of the child, the ability of the individual contends to meet those needs, the benefits and risks of each option and considering the need for security separately from the need for a change in status.

1.60　Whatever the answer for the individual child, the aim in each case is clear. As Baroness Hale of Richmond has written extra-judicially:

> 'The message for us all ... must be that the legal status should follow from the answers to the key questions about the child's future rather than the other way around. The legal status is a means and not an end. The end is the successful upbringing of the child.'[98]

Research: a warning

1.61　As Professors Douglas and Lowe have recently pointed out:[99]

> 'Empirical data and the insights of non-legal disciplines are used as a means of understanding how and why the law developed in the ways it has ... The socio-legal approach ... has come to be relied on to a major extent not only by legal scholars and policy makers but also by practitioners and the judiciary ... Research into how laws operate and how the family justice system operates plays an increasingly important role in influencing opinions and decision making.'

1.62　It is for this reason that the Handbook contains references not only to policy documents such as *Prime Minister's Review: Adoption* but also to

---

(Oxford University Press, 2000) chapter 14 at p 337 and *Adoption Now: Messages from Research* (Department of Health, 1999) at pp 128–129.
[97]　[2007] EWCA Civ 54, [2007] 1 FLR 819 per Wall LJ at [47].
[98]　Jordan and Lindley *Special Guardianship: What Does It Offer Children Who Cannot Live With Their Parents?* (Family Rights Group, 2006) Foreword at iv.
[99]　Ibid at p 2.

socio-legal research – for example *Supporting Adoption: Reframing the Approach*[100] – literature reviews of social research – notably *Adoption Now: Messages from Research*[101] and *What Works in Adoption and Foster Care?*[102] – as well as individual pieces of research. It is hoped that they will be found useful by readers and provide them with possibilities for further investigation. However, there must be warnings. This is a legal Handbook for practitioners and not a literature review. Not every important domestic – let alone foreign – study is included. Nor is it a substitute for expert evidence focused on the specific circumstances of the individual case. It will not provide a foundation for successfully asserting that 'judicial knowledge' will be taken of any 'fact' contained in it.

THE ADOPTION PROCESS – AN OVERVIEW

1.63   The substantive law relating to adoption is addressed in Chapter 2 and the procedural law in Chapter 17.

1.64   Prospective adopters can apply for an adoption order only when the child has had his home with them for a period of time, the length of which varies according to the circumstances (see **2.73** and following). Unless the prospective adopters are the child's relatives, it is unlawful for a parent to place their child with prospective adopters for adoption (see **7.22**). Instead, the services of an adoption agency (which includes local authorities as well registered societies) must be used. The functions of adoption agencies are described at **7.62**.

1.65   Before an agency can place a child for adoption

* The agency has to assess the child as being suitable for adoption (see Chapter 8 and **7.86**), assess the prospective adopters as being suitable adopters (see Chapter 8 and **7.92**) and approve the 'match between the two, (see **7.141**). In each instance, the agency must seek the views of its adoption panel (see **7.96**) and take its recommendation into account when reaching its decisions.

* The child's parents who have parental responsibility or guardians (see **3.5**) must consent to the child being placed (see **3.87**) or the child must be subject to a placement order (see **3.11**) obtained by a local authority.

1.66   A placement order can be made only if all parents with parental responsibility and guardians consent (see **3.91**) or the court dispenses with their consent on one of a number of grounds (see **3.101**).

---

[100]   Lowe and Murch and others op cit.
[101]   (Department of Health, 2000).
[102]   Sellick, Thoburn and Philpot (Barnados, 2004).

1.67   A child can be adopted only if all parents with parental responsibility and guardians consent (see **3.98**) or the child is subject to a placement order or the court dispenses with their consent on one of a number of grounds (see **3.101**).

1.68   Agencies have two other roles in addition to placing the child. They are under a duty to provide the child, the birth parents and prospective and adoptive parents with adoption support services (see Chapter 9) including assistance in seeking information about the child's origins when the child reaches adulthood (see **9.77**). Secondly, after an adoption application is made, the agency which placed the child or (if the child was not placed by an agency) the local authority for the area where the prospective adopters live have to report to the court on the circumstances of the placement and whether the adoption is in the best interests of the child (see **8.62**)

1.69   At all stages, the importance to the child of his birth family (see Chapter 12) and whether or not the child should remain in contact with family members (see **13.47**) has to be assessed and considered.

SPECIAL GUARDIANSHIP – AN OVERVIEW

1.70   The substantive law relating to special guardianship is addressed in Chapter 5 and the procedural law in Chapter 18.

1.71   The regulation of special guardianship is considerably lighter than for adoption. There are no restrictions on a child being placed with prospective special guardians unless the child is being looked after by a local authority in which case, the proposed placement has to be assessed and considered under the Placement of Children with Parents etc Regulations 1991 (see **15.68**).

1.72   Parental consent to making a special guardianship order is not required, the matter being governed by the welfare test provided by s 1 of the Children Act 1989.

1.73   An application for a special guardianship order cannot be made unless the applicants have given their local authority 3 months notice of their intention to apply (see **5.18**). The local authority will then to report to the court on the circumstances of the placement and whether special guardianship is in the best interests of the child (see **10.11**). The assessment of the suitability of the child and the applicants for a special guardianship order is covered in Chapter 10.

1.74   Local authorities are under a duty to provide the child, the birth parents and prospective and adoptive parents with special guardianship support services (see Chapter 11).

1.75 At all stages, the importance to the child of his birth family (see Chapter 12) and whether or not the child should remain in contact with family members (see **13.36**) has to be assessed and considered.

Chapter 2

ADOPTION

INTRODUCTION

2.1 Adoption gives parental responsibility for a child to the adopters or adopter and extinguishes the parental responsibility held by any other person. From the date of the order the adopted person is treated in law as if he was born as the legitimate child of the adopters and as not being the child of any other person save where his parent's partner adopts him in which case his relationship with that parent continues. The order therefore fundamentally interferes with the child's legal and, usually, social status, a birth parent's responsibilities and links with the child's extended birth family. For these reasons, an order cannot be made unless all those with parental responsibility consent or their consent is dispensed with on grounds which include their not being able to be found, being incapable of giving consent or that the child's welfare requires it. This latter ground needs more than a finding that adoption is in the child's best interests.

2.2 The Adoption and Children Act 2002 (ACA 2002) extends the categories of people who can adopt to include couples, whether in marriage, a civil partnership or who are living in an enduring family relationship, in part to widen the background from which adopters have previously been recruited in order to provide a permanent, alternative home for all children who require it.

THE MEANING OF ADOPTION

2.3 An adoption order is an order made by the court giving parental responsibility for a child to the adopters or adopter,[1] the making of which operates to extinguish the parental responsibility which any person other than the adopters or adopter has for the adopted child immediately before the making of the order,[2] save where the adopter is the partner of one of the child's parents.[3]

2.4 See also **2.96** for the status of the adopted child.

---

[1] ACA 2002, s 46(1).
[2] Ibid, s 46(2)(a).
[3] Ibid, s 46(3)(b).

BACKGROUND

2.5   The abandoned child, brought up by strangers as their own, has been a commonplace in literature for centuries[4] and a frequent occurrence in fact for the same period. It has been suggested[5] that children were abandoned throughout Europe to the end of the Middle Ages in great numbers by parents of every standing in a great variety of circumstances – poverty, disaster, because of their physical condition or ancestry (for example illegitimacy or incest) or because they believed that someone of greater means might bring them up in better circumstances. Society relied on the kindness of strangers to rear them but the increasing social significance of lineage meant in some strata of society at least, that families almost inevitably pretended the child was a biological member of the family. This practice continued until the twentieth century although, from the time of the Renaissance in Italy and the eighteenth century in Britain,[6] there was a public response to the problem in the form of foundling hospitals – with revolving doors (the *tour* or *ruota*) in a niche into which a parent or servant could place a child without being seen. However, such children, if they survived infancy, were seldom if ever adopted 'either [dying] among strangers[7] or [entering] society as strangers'.[8] There were other possibilities though. Children might be raised by either their immediate or extended family or non-family members while being supported and visited by one or other of their parents, albeit without the true relationship (although sometimes a half-open secret) being revealed to the child or society.[9] Where the lack of a birth tie was acknowledged, such arrangements might be referred to as 'adoptions'.

2.6   The Romans were unusual in the ancient Western world[10] in having a system of procedures – the main forms were *adoptio* and *adrogatio* – by which a child or adult could be adopted or treated in law as the child of someone other than his birth parent.[11] Although *adoptio* and *adrogatio* placed the adopted person for all legal purposes in the same position as he would have been had he been born into the family of the adopter, that is, under the *potestas* of the *paterfamilias*, and the State regulated *adrogatio*, they differed from the modern

---

4   For example, Sophocles, *Oedipus The King* (cir 430 BC); Shakespeare, *The Winter's Tale* (1611); Wilde, *The Importance of Being Earnest* (1895).

5   Boswell, *The Kindness of Strangers* (1988), chapter 12.

6   The Foundling Hospital was established in 1793 by Thomas Coram near Gray's Inn.

7   In Rheims in the eighteenth century, 46% of abandoned infants died in their first year – *The Kindness of Strangers* op cit, p 422, n 83. Before 1767, nearly all parish infants in London died in their first six years – Eden *The State of the Poor* (1797) vol 1, p 338 cited in Heywood *Children in Care: the Development of the Service for the Deprived Child* (3rd edn,1978) p 17, n 5. See also **8.2**.

8   *The Kindness of Strangers* op cit at 433.

9   For example, Eliza (born 1792–1859) the illegitimate daughter of the Duchess of Devonshire and Sir Charles Grey was reared by her paternal grandparents as a foundling, believing her mother to be only her godmother – Foreman, *Georgiana, Duchess of Devonshire* (1998), pp 268–270. Horatia Nelson (1801–1881) knew her father was Lord Nelson but was not convinced that Lady Hamilton was her mother – Gérin, *Horatia Nelson* (1970), p 287.

10   For the position in the Islamic world, see **6.157**.

11   Buckland: *A Text Book of Roman Law* (1967, Stein) pp 121–127.

concept of adoption in a number of important ways. They were not limited to a child: an independent, *sui juris* adult could be adopted. Nor were they primarily, if at all, concerned with the welfare of the adopted person,[12] but rather with rights of property and succession or, sometimes, political advantage. Finally, because *adrogatio* resulted in the transfer of everyone under the *potestas* of the adopted person into the *potestas* of the adopter, thereby extinguishing his legal family, it could directly involve others than just the adopted person.[13]

2.7 The Roman concept of legal adoption passed into Civil Law and influenced many Western European counties but in countries where the common law was practised, adoption was not recognised[14] and it was unknown for many centuries until introduced by statute.

The Adoption of Children Act 1926

2.8 After the first world war, which left so many children fatherless, it was realised that informal arrangements did not provide proper security for the 'adopted' child who did not become a full member of the new family, or the 'adopters' who feared the birth mother might reclaim the child when he was old enough to earn or the mother who might have to resume the care of the child if the adopters tired of their responsibility.[15] The 'Hopkinson' Committee[16] in 1921 reported in favour of legal adoption – adoption was legally recognised in 'almost all civilised states'[17] – and following further reports[18] in 1925 the Adoption of Children Act 1926 was passed. Cretney[19] describes the Act as important for 'making the "adoption" of children a legally recognised and sanctioned institution, providing for the permanent and irrevocable transfer of parentage' while commenting that it may be that it did little more than provide 'machinery for the registration (under minimal safeguards supervised by the courts) and recognition of a private civil contract'.

---

[12] Sometimes *adoptio* was used by a father to sell his child as a slave in order to discharge a debt. Boswell describes the later imperial proscription of such arrangements as a 'rare intrusion into family life' op cit at p 68.

[13] See also *The Kindness of Strangers* op cit pp 63–75 at note 40.

[14] *R v Secretary of State for the Home Department ex parte Brassey and another* [1989] 2 FLR 486 at 493; *Humphrys v Polak* [1901] 2 KB 385 per Stirling LJ at 390.

[15] *The Report of the Departmental Committee of the Adoption of Children* (1972) Cmnd 5107 para 10. Doubt has been cast on whether the War in fact resulted in an increase in informal adoptions – see Cretney, *Family Law in the Twentieth Century: A History* (2003) at p 599 and note 13.

[16] *Report of the Committee on Child Adoption* (1921) Cmd 1254.

[17] Ibid, para 4.

[18] *Child Adoption Committee First Report* ('The Tomlin Committee') (1925) Cmd 2410 and *Child Adoption Second Report* (1925) Cmd 2469.

[19] *Family Law in the Twentieth Century: A History* op cit at pp 605–606.

The development of adoption

2.9   The initial legislation was amended by subsequent Acts, each preceded by at least one report from a Departmental Committee.[20]

- The Adoption of Children (Regulation) Act 1939: The Horsburgh Report 1937.[21]

  The Act introduced an element of state regulation into what had hitherto been a process of private arrangement. See **7.3**.

- The Adoption of Children Act 1949: The Curtis Report 1946.[22]

  This Act followed the Children Act 1948 which reformed local authority care of children in need. The 1949 Act regulated both the giving of consent to adoption and allowed the adopters' identity to be withheld from the birth parents without prejudicing the court's ability to dispense with consent on the ground it was unreasonably withheld.

- The Children Act 1958: The Hurst Report 1954.[23]

  The Act, described by Cretney as 'mildly evolutionary',[24] allowed local authorities to arrange adoption for any child whether in care or not and, in a slight acknowledgement of the Committee's opinion that a child should be told he was adopted, gave the High Court and Westminster County Court the power to disclose some confidential adoption papers. In addition, the Act allowed a child to inherit under the terms of a will if the testator died after the order but did not affect life time settlements.

- The Children Act 1975, succeeded by the Adoption Act 1976: The Houghton Report.[25]

  The Act placed local authorities under a statutory duty to provide an adoption service – see **7.9**. It also introduced the concept of a 'freeing' order which allowed the issues of whether a child should, in principle, be adopted and parental consent to be resolved without the involvement of proposed adopters and even before they had been identified or elected.

2.10   Three stages of development can be traced in adoption legislation which reflect not only the growth of concern for the child to be adopted but also the rise of the social work profession with a body of knowledge about the assessment of social and personal problems.[26] The first stage, marked by the Adoption Act 1926 was concerned with the legality of adoption. The second

---

[20]   For a detailed account, see *Family Law in the Twentieth Century: A History* ibid chapters 17, and 20 (pp 736–737).

[21]   The Report of the Departmental Committee on Adoption Societies and Agencies (1937) Cmd 5499.

[22]   Report of the Care of Children Committee (1946) Cmd 9622.

[23]   Report of the Departmental Committee on the Adoption of Children (1954) Cmnd 9248.

[24]   op cit 615.

[25]   Report of the Departmental Committee on the Adoption of Children (1972) Cmnd 5107.

[26]   Heywood, *Children in Care: The Development of the Service for the Deprived Child* (1978), p 185.

stage (marked by the Adoption of Children (Regulations) Act 1939) first made provision for regulating the conduct of persons and societies who arranged or supervised adoptions. The third stage followed the historical changes in the welfare state in 1948. Starting with the Adoption of Children Act 1949 it was concerned with the welfare of the child and ensuring his integration into his new family. However, these three stages are in fact less well defined than the model might suggest and it was not until the Children Act 1975 that the framework of the modern system of regulation was created.

2.11 Legislation was influenced both by changes in social behaviour and attitudes and the development of professional knowledge, both in the United Kingdom and internationally. The Curtis Report in 1946 focused attention on the need to establish a national system of good care for children in need. As contraception became more effective and abortion was legalised, the number of babies being placed for adoption fell. At the same time, work by social workers such as Rowe and Lambert[27] and Tizard[28] drew attention to the urgent need of children in long term care for a permanent home, the misplaced optimism that this would be provided by birth parents if one waited long enough, the detrimental effects of early institutional care and the appropriateness of adoption for some older children albeit that they might have physical, emotional or behavioural problems. When older children started to be adopted, social workers needed to consider what contact, if any, there should be between the child and his birth family[29] and the concept of 'open' adoption (see **13.53**) became a familiar one.

2.12 Alongside these developments, other child care legislation, in particular the Children Act 1989, provided new legal structures for approaching the needs of children in an holistic manner.[30]

The Adoption and Children Act 2002

2.13 The Adoption and Children Act 2002 was preceded by The Review of Adoption Law: Report to Ministers of an Interdepartmental Working Group in 1992[31] and the Prime Minister's Review: Adoption[32] in 2000.

2.14 The recommendations of the Prime Minister's Review are discussed in detail throughout the Handbook. In summary, they aimed to tackle the major problem of delay in the child being adopted by removing restrictions on who can adopt thereby enabling the recruitment of adopters from a wider background than previously and including, for example, same sex couples;

---

[27] *Children Who Wait* (1973).
[28] *Adoption: A Second Chance* (1977).
[29] See, for example, Fratter, *Adoption With Contact* (1996) and work by John Triseliotis.
[30] The Review of Adoption Law: Report to Ministers of an Interdepartmental Working Group 1992 (op cit) was intended to be part of the Lord Chancellor's systematic review of family law and jurisdiction of which the main outcome was the 1989 Act – see the Report, para 16.
[31] (1992) Department of Health and Welsh Office.
[32] (2000) Performance and Innovation Unit.

reforming the freeing process; radically changing the grounds for dispensing with parental consent by placing the emphasis on the welfare requirements of the child (see **3.137**) and introducing national standards for practice.

Policy

2.15 The Review of Adoption Law: Report to Ministers of an Interdepartmental Working Group 1992 was clear that adoption, having the advantage of being universally understood,[33] will continue to have a valuable role for some children.

2.16 One of the main advantages of adoption is the permanent status it confers upon the relationship between the child and the adopters, giving security and stability to all and inviting a commitment from the adoptive parents.

> 'It makes a child permanently part of a new family and gives him or her the confidence that derives from knowing that no one can disrupt this arrangement. This may be particularly valuable for children who have spent many years in care and have lived with a succession of different carers, unsure at any time where their future lies and frightened of developing close emotional links with whoever is looking after them.'[34]

It is also special in that it creates a legal relationship between the child and all members of the adoptive family which continues beyond childhood and throughout the lives of all involved.[35]

2.17 The primary purpose of the Prime Minister's Review[36] was to address whether 'there should be more use of adoption as an option for looked after children and whether the process could be improved in the interests of children'.[37]

2.18 Its conclusion was even more positive and enthusiastic than that of the 1992 Report.

> 'Overall ... the government should promote an increase in adoption for looked after children, and that there is scope to increase the number of adoptions each year. The new Quality Protects initiative, directed specifically at children's services, is already improving the operation of adoption services. But a more fundamental and wide-ranging strategy is needed to deliver the service which children have a right to expect.
>
> This new approach must put the needs and rights of the child at the centre of the process. It should reflect the value we place on the commitment and skills of

---

33   *Adoption Guidance* op cit Annex A, para 3.5.
34   Ibid, para 3.3.
35   Ibid, para 3.4.
36   op cit.
37   Ibid, p 5.

people who are suitable and willing to care for these children, the Government's commitment to support them and a respect for the rights of birth families. The shifts in adoption trends need to be widely recognised and acknowledged; adoption of children from care in the 21st century is less about providing homes for relinquished babies and more concerned with providing secure, permanent relationships for some of society's most vulnerable children.'[38]

It underlined this approach by an open acceptance that for many children, state care was not 'good enough' (see **15.2**).

The current model of adoption

2.19   The legal concept and form of adoption has always applied without any limitation to all children regardless of their age. However, the understanding and approach of the courts to adoption has been strongly influenced by the way in which adoption is currently or has been[39] practised. Because adoption was initially concerned only with babies born in circumstances considered a disgrace by many, secrecy was the norm. It was a service for childless couples and this encouraged a pretense that the adopted child was in fact a child born to the adopters. Contact between the child and the birth parents was completely alien to this concept of a 'closed' or 'exclusive' adoption and even where it was sought, courts viewed adopters as possessing, if not absolute legal autonomy, something approaching it. *In Re C (A Minor) (Adoption Order: Conditions)*,[40] for example, Lord Ackner, while recognising the legal possibility of providing for contact, emphasised the near veto possessed by adopters.

'It seems to me essential that, in order to safeguard and promote the welfare of the child throughout his childhood, the court should retain the maximum flexibility given to it by the Act and that unnecessary fetters should not be placed upon the exercise of the discretion entrusted to it by Parliament. ... No doubt the court will not, except in the most exceptional case, impose terms or conditions as to access to members of the child's natural family to which the adopting parents do not agree. To do so would be to create a potentially frictional situation which would be hardly likely to safeguard or promote the welfare of the child.'

2.20   Such an approach was at odds with the interventionist stance taken in relation to children in care. This difference in approach became difficult to justify on the basis of the needs of adopted children because as adoption came to be considered as a way in which children in care could be found a permanent home, adopted children shared many characteristics with children in the population.

2.21   The 'traditional' approach to adoption was challenged by Professor Nigel Lowe in 1997.

---

[38]   Ibid.
[39]   'Popular beliefs about the character of adoption lag behind today's reality' – *Adoption Now: Messages from Research* (1999) Department of Health, p 129.
[40]   [1988] 2 FLR 159 per Lord Ackner at 167. See also **13.52**.

'The "mind set" which is, rightly or wrongly, associated with the adoption of babies, still permeates thinking not only behind the law and, possibly to a lesser extent, practice, but also the attitudes of the adopters themselves. Under this "mind set" ... [the "gift/donation" model], adoption is seen very much as the last and irrevocable act in a process in which the birth parent ... has "given away" her baby ... to the adopters who are left to their own devices and resources to bring up the child as their own ... This model however sits uneasily with the adoption of older children and ... in these instances, at least, a different model is needed in which it is recognized that adoption is not the end of the process but merely part of an ongoing and often complex process of family development.'[41]

Lowe argued that the State could not consider that its obligations towards children who had complex needs could be discharged by the making of a contact order.

'Its duty to support these needy children and those who take on the task of looking after them, must *prima facie* continue even after the adoption order has been made.'[42]

He pointed out that continuing support might mean a change in approach to the autonomy of adopters, many of whom still held onto the idea that upon adoption the child became 'theirs' and that there should be no further contact with the birth family. While adopters would remain legally in control of the child:

'It has to be asked whether the price to be paid for continuing support after the order should be to surrender some of that control.'[43]

2.22 The Adoption and Children Act 2002 introduced a detailed scheme of post-adoption support for families (see Chapter 9) but it remains to be seen how far the model of adoption, as viewed by the courts, will change. Some suggestion that it might can be found by two post-Act *dicta* of Baroness Hale of Richmond.

2.23 In *Re P (Adoption: Unmarried Couple)*[44] she noted the 'move to permanency' for children in care, many of whom 'had histories, sometimes very tragic histories, which left them with very special needs.'

'A rather different sort of adoptive family [is] required, perhaps a couple who had successfully brought up their own children, perhaps a couple who had been fostering the child, perhaps a single person who could give the child the one to one attention she required. Apart from the particular parenting problems these

---

[41] Lowe 'The changing face of adoption – the gift/donation model versus the contract/services model' [1997] CFLQ 371. See also Lowe 'English Adoption Law: Past, Present and Future' in Katz, Eekelar and Maclean (eds) *Cross Currents: Family Law and Policy in the US and England* (2000), ch 14 at 337 and *Adoption Now: Messages from Research* (1999) Department of Health pp 128–129.

[42] Ibid, p 383.

[43] Ibid, p 385.

[44] [2008] UKHL 38, [2008] 2 FLR 1084.

children might present, there might be … a need for continued contact of some sort between the child and the birth family.'

2.24   In *Down Lisburn Health and Social Services Trust v H*[45] Baroness Hale had earlier commented that:

'The court has to take into account the child's need for contact with the birth parents in deciding whether adoption is in the best interests of the child. These days, as already indicated, adoption can take many different forms. In many cases, particularly those where the child has a significant history, it is not enough for the court to decide in a vacuum whether "adoption" is in the best interests of the child. It must decide what sort of adoption will best serve her interests. If the court takes the view that some form of open adoption will be best, then it will have to take that into account in deciding whether it will accord with its most important consideration, the welfare of the child, to make an order freeing the child for adoption before there is any evidence available of the efforts made to secure the right sort of adoptive placement and to prepare both families for it.'

RESEARCH

2.25   There is much research both domestic and international on the 'success' of adoption placements but as both Sellick and Thoburn[46] and *Adoption Now Messages from Research* [47] point out, the task of evaluating child placement is difficult because of the 'discrete but interacting components of the placement'.[48] There are also questions of how a 'successful' placement can be defined, measured and the stage at which this should be done. For example, the child may leave his adoptive family but continue to have a supportive and enduring connection with them.[49]

2.26   Sellick and Thoburn suggest that whether or not children have a sense of permanence and of personal identity are particularly useful interim outcome measures but need to be considered with other matters relating to 'well-being' such as health, education, emotional and behavioural development and self-care, for example. Both they and the authors of *Adoption Now: Messages from Research* agree that 'disruption' of the placement is only a crude measure. Nor is it easy to correlate outcomes with practice. 'Long term outcomes' may be measured 20 or more years after the placement but the practice influencing these outcomes may have changed.

---

[45]   [2006] UKHL 36, [2007] 1 FLR 121 at [27].
[46]   Sellick, Thoburn and Philpot, *What Works in Adoption and Foster Care?* (2004) pp 8–14.
[47]   (1999) Department of Health pp 10–11.
[48]   Sellick and Thoburn, op cit p 8; see also Quinton and Selwyn 'Adoption: research, policy and practice' [2006] CFLQ 459.
[49]   *Adoption Now* at 10.

2.27   *Adoption Now Messages from Research* and *What Works in Adoption and Foster Care?* provide useful short summaries of recent research.[50]

Age at placement

2.28   Age at placement is generally reckoned to be an important factor in a 'successful' placement because it is a proxy for other variables.[51]

> 'Children who are older ... tend to have experienced more separations from people who were important to them, are more likely to have been maltreated and more likely to have emotional and behavioural problems.'[52]

2.29   Around 5 per cent of the placement of infants made at the request of birth parents will break down compared with an overall average of one in five placements for all children.[53]

2.30   For children placed for adoption as infants, success appears to rely on:

- the adopters' ability to accept the child's dual identity and the emotional significance to the child of the birth family; and

- their view of themselves as new parents.[54]

2.31   It cannot be assumed, however, that children placed as infants have no special difficulties. There may be inherited disorders or low intelligence. They may have neurological problems caused by alcohol or drug abuse by the mother during her pregnancy. They may have suffered deprivation in their early months, for example, children adopted from Romanian orphanages had suffered severe early deprivation. However, the various studies of the Romanian children demonstrate the benefits of permanent placements. Although some of the children showed continuing deficits, there was 'very considerable' cognitive catch up. At the ages of 4 and 6, the children were indistinguishable from early UK adopted children, none of whom had suffered deprivation. The rate of breakdown was 'remarkably low' and parental satisfaction was high.[55] Some other studies have found that adopted children with physical or learning difficulties do as well or better than children who are in other respects the same.[56]

---

[50]   For an earlier review of the literature, see Thoburn *The Review of Adoption Law* (1992) Appendix C.

[51]   Sellick and Thoburn p 57, *Adoption Now: Messages from Research* p 15.

[52]   Sellick and Thoburn p 59.

[53]   Ibid, p 108–109.

[54]   Ibid.

[55]   Various studies by Andersen-Wood and others cited in *Adoption Now: Messages from Research* pp 148–150.

[56]   Sellick and Thoburn at p 109.

Past experiences

2.32 Predicators of high risk may include:

• the longer children have been looked after;

• the greater the number of moves;

• early rejection by birth parents and other siblings or half-siblings remaining at home;

• abuse or severe deprivation.[57]

Children's behaviour

2.33 Behaviour problems of various kinds can be associated with high risk including:

• hyperactivity and restlessness;

• aggressive or sexualised behaviour;

• defiant behaviour.[58]

Composition of the adoptive household

2.34

• The presence of the adopters' birth children increases the risk of poorer outcomes but this factor may be sensitive to whether the children are close in age.[59]

• The presence of other unrelated children or the adopted child's siblings is not related to poor outcomes.[60]

Parenting styles

2.35 The parenting style of the adopters appears to be related to outcome.[61] One study[62] found that in particular, a responsive approach involving the expression of warmth, emotional involvement and sensitivity was a positive factor.

---

[57] *Adoption Now: Messages from Research* p 15; Sellick and Thoburn p 109.
[58] *Adoption Now: Messages from Research* p 16.
[59] *Adoption Now: Messages from Research* p 16; Sellick and Thoburn pp 88, 109.
[60] *Adoption Now: Messages from Research* p 16; Sellick and Thoburn p 109.
[61] Sellick and Thoburn p 89.
[62] Quinton, Rushton et al, *Joining New Families* (1998) cited in *Adoption Now: Messages from Research* pp 144–148 and Sellick and Thoburn at p 105.

Moderating factors

2.36   A number of moderating factors have been identified in the literature. These are discussed at **16.97**.

2.37   *Adoption Now: Messages from Research* points out that none of these predictive or moderating factors should be viewed in isolation. There is a considerable degree of interaction and predictions are not certainties.

> 'Simply checking through such factors will not be enough to ensure a successful placement but if not sufficient, it is certainly necessary.'[63]

The authors add:

> 'The satisfactions accompanying adoption for both children and adults should not be underestimated. They may serve to offset the risks.'[64]

2.38   The factors discussed above do not necessarily differentiate between the different types of permanent placements, for example, adoption or long term fostering. Sellick and Thoburn express the opinion that 'in summary, there is insufficient evidence on the desirability of adoption, permanent fostering or residence orders, from the child's point of view'.[65]

HOW MUCH ADOPTION IS THERE?

2.39   In 2006, 4,764 children were adopted, the lowest figure in the last 7 years which averaged 5,248.[66] The number of boys and girls adopted were almost identical.

2.40   In the year ending 31 March 2008, 3,200 children were adopted from care, of which 51% were boys. Their average age was 3 years 11 months. Four per cent were aged under 1, 70% between 1 and 4 years and 22% between 5 and 9 years. Just over nine in ten children were adopted by couples.[67]

---

[63]   *Adoption Now: Messages from Research.*
[64]   Ibid, p 18.
[65]   Ibid, p 86.
[66]   *Marriage, divorce and adoption statistics* ONS Series FM2 no 33. These figures are based on adoption orders by date of court order. Slightly different figures are obtained from dates of entry in the Adoption Children Register. There is a time lag in publishing statistics, the Office of National Statistics lagging behind the Department for Education and Skills which publishes statistics of 'looked after' children.
[67]   *Children looked after in England (including adoption and care leavers) year ending 31 March 2008* DFES http://www.dfes.gov.uk. The statistics are summarised by BAAF at http://www.baaf.org.uk/info/stats.

WHO CAN BE ADOPTED?

2.41 Any person under the age of 19[68] can be adopted provided:

- he was under the age of 18 at the date the application was made[69] even though he may have attained the age of 18 before the order is made;[70]

- he is not and has not been married or a civil partner;[71]

- the applicant has not made a previous application to adopt him in England and Wales, Scotland, Northern Ireland, the Isle of Man or any of the Channel Islands which was refused by any court unless it appears to the court that, because of a change in circumstances or for any other reason, it is proper to hear the application.[72]

There is no residential or domiciliary qualification and s 1 of the Family Law Act 1986 which governs jurisdiction for other orders relating to children is silent on adoptions within England and Wales. When the child is domiciled abroad, the court will usually require evidence as to whether the adoption will be recognised by the courts of his domicile.[73]

2.42 A person can be adopted even though he is already an adopted child.[74]

2.43 Because adoption confers a lifelong status and benefits, it does not matter that the child will shortly attain his majority or reach the age of 19. In *Re D (A Minor) (Adoption Order: Validity)*[75] the Court of Appeal upheld an adoption order made in favour of foster parents with whom the boy, who had severe mental difficulties, had lived since the age of 12, notwithstanding that he was only 6 days short of his eighteenth birthday. There was no requirement that benefit during minority should be a condition precedent to the making of an order whereas a benefit accruing after majority is a relevant factor.

2.44 However in *Re K (A Minor) (Adoption Order: Nationality)*[76] the Court of Appeal allowed an appeal by the Secretary of State against an adoption order made 8 days short of the girl's eighteenth birthday. Leaving aside the advantage of gaining nationality, the benefits which accrued to her after majority were minimal as compared to the considerations of public policy in relation to the acquisition of a right of abode.

---

[68] ACA 2002, s 47(9).
[69] Ibid, s 49(4).
[70] Ibid, s 49(5).
[71] Ibid, s 47(8), (8A).
[72] Ibid, s 48(1).
[73] *Re B (S) (An Infant) (No 2)* [1968] Ch 204. See **4.65**.
[74] Ibid, s 44(5).
[75] [1991] 2 FLR 66.
[76] [1994] 2 FLR 557.

WHO CAN ADOPT?

2.45   An adoption order may be made on an application by a couple (under s 50) or a sole person (under s 51). For the purposes of the Act, 'a couple' means:

- a married couple;

- two people who are civil partners; or

- two people (whether of different sexes or the same sex) living as partners in an enduring family relationship but excluding two people one of whom is the other's parent, grandparent, sister, brother, aunt or uncle.[77]

References to relationships in the last category are to relationships of the full blood or half blood or, in the case of an adopted person, such of those relationships as would exist but for adoption, and include the relationship of a child with his adoptive, or former adoptive, parents but do not include any other adoptive relationships.[78]

2.46   A person is the partner of a child's parent if the person and the parent are a couple but the person is not the child's parent.[79]

2.47   Two people who are married or in a civil partnership can adopt jointly even though they are separated.[80] However, a separated couple who are not married or in a civil partnership are excluded because they are no longer 'living as partners' in an enduring family relationship. Where there is separation the court will need to examine carefully whether it is appropriate to make a joint order. In *Re C (Foreign Adoption: Natural Mother's Consent: Service)*[81] the court made an adoption order notwithstanding that the couple had separated. The child had lived with them for 11 years, had been adopted by them in Papua New Guinea and the separation was 'a very civilised and orderly one' between two individuals who had managed to find a satisfactory *modus vivendi*.

Formal qualifications

2.48   Applicants must satisfy the following three conditions.

---

[77]   ACA 2002, s 144(4), (5) as amended.
[78]   Ibid, s 144(6).
[79]   Ibid, s 144(7).
[80]   *Re C (Foreign Adoption: Natural Mother's Consent: Service)* [2006] 1 FLR 318.
[81]   Ibid.

Residence

2.49

- At least one of the couple (or the sole applicant) must be domiciled in a part of the British Islands;[82] and

- both of the couple or the sole applicant must have been habitually resident in a part of the British Islands for a period of not less than one year ending with the date of the application.[83]

Age

2.50

- If the application is made by a couple, both must have attained the age of 21 on the date the order is made unless one of the couple is the child's birth parent and has attained the age of 18 and the other applicant, the age of 21.[84]

- If the application is made by a sole applicant, the applicant must have attained the age of 21.[85]

Marital/partnership status

2.51 If the sole applicant is married[86] or in a civil partnership[87] the court must be satisfied that:

- the person's spouse/civil partner cannot be found;

- the spouses/civil partners have separated and are living apart, and the separation is likely to be permanent; or

- the person's spouse/civil partner is by reason of ill-health, whether physical or mental, incapable of making an application for an adoption order;

- the person is the partner of a parent of the person to be adopted.[88]

2.52 An adoption order may not be made on an application solely by the mother or the father of the child unless the court is satisfied that:

---

82 ACA 2002, s 49(2).
83 Ibid, s 49(3).
84 Ibid, s 50(2).
85 Ibid, s 21 (1), (2).
86 Ibid, s 51(3).
87 Ibid, s 51(3A).
88 Ibid, s 51(2).

- the other natural parent is dead or cannot be found;

- by virtue of s 28 of the Human Fertilisation and Embryology Act 1990, there is no other parent;[89] or

- there is some other reason justifying the child being adopted by the applicant alone.[90]

2.53 Where the court makes an adoption order on such an application, it must record that it is satisfied as to the facts mentioned above and, in the case of 'some other reason', record the reason.[91]

Adoption by a single person

2.54 This is discussed at **8.38**.

Adoption by two people who are not a couple

2.55 Unless the two applicants are a couple as defined at **2.45** they cannot both adopt. A brother and sister may wish to adopt their nephew but would be precluded from doing so because they do not qualify as a couple. Although they are in a factually 'enduring relationship' they are legally excluded because they are siblings.[92] In such a case it may be possible for one to adopt and for the other to be granted parental responsibility by the making of a residence order. This was done in *Re AB (Adoption: Joint Residence)*[93] where, under the old law, a cohabiting heterosexual couple were precluded from adopting a child whom they had fostered because they were not married. However, the court may have reservations about making a residence order where it is not intended that the child will not be living with the non-adopter either under a joint residence or shared residence arrangement.

Adoption by same sex couples

2.56 This is discussed at **8.46**.

Adoption by a parent

2.57 There is no prohibition on a parent adopting his or her own child. Such an adoption can be made in favour of a parent either as part of a couple (see **2.45**) or solely. In the latter case, the requirements of s 51(4) (see **2.52**) must be

---

[89] Ie if at the time of the placing in her of the embryo or the sperm and eggs or of her insemination, the mother was married but her spouse did not consent and the embryo was not brought about with his sperm or the embryo or the sperm and eggs were placed in the mother, or she was artificially inseminated, in the course of treatment services provided for her alone.

[90] ACA 2002, s 51(4).

[91] Ibid.

[92] Ibid, s 144(5).

[93] [1996] 1 FLR 27.

satisfied. In addition, an adoption order made solely in favour of a partner of the birth parent, does not extinguish that parent's parental responsibility.[94]

2.58 The Houghton Committee[95] noted that there had been a few cases where a single mother adopted her own illegitimate child but commented that such an adoption added nothing to her status and if it was an attempt to hide the facts of his birth, as likely in the long run to be damaging. Likewise birth fathers had adopted their illegitimate child in order to confer legitimacy. This is less common now than in 1972. As Lord Nicholls of Birkenhead pointed out in *Re B (Adoption: Natural Parent)*:[96]

> 'The social and legal status of children born outside marriage has changed greatly in recent years. The social stigma and legal disabilities attendant upon "illegitimacy" have now largely gone.'

The committee expressed the view that adoption of a child by one birth parent had a very important legal effect: it cut out the other parent.

> 'In our working paper we put forward the view that it was undesirable that adoption should be used by a mother to cut the links between a child and his father or by a father to cut the links between a child and his mother ... Custody applications [are] the appropriate way of settling disputes between parents whether married or not ...'[97]

However, it was persuaded that there might be exceptional cases where adoption by a natural parent would be for the child's welfare but considered that the law should be changed to require the applicant to satisfy the court that there were special circumstances which justify the making of the order as an exceptional measure.[98]

2.59 These recommendations were not enacted and no 'exceptional' circumstances are required.[99]

2.60 In *Re B (Adoption: Natural Parent)*[100] the House of Lords held that circumstances in which it was in the best interests of a child to make an adoption order in favour of one birth parent are likely to be exceptional.

> 'On its face this permanent exclusion of the child's mother from the life of the child is a drastic and detrimental consequence of adoption so far as the child is

---

[94] ACA 2002, s 46(3)(a).
[95] Report of the Departmental Committee on the Adoption of Children (1972) Cmnd 5107.
[96] [2001] UKHL 70, [2002] 1 FLR 196 at [26].
[97] Ibid, para 100.
[98] Ibid, para 102.
[99] *Re B (Adoption By One Natural Parent To Exclusion of Other)* (CA) [2001] 1 FLR 589 per Hale LJ at 598. The decision was overturned by the House of Lords [2001] UKHL 70, [2002] 1 FLR 196.
[100] [2001] UKHL 70, [2002] 1 FLR 196, overturning the decision of the Court of Appeal at [2001] 1 FLR 589 which had allowed an appeal against an adoption order made by Bracewell J at [2000] 2 FLR 717.

concerned. How serious this loss is likely to be depends on the circumstances of the case. In deciding whether to make an order having this consequence the court must always be satisfied that this course is in the best interests of the child. There must be some reason justifying the exclusion of the other natural parent. The reason must be sufficient to outweigh the adverse consequences such an order may have by reason of the exclusion of one parent from the child's life. Consent of the excluded parent is not of itself a sufficient reason, but it is a factor to be taken into account. Its weight will depend on the circumstances.'

'An adoption order in favour of a single natural parent alone will also have the effect of permanently extinguishing any parental responsibility of the other natural parent ... This will afford the adoptive parent a measure of additional security. But it is important here to keep in mind the wide range of powers the court now has under the Children Act 1989 to restrict the possibility of inappropriate intervention in the child's life by the other natural parent. Adoption is not intended to be used simply as the means by which to protect the child's life with one natural parent against inappropriate intervention by the other natural parent.'[101]

2.61   Lord Nicholls explained that s 51(4)[102] imposed a prerequisite to the making of an adoption order on the application of the mother or father alone. One or other of the exceptions set out in paragraphs [a), b) and c)] must be satisfied. The three exceptions listed in paragraphs (a) [and (b)] are instances where the other natural parent cannot have, or is unlikely to have, any further part in the child's upbringing and life.

'But these three exceptions are not an exhaustive list of the circumstances in which a natural parent is unlikely in practice to have a further role in a child's life. Further, there may be other situations when the welfare of the child justifies the exclusion of a natural parent. Abandonment, or persistent neglect or ill-treatment of the child, could be instances.'[103]

Lord Nicholls could see no ground for importing into this exception that there is 'some other reason', an unexpressed limitation whereby that 'other reason' must be comparable with the death or disappearance of the other natural parent. All that is required is that the reason, whatever it be, must be sufficient to justify the exclusion of the other parent. Whether any particular reason satisfies this test depends on the circumstances.

2.62   This guidance has been criticised by Sonia Harris-Short as running 'counter to the strong and consistent view of commentators and policy makers' that because a change of legal status lay at the heart of adoption, adoption by a sole birth parent was not an appropriate mechanism simply to determine with which parent a child should live.[104]

---

[101]   Ibid at [25].
[102]   Lord Nicholls in fact discussed s 15(3) of the Adoption Act 1976 which was in identical terms.
[103]   *Re B (Adoption: Natural Parent)* op cit at [23].
[104]   Harris-Short '*Re B (Adoption: Natural Parent)* – Putting the child at the heart of adoption' (2002) CFLQ 325 at 331.

'Adoption by a sole natural parent does not sit easily with our current understanding of the social and legal purpose of adoption.'[105]

Examples

C (A Minor) (Adoption by a Parent)[106]

2.63   The child's parents divorced when the child was 12. Custody was granted to her mother (M) and her father (F) stopped having contact when she was 13. M remarried but her husband died after 4 months. She married for a third time and applied with her new husband to adopt. F did not consent but took no part in the proceedings. The order was refused on the grounds that the circumstances were not exceptional.

Re B (Adoption: Natural Parent)[107]

2.64   The mother (M) was not married to the father (F). She put the child (B) with a local authority for adoption without informing F of the pregnancy or the birth. By chance he found out about his daughter and the local authority placed B with him when she was 2 months old. When she was 3, F applied to adopt her. M had slight reservations about the adoption but did not oppose it. She said that she did not seek contact other than by way of an annual progress report and photograph and did not want to interfere with her life. At first instance Bracewell J made an adoption order on the ground that M had totally rejected B and wanted to play no part in her future. The Court of Appeal allowed an appeal by the Official Solicitor but the adoption order was reinstated as a result of F's successful appeal to the House of Lords relying on the principle in *G v G (Minors: Custody Appeal)*[108] that an appellate court should not interfere unless it can be shown that the trial judge erred in some relevant aspect (see **19.37**).

Adoption by step-parents

2.65   This is discussed at **14.100**.

Adoption by a relative

2.66   There is no prohibition on a child being adopted by relatives but caution has long been recommended because of the problems which may be caused by the dynamics of the family (see **16.73**). When the child's grandparents wish to adopt, there may be special problems, not least because of their age.

---

[105]   Ibid, at 339.
[106]   [1986] Fam Law 360 CC (HHJ Wooley).
[107]   [2000] 2 FLR 717 (first instance); [2001] 1 FLR 589 (Court of Appeal); [2001] UKHL 70, [2002] 1 FLR 196 (House of Lords).
[108]   [1985] FLR 894.

2.67 In *S v B and Newport City Council: Re K* Hedley J granted a special guardianship order of a 6-year-old boy to his grandparents with whom he had lived since he was 6 months old rather than adoption which was their preferred option. He pointed out that in familial placements adoption is not needed to give a lifelong status to carers because the existing family life already exists.

2.68 Adoption orders have been made in favour of grandparents in special circumstances – see, for example, *Re B (Adoption Order: Nationality)*[109] (at **2.93**).

2.69 Adoption orders in favour of uncles and aunts have been made under the 2002 Act. In *Re M-J (Adoption Order or Special Guardianship Order)*[110] the Court of Appeal refused to overturn an adoption order made in favour of an uncle and aunt where the trial judge had found that the child's welfare required greater long term stability and security than could be supplied by a special guardianship order. A similar decision was reached in *Re A-J (Adoption Order or Special Guardianship Order)*.[111]

2.70 The issues in any individual case are likely to centre on whether or not the child should be looked after within the family and, if he is, whether the legal relationship should be an adoptive one or secured, for example, by a special guardianship order. The advantages and disadvantages of kinship care is discussed in Chapter 12 and the practical problems and need for support, at **11.4**. Making the choice between the various orders is considered in Chapter 16.

2.71 Adoption by relatives is one of the situations where the making of arrangements for adoption other than by an adoption agency is not illegal under s 93 of the Act (see **7.2**).

PROCEDURAL REQUIREMENTS

2.72 A number of procedural requirements have to be satisfied before an adoption order can be made.

Having a home with the applicants

2.73 One of the following conditions must be met.

- If the child was placed for adoption with the applicant(s) by an adoption agency or in pursuance of an order of the High Court, or the applicant is a parent of the child, the child must have had his home with the applicant

---

[109] [1999] 1 FLR 907.
[110] [2007] EWCA Civ 56, [2007] 1 FLR 691.
[111] [2007] EWCA Civ 55, [2007] 1 FLR 507.

or, in the case of an application by a couple, with one or both of them at all times during the period of 10 weeks preceding the application.[112]

- If the applicant or one of the applicants is the partner of a parent of the child, the child must have had his home with the applicant or, as the case may be, applicants at all times during the period of 6 months preceding the application.[113]

- If the applicants are local authority foster parents, the child must have had his home with them at all times during the period of 1 year preceding the application or the court has given leave.[114]

- In any other case, the child must have had his home with the applicant or, in the case of an application by a couple, with one or both of them for not less than 3 years (whether continuous or not) during the period of 5 years preceding the application or the court has given leave.[115]

2.74 For a detailed discussion, see **17.17**.

Observation by the adoption agency or local authority

2.75 The court must be satisfied that sufficient opportunities to see the child with the applicant or, in the case of an application by a couple, both of them together in the home environment have been given where the child was placed for adoption with the applicant or applicants by an adoption agency to the agency, or, in any other case, to the local authority within whose area the home is.[116]

2.76 For a detailed discussion, see **7.21**.

Notice of intention

2.77 Where the child was not placed for adoption with the applicants by an adoption agency the proposed adopters must give notice to the appropriate local authority of their intention to apply for the adoption order not more than 2 years, or less than 3 months, before the date on which the application for the adoption order is made.[117]

2.78 If the child was not placed for adoption with the applicants by an agency or the applicants are not the parent or the partner of a parent of the child, but the requirements as to the length of time the child has had his home with the

---

[112] ACA 2002, s 42(1), (2).
[113] Ibid, s 42(1), (3).
[114] Ibid, s 42(1), (4), (6).
[115] Ibid, s 42(1), (4), (6).
[116] Ibid, s 42(7).
[117] Ibid, s 44(1).

applicants (see **2.73**) have not been met, the proposed applicants may not give notice of intention to adopt unless they have the court's leave to apply for an adoption order.[118]

2.79   For a detailed discussion, see **17.17**.

Consent

2.80   An adoption order requires the court to be satisfied that one of the following conditions has been met:

* each parent and guardian consents to the order;[119] or

* each parent has given advanced consent under s 20, *and* has not withdrawn the consent *and* does not oppose the making of the order;[120] or

* it should dispense with the parent's or guardian's consent;[121] or

* the child has been placed for adoption with the prospective adopters with the consent of each parent or guardian *and* that the consent of the mother was given when the child was at least 6 weeks old[122] *and* no parent or guardian opposes the adoption order; or

* the child has been placed for adoption under a placement order[123] *and* no parent or guardian opposes the adoption order; or

* the child is free for adoption by virtue of an order made in Scotland under s 18 of the Adoption (Scotland) Act 1978 or in Northern Ireland, under art 17(1) or 18(1) of the Adoption (Northern Ireland) Order 1987 or under the Adoption Act 1976.[124]

2.81   For a detailed discussion, see Chapter 3.

MAKING AN ADOPTION ORDER

The test

2.82   Whenever a court is coming to a decision relating to the adoption of a child, the paramount consideration of the court or adoption agency must be the child's welfare, throughout his life[125] (see **6.67**).

---

[118]   ACA 2002, s 44(4).
[119]   Ibid, s 47(2)(a) ('the first condition').
[120]   Ibid, s 47(2)(b): also ('the first condition').
[121]   Ibid, s 47(2)(c): also ('the first condition').
[122]   Ibid, s 47(4)(a) and (b)(i) ('the second condition').
[123]   Ibid, s 47(4)(a) and (b)(ii): also ('the second condition').
[124]   Ibid, s 47(6) ('the third condition').
[125]   Ibid, s 1(2).

2.83 In exercising its discretion the court or adoption agency must have regard to the matters (among others) in s 1(4) of the Act ('the adoption welfare checklist'). These are discussed in detail at **6.83**.

2.84 In addition, the court must:

- bear in mind at all times that, in general, any delay in coming to the decision is likely to prejudice the child's welfare[126] (discussed in detail at **6.18**);

- always consider the whole range of powers available to it in the child's case (whether under ACA 2002 or the Children Act 1989). It must not make any order under this Act unless it considers that making the order would be better for the child than not doing so[127] (see **6.37**);

- before making an adoption order, consider whether there should be arrangements for allowing any person contact with the child; and for that purpose the court must consider any existing or proposed arrangements and obtain any views of the parties to the proceedings[128] (discussed in detail at **13.111**).

Article 8

2.85 The jurisprudence of the European Court of Human Rights makes it clear that adoption proceedings constitute an interference with family life and require justification.[129] However, in *Re B (Adoption by One Natural Parent to Exclusion of Other)*,[130] Lord Nicholls, while agreeing that making an adoption order was a very serious step, said that there was no need to go beyond the Adoption Act 1976 which complied with Article 8 of the European Convention on Human Rights.

> 'On its face this permanent exclusion of the child's mother from the life of the child is a drastic and detrimental consequence of adoption so far as the child is concerned. How serious this loss is likely to be depends on the circumstances of the case. In deciding whether to make an order having this consequence the court must always be satisfied that this course is in the best interests of the child. There must be some reason justifying the exclusion of the other natural parent. The reason must be sufficient to outweigh the adverse consequences such an order may have by reason of the exclusion of one parent from the child's life. Consent of the excluded parent is not of itself a sufficient reason, but it is a factor to be taken into account. Its weight will depend on the circumstances ....'

---

[126] ACA 2002, s 1 (3)
[127] Ibid, s 1(6).
[128] Ibid, s 46(6).
[129] *Johansen v Norway* (1997) 23 EHRR 33, *Söderbäck v Sweden* (1998) EHRLR 342, [1999] 1 FLR 250, *Kuijper v Netherlands* (application No 64848/01) (unreported but noted in *Eski*) and *Eski v Austria* (Application No 21949/03), [2007] 1 FLR 1650.
[130] *Re B (Adoption: Natural Parent)* [2001] UKHL 70, [2002] 1 FLR 196 at [30].

This approach has been subject to criticism and the question of whether Article 8 adds anything to the provisions of the Act is discussed at **6.184**.

The approach of the courts

2.86   Even before the 2002 Act, it was made clear that the issue of whether a child should be adopted is more complicated than just a question of where the child should live. Adoption involves a change in status. The effects of this should be considered as well as whether some other order will adequately safeguard the child's welfare.[131] Thus in *Re M (Adoption or Residence Order)*[132] the Court of Appeal allowed an appeal against an adoption order made in respect a 12-year-old child (C) who had been placed with the applicant foster parents (the As) 3 years previously. M had contact with her birth family four times a year. Prior to the application the As had suggested that they would be content with a residence order provided the child's mother (M) did not apply for residence but when she offered to agree to a residence order in their favour and to submit to an order under s 91(14) preventing her from applying without leave, they changed their position stating that if they were not granted an adoption order, they would not be prepared to keep C. The Court of Appeal held that the trial judge had erred in not considering all the relevant matters. Having done so themselves they were satisfied that it was in C's interests to remain with the As and, on balance, to be adopted, but held they could not dispense with the consent of M on the ground it was unreasonably withheld. A residence order was made, coupled with a direction under s 91(14).

2.87   Notwithstanding the checklist factors, the court will not grant an adoption order unless it is satisfied that parental responsibility for the child is intended genuinely to pass to the adopters. In *Re O (A Minor) (Wardship: Adopted Child)*[133] M agreed to her 8-year-old son, O, being adopted by wealthy friend, A, somewhat older than she, who had taken a benevolent interest in the boy. At the time of the adoption M and A were living in the same household as O, but not as man and wife. She had the role of mother to O and housekeeper to A who had the role of father and educational tutor to O. When the arrangement broke down, M issued a summons in wardship seeking care and control of O. The Court of Appeal held that the interests of O required that the circumstances should be investigated as to their merits. Ormrod LJ described the adoption as 'an extraordinary situation and one which is gravely disturbing ... I hope that no adoption in such circumstances ever takes place again.'[134]

---

[131]   *Re M (Adoption Or Residence Order)* [1998] 1 FLR 570; see **16.60**.
[132]   Ibid.
[133]   [1978] 1 All ER 145, [1978] 2 All ER 27(CA).
[134]   Ibid, at 28d and 31g.

Immigration considerations

2.88 The issue of the genuineness of the arrangement and policy considerations most commonly arise when an application to adopt a child born abroad is made by relatives resident in the United Kingdom who hold British citizenship.

2.89 Making the order will result in the acquisition by a non-British child of British citizenship and the right of abode in the UK (see **2.101**).

2.90 Prior to the 2002 Act, the Courts adopted the following approach, founded to a great part, on the leading decision of the House of Lords in *Re B (Adoption Order: Nationality)*:[135]

- The court should ask whether the application is a genuine one (albeit tainted by deception), intended to create the psychological and legal relationship of parent and child rather than a sham whose purpose is solely designed to achieve immigration benefits ('an accommodation adoption').[136]

- An adoption order will not be made when the prospective adopters do not intend to exercise any parental responsibility but merely wish to assist the child to acquire a right of abode.[137]

- In the case of a genuine application, any benefit which will accrue to the child as a result of the adoption, during childhood or afterwards, is a relevant consideration.

- Considerations of immigration policy may also be relevant 'although it is not easy to see what weight they could be given'.[138]

- In such cases where it appears that adoption will confer real benefits to the child during its childhood, it is very unlikely that general considerations of immigration policy could justify refusal of an adoption order.[139]

- Benefits which will accrue only after the end of childhood are not welfare benefits during childhood to which first consideration must be given. If a right of abode will be of benefit only when the child becomes an adult, that benefit will ordinarily have to give way to the public policy of not usurping the Home Secretary's discretion.[140] In *Re K (A Minor)*

---

[135] [1999] 1 FLR 907.

[136] *Re J (Adoption: Non-Patrial)* [1998] 1 FLR 225; *Re B (Adoption Order: Nationality)* [1999] 1 FLR 907 per Lord Hoffman at 910.

[137] Ibid.

[138] Ibid.

[139] Ibid.

[140] *Re B (Adoption Order: Nationality)* [1999] 1 FLR 907 and *Re S and J (Adoption: Non-Patrials)* [2004] 2 FLR 111.

(Adoption Order: Nationality),[141] for example, the Court of Appeal set aside an adoption order made 8 days before the child reached her majority.

2.91   A two stage test, approved by the Court of Appeal,[142] in which a genuine motive to adopt should be balanced against the public policy considerations of upholding an immigration policy entrusted to the Secretary of State, was rejected by the House of Lords in *Re B (Adoption Order: Nationality)*.

> 'The two kinds of consideration are hardly commensurable so as to be capable of being weighed in the balance against each other.'[143]

When this approach was established and at the time of *Re B (Adoption Order: Nationality)*, the welfare test, set out in s 6 of the Adoption Act 1976 required the court to promote the welfare of the child throughout his *childhood* whereas s 1(2) of the 2002 Act refers to the child's welfare throughout his *life*. It is uncertain therefore to what extent benefits accruing solely after majority will now influence the decision.

Examples

Re H (Adoption: Non-Patrial)[144]

2.92   A boy, S, lived in Pakistan with his parents, being their sixth child. When he was 12 his father agreed that he could be adopted by distant relatives, the As, who lived in England. They applied to adopt him when he was 15. Holman J made an adoption order accepting that it was a genuine adoption application with genuine advantages for S. An appeal by the Secretary of State was dismissed. See also *Re I (Adoption: Nationality)*.[145]

Re B (Adoption Order: Nationality)[146]

2.93   When B was 14, she and her mother, who lived in impoverished circumstances in Jamaica, came to stay with her maternal grandparents, having been granted 6 months' leave to enter the UK. When her mother returned to Jamaica, B remained with her grandparents, who applied for an extension to her visa. When the request was rejected, the grandparents applied to adopt her. By the time of the hearing B was 16 and the application was opposed by the Secretary of State. The House of Lords allowed an appeal from the decision of

---

[141]   [1994] 2 FLR 557, approved on this point by the House of Lords in *Re B (Adoption Order: Nationality)*.
[142]   *Re H (Adoption: Non-Patrial)* [1996] 2 FLR 187.
[143]   op cit per Lord Hoffman at 910.
[144]   [1996] 1 FLR 717, [1996] 2 FLR 187 CA.
[145]   [1998] 2 FLR 997.
[146]   [1999] 1 FLR 907.

the Court of Appeal which had overturned an order for adoption. A genuine transfer of parental responsibility was contemplated and it was in B's best interests to be adopted.

Re S and J (Adoption: Non-Patrials)[147]

2.94 The As brought their two half-nephews to England from Bangladesh in breach of immigration control. They were later convicted of immigration offences but no steps were taken to deport the boys. When the boys were 17 and 15, the As applied to adopt them. Despite active opposition from the Secretary of State and the fact that the older boy was about 6 weeks short of his eighteenth birthday, adoption orders were made. The applications were not a mere sham nor motivated as a device to evade immigration control. The boys had integrated well into the As' family and there was no realistic prospect of the younger boy wishing to return to Bangladesh. Adoption would provide short and long term emotional benefits.

2.95 The entry of children into the United Kingdom for the purpose of being adopted here is considered in more detail at **4.43**.

THE STATUS OF THE ADOPTED CHILD

2.96 From the date of the adoption order, by virtue of s 67(3) the adopted person is to be treated in law as if:

- born as the legitimate child of the adopters or adopter;[148] and

- (if adopted by a couple, or one of a couple under s 51(2)) as the child of the relationship of the couple in question;[149]

- as not being the child of any person other than the adopters, or as the case may be, the adopter or, if adopted by one of a couple under s 51(2), the adopter and the other one of the couple.[150]

2.97 It is important to note that this provision applies only to how the child is to be treated *in law*. Section 67(3) does not affect any reference in the Act to a person's natural parent or to any other natural relationship.[151]

---

[147] [2004] 2 FLR 111.
[148] ACA 2002, s 67(1), (2).
[149] Ibid, s 67(2).
[150] Ibid, s 67(3).
[151] Ibid, s 67(3).

EFFECT OF ADOPTION

Parental responsibility

2.98 The order gives parental responsibility for a child to the adopters[152] and extinguishes the parental responsibility which any person other than the adopters or adopter has for the adopted child immediately before the making of the order[153] save where the adopter is the partner of one of the child's parents.[154]

Termination of orders

2.99 The order extinguishes:

• any order under the 1989 Act, for example, a contact or residence order, special guardianship order or care order;[155]

• any order under the Children (Northern Ireland) Order 1995;[156]

• any order under the Children (Scotland) Act other than an excepted order;[157],[158] and

• any duty arising by virtue of an agreement or an order of a court to make payments, so far as the payments are in respect of the adopted child's maintenance or upbringing for any period after the making of the adoption order.[159]

Restrictions on applications for section 8 orders under the Children Act 1989

2.100 Once the adoption order is made, the birth parents and relatives cease to be treated in law as the parents/relatives[160] and will require the leave of the court to make an application for an order, for example, for contact, under s 8 of the Children Act 1989. See **13.150**.

---

[152] ACA 2002, s 46(1).
[153] Ibid, s 46(2)(a).
[154] Ibid, s 46(3)(b).
[155] Ibid, s 46(2)(b).
[156] Ibid.
[157] That is, an order under s 9, 11(1)(d) or 13 of the Children (Scotland) Act 1995 or an exclusion order within the meaning of s 76(1) of that Act.
[158] ACA 2002, s 46(2)(c).
[159] Ibid, s 46(2)(d).
[160] Ibid, s 67(3).

Citizenship and nationality

2.101 The making of an adoption order by a court in the UK or a court qualifying territory or the making of a Convention adoption order (see **4.35**) in respect of a child who is not a British citizen confers British citizenship and nationality on the child provided:

- the adopter or, in the case of a joint adoption, one of the adopters is a British citizen; and

- in the case of a Convention adoption the adopter or, in the case of a joint adoption, both of the adopters are habitually resident in the UK or in a designated territory.[161]

The status of citizenship is not affected by any cessation of the adoption order whether 'by annulment' or otherwise.[162]

2.102 The making of an adoption order does not deprive the child of citizenship.

2.103 The importance of this benefit and the immigration considerations are discussed in more detail at **2.88**.

Property

2.104 Where a child is adopted by one of his birth parents as a sole adoptive parent, ACA 2002,s 67(3)(b) (which provides the child is to be treated as the child of the adopter and of no one else – see **2.96**) has no effect as respects an entitlement to property which depends on relationship to that parent, or as respects anything else depending on that relationship.[163]

2.105 Section 67(3) has implications for potential inheritances and interests under trusts. An adopted child will be treated as a child born to the adopter and so, for example, will inherit under the terms of a will made by an adoptive grandparent which refers to bequests 'to my grand children'.

2.106 In order to deal with such implications ss 69 to 74 contain detailed rules of interpretation for 'instruments' (for example, deeds and wills, and defined as including a private Act settling property[164]) so far as it contains a disposition of property,[165] and other provisions relating to dispositions which depend on the date of birth,[166] property devolving with peerages, dignities and titles of

---

[161] British Nationality Act 1981(as amended) s 1(5), (5A).
[162] Ibid, s 1(6).
[163] ACA 2002, s 67(4).
[164] Ibid, s 69(3).
[165] Ibid, s 69.
[166] Ibid, s 70.

honour,[167] the protection of trustees and personal representatives,[168] pensions in payment[169] and insurance with a friendly society for the payment on the death of the child of money for funeral expenses.[170]

2.107 For the purpose of these provisions, a 'disposition' includes the conferring of a power of appointment and any other disposition of an interest in or right over property and any discretionary power to transfer a beneficial interest in property without the furnishing of valuable consideration.[171]

2.108 The main provisions can be briefly summarised as follows.

• In a disposition which depends on the date of birth of a child or children of the adoptive parent or parents, the disposition is to be interpreted as if the adopted person had been born on the date of adoption.[172] For example, a phrase in wills on which this can operate is 'children of A living at my death or born afterwards'.[173]

• The provision under s 67(3) that a child is to be treated in law as not the child of anyone other than the adopter does not prejudice any interest vested in possession in the adopted person before the adoption (a 'qualifying interest') or any interest expectant upon such an interest.[174] Therefore where a child's (P) great-grandmother died before the date of the adoption leaving half her estate to be held in trust for the child's mother (M) with the remainder to M's children living at her death and attaining the age of 18, the adoption of P did not affect P's contingent interest which arose out of M's interest which was vested in possession.[175]

• Where a disposition depends on the date of birth of a person who was born illegitimate and who is adopted by one of the natural parents as sole adoptive parent, entitlement by virtue of Part 3 of the Family Law Reform Act 1987 is not affected.[176] For example where a testator dies in 2001 bequeathing a legacy to his 'eldest grandchild living at a specified time' and (a) his unmarried daughter has a child in 2002 who is the first grandchild (b) his married son has a child in 2003 and (c) subsequently his unmarried daughter adopts her child as sole adoptive parent, the status of the daughter's child as the eldest grandchild of the testator is not affected by the events described in paragraphs (b) and (c).[177]

---

[167] ACA 2002, s 71.
[168] Ibid, s 72.
[169] Ibid, s 75.
[170] Ibid, s 76.
[171] Ibid, s 73(2).
[172] Ibid, s 69(2)(1).
[173] Ibid, s 69(3).
[174] Ibid, s 69(4).
[175] *Staffordshire CC v B* [1998] 1 FLR 261.
[176] ACA 2002, s 70(1).
[177] Ibid, s 70(2).

- An adoption does not affect the descent of any peerage or dignity or title of honour.[178]

- An adoption does not affect the devolution of any property limited (expressly or not) to devolve (as nearly as the law permits) along with any peerage or dignity or title of honour in so far as a contrary intention is not expressed in the terms of the instrument.[179]

- A trustee or personal representative is not under a duty, by virtue of the law relating to trusts or the administration of estates, to enquire, before conveying or distributing any property, whether any adoption has been effected or revoked if that fact could affect entitlement to the property.[180]

CONDITIONS AND THE USE OF CHILDREN ACT 1989 SECTION 8

2.109 Under the provisions of s 7(3) of the Adoption Act 1958 and later s 12(b) of the Adoption Act 1976, courts could impose conditions when making an adoption order. Although this power was originally introduced to deal with issues relating to the child's religion[181] and was apparently commonly used for this purpose,[182] it could also be used for other purposes such as securing contact between the child and his birth parents.[183] There were problems though about how such conditions could be enforced. The Acts contained no express sanction and although courts could request undertakings to comply with the conditions, they were understandably reluctant to do so.[184] In *Re S (A Minor) (Blood Transfusion: Adoption Under Conditions)*[185] the Court of Appeal discharged an undertaking given by adopters who were Jehovah Witnesses that they would consent to their adopted child being given blood transfusions who felt they had given the undertaking under duress:

> 'The best thing for the child in the ordinary way is that he or she should become as near as possible the lawful child of the adopting parents .... I would not require it as in any way appropriate to impose a condition which derogated from that and which made very little difference as to what would in fact happen, in circumstances which were in any event unlikely to rise.'[186]

---

[178] ACA 2002, s 71(1).
[179] Ibid, s 71(2), (3).
[180] Ibid, s 72(1).
[181] See Maidment 'Access and Family Adoptions' (1977) 40 Mod Law Rev 293.
[182] See *Re J (a minor) (adoption order: conditions)* [1973] 2 All ER 410 per Rees J at 418. Prior to 1957 a judge when granting an adoption order to two active communists, made it a condition that the child should be sent regularly to church and that the London County Council should be consulted on his education – James 'The Illegitimate and Deprived Child: Legitimation and Adoption' in Graveson and Crane (eds) *A Century of Family Law* (1957) p 52 n 3.
[183] Ibid.
[184] Ibid at 418.
[185] [1994] 2 FLR 416.
[186] Ibid, per Staughton LJ at 421.

2.110 Another means of enforcing a condition was to permit the use of wardship proceedings in order to give the court power to make an enforceable order.

2.111 With the advent of the Children Act 1989, a failure to comply with a condition or agreement for contact could be met by granting the birth parent leave to apply for a contact order under s 8.[187]

2.112 The 2002 Act contains no power to impose conditions. Nor is any necessary now that s 8 orders under 1989 Act are available and can be exercised in adoption proceedings of the court's own motion even though no application for such an order has been made.[188] If there is an immediate or likely problem regarding disputed medical treatment for the child, for example, a specific issue order could be made requiring the child to receive treatment. Where the problem is less likely to occur, as, for example, in *Re S (A Minor) (Blood Transfusion: Adoption Under Conditions)*,[189] it can be left to be to be dealt with in the same way as for any child who had not been adopted. As Staughton LJ noted in that case, there is a well established procedure for doctors to use when an urgent blood transfusion is required.

2.113 An example of a case where the immediate use of a specific issue order might be the unusual case where adoption is in the best interests of the child but the proposed adopters refuse to tell the child the truth about her paternity. In 1987 in *Re S (A Minor) (Adoption by Step-Parents)*[190] a girl, S, was fostered from birth and then adopted by A and her first husband, B. They later divorced and A married C. S treated C as her step-father and believed A and B to be her birth parents. When S was 13, A and C applied to adopt her but made it plain that they did not want to tell her the truth. Allowing the appeal from a refusal at first instance to grant an adoption order, the Court of Appeal held that despite the risk to the child if she was not told the truth about her origins, this was outweighed by the advantages of adoption. Given the courts' current stance on children knowing the truth as soon as possible (see **14.41**) it is possible for the court to make a s 8 order that the child be told and either grant the adoption order or adjourn the adoption proceedings until she is told.

INJUNCTIONS

2.114 In adoption proceedings the High Court and county court but not the family proceedings courts have power to grant interim injunctions (including before proceedings are commenced if the matter is urgent or it is otherwise desirable in the interests of justice)[191] or after judgment has been given.[192]

---

[187] *Re T (Adoption: Contact)* [1995] 2 FLR 251.
[188] ACA 2002, s 10(1)(b); CA 1989, s 8(3).
[189] [1994] 2 FLR 416.
[190] [1988] 1 FLR 418.
[191] Family Procedure (Adoption) Rules 2005, r 119(2)(b).
[192] Ibid, r 119(1).

2.115 The scope of this power is uncertain. Certainly it can be used as an interim measure, for example, to restrain attempts by the birth parents to contact the child or the prospective adopters during pending proceedings including appeals[193] but there is some doubt about whether, by itself, it can be used to grant an indefinite injunction. In *Re F (A Minor) (Adoption Order: Injunction)*[194] against a background of the birth father threatening the prospective adopters, Douglas Brown J granted an injunction unlimited in time, purportedly under s 37(1) of the Supreme Court Act 1981, which restrained both birth parents from communicating with the child or coming within 300 yards of any place where she may live with her adoptive parents. In *Re D (A Minor) (Adoption Order: Validity)*[195] the Court of Appeal held *Re F* had been decided in error. Section 37(1) could not be used for this purpose but only for the purpose of protecting legal and equitable rights. It did not confer jurisdiction to make an order restrain contact. However, in *Re O (Contempt: Committal)*[196] a differently constituted Court of Appeal refused an appeal against a committal order imposed on birth parents for breaching an injunction restraining contact with their adopted child without commenting on whether the injunction had been validly granted.[197]

2.116 Both *Re D (A Minor) (Adoption Order: Validity)* and *Re O (Contempt: Committal)* were decided after the commencement of the 1989 Act but the provisions of the Act were not discussed in either case and it may be that in similar circumstances a prohibited steps order could be granted, strengthened by an injunction or penal notice.

REVOCATION

2.117 An adoption order will cease to have effect if the child is again adopted.[198]

2.118 Where a child adopted by one birth parent as sole adoptive parent subsequently becomes a legitimated person on the marriage of the natural parents, the court by which the adoption order was made may, on the application of any of the parties concerned, revoke the order.[199]

2.119 Other than this, adoption orders cannot be revoked other than by way of appeal and (as is discussed at **2.124**) the appellate courts are very reluctant to set aside adoption orders unless natural justice requires it. In *Re B (Adoption*

---

[193] See for example *Re R (Identification: Restriction on Publication)* [2007] EWHC 2742 (Fam), [2008] 1 FLR 1252 and **7.90**.

[194] [1990] 2 FLR 478.

[195] [1991] 2 FLR 66.

[196] [1995] 2 FLR 767.

[197] See *Re X (A Minor) (Adoption Details: Disclosure)* [1994] 2 FLR 450 and *Re W (Adoption Details: Disclosure)* [1998] 2 FLR 625 and **9.118** for a discussion of the power to prevent the disclosure of information from the Adoption Register by the Registrar General.

[198] ACA 2002, ss 46(2), 44(5).

[199] Ibid, s 55(1).

Setting Aside)[200] for example, the Court of Appeal refused to set aside an adoption order on an appeal brought by the adopted person more than 35 years earlier.

2.120 B had been adopted at the age of 3 months by an orthodox Jewish couple, and brought up as a Jew. In reality, his father was a Muslim Arab from Kuwait, and his mother was a Roman Catholic. The appellant wished to settle in Israel, but was suspected of being an Arab spy and was asked to leave. He was also unable to settle in Kuwait. Having discovered his true origins, he applied to have the adoption order set aside. Sir Thomas Bingham MR commented that 'the act of adoption has always been regarded in this country as possessing a peculiar finality'.[201] The order had been properly made and to invalidate it would undermine the whole basis of intended finality on which orders were made.

APPEALS

2.121 The general procedures relating to appeals (see Chapter 19) apply to adoption although appeals have to be brought within 14 days[202] as opposed to the usual 21 days. The court may extend the time for appealing.[203]

2.122 The appellate court has the same powers as and can affirm, set aside or vary any order made by the lower court.[204]

2.123 The jurisdiction of the appellate court is the same as for other cases. Every appeal is limited to a review of the decision of the lower court unless the court considers that in the circumstances of the individual appeal it would be in the interests of justice to hold a rehearing.

2.124 The Court of Appeal has stressed the special nature of adoption and this is borne in mind whenever an appeal against an adoption order is made.

> 'An adoption order has a quite different standing to almost every other order made by a court. It provides the status of the adopted child and of the adoptive parents. The effect of an adoption order is to extinguish any parental responsibility of the natural parents. Once an adoption order has been made, the adoptive parents stand to one another and the child in precisely the same relationship as if they were his legitimate parents, and the child stands in the same relationship to them as to legitimate parents. Once an adoption order has been

---

[200] [1995] 2 FLR 1. See also *Re M (Adoption or Residence Order)* [1998] 1 FLR 570 per Ward LJ at 589D.
[201] Ibid, at 10.
[202] Family Procedure (Adoption) Rules 2005, r 174.
[203] Ibid, r 176.
[204] See ibid, r 180.

made the adopted child ceases to be the child of his previous parents and becomes the child for all purposes of the adopters as though he were their legitimate child.'[205]

'The act of adoption has always been regarded in this country as possessing a peculiar finality. This is partly because it affects the status of the person adopted, and indeed adoption modifies the most fundamental of human relationships, that of parent and child. It effects a change intended to be permanent and concerning three parties. The first of these are the natural parents of the adopted person, who by adoption divest themselves of all rights and responsibilities in relation to that person. The second party is the adoptive parents, who assume the rights and responsibilities of parents in relation to the adopted person. And the third party is the subject of the adoption, who ceases in law to be the child of his or her natural parents and becomes the child of the adoptive parents.'[206]

2.125 To allow an appeal is to remove a status thought to be permanent, risking distress, confusion and uncertainty to the child and the adopters. Two matters flow from this consideration. Time limits for appealing will be more strictly observed and the court will be less willing to exercise the wide discretion given by CPR r 52(11) to allow the decision because it was 'wrong'. An error of law will provide proper grounds of appeal as will a failure of natural justice,[207] for example a person with a right to be heard, not being given notice of the hearing, or an order obtained by fraud.[208] However, an adoption order validly and regularly obtained will not be disturbed.[209] Strictly speaking, this proposition may be disregarded in such an exceptional case that the Court of Appeal may designate the decision as 'in no way a precedent'.[210]

2.126 *Re K (Adoption and Wardship)*[211] is an example of what can go wrong when the proper procedural steps are not followed. The case concerned a young girl, brought to the jurisdiction by an English couple from a Bosnian orphanage. By the time of the adoption she had a Bosnian guardian and it was known that the child's grandfather and aunt had wanted her returned to them. The Court of Appeal held that the procedure had been 'fatally flawed' and set aside the adoption order which had been made in the county court. The case should have been transferred to the High Court; the court should have appointed a guardian and the Bosnian guardian should have been contacted; the Home Office, having granted leave for the child to remain in England had not been served with the proceedings; there was no firm evidence that the child's parents had died; the adoption application did not set out in detail the process by which the child was brought to England nor was the history investigated. Butler-Sloss LJ observed that 'the procedural irregularities go far

---

[205] *Re B (Adoption Setting Aside)* [1995] 2 FLR 1 per Swinton Thomas LJ at 4.
[206] Ibid, per Sir Thomas Bingham MR at 10. See **2.119**.
[207] For example, *Re K (Adoption and Wardship* [1997 2 FLR 221.
[208] *Re B (Adoption: Setting Aside)* [1995] 2 FLR 1 per Sir Thomas Bingham MR at 10.
[209] *Webster v Norfolk County Council and the Children (By Their Children's Guardian)* [2009] EWCA Civ 59, [2009] 1 FLR 1378 per Wall LJ at at [160].
[210] *Re M (Minors) (Adoption)* [1991] 1 FLR 458 per Glidewell LJ at 459 and Butler-Sloss LJ at 460.
[211] [1997] 2 FLR 221.

beyond the cosmetic ... The welfare of the child herself dictated that proper steps should be taken to balance the natural family with the prospective adoptive family, at the very least.'[212]

2.127 In *Webster v Norfolk County Council and the Children (By Their Children's Guardian)*[213] the Court of Appeal refused to set aside care orders and placement orders made 4 years previously on the ground that one of the children, B, (then aged 2) had suffered fractures caused by one or other of his parents. At the time of the appeal the children were aged 8, 7 and 5 and had been adopted 3 years previously. Notwithstanding fresh evidence which might show that B's injuries had been caused by scurvy and that if this was correct, the parents had suffered a serious injustice, it was impossible to set the orders aside.

> 'In my judgment ... the public policy considerations relating to adoption, and the authorities on the point – which are binding on this court – simply make it impossible for this court to set aside the adoption orders even if, as Mr and Mrs Webster argue, they have suffered a serious injustice. This is a case in which the court has to go back to first principles. Adoption is a statutory process. The law relating to it is very clear. The scope for the exercise of judicial discretion is severely curtailed. Once orders for adoption have been lawfully and properly made, it is only in highly exceptional and very particular circumstances that the court will permit them to be set aside.[214]

2.128 In *Re M (Minors) (Adoption)*[215] the Court of Appeal set aside adoption orders made in favour of the mother of two girls aged 12 and 11 and her new husband with the consent of the girls' father. Three months later the mother died. Their step-father/adoptive father was unable to look after them whereas their birth father could. The father's consent had been given in ignorance of the mother's condition and it was in the girls' interests to set aside the orders. These were very exceptional circumstances and 'this is in no way a precedent for any other adoption case'.[216]

---

[212] [1997] 2 FLR 221 at 228.
[213] [2009] EWCA Civ 59, [2009] 1 FLR 1378.
[214] Ibid, per Wall LJ at [148]–[149].
[215] [1991] 1 FLR 458.
[216] Ibid, per Butler-Sloss LJ at 460.

Chapter 3

PLACEMENT ORDERS AND PARENTAL CONSENT

INTRODUCTION

3.1 A local authority or adoption agency may ('is authorised to') place a child for adoption or, where it has placed him with any persons, leave him with them as prospective adopters only if:

- the child is less than 6 weeks old;[1] or

- it is satisfied that each parent or guardian has consented to:
  - the child being placed with prospective adopters identified in the consent; or
  - has consented to the child being placed for adoption with any prospective adopters who may be chosen by the agency,
  - and has not withdrawn the consent;[2] or

- a placement order is in force.[3]

3.2 A placement order is one of the keys to simplifying the adoption process and reducing delays. It enables an agency to find prospective adopters for the child and to place him with them for adoption in the knowledge that, save in exceptional circumstances, the parents or guardian may not be able to oppose adoption.

3.3 A placement order can be revoked provided the application is made before the child is placed for adoption, but a parent or guardian will require leave to apply for revocation.[4] A parent or guardian who has previously consented to his child being adopted or whose child has been placed for adoption under a placement order is not allowed to oppose an adoption application without obtaining the court's leave, which can be granted only if it is in the child's interests and there has been a change in circumstances since the consent was given or placement order made.[5]

---

[1] Adoption and Children Act 2002 (ACA 2002), s 18(1).
[2] Ibid, s 19(1).
[3] Ibid, s 18(1).
[4] Ibid, s 24(2).
[5] Ibid, s 47(3), (5) and (7).

3.4 A child cannot be adopted without his parents or guardian having previously consented (or their consent being dispensed with and a placement order made) unless the court in the adoption proceedings dispenses with their consent.

'PARENTS OR GUARDIANS'

3.5 The various sections of the Act which deal with placement, placement orders and consent refer to 'the parent or guardian'. This phrase has a uniform meaning.

Parent

3.6 A 'parent' means a parent with parental responsibility.[6] If a father acquires parental responsibility at any time before an adoption order is made, his consent to adoption will be required. However, this is subject to an important exception. If the agency places the child for adoption under the 2002 Act, s 19, ie with the consent of Parent A, and the other parent (B) later acquires parental responsibility, B will be treated as if he had consented in the same terms as A.[7] This means that the acquisition of parental responsibility after the making of a placement order will not give B the right to refuse consent to an adoption (as opposed to opposing the order).[8]

3.7 Fathers without parental responsibility should therefore endeavour to obtain it under s 4 of the Children Act 1989 as soon as possible and in any event before the mother consents to the child being placed. Even if there is little prospect of parental responsibility being exercised, so long as the 1989 Act welfare test is satisfied[9] it may still be appropriate to grant it to enable a father to oppose the making of a placement or adoption order[10] but the court retains a discretion and a grant is not guaranteed.[11]

Guardian

3.8 A 'guardian' means a guardian appointed under s 5 of the Children Act 1989 ('the 1989 Act')[12] or a special guardian.[13]

---

[6] ACA 2002, s 52(6).
[7] Ibid, s 52(9) and (10).
[8] See ibid, s 47(4)(c).
[9] As explained in *Re H (Illegitimate Children: Parental Rights) (No 2)* [1991] 1 FLR 214.
[10] *Re H (Illegitimate Children: Father: Parental Rights) (No 2)* [1991] 1 FLR 214. Parental responsibility was granted by the Court of Appeal even though it in effect dispensed with his consent to the freeing order on the ground it was being unreasonably withheld.
[11] *W v Ealing London Borough Council* [1993] 2 FLR 788. The Court of Appeal dismissed an appeal against a refusal to grant parental responsibility.
[12] ACA 2002, s 144(1); CA 1989, s 105(1).
[13] ACA 2002, s 144(1).

3.9 The equivalent provision in the Adoption Act 1976[14] had included the words 'unless the context otherwise requires.' This was interpreted on a number of occasions at first instance[15] as including a person or organisation invested with parental rights under the law of the local jurisdiction[16] but not where the role was more akin to that of a local authority under a care order.[17] However, the words 'unless the context otherwise requires' do not occur in ACA 2002, s 144(1) and the earlier authorities may not apply. Bridge and Swindells[18] suggest that it may still be arguable that a broader construction of 'guardian' should be applied. Professor Lowe[19] is more definite. Relying both on Brussels II Revised[20] under which European Member States have to recognise and enforce, subject to a few exceptions, orders made (or legally binding agreements reached) in another Member State which concern parental responsibility and also on the wider considerations of comity, he argues that 'the 2002 Act should be interpreted as preserving the position that a foreign-appointed guardian is indeed a "guardian" for the purposes of adoption'. Had Parliament intended that a foreign-appointed guardian should be excluded from the definition, 'it would surely have done so by making a significantly more specific definition'.

3.10 In this chapter, the use of the word 'parent' will include 'guardian' unless the context makes it clear otherwise.

PLACEMENT ORDERS

3.11 A placement order is an order authorising a local authority (nb not a non-authority agency) to place a child for adoption with any prospective adopters it may chose.[21]

---

[14] ACA 2002, s 72(1).

[15] But not by Holman J in *Re D (Adoption Foreign Guardianship)* [1999] 2 FLR 865 – while it may be appropriate to give the word 'guardian' a wider definition, nothing in the wording of the Act required such a definition to be applied (Romanian hospital given parental rights under a Romanian court order was not a 'guardian').

[16] *Re AGN (Adoption: Foreign Adoption)* [2000] 2 FLR 431 (parental rights vested in an orphanage); *Re AMR (Adoption: Procedure)* [1999] 2 FLR 807 (great grand-mother appointed guardian by a Polish court). *Re J (Adoption: Consent of Foreign Public Authority)* [2002] EWHC 766 (Fam), [2002] 2 FLR 618 (Jordanian orphanage).

[17] *Re J (Adoption: Consent of Foreign Public Authority)* [2002] EWHC 766 (Fam), [2002] 2 FLR 618. Child in Jordanian orphanage, not placed as a result of a court order. The court dispensed with the consent of the natural parents on the ground that they could not be found.

[18] *Adoption: the Modern Law* (2003) at para 15.64.

[19] *Do Foreign-Appointed Guardians Qualify as 'Guardians' for the Purposes of the Adoption and Children Act 2002?* [2008] Fam Law 163.

[20] Regulation (EC) No 1347/2000 (2003) OJ L 338/1.

[21] ACA 2002, s 21(1).

Effect of a placement order

Parental responsibility

3.12

- Parental responsibility is given to the local authority.[22]

- The child is to be treated as if it is being looked after by the authority under CA 1989, s 22.[23]

- The authority may decide that the parental responsibility of a parent, guardian, special guardian or prospective adopter is restricted to the extent it may specify.[24]

- A guardian may not remove the child from the UK.[25]

Orders ceasing to have effect

3.13

- Any order made under CA 1989, s 8, ie a residence, contact, specific issue or prohibited steps order, ceases to have effect.[26]

- Any supervision order ceases to have effect.[27]

- Any care order ceases to have effect while the placement order is in force.[28]

- Any order for contact made under CA 1989, s 34(2).[29]

Restrictions on orders which may be made

3.14

- No prohibited steps, specific issue, supervision or child assessment order may be made.[30]

- A residence order may be made only if an adoption application has been made and the application is made by a parent or guardian who has

---

[22]   ACA 2002, s 25(1)(b).
[23]   Ibid, s 18(3).
[24]   Ibid, ss 25(4), 29(6).
[25]   Ibid, s 29(7)(b).
[26]   Ibid, s 29(2).
[27]   Ibid, s 29(2).
[28]   Ibid, s 29(1).
[29]   Ibid, s 26(1). The making of a freeing order terminated any care order – Adoption Act 1976, s 20(3A), *Re G (Adoption: Freeing Order)* [1997] 2 FLR 202.
[30]   ACA 2002, s 29(3).

obtained leave to oppose an adoption order under ACA 2002, s 47(3) or (5) or by anyone who has obtained leave under s 29(5).[31]

- A special guardianship order may only be made if an application has been made for an adoption order and the person applying for the special guardianship order has obtained the leave of the court under s 29(5) or, if a guardian, has obtained leave under s 47(5).[32]

Placement for adoption

3.15 The local authority or an agency may place the child for adoption with prospective adopters without the consent of his parents.[33] 'Place for adoption' includes placing a child with a view to his being adopted outside England and Wales[34] although the proposed adopters will need to be granted parental responsibility under s 84(1) in order to avoid committing an offence under s 85. In addition, if the child is to leave the jurisdiction for more than one month, the agency also requires the consent of the court under s 28(3) unless all parents and guardians consent, and the proposed adopters. Upon placement, the proposed adopters acquire parental responsibility[35] – see **7.195**.

Contact

3.16

- Any order for contact made under s 8[36] or s 34(2)[37] of CA 1989 ceases to have effect.

- The requirement imposed under s 34 of the 1989 Act on a local authority to allow parents, guardians and specified others reasonable contact with a child subject to a care order ceases to have effect.[38]

- No application for a s 8 contact order may be made.[39]

- The following people may apply for a contact order under ACA 2002, s 26(3) or such an order may be made by the court of its own initiative when making a placement order:[40]
  - the child or the agency;

---

[31] ACA 2002, s 29(5).
[32] Ibid. The applicant has to give notice of an intention to apply under CA 1989, s 14A(7) but not 3 months' notice – ACA 2002, s 29(6).
[33] Ibid, s 18(1).
[34] *Re S (Freeing for Adoption)* [2002] EWCA Civ 798, [2002] 2 FLR 681, *Re A (Adoption: Placement Outside Jurisdiction)* [2004] EWCA Civ 515, [2004] 2 FLR 337.
[35] ACA 2002, s 25(3).
[36] Ibid, s 29(2).
[37] Ibid, s 26(1).
[38] Ibid, s 29(1).
[39] Ibid, s 26(2).
[40] Ibid, s 26(4).

- a parent, guardian or relative;[41]
- any person in whose favour a section 8 contact order had been in force which ceased to have effect because of s 26(10);
- the person in whose favour a residence order was in force immediately before an agency as authorised to place the child for adoption (ie under a placement order or with the consent of the parents) or, if the child as under the age of 6 weeks, the child as placed for adoption;
- the person who had the care of the child under the High Court's inherent jurisdiction immediately before an agency as authorised to place the child for adoption;
- any person with leave.

3.17   Contact orders under s 26 are discussed in detail at **13.112**.

Effect when an adoption application is made

3.18

• The consent of the parents to the application being granted is not required.[42]

• The parents are made respondents to the application.[43]

• However, they may not oppose the making of the order without leave,[44] see **3.145**.

Background

3.19   Until the Children Act 1975, there was no way in which the issue of a parent's consent or opposition to adoption could be resolved prior to the issue of an adoption application, much less the child being placed with a prospective couple.

3.20   In 1972 the *Report of the Departmental Committee on the Adoption of Children*[45] recorded 'considerable dissatisfaction' with the situation. Although there was never a period when the child was not the legal responsibility of either birth or adoptive parents, the procedure imposed unnecessary confusion and strain on the birth mother and might encourage her to be indecisive and prevent her from facing the reality of her decision. There were also obvious disadvantages for the adoptive parents. The child's future remained in doubt

---

[41]   Defined as a grandparent, brother, sister, uncle or aunt whether of the full-blood or half-blood or by marriage – ACA 2002, s 144(1).
[42]   Ibid, s 47(4).
[43]   Family Procedure (Adoption) Rules 2005 (FP(A)R 2005), SI 2005/2795, r 23, Table 2.
[44]   ACA 2002, s 47(5).
[45]   'The Houghton Committee' Cmnd 5107 (1972) at paras 168–172.

and although the risks of his being removed were small, the knowledge that this was possible could make them anxious and even make them hesitate to give the child total commitment.

3.21 In addition, the Committee noted the growing belief that adoption could provide a secure permanent future for a sizeable number of children who were in care either of local authorities or voluntary agencies for whom no such future could currently be arranged because parents could not bring themselves to make a plan or refused to consent to adoption even though they were unable to look after the child. Under the existing law there was no way of testing whether the parents' refusal of consent was unreasonable without first placing the child with prospective adopters and taking the risk that parents might remove the child.[46]

3.22 The Committee therefore recommended that:

- parents should be able to relinquish their rights by an application to the court made jointly with an adoption agency,[47] the rights then vesting in the agency;

- a local authority or agency should be able to apply to a court for the transfer of parental rights to the agency with a view to the child's adoption.[48]

3.23 The Recommendations were accepted and s 14–16 of the Children Act 1975 created a 'freeing order'.

3.24 Experience of the procedure revealed a number of problems. The process of 'freeing' was not mandatory. Some authorities were reluctant to use it because, if the child had not been placed for adoption they could not give evidence about the stability of the relationship between prospective adopters and the child. Others issued freeing applications even after the child had been placed for adoption. Prospective adopters in such cases had the double disadvantage of possibly being called as a witness but without party status or their own legal representation. Procedural rules made it difficult for courts to consider contact at the same time as a freeing application. The status of the freed child was unclear and might be described as being in a 'legal limbo'. At the same time, researchers found there were advantages to freeing, most notably that it removed worry and anxiety about the adoption process from adopters.[49]

---

[46] The Houghton Committee op cit at paras 221–224.
[47] Ibid, para 191.
[48] Ibid, para 225.
[49] *Interdepartmental Review of Adoption Law: Discussion Paper Number 2: Agreement and Freeing* (Department of Health, 1991) at paras 106–179.

3.25   In 1992 *The Review of Adoption Law*[50] recommended that freeing should be abolished and replaced by a placement order which would be a compulsory pre-requisite to a child being placed for adoption in all cases where parents were opposing adoption. The process would enable the court to examine the options available before it became effectively too late for alternative arrangements to be made. However, in an important aspect it differed from the concept of placement orders introduced by the 2002 Act. The court was to examine the issues in the context of a particular proposed placement to prevent the court contrasting 'the readily apparent shortcomings' in the care offered or likely to be offered by the parents with the care likely to be offered by 'hypothetically perfect adoptive parents'. This feature was missing from the Adoption Bill submitted for consultation.[51]

3.26   The *Prime Minister's Review: Adoption*[52] identified inconsistent use of freeing orders as one of the causes of delay in the adoption process.

> 'Freeing can speed the eventual adoption proceedings but it can be a lengthy legal process in itself. It is therefore clearly preferable that, where Freeing is appropriate, it should, wherever possible, happen simultaneously with the Care order rather than sequentially.'[53]

Moreover the current legal framework did not allow consent to be handled in the most effective way. Three-quarters of freeing applications were formally contested although only a fifth (22%) were actively opposed.[54] More sensitively worded consent forms could help parents to agree to their child being adopted and where they did so, the child could be placed for adoption without a placement order.

3.27   The White Paper – *Adoption: A New Approach*[55] did not discuss placement orders but the proposals in the Adoption and Children Bill were recognised as 'probably the most significant change' in adoption law which would make it commonplace for applications for placement orders to be brought within care proceedings.[56]

Article 8

3.28   Provided the statutory procedure had been observed, the grant of a freeing order could be justified under Art 8(2) of the European Convention as

---

[50]   *Report to Ministers of an Interdepartmental Working Group* (Department of Health, 1992) paras 14.3–17.7.
[51]   *Adoption – A Service for Children* (Department of Health, 1996). The *Prime Minister's Review* (see below) firmly stamped on this suggestion – at para 7.7.
[52]   Performance and Innovation Unit (2000).
[53]   Ibid, para 3.59.
[54]   Ibid, para 3.64.
[55]   Cm 5017 (2000).
[56]   Cullen 'Adoption – a (fairly) new approach' [2005] CFLQ 475 at pp 482–483.

necessary in a democratic society.[57] There is no reason to suppose that the position is any different for a placement order.

The duty of an authority to apply for a placement order

3.29 A local authority must apply to the court for a placement order in respect of a child if it is satisfied that the child ought to be placed for adoption and either:

- the child is placed for adoption by them or is being provided with accommodation by them; or

- no adoption agency is authorised to place the child for adoption; or

- the child has no parent or guardian or the authority consider that the conditions in CA 1989, s 31(2) are met;[58] or

- an application has been made (and has not been disposed of) under CA 1989, s 31; or

- a child is subject to a care order and the appropriate local authority are not authorised to place the child for adoption.[59]

3.30 If a child is subject to a care order and the appropriate local authority[60] are authorised to place the child for adoption under ACA 2002, s 19, the authority may apply to the court for a placement order.[61]

3.31 However, the above provisions of s 22 do not apply if:

- any person has given notice of intention to adopt the child unless the period of 4 months beginning with the giving of the notice has expired without them applying for an adoption order or their application for such an order has been withdrawn or refused; or

- an application for an adoption order has been made and has not been disposed of.[62]

3.32 Conversely, an authority may not apply for a placement order until it is satisfied that the child ought to be placed for adoption. It can only be satisfied after the matter has been referred to the authority's adoption panel under

---

[57]   *Scott v UK* ECHR Case 34745/97, [2000] 1 FLR 958. *Down Lisburn Health and Social Services Trust v H* [2006] UKHL 36, [2007] 1 FLR 11 per Baroness Hale of Richmond at [34] – see **3.139**.

[58]   ACA 2002, s 22(1).

[59]   Ibid, s 22(2).

[60]   Defined in ibid, s 22(7) as the authority to whom the care order has been made or who is making a s 31 application.

[61]   Ibid, s 22(3).

[62]   Ibid, s 22(5).

reg 17 of the Adoption Agencies Regulations 2005 and the authority has taken the panel's recommendation into account under reg 19(1).[63] The Panel must also be supplied with all relevant information including expert reports or an accurate summary of such reports.[64] Whether or not a failure to comply with the Regulations will render any placement order void or lead inevitably to it being set aside on appeal is uncertain.[65] It will certainly render it vulnerable to appeal. In *Re B (Placement Order)*[66] the authority failed to provide the Panel with paediatric, child psychiatric and psychological reports, one of which had indicated that the children had responded well to foster care and stated that it was not possible to be prescriptive about contact arrangements. The summary of the reports which was given to the Panel mistakenly misrepresented that adoption had been recommended. Despite misgivings because of the delay which would result, the order was set aside and the application adjourned for the matter to be considered properly by the Panel.

3.33   The involvement of the Panel is discussed in detail at **7.104**.

The child's position pending the hearing

3.34   If a local authority is under a duty to apply for a placement order or has applied and the application has not been disposed of, the child is to be treated as if it is being looked after by the authority under CA 1989, s 22.[67]

Requirements for placement orders

3.35   The court may not make a placement order in respect of a child unless:

• the child is subject to a care order;

• the court is satisfied that the conditions in section 31(2) of the Children Act 1989 (conditions for making a care order) are satisfied; or

• the child has no parent[68] or guardian;[69,70] *and*

• the court is satisfied that:

---

[63]   *Re P-B (Placement Order)* [2006] EWCA Civ 1016, [2007] 1 FLR 1106, *Re S (Placement Order: Revocation)* [2008] EWCA Civ 1333, [2009] 1 FLR 503.

[64]   *Re B (Placement Order)* [2008] EWCA Civ 835, [2008] 2 FLR 1404 at [81].

[65]   *Re P-B (Placement Order)* [2006] EWCA Civ 1016, [2007] 1 FLR 1106 per Arden LJ at [37] and *Re B (Placement Order)* [2008] EWCA Civ 835, [2008] 2 FLR 1404 per Wall LJ at [36].

[66]   Ibid.

[67]   ACA 2002, s 22(4).

[68]   ACA 2002, s 52(6) does not apply so the word has its normal meaning and is not restricted to only a parent with parental responsibility.

[69]   'Guardian' includes special guardian: ACA 2002, s 144(1).

[70]   Ibid, s 21(2).

- each parent[71] has consented to the child being placed for adoption with any prospective adopters who may be chosen by the authority *and* has not withdrawn the consent; or
- it should dispense with the parent's consent.[72]

Applications for care orders and placement orders

3.36 Save where certain conditions are met, a placement order may not be made unless the child is subject to a care order[73] and in many cases applications for care orders and placement orders are and, in order to avoid unnecessary delay, should be heard together. The application for a care order will be the primary application.[74] The Family Justice Council has provided guidance on linked care and placement order applications.[75] Care and placement order proceedings are likely to be inappropriate in cases where the only parent with parental responsibility is willing to consent to placement for adoption.[76]

3.37 Because the care proceedings may have been listed for hearing shortly after the filing of assessment reports and the recommendation of the adoption panel, the application for a placement order may be issued only days before the hearing. There is normally no objection to this provided the guardian has had an opportunity of considering the matter and the parents have been given proper notice of the authority's intention. In *Re P-B (Placement Order)*,[77] for example, the Court of Appeal held that because the authority had clearly signalled their intention to pursue adoption and to issue an application for a placement order if and when the Panel approved the plan, it was hard to identify what benefit would be denied the mother or prejudice be caused by hearing the application as soon as it was issued, on the third day of the hearing of the care application.

3.38 Although a single judgment is often given at a joint hearing, the Court will need to ensure that the correct statutory tests, which differ, are applied correctly to each application. The following issues should be considered:[78]

- Is the section 31 Children Act 1989 test satisfied?

---

[71] For the purpose of this 'parent' means a parent with parental responsibility – ACA 2002, s 21(3) and s 52(6). See **3.6**.

[72] Ibid, s 21(3).

[73] Ibid, s 21(2).

[74] *Re D (Simultaneous Applications for Care Order and Freeing Order)* [1992] 2 FLR 49 and *Re M (Care Order: Freeing Application)* [2003] EWCA Civ 1874, [2004] 1 FLR 826.

[75] *Linked Care and Placement Order Applications: Updated Guidance* July 2007 at http://www.family-justice-council.org.uk/docs/ 080707_Linked_Care_and_Placement_Order_Proceedings.pdf.

[76] *C v XYZ County Council* [2007] EWCA Civ 1206, [2008] 1 FLR 1294 at [6], [22], [68]–[69].

[77] [2006] EWCA Civ 1016, [2007] 1 FLR 1106.

[78] *Re M (Care Order: Freeing Application)* [2003] EWCA Civ 1874, [2004] 1 FLR 826 per Ward LJ at [21]. The order of steps given in the judgment has been slightly amended to include questions which were implied in the judgment.

- Where should the child live? ('The essential question').

- If a ready and convincing answer to the preceding question is not available on the current evidence, would an adjournment secure evidence which would resolve any doubts and difficulties?[79]

- Applying the CA 1989, s 1 test, what order, if any, should be made:
  - care order;
  - supervision order;
  - s 8 residence order;
  - special guardianship order; or
  - no order?

- Should the care plan be approved?

3.39 If a care order is made:

- In the light of the circumstances both in which the care order was made and generally, is it in the child's best interests, applying the ACA 2002, s 1(2) test, to be placed for adoption?

- Do the parents consent or should the court dispense with their consent?

3.40 The available possible options for the court (for example, living with a member of the extended family) should be considered as early in the proceedings as possible so that assessments of viable carers can take place without delaying the decision (see **12.65**). Where proposals are made late (even at the final hearing itself), the court should consider adjourning the proceedings for the assessment to take place and may be required to do so notwithstanding the delay which will be caused.[80] In other cases the judge may have sufficient objective evidence to show that the proposal is not viable.[81]

The test

3.41 The test is the welfare test set out in ACA 2002, s 1(1). The paramount consideration of the court or adoption agency must be the child's welfare throughout his life (see **6.9**). The court has to consider all the circumstances including the matters set out in the s 1(4) checklist (see **6.42**). In addition it must bear in mind at all times that, in general, delay in coming to a decision is likely to prejudice the child's welfare[82] (see **6.18**).

---

[79]   Logically, this is the second question and not the third (as given in *Re M (Care Order: Freeing Application)*).

[80]   For example, *Re A (a child) (care order)* [2006] All ER (D) 247 (Oct) and *Re M-H (Assessment: Father of Half-Brother)* [2006] EWCA Civ 1864, [2007] 1 FLR 1715.

[81]   For example, *G and B (Children)* [2007] EWCA Civ 358, [2007] 2 FLR 140.

[82]   ACA 2002, s 1(3).

3.42 On occasions the extreme difficulties of the child and his need for 'extraordinary' care may make it uncertain whether the authority will be able to find suitable adopters, notwithstanding that adoption is the ideal solution. Mere uncertainty as to whether adoption is possible or even a real possibility that it is not, is not a reason for refusing a placement order. It can be made even if much investigation and preparation are needed before a family can be found and approved and the child placed with them.[83]

3.43 This is to be distinguished though from the situation where the child is not currently suitable for adoption. Where this is so, a placement order cannot be made.[84]

> '[It] is an insufficient foundation for a placement order that the long-term aim of the court is that the child should be adopted. The necessary foundation is that – broadly speaking – the child is presently in a condition to be adopted and is ready to be adopted, even though in some cases the court has to countenance the possibility of substantial difficulty and thus delay in finding a suitable adoptive placement or even of failure to find one at all.'[85]

3.44 Whilst there are 'very substantial differences – both philosophical and practical' between adoption and long-term fostering, the Court of Appeal in *Re P (Placement Orders: Parental Consent)*[86] said that a local authority can be 'satisfied that the child ought to be placed for adoption'[87] even though it recognises the reality that a search for adoptive parents may be unsuccessful and that, if it is, the alternative plan will have to be for long-term fostering. There can moreover, be compelling pragmatic reasons for adopting 'dual planning' in appropriate cases.

3.45 Peggy Ray[88] has criticised such an approach, drawing attention to the significant differences between a care order and a placement order in relation to the exercise of parental responsibility, contact, the ability to apply for a revocation of a care order, the framework of 'Looked After' Reviews and the involvement of Independent Reviewing Officers ('IRO') (see **15.59**). She suggests the following:

- a preamble to the placement order to the effect that if the search for an adoptive placement is given up or at the end of a stated period without a placement being identified, the agency will consider applying to revoke the placement order;

---

[83]   *Re T (Placement Order)* [2008] EWCA Civ 248, [2008] 1 FLR 1721.

[84]   Ibid. The facts and decision in *Re T* can be contrasted with those in *Re P (Placement Orders: Parental Consent)* [2008] EWCA Civ 535, [2008] 2 FLR 625.

[85]   *NS-H v Kingston Upon Hull City Council and MC* [2008] EWCA Civ 493, [2008] 2 FLR 918 per Wilson LJ at [28].

[86]   [2008] EWCA Civ 535, [2008] 2 FLR 625 per Wall LJ at [135]–[140]. See also *Cardiff County Council v M* (unreported) 26 July 2008, [2008] Fam Law 75.

[87]   ACA 2002, s 22(1)(d).

[88]   *Placement Orders After Re P* (Lime Legal, 2008).

- making sure the care plan incorporates full participation by parents pending matching of an adoptive placement, as though under a care order;

- ensuring that the care plan and a transcript of the judgment is sent to the IRO.

Varying or revoking placement orders

Variation

3.46   A court may vary a placement order to substitute another local authority for the named one.[89] The application has to be made by both local authorities.[90]

Revocation

3.47   A court may revoke a placement order on an application made by:

- the child;[91]

- the local authority authorised by the order to place the child;[92]

- anyone else provided:
    - the child is not placed for adoption;[93]
    - the court is satisfied there has been a change of circumstances since the order was made;[94] and
    - the court has given leave.[95]

3.48   The court may also revoke the order if it has decided not to make an adoption order.[96]

3.49   The High Court had an inherent jurisdiction to revoke a freeing order even if there was no one entitled to apply for revocation.[97] There is no reason to suppose that the same power does not exist for placement orders even though there are fewer restrictions on applications than for revocation of freeing orders.

3.50   Mere placement of a child with foster carers who might decide to apply to adopt the child does not equate with the child being 'placed for adoption'. For that to be the case the prospective adopters have to be considered by the

---

[89]   ACA 2002, s 23(1).
[90]   Ibid, s 23(2).
[91]   Ibid, s 24(2).
[92]   Ibid.
[93]   Ibid, s 24(2)(b).
[94]   Ibid, s 24(3).
[95]   Ibid, s 24(2)(a).
[96]   Ibid, s 24(4).
[97]   *Re C (Adoption Freeing Order)* [1999] 1 FLR 348. See **3.57–3.59**.

Panel and approved by the agency as prospective adopters and the child's matching with them must likewise be considered and approved.[98]

3.51 If an application to revoke the order has been made and has not been disposed of, the child may not be placed for adoption without the leave of the court.[99] However, this does not preclude a placement where an application to apply for leave to apply for revocation is pending.[100] If such an application is pending it is normally good practice for a local authority either to agree not to place the child pending the application or at least give notice, say, of 14 days, of the intended placement to the applicant so that he can either take steps to challenge the decision to place by way of judicial review or, probably more easily, to seek to expedite the hearing of the application for leave.[101] To do otherwise risks the local authority's actions being condemned as 'disgraceful', 'an abuse of power' 'arrogant' and 'shoddy'.[102] The decision to place may very well be quashed on judicial review.[103]

Applying for leave

3.52 The welfare test does not govern the court's discretion to grant leave to apply for revocation.[104] The welfare of the child and the prospect of the application succeeding should both be weighed. In the vast majority of cases the court may usefully apply the test applicable to permission to appeal: does the application have 'a real prospect of success'? However, the required analysis of success might not always be carried out within an analysis of the prospects of success.[105]

Examples

M v Warwickshire CC[106]

3.53 On being informed that her children, aged 5 and 3, were about to be placed for adoption a year after placement orders had been made and 3 years after they had moved to short-term foster care, their mother, M, applied for leave. The Court of Appeal allowed an appeal against the order granting leave. Revocation would amount to a wholesale reversal of the care plan. Even if M were able to show she was no longer addicted to drugs, a full assessment of her

---

[98] *Re S (Placement Order: Revocation)* [2008] EWCA Civ 1333, [2009] 1 FLR 503.
[99] ACA 2002, s 24(5).
[100] *M v Warwickshire CC* [2007] EWCA Civ 1084, [2008] 1 FLR 1093, *Re F (Placement Order)* [2008] EWCA Civ 439, [2008] 2 FLR 550.
[101] *M v Warwickshire CC* [2007] EWCA Civ 1084, [2008] 1 FLR 1093 at [14].
[102] *Re F (Placement Order)* [2008] EWCA Civ 439, [2008] 2 FLR 550 at [37], [44], [79] and [102].
[103] Ibid at [36] The Court of Appeal did not consider the possibility that the child could be made a ward, thereby requiring the proposed adopters to seek leave to commence adoption proceedings. For a discussion of the possible use of the inherent jurisdiction when there is a placement order, see *NS-H v Kingston Upon Hull City Council and MC* [2008] EWCA Civ 493, [2008] 2 FLR 918 at [33].
[104] *M v Warwickshire CC* [2007] EWCA Civ 1084, [2008] 1 FLR 1093 at [22].
[105] Ibid.
[106] Ibid.

ability to look after them would be required. However, it was overwhelmingly unlikely that the court would adjourn the revocation proceedings to enable the assessment to take place because delay would be prejudicial to the children.

NS-H v Kingston Upon Hull City Council and MC[107]

3.54 When T was just over 2 years old he was removed from the care of his mother, M, because of his very low weight, thought to have been caused by profound psychological mistreatment by M. A placement order was made. T lost weight in his short term foster home and the authority decided to move him to another home, accepting that he could only be placed for adoption if he began to thrive. The Court of Appeal granted M leave to apply for the placement order to be revoked. It would occasionally be proper for the court to grant a parent leave to apply to revoke a placement order, notwithstanding the absence at present of any real prospect that a court would find it to be in the interests of the child to return to live with his parent. The question was whether in all the circumstances, including M's prospect of success in securing revocation of the placement order and T's interests, leave should be given. There was a real prospect that M could persuade the court that it was not currently appropriate for the placement order to remain in being. See also *Re S (Placement Order: Revocation)*.[108]

Test for revocation

3.55 The test to be applied when deciding whether to revoke the placement order is the s 1(2) welfare test. Unlike the position with freeing orders, when an application to revoke could be made only after a year from the making of the order, there is no such restriction in respect of placement orders.

3.56 In *Re G (Adoption: Freeing Order)*[109] the House of Lords made it clear that circumstances may change after an order is made and children should not remain in limbo.

> 'If the proposed adoption giving rise to the freeing order fails to materialise and there is no other proposed adoption pending, it is hard to accept that Parliament could have intended that the parent should continue to be deprived of all [parental rights] leaving the child in an indefinite adoptive limbo ... Circumstances may change. For example, if there has been continuing contact between the parent and child notwithstanding the freeing order, a bond may have developed between them. The situation may have developed in which some third party is prepared to provide satisfactory day-to-day care for the child whilst maintaining beneficial contact between the child and the parent.'[110]

---

[107] [2008] EWCA Civ 493, [2008] 2 FLR 918.
[108] [2008] EWCA Civ 1333, [2009] 1 FLR 503.
[109] [1997] 2 FLR 202.
[110] Ibid, per Lord Browne-Wilkinson at 208.

Examples

Re C (Adoption Freeing Order)[111]

3.57 C was freed for adoption when aged 7. By the time he was 15, he was living in a residential home, had not been adopted and there was no prospect of adoption. On the application of the local authority, the freeing order was revoked. 'It is clearly in C's best interests that his birth mother should regain her legal status as his mother.'

Re J (Freeing for Adoption)[112]

3.58 J had spent his life with a number of carers. Following a care order made when he was 6, a freeing order was made the following year. No adoptive family was found but when he was 8 the local authority found suitable permanent foster carers who lived in Scotland. His mother was unlikely to apply for the order to be revoked. On an application by the local authority (who could not apply for revocation because of the terms of the Adoption Act 1976), the order was revoked under the inherent jurisdiction, the prospect of adoption having been abandoned. It was clearly in J's interests to revive his legal relationship with his birth family. A care order would enable the local authority to provide a permanent placement by way of foster care.

Oldham MBC v D[113]

3.59 A freeing order was made in respect of M when he was a baby. Shortly afterwards, his father, who did not have parental responsibility, presented himself as a carer. The order was revoked under the inherent jurisdiction and a care order made to enable M to be placed with his father.

Effect of revocation

3.60

- Any care order which was in force when the placement order was made, revives.[114]

- Section 8 orders and supervision orders are not revived.[115]

---

[111] [1999] 1 FLR 348.
[112] [2000] 2 FLR 58.
[113] [2000] 2 FLR 382.
[114] ACA 2002, s 29(1). This was not the position with freeing orders – Adoption Act 1976, s 20(3A), *Re G (Adoption: Freeing Order)* [1997] 2 FLR 202.
[115] ACA 2002, s 29(2).

Termination of placement order

3.61 A placement order ends:

- on the making of an adoption order;

- when the order is terminated;

- when the child reaches the age of 18.

PARENTAL CONSENT

3.62 The consent of the child's parent or guardian is relevant at a number of stages of the adoption process:

- when the child is placed for adoption;

- when the court is considering making a placement order;

- when the court is considering making an adoption order.

3.63 A placement order may be made only if the court is satisfied that:

- each parent or guardian has consented to the child being placed for adoption with any prospective adopters who may be chosen by the authority *and* has not withdrawn the consent;[116] or

- it should dispense with the parent's or guardian's consent.[117]

3.64 An adoption order requires the court to be satisfied that one of three conditions is satisfied. These are summarised as:

- each parent and guardian consents to the order;[118] or

- each parent has given advanced consent under s 20, *and* has not withdrawn the consent *and* does not oppose the making of the order;[119] or

- it should dispense with the parent's or guardian's consent;[120] or

- the child has been placed for adoption with the prospective adopters with the consent of each parent or guardian *and* that the consent of the mother

---

[116] ACA 2002, s 21(3)(a).
[117] Ibid, s 21(3)(b).
[118] Ibid, s 47(2)(a) ('the first condition').
[119] Ibid, s 47(2)(b): also 'the first condition'.
[120] Ibid, s 47(2)(c): also 'the first condition'.

was given when the child was at least 6 weeks old[121] *and* no parent or guardian opposes the adoption order; or

• the child has been placed for adoption under a placement order[122] *and* no parent or guardian opposes the adoption order.[123]

3.65 The consent which is required is that of each 'parent and guardian'.

Consent of the child

3.66 The Departmental *Review of Adoption Law*[124] in 1992 recommended that the court should not grant an adoption order unless the child, if aged 12 or over, had consented or the court had dispensed with his consent. This did not attract much support. The British Agencies for Adoption and Fostering (BAAF), for example, found it difficult to reach a consensus on the questions. Although it would be quite wrong for an adoption order to be made against the wishes of a child who had sufficient understanding, for some children it could be difficult either to 'renounce' their birth families or to feel constrained to consent when they were living with prospective adopters who, they knew, wanted to adopt them.[125] Fortin[126] made the point that most children being placed from care were probably very vulnerable and it was arguable that they should not be given a veto. Piper[127] took an opposing view. She drew on Russian experience (where, save for one exception, the consent of children aged 10 and over is required) and argued that requiring the consent of the child would affirm him as a 'current rights holder' whose views must be respected and would enhance his welfare and autonomy.

3.67 The recommendation of the Departmental Review, was 'conspicuous by its absence from official policy documents'[128] and the Act does not require the child to consent to the making of the adoption order. However, his wishes and feelings have to be ascertained and considered by the agency or local authority at various planning stages and by the court.[129]

---

[121] ACA 2002, s 47(4)(a) and (b)(i) ('the second condition').
[122] Ibid, s 47(4)(a) and (b)(ii): also 'the second condition'.
[123] The third condition relates to Scotland and Northern Ireland.
[124] op cit paras 9.5–9.6.
[125] *Response to the Draft Adoption Bill* (1996) para 6.4.
[126] *Children's Rights and the Developing Law* (Cambridge University Press, 2nd edn, 2003) p 266.
[127] See Piper and Miakishev 'A Child's Right to Veto in England and Russia: Another Welfare Ploy?' [2003] CFLQ 57.
[128] op cit p 5.
[129] See **6.51**.

Giving consent

The meaning of 'consent'

3.68 'Consent' means consent given unconditionally and with full understanding of what is involved.[130]

3.69 Other than being able to limit consent to a placement with or adoption by identified adopters, parents cannot stipulate that the child must or must not be adopted by adopters of a particular religion persuasion[131] or sexual orientation. However, the agency is under a duty to ascertain their views and wishes about a placement.[132] These should be recorded on the child's case record and will need to be taken into account when a decision is taken to match the child with prospective adopters.[133]

Form of consent

3.70 The Family Procedure (Adoption) Rules 2005 (FP(A)R 2005) require specific forms to be used for consents and makes provisions for these to be witnessed by CAFCASS where the parent or guardian is in England and Wales. These forms and provisions are discussed below.

3.71 Where the relevant form is executed in Scotland it must be witnessed by a Justice of the Peace or Sheriff[134] or in Northern Ireland it must be witnessed by a Justice of the Peace.[135]

3.72 Any form of consent executed outside the UK must be witnessed by:

- any person for the time being authorised by law in the place where the document is executed to administer an oath for any judicial or other legal purpose;

- a British Consular officer;

- a notary public; or

- if the person executing the document is serving in any of the regular armed forces of the Crown, an officer holding a commission in any of those forces.[136]

---

[130] See **3.74**.
[131] As was the position until the Children Act 1975 – see the Report of the Houghton Committee op cit paras 228–231.
[132] Adoption Agencies Regulations 2005 (AAR 2005), SI 2005/389, reg 14.
[133] *Adoption Guidance* (Department for Education and Skills, 2002) ch 2, para 31.
[134] FP(A)R 2005, r 28(4).
[135] Ibid, r 28(5).
[136] Ibid, r 28(6).

3.73 Rule 28 of the FP(A)R 2005 states that consent to any adoption order, but not to placement under s 19 or an advanced adoption order under s 20, 'may' be given in this way. In *Re D (Adoption: Freeing Order)*[137] a mother gave written consent to the making of an adoption order but this was not witnessed by the reporter whom she refused to see. She had discussed the matter on a number of occasions, seemingly with a worker employed by the adoption agency. The court was prepared to accept that she fully and with full understanding of what was involved, agreed to the order.

3.74 It is important to ensure that there is compliance with the formal requirements, that a full and proper explanation of what is involved is given to parents and that the procedure is not rushed. In *Re A (Adoption: Agreement: Procedure)*[138] a freeing order was set aside, in part because a 15-year-old mother from Kosovo had been mislead by a consent form which failed to distinguish adequately between freeing and adoption and which had led her to believe that she could change her mind. Furthermore it had not been established that her agreement was sufficiently informed, unequivocal, mature and stable. 'The course for adoption was set ... at too rapid a pace and with too little consideration of what alternative managements were open.'[139]

Withdrawing consent

3.75 Although consent may be withdrawn (see **3.89** and **3.98**), withdrawal of consent to a child being placed for adoption will be ineffective once an adoption application has been issued. Once the child has been placed for adoption, the parent may oppose the adoption only with the consent of the court. In addition, the longer the time which passes before a parent withdraws her consent, the greater will be the difficulties in persuading the court or agency that the child should be returned, especially if already placed with prospective adopters. Any psychological tie with the parent will have diminished and a corresponding tie with the prospective adopters, strengthened. In addition, any child old enough to understand what adoption entails will have been prepared for adoption and introduced to the idea that this will be permanent.

3.76 *Re J (Adoption: Mother's Objections)*[140] is an example of the difficulties which can occur. An 18-year-old woman (M) with an eating disorder became pregnant and said that she wanted her baby, L, adopted. Three days after his birth, he was placed with foster parents and, at the age of 8 weeks, with prospective adopters. Five weeks later the adoption application was issued. When he was 20 weeks old, M changed her mind. The adoption application was heard a few days before his first birthday and an order was made dispensing with M's consent on the ground it was unreasonably withheld. 'L

---

[137] [2001] 1 FLR 403 decided under the former Rules.

[138] [2001] 2 FLR 455.

[139] Ibid per Thorpe LJ at 463. See also *Kearns v France Application No 35991/04* [2008] 1 FLR 888 for a discussion by the European Court of Human Rights of the comparative approaches of different countries to the time allowed for withdrawing consent.

[140] [2000] 1 FLR 665.

sadly has no knowledge of his mother, he has no bond or attachment to her ... There is a real risk of disturbance and lasting damage if L were now to move'.[141]

Counselling parents

3.77   The importance of parents being given the opportunity of making a fully informed decision about placement and adoption is underlined by the Departmental *Adoption Guidance*[142] and the requirements for agencies to provide a counselling service for the parents of the child[143] which should be sensitive to the parents' ethnic origins and religious beliefs. If English is not their first language, the agency should ensure that it is either provided by or assisted by a person who can communicate effectively with them.[144]

3.78   During the counselling, the agency is required – so far as is reasonably practicable – to explain and provide the parents with written information about:

- the procedures for placement for adoption and adoption;

- the legal implications of giving consent:
    - to placement for adoption under s 19;
    - to the making of a future adoption order under s 20;
    - a placement order;

- the legal implications of adoption.

3.79   When explaining these matters the agency needs to be clear about why it considers the child should not be returned to the parent and should be placed for adoption. The consequences of the adoption process for parental responsibility, for contact with the child and how this will change if the agency is given authority to place the child for adoption should also be made clear. As well as providing an oral explanation, the agency should provide the parents with clearly written explanations initially and whenever they seek this information later in the process.[145]

> 'It is essential that the agency provides the parent or guardian with opportunities to discuss matters fully. It should offer the services of an independent support worker: someone who can provide advice and support and is either from another agency or, at least, not a member of the team of social workers who are responsible for the child's case.[146]

---

[141]   [2000] 1 FLR 665 per Sumner J at 693.
[142]   op cit.
[143]   AAR 2005, reg 14.
[144]   op cit para 30.
[145]   Guidance op cit ch 2, para 23.
[146]   Guidance op cit ch 2, para 25.

3.80   The agency should encourage the parents to consult their own solicitor as soon as possible, particularly where they are not prepared to accept that adoption is the preferred option for their child.[147]

3.81   Where the parent refuses to consider the proposal of adoption for the child, they may decide to decline counselling from the agency, in which case the agency should take all reasonable steps to ensure the parent is provided with the opportunity to receive counselling through another agency. Where counselling is refused, the agency should record this, together with a record of its actions, on the child's case record. The agency should also write to the parent's solicitor and independent support worker to ensure that they are aware of the situation and are able to receive essential information about the legal implications of the adoption process and the rights of the parent or guardian.[148]

3.82   The agency should, wherever practicable, maintain contact with the parent or guardian throughout the adoption process, through their solicitor if necessary, and should be ready to provide counselling to the parents if they change their mind. Where the agency is able to maintain contact with the child's parents it is more likely to be aware whether they intend to attend the adoption order hearing.[149]

Children under the age of 6 weeks

Placement

3.83   All parents or guardians, may, as a matter of law, give effective consent to the making of a placement order or, under s 18(1) or s 19, to the child being placed for adoption. However, the statutory *Adoption Guidance*[150] states the agency should not seek to obtain the consent of the mother under s 19 but should proceed under s 18(1). This was endorsed by the High Court in *A Local Authority v GC*.[151]

3.84   Consent to a placement under s 18(1) must be in writing.[152] The Guidance recommends using the agreement form set out in Annex B to the Guidance. In addition the agency should provide counselling for the parent or guardian. It should make it clear orally and in writing that:

- the parent or guardian retains full parental responsibility until:
  - they give their consent under ACA 2002, s 19, after the child reaches the age of 6 weeks;
  - a placement order is made;

---

147   Ibid, para 26.
148   Ibid, para 28.
149   Ibid, para 29.
150   op cit ch 2, para 65.
151   [2008] EWHC 2555 (Fam), [2009] 1 FLR 299 at [36].
152   AAR 2005, reg 35(3).

> – or an adoption order is made;

- the parent or guardian may only have contact with the child by agreement with the agency or by order of the court;

- if the parent or guardian asks for the child to be returned, the child must be returned by the agency unless any of the following orders are applied for or made in relation to the child:
  - an emergency protection order or a care order under the 1989 Act;
  - a placement order or an adoption order under the 2002 Act;

- after the child is 6 weeks old, the agency will seek to arrange for them to give their formal consent to the child being placed for adoption.[153]

3.85 Thereafter the agency should try to maintain contact with the child's parent and ascertain when the child reaches the age of 6 weeks whether they are prepared to consent to a placement of the child for adoption under s 19, with or without advanced consent (see **3.95**) under s 20.[154]

Adoption

3.86 The mother may not give effective consent for the adoption of her child while the child is under the age of 6 weeks.[155] This accords with the requirements of the European Convention on the Adoption of Children 1967.[156] This does not apply to a father or guardian.

Children over the age of 6 weeks

Placement

3.87 An authority is only able to place a child for adoption under s 19 if there is no application pending in which the court may make a care order and no care order has been made.[157] If either of these two situations apply, the route for placement must be by way of a placement order.

3.88 Consent to the placement of a child with any prospective adopters chosen by the agency must be in Form A100 of the Family Procedure (Adoption) Rules 2005, to the placement of the child with identified adopters, in Form A101 and to placement with identified adopters and, if the placement breaks down, with any prospective adopters, in Form A102.[158] The agency must request CAFCASS to appoint an officer for the purpose of signification,

---

[153] Guidance, ch 2, para 67.
[154] Ibid, para 68.
[155] ACA 2002, s 52(3).
[156] See *A Local Authority v GC* [2008] EWHC 2555 (Fam), [2009] 1 FLR 299 at [26].
[157] ACA 2002, s 19(3).
[158] FP(A)R, r 28(1).

sending to CAFCASS the information specified in Sch 2 to the Adoption Agencies Regulations 2005.[159] The agency should also inform the parents or guardian in writing that:

- they may withdraw their consent, but that withdrawal of consent is ineffective if made after an application for an adoption order has been made; and

- where the parent or guardian gives consent under s 20, they may at the same time or subsequently – through a notice given in writing to the agency:
  - state that they do not wish to be informed of any application for an adoption order; or
  - withdraw such a statement.[160]

3.89 Consent may be withdrawn but will be ineffective if given after an application for an adoption order is made.[161] In addition, if the second condition in ACA 2002, s 47 is relied on, once the child has been placed for adoption, the parent may only oppose the adoption with the permission of the court.[162]

3.90 Consent is withdrawn by notice to the agency or in Form 106 or a form 'to like effect'.

Advanced consent

3.91 A parent or guardian who has consented to the child being placed with prospective adopters identified in the consent, may consent to adoption by them or may consent to any prospective adopters chosen by the agency.[163] The consent may be withdrawn at any time[164] before the issue of an adoption application[165] by notice to the agency or in Form 106 or a form 'to like effect'.

3.92 Advanced consent is given in Form A103. The agency must request CAFCASS to appoint an officer for the purpose of signification, sending to CAFCASS the information specified in Sch 2 to the Adoption Agencies Regulations 2005.[166] For consent to be effective, a CAFCASS officer will need to be satisfied that the parent or guardian fully understands the consequences of giving consent and that they are willing to do so unconditionally.[167] Where the CAFCASS officer is not satisfied that the parents wish to give their full consent, or has doubts that they fully understand its implications, or considers

---

[159] AAR 2005, reg 20.
[160] Guidance op cit ch 2, para 67.
[161] ACA 2002, s 52(4).
[162] Ibid, s 47(5). See **3.146**.
[163] Ibid, s 20(2).
[164] Ibid, s 20(3).
[165] Ibid, s 52(3).
[166] AAR 2005, reg 20.
[167] ACA 2002, s 52(5).

that they are not competent to give consent, he or she will be directed by CAFCASS guidance to notify the agency. In these circumstances consent cannot be given.[168]

3.93 A parent who gives or has given advanced consent may state that they do not wish to be informed of any application for an adoption order[169] in which case they will not be made a respondent to the application.[170] The notice may be withdrawn[171] by notice to the agency.

Placement order

3.94 Consent to a placement order is in Form 100. It will be witnessed by the reporting officer if one has been appointed.[172] See **17.113** for the duties of the reporting officer.

3.95 Although the Rules provide that the court 'will' appoint a reporting officer if it appears that the parent or guardian who is in England and Wales is willing to consent to the child being placed for adoption,[173] in cases where parents initially object to a placement order and then later consent, the court may take evidence of consent directly from the parent without appointing a reporting officer. It is suggested that as a matter of good practice this should be done only where the parent is legally represented and even then it may be desirable to invoke the assistance of CAFCASS. There is no legal reason why the child's guardian cannot be appointed as a reporting officer, but the guardian's duties relate specifically to the child and she may not be perceived as being wholly independent.

Adoption

3.96 There are two ways to consent to the making of an adoption order: consent under s 20 to the making of a future adoption order – 'advanced consent' – or to the making of an actual adoption order. Advanced consent is not available for the making of a placement order. If a parent consents, then he or she will consent to the child being placed.

3.97 A person may consent to adoption without knowing the identity of the persons in whose favour the order will be made.[174]

---

[168]   Guidance op cit para 77.
[169]   ACA 2002, s 20(4).
[170]   FP(A)R 2005, r 23, Table 2.
[171]   ACA 2002, s 20(4).
[172]   FP(A)R 2005, r 71.
[173]   Ibid, r 69.
[174]   ACA 2002, s 52(5).

Consent to adoption

3.98 Consent is given in Form 104 and, unlike advanced consent, may be withdrawn at any time. It will be witnessed by the reporting officer if one has been appointed.[175]

3.99 The reporting officer has to ensure so far as reasonably practicable that the parent or guardian is giving consent unconditionally and with full understanding of what is involved[176] and has to investigate all the circumstances relevant to a parent's or guardian's consent.[177]

3.100 As noted at **3.73** consent can be given other than in Form 104. In *Re C (Foreign Adoption: Natural Mother's Consent: Service)*[178] a mother, M, consented to the applicants adopting her child in Papua New Guinea. The adoption order was not recognised in the UK and the applicants issued new proceedings in England and Wales. The court held that M's signed and witnessed consent given to the Papua New Guinea adoption sufficed as consent to an English adoption by the same adopters and in the circumstances of the case it was not necessary for her to be given notice of the proceedings.

Dispensing with consent

Background

3.101 The Adoption Act 1926 required parental consent except where the parent had abandoned the child, could not be found, was incapable of giving consent or where the court had dispensed with the consent of 'any person whose consent ought, in the opinion of the court and in all the circumstances, to be dispensed with'.[179] The power to dispense with consent was little used.[180]

3.102 The Adoption of Children Act 1949 added two new grounds – that of 'neglect' and 'persistent ill-treatment'. It varied the 'dispensing' ground to enable a court to dispense with consent if it was satisfied that it was 'unreasonably withheld'.[181]

3.103 The Act also introduced far greater formality into the giving of consent. To be effective it could not be given before the child was born or for a mother to give it within 6 weeks of the child being born. In addition it had to be in writing and witnessed by a Justice of the Peace.[182]

---

[175] FP(A)R 2005, r 71.
[176] See **3.124**.
[177] FP(A)R 2005, r 71 and see **17.113**.
[178] [2006] 1 FLR 318.
[179] ACA 2002, s 2(3).
[180] *Interdepartmental Review of Adoption Law* Discussion Paper Number 2: Agreement and Freeing (Department of Health, 1991) para 31.
[181] ACA 2002, s 3(1).
[182] Ibid, s 3(3).

3.104   The Adoption Act 1958 added a ground of persistent failure without reasonable cause to discharge the obligations of a parent.[183]

3.105   Finally, the Adoption Act 1975 added a yet further ground: that the parent concerned had seriously ill-treated the child.

3.106   In summary, by 2002 the consent of each parent with parental responsibility was required but the court could dispense with this consent on objective grounds relating to parental culpability or on the ground it was unreasonably withheld.

3.107   There was increasingly heavy reliance on the 'unreasonably withheld' ground. In 1979, for example, it was the sole ground in a quarter of all cases and one of a number of grounds in just under two-fifths of all cases where the court dispensed with consent. The proportion increased to 45% (sole ground) or three in five cases (multiple grounds) by 1985.[184] In contrast, the grounds which relied on parental culpability were seldom used.

3.108   The ground was difficult to interpret and to apply. In 1954 the report of the Departmental Committee on the Adoption of Children[185] (the 'Hurst Committee') thought that it had been intended to place greater weight on the child's welfare whereas the courts concentrated on whether the parent was acting unreasonably as a parent.[186] In *Re W (An Infant)*[187] the House of Lords made it clear the ground required unreasonableness but not culpability.

> 'The test is reasonableness and not anything else. It is not culpability. It is not indifference. It is not failure to discharge parental duties. It is reasonableness and reasonableness in the context of the totality of the circumstances ... Two reasonable parents can perfectly reasonably come to the opposite conclusions on the same set of facts without forfeiting their title to be regarded as reasonable. The question in any given case is whether a parental veto comes within the band of possible reasonable decisions and not whether it is right or wrong. Not every reasonable exercise of judgment is right and not every mistaken exercise of judgment is unreasonable. There is a band of decisions within which no court should seek to replace the individual's judgment with his own.'

3.109   Although this clarified the test, it remained difficult to apply. Lawyers had to wrestle with what Wall LJ has called 'the intellectual complexities imposed by the test'[188] and Steyn and Hoffman LJJ, 'the embarrassment at having to consult the views of so improbable a legal fiction' as the reasonable hypothetical parent.[189] What were the characteristics and beliefs of such a

---

[183]   ACA 2002, s 18(3).
[184]   *Interdepartmental Review of Adoption Law* Discussion Paper Number 2 paras 34–36.
[185]   Cmnd 9284 (1954) para 117.
[186]   Cretney comments that the Committee may have been wrong in this supposition: *Family Law in the Twentieth Century: A History* (Oxford University Press, 2003) at p 619.
[187]   [1971] AC 682 per Lord Hailsham LC at 699, 698.
[188]   *SB v County Council: P (A Child)* [2008] EWCA Civ 535 at [76].
[189]   *Re C (A Minor)* [1993] 2 FLR 260 at 272.

parent? When, for example, a homosexual father refused to consent to the adoption of his son by his former wife's new husband, should the reasonable hypothetical parent be deemed to be heterosexual or homosexual?[190]

3.110 Nor was the test fair on parents. It could create an almost insurmountable problem for them because by the time the matter had to be considered, it was inextricably linked to a number of other issues such as the view taken on open adoption and at this stage 'it [was] clear to all what will be the best for the child and the parents appear almost powerless to prevent it'.[191]

3.111 In 1992 the issue was considered by the *Review of Adoption Law*[192] and the Committee concluded that the 'unreasonably withholding' test was unsatisfactory because it was unclear how much weight the reasonable hypothetical parent would be expected to place on the welfare of the child. Most of the other grounds were also unsatisfactory in that they related to parental shortcomings which did not necessarily mean that adoption was a suitable option for the child. It therefore recommended that all grounds other than that a parent cannot be found or is incapable of giving consent should be revoked.

3.112 The Committee had commissioned a literature review by Thorburn.[193] She advised that professionals were clearly divided about what was likely to be in the best interests of the child, especially in the area of contact. It would be risky to move towards a total reliance on the paramountcy principle which itself relied on the assumption that there would be a clear view about where the child's welfare lay.[194] However, the Committee recommended a single test which addressed the question of the advantages of having a new status, focused on the needs of the child and required the court to be satisfied that adoption was significantly better than the other available options.

> 'Where adoption would only be marginally better than another option, the court should allow the fact that a parent does not agree to adoption to tip the balance in favour of the other option.'[195]

3.113 In *Re C (A Minor)*[196] Balcombe LJ expressed doubts as to whether, despite the difficulties in the 'unreasonably withholding' test, the recommendation would provide 'the right answer to what is undoubtedly a difficult legal, moral and social problem: the balance between the welfare of the child and the rights of the parents in the context of adoption.'

---

[190] *Re D (An Infant) (Adoption: Parent's Consent)* [1977] AC 602. Lord Simon thought this an 'unreal 'question.

[191] *Interdepartmental Review of Adoption Law* Discussion Paper Number 2 op cit para 74.

[192] Report to Ministers of an Interdepartmental Working Group (Department of Health, 1992) para 12.6.

[193] Ibid Appendix C para 158.

[194] See, for example, Herring 'Parents and Children' in Herring (ed) *Family Law: Issues, Debates and Policy* (Willan Publishing, 2001) at pp 164–166.

[195] Report to Ministers of an Interdepartmental Working Group op cit at para 12.8.

[196] [1993] 2 FLR 260 at 270.

3.114   The consultative Adoption Bill[197] in 1996 included a clause similar to ACA 2002, s 52(1), as originally enacted. The terms were adopted into the 2002 Bill without significant comment in The Prime Minister's Review[198] or the White Paper, *Adoption: A New Approach*.[199]

Research

3.115   In many cases birth parents only passively oppose adoption applications, neither giving consent, perhaps avoiding appointments with social workers or the reporting officer, nor actively opposing it by contesting the matter in court.[200] Even when they go to court, opposition to the order often quickly evaporates.[201] Whether contested or not, virtually all 'public' law adoptions and (in the past) freeing applications are successful.[202]

3.116   Three reasons for active opposition have been identified:[203]

- objection to the very idea of the child being adopted;

- disputes about the arrangements for contact; and

- parents not approving the specific adopters.

3.117   *Adoption Now: Messages from Research*[204] recommends that it is important for social workers to distinguish between passive opposition which may be essentially concerned with negotiation and active opposition.

The test

3.118   The court may dispense with the consent of a parent or guardian if the court is satisfied that:

- the parent or guardian cannot be found;[205] or

- the parent or guardian lacks capacity within the meaning of the Mental Capacity Act 2005 to give consent;[206] or

---

[197]   *Adoption – A Service For Children* (Department of Health, 1996) clause 46.
[198]   op cit.
[199]   op cit.
[200]   Murch, Lowe et al *Pathways to Adoption* (HMSO, 1993) para 3.1(b); Malos and Milsom *Delays and Difficulties in the Judicial Process in Adoption*, both noted in Parker (ed) *Adoption Now: Messages from Research* (Department of Health, 1999) at pp 68–70.
[201]   Lowe and Murch *Supporting Adoption: Reframing the Approach* (BAAF, 1999) at p 249.
[202]   *Adoption Now: Messages from Research* op cit at p 70.
[203]   *Delays and Difficulties in the Judicial Process in Adoption* op cit, noted in *Adoption Now: Messages from Research* op cit at pp 68–70.
[204]   op cit at p 70.
[205]   ACA 2002, s 52(1)(a).
[206]   Ibid.

- the welfare of the child requires the consent to be dispensed with.[207]

3.119 If these grounds are proved, the court has a discretion to dispense with consent and the welfare test applies to the exercise of the discretion.[208]

3.120 Where the Act or Regulations require the consent of someone for something other than a placement order or adoption, for example, to place a child, the requirement for consent cannot be disregarded or dispensed with on any of the above grounds.

'Cannot be found'

3.121 All reasonable steps must be taken to find the parent and if even one reasonable step is omitted, it cannot be said that the person cannot be found.[209] To be reasonable, the steps must be practical.[210]

3.122 Depending on the circumstances of the case, 'all reasonable steps' may include:

- writing to the parent's last known address;

- making enquiries of any known relatives;

- the court requesting information from government departments, for example, the Department for Work and Pensions;[211]

- advertising in discreet terms in a newspaper in an area where the parent was last known to live;

- making enquiries of local authority housing and housing benefit departments.

Examples

Re F (R) (An Infant)[212]

3.123 The parents had separated. The father, F, consented to the child being adopted. The adopters wrote to the mother, M, at her last known address but the letter was returned as 'gone away'. They advertised in a local paper to no

---

[207] ACA 2002, s 52(1)(b).
[208] *Re P (Placement Orders: Parental Consent)* sub nom *SB v County Council: P (A Child)* [2008] EWCA Civ 535, [2008] 2 FLR 625 per Wall LJ at [114].
[209] *Re F (R) (An Infant)* [1970] 1 QB 385 per Salmon LJ at 389; followed by the Scottish Court of Session (Inner House) *Re S (Adoption)* [1999] 2 FLR 374.
[210] *Re R (Adoption)* [1967] 1 WLR 34; *Re A (Adoption of Russian Child)* [2000] 1 FLR 539.
[211] NICB, Special Section A, Newcastle-Upon-Tyne NE98 1YU. *Practice Direction of 20 July 1995* which relates inter alia to Her Majesty' Revenue and Customs may not assist because the inquiry does not relate to tracing a missing child.
[212] [1970] 1 QB 385.

avail. However, although they knew that F was in contact with M, they did not ask him to inform her of the adoption application. M learned of the adoption order two months after it was made. Her appeal was allowed, the adoption order was set aside and a rehearing directed.

Re A (Adoption of Russian Child)[213]

3.124   The child was born in Russia and after her mother, M, agreed to her being adopted, she was placed in an orphanage. An English couple, Mr and Mrs B, obtained an adoption order from a Russian court but later applied to adopt in England. The address of M was unknown. Charles J held that the legal difficulties in Russia if an attempt was made to trace M and the possible serious consequences for Mr B's commercial interests in Russia which these would cause made it impractical and unreasonable for such steps to be taken.

'Lacks capacity within the meaning of the Mental Capacity Act 2005'

3.125   For the purposes of Mental Capacity Act 2005, a person lacks capacity in relation to a matter if at the material time he is unable to make a decision for himself in relation to the matter because of an impairment of, or a disturbance in the functioning of, the mind or brain. It does not matter whether the impairment or disturbance is permanent or temporary.[214] When deciding whether someone has capacity, the court has to have regard to the following principles:

- A person must be assumed to have capacity unless it is established that he lacks capacity[215] and any question whether a person lacks capacity within the meaning of the Mental Capacity Act 2005 must be decided on the balance of probabilities.[216]

- A person is not to be treated as unable to make a decision unless all practicable steps to help him to do so have been taken without success.

- A person is not to be treated as unable to make a decision merely because he makes an unwise decision.[217]

3.126   A person is not to be regarded as unable to understand the information relevant to a decision if he is able to understand an explanation of it given to him in a way that is appropriate to his circumstances (using simple language,

---

[213]   [2000] 1 FLR 539.
[214]   Mental Capacity Act 2005, s 2(1), (2).
[215]   Ibid, s 1(2).
[216]   Ibid, s 2(4).
[217]   Ibid, s 1. Subsections 1(5) and (6) do not apply because under the ACA 2002 there is no power for anyone to give consent on behalf of the person whose consent is required. And see s 27(1)(e) and (f) of the Mental Capacity Act 2005.

visual aids or any other means).[218] The fact that a person is able to retain the information relevant to a decision for a short period only does not prevent him from being regarded as able to make the decision.[219]

3.127 A person is unable to make a decision for himself if he is unable:

- to understand the information relevant to the decision;[220]

- to retain that information;

- to use or weigh that information as part of the process of making the decision; or

- to communicate his decision (whether by using sign language or any other means).[221]

3.128 The information relevant to a decision includes information about the reasonably foreseeable consequences of:

- deciding one way or another; or

- failing to make the decision.[222]

3.129 The High Court and the Court of Appeal have not considered the information which a person needs to have when his or her consent to adoption is being sought. CAFCASS explains the meaning of adoption to children thus:

> 'Adoption is when a court makes the adults who are looking after a child or young person their legal parents. The child's last name usually changes to become the same as theirs. The people who adopt a child are given 'parental responsibility' for that child and can make decisions for them. Adoption is permanent and means that from then on a child or young person is legally part of that family.'[223]

3.130 A lack of capacity cannot be established merely by reference to:

- a person's age or appearance; or

- a condition of his, or an aspect of his behaviour, which might lead others to make unjustified assumptions about his capacity.[224]

---

[218] Mental Capacity Act 2005, s 3(2).
[219] Ibid, s 3(3).
[220] Ibid, s 3(1)(a). See s 3(4).
[221] Ibid s 3(1). See also *Re MB* [1997] 2 FLR 426.
[222] Ibid, s 3(4).
[223] www.cafcass.gov.uk/cafcass_and_you/info_for_teenagers/adoption
[224] Mental Capacity Act 2005, s 2(3).

Need for a litigation friend

3.131 Separate from the issue of whether someone is incapable of giving consent is the issue of whether they require a litigation friend to act for them. Someone who is a 'protected party' must have a litigation friend to conduct proceedings on his behalf.[225]

3.132 In addition to the general principles for deciding capacity, the common law test set out in *Masterman-Lister v Brutton & Co and Jewell & Home Counties Dairies*[226] still applies when a court is considering capacity to conduct proceedings:

> '... The test to be applied ... is whether the party to legal proceedings is capable of understanding, with the assistance of such proper explanation from legal advisers and experts in other disciplines as the case may require, the issues on which his consent or decision is likely to be necessary in the course of those proceedings. If he has capacity to understand that which he needs to understand in order to pursue or defend a claim, I can see no reason why the law – whether substantive or procedural – should require the interposition of a ... litigation friend.'

3.133 In *R P v Nottingham City Council and the Official Solicitor (Mental Capacity of Parent)*[227] Wall LJ gave guidance on the steps which should be taken if a local authority thinks that a parent will require a litigation friend.

- The question of adult capacity to give instructions needs to be addressed at the earliest opportunity. The local authority will be expected, in the pre-proceedings phase of the case, to be on the alert for the possibility that a parent in particular may be a protected person and may not have the capacity to give instructions in the proceedings.

- In many cases, the local authority will be working with the child's parents in an attempt to keep the family together. In these circumstances the parent in question should probably be referred to the local authority's adult learning disability team (or its equivalent) for help and advice. If that team thinks that further investigations are required, it can undertake them. It should have the necessary contacts and resources to commission a report so that as soon as the pre-proceedings letter is written, and proceedings are issued, the legal advisers for the parent can be in a position, with public funding, to address the question of a litigation friend.

- It is important that judgments on capacity are not made by the social workers from the child protection team.

---

[225] FP(A)R 2005, r 50(1). A 'protected party' means someone who lacks capacity under the Mental Capacity Act 2005 to conduct the proceedings: ibid r 6(1).

[226] [2002] EWCA Civ 1889, [2003] 3 All ER 162 per Chadwick LJ at [75].

[227] [2008] EWCA Civ 462, [2008] 2 FLR 1516 per Wall LJ at [174]–[178].

- A litigation friend, whether the Official Solicitor or otherwise, cannot become involved unless and until proceedings are issued.

- Prior to the institution of proceedings, the local authority should feel free to offer whatever advice is appropriate, although any advice given to the parent in question should come from the local authority's adult learning disability team.

- Once proceedings are issued, the question of the parent's representation becomes and remains a matter for the parent's legal advisers.

- The question of ensuring that a parent during proceedings is properly informed and understands the role of the litigation friend – and, in particular the role of the Official Solicitor – must be a matter for that parent's legal team, and for the Official Solicitor himself. The child protection team would have a clear conflict of interest were it to seek to ensure that the parent in question fully understood the role of his or her litigation friend.

3.134 There is no reason in most civil litigation why a lay person – with appropriate legal advice – should not be the litigation friend of the claimant but it is of the essence of such an appointment that the litigation friend has no conflict of interest with the protected party.[228] In *R P v Nottingham City Council and the Official Solicitor (Mental Capacity of Parent)*,[229] for example, there were clear conflicts. Both the maternal grandparents and the maternal uncle put themselves forward to care for the child. Had those applications been pursued, each would have had to become involved in the proceedings, acting directly in opposition to the mother's assertion that she was fully capable of caring for the child. It was clear that no family member could advance RP's case whilst putting themselves forward as carers in opposition to the mother's wishes. In addition, the mother's lack of capacity to give instructions was based on her fundamental learning difficulties. She needed clear and objective professional advice, and advice which none of her family was capable of giving.

3.135 The Procedure relating to litigation friends is contained in Part 7 of FP(A)R 2005.[230]

Dispensing with consent

3.136 In *R P v Nottingham City Council and the Official Solicitor (Mental Capacity of Parent)*[231] the Court of Appeal held that a litigation friend could not advance an unarguable case against adoption. In the instant case, the evidence was overwhelmingly in favour of care and placement orders.

---

228 [2008] EWCA Civ 462, [2008] 2 FLR 1516 per Wall LJ at [130].
229 Ibid.
230 SI 2005/2795.
231 [2008] EWCA Civ 462, [2008] 2 FLR 1516 per Wall LJ at [160], [162].

The welfare of the child requires the consent to be dispensed with

Article 8

3.137 An order allowing a child to be placed for adoption will inevitably interfere with the rights of the child under Art 8 of the European Convention on Human Rights and Fundamental Freedoms to a family life. It is the most draconian interference with family life possible and will therefore need to be justified as necessary in a democratic society.[232]

3.138 Because Art 8 is engaged any placement or adoption order made without parental consent in accordance with s 52(1)(b) must be proportionate to the legitimate aim of protecting the welfare and interests of the child. If the state was to interfere with the child's right to family life, the interference has to be in accordance with the law, to be for a legitimate aim (in this case the protection of the welfare and interests of the children); and be 'necessary in a democratic society.'[233]

3.139 The European Court of Human Rights has not questioned the practice of dispensing with consent to adoption and the UK is unusual amongst members of the Council of Europe in permitting the total severance of family ties without parental consent.[234] In *Down Lisburn Health and Social Services Trust v H*[235] Baroness Hale of Richmond added:

'That is not to say that it can never be justified in the interests of the child. The European Court has said that where the interests of the child and the interests of the adults conflict, the interests of the child must prevail: e g *Yousef v The Netherlands.*[236] But it can be expected that the European Court would scrutinise the relevance and sufficiency of the reasons given for such a drastic interference with the same intensity with which it has scrutinised severance decisions in other care cases: see, in particular, *P, C and S v United Kingdom.*[237] The margin of appreciation accorded to the national authorities is correspondingly reduced. In a freeing application, the question must be whether it is necessary and proportionate to sever the links with the family of birth if a new family has not yet been identified.'

---

[232] See *Söderbäck v Sweden* [1999] 1 FLR 250 at para 26.
[233] *Re C and B (Care Order: Future Harm)* [2001] 1 FLR 611 per Hale LJ at [33]. And see also *Re B (Care: Interference with Family Life)* [2003] EWCA Civ 786, [2003] 2 FLR 813, per Thorpe LJ at [34]: both cited with approval in relation to s 52(1)(b) by the Court of Appeal in *Re P (Placement Orders: Parental Consent)* op cit per Wall LJ at [119]–[124].
[234] *Down Lisburn Health and Social Services Trust v H* [2006] UKHL 36, [2007] 1 FLR 121 at [34]. Baroness Hale noted that an expert witness in the case, Professor Triseliotis, thought that only Portugal and perhaps one other European country allowed this.
[235] Ibid.
[236] [2003] 1 FLR 210 at para 73.
[237] [2002] 2 FLR 631 at para. 118.

Domestic law

3.140 The legislature clearly had the requirements of Art 8 in mind when drafting s 52(1)(b).

3.141 In *Re S (Special Guardianship)*[238] the Court of Appeal referred to the new test as constituting 'a major change'.

'At first blush it would appear likely to be the case that once the court has reached the conclusion that adoption is in the best interests of the child, it will follow that his or her welfare will require the court to dispense with parental consent to adoption ... We do not, however, think it appropriate to express a final decision on the point until it arises in a case in which it is pivotal to outcome.'

3.142 In *Re P (Placement Orders: Parental Consent)*[239] it considered the matter in more detail but pointed out that the guidance it gave was 'simple enough'.

- Judges should apply the statutory language with care to the facts of the particular case.

- Judges should be aware of the importance to the child of the decision being taken and 'there is, perhaps, no more important or far-reaching decision for a child than to be adopted by strangers'.[240]

- What has to be shown is that the child's welfare 'requires' *adoption* as opposed to something short of adoption.

  'A child's circumstances may "require" statutory intervention, perhaps may even "require" the indefinite or long-term removal of the child from the family and his or her placement with strangers, but that is not to say that the same circumstances will necessarily "require" that the child be adopted. They may or they may not. The question, at the end of the day, is whether what is "required" is adoption.'

- The word 'requires' is a perfectly ordinary English word. Judges should approach the question of dispensation by asking themselves whether the welfare of the child required adoption and answering it by reference to s 1 and in particular by a careful consideration of all the matters identified in s 1(4).

- 'Requires' is to be equated with 'necessary' in Art 8. 'It is a word which was plainly chosen as best conveying ... the essence of the Strasbourg jurisprudence.' While taking its colour from the statutory context, in the Strasbourg jurisprudence its meaning lies somewhere between 'indispensable' on the one hand and 'useful', 'reasonable' or 'desirable' on the other.

---

[238] [2007] EWCA Civ 54, [2007] 1 FLR 819 per Wall LJ at [69]–[72].
[239] [2008] EWCA Civ 535, [2008] 2 FLR 625 at [117]–[129].
[240] And see *Johansen v Norway* [1996] 23 EHRR 33 at [78].

It implies the existence of what the Strasbourg jurisprudence calls a 'pressing social need.' It has 'the connotation of the imperative, what is demanded rather than what is merely optional or reasonable or desirable'.

- Dispensing with parental consent is 'an extreme – indeed the most extreme' interference with family life. It has to be proportionate to the aim to be achieved. The court should begin with a preference for the less interventionist approach which should be considered to be in the better interests of the children unless there are cogent reasons to the contrary.[241] Cogent justification must therefore exist if parental consent is to be dispensed with in accordance with s 52(1)(b).

Examples

Re M-J (Adoption Order or Special Guardianship Order)[242]

3.143 A child was placed with foster carers at the age of about 6 months because of concerns about his parents' drug and alcohol dependency. Although his mother, M, initially made good progress with her treatment, there was a relapse following which the child was placed with his maternal aunt with a view to adoption. M accepted that he should remain there but opposed the adoption. The trial judge decided that although many of the child's needs could be met by a special guardianship order, this did not give total security and nothing less than adoption was required. The Court of Appeal upheld the decision.

Re P (Placement Orders: Parental Consent)[243]

3.144 The case concerned four children aged between nearly 6 and 2. The elder two, D and S, were seriously damaged children and it was likely that they would be placed separately for adoption. S had a positive relationship with his mother, M, and contact between D and M might be required once she had settled into a permanent placement. The trial judge made a s 26 order, unlimited in time, for contact between both children, seven times a year. The trial judge found that although there was a small risk that post-adoption contact would not take place, the welfare of the children required adoption. The Court of Appeal dismissed M's appeal.

---

[241] Citing *Re O (Care or Supervision Order)* [1996] 2 FLR 755 per Hale LJ at 760.
[242] [2007] EWCA Civ 56, [2007] 1 FLR 691.
[243] [2008] EWCA Civ 535, [2008] 2 FLR 625.

SEEKING LEAVE TO OPPOSE AN ADOPTION APPLICATION

3.145 Absent any statutory exception a parent with parental responsibility or guardian will be made a respondent to an adoption application[244] and may oppose it.

3.146 The statutory exceptions are:

- a parent or guardian who has given advance consent to adoption (see **3.91**) and has not withdrawn it before the application is made;[245]

- the child has been placed for adoption by an agency with the consent of each parent or guardian;[246]

- the child has been placed for adoption by an agency under a placement order.[247]

3.147 Where these exceptions apply, the Court may give leave to the parents and guardians to oppose the making of an adoption order if it is satisfied 'that there has been a change in circumstances since the consent of the parent or guardian was given or, as the case may be, the placement order was made'.[248]

The test

3.148 The application involves a two stage process:

- Has there been a change in circumstances?

- If there has been, should the court's discretion be exercised?[249]

Change of circumstances

3.149 Whether or not there has been a relevant change in circumstances must be a matter of fact to be decided by the good sense and sound judgment of the tribunal hearing the application. The change in circumstances whilst not having to be 'significant' must be of a nature and degree sufficient, on the facts of the particular case, to open the door to the exercise of the judicial discretion to permit the parents to defend the adoption proceedings. It can embrace a wide range of different factual situations. It is not limited to a change to the circumstances of the parents and the only limiting factor is that it must be a change in circumstances 'since the placement order was made'. The test should

---

[244] FP(A)R 2005, r 23, Table 2.
[245] ACA 2002, ss 20(4), 52(4), 47(3).
[246] Ibid, ss 47(4)(b)(i), 47(5).
[247] Ibid, ss 47(4)(b)(ii), 47(5).
[248] Ibid, s 47(7).
[249] *Re P (Adoption: Leave Provisions)* [2007] EWCA Civ 616, [2007] 2 FLR 1069.

not be set too high, because parents should not be discouraged either from bettering themselves or from seeking to prevent the adoption of their child by the imposition of a test which is unachievable.[250]

Exercise of discretion

3.150 The s 1(2) welfare test and the s 1(4) checklist apply to a decision to grant leave. Even if the parents are able to identify a change in circumstances sufficient to make it appropriate for the judge to consider whether or not to exercise his discretion to permit them to opposed the adoption proceedings, the paramount consideration of the court in the actual exercise of the discretion must be the welfare of the child throughout her life, and in that context the court must have regard in particular to the matters set out in s 1(4).[251]

Nature of the hearing

3.151 The judge does not need to conduct a full welfare hearing with oral evidence and cross-examination in order to reach a conclusion and may conclude that the hearing can fairly be conducted on submissions. However, there may be cases in which a particular factual issue requires oral evidence.[252]

Example

Re P (Adoption: Leave Provisions)[253]

3.152 Both parents abused alcohol and drugs and the father inflicted serious violence on the mother. A care order was made when S was one and shortly after, a placement order was made with her parents' consent. One month later S was placed for adoption and thrived. Five months later an adoption application was issued. The parents sought leave to oppose the proceedings, arguing that they had successfully addressed their problems and, following a positive parenting assessment, were looking after a subsequent child. The Court of Appeal dismissed their appeal against the refusal of leave. There had been a sufficient change in circumstances but the trial judge had been entitled to conclude that S's welfare continued to require her to be adopted by the applicants.

Effect of granting leave to oppose

3.153 If leave is granted, the parent becomes a party and is entitled to play a full part in his proceedings. The applicants will no longer be able to rely on condition 2 of s 47 (see **3.64**) but will have to satisfy the court that it should dispense with the consent of the parent under s 52(1)(a).[254]

---

[250] [2007] EWCA Civ 616, [2007] 2 FLR 1069 at [30]–[32].
[251] Ibid at [35].
[252] Ibid at [54].
[253] Ibid.
[254] ACA 2002, s 47(1), (2), (4).

Chapter 4

INTERNATIONAL ASPECTS OF ADOPTION

INTRODUCTION

4.1   The limited number of babies for available for adoption means that some prospective adopters seek to adopt children who are living abroad. The awareness of the importance of considering whether children who cannot remain with their families should live with members of their extended family may mean the local authority or agency investigating families who live abroad. Furthermore, the increase in immigration, emigration and movement across borders for the purpose of employment has meant that adopters may not be permanently resident in one country throughout the life of the child and the question of the recognition of any adoption in other countries is a real and significant one. As a result of this internationalisation of adoption, domestic courts have regularly to deal with cases where children are brought into England and Wales from abroad for the purpose of adoption or where local authorities seek to remove children for the purpose of adoption abroad.

4.2   Cross-border movement of children can result in trafficking. Even where the movement of children is genuine and humanitarian in its purpose, important matters arise such as the assessment of the needs of the child and the suitability of the proposed adopters and the placement.

4.3   The Hague Convention on Protection of Children and Co-operation in Respect of Intercountry Adoption 1993 with 78 signatories[1] including the UK – one of 'an important trilogy of child protection instruments'[2] (the other two being the Hague Abduction Convention 1980 and the Hague Convention on the Protection of Children 1996) – plays an increasingly important role in regulating these issues and underpins detailed domestic regulation in England and Wales. It governs the adoption of children resident in a signatory state by the courts in another signatory state.

4.4   The thrust of domestic regulation is concerned with:

*   the entry of children into the UK for the purpose of adoption here;

---

[1]   As at 19 February 2009.
[2]   G Douglas and N Lowe, *The Continuing Evolution of Family Law* (Family Law, 2009) at p 276.

- the adoption of such children in the UK whether as a Convention or normal adoption;

- the removal of children from the UK for the purpose of adoption abroad whether under the Convention or otherwise.

In each instance, it is important to distinguish between cases where the Convention applies and those when it does not. In addition it is important not to overlook the provisions of the Immigration Rules.[3]

BACKGROUND

4.5   Intercountry adoption has been known since the post-War years, initially as a humanitarian movement in response to displaced children. More recently, it became a way of providing children for childless couples, perhaps unable to adopt through agencies because of a shortage of children available for adoption within their own country. During 1990–91, Romania, after the fall of Ceauşescu and following international publicity about the plight of children in its institutions, became the international focal point of intercountry adoption. One report estimated that about 4,000 children were adopted in the UK in seven months in 1990/91.[4] In 2001 the Romanian government imposed a moratorium on international adoption from the country[5] and followed this by an adoption law, effective from 1 January 2005, which effectively banned all intercountry adoptions from the country.

4.6   Children from other states, for example, Bosnia, were also brought into the UK for adoption.[6] Nevertheless the number of intercountry adoptions in the UK has appeared historically to be low compared to the majority of European countries (in which they form the majority of adoptions) and in the United States.[7]

4.7   Concern about the number of children being adopted outside their country of origin and about the effects of intercountry adoption on the children themselves and on their country of origin, gave an impetus to international initiatives to develop a convention on international adoption,

---

[3]   HC 395, available at http://www.ukba.homeoffice.gov.uk/policyandlaw/immigrationlaw/immigrationrules/.

[4]   *Inter-Departmental Review of Adoption Law: Discussion Paper Number 4: Intercountry Adoption* paras 1–11. For an example of the difficulties encountered, see *R v Secretary of State for Health Ex Parte Luff* [1992] 1 FLR 59, *Re R (No 1) (Intercountry Adoption)* [1999] 1 FLR 1014 and *Re R (Intercountry Adoption)* [1999] 1 FLR 1042.

[5]   Bainham *International adoption from Romania – why the moratorium should not be ended* (2003) CFLQ 223.

[6]   See, for example, *Re K (Adoption and Wardship)* [1997] 2 FLR 221.

[7]   Lowe 'English Adoption Law: Past, Present and Future' in Katz, Eekelaar and Maclean (eds) *Cross Currents – Family Law and Policy in the US and England* (Oxford University Press, 2000) at p 332.

This resulted in the Hague Convention on Protection of Children and Co-operation in respect of Intercountry Adoption 1993.[8]

4.8　In 1992, the Review of Adoption Law: Report to Ministers of an Interdepartmental Working Group[9] commented that while intercountry adoption cannot be regarded as a solution to the problems associated with world poverty, it may provide the only opportunity of a family life for some children who have no family and are living in circumstances of deprivation and poverty. Research at that time suggested that the majority of intercountry adoptions were successful in terms of the child's development and the 'satisfaction' rate of them and their adoptive parents. Subsequently, studies of 165 6-year-old Romanian children adopted under the age of $3\frac{1}{2}$ in the UK[10] suggested that some risks may have been over-emphasised. Findings by 1999 provided no evidence that families who might have fallen outside the guidelines regarding intercountry adoption were prone to a greater risk of the 'placement' breaking down. In any event, the rate of breakdown was 'remarkably low' and the satisfaction of the adoptive parents was high. See also **2.101**. Between the ages of 6 and 11, only one adoption had broken down.[11]

4.9　There are, however, concerns about a number of aspects of intercountry adoptions. They were and, in some parts of the world, still are arranged without professional supervision, support and safeguards which are required by the domestic adoption laws of the receiving country. At its worst, unregulated activity may give rise to corruption, abuse, child-stealing and trafficking.[12]

4.10　Even where corruption is not involved, there is a risk that insufficient attention may be paid to the needs of the child, particularly in terms of possible risks associated with transracial and transcultural adoption[13] (see also **6.103**). However, as *Adoption Now: Messages from Research*[14] pointed out in 1999, some of the adopters of Romanian children suggested that the children may not have had a cultural identity in Romania as they were destined to live in very poor institutional care without an alternative domestic family placement and their only opportunity was overseas adoptions. This may be specific to the

---

[8]　For a discussion of the Convention, see Silberman 'The Hague Children Conventions' in *Cross Currents – Family Law and Policy in the US and England* op cit, at pp 606–615 and 'Where in the world is International Family Law Going Next?' in Douglas and Lowe *The Continuing Evolution of Family Law* op cit, at pp 261–276.

[9]　(Department of Health and Welsh Office, 1992) paras 46.2, 47.1.

[10]　The English and Romanian Adoptees Study Team, Rutter and others at the Institute of Psychiatry, London, summarised in *Adoption Now: Messages from Research* (Department of Health, 1999) Appendix 1.

[11]　Castle et al 'Service Use by Families with Children Adopted from Romania' (2006) *Journal of Children Services* 1(1) 5.

[12]　*Review of Adoption Law: Report to Ministers of an Interdepartmental Working Group* op cit para 46.3.

[13]　Ibid.

[14]　op cit at p 127.

Romanian situation and not applicable to all intercountry adoptions.[15] According to the researchers, most of the adopters were aware of the importance of the children's heritage and identity.

4.11 A further question relates to the provision of post-adoption services. Intercountry adopted children may have a greater than average need for medical and other support[16] but their adopters may have had little or no contact with agencies and may be unable to access non-medical support.[17] The Romanian study, carried out when the children were 6 years old commented that there was a considerable variation in the types of services provided and their effectiveness and the services which were provided were poorly coordinated.[18]

4.12 These problems are tackled both internationally by the Hague Convention and domestically by the use both of immigration and adoption law. Home study reports now ensure that there will be pre-immigration assessment. The general adoption support provisions of ACA 2002 (see Chapter 11) are available for all adoptions regardless of where the adopted person may be habitually resident and whether the adoption was effected in the UK or elsewhere.[19] Nevertheless the problem of attempts to evade the requirements of the legislation is ever present.[20]

POLICY

International policy

4.13 A number of international instruments provide a framework for the operation of intercountry adoption which keep the interest of the child central to the process and any decisions that are made.[21]

4.14 These include:

- the UN Declaration on Social Legal Principles relating to the Protection and Welfare of Children, with special reference to Foster Placements and Adoption nationally and internationally (1983);

- the UN Convention on the Rights of the Child 1989;

---

[15]   However, for conditions in the former USSR at the time, see Dyuzheva 'Adoption and the Abandonment of Children in the Former Soviet Union' [1992] Fam Law 389.

[16]   Nearly a third of the Romanian children adopted in the UK after the age of 6 months had received mental health provision by the age of 11, a far higher rate than the 11 to15% adopted before that age – 'Service Use by Families with Children Adopted from Romania' op cit.

[17]   *Adoption Now: Messages from Research* op cit at p 127.

[18]   *Adoption Now: Messages from Research* op cit at p 150.

[19]   ACA 2002, s 2(8).

[20]   See, for example, *Flintshire County Council v K* [2001] 2 FLR 476, *Re M (Adoption: International Adoption Trade)* [1993] 1 FLR 947 and **7.57**.

[21]   *Adoption Guidance: Adoption and Children Act 2002* (DfES, 2002) Annex C para 2.

- the Hague Convention on Protection of Children and Co-operation in respect of Intercountry Adoption 1993 Recommendation 1443 (2000);

- International adoption: respecting children's rights (2000);

- The European Parliament's Resolution on improving the law and co-operation between the Member States on the adoption of minors (1996).

4.15 The instruments support the following principles:

- Children who cannot live with their birth parents should be either found a placement with a family member or given the opportunity to live with a family within their State of origin.

- Intercountry adoption may be considered as an alternative means of providing a permanent family for children who cannot be cared for in a suitable family in their own country.

- Intercountry adoption should take place in the best interests of the child and with respect for his or her fundamental rights.

- Safeguards and standards equivalent to those which apply in domestic adoption should be applied in intercountry adoption to protect the welfare of the child.

- Profit should not be made from the process.[22]

4.16 The 1993 Hague Convention on Protection of Children and Co-operation in Respect of Intercountry Adoption aims to establish safeguards to protect the best interests of the child and put in place a system of co-operation between countries to prevent the abduction or sale of or traffic in children. The UK implemented the Convention with effect from 1 June 2003.

4.17 Key requirements of the Convention are:

- The child's home country must ensure that the child has been freely given up for adoption and that this has not been induced by payment or compensation of any kind.

- Attempts must be made to place the child in a family in their country of origin. If this is not possible, it must be confirmed that intercountry adoption is in the child's best interests.

- An adoption can take place only if the adopters have been approved as suitable to become adopters in the receiving State (ie in the country where

---

[22] *Adoption Guidance: Adoption and Children Act 2002*, op cit, para 3.

the adoption will take place) and the receiving country confirms that the child will be allowed to reside permanently in that country.

- All appropriate measures must be taken by contracting States to prevent improper financial or other gain in connection with adoption and to deter all practices contrary to the objects of the Convention.

- Each State may accredit bodies to work as adoption agencies. These bodies must be non-profit making.

- Adoptions made in countries which have ratified or acceded to the Convention, if certified in accordance with Art 23(1), are recognised in other Hague Convention contracting States.[23]

Domestic policy

4.18   The principles and aims set out above find their domestic expression in the provision of the Adoption and Children Act 2002 and Regulations made under the Act. Effect to the Hague Convention is also given by the Act.

4.19   The Local Authority Circular, *Adoption – Achieving the Right Balance*,[24] states that:

'The primary purpose of intercountry adoption is to provide a child with a family where this cannot be provided in the child's own country; it is not about improving the material quality of life of children from overseas, although this is likely to be one of its effects. Intercountry adoption is now a major feature of adoption in the UK ... The Government recognises and understands the humanitarian and altruistic response of some people who wish to adopt children living overseas, particularly those described as orphaned or abandoned.'

It continues by pointing out that:

'Most intercountry adoption applications involve a child leaving his or her own country to live permanently with families in the UK. This necessarily brings radical changes to the life of a child in many ways. Intercountry adoption also brings profound changes to the lives of the adopters and affects not only their immediate families but their relatives and friends ... Adoption agencies need to be satisfied that prospective adopters are not only equal to the task of adopting a child from overseas but that they fully appreciate the implications of bringing an unrelated child from abroad into their own family. Prospective adopters also need to understand the implications for a child to be taken from his or her own country, family, friends, familiar environment etc. and begin life afresh in a totally unfamiliar setting. Assessments and checks are necessarily thorough to ensure that prospective adopters are equal to the task in the very serious commitment they wish to undertake and, so far as possible, avoid future disruption of a placement. Such assessments and checks are also important to the countries from which the

---

[23]   *Adoption Guidance: Adoption and Children Act 2002*, op cit, para 5.
[24]   LAC(98)20 at paras 51 and 52. See Appendix 3.

children originate; countries seek the assurance of the UK that prospective adopters have been assessed as suitable by agencies authorised to do so.'[25]

4.20 In line with the general principle that safeguards and standards equivalent to those which apply in domestic adoption should be applied in intercountry adoption the Circular points out that:

'The standards and criteria applied in domestic adoption concerning the assessment of prospective adopters are to be applied to families seeking to adopt a child from overseas. To do less would leave the UK open to accusations of applying double standards in their assessment process. These standards and associated criteria allow agencies to apply sufficient measures of flexibility and discretion to reflect conditions of children commonly encountered in intercountry adoption.'[26]

STRUCTURE OF DOMESTIC LEGISLATION

4.21 The main legal framework for intercountry adoption in England and Wales is set out in the following primary and secondary legislation:

- Adoption and Children Act 2002 (ACA 2002);

- Adoption (Intercountry Aspects) Act 1999 (gives power to make Regulations);

- Adoption Agencies Regulations 2005 (AAR);[27]

- Adoptions with a Foreign Element Regulations 2005 (AFER 2005);[28]

- Suitability of Adopters Regulations 2005 (SAR 2005);[29]

- Restriction on the Preparation of Adoption Reports Regulations 2005 (RPARR 2005).[30]

4.22 Statutory Guidance on the regime is provided by *Adoption Guidance: Adoption and Children Act 2002* (*the Guidance*) which is issued under s 7 of the Local Authority Social Services Act 1970. This is supplemented by the Local Authority Circular, *Adoption – Achieving the Right Balance*.[31]

---

[25] LAC(98)20 at paras 51 and 52. See Appendix 3.
[26] Ibid, para 53.
[27] SI 2005/389.
[28] SI 2005/392.
[29] SI 2005/1712.
[30] SI 2005/1711.
[31] op cit.

Failure to comply with the regime

4.23   *The Guidance*[32] states that as a public authority, a local authority has a duty to notify the police and provide them with such information as they may require if they are made aware that a person has:

- made an application to adopt a child who was brought into the UK in contravention of the provisions on intercountry adoption in the Act; or

- brought, or has caused someone else to bring, a child into the UK without complying with the conditions or requirements included in the AFER 2005; or

- brought a child into the UK with the immigration status of a visitor but with the actual intention of adopting the child; or

- removed a child from the UK for the purposes of adoption in a country outside the British Islands without complying with s 85 of the Act (see **4.126**).

4.24   The police will then investigate the case and, where relevant, refer it to the Crown Prosecution Service to determine whether or not to prosecute the alleged offender.

4.25   In *Re M (Adoption: International Adoption Trade)*[33] Munby J said that any local authority faced with a situation where an adoption was proceeding overseas on the basis of an illegal home study report must not hesitate to inform the foreign court and any other agencies involved, and in the clearest possible terms ('clearly, loudly and explicitly'), that the provision of 'home study reports' other than by an adoption agency or its agent is a criminal offence and of matters within its knowledge suggesting that the prospective adoptive parents are not suitable either to adopt at all or (as the case may be) to adopt the particular child involved.

ADOPTIONS WITHIN ENGLAND AND WALES

4.26   There is a clear distinction between adoption orders made in England and Wales under the Hague Convention in terms of:

- the recognition which will be afforded the order in countries which have implemented the Convention;[34]

- the pre-application procedure;

---

[32]   Annex C, para 10.
[33]   [2003] EWHC 219 (Fam), [2003] 1 FLR 1111 at [65].
[34]   Hague Convention on Protection of Children and Co-operation in Respect of Intercountry Adoption 1999, Art 23.

• the court procedure.

Recognition

4.27 Under Art 23 of the Convention an adoption certified by the competent authority of the State of the adoption as having been made in accordance with the Convention shall be recognised by operation of law in the other contracting States. However, the recognition of an adoption may be refused in a contracting State but only if the adoption is manifestly contrary to its public policy, taking into account the best interests of the child.[35]

4.28 The recognition of an adoption under the Convention includes recognition of:

• the legal parent-child relationship between the child and his or her adoptive parents;

• the parental responsibility of the adoptive parents for the child;

• the termination of a pre-existing legal relationship between the child and his or her mother and father, if the adoption has this effect in the contracting State where it was made.[36]

4.29 The Convention also provides that in the case of an adoption having the effect of terminating a pre-existing legal parent-child relationship, the child shall enjoy in the receiving State, and in any other contracting State where the adoption is recognised, rights equivalent to those resulting from adoptions having this effect in each such State. This provision does not prejudice the application of any provision more favourable for the child, in force in the contracting State which recognises the adoption.[37]

4.30 Recognition is discussed further at **4.192**.

4.31 The Convention can be found in the Adoption (Intercountry Aspects) Act 1999, Sch 1.

4.32 A list of countries which have ratified or acceded to the Hague Convention can be found at http://www.hcch.net/index_en. php?act=conventions.text&cid=69.

---

[35] Hague Convention on Protection of Children and Co-operation in Respect of Intercountry Adoption 1999, Art 24.
[36] Ibid, Art 26.
[37] Ibid.

4.33   The UK has the power to suspend adoptions from signatory states. As from 23 July 2003, Cambodia is treated as a non-Convention country as far as the UK is concerned.[38]

4.34   The Permanent Bureau at the Hague has issued a *Guide to Good Practice on Implementation* which includes guidance on adoption support.[39]

Qualifying conditions for the grant of a Convention adoption order

4.35   An adoption order cannot be made as a Convention adoption order unless:

- in the case of an application by a couple, both members of the couple have been habitually resident in any part of the British Islands for a period of not less than one year ending with the date of the application; or

- in an application by one person, the applicant has been habitually resident in any part of the British Islands for a period of not less than one year ending with the date of the application;[40]

and

- the child to be adopted was, on the date on which the Art 17(3) agreement (the agreement of the Central Authorities for the state of origin and the receiving state that the adoption may proceed), habitually resident in a Convention country outside the British Islands; and

- where one member of a couple (in the case of an application by a couple) or the applicant (in the case of an application by one person) is not a British citizen, the Home Office has confirmed that the child is authorised to enter and reside permanently in the UK.[41]

4.36   The Central Authority for England is the Secretary of State for the Department for Education and Skills[42] and, in Wales, the National Assembly for Wales. In this chapter, references to the DfES should be read as referring to the National Assembly where applicable.

---

[38]   See *R (Charlton Thomson And Others) v Secretary of State for Education and Skills* [2005] EWHC 1378 (Admin), [2006] 1 FLR 175.
[39]   *The Implementation and Operation of the 1993 Hague Intercountry Adoption Convention: A Guide to Good Practice* (2008) available at http://www.hcch.net.
[40]   AFER 2005, reg 31.
[41]   Ibid.
[42]   Adoption (Intercountry Aspects) Act 1999, s 2(1).

4.37 'Habitual residence' under the Regulations has the same meaning as 'ordinarily resident' under the 1989 Act:[43]

'A person may cease to be habitually resident in country A in a single day if he or she leaves it with a settled intention not to return to it but to take up long-term residence in country B instead. Such a person cannot, however, become habitually resident in country B in a single day. An appreciable period of time and a settled intention will be necessary to enable him or her to become so ... where the habitual residence of a young person is in question, the element of volition will usually be that of the person or persons, who has or have parental responsibility for that child.'[44]

In *Greenwich London Borough Council v S*[45] Sumner J held that children in the care of a London Borough who had been placed with an aunt in Canada for what was regarded as an extended holiday remained habitually resident in England and Wales. The court was therefore able to entertain applications for adoption orders under the Convention.

REGULATORY OFFENCES

4.38 As well as the offences created under ACA 2002, s 83 (bringing children into the UK for the purpose of adoption – see **4.43**), s 85 (taking children out – see **4.123**) and AFER 2005, reg 59 (see **4.61**) the prohibitions backed by criminal sanction which are discussed in Chapter 7, have relevance for adoptions with an international element.

4.39 These are:

• illegal placements – ACA 2002, ss 92 and 93 (see **7.22**);

• restrictions on who can prepare reports – ACA 2002, s 94 (see **7.41**);

• prohibition on payments – ACA 2002, s 95 (see **7.31**);

• prohibitions on advertisements – ACA 2002, s 123 and 124 (see **7.13**).

4.40 The effect of the illegality on the adoption is discussed at **7.50**.

WHICH COURT?

4.41 Proceedings for adoption for a Convention adoption order, or one under the 2002 Act where s 83 applies (see **4.47**) must be started in or, if transferred to

---

[43] *Greenwich London Borough Council v S* [2007] EWHC 820 (Fam), [2007] 2 FLR 154 per Sumner J at [21].

[44] *Re J (A Minor) (Abduction: Custody Rights)* 2 AC 562 per Lord Brandon at 578.

[45] op cit.

a county court, must be transferred to an intercountry adoption centre.[46] These are: the Principal Registry of the Family Division[47] and the following county courts: Birmingham, Bournemouth, Bristol, Cardiff, Chester, Exeter, Leeds, Liverpool, Manchester, Newcastle-upon-Tyne, Nottingham, Portsmouth, Wrexham.[48]

4.42   When a court is considering under the Allocation and Transfer of Proceedings Order 2008[49] whether the proceedings ought to be heard in the High Court, in addition to the general factors in paragraph 5 of the Practice Direction – Allocation and Transfer of Proceedings,[50] it will take into account the following factors:

- whether an adoption order is sought in relation to a child who has been adopted abroad in a country whose adoption orders are not recognised in England and Wales;[51]

- whether an adoption order is sought in relation to a child who has been brought into the UK in circumstances where ACA 2002, s 83 applies and:
    - the person bringing the child, or causing the child to be brought has not complied with any requirement imposed by regulations made under s 83(4); or
    - has not met any condition required to be met by regulations made under s 83(5) within the required time; or

- whether there are complicating features in relation to the application.[52]

NON-CONVENTION ADOPTIONS

Section 83

4.43   It is an offence for any person who is habitually resident in the British Islands (the 'British resident') to

- bring, or cause another to bring, a child who is habitually resident outside the British Islands into the UK for the purpose of adoption by the British resident or by the British resident and another person; or

- at any time to bring, or cause another to bring, into the UK a child adopted by the British resident under an external adoption effected within the period of 6 months ending with that time;

---

[46]   Family Law: The Allocation and Transfer of Proceedings Order 2008 (SI 2008/2836), arts 11(1), 21(2).
[47]   Ibid, art 3.
[48]   Ibid, Sch 1.
[49]   SI 2008/2836.
[50]   3 November 2008.
[51]   Ibid, para 5.1(3).
[52]   Ibid, para 5.1(4).

unless the child is intended to be adopted under a Convention adoption order.[53]

4.44 An 'external adoption' means an adoption, other than a Convention adoption, of a child effected under the law of any country or territory outside the British Islands, whether or not the adoption is:

- an adoption within the meaning of ACA 2002, s 66 or

- a full adoption (within the meaning of ACA 2002, s 88(3)).[54]

4.45 A person guilty of an offence under this section is liable on summary conviction to imprisonment for a term not exceeding 6 months, or a fine not exceeding the statutory maximum, or both or, on conviction on indictment, to imprisonment for a term not exceeding 12 months, or a fine, or both.[55]

Entry requirements under Adoption Regulations

4.46 Part 2, Chapter 1 of AFER 2005 govern both the pre- and post-entry requirements where it is not intended that the child should be adopted under the Convention.

4.47 A person intending to bring, or to cause another to bring, a child into the UK in circumstances where s 83(1) of the Act applies must:

- apply in writing to an adoption agency for an assessment of his suitability to adopt a child; and

- give the agency any information it may require for the purpose of the assessment.[56]

4.48 Prior to the child's entry into the UK, the prospective adopter must:

- receive written notification from the Secretary of State that she has issued a certificate confirming to the relevant foreign authority:
  - that the person has been assessed and approved as eligible and suitable to be an adoptive parent in accordance with Part 4 of AAR 2005 or corresponding Welsh provision; and
  - that if entry clearance and leave to enter and remain, as may be necessary, is granted and not revoked or curtailed, and an adoption order is made or an overseas adoption is effected, the child will be authorised to enter and reside permanently in the UK;
  (A 'relevant foreign authority' means a person, outside the British Islands performing functions in the country in which the child is, or in

---

[53] ACA 2002, s 83(1), (2).
[54] ACA 2002, s 83(3).
[55] Ibid, s 83(8).
[56] AFER 2005, reg 3.

which the prospective adopter is, habitually resident which correspond to the functions of an adoption agency or to the functions of the Secretary of State in respect of adoptions with a foreign element.[57])

- before visiting the child in the State of origin:
    - notify the agency of the details of the child to be adopted;
    - provide the agency with any information and reports received from the relevant foreign authority; and
    - meet the agency to discuss the proposed adoption and information received from the relevant foreign authority;

- visit the child in the State of origin (and where the prospective adopters are a couple each of them must do so); and

- after that visit:
    - confirm in writing to the agency that he has done so and wishes to proceed with the adoption;
    - provide the agency with any additional reports and information received on or after that visit; and
    - notify the agency of his expected date of entry into the UK with the child.[58]

Home Study Reports

4.49 The reports as to the prospective adopters' suitability to adopt must be prepared by an adoption agency, that is, a local authority or registered adoption society.[59]

4.50 It an offence punishable on summary conviction to imprisonment for a term not exceeding 6 months, or a fine not exceeding level 5 on the standard scale, or both for a person to prepare a report for any person, to cause a person to prepare a report, or to submit to any person a report which has been prepared about the suitability of a child for adoption or of a person to adopt a child or about the adoption, or placement for adoption, of a child.[60] See **7.13** and following.

4.51 The report will cover the matters set out in Part 4 of AAR 2005 (see **7.119**).

---

[57] Ibid, reg 2.
[58] AFER 2005, reg 4(2).
[59] ACA 2002, s 2(1).
[60] Ibid, s 94(1), (5). See also *Re C (Adoption: Legality)* [1999] 1 FLR 370.

Entry requirements under the Immigration Rules

4.52 The UK Border agency has issued a very useful guide, *Inter-country Adoption and the Immigration Rules.*[61]

4.53 The prospective adopter or the child must show that he:

- is seeking limited leave to enter to accompany or join a person or persons who wish to adopt him in the UK (in one of the following circumstances):
    - both prospective adopters are present and settled in the UK;
    - both prospective adopters are being admitted for settlement on the same occasion that the child is seeking admission;
    - one prospective adopter is present and settled in the UK and the other is being admitted for settlement on the same occasion that the child is seeking admission;
    - one prospective adopter is present and settled in the UK and the other is being given limited leave to enter or remain in the UK with a view to settlement on the same occasion that the child is seeking admission, or has previously been given such leave;
    - one prospective adopter is being admitted for settlement on the same occasion that the other is being granted limited leave to enter with a view to settlement, which is also on the same occasion that the child is seeking admission;
    - one prospective adopter is present and settled in the UK or is being admitted for settlement on the same occasion that the child is seeking admission, and has had sole responsibility for the child's upbringing; or
    - one prospective adopter is present and settled in the UK or is being admitted for settlement on the same occasion that the child is seeking admission, and there are serious and compelling family or other considerations which would make the child's exclusion undesirable, and suitable arrangements have been made for the child's care; and
    - the child is under the age of 18;
    - the child is not leading an independent life, is unmarried, and has not formed an independent family unit;
    - the child can, and will, be maintained and accommodated adequately without recourse to public funds in accommodation which the adopters own or occupy exclusively;
    - the child will have the same rights and obligations as any other child of the marriage;
    - the child is being adopted due to the inability of the original parents or current carers (or those looking after him immediately prior to him being physically transferred to his prospective parent or parents) to care for him, and there has been a genuine transfer of parental responsibility to the prospective parent or parents;

---

[61] http://www.bia.homeoffice.gov.uk/sitecontent/documents/residency/intercountryadoption.pdf accessed on 24 May 2009.

- the child has lost or broken or intends to lose or break his ties with his family of origin; and
- the child will be adopted in the UK by the prospective adopters, but the proposed adoption is not one of convenience arranged to facilitate his admission to the UK.[62]

4.54 Prior Entry Clearance for admission is mandatory.

4.55 Although European Economic Area nationals can reside and exercise EEC Treaty rights in the UK, they are not 'settled' for the purpose of the Immigration Rules and cannot sponsor the entry of the child. *Inter-country Adoption and the Immigration Rules* provides further guidance.

4.56 Children will be admitted for a period of 24 months to allow the adoption to proceed.[63]

Post-entry requirements

4.57 The prospective adopter must accompany the child on entering the UK unless, in the case of a couple, the agency and the relevant foreign authority have agreed that it is necessary for only one of them to do so.[64]

4.58 Except where an overseas adoption is or is to be effected, the prospective adopter must within the period of 14 days beginning with the date on which the child is brought into the UK give notice to the relevant local authority:

- of the child's arrival in the UK; and

- of his intention:
    - to apply for an adoption order in accordance with ACA 2002, s 44(2); or
    - not to give the child a home.[65]

4.59 Where a prospective adopter has given notice and subsequently moves his home into the area of another local authority, he must within 14 days of that move confirm in writing to that authority, the child's entry into the UK and that notice of his intention to apply for an adoption order or not to give the child a home has been given to another local authority.[66]

---

[62] Ibid, Appendix 1 p 18. Immigration Rules HC 395.
[63] *Inter-country Adoption and the Immigration Rules*, op cit Appendix 1, p 13.
[64] AFER 2005, reg 4(3).
[65] Ibid, reg 4(4).
[66] Ibid, reg 4(5).

4.60 The 'relevant local authority' means in the local authority within whose area the prospective adopter has his home or in the case where he no longer has a home in England or Wales, the local authority for the area in which he last had his home.[67]

4.61 If a person brings, or causes another to bring, a child into the UK at any time in circumstances where this section applies, he is guilty of an offence if he has not complied with any requirement imposed by reg 4 of AFER 2005 (see **4.61**) or failed to meet any condition before that time, or before any later time.[68] A person guilty of an offence under this section is liable on summary conviction to imprisonment for a term not exceeding 6 months, or a fine not exceeding the statutory maximum, or both or on conviction on indictment, to imprisonment for a term not exceeding 12 months, or a fine, or both.[69]

4.62 AFER 2005 impose detailed functions on the local authority which include:

- setting up a case record;

- notifying the child's general practitioner, Primary Care Trust and, where the child is of compulsory school age, the local education authority;

- ensuring that the child and the prospective adopter are visited within 1 week of receipt of the notice of intention to adopt and thereafter not less than once a week until the initial review and thereafter at such frequency as the authority may decide;

- carrying out a review of the child's case not more than 4 weeks after receipt of the notice of intention to adopt and visit and, if necessary, review not more than 3 months after that initial review and thereafter not more than 6 months after the date of the previous visit;

- ensuring that:
  - advice is given as to the child's needs, welfare and development;
  - written reports are made of all visits and reviews of the case and placed on the child's case record; and
  - on such visits, where appropriate, advice is given as to the availability of adoption support services.[70]

Substantive law

4.63 The normal substantive law (see Chapter 2) applies with the following amendments.

---

[67] Ibid, reg 2.
[68] ACA 2002, s 83(7).
[69] ACA 2002, s 83(8).
[70] AFER 2005, reg 5.

- The notice of intention to adopt must not only be given to the relevant local authority not more than 2 years or less than 3 months before the adoption application is made,[71] it must be given within 14 days of the child's entry to the UK.

- Where the requirements imposed by ACA 2002, s 83(4) and the conditions required by s 83(5) have been complied with, the period under s 42(5) for which the child is required to have his home with at least one of the applicants ('in any other case' – see **6.71**) for 3 years in the period of 5 years preceding the application, is amended to 6 months. Where they are not met, the period of 12 months is substituted.[72]

- Other minor amendments are made to s 28(2) (change of name and removal from the UK)[73] and s 35 (return of child)[74] (see **7.252**).

4.64   Matters of particular relevance in the substantive law are:

- the habitual residence of the applicants and their having a home in the area of a local authority (see **17.17**);

- the consent of the birth parents or guardian especially where they have already adopted the child abroad (see **3.8** and **3.121**);

- adoption conferring British citizenship (see **2.88**).

4.65   When deciding whether to make an adoption order in respect of a child not domiciled in the UK, the court should consider whether its order will be recognised by the courts of the child's domicile.

> 'Evidence should be furnished to show that the order, if made, will be recognised by the foreign court ... If so, then the English court is free to proceed regardless of any question of foreign law or procedure but if not, the court will have to weigh the disadvantages of the child having one status here and another in other countries ... against the other considerations there may be in favour of adoption.'[75]

Procedure

4.66   The usual procedure for adoption applies (see Chapter 17) with the following additional provisions.

---

[71]   ACA 2002, s 44.
[72]   AFER 2005, reg 9.
[73]   AFER 2005, reg 7.
[74]   Ibid, reg 8.
[75]   *Re B(S) (An Infant)* [1968] Ch 204 per Goff J.

Which form?

4.67 The application for an adoption order is made in Form A60 where the child is habitually resident outside the British Islands and is brought into the UK for the purpose of adoption.[76]

The first directions hearing

4.68 At the first directions hearing in applications for:

- a Convention adoption order;

- a s 84 order;

- a s 88 direction;

- a s 89 order; and

- an adoption order where the child has been brought into the UK in the circumstances where s 83(1) of the Act applies,

the court will, in addition to any matters referred to in FP(A)R, r 26(1) (see **17.120**):

- consider whether the requirements of the Act and AFER 2005 appear to have been complied with and, if not, consider whether or not it is appropriate to transfer the case to the High Court;

- consider whether all relevant documents are translated into English and, if not, fix a timetable for translating any outstanding documents;

- consider whether the applicant needs to file an affidavit setting out the full details of the circumstances in which the child was brought to the UK, of the attitude of the parents to the application and confirming compliance with the requirements of AFER 2005;

- give directions about:
  - the production of the child's passport and visa;
  - the need for the Official Solicitor and a representative of the Home Office to attend future hearings;
  - personal service on the parents (via the Central Authority in the case of an application for a Convention Adoption Order) including information about the role of the Official Solicitor and availability of legal aid to be represented within the proceedings; and
  - consider fixing a further directions appointment no later than 6 weeks after the date of the first directions appointment and timetable

---

[76] Family Procedure (Adoption) Rules 2005 (FP(A)R 2005), r 17.

a date by which the Official Solicitor should file an interim report in advance of that further appointment.[77]

4.69   The Official Solicitor has to be considered because of his functions as the Central Authority in England and Wales for the Hague Convention on the Civil Aspects of International Child Abduction (the Abduction Convention), the Council Regulation[78] (Revised Brussels II) and the European Convention on Recognition and Enforcement of Decisions Concerning Custody of Children and on Restoration of Custody of Children (the European Convention). These functions are carried out by the International Child Abduction and Contact Unit.

4.70   The Home Office needs to be considered because an adoption order will result in the child being granted British citizenship (see **2.101**). The Secretary of State can apply to be joined as a party under Part 9 of FP(A)R 2005 (see **17.87**). It is the Secretary of State's policy to apply to be joined unless:

- the child is being adopted by a couple one of whom is the child's natural parent;

- the child was admitted in possession of an entry clearance marked 'for adoption';

- the child has been granted or would qualify for indefinite leave to remain or leave in some other capacity where it is accepted that his birth family is unable to care for him; or

- the child has been granted or would qualify for leave to remain for the purpose of adoption.[79]

4.71   In *Re R (Inter-Country Adoptions: Practice)*[80] Bracewell J gave the following guidance if a guardian is appointed – and it is suggested that one should be appointed. They must be pro-active. Priority should be given to interviewing the birth parents and early consideration also be given as to whether there is any need for expert evidence.

CONVENTION ADOPTIONS

Section 83

4.72   Section 83 does not apply if the child is intended to be adopted under a Convention adoption order.[81]

---

[77]   FP(A)R 2005, Practice Direction 5B.
[78]   (EC) No 2201/2003.
[79]   IDI (July/01) Ch 8, Annex 5, para 5.
[80]   [1999] 1 FLR 1042.
[81]   ACA 2002, s 83(2).

Entry requirements under Adoption Regulations

4.73 Part 3 Chapter 1 of AFER 2005 governs both the pre- and post-entry requirements where it is intended that the child should be adopted under the Convention.

4.74 Applicants who wish to adopt a child habitually resident in a Convention country outside the British Islands must:

- apply in writing to an adoption agency for a determination of eligibility, and an assessment of his suitability, to adopt; and

- give the agency any information it may require for the purposes of the assessment.[82]

The adoption agency

4.75 An agency may not consider an application unless at the date of that application:

- in the case of an application by a couple, they have both:
    - attained the age of 21 years; and
    - been habitually resident in a part of the British Islands for a period of not less than 1 year ending with the date of application;

- in the case of an application by one person, he has:
    - attained the age of 21 years; and
    - been habitually resident in a part of the British Islands for a period of not less than 1 year ending with the date of application.[83]

4.76 The agency must, unless it is satisfied another agency has done so, provide a counselling service for the prospective adopters in accordance with reg 21(1)(a) of AAR 2005 (see **7.97**) and explain to them and provide them with written information about the procedure and legal implications of adopting a child from the State of origin from which the prospective adopter wishes to adopt.[84]

4.77 The requirements for assessment and reports in AAR 2005, regs 22–25 apply (see **8.93**). In addition, the agency must include in the prospective adopter's report:

- the State of origin from which the prospective adopter wishes to adopt a child;

---

[82] AFER 2005, reg 13(1).
[83] AFER 2005, reg 13(2).
[84] Ibid, reg 14.

- confirmation that the prospective adopter is eligible to adopt a child under the law of that State;

- any additional information obtained as a consequence of the requirements of that State; and

- the agency's assessment of the prospective adopter's suitability to adopt a child who is habitually resident in that State.[85]

4.78   The advice of the agency's adoption panel under AAR 2005, reg 26 (see **7.119**) must be taken[86] and following the Panel's recommendation the agency must make a decision about whether the prospective adopter is suitable to adopt a child.

4.79   The review provisions under AAR 2005, reg 29 apply (see **7.124**) unless the agency has received written notification from the relevant Central Authority that the agreement under Art 17(c) (see **4.91**) of the Convention has been made.[87]

4.80   Where the agency has made a decision that the prospective adopter is suitable to adopt a child it must send to the DfES:

- written confirmation of the decision and any recommendation the agency may make in relation to the number of children the prospective adopter may be suitable to adopt, their age range, sex, likely needs and background;

- the enhanced criminal record certificate;

- all the documents and information which were passed to the adoption panel in accordance with AAR 2005, reg 25(9) or corresponding Welsh provision;

- the record of the proceedings of the adoption panel, its recommendation and the reasons for its recommendation; and

- any other information relating to the case as the DfES or the Central Authority of the State of origin may require.[88]

The Central Authority

4.81   If the DfES is satisfied that the agency has complied with the duties and procedures imposed by the AAR 2005 or corresponding Welsh provision, and

---

[85]   Ibid, reg 15 (1), (2).
[86]   Ibid, reg 15(3).
[87]   AFER 2005, reg 17.
[88]   Ibid, reg 18(1).

that all the relevant information has been supplied by that agency, it will send to the Central Authority of the State of origin:

- the prospective adopter's report;

- the enhanced criminal record certificate;

- a copy of the adoption agency's decision and the adoption panel's recommendation;

- any other information that the Central Authority of the State of origin may require; and

- a certificate in the form set out in Schedule 1 to the AFER 2005 confirming that:
  - the prospective adopter is eligible to adopt;
  - the prospective adopter has been assessed in accordance with this Chapter;
  - the prospective adopter has been approved as suitable to adopt a child; and
  - the child will be authorised to enter and reside permanently in the UK if entry clearance, and leave to enter or remain as may be necessary, is granted and not revoked or curtailed and a Convention adoption order or Convention adoption is made.[89]

Matching

4.82 If the relevant authority in the State of origin approves the application, the prospective adopters will be added to the waiting list of approved adopters until the authority can match them with a child. *The Guidance*[90] states that prospective adopters should be made aware that it can take some time to know what decision has been made by the authority in the State of origin. In some countries it is unlikely a decision will be made until the case comes to the top of the waiting list.[91]

4.83 If the application is not accepted or there are no suitable children, the Guidance states that the agency should arrange to discuss the outcome with the prospective adopter, provide counselling and support, and assist them in deciding what they would like to do.[92]

4.84 When prospective adopters are found eligible and suitable to adopt, their report will relate to a specific country. If they wish to apply to a different country after they have been approved the Guidance recommends that they should discuss this with the agency. They will need to demonstrate that they

---

[89] AFER 2005, reg 18(2).
[90] op cit Annex C, para 25.
[91] Ibid, para 27.
[92] Ibid, para 26.

fully understand the cultural and other needs of a child from the 'new' country, and that they also meet the eligibility criteria of that country. An addendum report should be produced and returned to the Panel and agency decision maker to obtain a new approval. This should then be forwarded to the DfES which should be informed at the earliest opportunity if the prospective adopter decides on a change of country, so that the authorities in the country concerned can be notified and the original application can be withdrawn. The applicants should also be warned that further expenses may be incurred.[93]

4.85 Where the relevant authority in the State of origin accepts the application it will consider the reports on the prospective adopters prior to making a match with a child. It will then either send the proposed match with information collated under Art 16 of the Convention about the child to the DfES, who will forward it to the prospective adopter and the agency or send the proposed match and information about the child to the prospective adopter directly. Where this is the case, the prospective adopter must send a copy of the reports to the agency. When the adoption agency receives details of the proposed match it must meet the prospective adopter to discuss the proposed adoption.[94]

4.86 The Art 16 information is:

- the report referred to in Art 16(1) of the Convention including information about the child's identity, adoptability, background, social environment, family history, medical history including that of the child's family and any special needs of the child;

- proof of confirmation that the consents of the persons, institutions and authorities whose consents are necessary for adoption have been obtained in accordance with Art 4 of the Convention; and

- the reasons for the Central Authority of the State of origin's determination on the placement.[95]

4.87 If at any time the prospective adopters decide not to go ahead the agency should:

- notify the DfES of this decision; and

- return all the papers to the DfES for return to the relevant authority in the State of origin.[96]

---

[93]   Ibid, paras 46–48; AFER 2005, reg 19 (1), (2).
[94]   *The Guidance*, para 27.
[95]   AFER 2005, reg 19(6).
[96]   *The Guidance*, Annex C, para 29; AFER 2005, reg 20.

4.88   The Guidance states that it is good practice for the adoption agency to offer the prospective adopters counselling, advice and support as well as discussing with them what options are now open to them and how they would like to proceed.[97]

4.89   If the prospective adopters decide that they would like to proceed further with the proposed match, they must visit the child in the State of origin.[98] The Guidance states that because a couple will be parenting the child together, they should be strongly encouraged to go together.[99]

4.90   If after meeting the child the prospective adopters wish to proceed with the adoption they must notify the agency in writing that:

- they have visited the child;

- they have provided the agency with additional reports and information received on or after that visit; and

- they wish to proceed to adopt the child.

4.91   The agency must then notify the DfES in writing that the requirements specified above have been satisfied and at the same time it must confirm that it is content for the adoption to proceed.[100] The DfES will then notify the Central Authority of the State of origin that:

- the prospective adopter wishes to proceed to adopt the child;

- it is prepared to agree with the Central Authority of the State of origin that the adoption may proceed; and

- confirm to the Central Authority of the State of origin that:
    - in the case where the requirements specified in s 1(5A) of the British Nationality Act 1981 are met that the child will be authorised to enter and reside permanently in the UK; or
    - in any other case, if entry clearance and leave to enter and remain, as may be necessary, is granted and not revoked or curtailed and a Convention adoption order or a Convention adoption is made, the child will be authorised to enter and reside permanently in the UK.[101]

---

[97]   *The Guidance*, Annex C, para 30; AFER 2005, reg 3.
[98]   AFER 2005, regs 4(2)(b), 19(3).
[99]   *The Guidance*, Annex C, para 32.
[100]   AFER 2005, reg 19(3).
[101]   Ibid, reg 19(4).

The two States will then reach an agreement about the adoption under Art 17(3) following which DfES must inform the adoption agency and the prospective adopter when the agreement under Art 17(c) of the Convention has been made.[102]

4.92   Following the agreement the prospective adopters must:

- notify the agency of their expected date of entry into the UK with the child;

- confirm to the agency when the child is placed with them by the competent authority in the State of origin; and

- accompany the child on entering the UK unless, in the case of a couple, the agency and the Central Authority of the State of origin have agreed that it is necessary for only one of them to do so.[103]

4.93   Where the agency is informed by the DfES that the agreement under Art 17(c) has been made and the adoption may proceed, it must, before the child enters the UK:

- send the prospective adopter's general practitioner written notification of the proposed placement and a written report of the child's health history and current state of health, so far as it is known;

- send the local authority (if that authority is not the adoption agency) and the Primary Care Trust or Local Health Board (Wales), in whose area the prospective adopter has his home, written notification of the proposed arrival of the child into England or Wales; and

- where the child is of compulsory school age, send the local education authority, in whose area the prospective adopter has his home, written notification of the proposed arrival of the child into England or Wales and information about the child's educational history if known and whether he is likely to be assessed for special educational needs under the Education Act 1996.[104]

Entry requirements under Immigration Regulations

4.94   Entry clearance for admission is mandatory.

---

[102]   Ibid, reg 19(5).
[103]   Ibid, reg 21.
[104]   AFER 2005, reg 22.

4.95 The prospective adopter or the child must show that the child:

- is seeking limited leave to enter to accompany one or two people each of whom are habitually resident in the UK and who wish to adopt him under the Hague Convention ('the prospective parents') in a UK court;

- is the subject of an agreement made under Art 17(c) of the Hague Convention (see **4.91**);

- has been entrusted to the prospective parents by the competent administrative authority of the country from which he is coming to the UK for adoption under the Hague Convention;

- is under the age of 18;

- can, and will, be maintained and accommodated adequately without recourse to public funds in accommodation which the prospective parent or parents own or occupy exclusively; and

- holds a valid UK entry clearance for entry in this capacity.[105]

4.96 If these requirements are met, entry clearance will be granted. The child will be admitted for a period of 24 months to allow the adoption to proceed.[106]

Post-entry requirements

4.97 The prospective adopters must within the period of 14 days beginning with the date on which the child enters the UK give notice to the relevant local authority:

- of the child's arrival in the UK; and

- of his intention:
    - to apply for an adoption order in accordance with ACA 2002, s 44(2) of the Act; or
    - not to give the child a home.[107]

The 'relevant local authority' means in the local authority within whose area the prospective adopter has his home or in the case where he no longer has a home in England or Wales, the local authority for the area in which he last had his home.[108]

4.98 Where prospective adopters have given notice and subsequently move home into the area of another local authority, they must within 14 days of that

---

[105] *Inter-country Adoption and the Immigration Rules* op cit at Sch 1, p 21.
[106] *Inter-country Adoption and the Immigration Rules* op cit at p 13.
[107] AFER 2005, reg 24(1).
[108] Ibid, reg 2.

move confirm to that authority in writing the child's entry into the UK and that notice has been given under AAR 2005, reg 24(1).[109]

4.99 The AFER 2005 impose detailed functions on the local authority which, subject to minor amendments are the same as imposed by reg 5 in respect of non-Convention adoptions (see **4.62**).[110]

Removal

4.100 Where the prospective adopter gives notice to the relevant local authority that he does not wish to proceed with the adoption and no longer wishes to give the child a home, the authority must:

- receive the child from him before the end of the period of 7 days beginning with the giving of the notice; and

- give notice to the DfES of the decision of the prospective adopter not to proceed with the adoption.[111]

4.101 Where the relevant local authority are of the opinion that the continued placement of the child is not in the child's best interests:

- the authority must give notice to the prospective adopter of their opinion and request the return of the child to them; and

- the prospective adopter must, not later than the end of the period of 7 days beginning with the date on which notice was given, return the child to the authority.[112]

4.102 However, if an application for a Convention adoption order was made prior to the giving of the notice and the application has not been disposed of, the prospective adopter is not required to return the child unless the court so orders.[113]

4.103 Where the relevant local authority has given notice, at the same time it must notify the DfES that it has requested the return of the child.[114]

4.104 This provision does not affect the exercise by any local authority or other person of any power conferred by any enactment or the exercise of any power of arrest.[115]

---

[109] Ibid, reg 24(2).
[110] Ibid, reg 25.
[111] Ibid, reg 27.
[112] AFER 2005, reg 27(1).
[113] Ibid, reg 27(3).
[114] Ibid, reg 27(2).
[115] Ibid, reg 27(4).

4.105 See also **4.116**.

Substantive law

4.106 The normal substantive law (see Chapter 2) applies with amendments discussed at **4.63**.

4.107 Matters in the substantive law of particular relevance to all international adoptions are discussed at **4.64**.

4.108 In addition:

• the qualifying conditions for the grant of a Convention adoption order (see **4.35**) must be met;

• any consent to a Convention adoption order must be in a form which comes with the internal law relating to adoption of the Convention country in which the child is habitually resident.[116]

Procedure

4.109 The usual procedure for adoption applies (see Chapter 17) with the additional provisions discussed at **4.66**.

4.110 There are the following additional provisions of relevance to Convention adoptions.

Which form?

4.111 The application for a Convention adoption order is made in Form A59.

Local authority report

4.112 The report of the investigation which a local authority must submit to the court in accordance with ACA 2002, s 44(5) must include:

• confirmation that the Certificate of eligibility and approval has been sent to the Central Authority of the State of origin in accordance with AFER 2005, reg 18 (see **4.81**);

• the date on which the agreement under Art 17(c) of the Convention was made; and

• details of the reports of the visits and reviews made in accordance with AFER 2005, reg 5 as modified by reg 25.[117]

---

[116] FP(A)R 2005, r 28(3).
[117] AFER 2005, reg 30.

The order

4.113 Within 7 days beginning with the date on which the final order was made in proceedings or such shorter time as the court may direct a court officer will send a copy of a Convention adoption order to the relevant Central Authority.[118]

4.114 When the DfES receives a copy of a Convention adoption order it must issue a certificate in the form set out in Sch 2 to AFER 2005 certifying that the adoption has been made in accordance with the Convention.[119] A copy of the certificate must be sent to:

- the Central Authority of the State of origin;

- the adoptive parent; and

- the adoption agency and, if different, the relevant local authority.[120]

Refusal of an order

4.115 Where an application for a Convention adoption order is refused by the court or is withdrawn, the prospective adopter must return the child to the relevant local authority within the period determined by the court.[121]

Breakdown of the placement

4.116 Where:

- notification is given by the prospective adopter under AFER 2005, reg 26 (unable to proceed with adoption);

- the child is withdrawn from the prospective adopter under AFER 2005, reg 27 (withdrawal of child from prospective adopter);

- an application for a Convention adoption order is refused;

- a Convention adoption which is subject to a probationary period cannot be made; or

- a Convention adoption order or a Convention adoption is annulled pursuant to ACA 2002, s 89(1),

the following provisions set out in AFER 2005, reg 28 apply.[122]

---

[118] FP(A)R, r 112(1)(c).
[119] AFER 2005, reg 32(1).
[120] Ibid, reg 32(2).
[121] AFER 2005, reg 33.
[122] Ibid, reg 28.

4.117 Where the relevant local authority (see **4.60**) is satisfied that it would be in the child's best interests to be placed for adoption with another prospective adopter habitually resident in the UK, it must take the necessary measures to identify a suitable adoptive parent for that child.

4.118 Where the relevant local authority have identified and approved another prospective adopter who is eligible, and has been assessed as suitable, to adopt in accordance with AFER 2005:

- that authority must notify the DfES in writing that:
  - another prospective adopter has been identified; and
  - the provisions in AFER, regs 14, 15 and 16 have been complied with; and

- the requirements specified in AFER 2005, regs 18 and 19 have been complied with.[123]

4.119 Where the DfES has been notified:

- it shall inform the Central Authority of the State of origin of the proposed placement; and

- it shall agree the placement with the Central Authority of the State of origin.

4.120 Where the relevant local authority is not satisfied it would be in the child's best interests to be placed for adoption with another prospective adopter in England or Wales, it must liaise with the DfES to arrange for the return of the child to his State of origin.[124]

4.121 Before coming to any decision under AFER 2005, reg 28, the relevant local authority must have regard to the wishes and feelings of the child, having regard to his age and understanding, and where appropriate, obtain his consent in relation to measures to be taken under reg 28.[125]

Offences

4.122 Any person who contravenes or fails to comply with:

- AFER 2005, reg 26 (requirement to notify relevant local authority) (see **4.97**);

- AFER 2005, reg 27 (withdrawal of child by local authority) (see **4.101**); or

---

[123] Ibid, reg 28(3).
[124] AFER 2005, reg 28(5).
[125] Ibid, reg 28(6).

- AFER 2005, reg 33 (return following a refusal of court to make Convention adoption order) (see **4.115**),

is guilty of an offence and liable on summary conviction to imprisonment for a term not exceeding 3 months, or a fine not exceeding level 5 on the standard scale, or both.[126]

REMOVAL OF CHILDREN OUTSIDE ENGLAND AND WALES FOR THE PURPOSE OF ADOPTION

Prohibition on removal

4.123 A child who is a Commonwealth citizen or is habitually resident in the UK, must not be removed from the UK to a place outside the British Islands for the purpose of adoption unless:

- the prospective adopters have parental responsibility for the child by virtue of an order under ACA 2002, s 84 (see **4.132**); or

- the child is removed under the authority of an order under s 49 of the Adoption (Scotland) Act 1978 or art 57 of the Adoption (Northern Ireland) Order 1987.[127, 128]

4.124 'Removing a child' from the UK includes arranging to do so. The circumstances in which a person arranges to remove a child from the UK include those where he:

- enters into an arrangement for the purpose of facilitating such a removal of the child;

- initiates or takes part in any negotiations of which the purpose is the conclusion of an arrangement within the above paragraph; or

- causes another person to take any step mentioned in either of the above two paragraphs.[129]

4.125 'An arrangement' includes an agreement (whether or not enforceable).[130]

4.126 A person who removes a child from the UK in contravention of subs 85(1) is guilty of an offence and liable on summary conviction to imprisonment for a term not exceeding 6 months, or a fine not exceeding the

---

[126] Ibid, reg 59.
[127] SI 1987/2203 (NI 22).
[128] ACA 2002, s 85(1), (2).
[129] Ibid, s 85(3).
[130] Ibid, s 85(3).

statutory maximum, or both and on conviction on indictment, to imprisonment for a term not exceeding 12 months, or a fine, or both.[131]

4.127 A person is not guilty of an offence of causing a person to take any step mentioned in subs 85(3)(a) or (b) unless it is proved that he knew or had reason to suspect that the step taken would contravene subs 85(1).

4.128 However, this defence applies only if sufficient evidence is adduced to raise an issue as to whether the person had the knowledge or reason mentioned.[132]

4.129 In any proceedings under ACA 2002, s 85, a report by a British consular officer or a deposition made before a British consular officer and authenticated under the signature of that officer is admissible, upon proof that the officer or the deponent cannot be found in the UK, as evidence of the matters stated in it. It is not necessary to prove the signature or official character of the person who appears to have signed any such report or deposition.[133]

4.130 Although a local authority may arrange for a child in its care to live outside England and Wales,[134] this power is expressly excluded if the placement is for adoption outside the UK.[135] However, in *Re A (A Child) (Adoption: Assessment Outside Jurisdiction)*[136] a distinction was drawn between a child being placed with potential adopters, in that case an uncle and aunt living in the United States, for the purpose of assessing whether it might be appropriate for the child to live there permanently, possibly but not necessarily under an adoption order, and the child being placed there for adoption.[137] In the former instance, the local authority can proceed under Sch 2, para 19 to the CA 1989 but in the latter, an order under ACA 2002, s 84 is required.

4.131 A placement for adoption abroad in breach of s 85 is still an effective placement.[138]

---

[131] Ibid, s 85(4), (6).
[132] Ibid, s 85(5).
[133] ACA 2002, s 85(7).
[134] CA 1989, Sch 2, para 19.
[135] Ibid, Sch 2, para 19(9).
[136] [2009] EWCA Civ 41, [2009] 2 FCR 123.
[137] Ibid per Wall LJ at [97]. See also *ECC v M* [2008] EWHC 332 (Fam) and *Plymouth City Council v CR* 13 June 2006 (unreported) Coleridge J.
[138] *Re A (Adoption: Placement Outside the Jurisdiction)* [2004] EWCA Civ 515 – decided under the provisions of the 1976 Act.

GIVING PARENTAL RESPONSIBILITY PRIOR TO ADOPTION ABROAD

4.132 The High Court may, on an application by persons who the court is satisfied intend to adopt a child under the law of a country or territory outside the British Islands, make an order giving parental responsibility for the child to them.[139]

Requirements as to residence etc

4.133 A section 84 order cannot be made where the court is satisfied the proposed adopters meet the requirements as to domicile, or habitual residence, in England and Wales which have to be met if an adoption order is to be made in favour of those persons.[140] Instead they have to apply for an adoption order in the UK.

4.134 The Act and the Regulations have to balance the purpose of the removal of the child, namely that he should be adopted abroad by adopters who will usually be living abroad, and the need to ensure that before the order is made, there has been an adequate opportunity for the agency or local authority to observe the child with the applicants and to ensure that adoption by them will meet its best interests. They attempt to strike this balance by a number of provisions.

- An application for a s 84 order cannot be made unless at all times during the preceding 10 weeks the child's home was with the applicant or, in the case of an application by two people, both of them.[141] However, the applicant's home during the 10 weeks preceding the application need not be in England and Wales.[142] Nor does s 84(4) require the physical presence of each applicant throughout the 10-week period.[143]

- An order under s 84 may not be made unless the court is satisfied that sufficient opportunities to see the child with the applicant or, in the case of an application by a couple, both of them together in the home environment have been given:
    - where the child was placed for adoption with the applicant or applicants by an adoption agency, to that agency;
    - in any other case, to the local authority within whose area the home is.[144]

---

[139]   ACA 2002, s 84(1).
[140]   Ibid, s 84(2).
[141]   ACA 2002, s 84(4).
[142]   *Re A (A Child) (Adoption: Assessment Outside Jurisdiction)* [2009] EWCA Civ 41, [2009] 2 FCR 123, allowing an appeal against the judgment at first instance at [2008] EWHC 1722 (Fam), reported as *Haringey LBC v MA, JN, IA* [2008] 2 FLR 1857.
[143]   *Re G (Adoption: Placement Outside Jurisdiction)* [2008] EWCA Civ 105, [2008] 1 FLR 1484.
[144]   AFER 2005, reg 11(1)(i), applying s 42(7).

4.135 The difficulties which can arise are illustrated by *Re A (A Child) (Adoption: Assessment Outside Jurisdiction)*.[145] A local authority wanted to assess Mr and Mrs N, who lived in the United States, as potential adopters for their niece, A. Mr and Mrs N were unable to come to England to stay for a period of 10 weeks. Therefore a s 84 order could not be made unless the child was placed with them for adoption. However, her parents had not yet given their consent to the placement and no placement order had been made. Before it could be made, an assessment of the Ns and their relationship with A was needed. The Court of Appeal cut the knot by stating that A could be placed with the Ns under CA 1989, Sch 2, para 19 ('arrangements to assist children to live abroad'). An assessment could then be carried out and thereafter a placement order sought (if the parents did not consent to the placement). If granted, A could be placed with the Ns for adoption during a short stay in England and Wales. Although A had to have her home with the Ns for 10 weeks preceding the placement, that home did not have to be in the jurisdiction nor did the sufficient opportunity to observe A with the Ns have to post-date the placement.

Substantive law

4.136 The requirements of the substantive law concerning the making of a placement order (see Chapter 3) and adoption (including consent or dispensing with consent) (see Chapter 2) must be met.[146]

Procedure

4.137 The procedure is governed by AFER 2005, Part 2, Chapter 2, regs 10–11 for non-Convention countries and Part 3, Chapter 2, regs 35–51 for removal to Convention countries.

Child placed by an adoption agency

Removal to non-Convention countries

4.138 *The Guidance* states that where a local authority decides that a looked after child's best interests may be served by being adopted by a known person in another country (for example, a relative) they must satisfy themselves of the individual's suitability to adopt the child. The assessment should usually be carried out in the individual's State of origin and be sent to the agency for consideration in the same way as for any other prospective adopter.[147]

4.139 Where the child was placed with the applicants by an adoption agency, the agency must:

---

[145] op cit.

[146] ACA 2002, s 84(3); AFER 2005, reg 11.

[147] op cit Annex C, para 68.

- confirm to the court that it has complied with the requirements imposed in accordance with Part 3 of the Agencies Regulations or corresponding Welsh provision;

- submit to the court:
  - the reports and information prepared for the adoption panel under AAR 2005, reg 17 (see **7.73**);
  - the recommendations made by the adoption agency (see **7.149**);
  - the adoption placement report;
  - the reports and information obtained in respect of the post-placement visits and reviews referred to in AAR 2005, reg 36 (see **7.206** and **7.215**);
  - the report referred to in ACA 2002, s 43 (see **8.65**).[148]

4.140 In addition the relevant foreign authority must:

- confirm in writing to the agency that the prospective adopter has been counselled and the legal implications of adoption have been explained to him;

- prepare a report on the suitability of the prospective adopter to be an adoptive parent;

- determine and confirm in writing to the agency that he is eligible and suitable to adopt in the country or territory in which the adoption is to be effected; and

- confirm in writing to the agency that the child is or will be authorised to enter and reside permanently in that foreign country or territory.[149]

4.141 The 'relevant foreign authority' will be the foreign equivalent of the English adoption agency, not a governmental body.[150] The confirmation of the matters set out in AFER 2005, reg 10(b) need not be in absolute, unconditional or unqualified terms.

> 'We read it as requiring confirmation from the foreign body equivalent to an English adoption agency to the effect that, provided that all relevant procedures in the UK, and any adoption-related procedures under the law of the foreign state which are prerequisites to the child being allowed into that state are followed, then, from its knowledge and experience, the child will be authorised to enter the foreign state.'[151]

---

[148] AFER 2005, reg 10(1)(a).

[149] AFER 2005, reg 10(1)(b).

[150] *Re G (Adoption: Placement Outside Jurisdiction)* op cit at [32]. See also *Re G (Adoption: Placement Outside Jurisdiction) (No 2)* [2008] EWCA Civ 105 2, [2008] 1 FLR 1497.

[151] Ibid, per Sir Mark Potter P at [32].

4.142 The non-statutory guidance, *Preparing and Assessing Prospective Adopters*[152] notes that some prospective intercountry adopters may be ineligible to adopt a child from another country if they do not meet the legal requirements of that country and adds that the agency is responsible for checking the eligibility of prospective adopters in such cases.

4.143 Information about the legal requirements of other countries may be obtained from www.dfes.gov.uk/intercountryadoption/countries.shtml

4.144 The prospective adopter must confirm in writing to the agency that he will accompany the child on taking him out of the UK and entering the country or territory where the adoption is to be effected, or in the case of a couple, the agency and relevant foreign authority have confirmed that it is necessary for only one of them to do so.[153]

4.145 The court apparently has no power to dispense with these requirements and, unless they are complied with, no order can be made.[154]

Removal to Convention countries

4.146 Where an adoption agency is considering whether a child is suitable for an adoption in accordance with the Convention, it must, unless the agency is satisfied that the requirements have been carried out in respect of the prospective adopter by another agency, provide a counselling service for and information to that child and for the parent or guardian of the child in accordance with AAR 2005, regs 13 and 14[155] and explain to them in an appropriate manner the procedure in relation to, and the legal implications of, adoption under the Convention for that child by a prospective adopter habitually resident in the receiving State; and provide them with written information about those matters.[156]

4.147 The child's permanence report which the agency is required to prepare in accordance with AAR 2005, reg 17 must include a summary of the possibilities for placement of the child within the UK and an assessment of whether an adoption by a person in a particular receiving State is in the child's best interests.[157]

---

[152] (DfES, 2006) para 10.
[153] AFER 2005, reg 10(c).
[154] Ibid, reg 10(1).
[155] Every reference to the Regulations is also a reference to 'or corresponding Welsh provision'.
[156] AAR 2005, regs 36 and 37.
[157] Ibid, reg 38(1).

4.148 The agency must send, if received, the Art 15 Report and their observations on that Report, together with the above reports and information referred to in AAR 2005, reg 17(2) to the adoption panel[158] which must take them into account.[159]

4.149 Where the agency decides, following the Panel recommendation, that the child should be placed for an adoption in accordance with the Convention it must notify the DfES of:

• the name, sex and age of the child;

• the reasons why they consider that the child may be suitable for such an adoption;

• whether a prospective adopter has been identified and, if so, provide any relevant information; and

• any other information that the DfES may require.[160]

4.150 The DfES has to maintain a Convention list of children who are notified to that Authority under AAR 2005, reg 40 and shall make the contents of that list available for consultation by other Authorities within the British Islands.[161]

4.151 Where a local authority places for adoption a child whose details have been notified to the DfES or determines that an adoption in accordance with the Convention is no longer in the best interests of the child, it must notify the DfES accordingly and the DfES must remove the details relating to that child from the Convention list.[162]

4.152 When the DfES receives a report from the Central Authority of the receiving State which has been prepared for the purposes of Art 15 which relates to a prospective adopter who is habitually resident in that receiving State; and the prospective adopter named in the report wishes to adopt a child who is habitually resident in the British Islands, the Department if it is satisfied that the prospective adopters:

• meet the age requirements as specified in ACA 2002, ss 50 and 51; and

• in the case of a couple, both are, or in the case of adoption by one person, that person is habitually resident in a Convention country outside the British Islands,

---

[158] Ibid, reg 38(2).
[159] Ibid, reg 39.
[160] Ibid, reg 40.
[161] AAR 2005, reg 41(1).
[162] Ibid, reg 41(2).

must consult the Convention list and may, if it considers it appropriate, consult any Convention list maintained by another Central Authority within the British Islands.[163]

4.153 Where the DfES identifies a child on the Convention list who may be suitable for adoption by the prospective adopter, the Department must send the Art 15 report to the local authority which referred the child's details to it.[164]

4.154 Where a prospective adopter has already been identified in relation to a proposed adoption of a particular child, the Department need not consult the Convention list but must send the Art 15 Report to the local authority.[165]

4.155 On receipt of the Art 15 report the agency must, unless it has already done so refer the report to the panel and consider its recommendations before deciding whether a Convention adoption by the prospective adopter is in the child's best interests.[166]

4.156 If the agency decides that the proposed placement should proceed, it must prepare a report for the purposes of Art 16(1) which must include:

- the information about the child which is specified in Sch 1 to AAR 2005; and

- the reasons for their decision.[167]

4.157 The agency must send the DfES:

- the report;

- details of any placement order or other orders, if any, made by the courts; and

- confirmation that the parent or guardian consents to the proposed adoption.[168]

4.158 The DfES must then send the documents referred to above to the Central Authority of the receiving State.[169]

4.159 The DfES may notify the Central Authority of the receiving State that it is prepared to agree that the adoption may proceed, provided that the Central Authority has confirmed that:

---

[163] Ibid, reg 42(1), (2) (4).
[164] Ibid, reg 42(2), (5).
[165] Ibid, reg 42 (3).
[166] Ibid, regs 43, 44, 45 and 48.
[167] AAR 2005, reg 46(1).
[168] Ibid, reg 46(2).
[169] Ibid, reg 46(3).

- the prospective adopter has agreed to adopt the child and has received such counselling as may be necessary;

- the prospective adopter has confirmed that he will accompany the child to the receiving State, unless in the case of a couple, the adoption agency and the Central Authority of the receiving State have agreed that it is only necessary for one of them to do so;

- it is content for the adoption to proceed;

- in the case where a Convention adoption is to be effected, it has explained to the prospective adopter the need to make an application under s 84(1) of the Act; and

- the child is or will be authorised to enter and reside permanently in the Convention country if a Convention adoption is effected or a Convention adoption order is made.[170]

4.160 However the DfES may not make an agreement under Art 17(c) with the Central Authority of the receiving State unless:

- confirmation has been received in respect of the matters referred to above;

- the agency has confirmed to the DfES that:
    - it has met the prospective adopters and explained the requirement to make an application for an order under s 84 of the Act before the child can be removed from the UK;
    - the prospective adopters have visited the child; and
    - the prospective adopters are content for the adoption to proceed.[171]

4.161 An agency may not place a child for adoption unless the agreement under Art 17(c) has been made and the DfES must advise the agency when that agreement has been made.[172]

4.162 In the case of a proposed Convention adoption, the following requirements have to be met to satisfy s 84(3).[173]

4.163 The competent authorities of the receiving State must have:

- prepared a report for the purposes of Art 15;

- determined and confirmed in writing that the prospective adoptive parent is eligible and suitable to adopt;

---

[170]   Ibid, reg 47(1).
[171]   AAR 2005, reg 47(2) and (4).
[172]   Ibid, reg 47(3).
[173]   Ibid, reg 48.

- ensured and confirmed in writing that the prospective adoptive parent has been counselled as may be necessary; and

- determined and confirmed in writing that the child is or will be authorised to enter and reside permanently in that State.

AFER 2005, reg 10(b), which deals with non-Convention orders, refers to 'the relevant foreign authority' whereas reg 48 refers to the 'competent authority', for which see Art 22(2). In practice the two expressions would seem to mean the same.

4.164 The agency must have:

- prepared the report required for the purposes of Art 16(1);

- confirmed in writing that it has complied with the requirements imposed upon it under Part 3 of AAR 2005 and Part 3, Chapter 2 of AFER 2005;

- has obtained and made available to the court:
  – the reports and information referred to in AAR 2005, reg 17(1) and (2);
  – the recommendation made by the adoption panel in accordance with AAR 2005, reg 18; and
  – the adoption placement report prepared in accordance with AAR 2005, reg 31(2);

- included in their report submitted to the court in accordance with ACA 2002, s 43(a) or s 44(5) as modified respectively by AAR 2005, reg 11, details of any reviews and visits carried out as a consequence of Part 6 of the AAR 2005.

4.165 The prospective adopters must have confirmed in writing that they will accompany the child on taking the child out of the UK to travel to the receiving State unless, in the case of a couple, the agency and competent foreign authority have confirmed that it is necessary for only one of them to do so.

4.166 In the case of a proposed application for a Convention adoption order, the report which a local authority must submit to the court in accordance with ACA 2002, s 43(a) or s 44(5) must include a copy of the:

- Art 15 Report;

- report prepared for the purposes of Art 16(1); and

- written confirmation of the agreement under Art 17(c) of the Convention.[174]

---

[174] AAR 2005, reg 49.

Return of the child to the adoption agency

4.167 Where an agency gives notice to the prospective adopters that they require the return of the child under ACA 2002, s 35(2) in respect of the child (see **7.255**) and before the notice was given, an application for a s 84 order, special guardianship order or residence order, or for leave to apply for a special guardianship order or residence order, has been made and the application (and, in a case where leave is given on an application to apply for a special guardianship order or residence order, the application for the order) has not been disposed of, the prospective adopters are not required by virtue of the notice to return the child to the agency unless the court so orders.[175]

The test

4.168 The welfare test and checklist apply.

Court procedure

Which court?

4.169 An application for a s 84 order must be heard in the High Court.[176]

Which form?

4.170 The application is made in Form A61.

Who are the parties?

4.171 The applicants are the prospective adopters.[177]

4.172 The respondents are the same as for an adoption order (see **17.46**).[178]

General procedure

4.173 The general rules of procedure apply as for an adoption order. In addition, Practice Direction 5B makes provision for certain matters to be considered at the first direction hearing.

---

[175] ACA 2002, s 35(5) as applied and amended by AFER 2005, reg 11(2).
[176] ACA 2002, s 84(1).
[177] FP(A)R 2005, r 22(3), Table 1.
[178] Ibid, Table 2.

The effect of the order

4.174 The order grants parental responsibility to the applicants[179] and enables them to remove the child from the UK for the purpose of being adopted abroad.[180]

4.175 The making of the order operates to extinguish:

- the parental responsibility which any person other than the applicants or applicant has for the child immediately before the making of the order;

- any order under the CA 1989 or the Children (Northern Ireland) Order 1995;[181]

- any order under the Children (Scotland) Act 1995 other than an excepted order; and

- any duty arising by virtue of an agreement or an order of a court to make payments, so far as the payments are in respect of the adopted child's maintenance or upbringing for any period after the making of the adoption order.

4.176 The order:

- does not affect parental responsibility so far as it relates to any period before the making of the order; and

- in the case of an order made on an application by the partner of a parent of the adopted child, does not affect the parental responsibility of that parent or any duties of that parent within subsection 52(2)(d) not being a duty arising by virtue of an agreement which constitutes a trust, or which expressly provides that the duty is not to be extinguished by the making of an adoption order.[182]

Revocation

4.177 The order can be revoked but only apparently if the court determines, on an application for an adoption order, not to make the order.[183]

---

[179] ACA 2002, s 84(1).
[180] Ibid, s 85(1),(2).
[181] SI 1995/755 (NI 2).
[182] ACA 2002, s 84(5) which applies s 46(2)–(4).
[183] Ibid, s 24(4) applied by AFER 2005, reg 11(1)(e).

MODIFICATION OR ANNULMENT OF OVERSEAS AND CONVENTION ADOPTIONS

Modification of a Convention adoption order

4.178   Some countries, like the UK, completely sever the legal tie between the child and his birth parents. Such an adoption is referred to as a 'full adoption'.[184] For example, ACA 2002, s 67(3) provides that an adopted person is to be treated in law as not being the child of any person other than the adopter and (in the case where s 51(2) applies), the adopter's partner. See **2.96**.

4.179   In other countries the tie is not completely severed and these orders are referred to as 'simple adoptions'. Only the State of origin which makes a Convention adoption order can decide whether the legal relationship has been severed.[185] This creates potential difficulties when the UK authorities have to decide how a Convention adoption order, made by another Convention country is to be applied in domestic law.

4.180   Section 88 therefore provides that if the High Court is satisfied, on an application, that each of the following conditions is met in the case of a Convention adoption, it may direct that ACA 2002, s 67(3) does not apply, or does not apply to any extent specified in the direction.[186]

4.181   The conditions are:

- that under the law of the country in which the adoption was effected, the adoption is not a full adoption;

- that the consents referred to in Art 4(c) and (d) of the Convention have not been given for a full adoption or that the UK is not the receiving State (within the meaning of Art 2 of the Convention); and

- that it would be more favourable to the adopted child for a direction to be given under ACA 2002, s 88(1).[187]

Procedure

4.182   The appropriate form is Form A62.

4.183   The applicants may be:

- the adopted child;

---

[184]   ACA 2002, s 88(3).
[185]   1993 Hague Convention on Protection of Children and Co-operation in Respect of Intercountry Adoption 1999, Art 26(1).
[186]   ACA 2002, s 88(1).
[187]   Ibid, s 88(2).

- the adopters;

- any parent;

- any other person.[188]

4.184 The respondents are:

- the adopters;

- the parents;

- the adoption agency;

- the local authority to whom notice under ACA 2002, s 44 has been given;

- the Attorney General.[189]

Annulment of an overseas or Convention adoption order

4.185 The High Court may, on an application:

- annul a Convention adoption order on the ground that the adoption is contrary to public policy;

- direct that an overseas adoption or a determination under s 91 shall cease to be valid on the ground that the adoption or determination is contrary to public policy or that the authority which purported to authorise the adoption or make the determination was not competent to entertain the case; or

- decide the extent, if any, to which a determination under s 91 has been affected by a subsequent determination under that section.[190]

4.186 'A determination' under s 91 is an authorisation or review of an authorisation by an authority in a Convention country of an adoption order made in that country or territory or the revocation or annulment or the review of a revocation or annulment of such an adoption order or a Convention adoption.[191]

4.187 'An overseas adoption' means an adoption of a description specified in an order made by the Secretary of State, being a description of adoptions

---

[188] FP(A)R 2005, r 23, Table 1.
[189] op cit, Table 2.
[190] ACA 2002, s 89 (1), (2).
[191] Ibid, s 91(1).

effected under the law of any country or territory outside the British Islands, but does not include a Convention adoption.[192]

4.188 The High Court may, in any proceedings, decide that an overseas adoption or a determination under s 91 is to be treated, for the purposes of those proceedings, as invalid on either of the grounds mentioned in s 89(2)(a).[193]

4.189 Subject to the above provisions, the validity of a Convention adoption, Convention adoption order or overseas adoption or a determination under s 91 cannot be called in question in proceedings in any court in England and Wales.[194]

4.190 No application may be made under ACA 2002, s 89(1) (invalidity) in respect of an adoption unless immediately before the application is made:

• the person adopted, or

• the adopters or adopter

are habitually resident in England and Wales.[195]

4.191 In deciding under s 89 whether such an authority as is mentioned in s 91 was competent to entertain a particular case, a court is bound by any finding of fact made by the authority and stated by the authority to be so made for the purpose of determining whether the authority was competent to entertain the case.[196]

RECOGNITION OF OVERSEAS ADOPTIONS

4.192 The recognition of overseas adoptions is largely but not wholly concerned with matters of immigration law. Reference should therefore be made to such textbooks as *Macdonald Immigration Law and Practice*[197] or *Dicey, Morris and Collins on the Conflict of Laws*.[198]

4.193 In summary, Courts in England and Wales give recognition to the following adoptions made overseas.

---

[192] Ibid, s 7(1).
[193] Ibid, s 89(3).
[194] Ibid, s 89(4).
[195] ACA 2002, s 90(2).
[196] Ibid, s 90(3).
[197] (Butterworths, 7th revised edn, 2009).
[198] (Sweet & Maxwell, 14th edn, 2008). The Immigration Rules and the four avenues for obtaining entry clearance were discussed in *MN (India) v Entry Clearance Officer (New Delhi)* [2008] EWCA Civ 38, [2008] 2 FLR 87 per Ward LJ at [13]–[18].

Convention adoption

4.194 Full recognition is granted (see **4.27**).

Overseas adoptions

4.195 Overseas adoptions as defined in s 87(1) (see **4.187**) are recognised[199] but the adoption has to be proved by evidence which may include a certified copy of an entry made in a public register or certificate as provided by art 4 of the Adoption (Designation of Overseas Adoptions) Order 1973. However, the adoption will not confer UK citizenship.[200]

Other adoptions

4.196 These may be recognised if the adopting parties were domiciled in the country where the order was made at the time it was made but equally domestic courts may refuse to recognise them on grounds of public policy.[201]

4.197 In *Re Goodman's Trusts*,[202] James LJ said that:

'The family relation is at the foundation of all society, and it would appear almost an axiom that the family relation, once duly constituted by the law of any civilised country, should be respected and acknowledged by every other member of the great community of nations.'

4.198 Later, in *Re Valentine's Settlement*[203] Lord Denning MR commented that *Re Goodman's Trusts* was a legitimation case but 'the like principle applies to adoption'. He continued:

'But when is the status of adoption duly constituted? Clearly it is so when it is constituted in another country in similar circumstances as we claim for ourselves. Our courts should recognise a jurisdiction which *mutatis mutandis* they claim for themselves: see *Travers v Holley*.[204] We claim jurisdiction to make an adoption order when the adopting parents are domiciled in this country and the child is resident here. So also, out of the comity of country when the adopting parents are domiciled there and the child is resident there.

Apart from international comity, we reach the same result on principle. When a court of any country makes an adoption order for an infant child, it does two things: (1) it destroys the legal relationship theretofore existing between the child and its natural parents, be it legitimate or illegitimate; (2) it creates the legal relationship of parent and child between the child and its adopting parents, making it their legitimate child. It creates a new status in both, namely, the status of parent and child. Now it has long been settled that questions affecting status

---

[199]   ACA 2002, ss 66(1), 67(1).
[200]   Ibid, s 74(2).
[201]   *Re Valentine's Settlement* [1965] 1 Ch 832.
[202]   (1881) 17 Ch.D. 266 at 297.
[203]   [1965] 1 Ch 832 at 842. See also Danckwerts LJ at 846.
[204]   [1953] P 246 at 257.

are determined by the law of the domicile. This new status of parent and child, in order to be recognised everywhere, must be validly created by the law of the domicile of the adopting parent. You do not look to the domicile of the child: for that has no separate domicile of its own. It takes its parents' domicile. You look to the parents' domicile only. If you find that a legitimate relationship of parent and child has been validly created by the law of the parents' domicile at the time the relationship is created, then the status so created should be universally recognised throughout the civilised world, provided always that there is nothing contrary to public policy in so recognising it.'

4.199 In *D v D (Foreign Adoption)*,[205] Ryder J granted a declaration that adoptions in India under the Hindu Adoption and Maintenance Act 1956 of two orphans by a couple who were Indian citizens but with indefinite leave to enter and remain in the UK were recognised in English law and had resulted in adoptions as defined by ACA 2002, s 66(1)(e).

De facto adoptions

4.200 These are not recognised as creating in domestic law the relationship of parent and child but may be given effect as the basis for entry and stay in the UK.[206] There is no obligation in international law to recognise *de facto* adoption.

> 'In my judgment ... at best [*UNHCR's Global Consultations on International Protection*[207]] illustrate an increasing awareness of the need for a flexible approach to the concept of family but they do not address in terms the question of de facto adoption which, because of its very lack of formality, presents a receiving state with obvious problems of verification. ... Whilst there is a perceptible concern that the concept of family, in the context of family reunion, should not be resistant to social and cultural change, I do not consider that there is a precise, identifiable obligation of customary international law that is prescriptive of the national approach to de facto adoption.'[208]

However, for some purposes of domestic immigration law, a *de facto* adoption is treated as giving rise to a parent/child relationship.

4.201 Paragraph 310 of the Immigration Rules[209] provides that:

> 'The requirements to be met in the case of a child seeking indefinite leave to enter the UK as the adopted child of a parent or parents present and settled in the UK are that he ... (ix) was adopted due to the inability of the original parent(s) or current carer(s) to care for him, and there has been a genuine transfer of parental responsibility to the adoptive parents.'

---

[205] [2008] EWHC 403 (Fam), [2008] 1 FLR 1475.
[206] Macdonald op cit, Supp to 7th edn, para 11.04.
[207] (2001) – see Feller, Türk and Nicholson (eds) Refugee Protection in International Law (Cambridge University Press, 2003).
[208] *MK (Somalia) v Entry Clearance Officer, Joint Council for the Welfare of Immigrants Intervening* [2008] EWCA Civ 1453, [2009] 2 FLR 138 per Maurice McKay LJ at [12].
[209] HC 395.

'Parent' is defined as including:

> 'an adoptive parent, where a child was adopted in accordance with a decision taken by the competent administrative authority or court in a country whose adoption orders are recognised by the UK or *where the child is the subject of a de facto adoption in accordance with the requirements of paragraph 309A of these Rules ...*'[210]

4.202 Paragraph 309A of the Immigration Rules provides:

> 'For the purposes of adoption under paragraphs 310–316C a *de facto* adoption shall be regarded as having taken place if:
>
> (a) at the time immediately preceding the making of the application for entry clearance under these Rules the adoptive parent or parents have been living abroad (in applications involving two parents both must have lived abroad together for at least a period of time equal to the first period mentioned in sub-paragraph (b)(i)) and must have cared for the child for at least a period of time equal to the second period material in that sub-paragraph and
> (b) during their time abroad the adoptive parent or parents have:
>   (i) lived together for a minimum of 18 months, of which the 12 months immediately preceding the application for entry clearance must have been spent living together with the child and
>   (ii) assumed the role of the child's parents, since the beginning of the 18 month period, so that there has been a genuine transfer of parental responsibility.'

4.203 In *Singh v Entry Clearance Officer, New Delhi*[211] two Indian born British citizens, living in the UK, had one child and decided in accordance with their cultural and religious custom to adopt another child from within their family. Having chosen a baby of a cousin who lived in India, they participated in a religious adoption ceremony and then executed a deed of adoption which, having been registered was recognised by the Indian courts. The Court of Appeal held that the child was entitled to entry clearance to enter the UK. The fact that an adoption did not meet the requirements of relevant international instruments such as the *Declaration on Social and Legal Principles relating to the Protection and Welfare of Children, with special reference to Foster Placements and Adoption Nationally and Internationally*[212] should not invariably be a reason for according little weight to it in determining whether family life exists or not.

> 'Such a rigid and formulaic approach is in my view not justified. The significance of the failure to satisfy the requirements of relevant international instruments will vary from case to case. Of considerable importance will be the nature of the departure from the provisions of a relevant instrument. If the departure is one of

[210] Ibid, para 6.
[211] [2004] EWCA Civ 308, [2005] 1 FLR 308.
[212] Adopted by the UN General Assembly in Resolution 41/85 of 3 December 1986.

substance rather than procedure and it goes to the heart of the safeguards that the instrument is intended to promote, then it may well be appropriate to give the adoption order little weight.'[213]

4.204   Dyson LJ continued:

'I would accept that an inter-country adoption which has come about in circumstances in which little or no regard has been had to the best interests of the child must be viewed with great caution. An adoption order made in those circumstances should not, of itself, be given much weight in deciding whether family life has been established. But, there will be cases in which, although the order was made without regard to the best interests of the child, it can be seen, with hindsight, that adoption was, in fact, in the child's best interests; and that the fact that the order was made, and has been recognised in the jurisdiction in which the child has been living, has enabled a family relationship to develop. In such circumstances the fact that the order was made without regard to the child's best interests is not a reason to refuse recognition to the family life which has, in fact, developed as a result of the order.'[214]

4.205   In comparison, in *RS v Entry Clearance Officer (New Delhi)*[215] the Court of Appeal held that there had been no genuine transfer of parental responsibility. The natural parents lacked neither the means, the skill nor the opportunity to care for the child but did not wish to do so.[216]

4.206   Even where cases fall outside the test for *de facto* adoption, there may still be an argument under Art 8 of the European Convention on Human Rights to support the grant of a right of entry.[217] However, such an argument failed on its facts in *MN (India) v Entry Clearance Officer (New Delhi)*.[218] A couple with the right to enter the UK adopted a child in India, the adoption being recognised in Indian law. However, because they had not lived with the child for 12 months as required by Rule 309A of the Immigration Rules, the adoption could not at the present time be treated as a *de facto* one under the Rules. The Court of Appeal held that although there was good evidence that the couple were serving the interests of the child well in India, there was no independent evidence that it would be conducive to her welfare to move to the UK. The interference with her right to a family life under Art 8 could not be said to be unjustified or disproportionate.

4.207   India is now a signatory to the Hague Convention.

---

[213]   Per Dyson LJ at [33].
[214]   Ibid, at [34].
[215]   [2005] EWCA Civ 89, [2005] 2 FLR 219.
[216]   Per Pill LJ at [20].
[217]   See, for example, *MK (Somalia) and others v Entry Clearance Officer, Joint Council for the Welfare of Immigrants Intervening* [2008] EWCA Civ 1453, [2009] 2 FLR 138.
[218]   [2008] EWCA Civ 38, [2008] 2 FLR 87.

Chapter 5

SPECIAL GUARDIANSHIP ORDERS

INTRODUCTION

5.1 Parental responsibility is the keystone to the private law relating to children. Usually, it can be gained permanently only by parents and step-parents. However, if the child's need for permanence cannot be met by adoption, special guardianship enables it to be granted to someone who is not the child's parents.

5.2 The provisions relating to special guardianship orders (SGOs) are contained in ss 14A–14G of the Children Act 1989, inserted by the Adoption and Children Act 2002 (ACA 2002), s 115(1) which came into effect on 30 December 2005. Arising from a major review of adoption law, the status of special guardianship is one which belongs in private law proceedings whilst applications for SGOs can arise in both public and private law proceedings.

Background

Custodianship

5.3 The problem of how to provide a permanent family placement for older children in local authority care or living with relatives for whom adoption is not an option has been recognised for over 30 years. In 1972 the Departmental Committee on the Adoption of Children ('the Houghton Committee') reported that:

> 'There are many children not being brought up by their natural parents but who are in the long-term care of foster parents or relatives. These people normally have no legal status in relation to the child, and the law provides no means by which they can acquire it without cutting his links with his natural family by adoption. They are faced with the choice of doing without legal security, which may be damaging to the child or applying for an adoption order. This is one reason why ... adoption is frequently applied for in inappropriate circumstances, particularly by relatives.'[1]

5.4 The Committee recommended that the right to apply for 'guardianship' should be granted to relatives and (although it had some reservations) to foster parents. It might be appropriate for foster parents where the parents were out of

---

[1] *Report of the Departmental Committee on the Adoption of Children* (Cmnd 5107, 1972) at para 116.

the picture, the foster parents and the child wanted to secure their relationship and be independent of the local authority but the child was old enough to have a sense of identity and wished to keep this and retain his own name. It might also be appropriate in a few cases where the natural parents were in touch with the child and their bond with the child was secure, but they recognised they would never be able to provide him with a home. In other cases, foster parents might be precluded from applying for adoption because of financial constraints.[2]

5.5   The order would differ from adoption in a number of ways.[3]

- It would not be irrevocable.

- It would not permanently extinguish parental rights although these would be suspended.

- It would not alter the child's relationship with the members of his natural family.

- The child's natural parents could have contact with him but under the control of the court.

- The child would retain his own name unless he wanted to change it.

- There would be no right to inherit under intestacy.

These are all features of special guardianship.

5.6   The proposals of the Houghton Committee were enacted in Part II of the Children Act 1975 with the status being referred to as 'custodianship' rather than 'guardianship'. Stephen Cretney has commented that had the provisions actually been brought into force with minimal delay 'it would have been seen as a landmark in the history of child law'.[4] Unfortunately, there was delay in its coming into force because of lack of resources, both staffing and financial, including the cost of providing for Legal Aid.[5] In the event, it did not come into force until 1 December 1985 and even then, the provisions of the Act which required local authorities to establish a comprehensive adoption service were delayed for another 3 years. One contemporary commentator, Professor Bevan, wrote in 1988, 'waiting for something for over a decade may diminish one's enthusiasm for it'.[6] In fact, by 1985, 'it was all but dead on arrival'.[7] It was given its quietus by being repealed by Sch 15 of the Children Act 1989. An

---

[2]   *Report of the Departmental Committee on the Adoption of Children*, op cit, para 121.

[3]   Ibid, para 123.

[4]   Cretney *Family Law in the Twentieth Century* (2004) at p 707.

[5]   *The Cost of Operating the Unimplemented Provisions of the Children Act 1975* (DHSS, 1980); Cretney (above) at p 707.

[6]   Bevan *Child Law* (1989) at para 6.94.

[7]   Cullen 'Adoption – a (fairly) new approach' (2005) CFLQ 476 at 478.

official verdict was that the legislation was 'complicated and technical and its impact appears to have been small. This was probably due to its complexity and late implementation.'[8]

Judicial attitudes to custodianship

5.7   Judicial attitudes towards custodianship were on the whole supportive.[9] It was welcomed in advance of enactment as filling a gap in the existing law[10] and Balcombe LJ in *Re C*[11] stated that 'when the custodianship provisions of Part II of the Children Act are brought into force ... in some cases at any rate, contested applications for adoption may become things of the past'. In cases where parents opposed adoption on the ground that custodianship would be available, courts took this into account. In *Re H*[12] the foster parents of children aged 11 and 9 who had continuing contact with their father and paternal grandmother commenced adoption proceedings to prevent their feared removal by the local authority. The Court of Appeal held that this was a misuse of the procedure and Sir John Arnold P commented that 'if ever there was a case which cried out for the consideration of custodianship [yet to be brought into force] this is that case'. The possibility of custodianship meant that the father could not be said to be unreasonably withholding his consent to adoption. On the other hand there were cases where the absolute security of adoption was seen as being important for the child concerned and the possibility of custodianship was rejected in favour of adoption.[13] One difficulty in drawing much guidance from this experience is that courts in the main were dealing with adoption applications being made in advance of the custodianship provisions coming into force and the practicalities of the status did not have to be examined critically against the factual background of the cases.

Adoption – a new approach

5.8   The problem of what to do with children in need of a permanent home did not go away. In 1993, another White Paper, *Adoption: The Future*[14] proposed introducing a 'new guardianship order' to be known as 'Inter-Vivos Guardianship'.[15] It would extend to the age of 18 and allow a guardian to appoint another in the event of his death. Foster parents who obtained an order might regard it as giving them 'Foster-plus' status. However, the idea

---

[8]   *Inter-Departmental Review of Adoption Law – Discussion Paper Number 1: The Nature and Effect of Adoption* (Department of Health, 1990) para 42. See also Bullard, Malos and Parker *Custodianship Research Project: a report to the Department of Health* (Socio-Legal Centre for Family Studies, University of Bristol, 1990).

[9]   See Montgomery 'Custodianship: Twelve Months On' [1987] Fam Law 214; Hershman and McFarlane 'Child in Care: Adoption, Custodianship, Access' [1988] Fam Law 31.

[10]   See, for example, *Re M (Minors) (Adoption: Parents' Agreement)* [1985] FLR 921.

[11]   [1986] 1 FLR 315 at 318.

[12]   [1985] FLR 519.

[13]   *Re J (a minor)* [1987] 1 FLR 455; *Re S (a minor)* [1987] 2 FLR 331.

[14]   Cm 2288.

[15]   Above paras 5.23–5.27.

never reached the statute book. It was revived again in 2000 by the *Prime Minister's Review of Adoption*[16] which made comments similar to those of the Houghton Committee 28 years earlier.

> 'One specific message to be voiced during the study was that the range of legal options to provide the spectrum of permanence is at present not complete. In particular, there was a need identified for an intermediate legal status for children that offered greater security than long term fostering without the absolute legal severance from the birth family associated with adoption.
>
> While planned long term fostering could offer some degree of security, and might suit some children, it still lacks real security and a proper sense of permanence in a family. Children are still subject to monthly visits by social workers and annual medical inspections, and permission from a social worker is needed, for example, before a child can 'sleep over' at a friend's house. Residence Orders were acknowledged to provide some of what was required, but are still open to legal challenge at any time, and usually ended when the child was 16. Those consulted were of the view that a new option would in particular fulfil the needs of a distinct group of older children who did not wish to be adopted. The precise nature of a new option will need careful consideration.'[17]

5.9   A further White Paper in the same year, *Adoption – a new approach*,[18] adopted and widened this.

> 'Adoption is not always appropriate for children who cannot return to their birth parents. Some older children may not wish to be legally separated from their birth families. Adoption may not be best for some children being cared for on a permanent basis by members of their wider birth family. Some minority ethnic communities have religious and cultural difficulties with adoption as it is set out in law. Unaccompanied asylum-seeking children may also need secure, permanent homes, but have strong attachments to their families abroad. All these children deserve the same chance as any other to enjoy the benefits of a legally secure, stable permanent placement that promotes a supportive, lifelong relationship with their carers, where the court decides that is in their best interests...
>
> In order to meet the needs of these children where adoption is not appropriate, and to modernise the Government believes there is a case to develop a new legislative option to provide permanence short of the legal separation involved in adoption. ...
>
> The Government will legislate to create this new option, which could be called "special guardianship". It will be used only to provide permanence for those children for whom adoption is not appropriate, and where the court decides it is in the best interests of the child or young person. It will
>
> •   give the carer clear responsibility for all aspects of caring for the child or young person, and for taking the decisions to do with their upbringing. The child or young person will no longer be looked after by the council;

---

[16]   *Prime Minister's Review of Adoption* (PIU, 2000).

[17]   Ibid, paras 8.5–8.7.

[18]   Cm 5017.

- provide a firm foundation on which to build a lifelong permanent relationship between the carer and the child or young person;
- be legally secure;
- preserve the basic legal link between the child or young person and their birth family;
- be accompanied by proper access to a full range of support services including, where appropriate, financial support.[19]

These proposals were enacted by the Adoption and Children Act 2002, adding ss 14A–14G to the Children Act 1989.

Special guardianship – the future

5.10 In 1988 Professor Bevan had prophesied that 'four closely integrated factors' would determine the future of custodianship: its attractiveness as an alternative to adoption, the crucial role of the local authority, judicial attitudes and the availability of advice and resources.[20] The *Prime Minister's Review* reported that those consulted were of the view that special guardianship would fulfil a need[21] and the White Paper, that it was 'strongly supported'.[22] Whether it will prove to be popular in practice, falling short of adoption which has a psychological resonance both with children and carers, will be seen in time. The provision of resources will play an important role and unlike custodianship, regulations will set out the services which local authorities must provide, not only for the duration of the order but also after the child reaches the age of 18. When the provisions of s 14A came into force Deborah Cullen[23] commented that 'if properly publicised and supported by local authorities, it could be a really important option for some children'. However 'there is detectable some ambivalence in the government, perhaps a fear that special guardianship will be too readily seen by the courts as a less controversial option than adoption'. As for custodianship, special guardianship is likely to be welcomed by the judiciary as an additional option, especially as there is greater awareness of the disadvantages of growing up in care[24] and the importance of the child's autonomy.[25]

THE STATUS OF SPECIAL GUARDIANSHIP

5.11 The order lasts until the child's 18th birthday.

---

[19] Ibid, paras 5.8–5.10. Cited in *Re S (Adoption Order or Special Guardianship Order)* [2007] EWCA Civ 54 [2007] 1 FLR 819 at [11].

[20] *Child Law* (1989) para 6.94.

[21] *Prime Minister's Review of Adoption* (The Cabinet Office, 2000) para 8.6.

[22] Cm 5017 para 5.9.

[23] Then Secretary to the Legal Group of the British Association for Adoption and Fostering (BAAF) *Adoption – a (fairly) new approach*. See also Johnstone 'Special Guardianship Orders: A Guide' (2006) Fam Law 116.

[24] See, for example, *People Like Us* (Utting Stationery Office, 1997) and Chapter 15.

[25] For example, *Mabon v Mabon* [2005] EWCA Civ 634, [2005] 2 FLR 1011.

5.12   The effect of the order is that while the order is in force:

- the special guardian has parental responsibility for the child;[26]

- subject to any other order, the special guardian is entitled to exercise parental responsibility to the exclusion of any other person with parental responsibility apart from another special guardian,[27] unless any enactment or rule of law requires the consent of more than one person with parental responsibility.[28] In the absence of judicial guidance it is uncertain whether a special guardian needs the agreement of all with parental responsibility before authorising a non-therapeutic operation such as circumcision;

- making the order discharges any care order which is in force;[29]

- no person may cause the child to be known by a new surname or to remove him from the United Kingdom (save in the case of a special guardian, for less than 3 months[30]) without either the written consent of every person who has parental responsibility or the leave of the court.[31] This may create a difficulty where there are two special guardians and a residence order has been made in respect of one. Can the special guardian with residence remove the child for more than 1 but less than 3 months without the consent of the other?

- if the child dies, the special guardian must take reasonable steps to give notice of the fact to each parent with parental responsibility and each guardian;[32]

- no application may be made for a residence order made without leave whether or not the applicant would otherwise require leave;[33]

- the consent of the special guardian is needed before the child can be adopted.[34]

5.13   The order does not affect any rights which a parent has in relation to the child's adoption or placement for adoption.[35] Nor does it affect rights held by a

---

[26]   CA 1989, s 14C(1)(a).

[27]   Ibid, s 14C(1)(b).

[28]   Ibid, s 14C(2)(a).

[29]   Ibid, s 91(5A).

[30]   Compare ibid, s 13 where a person with a residence order may remove the child for less than 1 month.

[31]   Ibid, s 14C(3) and see below **5.31**.

[32]   Ibid, s 14C(5).

[33]   Ibid, s 10(7A).

[34]   Ibid, s 52(1); ACA 2002, s 144(1).

[35]   CA 1989, s 14C(2)(b).

parent as parent and not just as someone with parental responsibility, for example the right to apply for a residence order without first seeking leave.[36]

5.14   The courts view special guardianship as:

'an issue of very great importance to everyone concerned with it, not least, of course, the child who is its subject. It is plainly not something to be embarked upon lightly or capriciously, not least because the status it gives the special guardian effectively prevents the exercise of parental power on the part of the child's natural parents and terminates the parental authority given to a local authority under a care order (whether interim or final). In this respect it is substantially different from a residence order which, whilst it also brings a previously subsisting care order in relation to the same child to an end, does not confer on any person who holds the order the exclusivity in the exercise of parental responsibility which accompanies a special guardianship order'.[37]

5.15   In addition:

'The carefully constructed statutory regime (notice to the local authority, leave requirements in certain cases, the role of the court and the report from the local authority – even where the order is made by the court of its own motion) demonstrates the care which is required before making a special guardianship order, and that it is only appropriate if, in the particular circumstances of the particular case, it is best fitted to meet the needs of the child or children concerned.'[38]

WHO CAN BE A SPECIAL GUARDIAN?

5.16   A special guardian(s) can be:

- one or more individuals, who

- must be aged 18 or over, but

- who is not a parent of the child in question.[39]

APPLICATIONS

5.17   An SGO can be made only on an application made by someone who does not require leave or who has leave. In addition, the court may make an

---

[36]   CA 1989, s 10(4)(a).
[37]   *Birmingham City Council v R* [2006] EWCA Civ 1748, [2007] 1 FLR 564 per Wall LJ at [78].
[38]   *Re S (Adoption Order or Special Guardianship Order)* [2007] EWCA Civ 54, [2007] 1 FLR 819 per Wall LJ at [47].
[39]   CA 1989, s 14A(1) and (2).

order without an application in any family proceedings[40] in which a question arises with respect to the welfare of the child.[41]

Notice to the local authority

5.18   No one may apply for an SGO unless, before the beginning of a period of 3 months ending with the date of the application he has given written notice of his intention to make the application to any local authority looking after the child[42] or, if the child is not being looked after, to the local authority in whose area he normally resides.[43] See also **18.20** and **17.18**.

5.19   There is no discretion to waive this requirement[44] but it does not apply when an SGO is being made by the court on its own initiative.

Who can apply?

Applicants who do not need leave

5.20   These are:[45]

- any guardian of the child;

- any individual in whose favour a residence order is in force;

- any person with whom the child has lived for a period of at least 3 years. This need not be continuous but must not have begun more than 5 years before or ended more than 3 months before the making of the application;[46]

- any person who in a case where a residence order is in force has the consent of each person in whose favour the order was made;

- any person who in a case where the child is in the care of the local authority,[47] has the consent of that authority;[48]

- any person who has the consent of each person who has parental responsibility for the child;

---

[40]   Defined in CA 1989, s 8(3) and includes proceedings under the ACA 2002.
[41]   CA 1989, 14A(3).
[42]   Ie accommodating the child or who has a care order in respect of the child: ibid, s 22(1).
[43]   Ibid, s 14(7).
[44]   *Birmingham City Council v R* [2006] EWCA Civ 1748, [2007] 1 FLR 564 at [92].
[45]   CA 1989, s 14A(5).
[46]   Ibid, s 14A(12) and s 10(10).
[47]   Ie is subject to a care order: ibid, s 31(1).
[48]   It may be that this does not apply to a child who is subject to a freeing order because while such an order is in existence, the care order is no longer in force (see ibid, s 105(1) and ACA 2002, s 29(1)).

- a local authority foster parent with whom the child has lived for a period of at least 1 year preceding the application.

Applicants who need leave

5.21 Anyone else, including the child, requires leave and s 9(3) applies in relation to an application for permission.[49] Taking into account s 10(5) this means that a person who is or was at any time in the last 6 months a local authority foster parent of the child who does not qualify under s 14A(5)(d) has to apply for leave unless:

- if the child is being looked after, he has the consent of those with parental responsibility to apply;

- if the child is subject to a care order and the local authority consents to the order being granted[50]); or

- he is a relative of the child.

Where the applicant is the child concerned, the court may grant leave only if it is satisfied that he has sufficient understanding to make the proposed application.[51]

5.22 Where the applicant is not the child concerned the court must have particular regard to:

- the nature of the proposed application;

- the applicant's connection with the child;

- any risk there might be of the application disrupting the child's life to such an extent that he would be harmed by it; and

- where the child is being looked after by the local authority:
  - the authority's plans for the child; and
  - the wishes and feelings of the child's parents.[52]

The welfare checklist does not apply to applications for leave and the child's welfare is not the primary consideration.[53]

---

[49] CA 1989, s 14A(4).
[50] Ibid, s 14A(5)(c); s 10(5)(c)(ii).
[51] Ibid, s 14A (12) and s 10(8). See also Chapter 11.
[52] Ibid, s 14A(12) and s 10(9). See also Chapter 11.
[53] *Re and W (Minors) (Residence Order: Leave to Apply)* [1992] 2 FLR 154.

5.23 Applicants do not have to show that they have 'a good arguable case'[54] but this does not prohibit the court considering 'a broad assessment of the case' as opposed to a determination of the application on a 'no reasonable prospect of success' criterion.[55]

5.24 A person who requires leave cannot make the application for an SGO or give notice to their local authority under s 14A(7) of their intention to do so until he has obtained the court's permission.[56]

Orders without an application

5.25 The court may make an SGO in any family proceedings[57] in which a question arises as to the welfare of the child, if it considers that it should be made even though no application has been made.[58] However, it must first receive a report dealing with the matters referred to in s 14A(8).[59] When the court is considering making the order without an application, under s 14A(9) it can direct the local authority to investigate and prepare a report and, in such a case, the 3-month notice required under s 14A(7) is not required.

5.26 If no application for an SGO has been made by any party, a common reason may be that no party wants it. As Wall LJ stated in *Re S (Adoption Order or Special Guardianship Order)*[60] the statute therefore envisages an order being made against the wishes of the parties.

> 'Whether or not it will do so will depend upon the acts of the individual case including the nature of the refuser's case and its interrelationship with the welfare of the particular child. What seems to us clear is that if the court comes to the view on all the facts and applying the welfare checklist under the 1989 Act (including the possible consequences to the child of the refuser implementing the threat to refuse to be appointed a special guardian) that a special guardianship order will best serve the welfare interests of the child in question, that is the order the court should make.'[61]

In *Re S (Adoption Order or Special Guardianship Order)*, the Court rejected the appeal of a foster mother who had not agreed to being granted an SGO, preferring an adoption order.

---

[54]   *Re J (Leave to Issue Applications for a Residence Order)* [2003] 1 FLR 114.

[55]   *Re R (Adoption: Contact)* [2005] EWCA Civ 1128, [2006] 1 FLR 373 per Wall LJ at [46]. See also *Re H* [2003] EWCA Civ 369.

[56]   *Birmingham City Council v R* [2006] EWCA Civ 1748 at [93].

[57]   As defined by CA 1989, s 8(3).

[58]   Ibid, s 14A(6)(b).

[59]   Ibid s 14A(11). *Re S (Adoption Order or Special Guardianship Order)* [2007] EWCA Civ 54, [2007] 1 FLR 819 at [73].

[60]   Ibid, at [73].

[61]   Ibid, at [77].

THE TEST

5.27 The test is the welfare test,[62] but in addition to the usual checklist the court must also consider whether, if the SGO is made, a contact order should also be made with respect to the child and whether any section 8 order in force should be varied or discharged.[63] For a detailed discussion of the test, see Chapter 6.

5.28 As the order inhibits the exercise of parental responsibility, making the order as opposed to merely granting a residence order will have to be justified under Art 8 of the European Convention for the Protection of Human Rights and Fundamental Freedoms. In particular, it must be necessary and proportionate.[64] Parents will still be able to apply for a residence order or specific issue or prohibited steps order (albeit with leave), and therefore the permanency and freedom of action offered by the order is limited and not absolute. In addition, residence orders can now be made until the child is 18 without the need for exceptional circumstances.[65] Therefore the essential benefit of the order (as compared with a residence order) is the limited protection from parental interference provided by the need for anyone other than the special guardian to have leave to apply for a residence order or to vary or discharge the order, and the ability to apply for special guardian support services (see below and Chapter 11).

EXERCISE OF PARENTAL RESPONSIBILITY

5.29 Subject to any other order, the special guardian is entitled to exercise parental responsibility to the exclusion of any other person with parental responsibility apart from another special guardian,[66] unless any enactment or rule of law requires the consent of more than one person with parental responsibility.[67] If there is a dispute in relation to any exercise of parental responsibility, the parent or special guardian or anyone with a residence order[68] (and others who have obtained leave under s 10(8)) may apply under s 10 for a specific issue or prohibited steps order.

5.30 The absence of a requirement that parents obtain leave may seem surprising because SGOs are designed to promote finality. One might expect similar considerations to apply to other forms of orders under s 8. An essential component of the advantages produced by an adoption order for both adopters and children is that they are in most cases then free from the threat of

---

[62] CA 1989, s 1(1).
[63] Ibid, s 14B(1).
[64] See Chapter 3.
[65] CA 1989, s 12(5) inserted by ACA 2002, s 139(1), (3), Sch 3.
[66] CA 1989, s 14C(1)(b) and see **5.12**.
[67] Ibid, s 14C(2)(a).
[68] Ibid, s 10(2).

future litigation. If the same protection is not available in respect of SGOs, this may be a substantial derogation from the security provided.[69]

LEAVE TO REMOVE FROM THE JURISDICTION AND A CHANGE OF NAME

5.31 In addition to making the order the court may give leave for the child to be known by a new surname and also order as to whether the guardian should be given leave to remove the child from the United Kingdom without the consent of others for a period of 3 months or more (either generally or for specified purpose).[70]

Leave to permit removal from the jurisdiction

5.32 The reports contain many decisions relating to the question of whether a parent should be granted permission to remove a child. Although the matter is governed by the welfare test, the cases rest on dicta of the Court of Appeal in *Poel v Poel*:[71]

> 'When a marriage breaks up, a situation normally arises when a child of that marriage, instead of being in the joint custody of both parents, must of necessity become one who is in the custody of a single parent. Once that position has arisen and the custody is working well, this court should not lightly interfere with such reasonable way of life as is selected by that parent to whom custody has been rightly given. Any interference may, as my Lord has pointed out, produce considerable strains which would not only be unfair to the parent whose way of life is interfered with but also to any new marriage of that parent. In that way it might well in due course reflect on the welfare of the child. The way in which the parent who properly has custody of a child may choose in a reasonable manner to order his or her way of life is one of those things which the parent who has not been given custody may well have to bear, even though one has every sympathy with the latter on some of the results.'

5.33 Although an application of this dicta meant that leave to remove the child was granted in almost all the reported cases in the 30 years after 1970, the Court of Appeal in *Payne v Payne*[72] was careful to point out that there was no presumption in favour of the parent who wanted to emigrate. However, 'the underlying principles in *Poel*, as explained in *Chamberlain*,[73] have stood the test of time and give valuable guidance as to the approach the court should adopt in those most difficult cases'.[74] The court summarised the position as follows.

---

[69]   *Re S (Adoption Order or Special Guardianship Order)* [2007] EWCA Civ 54, [2007] 1 FLR 819 per Wall LJ at [65].
[70]   CA 1989, s 14B(2).
[71]   [1970] 1 WLR 1469, per Sachs LJ at 1473.
[72]   [2001] EWCA Civ 166, [2001] 1 FLR 1052. For a critical assessment of *Payne*, see the case note by Perry in [2001] 4 CFLQ 455.
[73]   *Chamberlain v de la Mare* (1983) 4 FLR 434.
[74]   [2001] EWCA Civ 166, [2001] 1 FLR 1052, per Dame Elizabeth Butler-Sloss P at [83].

Where there is a real dispute as to which parent should be granted a residence order, and the decision as to which parent is the more suitable is finely balanced, the future plans of each parent are relevant. If one parent intended to emigrate and to remove the child from school, surroundings, the other parent and family, it may in some cases be an important factor to weigh in the balance. But where the balance clearly lay in favour of the emigrating parent or residence was not a live issue, the following considerations would be relevant:

- the welfare of the child is always paramount;

- there is no presumption granted by CA 1989, s 13(1)(b);

- the reasonable proposals of the parent with a residence order wishing to live abroad carry great weight;

- consequently the proposals have to be scrutinised with care and the court needs to be satisfied there is a genuine motivation for the move and not the intention to bring contact between the child and the other parent to an end;

- the effect upon the applicant parent and the new family of the child of a refusal of leave is very important;

- the effect upon the child of the denial of contact with the other parent and in some cases his family is very important;

- the opportunity for continuing contact between the child and the parent left behind may be very significant.

5.34   The President added:

'[These] are not and could not be exclusive of the other important matters which arise in the individual case.'[75]

Indeed, the wishes and feelings of the child, for example, need to be considered,[76] as will the question of whether the child's residence should be transferred to the parent who is not emigrating.

5.35   In *Payne* Thorpe LJ added that there was a danger that if the reasonable proposals of the primary carer were elevated into a legal presumption then there would be an obvious risk of the breach not only of the respondent's rights under Art 8 but also his rights under Art 6 to a fair trial. To guard against this he suggests the following approach.

---

[75]   [2001] EWCA Civ 166, [2001] 1 FLR 1052 at [85]. See, for example, *M v M (Removal from Jurisdiction)* [1993] 1 FCR 5.

[76]   See Perry 'Payne v Payne: Leave to Remove Children From the Jurisdiction' [2001] 13 CFLQ 455.

'(a) Pose the question: is the mother's application genuine in the sense that it is not motivated by some selfish desire to exclude the father from the child's life? Then ask: is the mother's application realistic, by which I mean founded on practical proposals both well researched and investigated? If the application fails either of these tests refusal will inevitably follow.

(b) If however the application passes these tests then there must be a careful appraisal of the father's opposition: is it motivated by genuine concern for the future of the child's welfare or is it driven by some ulterior motive? What would be the extent of the detriment to him and his future relationship with the child were the application granted? To what extent would that be offset by extension of the child's relationships with the maternal family and homeland?

(c) What would be the impact on the mother, either as the single parent or as a new wife, of a refusal of her realistic proposal?[77]

(d) The outcome of the second and third appraisals must then be brought into an overriding review of the child's welfare as the paramount consideration, directed by the statutory checklist insofar as appropriate.'[78]

5.36 There are a variety of reasons why a parent with care seeks to relocate. Glenn Brasse[79] usefully categorised these into Re-marriage cases,[80] the Career/Lifestyle choice[81] and a Return to Family Roots.[82] There is, however, no difference in the principles to be applied.[83]

5.37 Is there any reason why a similar approach should not be adopted where the child has a special guardian? Section 14B(2) merely provides an occasion when the court may grant permission. The guidance in *Payne* will be the starting point but it remains to be seen whether the increased status given to guardians over others with parental responsibility will add any greater weight to their reasonable wishes.

Leave to permit a change of name

5.38 Change of name already seems to be an area where no clear guidance can be given as to when a change of name will be permitted when a child has grown up with the special guardians from an early age. The matter has,

---

[77] In *Re B (Leave to Remove: Impact of Refusal)* [2004] EWCA Civ 956, [2005] 2 FLR 239 the Court of Appeal ordered a retrial because this had not adequately been investigated by the trial judge.

[78] [2001] EWCA Civ 166, [2001] 1 FLR 1052 at [40].

[79] Brasse 'The Payne Threshold: Leaving the Jurisdiction' [2005] Fam Law 780.

[80] Eg *Poel v Poel* [1970] 1 WLR 1469, *Re H (Application to Remove from the Jurisdiction)* [1998] 1 FLR 848, *Re B (Removal from Jurisdiction); Re S (Removal from Jurisdiction)* [2003] EWCA Civ 1149, [2003] 2 FLR 1043, *L v L (Leave to Remove from Jurisdiction: Effect on Children)* [2002] EWHC 2577 (Fam), [2003] 1 FLR 900.

[81] Eg *Re B (Leave to Remove: Impact of Refusal)* [2004] EWCA Civ 956, [2005] 2 FLR 239.

[82] Eg *A v A (Child: Removal from the Jurisdiction)* (1980) 1 FLR 380, *Payne v Payne* [2001] EWCA Civ 166, [2001] 1 FLR 1052, *Re G (Removal from Jurisdiction)* [2005] EWCA Civ 170, [2005] 2 FLR 166, *Re C (Permission to Remove from Jurisdiction)* [2003] EWHC 596 (Fam), [2003] 1 FLR 1066.

[83] *Re B (Leave to Remove: Impact of Refusal)* [2004] EWCA Civ 956, [2005] 2 FLR 239 per Thorpe LJ at [17].

however, been the subject of considerable guidance in children cases generally. The approach of the courts to issues of change of surnames was summarised by the Court of Appeal in *Re W, Re A, Re B (Change of Name).*[84]

- If parents are married, they both have the power and the duty to register their child's name.

- If they are not married, the mother has the sole duty and power to do so.

- After registration of the child's names, the grant of a residence order obliges any person wishing to change the surname to obtain the leave of the court or the written consent of all those who have parental responsibility.

- In the absence of a residence order, the person wishing to change the surname from the registered name ought to obtain the relevant written consent or the leave of the court by making an application for a specific issue order.

- On any application, the welfare of the child is paramount and the judge must have regard to the s 1(3) criteria.

- Among the factors to which the court should have regard is the registered surname of the child and the reasons for the registration, for instance, recognition of the biological link with the child's father. Registration is always a relevant and important consideration but is not in itself decisive. The weight to be given to it by the court will depend on the other relevant factors or valid countervailing reasons which may tip the balance the other way.

- The relevant considerations should include factors which may arise in the future as well as the present situation.

- Reasons given for changing or seeking to change a child's name based on the fact that the child's name is or is not the same as the parent making the application do not generally carry much weight.

- The reasons for an earlier unilateral decision to change a child's name may be relevant.

- Any change of circumstances of the child since the original registration may be relevant.

- In the case of a child whose parents were married to each other, the fact of the marriage is important and there would have to be strong reasons to change the name from the father's surname if the child were so registered.

---

[84] [1999] 2 FLR 930.

- Where the child's parents were not married to each other, the mother has the control over registration. Consequently, on an application to change the surname of the child, the degree of commitment of the father to the child, the quality of the contact, if it occurs, between father and child, and the existence or absence of parental responsibility are all relevant factors to take into account.

5.39 Dame Elizabeth Butler-Sloss P added:

'I cannot stress too strongly that these are only guidelines which do not purport to be exhaustive. Each case has to be decided on its own facts with the welfare of the child the paramount consideration and all the relevant factors weighed in the balance by the court at the time of the hearing.'[85]

5.40 Other cases make the following points:

- an order for a change of name ought not to be made unless there is some evidence that this will lead to an improvement from the point of view of the welfare of the child;[86]

- bearing the father's name preserves a link between the child and the non-resident parent. This link is as important when there is good contact as when there is none;[87]

- the time which has passed between the original change of name and the application is likely to be an important consideration because a further change may confuse the child;[88]

- the wishes of the child are not decisive.[89]

There has been a recent trend in courts seeking a middle way of allowing a child to use a new name informally while retaining the registered name[90] or combining the names of both parents.[91]

5.41 Early indications seem to show that when making an SGO courts will exercise the power to permit a change of name very cautiously. In *S v B and Newport City Council: Re K*[92] Headley J made an SGO in favour of maternal grandparents who had been looking after their 6-year-old grandson since he was 6 months old. He rejected the grandparents' preference for an adoption order on the ground that it would skew familial relationships (and see

---

[85] [1999] 2 FLR 930 at [10].
[86] *Dawson v Wearmouth* [1999] AC 308, per Lord Mackay of Clashfern.
[87] *Re C (Change of Surname)* [1998] 2 FLR 656.
[88] Ibid and *Re PC (Change of Surname)* [1997] 2 FLR 730.
[89] *Re B (Change of Surname)* [1996] 1 FLR 791.
[90] *Re PC (Change of Surname)* [1997] 2 FLR 730, *Re S (Change of Names: Cultural Factors)* [2001] 2 FLR 1005.
[91] *Re R (Surname: Using Both Parents')* [2001] EWCA Civ 1344, [2001] 2 FLR 1358.
[92] [2007] 1 FLR 1116.

Chapter 17) but he nevertheless gave permission for the child to be known by their surname. In contrast, in *Re L (Special Guardianship: Surname)*[93] the Court of Appeal upheld a refusal by the trial judge to allow maternal grandparents in very similar circumstances to change the 3-year-old's surname. The two cases might be distinguished by the fact that the grandparents in *S v B* may (it is not clear) have been bringing the child up as their grandchild whereas in *Re L* the grandparents, at least in the past, had been perceived as being reluctant to clarify to the child who her biological parents were. On the other hand, the difference might have been that the two cases were heard by different judges who had formed their own assessment of the different parties.

5.42 In *Re L (Special Guardianship: Surname)* the trial judge found that:

'In a case where there is as much anxiety as there is here about the way in which [E's] identity is dealt with, it would be completely contrary to her interests, in my view, for her now to be known by a different surname. Her welfare is most likely to be secured, it seems to me, by keeping her circumstances as faithful to reality and the truth of the situation as possible. Whilst I accept that some explanation of names will be required, for instance, doctors and schools, I do not consider that would an insuperable problem in the context of a special guardianship order.'[94]

5.43 In the Court of Appeal Ward LJ added:

'Sympathetic as I am to [the predicament of the grandparents] and their hurt, their concerns overlook the value of the lesson ...: honesty is the best policy ... It avoids the much more difficult questions that will be asked when [E] wishes to know, "why am I S if my parents are L?".'[95]

RESTRAINING FURTHER APPLICATIONS

5.44 Section 91(14) of the Children Act enables a court to control further applications in respect of a child by ordering that 'no application for an order under the Act of a specified kind may be made in respect of the child concerned by any person named in the order without leave of the court.'

5.45 The test to be applied when considering whether to make a section 91(14) order is the welfare test. In *Re P (Section 91(14) Guidelines) (Residence and Religious Heritage)*[96] the Court of Appeal summarised existing authority.

(1) Section 91(14) should be read in conjunction with s 1(1) which makes the welfare of the child the paramount consideration.

---

[93] [2007] EWCA Civ 196, [2007] 2 FLR 50.
[94] Ibid, at [36] per Black J.
[95] At [39].
[96] [1999] 2 FLR 573.

(2)   The power to restrict applications to the court is discretionary and in the exercise of its discretion the court must weigh in the balance all the relevant considerations.

(3)   An important consideration is that to impose a restriction is a statutory intrusion on the right of a party to bring proceedings before the court and to be heard in matters affecting his/her own child.

(4)   The power therefore has to be used with great care and sparingly – the exception and not the rule.

(5)   It is generally to be seen as a useful weapon of last resort in cases of repeated and unreasonable applications.

(6)   In suitable circumstances (and on clear evidence) a court may impose the leave restriction in cases where the welfare of the child requires it although there is no past history of making unreasonable applications.[97]

(7)   In cases under para (6) the court will need to be satisfied, first that the facts go beyond the commonly encountered need for time to settle a regime ordered by the court and the all too common situation where there is animosity between the adults in dispute or between the local authority and the family and secondly that there is a serious risk that without the imposition of the restriction, the child or the primary carers will be subject to unacceptable strain.

(8)   A court may impose the restriction on making applications in the absence of a request from any of the parties, subject, of course, to the rules of natural justice such as an opportunity for the parties to be heard on the point.

(9)   A restriction may be imposed without limitation of time.

(10) The degree of restriction should be proportionate to the harm it is intended to avoid. Therefore the court imposing the restriction should carefully consider the extent of the restriction to be imposed and specify, where appropriate, the type of application to be restrained and the duration of the order.

(11) It would be undesirable in other than the most exceptional cases to make the order without notice.

5.46 In *Re P (Section 91(14) Guidelines) (Residence and Religious Heritage)* Butler-Sloss P held that s 91(14) does not breach the right to a fair trial

---

[97]   Eg *Re F (Children) (Restriction on Applications)* [2005] EWCA Civ 499, *Re M (A Child) (Restriction on Applications)* [2005] All ER (D) 84 (Dec CA).

guaranteed by Art 6(1) of the European Convention for the Protection of Human Rights and Fundamental Freedoms 1950.

> 'The applicant is not denied access to the court. It is a partial restriction in that it does not allow him the right to an immediate inter partes hearing. It thereby protects the other parties and the child from being drawn into the proposed proceedings unless or until a court has ruled that the application should be allowed to proceed. On an application for leave, the applicant has to persuade a judge that he has an arguable case with some chance of success. That is not a formidable hurdle to surmount. If the application is hopeless and is refused the other parties and the child will have been protected from unnecessary involvement in the proposed proceedings and unwarranted investigations into the present circumstances of the child.'[98]

5.47 In *Re S (Adoption Order Or Special Guardianship Order)*[99] Wall J, having discussed the anomaly that natural parents do not need the leave of the court to apply for a s 8 order (see **5.29** above) said that 'The need to invoke s 91(14) to protect special guardians and children from the anxiety imposed by the prospect of future litigation is a possible weakness in the scheme.' It remains to be seen whether courts will be more willing to grant applications for a s 91(14) order when making an SGO than in other cases.

5.48 In *S v B and Newport City Council: Re K*[100] Headley J made a s 91(14) order without limitation of time preventing the parents applying for contact on the grounds that the needs of the child required it and a failure to do so, having regard to the volatile behaviour of the parents, would impose an intolerable strain on the special guardian grandparents.

COURT APPLICATIONS

5.49 Research by Ananda Hall into the first year in which special guardianship was available found that 372 orders were made in England and Wales in 2006 excluding orders made in Family Proceedings Courts.[101] Nearly three-quarters (74%) were made in care proceedings and a quarter (26%) in private law proceedings.

5.50 An analysis of a sample of 70 cases found that kinship carers were by far the most common special guardians (87%) compared to local authority foster parents (12%). Of the kinship carers just over two-thirds (68%) were of the 'grandparent' generation, 17% were aunts and uncles and the remaining 15%, cousins, step-parents or siblings. A quarter of the special guardians had not previously cared for the child. The children in the sample ranged from 6

---

[98] At 593.
[99] op cit at [67].
[100] [2007] 1 FLR 1116.
[101] 'Special Guardianship: A Missed Opportunity – Findings From Research' [2008] Fam Law 148 and 'Special guardianship and permanency planning: unforeseen circumstances and missed opportunities' [2008] CFLQ 359.

months to 17 years and Hall found no evidence that special guardianship was being used for older children. Contact orders were made in 30% of cases and orders permitting a change of name in 10%.

5.51   In 2007 it is estimated that 826 applications were made of which 95% were made in private law proceedings. However, 1,594 orders were granted of which over 68% were made in public law proceedings.[102] If these estimates are correct the explanation must either be that a large number of applications were pending from 2006 or that a considerable number of orders were being made of the court's own volition under s 14A(6)(b).

THE PROCEDURE

Notice

5.52   For the requirement as to notice, see **5.18**.

Local authority report

5.53   No SGO can be made without the court considering a report from the relevant local authority.[103] If the applicants have given notice under s 14A(7) the local authority must investigate and provide the court with a report dealing with:

(a)   the suitability of the applicant to be a special guardian;

(b)   such other matters as may be prescribed by the Secretary of State;[104] and

(c)   such other matter as the local authority considers relevant.[105]

If no application has been made but the court is considering making the order under its powers under s 14A(6), it will have to order a report under s 14A(9).[106]

> 'There is no provision either in the statute or the regulations for any restriction, reduction or alteration in the information which the local authority is required to cover. We do, however, think it important to pause to reflect why this is so. In our judgment it is because special guardianship is an issue of very great importance to everyone concerned with it, not least, of course, the child who is its subject. It is plainly not something to be embarked upon lightly or capriciously, not least

---

[102]   *Judicial Statistics 2007.*

[103]   CA 1989, s 14A(11); *Re S (Adoption Order or Special Guardianship) (No 2)* [2007] EWCA Civ 90, [2007] 1 FLR 855 at [4].

[104]   Prescribed by virtue of the Special Guardianship Regulations 2005 (SI 2005/1109), reg 21 and the Schedule.

[105]   Ibid, s 14A(8).

[106]   *Birmingham City Council v R* [2006] EWCA Civ 1748, [2007] 1 FLR 564 at [97] and *Re S (Adoption Order or Special Guardianship) (No 2)* op cit at [11].

because the status it gives the special guardian effectively prevents the exercise of parental responsibility on the part of the child's natural parents, and terminates the parental authority given to a local authority under a care order (whether interim or final). In this respect, it is substantially different from a residence order which, whilst it also brings a previously subsisting care order in relation to the same child to an end, does not confer on any person who holds the order the exclusivity in the exercise of parental responsibility which accompanies a special guardianship order.'[107]

However, a judge should not use s 14A(9) to compel an authority to perform its obligations under s 14(8) at the instance of a person who needs but has not obtained permission to apply unless s 14A(6) applies.[108]

5.54 When it is considering whether to invoke s 14A(6) the court should consider carefully the manner in which it should use its powers under s 14A(9). In some cases the information which is required under the Special Guardianship Regulations 2005[109] will be before it in a different form, for example in adoption proceedings. In such a case the court should adopt a commonsense approach. The material can be cross-referenced and need not be duplicated in a different format. In other cases the information may not be before the court and the authority may well be required to conduct a fresh application and prepare a fresh report without preconceptions.[110] However, the court cannot define or limit the requirements of a local authority to investigate and report.[111]

5.55 If the child is subject to a placement order, ss 25(5), (6) and (7) of the Adoption and Children Act 2002 apply.

5.56 For a detailed discussion of the contents of the report and the assessment of the child and the applicants, see Chapter 10.

THE ROLE OF THE LOCAL AUTHORITY

5.57 As well as reporting to the court, the relevant local authority will have duties after the order is made, regardless of whether the child was in care or was being looked after. It must make arrangements to provide special guardianship support services which are counselling, advice and information as well as such other services as may be prescribed,[112] including the provision of

---

[107] *Birmingham City Council v R* [2006] EWCA Civ 1748, [2007] 1 FLR 564 per Wall LJ at [77]–[78].

[108] *Birmingham City Council v R* [2006] EWCA Civ 1748, [2007] 1 FLR 564 at [103].

[109] SI 2005/1109.

[110] *Re S (Adoption Order or Special Guardianship) (No 2)* op cit at [14].

[111] *Birmingham City Council v R* op cit at [77] and *Re S (Adoption Order or Special Guardianship) (No 2)* op cit at [17]–[18].

[112] CA 1989, s 14F(1).

financial support.[113] This could therefore include continuing foster allowances to former foster parents under a different guise. At the request of the child, his parent, a special guardian or any other prescribed person, the local authority may carry out an assessment of that person's needs for special guardianship support services and must carry out an assessment in prescribed circumstances.[114] For a detailed discussion of Special Guardianship Support, see Chapter 11.

5.58 Under s 14G every local authority has to establish a procedure for considering representations made to it in relation to its functions under s 14F.

VARIATION AND DISCHARGE

Application without leave

5.59 The court may vary or discharge an SGO on an application by:

(1) the special guardian;

(2) any individual in whose favour a residence order is in force;

(3) a local authority designated in a care order with respect to the child.[115]

Application with leave

5.60 The following applicants require leave:

(1) the child himself;

(2) any parent or guardian;

(3) any step-parent who has acquired and not lost parental responsibility;

(4) any individual not being the child's special guardian, parent or guardian or a person in whose favour a residence order is in force who has or immediately before the making of the SGO had parental responsibility for the child.[116]

No other person may apply.

5.61 Where the applicant is the child concerned, the court may grant leave only if it is satisfied that he has sufficient understanding to make the proposed

---

[113] Ibid, s 14F(2). And see Special Guardianship Regulations 2005 (SI 2005/1109) and *Special Guardianship Guidance* (DfES, 2005).

[114] CA 1989, s 14F(3).

[115] Ibid, s 14D(2).

[116] Ibid, s 14D(3).

application.[117] The court may not grant leave to anyone other than the child if it is satisfied that there has been a significant change in circumstances since the making of the order.[118]

Orders without an application

5.62 The court may vary or discharge an SGO in any family proceedings[119] in which a question arises as to the welfare of the child if it considers that it should be varied or discharged even though no application has been made.[120]

---

[117] CA 1989, s 14D(4).
[118] Ibid, s 14D(5).
[119] As defined by s 8(3).
[120] Ibid, s 14D(2).

Chapter 6

THE WELFARE TEST AND HUMAN RIGHTS

INTRODUCTION

6.1   Section 1 of the Children Act 1989 (CA 1989) and s 1 of the Adoption and Children Act 2002 (ACA 2002) govern the approach of the court to applications for the grant and revocation of special guardianship orders and adoption and placement orders respectively. They are in similar but not identical terms. In addition s 1 of the 2002 Act governs any consideration by an adoption agency of a decision relating to the adoption of a child.

6.2   The child's welfare has to be the court's paramount consideration ('the paramountcy principle'). In deciding what is in the best interests of the child, the court has to have regard to all the circumstances including those in what is known as 'the s 1 checklist'. Again, the checklist in the 2002 Act is similar but not identical to the checklist in the 1989 Act.

6.3   The decision has to be based on the circumstances of the individual child and there are no presumptions. In addition, the court has to have regard to two matters of general application: the 'no delay' and the 'no order' principles. First, there is the principle that any delay in determining the question is likely to prejudice the welfare of a child. Secondly, the court must not make an order unless it considers that doing so would be better for the child than making no order at all.

6.4   Article 8 of the European Convention for the Protection of Human Rights and Fundamental Freedoms 1950 requires respect for the family life of the child and his parents. Any interference with family life, particularly in such a permanent way as adoption, has to be necessary and proportionate.

THE WELFARE TEST

Children Act 1989, s 1

6.5

'When a court determines any question with respect to –

(a)   the upbringing of a child or

(b)   the administration of a child's property or the application of any income arising from it

the child's welfare shall be the court's paramount consideration.'[1]

Adoption and Children Act 2002, s 2

6.6   This section applies whenever a court or adoption agency is coming to a decision relating to the adoption of a child.

6.7   The paramount consideration of the court or adoption agency must be the child's welfare throughout his life.'[2] The section is similar to s 1 of the CA 1989 but there are important differences.

6.8   First, the test governs decisions made not just by the court but also by any adoption agency. It governs not only their exercise of their statutory powers but also decisions made under statutory regulations many of which form the procedural background to the statutory powers. For example, the Adoption Agencies Regulations 2005,[3] reg 19 governs the consideration of whether a child should be placed for adoption and s 18, the actual placing of the child.

6.9   Second, ACA 2003, s 1(2) specifically requires that the child's welfare must be considered in the context of his whole life and not just his childhood. Courts when applying CA 1989, s 1 will of course have regard to the long term implications of any order, for example, a decision about contact may have implications for the relationship between a child and his father throughout their mutual lives. However, such orders can be varied whereas the making of an adoption order places practical and legal difficulties in the way of anyone seeking a contact order or to challenge the exercise of parental responsibility by the adopters. In addition the order has legal effects which will not cease when the child reaches 18, for example, succession rights on intestacy. An adoption order makes such fundamental and permanent changes to the status of the child, the natural parents and the adopters that it is appropriate that the courts and agencies should be specifically required to look beyond the immediate present. The *Review of Adoption Law*[4] pointed out that:

> 'One of the special features of adoption is that it has a significant effect on a person's identity and family relationships not just during childhood but after the age of 18. It is known that some adopted people who have no great difficulties during childhood coming to terms with the fact that they are adopted and have enjoyed a close relationship with their adopted parents subsequently experience difficulties in the area of personal identity. We recommend that the legislative framework should underline the long-term significance of an adoption order and

---

[1]   CA 1989, s 1(1).
[2]   ACA 2002, s 1(1), (2).
[3]   SI 2005/389.
[4]   *Report to Ministers of an Interdepartmental Working Group* (Department of Health and Welsh Office, 1992), para 7.2.

that the welfare test should refer not only to the welfare of the child throughout childhood but his welfare in adult life as well.'

6.10 The more remote the possible effect of a decision, the more difficult it will be to weigh the possibility. The section does not however require the court to prophesy what *will* happen but rather to have regard to the fact that the decision *may* have long term implications and to refrain from too readily making the decision based on what appears to be in the short- or medium-term interests of the child.

6.11 Section 1 of the 2002 Act differs significantly from its immediate predecessors which required the welfare of the child, rather than being the 'paramount consideration' (ie outweighing all others) to be the 'first' consideration (ie outweighing any other consideration).[5] In *Re B (A Minor) (Adoption)*[6] Cumming-Bruce LJ described the difference as 'manifestly fine' but a difference there was. It could be argued that the difference was an appropriate one given the permanency of adoption.

> 'More than any other area of family law, adoption requires the balancing of the interests of family members ... The paramountcy principle has greater implications for adoption than in other areas of child law. If consistency were introduced, where would this leave the natural parent in the face of highly competent and mature adopters, for example? Would it be harder for the natural parent to oppose adoption? Alternatively, would children be placed for adoption more readily, this minimizing the emotional damage that delay can bring? The issues raised by adoption arguably sit less easily with paramountcy than do other matters of upbringing.'[7]

6.12 Nevertheless the attractions of the test being the same as in other child litigation, the illogicality of the court having to apply different tests in the same case where issues of adoption and contact arose[8] and the importance of the child's welfare being central to all decisions resulted in nearly all responses to the *Departmental Review of Adoption Law* in 1992 being in favour of the paramountcy principle being adopted in the Act.[9] In most individual cases the change will make little or no direct difference, there being few if any reported cases where the decision about adoption – as opposed to whether or not the court could dispense with the consent of the parents to adoption on the ground that it was being unreasonably withheld – turned on the words of the test, but where it may make a difference is in the psychological approach of the courts and the professionals.

---

[5] In *Re D (An Infant) (Adoption: Parent's Consent)* [1977] AC 602.

[6] [1984] FLR 402.

[7] Bridge 'Adoption Law: A Balance of Interests' in Herring (ed) *Family Law: Issues, Debates and Policy* (2001) at pp 212 and 216.

[8] See *Inter-Departmental Review of Adoption Law Discussion Paper No 1: The Nature and Effect of Adoption* (Department of Health, 1990), para 86.

[9] *Review of Adoption Law* op cit para 7.1; *Prime Minister's Review: Adoption* (Cabinet Office, 2000) para 8.1; *Adoption: A New Approach* Cm 5017 (2000), para 4.14.

The meaning of welfare

6.13 'Welfare' has to be construed in the widest sense. It has to be measured not only by material standards but also in terms of the child's moral and emotional well-being.[10] The classic exposition of the paramountcy principle was given by Lord MacDermott in *J (and Another) v C (and Others)*:[11]

> 'Reading these words in their ordinary significance and relating them to the various classes of proceedings [in which they are to be applied], it seems to me that they must mean more than that the child's welfare is to be treated as the top item in a list of items relevant to the matters in question. I think they connote a process whereby, when all the relevant facts, relationships, claims and wishes of parents, risks, choices and other circumstances are taken into account and weighed, the course to be followed will be that which is most in the interests of the child's welfare as that term now has to be considered. That is the first consideration because it is of first importance and the paramount consideration because it rules upon or determines the course to be followed.'

6.14 The process is not one of precision, with values being attributed to the different factors, but rather calls for a quality of judgment and this is not susceptible to detailed analysis. In *Re F (An Infant)* Megarry J commented:[12]

> 'There is a limit to the extent to which the court can fairly be expected to expound the process which leads to a conclusion, not least in the weighing of imponderables. In matters of discretion it may at times be impossible to do much more than ensure that the judicial mind is brought to bear, with a proper emphasis on all that is relevant to the exclusion of all that is irrelevant.'

6.15 The wishes of the parent, whether what used to be called the 'unimpeachable parent'[13] or otherwise, cannot dictate the course to be followed:

> 'The role of the court is to exercise an independent and objective judgment. If that judgment accords with that of the devoted and responsible parent, well and good. If not, then it is the duty of the court, after giving due weight to the view of the devoted and responsible parent, to give effect to its own judgment ... Once the jurisdiction of the court is invoked, its clear duty is to reach and express the best judgment it can.'[14]

6.16 Procedural issues rather than substantive ones do not involve questions of a child's upbringing.[15] The test does not apply when the court is considering an application for leave to apply to be joined as a party,[16] or for the ordering of

---

[10]   *Re McGrath (Infants)* [1893] 1 Ch 143.
[11]   [1970] AC 668 at 710.
[12]   [1969] 2 All ER 766 at 768.
[13]   Ormrod LJ commented in *S (BD) v S (DJ) (Infants: Care and Consent)* [1977] 1 All ER 656 at 661: 'I have never known and still do not know what [the phrase] means', discussed in Chapter 8.
[14]   *Re Z (A Minor) (Freedom of Publication)* [1996] 1 FLR 191, per Sir Thomas Bingham at 217.
[15]   *Re A and W (Minors) (Residence Order: Leave to Apply)* [1992] 2 FLR 154.
[16]   *G v Kirklees Metropolitan Borough Council* [1993] 1 FLR 805.

a blood test.[17] However, even when the test does not apply, the court will still regard the welfare of the child as one of the factors to be taken into account.

The welfare test and Article 8

6.17 There is potential for conflict between s 1 and Art 8 of the European Convention for the Protection of Human Rights and Fundamental Freedoms 1950. This is discussed at **6.186**.

DELAY

6.18 Both statutes direct the decision-maker to have regard to the fact that delay is likely to prejudice the child's welfare. The CA 1989 provides that:

> 'In any proceedings in which any question with respect to the upbringing of a child arises, the court shall have regard to the general principle that any delay in determining the question is likely to prejudice the welfare of the child.'[18]

Similarly, under the ACA 2002:

> 'The court or adoption agency must at all times bear in mind that in general, any delay in coming to the decision is likely to prejudice the child's welfare.'[19]

6.19 In addition, Art 6(1) of the European Convention for the Protection of Human Rights and Fundamental Freedoms 1950 requires that proceedings should be determined 'within a reasonable time'. The European Court of Human Rights has recognised that the reasonableness of the length of proceedings must be assessed in the light of the circumstances of the particular case, in particular to its complexity, the conduct of the applicant and to the importance to the applicant of what is at stake but it is essential for custody cases to be dealt with speedily.[20]

The importance of avoiding delay

6.20 In its Working Paper which eventually resulted in the CA 1989,[21] the Law Commission proposed that any dispute about a child's upbringing should be heard within a maximum of 3 months. The final report reluctantly drew back from stipulating a time-limit because it recognised the resource implications but nevertheless emphasised the importance of the principle:

---

[17] *S (An Infant, by her Guardian ad Litem the Official Solicitor to the Supreme Court) v S; W v Official Solicitor (acting as Guardian ad Litem for a Male Infant named PHW)* [1972] AC 24.
[18] CA 1989, s 1(2).
[19] ACA 2002, s 1(3).
[20] *Nuutinen v Finland* (2002) 34 EHRR 15.
[21] *Care, Supervision and Interim Orders in Custody Proceedings* (1987) Working Paper No 100.

'The case for a scheme along these lines is very strong indeed. Prolonged litigation about their future is deeply disturbing [to children] not only because of the uncertainty it brings for them but because of the harm it does to the relationship between the parents and their capacity to cooperate with one another in the future. Moreover, a frequent consequence is that the case of the parent who is not living with the child is severely prejudiced by the time of the hearing. Regrettably it is almost always to the advantage of one of the parties to delay the proceedings as long as possible and, what may be worse, to make difficulties over contact in the meantime.'[22]

6.21 A sense of time is relative. What may be a short period for an adult may seem an eternity for a young child; delay in the resolution of disputes therefore has to be viewed not just in terms of objective measurements of weeks and months but according to what has been called 'the child's sense of time':[23]

'Too often adults forget how things look to children. They think about systems, what is logical and what are acceptable timescales from an adult's point of view. Adults forget how time appears to pass more slowly to children. Adults tend no longer to remember the confusion of entirely new issues and the worry of questioning those who are grownup and logical.'[24]

6.22 Thirty years ago Goldstein, Freud and Solnit[25] commented that:

'For most children under the age of five years, an absence of parents for more than two months is ... beyond comprehension. For the younger school-age child, an absence of six months or more may be similarly experienced. More than one year of being without parents and without evidence that there are parental concerns and expectations is not likely to be understood by the older school-age child and will carry with it the detrimental implications of the breaches in continuity ... After adolescence is fully launched an individual's sense of time closely approaches that of most adults.'

Rowe and Lambert put it more shortly.

'Children cannot be put into cold storage while adults argue about what to do with them or pay attention to the needs of other adults.'[26]

6.23 The point in the child's development at which the unresolved dispute occurs is also significant. Growth in different areas – physical, intellectual, emotional and social and educational – does not take place at an even pace. Although, in most areas of development, the period of most rapid growth occurs in the first 6 years with a 'spurt' at puberty, for some characteristics there is as much quantitative growth in a single year as there are in 8 or 10 years at other stages. Studies suggest that there are periods when children respond

---

[22] *Family Law Review of Child Law: Guardianship and Custody* (1988) Law Com No 172, para 4.55.

[23] Goldstein, Freud, Solnit *Beyond the Best Interests of the Child* (Macmillan, 1973).

[24] *Adoption: A New Approach* (Department of Health, 2000).

[25] Goldstein, Freud, Solnit *Beyond the Best Interests of the Child* (Macmillan, 1973) at p 41.

[26] *Children Who Wait* (Association of British Adoption Agencies, 1973) at p 114.

more readily to various environmental opportunities and setbacks during these periods may have a lasting, although not necessarily irreversible, effect on the child's development.[27]

6.24 Disputes often adversely affect the child, his parents and other involved adults, not only during the course of the litigation but for some time afterwards. One study, *Families in Conflict*,[28] measured the well-being of parents and children both at the end of disputed residence or contact proceedings and one year later. They found that, after the proceedings, nearly nine in ten parents were experiencing disruption in the way in which they normally functioned. Just under half of all of the children had borderline or abnormal scores on a Strengths and Difficulties questionnaire (SDQ), indicating a significant level of emotional and behavioural difficulties.[29] One year later, the well-being of parents had improved but just under half of fathers and a third of mothers were still experiencing emotional problems. The well-being of the children, on the other hand, had deteriorated during the year, more than half having borderline or abnormal SDQ scores. Over a third of girls still had significant difficulties (nearly twice that expected in the general population) but the percentage of boys in these ranges had increased to nearly two-thirds, three times that expected. Overall, younger children were more likely to be affected than older ones.

6.25 There is no reason to believe that involvement in adoption proceedings affects children and their parents less. Proposed adopters too are likely to be affected. The review of studies of the adoption process – *Adoption Now: Messages from Research*[30] found that

> 'There is a good deal of evidence in the studies about how delay – especially unexplained delay – causes uncertainty, anxiety and stress, both for children and prospective adopters ... Adopters could face the prospect of a long wait until a child was placed with them after they had been approved and because of this, some said that they felt unduly pressured into accepting a child about whom they had certain reservations. Others felt let down, frustrated or ignored as time passed without a placement being made.'

Causes of delay

6.26 *The Prime Minister's Review: Adoption*[31] found delay both in the local authority procedure and in the courts.

---

[27] Pringle *The Needs of Children* (3rd edn, 1986), pp 19–24.
[28] Buchanan and Others *Families in Conflict* (The Policy Press, 2001) summarised in Buchanan and Others 'Families in Conflict – Perspectives of Children and Parents on the Family Court Welfare Service' [2001] Fam Law 900.
[29] In the general population of children, it would be expected that 80% would score in the normal range, 10% in the borderline and 10% in the abnormal range.
[30] (Department of Health, 1999) at p 121.
[31] op cit chapter 3.

'The ... whole process is subject to unjustified delay to the detriment of all parties involved but especially the child.'

According to the report, in 1999 it took on average 6 months between a decision that adoption was in the child's best interest and a match with prospective adopters being made. While the average time between match and placement was only one month, the average between placement and adoption was a further 14 months. Older children took longer to place and waited longer to be adopted once placed.

6.27   Delay in the process was associated with:

• A 'lack of grip' on the process. 'There can often be a relaxation of effort once the Care Order has been secured as the child is perceived to be safe, and social workers' attention can often be diverted to more urgent matters.'

• Delay in identifying prospective adoptive parents. The Report noted that 'judges' experience of placement for adoption being delayed can and does influence their willingness to approve Care plans with adoption as the plan.'

• Delays associated with adoption panels. Some authorities reported that progress could be held up by a failure to secure a timely slot at the Adoption Panel.

• Delay in completing reports. Often reports were not completed within the (then) 6-week statutory time limit and this would have a 'knock on' effect on the guardian's report and the hearing.

6.28   Adoption proceedings took 6.3 months on average from the issue of the application to the final order. Contested cases took 7.9 months compared to 4.5 months for uncontested cases. Freeing orders took longest, on average 9.3 months because 75% were contested compared to 25% of adoption applications. Step-parent adoptions took the longest because both local authorities and the courts saw them as being less urgent, the child already living with one birth parent and not being perceived to be at risk of harm.

6.29   Delay in the court process was associated with:

• delays in securing court time;

• delays in resolving legal aid;

- a general 'lack of grip'. 'In many cases the pace of the process is driven by the speed at which the various parties chose to complete their tasks with no central drive or focus.'[32]

6.30 Delay in the court process has also been a matter of complaint in 'private law' proceedings – mainly residence and contact applications.

6.31 Two studies commissioned by the Lord Chancellor's Department, the first by Dame Margaret Booth in 1996[33] and a scoping study in 2002,[34] have examined the causes of delay in cases involving children. They identified a number of causes, aggravated by the unpredictable number of applications being made each year. These included:

- a lack of adequate resources, including what the scoping study called 'not having the right judges in the right place at the right time';

- poor administration;

- lax procedures on transfer from the family proceedings courts;

- lack of proper control by the courts through case management;

- too many parties being joined;

- overuse of experts and insufficient experienced experts of the level required.

6.32 The importance of avoiding unnecessary delay is reflected throughout *Adoption Guidance*[35] issued by the Department for Education and Skills under s 7 of the Local Authority Social Services Act 1970. For example, a proposed placement with a suitable prospective adopter should be identified and approved by the adoption panel within 6 months of the agency deciding that the child should be placed for adoption. However, although the timescales should generally be adhered to, 'the paramount consideration must always be the welfare of a child' and the agency may depart from the timescales if the agency considers that in a particular case compliance would not be in the child's interests.

---

[32] op cit at para 3.55.

[33] *Avoiding Delay in Children Act Cases* (Lord Chancellor's Department, 1996).

[34] *Scoping Study on Delay in Children Act Cases* (Lord Chancellor's Department, 2002), summarised in [2002] Fam Law 492. See also Finlay 'Delay and the Challenges of the Children Act' in Thorpe and Cowton (eds) *Delight and Dole – The Children Act 10 Years On* (Family Law, 2002).

[35] (DfES, 2002) paras 4.1–4.2.

Acceptable delay

6.33 Not all delay prejudices the child. Both the courts and professionals recognise that 'delay' can be acceptable and even necessary, provided it furthers the child's interests.

> 'Delay is ordinarily inimical to the welfare of the child, but ... planned and purposeful delay may well be beneficial. A delay of a final decision for the purpose of ascertaining the result of an assessment is proper delay and is to be encouraged.'[36]

Likewise, in *Re S (Adoption Order or Special Guardianship Order)*[37] Wall LJ said that:

> 'In most cases ... the issue will be, not the actual placement of the child, but the form of order which should govern the future welfare of the child: in other words, the status of the child within the particular household. ... The risk of prejudice caused by delay (to which section 1(2) of the 1989 Act rightly draws attention) may be of less pivotal importance. Indeed, in many cases, it may be appropriate to pause and give time for reflection, particularly in those cases where the order in being made of the court's own motion.'

6.34 *Adoption Now: Messages from Research*[38] also states:

> 'There is obviously a proper pace at which matters should proceed for each child, a pace that provides enough time for the necessary assessments to be made, agreements to be obtained and reports submitted. Furthermore the right family for a child may not be readily available and, when it is, it will be necessary for the period of introduction to be adjusted for different children. Certainly the studies indicated that placements can be made too hurriedly as well as too slowly.'

6.35 For example, ordering an expert report may delay the final hearing of an application for a placement order, but the child will benefit by the court having more information about the risks and benefits of various options. Conversely, the evidence may be likely to add nothing to what is already known:[39]

> 'Delay is always to be regarded as in some degree likely to prejudice the child's welfare ... Parliament here has made a value judgment about the likely impact of delay and it is not open to the court or the adoption agency to quarrel with that basic value judgment.'[40]

---

[36]   *C v Solihull Metropolitan Borough Council* [1993] 1 FLR 290, per Ward J at 304.
[37]   [2007] EWCA Civ 54, [2007] 1 FLR 819 at [48].
[38]   op cit at p 121.
[39]   See, for example, *Re C (A Child) v XYZ County Council* [2007] EWCA Civ 1206, [2008] 1 FLR 1294.
[40]   Ibid, per Arden LJ at [17].

THE NO ORDER PRINCIPLE

6.36 Section 1(5) of the CA 1989 provides that:

'Where a court is considering whether or not to make one or more orders under the Act with respect to a child, it shall not make the order or any of the orders unless it considers that doing so would be better for the child than making no order at all.'

6.37 Section 1(6) of the ACA 2002 conflates subss 1(5) and 1(3)(g) of the 1989 Act and provides that:

'The court or the adoption agency must always consider the whole range of the powers available to it in the child's case (whether under this Act or the Children Act 1989); and the court must not make any order under this Act unless it considers that making the order would be better for the child than not doing so.'

6.38 In *Re G (Children)*[41] Lord Justice Ward noted that although there seemed to be considerable academic learning on the subsection, the provision was 'perfectly clear'. It did not create a presumption one way or the other. 'It merely demanded of the court that it ask itself the question whether to make an order would be better for a child than making no order at all.'

6.39 In contested cases 'no order' is often not an option, especially where there are cross-applications. In uncontested cases, orders may still be necessary – for example, residence orders being granted to a parent and step-parent in order to give the step-parent parental responsibility.[42] In *Re S (Adoption Order or Special Guardianship Order)*[43] Wall LJ commented that:

'In most cases (the issue will be, not the actual placement of the child, but the form of order which should govern the future welfare of the child ... It is unlikely that the court need be concerned with the alternative of making "no order" under section 1(5) of the 1989 Act and 1(6) of the 2002 Act ... although the "no order" principle as such is unlikely to be relevant ...'

6.40 If the court has to make an order, it should begin with a preference for the less interventionist rather than the more interventionist approach. 'This should be considered to be in the better interests of the children, again unless there are cogent reasons to the contrary.'[44]

---

[41] [2005] EWCA Civ 1283, [2006] 1 FLR 771 at [10].
[42] *G v F (Contact and Shared Residence: Applications for Leave)* [1998] 2 FLR 799 but otherwise in *Re WB (Residence Orders)* [1995] 2 FLR 1023.
[43] [2007] EWCA Civ 54, [2007] 1 FLR 819 at [48].
[44] *Re O (Care or Supervision Order)* [1996] 2 FLR 755 per Hale J at 759. See also *Oxfordshire CC v L (Care or Supervision Order)* [1998] 1 FLR 70 per Hale J at 74.

THE WELFARE CHECKLIST

6.41   A court, when considering whether to make, vary or discharge a special guardianship order in contested proceedings, must have regard in particular to a number of matters listed in s 1(3) of the CA 1989. These have become known as 'the welfare checklist'.

6.42   Under the ACA 2002, a checklist was introduced in adoption proceedings. Whenever a court or adoption agency is coming to any decision, whether contested or not, relating to the adoption of a child, it has to have regard (among others) to the matters set out in ACA 2002, s 1(4).

6.43   As for the welfare tests, both checklists are similar but not identical. In addition the CA 1989, s 1(3) test applies only to contested special guardianship proceedings unlike the ACA 2002, s 1(4) test which applies to all adoption matters.

6.44   As stated by the Law Commission in relation to the 1989 Act,[45] the purpose of the checklists is to assist greater consistency, clarity and a more systematic approach to decisions:

> 'Perhaps most important of all, we are told that such a list could assist both parents and children in endeavouring to understand how judicial decisions are made. At present, there is a tendency for advisers and clients (and possibly even courts) to rely on "rules of thumb" as to what the court is likely to think best in any given circumstances. A checklist would make it clear to all what, as a minimum would be considered by the court.'

> 'While the checklist may provide a clear statement of what society considers the most important factors in the welfare of children, it must not be applied too rigidly or be so formulated as to prevent the court from taking into account everything which is relevant in the particular case.'

6.45   However, it can only be practicable if it is 'confined to major points leaving others to be formulated elsewhere'. Because knowledge and understanding of children and their needs are progressing all the time, courts have to be able to keep pace with change and be free of fetters imposed by too detailed or rigid a list.

6.46   The checklists contain no hierarchy:

> 'It is one of the functions of the Court of Appeal, in appropriate cases, to lay down general guidelines on the relative weights to be given to various factors in different circumstances ...These guidelines, not expressly stated by Parliament, are derived by the courts from values about family life which it considers would be widely accepted in the community. But there are many cases which involve value judgements on which there are no such generally held views ... Since judges are

---

[45]   *Family Law Review of Child Law: Guardianship and Custody* Law Com No 172 (HMSO, 1988).

also people, this means that some degree of diversity in their application of values is inevitable and, within limits, an acceptable price to pay for the flexibility of the discretion conferred by the ... Act. The appellate court must be willing to permit a degree of pluralism in these matters.'[46]

6.47 As noted by the Law Commission guidance is a reflection of the values sought to be expressed at the time it is given and may and will change as the values or their weight change. In *Re J (Child Returned Abroad: Convention Rights)*[47] Baroness Hale of Richmond pointed out that:

> 'In a world which values difference, one culture is not inevitably to be preferred to another. Indeed, we do not have any fixed concept of what will be in the best interests of the individual child. Once upon a time it was assumed that all very young children should be cared for by their mothers, but that older boys might well be better off with their fathers. Nowadays we know that some fathers are very well able to provide everyday care for even their very young children and are quite prepared to prioritise their children's needs over the demands of their own careers. ... Once upon a time it may have been assumed that there was only one way of bringing up children. Nowadays we know that there are many routes to a healthy and well-adjusted adulthood. We are not so arrogant as to think that we know best.'

6.48 The matters do not form an exhaustive list and, provided they are considered, it is for the court or the local authority to weigh the factors in the circumstances of the particular case.

> 'Section 1[of the Adoption and Children Act 2002] stipulates that particular matters are to be taken into account, but does not provide any express machinery for ascertaining those matters. The means of ascertaining those matters is left to the inherent powers of the court or statutory powers of the adoption agency. The legislation is not prescriptive, and it has been left to the exercise of discretion as to whether any means available as a matter of inherent jurisdiction or under statutory powers is actually employed. Finally, with one exception [that of delay], s 1 does not establish any preference for any particular result or prescribe any particular conclusion. Importantly ... it does not express a preference for following the wishes of the birth family or placing a child with the child's birth family, though this will often be in the best interests of the child.[48]

6.49 The s 1 test is founded on the welfare of a specific child, the child who is the subject of the adjudication. 'The focus [of the trial judge] has to be on the individual child in the particular circumstances of the case'[49] and general propositions of policy, must give way to the interests of the individual child.

---

[46] *Piglowska v Piglowski* [1999] 2 FLR 763, per Lord Hoffmann at 785–786, discussing the financial relief checklist in the Matrimonial Causes Act 1973, s 25.

[47] *Re J (Child Returned Abroad: Convention Rights)* [2005] UKHL 40, [2005] 2 FLR 802 at [38].

[48] *Re C (A Child) v XYZ County Council* op cit per Arden LJ at [17].

[49] *Re J (Child Returned Abroad: Convention Rights)* [2005] UKHL 40, [2005] 2 FLR 802 per Baroness Hale at [29].

CHECKLIST – SPECIAL GUARDIANSHIP

6.50 Sections 1(3) and (4) of the Children Act 1989 provide that when the court is considering whether to make, vary or discharge a special guardianship order it shall have regard in particular to:

(a) the ascertainable wishes and feelings of the child concerned (considered in the light of his age and understanding);

(b) the child's physical, emotional and educational needs;

(c) the likely effect on him of any change in his circumstances;

(d) his age, sex, background and any characteristics of his which the court considers significant;

(e) any harm which he has suffered or is at risk of suffering;

(f) how capable each of his parents, and any other person in relation to whom the court considers the question to be relevant, is of meeting his needs;

(g) the range of powers available to the court under the Act in the proceedings in question.

The ascertainable wishes and feelings of the child concerned (considered in the light of his age and understanding)

6.51 Those wishes and feelings will be set out in in the s 14A(8) report[50] (see **10.11**) and in any s 7 report. In appropriate but exceptional cases, the child may be joined as a party and represented by a guardian or next friend (see **18.70**). In rare cases, when the child is able, having regard to his understanding, to give instructions in relation to the proceedings, he may be allowed to act without a guardian/next friend.

6.52 The approach of the Law Commission in 1988[51] offers a good summary of the current position of courts:

> 'The opinion of our respondents was almost unanimously in favour of the proposal to give statutory recognition to the child's views. Obviously there are dangers in giving them too much recognition. Children's views have to be discovered in such a way as to avoid embroiling them in their parents' disputes, forcing them to "choose" between their parents or making them feel responsible for the eventual decision. This is usually best done through the medium of a court welfare officer's report although most agreed that courts should retain their present powers to see children in private. Similarly, for a variety of reasons the

---

[50] The Special Guardianship Regulations 2005 (SI 2005/1109), Sch, para 3(a).

[51] *Family Law: Review of Child Law: Guardianship and Custody* Law Com No 172.

child's views may not be reliable, so that the court should only have to take due account of them in the light of his age and understanding. Nevertheless, experience has shown that it is pointless to ignore the clearly expressed views of older children. Finally, however, if the parents have agreed on where the child will live and made their arrangements accordingly, it is no more practicable to try to alter these to accord with the child's views than it is to impose the views of the court. After all, united parents will no doubt take account of the views of their children in deciding upon moves of house or employment but the children cannot expect their wishes to prevail.'[52]

Why should wishes and feelings be ascertained?

6.53   There are three reasons for a child's wishes being ascertained and then considered. The first is protective, the second, utilitarian and the third, rights-based.

> 'Any order which causes a child harm by reason of emotional disturbance needs to be avoided. Second, the wishes and feelings of the child may be relevant to the effectiveness of the order proposed. A 2-year-old child removed from the care of his mother and placed with someone who is a psychological stranger for a day's contact may become distraught, protest and, irrespective of the distress suffered by the child, contact will not be successful. Likewise, forcing a course of action on an unwilling teenager may be doomed to failure.[53] Lastly is the growing recognition that it is important that children as individuals ought to be able to contribute to decisions about their futures, whether or not this can be termed a 'right'.[54]

6.54   The European Court of Human Rights has recognised that courts should take into account the wishes and feelings of children. In *Hokkanen v Finland*,[55] for example, it held that the wish of a mature 10-year-old of an above-average intelligence to remain with her grandparents, with whom she had lived since she was 2, and her feeling that their home was her home were not only relevant but were sufficient to justify dismissing her father's application for custody.

6.55   However, the current emphasis placed by the European Court of Human Rights is not so much on the right of the child to be heard in the sense of his wishes being taken into account but on the need to investigate all relevant circumstances before deciding whether any interference with family life was justified. Nor has the Court prescribed steps which must be taken in every case. In *Sahin v Germany; Sommerfeld v Germany*[56] the Fourth Section of the Court held that in a contact case a domestic court's failure to hear directly from the

---

[52]   *Family Law: Review of Child Law: Guardianship and Custody* Law Com No 172, para 3.23.
[53]   See for example *Re P (A Minor) (Education)* [1992] 1 FLR 316.
[54]   For summaries of the argument, see Fortin *Children's Rights and the Developing Law* (2nd edn, 2003) chap 7, Lowe and Murch 'Children's Participation in the Family Justice System – Translating Principles into Practice' [2001] CFLQ 137 and Piper 'Barriers to Seeing and Hearing Children in Private Law Proceedings' [1999] Fam Law 394.
[55]   (1994) 19 EHRR 139, [1996] 1 FLR 289.
[56]   [2002] 1 FLR 119.

child in the first case (although there had been a psychological report) and to direct a report by a psychologist in the second infringed the *father's* right to be sufficiently involved in the proceedings. However, the Grand Chamber[57] took a different view, recognising that domestic courts had a margin of appreciation when deciding what was required by the circumstances of the particular case.

'[As] a general rule it is for the national courts to assess the evidence before them, including the means to ascertain the relevant facts (see *Vidal v Belgium* (22 April 1992), Series A, No 235-B 17 at para 33). It would be going too far to say that domestic courts are always required to hear a child in court on the issue of access to a parent not having custody, but this issue depends on the specific circumstances of each case, having due regard to the age and maturity of the child concerned.'[58]

Furthermore any requirement that a child's views should be considered, does not equate with the child having a right to be a party.[59]

6.56   There are other international Conventions which acknowledge that the views of children should be considered and given due weight and that when a child is capable of forming its own views, the child should have the opportunity of being heard by the court either directly or indirectly.

6.57   Article 12 of the UN Convention on the Rights of the Child 1989 provides that:

'States parties shall assure to the child who is capable of forming his or her own views the right to express those views freely in all matters affecting the child, the views of the child being given due weight in accordance with the age and maturity of the child ... the child shall in particular be provided the opportunity of being heard in any judicial and administrative proceedings affecting the child either directly or through a representative or appropriate body, in a manner consistent with procedural rules of national law.'

6.58   Article 3 of the European Convention on the Exercise of Children's Rights 1996 (which has not yet been ratified by the United Kingdom) provides that a child:

'... considered by internal law as having sufficient understanding shall in judicial proceedings affecting him be granted and be entitled to request the following rights:

(a)   to receive all relevant information;
(b)   to be consulted and express his or her own views;
(c)   to be informed of the possible consequences of compliance with these views and the possible consequences of any decision.'

---

[57]   [2003] 2 FLR 671.
[58]   Para [73].
[59]   *M v United Kingdom* [1985] 52 DR 269.

6.59 Article 4 provides the further right:

'to apply, in person or through other persons or bodies, for a special representative in proceedings before a judicial authority affecting the child where internal law precludes the holders of parental responsibilities from representing the child as a result of conflict of interests with the latter.'

6.60 Both domestic and Convention law agree therefore that courts should consider the wishes and feelings of children, that these should be given weight according to the age and maturity of the child and that, in order to protect rights, it may be necessary for them to be allowed to be parties. The existence of Convention rights, however, has encouraged courts in England and Wales to revisit their traditional approach that children should not be made parties in private law cases. In *Re A (Contact: Separate Representation)*,[60] Butler Sloss P said:

'There are cases when they do need to be separately represented and I suspect as a result of the European Convention for the Protection of Human Rights and Fundamental Freedoms 1950 becoming part of domestic law and the increased view of the English courts, in any event, that the children should be seen and heard in child cases and not always sufficiently seen and heard by the use of a court welfare officer's report, there will be an increased use of guardians in private law cases. Indeed, in the right case I would welcome it.'

However, she added that, 'in the majority of cases, in private law proceedings, children do not need to be separately represented'.

6.61 In contested adoption proceedings, the child will be represented by a guardian. In special guardianship proceedings the court has a discretionary power to join the child as a guardian and to appoint a guardian. See **18.70**.

The weight to be given to a child's wishes and feelings

6.62 The weight to be given to the wishes and feelings has to be ascertained according to the child's age or understanding.[61] Although, in the past, courts have commented on the weight to be given to the wishes of a child of a particular age, the current approach is to consider the maturity and understanding of the particular child rather than to adopt the assumed understanding of a hypothetical child of the particular child's age. Allowance has to be made for the possibility that the wishes and feelings may have been influenced, whether indirectly or intentionally, by an adult but remembering that such wishes and feelings are nevertheless real. What may be of greater importance is whether those wishes are based on a substratum of supporting fact, how carefully the child has considered the situation, how much the child can appreciate the benefits and demerits of alternative possibilities, long as well as short term, and how far those wishes and feelings may change.

---

[60] [2001] 1 FLR 715 at [22].
[61] See *Re H (Care Order: Contact)* [2008] EWCA Civ 1245, [2009] 2 FLR 55.

6.63 In *Re T (Abduction: Child's Objection to Return)*,[62] a case brought under the Hague Convention on the Civil Aspects of International Child Abduction 1980 the Court of Appeal gave general guidance on the weight to be accorded to a child's wishes:

'It seems to me [said Thorpe LJ] that the matters to establish are:

(1)   Whether the child objects [to a particular course of conduct].
(2)   The age and degree of maturity of the child. Is the child more mature or less mature than or as mature as her chronological age? ...
(3)   ... the strength and validity of those views [need to be ascertained] which will call for an examination of the following matters among others:
    (a)   What is the child's own perspective of what is in her interests, short, medium and long term? Self-perception is important because it is *her* views which have to be judged appropriate.
    (b)   To what extent, if at all, are the reasons for objection rooted in reality or might reasonably appear to the child to be so grounded?
    (c)   To what extent have those views been shaped or even coloured by undue influence and pressure, directly or indirectly exerted by the abducting party?
    (d)   To what extent will the objections be mollified on return and, where it is the case, on removal from any pernicious influence from the abducting parent?'

6.64 One matter is clear as a matter of principle. The child's wishes and feelings are never the sole consideration. All the other s 1 factors have to be considered as well and the course to be taken must be in the child's best interests. However, in some cases the strength of the wishes may be such as to effectively determine the matter.

The child's physical, emotional and educational needs

6.65 Physical and educational needs require little elaboration. A child needs adequate nutrition, hygiene and safety from injury, whether caused deliberately or by neglect.

6.66 The Department of Health in its *Framework for the Assessment of Children in Need and their Families*[63] defines 'health' including growth and development as well as physical and mental wellbeing.

'The impact of genetic factors and of any impairment should be considered. It involves receiving appropriate health care when ill, an adequate and nutritious diet, exercise, immunisations where appropriate and developmental checks, dental and optical care and, for older children, appropriate advice and information on issues that have an impact on health, including sex education and substance misuse.'

---

[62]   [2000] 2 FLR 192, per Ward LJ at 203. See also *Re J (Abduction: Child's Objections to Return)* [2004] EWCA Civ 428, [2004] 2 FLR 64.
[63]   (HMSO, 2000) ch 2.

6.67 Parents are under a duty to cause their child of compulsory school age to receive efficient full-time education suitable to his age, ability and aptitude and to any special educational needs he may have whether by ensuring he attends school 'or otherwise'.[64] The *Framework* adds that education 'covers all areas of a child's cognitive development which begins from birth'. The child's needs include:

> 'opportunities: for play and interaction with other children; to have access to books; to acquire a range of skills and interests; to experience success and achievement ... an adult interested in educational activities, progress and achievements, who takes account of the child's starting point and any special educational needs.'

6.68 Emotional needs are less obvious. There are four basic emotional needs which have to be met from the very beginning of life to enable a child to grow 'from helpless infancy to mature adulthood'.[65] These are:

- The need for love and security:

> 'The security of a familiar place and a known routine make for continuity and predictability in a world in which the child has to come to terms with so much that is new and changing. Also, a stable family life provides him with a sense of personal continuity, of having a past as well as a future, and of a coherent and enduring identity.'

- The need for new experiences.

- The need for praise and recognition.

- The need for responsibility to enable the child to gain personal independence.

6.69 The *Framework* provides the following analysis.

- *Emotional and Behavioural Development* – 'the appropriateness of response demonstrated in feelings and actions by a child, initially to parents and caregivers and, as the child grows older, to others beyond the family'; it includes 'nature and quality of early attachments, characteristics of temperament, adaptation to change, response to stress and degree of appropriate self control'.

- *Identity* – involves the child's growing sense of self as a separate and valued person and includes 'the child's view of self and abilities, self image and self esteem, and having a positive sense of individuality' with contributions from race, religion, age, gender, sexuality and disability.

---

[64] Education Act 1944, s 36, as amended.
[65] Pringle *The Needs of Children* (3rd edn, 1986) ch 7.

Also included are feelings of belonging and acceptance by family, peer group and wider society, including other cultural groups.

- *Family and Social Relationships* – development of empathy and the capacity to place self in someone else's shoes. They include 'a stable and affectionate relationship with parents or caregivers, good relationships with siblings, increasing importance of age appropriate friendships with peers and other significant persons in the child's life and response of family to these relationships'.

- *Social Presentation* – a child's 'growing understanding of the way in which appearance, behaviour, and any impairment are perceived by the outside world and the impression being created'. Included are 'appropriateness of dress for age, gender, culture and religion; cleanliness and personal hygiene; and availability of advice from parents or caregivers about presentation in different settings'.

- *Self Care Skills* – the acquisition by a child of practical, emotional and communication competencies required for increasing independence. His needs include 'early practical skills of dressing and feeding, opportunities to gain confidence and practical skills to undertake activities away from the family and independent living skills as older children'. Encouragement is needed to enable the child to acquire social problem solving approaches. 'Special attention should be given to the impact of a child's impairment and other vulnerabilities, and on social circumstances affecting these in the development of self care skills.'

6.70   The court has to consider both the child's temporary and long-term needs and these may differ. For example, in *Re H (A Minor) (Custody: Interim Care and Control)*,[66] a 9-year-old child was living with her terminally ill mother who, a week before she died, arranged for her to go to live with her maternal grandmother. The girl's father applied for an order that she should live with him. The Court of Appeal held that she should remain with her grandmother pending a final hearing in 3 months' time when the trial judge would have the benefit of a welfare report:

> 'There is some danger in this case of confusing the long-term and the short-term needs of this child ... at this moment of time, with the devastation to her of the tragic loss of her mother, her grandmother ... is a very good person with whom to live. She will find, no doubt, the period of bereavement a great deal easier with grandmother.'[67]

The likely effect on him of any change in his circumstances

6.71   The extent and possible effect of any change should not be underestimated. For example, a residence order causing a child to move from

---

[66]   [1991] 2 FLR 109.
[67]   Ibid, per Butler-Sloss LJ at 111–112.

one parent to another will not only involve a change in carer but possibly a change of home, school, neighbourhood and friends:[68]

'Some of the authorities convey the impression that the upset caused to a child by a change of custody is transient and a matter of small importance. For all I know that may have been true in the cases containing dicta to that effect. But I think a growing experience has shown that it is not always so and that serious harm even to young children may, on occasion, be caused by such a change ... a child's future happiness and sense of security are always important factors and the effect of a change of custody will often be worthy of ... close and anxious attention ...'[69]

6.72 Courts favour the status quo which one of the most experienced family judges of the twentieth century,[70] Ormrod LJ, called 'one of the most important single factors in deciding what is in the best interests of young children'.[71] Clear evidence is required to show that a change of carer is in the child's interests.[72]

His age, sex, background and any characteristics of his which the court considers significant

6.73 There are no universal guidelines and each child has to be considered as an individual. Nor is there, any longer, any presumption or assumption that a child (as opposed to a young baby)[73] should be with its mother.[74] Nor is there a general assumption that girls should be raised by their mothers.[75]

6.74 The factor includes the child's cultural, racial and religious background.[76] In *Re M (Section 94 Appeals)*,[77] the Court of Appeal held that the court below should have taken account of the fact that a child, living with her white mother, and who was of mixed race, was confused about her racial identity when deciding an application for contact by her black father. In considering these issues, courts act pragmatically rather than having regard to niceties, for example, of religious law.

6.75 The issues of race, religion and culture are considered more fully at **6.107**.

---

[68] For a more detailed discussion in relation to residence orders, see Chapter 8.
[69] *J and Another v C and Others* [1970] AC 668, per Lord MacDermott at 715.
[70] He qualified as a doctor as well as a barrister.
[71] *S (BD) v S (DJ) (Infants: Care and Consent)* [1977] 1 All ER 656 at 663.
[72] See, for example, *Re A (A Minor) (Custody)* [1991] 2 FLR 394.
[73] *K and T v Finland* [2001] 2 FLR 707, ECHR at 737 and *Re W (A Minor) (Residence Order)* [1992] 2 FLR 332.
[74] *Re S (A Minor) (Custody)* [1991] 2 FLR 388 but see *Brixey v Lynas* [1996] 2 FLR 499.
[75] *Re A (A Minor) (Custody)* [1991] 2 FLR 394.
[76] *Re P (Section 91(14) Guidelines) (Residence and Religious Heritage)* [1999] 2 FLR 573.
[77] [1995] 1 FLR 546.

Any harm which he has suffered or is at risk of suffering

6.76 'Harm' means ill-treatment or the impairment of health or development. 'Ill-treatment' includes sexual abuse and forms of ill-treatment which are not physical. 'Health' means physical or mental health, including harm a child 'has suffered or is at risk of suffering as a result of seeing or hearing the ill-treatment of another person'.[78] 'Development' means physical, intellectual, emotional, social or behavioural development. When the court considers whether harm suffered by a child is significant to the child's health or development, his health or development has to be compared with what could reasonably be expected of a similar child.[79]

6.77 Included in this factor may be the harm a child may suffer if his primary carer does not have parental responsibility or he remains in care (for example, with a foster carer and not a special guardian) or if parental responsibility is shared fully with a natural parent or if his home is disrupted by repeated applications by a natural parent seeking contact. If there is an issue of whether or not a child should be rehabilitated to the care of a parent, the degree of risk associated with the attempt must be properly ascertained.[80] Conversely the risk of harm to the child in moving from a settled foster home to an adoptive home must also be considered. In *Re F (Adoption: Welfare of Child: Financial Considerations)*[81] three children aged between 7 and 4 years old had been in an 'excellent' foster home for a year. The authority applied to free them for adoption. Black J rejected the application on the basis the boys should remain in their current home as foster children.

> 'As a general principle, … adoption has more to offer children, and particularly younger children, in all sorts of ways than long-term foster care, but every recommendation bar one [in this case] is to the effect that that general principle does not apply in this case, and that these children's welfare would best be served by staying where they are.'[82]

6.78 When a court is considering whether a child is 'likely' to suffer harm, it does not have to be satisfied that it is more likely than not to suffer harm. Rather, it has to be satisfied on evidence (as opposed to suspicion) that there is a real possibility of harm, 'a possibility that cannot sensibly be ignored having regard to the nature and gravity of the feared harm in the particular case'.[83] The assessment of risk must be based on evidence.[84]

---

[78] CA 1989, s 105(1) and s 31(9) inserted by Adoption and Children Act 2002, s 120.
[79] CA 1989, ss 105(1), 31(9) and (10).
[80] *Re G (A Minor) (Adoption: Parental Agreement)* [1990] 2 FLR 429.
[81] [2003] EWHC 348 (Fam), [2004] 2 FLR 440.
[82] Ibid, per Black J at [77].
[83] *Re H and R (Child Sexual Abuse: Standard of Proof)* [1996] 1 FLR 80, per Lord Nicholls of Birkenhead at 95.
[84] *Re B (Children)* [2008] UKHL 35, per Baroness Hale of Richmond at [44]. See also *Re M and R (Minors) (Abuse: Expert Evidence)* [1996] 2 FLR 195 per Butler Sloss LJ at 203.

How capable each of his parents, and any other person in relation to whom the court considers the question to be relevant, is of meeting his needs

6.79 There is no room for stereotypical judgments. A father may be more able to meet a child's needs than the mother.[85] The court has to consider *this* person in relation to the needs of *this* child. The strain which parents may be under at the time of the hearing or following a separation from a former partner may temporarily affect or disguise his or her parenting ability. This may cause difficulties in assessing the parent's ability to meet both the child's long-term and short-term needs.

6.80 The Department of Health's *Framework for the Assessment of Children in Need and their Families* lists various dimensions of parenting capacity.[86]

- *Basic care* – providing for the child's physical needs, and appropriate medical and dental care including provision of food, drink, warmth, shelter, clean and appropriate clothing and adequate personal hygiene.

- *Ensuring safety* – ensuring the child is adequately protected from harm or danger, including providing protection from significant harm or danger, and from contact with unsafe adults/other children and from self-harm. Recognition of hazards and danger both in the home and elsewhere.

- *Emotional warmth* – ensuring the child's emotional needs are met, giving the child a sense of being specially valued and a positive sense of own racial and cultural identity. This includes:

  > 'ensuring the child's requirements for secure, stable and affectionate relationships with significant adults, with appropriate sensitivity and responsiveness to the child's needs. Appropriate physical contact, comfort and cuddling sufficient to demonstrate warm regard, praise and encouragement.'

- *Stimulation* – promoting the child's learning and intellectual development through encouragement and cognitive stimulation and promoting social opportunities. Facilitating the child's cognitive development and potential through interaction, communication, talking and responding to the child's language and questions, encouraging and joining the child's play, and promoting educational opportunities. Enabling the child to experience success and ensuring school attendance or equivalent opportunity. Facilitating the child to meet the challenges of life.

- *Guidance and boundaries* – enabling the child to regulate their own emotions and behaviour.

---

[85] *Re S (A Minor) (Custody)* [1991] 2 FLR 388.
[86] op cit chapter 2. See also Balbernie 'Law and Child Development' [2003] Fam Law 508.

'The key parental tasks are *demonstrating and modelling* appropriate behaviour and control of emotions and interactions with others, and *guidance* which involves setting boundaries, so that the child is able to develop an internal model of moral values and conscience, and social behaviour appropriate for the society within which they will grow up. The aim is to enable the child to grow into an autonomous adult, holding their own values, and able to demonstrate appropriate behaviour with others rather than having to be dependent on rules outside themselves. This includes not overprotecting children from exploratory and learning experiences.'

- *Skills* – 'social problem solving, anger management, consideration for others, and effective discipline and shaping of behaviour'.

- *Stability* – providing a sufficiently stable family environment to enable a child to develop and maintain a secure attachment to the primary caregiver(s) in order to ensure optimal development and ensuring children keep in contact with important family members and 'significant others'. This requires ensuring secure attachments are not disrupted, 'providing consistency of emotional warmth over time and responding in a similar manner to the same behaviour'.

The guidance notes that parental responses change and develop according to a child's developmental progress.

6.81 Not infrequently a party seeks to adduce evidence of parental skills by relying on psychometric testing. While such tests may be of benefit when ascertaining a person's intellectual capacity and skills, the results of personality testing should be approached with great caution.

'The principal issue for the judge was the mother's parenting skills. If the judge was (exceptionally) minded to rely on the results of the personality tests, he had first to assess their validity, both generally and for the purpose of this case. The qualifications to the test results properly made by [the psychologist] in his evidence, to my mind, demonstrate that personality testing of this kind cannot be used to resolve issues such as parenting skills unless they are validated by other evidence.'[87]

The range of powers available to the court under the Act in the proceedings in question

6.82 When a court is considering an application in any family proceedings[88] it can make any s 8 order – a residence order, contact order, specific issue order or prohibited steps order – under the CA 1989, a contact order under s 26 of the ACA 2002 or ouster/occupation and non-molestation orders under Part IV of

---

[87]   *Re S (Care: Parenting Skills: Personality Tests)* [2004] EWCA Civ 1029, [2005] 2 FLR 658 per Arden LJ at [68].

[88]   Which include adoption proceedings: CA 1989, s 8(3).

the Family Law Act 1986 without an application needing to be made.[89] In addition, in s 8 proceedings under the CA 1989, the court can make a family assistance order in order to provide help to the family from CAFCASS or a local authority.[90]

CHECKLIST – ADOPTION

6.83 Section 1(4) of the ACA 2002 provides that when a court or adoption agency is coming to a decision relating to the adoption of a child it must have regard to the following matters (amongst others):

(a)   the child's ascertainable wishes and feelings regarding the decision (considered in the light of the child's age and understanding);

(b)   the child's particular needs;

(c)   the likely effect on the child (throughout his life) of having ceased to be a member of the original family and become an adopted person;

(d)   the child's age, sex, background and any of the child's characteristics which the court or agency considers relevant;

(e)   any harm (within the meaning of the Children Act 1989) which the child has suffered or is at risk of suffering;

(f)   the relationship which the child has with relatives and with any other person in relation to whom the court or agency considers the relationship to be relevant, including:
   (i)   the likelihood of any such relationship continuing and the value to the child of its so doing;
   (ii)   the ability and willingness of any of the child's relatives or of any such person to provide the child with a secure environment in which the child can develop, and otherwise to meet the child's needs;
   (iii) the wishes and feelings of any of the child's relatives or of any such person, regarding the child.

6.84 Section 1(5) adds that 'In placing the child for adoption, the adoption agency must give due consideration to the child's religious persuasion, racial origin and cultural and linguistic background'.

6.85 Section 1(6) states that the court or agency must always consider the whole range of powers available to it whether under the ACA 2002 or the CA 1989.

---

[89]   CA 1989, s 10(1), ACA 2002 s 26(4), Family Law Act 1996, ss 39(2) and 42(2).
[90]   CA 1989, s 16. See Chapter 13.

6.86   These are key factors which should always be taken into consideration. The local authority/agency and the guardian are expected to explore them with the child, family and adoption applicants prior to the hearing.[91] In addition to any other evidence, they have to be addressed in the report filed by the local authority or agency under the Family Procedure (Adoption) Rules 2005 (FP(A)R 2005).[92] These are also discussed in Chapters 8 and 10 in relation to assessment.

The child's ascertainable wishes and feelings regarding the decision (considered in the light of the child's age and understanding)

6.87   This is discussed at **6.51**. The child's wishes will be set out in the report filed by the local authority or agency under FP(A)R 2005, r 29 in the proceedings for adoption[93] or for a placement order[94] as well as in the report of any guardian[95] or children and family reporter.[96]

6.88   The importance of ascertaining wishes and feelings is even more important when the court or agency is considering adoption. The White Paper, *Adoption: A New Approach*, recognised that some older children do not wish to be legally separated from their birth families and for these children, special guardianship may be more appropriate.[97]

The child's particular needs

6.89   This is discussed at **6.65**.

The likely effect on the child (throughout his life) of having ceased to be a member of the original family and become an adopted person

6.90   This is the first of the factors in the adoption checklist which is not in the CA 1989 checklist.

6.91   After noting that one of the special features of adoption is that it has a significant effect on a person's identity and family relationships throughout his life the *Review of Adoption Law*[98] recommended that one of the factors which must be taken into account should be the likely effect on the child's adult life of any change in his legal status.

---

[91]   *Review of Adoption Law* op cit 7.4.
[92]   SI 2005/2795.
[93]   FP(A)R 2005, Practice Direction 5C, Annex A, Section B, Part 2 (c).
[94]   Ibid.
[95]   Ibid, r 65(2)(b).
[96]   Ibid, r 74(3)(c).
[97]   Cm 5017 at para 5.8.
[98]   op cit at para 7.2.

'This may, for instance, lead the court to ascertain whether the birth family and adoptive family have considered what would be the most appropriate way of making contact if the child should wish to re-establish contact at an older age.'

6.92 Under the law as it was before the Act came into force, the court could consider benefits accruing after majority.[99] The Court of Appeal approved the opinion of the trial judge, Thorpe J, that:

'I am in no doubt that ... in an appropriate case the court is entitled to have regard to considerations which will inure to the benefit of the child beyond minority and for the rest of his life.'

6.93 The child may be affected by losing or gaining a pecuniary benefit. For example, by being treated in law from the date of adoption as if born as the child of the adopter and no one else[100] he would lose the right to claim upon the intestacy of a natural parent and under any instrument, for example a will or trust deed which confers an unvested benefit on a class of which he was a member. Conversely he would acquire a similar right in relation to the adopter's estate and may gain a benefit in becoming a member of a class of beneficiaries. If a disposition depends on the date of a birth of a child, the disposition is to be interpreted as if the child as born on the date of the adoption (see **2.104**).[101] Citizenship may also be gained (see **2.101**).

6.94 There may also be psychological gains or losses including the loss of a relationship with parents or siblings. See Chapter 12.

The child's age, sex, background and any of the child's characteristics which the court or agency considers relevant

6.95 This is discussed at **6.73**.

Any harm (within the meaning of the Children Act 1989) which the child has suffered or is at risk of suffering

6.96 This is discussed at **6.76**.

6.97 This may include the harm caused by a child growing up without a permanent home. The factor is not, however, confined to the risk to the child if an adoption order is not made. Making the order may also involve a risk of harm if, for example, the placement breaks down or the needs of the child are not met.

'The issue of risks that may accompany [the children's] placements must be confronted. [The] issue has several dimensions. When we endeavour to estimate

---

[99] *Re D (A Minor) (Adoption Order: Validity)* [1991] 2 FLR 66 at 73E–73F.
[100] ACA 2002, s 67(1)–(3); but note that this does not affect the child's relationship with a natural parent who adopts him as a sole adopter (ibid, s 67(4)).
[101] Ibid, s 69(2).

risks, what do we have in mind? ... Furthermore, who runs the risks? Obviously, the principle concern is with the child but there is evidence that others in the adoptive family may also be exposed to a variety of risks. The [adopting] parents may risk long periods of stress, frustration or despair.[102] Other children in the family may be put at risk of unhappiness or even abuse. They may feel that they risk the loss of their parents' attention or affection. The family as a whole may risk turbulence, upheaval and discord.'[103]

At the same time, the satisfactions arising from adoption for both children and adults should not be underestimated and may serve to mitigate the risk.[104]

The relationship which the child has with relatives and with any other relevant person

6.98 The court and agency must have regard to the relationship which the child has with relatives and with any other person in relation to whom the court or agency considers the relationship to be relevant, including:

- the likelihood of any such relationship continuing and the value to the child of its so doing;

- the ability and willingness of any of the child's relatives or of any such person to provide the child with a secure environment in which the child can develop, and otherwise to meet the child's needs;

- the wishes and feelings of any of the child's relatives or of any such person, regarding the child.

This is the second factor in the checklist which is not in the CA 1989 checklist and, like s 1(3)(c) is concerned with the wide-ranging and permanent effect of adoption.

6.99 References to 'relationships' are not confined to legal relationships – they may, for example, included a foster carer – and references to a relative includes the child's parents.[105] The importance of sibling relationships is recognised both in domestic law[106] and under Art 8(1) of the European Convention for the Protection of Human Rights and Fundamental Freedoms.

---

[102] See, for example, *A v Essex County Council* [2003] EWCA Civ 1848, [2004] 1 FLR 749 where adopters recovered damages including damages for psychiatric illness from a local authority who placed a boy with them with a view to adoption without warning them of his serious behavioural difficulties.

[103] *Adoption Now: Messages from Research* (Department of Health, 1999) at p 17.

[104] Ibid, at p 18.

[105] ACA 2002, s 1(8).

[106] For example *B v B (Residence Order: Restricting Applications)* [1997] 1 FLR 139 per Butler-Sloss LJ at 144 and *C v C (Minors: Custody)* [1988] 2 FLR 291 per Purchas LJ at 302.

6.100 These considerations affect not just the decision of whether or not a child should be adopted or placed for adoption but also whether there should be contact between the child and the other person. These issues are considered more fully in Chapters 12 and 13.

6.101 There are two distinct features of this factor. The first is directly concerned with the child's welfare: what is the importance of any relationship to the child, what implications does this have for the decision and can the other person offer the child a home?[107]

6.102 The second is more tangential: what are the wishes of that other person? This second feature might be thought to deal, at least in part, with the concern identified by Caroline Bridge[108] that supplanting the test that the child's welfare is the *first* consideration by the paramountcy principle (see **6.11**) lessened the scope for giving weight to the competing interests of the other parties. Whether in practice it does more than ensure that all possibilities are explored during the assessment or hearing remains to be seen. Arguments put forward by the other person in opposition to adoption will have to be considered when applying the checklist but it is doubtful whether they can be given extra weight merely because they are being urged by a parent or relative. In *Re S: Newcastle City Council v Z*[109] the mother of a Muslim child of Pakistani origin opposed the making of a freeing order, it being intended the child should be adopted by a Pakistani Muslim family on the ground that adoption was prohibited by Islam. Munby J dispensed with her consent on the ground it was being unreasonably withheld.

> 'All [religious beliefs] are entitled to equal respect ... but however much respect one pays to religion or to any particular religion and whatever the religion and the nature of religious beliefs in the issue in a particular case, a parental view based on religious belief, however profound, cannot be determinative when it comes to considering what is to be done in relation to a child.'[110]

THE CHILD'S RELIGIOUS PERSUASION, RACIAL ORIGIN AND CULTURAL AND LINGUISTIC BACKGROUND

6.103 Section 1(5) of the ACA 2002 requires that 'In placing the child for adoption, the adoption agency must give due consideration to the child's religious persuasion, racial origin and cultural and linguistic background'. As drafted, this factor apparently applies only to a placement decision by the agency and not to a decision by the court. However, although it is not expressly

---

[107] *Review of Adoption Law* op cit at para 7.6.
[108] *Adoption Law: A Balance of Interests* op cit at p 212.
[109] [2005] EWHC 1490 (Fam), [2007] 1 FLR 861.
[110] Ibid, at 877.

included in the CA 1989 checklist or elsewhere in the ACA 2002 checklist, it falls within 'the background and any characteristics of his which the court considers significant'.[111]

6.104　When the court is considering an application for a placement order there is usually no assurance that the child will be placed with an identified adopter. It cannot impose conditions, for example that the child is placed with adopters of his or her race or religion. Whether or not a prospective adopter has been identified, in some cases the decision may be fairly evenly balanced and in some cases, the likelihood of the agency finding suitably matched adopters may be decisive.

6.105　The importance of this factor to the particular child cannot always be foreseen. In *Re B (Adoption: Setting Aside)*[112] a child with an English Roman Catholic mother and a Kuwaiti Muslim father was adopted by a Jewish couple who at first believed he was Jewish by birth. After they discovered that he was not, brought him up as a Jew. When he was an adult he emigrated to Israel but was asked to leave because he was considered to be an Arab. He was also prevented from entering Kuwait to see his father because of his previous travels to Israel.

Race and culture

Background

6.106　As has been noted by a number of authors, 'there are few areas of the adoption debate which are more controversial than trans-racial adoption, or the adoption by one racial group (usually white) of children from another group or groups'.[113] The importance of the issue justifies this factor being discussed in some detail.

6.107　In very general terms, the argument which has been running for at least 35 years in Britain is between two points of view. The first argues that because may there be an actual or perceived difficulty in finding adopters of the same racial background as the child it is better for children to be adopted by someone not of their racial background rather than to remain in care indefinitely. The second argues that it is essential for a proper development of a child's identity and ability to cope with a society where racial prejudice might/will be encountered to be brought up in a family of the same racial background. The two are not inconsistent. The difficulty lies in deciding how long a child should wait for a suitable match.

---

[111]　CA 1989, s 1(3)(d), ACA 2002, s 1(4)(d). See *Re P (Section 91(14) Guidelines) (Residence and Religious Heritage)* [1999] 2 FLR 573.

[112]　[1995] 1 FLR 1. Despite having sympathy for the situation in which he found himself the court declined to set aside the adoption order which had been regularly made.

[113]　*Adoption and the Care of Children: The British and American Experience* (Morgon IEA Health and Welfare Unit, 1998) at p 105.

6.108 The arguments – and the way courts viewed the matter – cannot be understood without taking into account the changes there have been in society. The racial mix of society has changed with an increase in both the numbers of non-white children thought suitable for adoption and of potential adopters who are non-white. Adoption is no longer concerned primarily with babies who have left their mothers shortly after birth but rather with older children in care who have lived with their natural family. The importance of a child's heritage has increasingly been understood.

6.109 As the racial picture became more complex, professionals became increasingly aware that the issue was not just one of colour but also race, culture and religion. This increasing complexity, especially where the child has a mixed heritage may make it harder to 'match' children with adopters who share the same background.

6.110 In the 1970s, the problem was seen as there being insufficient ethnically appropriate adopters for children, not babies, who could be adopted. The importance of adoption to the child was judged to override any cultural needs of the child, insofar as they were considered. For example, in 1970 *A Guide to Adoption Practice*[114] stated that

> 'There are generally insufficient applications from adopters for older, coloured or handicapped children or for families of several children ... It is important that the child's particular problem (sic) should not be allowed to loom so large that it distorts the picture and other aspects of personality and needs are forgotten ... In placing children of mixed British and African or Asian backgrounds, it is important to remember that they are half white and therefore white families are as appropriate for them as are Asian or African families. Adoption across racial lines is a relatively new development but studies in this country and North America seem to show that contrary to lay opinions, non-white children may be more easily assimilated in areas where there are a few non-white people than in places where they are numerous.'

6.111 Two years later the Houghton Report[115] stated that although some progress had been made in placing children who were non-white 'there are still reports from certain areas of parents who want their children adopted being told there is little hope of placing a coloured (sic) child'. The Report did not address the question of whether it was important for children to be adopted by couples from the same background but noted that it was increasingly recognised that at some stage the child would need to know about his origins in order to help a proper development of a sense of identity.

6.112 In 1973 Rowe and Lambert published *Children Who Wait*[116] which came to play an important role in changing professional views about adoption from being a service for placing babies with childless couples to one for

---

[114] (The Advisory Council on Child Care, HMSO, 1970) at paras IV.23-4, IV.19.
[115] *Report of the Departmental Committee on the Adoption of Children* (Cmd 5107, 1972) at paras 23-4 and 28.
[116] (Association of British Adoption Societies, 1973).

securing permanent homes for children in care, many of whom were living in residential care. Although they noted that 'the public has come forward to offer homes for Asian, African and West Indian *babies*',[117] in a sample of those *children* thought to be in need of a permanent home, the child's colour was thought to be a 'problem' for adoption in just under a quarter of the cases, higher than behavioural problems (13%) or the child's age (20%). Four years later, Tizard[118] argued although there were special problems in adopting non-white children, not least a shortage of black families with the resources to adopt:

> 'the case-work alternative of attempting to restore the child to "his own kind", almost irrespective of whether the family to which he is sent can meet his needs, often appears to derive not only from a belief in blood ties, but also in the over-riding importance of skin colour.'

6.113 In the 1980s and the 1990s there was a reaction against trans-racial adoption, in part informed by experience from North America. For example, in 1987, a guide for adoptive parents published by the British Agencies for Adoption and Fostering – *Explaining Adoption*[119] – advised that 'the black child in a white family is not only a minority in society but in their own family'. White adoptive families were ignorant and helpless when enabling their adoptive child to deal with the wider world and needed the support of black people.

6.114 The evidence though was not conclusive. In 1983 Gill and Jackson[120] looked in detail at the effects of trans-racial adoption and talked to a number of teenage children about their experience of being adopted before the age of 2. Generally they were doing well and were perceived to be experiencing few difficulties but the authors found that a large majority of adopters had made only limited or very limited attempts to give the children a sense of racial pride and awareness of their racial origin.

> 'The children in turn saw themselves as "white" in all but skin colour and had little knowledge or experience of their counterparts growing up in the black community. There was no general evidence however that the absence of racial pride or identity was, at this stage, associated with low self-esteem or behavioural disorder.'[121]

6.115 By the 1990s there had been progress towards same-race adoption but there were still problems in practice. In 1995 a survey of all children adopted from care in that year found that 24% of adoptions recorded by local authorities and 6% by agencies were adopted trans-racially.[122]

---

[117] *Children Who Wait*, op cit, at p 101.
[118] *Adoption a Second Chance* (Open Books, 1977) at p 241.
[119] P Chennells (1987).
[120] *Adoption and Race* (Batsford, 1983).
[121] Ibid, at p 130.
[122] *Focus on Adoption: a Snapshot of Adoption Patterns in England – 1995* (British Agencies for Adoption and Fostering, 1997).

6.116 In 1999 Lowe and Murch[123] found that many agencies had a 'same race' matching policy[124] and where one agency did not have such a policy, one of its workers told the researchers that 'we pursue it in practice'.

'The views expressed by some adopters and social workers about ethnicity in matching can be regarded as sensitive and controversial. Pejorative terms such as "problem" and "racist" were used. Some agency workers appear to be negative and defensive about this aspect of their work, their views and language reflecting the wider social context of racism and discrimination.'[125]

6.117 Lowe and Murch found that the 'ideal' expressed by such a policy was not always possible to achieve in practice, partly because of difficulties in finding appropriate matches but also because of the time this would take. Matching with adopters where at least one was black or of mixed heritage was seen as a solution in many cases.[126]

Research reviews

6.118 In 1990 the Interdepartmental Working Group, *Reviewing Adoption Law*, commissioned Thoburn to carry out a literature review of research relating to adoption.[127] Having examined a number of British and North American studies into trans-racial adoption, she wryly commented that:

'These authors pose, but do not answer, the question as to whether it is better to place a child early, trans-racially, or to delay placement in order to make the same race placement.'[128]

6.119 The authors of a further review in 1999, *Adoption Now: Messages from Research*,[129] concluded that:

'Placements may give the impression of being ethnically matched when colour is treated as the pre-eminent consideration but placements matched for colour are not necessarily matched for race or culture. The grounds for matching black with black may lie elsewhere than simply in ethnicity, most notably in the nurturing of a black identity and in defence against racism. The large proportion of mixed-parentage children (particularly those brought up by white birth mothers) amongst those being adopted from care can create a dilemma for placement policy and practice. However older children are likely to have a view about what should happen and this should be respected.'

---

[123] Lowe, Murch and others *Supporting Adoption: Reframing the Approach* (BAAF, 1999) at p 164.

[124] For criticisms of this policy, see *Adoption and the Care of Children* op cit, ch11 and Hayes 'Giving due consideration to ethnicity in adoption placements – a principled approach' [2003] CFLQ 255.

[125] *Supporting Adoption: Reframing the Approach* op cit, at p 189.

[126] Ibid, at p 165.

[127] Published as Appendix C to the *Review of Adoption Law* op cit.

[128] Ibid, at para 115.

[129] op cit at p 44.

6.120   Sellick, Thoburn and Philpot carried out a third Review in 2004.[130] They identified a number of pointers.[131]

- There is general agreement between UK and American researchers that some white parents, especially those living in mixed race communities, can successfully parent black children.

- Some young people consider they have lost out by being placed trans-racially.

- When parents and children are visibly different, there are extra obstacles to be overcome in adapting to the adoptive family and white families have additional challenges in ensuring that black children have a positive sense of their racial and cultural identity.

- Agencies determined to recruit new black parents succeed in doing so.

- It is now unusual for children with two black or Asian parents to be placed with white families although children with one black or Asian grandparent are still as likely as not to be placed with a white family.

The approach of the courts

6.121   See **6.143** below.

Religion

Background

6.122   The issue of religion is a particularly sensitive matter especially because of religious persecution, the arrival in the UK of other religions with different cultural and social dimensions, the resulting pluralism of society and the right to freedom of religion guaranteed by Art 9(1) of the European Convention on Human Rights.

6.123   There are differing concepts of religion. For Christianity, at least in Western Europe, 'religion' means primarily a system of beliefs to which the believer is required to assent. One becomes a Christian by choice or conversion. This is, as Douglas and Lowe put it:

> 'a view of religion ... as something that must be positively embraced through conscious acceptance, rather than something that is an inherent part of child's identity based on his or her family background.'[132]

---

[130]   *What works in adoption and foster care?* (Barnados, 2004).
[131]   Ibid, at p 82.
[132]   Douglas and Lowe (eds) *The Continuing Evolution of Family Law* (Family Law, 2009) p 14.

In comparison, to be a Jew means first and foremost to belong to a group, the Jewish people, and religious beliefs are secondary.[133] Like Judaism, Islam means much more that what is usually meant by the Western concept of religion but unlike Judaism, it is not necessarily primarily a matter of birth. Whether one is a Muslim appears to depend on a combination of belief and practice and how one sees oneself and is seen by others.[134]

6.124 In practice though the distinction between Western and non-Western religions is not clear cut and in practice there are similarities. A child may become a Christian through infant baptism but for his believing parents, his Christianity may be as much a part of his identity as if a Christian by birth. One study[135] which examined a group of parents who were predominantly from Christian and Muslim backgrounds found that most thought that religion was a way of life, transmitted between generations and believed that it was part of their parenting responsibility to pass on their faith. In both groups of believers, the prospect of the child being adopted outside the faith may cause considerable distress. In practice therefore it has been assumed that a child shares his parents' religion or cultural identity from birth, regardless of whether the child has undergone any rite of acceptance.

6.125 Irrespective of whether the child is born into a religion, background of parental influence is obviously important in producing religious attitudes, belief and behaviour. Young children, up to about the age of 12, readily take to religion and accept what they are told without difficulty.[136] Their beliefs are therefore likely to mirror those of their parents. It is with the onset of adolescence that the young person starts to take an independent stance.[137] The phase starts with a high level of religious activity, followed typically by a period of questioning and doubt in which overt religious activity may decline. Many may 'drop out' from the church in which they were brought up and many are converted to a new faith. 'This is an age of both conversion and deconversion'.[138]

6.126 Section 7 of the Adoption Act 1976 provided that an agency placing a child for adoption had to have regard 'so far as is practicable' to any wishes of the child's parent or guardian as to the religious upbringing of the child. This provision was repealed by the Adoption and Children Act 2002 and has not been re-enacted.

---

[133] de Lange *Judaism* (Oxford University Press, 1986) pp 3–4. Conversion is recognised but there can be problems: see, for example, *R (E) v The Governing Body of JFS* [2009] EWCA Civ 626.

[134] Pearl and Menski *Muslim Family Law* (3rd edn, 1998) ch 5.

[135] Howarth, Lees et al *Religion, beliefs and parenting practices* (Joseph Rowntree Foundation, 2008) Summarised Findings 2265.

[136] Argyle *Psychology and Religion* (Routledge, 2000) pp 25–29.

[137] See, for example, *Re S (Minors) (Access: Religious Upbringing)* [1992] 2 FLR 313 at 320.

[138] Argyle op cit at p 26.

Article 9

6.127   Article 9(1) of the European Convention on Human Rights guarantees:

'... the right to freedom of thought, conscience and religion; this right includes freedom to change his religion or belief and freedom, either alone or in community with others and in public or private, to manifest his religion or belief, in worship, teaching, practice and observance.'

6.128   Article 9(2) provides that

'Freedom to manifest one's religion or beliefs shall be subject only to such limitations as are prescribed by law and are necessary in a democratic society in the interests of public safety, for the protection of public order, health or morals or for the protection of the rights and freedoms of others.'

The approach to justification under Art 9(2) is the same as under Art 8(2) for which see **6.183**.

The approach of the English courts

6.129   Courts recognise both the need to respect religious beliefs and the tolerance required in a pluralistic society. However, judges are anxious not to stray into areas either of religious controversy or of deciding between competing faiths.

6.130   In *Re S; Newcastle City Council v Z*[139] Munby J said that:

'There have been enormous changes in the social and religious life of our country. We live in a secular and pluralistic society. But we also live in a multicultural community of many faiths ... on which men and woman of different faiths or no faith at all hold starkly differing views. All of those views are entitled to the greatest respect but it is not for a judge to choose between them ... Religion – whatever the particular believer's faith – is no doubt something to be encouraged but it is not the business of government or of the secular courts, though the courts will, of course, pay every respect and give great weight to a family's religious principles. Article 9 of the European Convention, after all, demands no less. So the starting point of the law is a tolerant indulgence to cultural and religious diversity and an essentially agnostic view of religious beliefs. A secular judge must be wary of straying across the well recognised divide between church and state. It is not for a judge to weigh one religion against another. The court recognises no religious distinctions and generally speaking passes no judgment on religious beliefs or on the tenets, doctrines or rules of any particular section of society. All are entitled to equal respect ...'

6.131   The current religious practices of the child will need to be considered as will the child's wishes. The older the child, especially where he has made an

---

[139]   [2005] EWHC 1490(Fam), [2007] 1 FLR 861 at [54].

independent decision to adhere to a particular faith, the more weight is likely to be given to his wishes and the effect of any change.

6.132 However weight accorded to religion may be outweighed by other considerations.[140] It is not given a pre-eminent place in the checklist. 'The safeguarding of the welfare of vulnerable children ... ought not to be subordinated by the court to any particular religious belief'.[141] It has been argued that if too much consideration is given to ethnicity, then the obligation to give paramount consideration to the child's welfare may be compromised. 'To resolve this problem, ethnicity should be considered only where all factors relating to a child's needs and wishes leave the decision maker with equally acceptable placement choices.'[142] However, s 1(3) seems to require that all the factors are considered together rather than some being weighed together and others considered sequentially.

6.133 The wishes of parents are not determinative.

> '[A] parental view based on religious belief, however profound, can never be determinative when it comes to considering what is to be done in relation to a child. ... The mother's rights under Art 9, in other words, are qualified by S's rights, for example his right under Art 8 to "family life" in an albeit substitute family: see the discussion by Wall J in *Re J (Specific Issue Orders: Muslim Upbringing and Circumcision)*[143] approved by the Court of Appeal in *Re J (Specific Issue Orders: Child's Religious Upbringing and Circumcision)*.[144] And s 7 of the Adoption Act 1976, as we have seen, requires regard to be had to the parent's religious views only "so far as is practicable". The point was put very clearly by Rutledge J in the United States Supreme Court in *Prince v Massachusetts:*[145]
>
>> "Parents may be free to become martyrs themselves. But it does not follow that they are free in identical circumstances to make martyrs of their children before they have reached the age of full and legal discretion when they can make choices for themselves".'[146]

Policy guidance

6.134 Against the background of limited research knowledge and political disagreement about trans-racial adoption, the Department of Health issued guidance to local authorities in a Circular, *Adoption – Achieving the Right Balance*[147] in 1998 which remains in force.[148]

---

[140] See, for example, *Re M (Section 94 Appeals)* [1995] 1 FLR 546.
[141] *Haringey LBC v C, E and others* [2006] EWHC 1620, [2007] 1 FLR 1035 per Ryder J at [36].
[142] Hayes 'Giving due consideration to ethnicity in adoption placements – a principled approach' [2003] CFLQ 255.
[143] [1999] 2 FLR 678, at 700–701.
[144] [2000] 1 FLR 571.
[145] (1944) 321 US 158, at 170.
[146] *Re S ; Newcastle City Council v Z* [2005] EWHC 1490 (Fam), [2007] 1 FLR 861 at [54]. See also Fortin *Children's Rights and the Developing Law* (2nd edn, 2003) ch 11.
[147] LAC(98)20; see Appendix 3.

6.135   It began by noting that although agencies had made significant progress in learning about the particular needs of children from minority ethnic backgrounds and the need to take account of their heritage when making decisions about their future, more work needed to be done. It pointed out that the structure of minority ethnic groups was often complex and their heritage diverse, where the race, religion, language and culture of each community had varying degrees of importance in the daily lives of their members.

> 'Families from these communities should have confidence that their local social services understands, appreciates and is respectful of their particular racial, cultural, and religious values.'

6.136   It continued by stating that:

> 'A child's ethnic origin, culture, language and religion are significant factors ["a principal tenet"] to be taken into account when adoption agencies are considering the most appropriate placement for a child; however, such consideration has to take account of all the child's needs. Simply identifying a child's ethnic background is not sufficient in itself. Adoption agencies need to go further and be aware of the implications for a child of these cultural elements – how the culture of a family, community or society can influence the way a child sees the world; the significance of religion in a child's daily life and the importance of maintaining a knowledge of his history, culture and language.'

6.137   The Circular makes the following points.

- The choice of placement had to take into account the child's previous experience and wishes and feelings whilst recognising that the latter may be restrictive or unrealistic.

- Placement with a family of similar ethnic origin and religion is very often most likely to meet the child's needs as fully as possible. But this is only one amongst a number of other significant factors and should not of itself be regarded as decisive.

- Where no family can be identified which matches significantly closely the child's ethnic origin and cultural heritage, the agency should be pro-active and work to a realistic timetable to find an alternative family.

  > 'The Government has made it clear that it is unacceptable for a child to be denied loving adoptive parents solely on the grounds that the child and adopters do not share the same racial or cultural background.'

- Families should assist children to understand and appreciate their background and culture and to this end enlist the help and support of others. This can include providing opportunities for children to meet others from similar backgrounds, to practice their religion in a formal place of worship and in the home. Maintaining continuity of the heritage

---

[148]   It was considered, for example, in *Re C (Adoption; Religious Observance)* [2002] 1 FLR 1119.

of their birth family in their day-to-day life is important to most children as a means of retaining knowledge of their identity and feeling that although they have left their birth family they have not abandoned important cultural, religious or linguistic values of their community. This will be of particular significance as they reach adulthood.

- The issue of racism will inevitably arise at some stage in the life of a child from a minority ethnic group and the adoptive family has the responsibility of preparing the child to deal with it when it occurs. They may need help in this.

- It is important that social workers should avoid 'labeling' a child and ignoring some elements of his background.

- Children of mixed origin should be helped to understand and take pride in all elements in their racial heritage and feel comfortable about their origins.

- The increase in the number of couples who are not of the same ethnic origin or who are of mixed origin provides agencies with an opportunity to address more effectively the needs of a range of children who are themselves from different backgrounds including mixed and minority ethnic backgrounds. 'Any practice which classifies such couples in a way that effectively rules out the adoption of a child whose origins differ from either or both prospective adopters is unacceptable.'

- In every case, regardless of the ethnic origin of the prospective adopters, the issue is whether they are sympathetic to and understand the issues to be confronted by a child of minority ethnic or mixed race origins who, growing up, will face discrimination and racism.

6.138 In 2003 the Department of Health issued *Adoption: Regulations: National Minimum Standards* against which the authority or agency will be judged by the registration authority. Standard 2.2 states that:

'Children are matched with adopters who best meet their assessed needs. Wherever possible this will be with a family which:

a. reflects their ethnic origin, cultural background, religion and language; and
b. allows them to live with brothers and sisters unless this will not meet their individually assessed needs.

Where the child cannot be matched with a family which reflects their ethnic origin, cultural background, religion and language, the adoption agency makes every effort to find an alternative suitable family within a realistic timescale to ensure the child is not left waiting indefinitely in the care system. Where children cannot live with a family as set out in (a) and (b) above, a clear explanation will be given to them, having regard to their age and understanding, and be recorded.'

6.139   Guidance on assessing the needs of children in relation to religion race and culture is given in *The Children Act 1989 Guidance and Regulations: Vol 3 Family Placements*.[149]

> 'It may be taken as a guiding principle of good practice that other things being equal and in the great majority of cases, placement with a family of similar ethnic origin and religion is most likely to meet a child's needs as fully as possible and to safeguard his or her welfare most effectively. Such a family is most likely to be able to provide a child with continuity in life and care and an environment which the child will find familiar and sympathetic and in which opportunities will naturally arise to share fully in the culture and way of life of the ethnic group to which he belongs ... Families of similar ethnic origin are usually best placed to prepare children for life as members of an ethnic minority group in a multi-racial society, where they may meet with racial prejudice and discrimination, and to help them with their development towards independent living and adult life'.[150]

6.140   However, the circumstances of the individual case must be considered and there may be circumstances where placement with a family of different ethnic origin is the best choice for the particular child. Likewise the importance of religion 'as an element of culture' should not be overlooked and may be the dominant factor.[151] For a child whose parents are of different ethnic groups, placement in a family which reflects the natural family as near as possible is likely to be the best choice in most cases although choice will be influenced by the child's previous family experience.[152]

6.141   Caballero and others have carried out a small study of 'mixed' families in the general community.[153] They found that mixed-parent couples in Britain were often in sustained relationships and a high proportion were middle class. The couples interviewed used three typical approaches to instil a sense of belonging in their children; particular approaches were not associated with particular racial or faith combinations:

- *Individual*: The children's sense of belonging was not seen as rooted in their mixed background.

- *Mix*: The children's mixed background was understood as a factual part of their identity; all aspects were emphasised.

- *Single*: One aspect of the children's mixed background was stressed.

---

[149]   (Department of Health, HMSO, 1991). This was issued under s 7 of the Local Authority Social Services Act 1970.
[150]   Ibid, para 2.40.
[151]   Ibid, para 2.41.
[152]   Ibid, para 2.42.
[153]   Caballero, Edwards and Puthussery *Parenting 'mixed' children: Negotiating difference and belonging in mixed race, ethnicity and faith families* (Joseph Rowntree Foundation, 2008) noted in Findings 2232.

- *Couples:* whose approach differed in giving their children a sense of belonging were not necessarily in conflict. For some, divergent approaches were complementary. Others saw difficulties between them as humanistic, political or personality choices.

The researchers concluded that it was important that family support, health, education and social services do not make assumptions about mixed families. Families who seem to share a form of mixing can differ from each other. 'Mixedness' may be insignificant for some, compared to other issues.

6.142 The impact of race on the chances of a child being adopted is discussed at **15.23**.

The approach of the courts

6.143 The changes in society during the past three decades have influenced the attitude of the courts as well as professional practice. As early as 1990, the judges in the High Court were well aware of the debate summarised above[154] and it was established that where the issue of a child's racial, cultural and religious identity is relevant, it must be considered.[155]

6.144 A number of factors are relevant when considering whether a placement is appropriate:

- the child's current religious identity and practices (if any);

- the length of time the child has been in his current placement in including the age of the child and the likely effect on the child of a move and/or waiting for a move;

- the identity of a culturally appropriate family for the particular child;

- the availability or likely availability of a culturally appropriate family.

6.145 The factors will need to be balanced against the context of needs and circumstances of the individual child. In *Re P (A Minor) (Adoption)*[156] a child born of an African/Caribbean mother and white European father was placed with a white foster mother at birth. The local authority had a policy that children should be brought up by a family of the same race and ethnic group and a year later decided that P should be adopted. It rejected an application by the foster mother to be approved as his adopter in favour of placing P with a family who originated from the Caribbean. The trial judge dismissed a challenge brought by the foster mother and the Court of Appeal dismissed her

---

[154] See *Re N (A Minor) (Adoption)* [1990] 1 FLR 58 per Bush J at 61H–63H.

[155] *Re M (Section 94 Appeals)* 546 [1995] 1 FLR 546. The Court of Appeal held that the magistrates hearing an application for contact by a black father in relation to his child by a white mother should have considered the child's racial identity.

[156] [1990] 1 FLR 96.

appeal. The trial judge had balanced the impact on P of moving him against the benefits of being brought up in a black family and the decision he reached was not 'plainly' wrong.

6.146 In some cases, the competition between the child's needs for continuity and identity can be reframed by considering an order short of adoption.[157] Relevant issues may include whether it is important that the child should continue to have contact with his natural parents. Where this occurs it may help the child with his racial or cultural identity but in other cases this help will be available because of the origins of the adopters or in other ways. For a further discussion see Chapters 14 and 17.

The importance of stability

6.147 The weight to be given to the child's racial and cultural identity is particularly difficult when the factor is weighed against the status quo. The lengthy of the time the child has been with his current carers and the strength of his attachment to them are important considerations as is the likelihood of suitable adopters being found or the possibility of living with parents' relatives.

Examples

Re A (A Minor) (Cultural Background)[158]

6.148 A Nigerian child, born in Nigeria went to live with her grandmother at the age of 14 months after her father had died. When she was just 4 her grandmother who by that time was living in England could not look after her and she went to live with white foster parents, coming to regard them as her own family. Four years later her grandmother sought her return. A social worker from the local authority recommended her immediate return because she took the view that any child of West African background must be placed with a West African family regardless of the time she had been in her present family. Swinton-Thomas J disagreed and directed that she remain with her foster parents.

> 'I do not in anyway underestimate the loss to a degree of M's Nigerian culture and background and her own family if she were to remain with Mr and Mrs N. However I am quite sure that to remove M now from the family with whom she has lived for, in her life, many years, would have a quite devastating effect on her.'[159]

---

[157] See, *Re N (A Minor) (Adoption)* [1990] 1 FLR 58.
[158] [1987] 2 FLR 429.
[159] Ibid, at 437F.

Re JK (Adoption: Transracial Placement)[160]

6.149 An illegitimate child born to a Sikh mother was placed at birth with short-term, (presumably white) foster parents. The local authority were unable to find culturally appropriate adopters, in part because it was said adoption in the Sikh community was very rare and also even more rare if the child was illegitimate. They proposed moving the child (now 3 years old) to a bridging family while they continued their search. In care proceedings Stephen Brown P held that the child should remain with her foster parents who wanted to adopt her and with whom she was well integrated and secure. He took into account that she lived in a mixed racial community and the willingness of the foster-parents to assist her to follow her Sikh traditions and culture and to seek help if necessary. It was not possible to place her with a Sikh family and furthermore there was psychiatric evidence that she would probably suffer psychological harm if she were to be moved.

Re P (Section 91(14) Guidelines) (Residence and Religious Heritage)[161]

6.150 Orthodox Jewish parents, the father being a Rabbi, applied for a residence order in respect of their 8-year-old daughter who suffered from Down's Syndrome and serious respiratory problems which required constant attention. She had been cared for by non-practising Roman Catholic foster parents since she was 17 months old to whom she was more strongly attached than a normal child to her parents. The Court of Appeal dismissed the parents' appeal against the dismissal of their application. A move from them carried not only a certainty of short-term emotional harm but also a grave risk both of long-term harm and a deterioration in her physical health.

'[A child's religious heritage] is a relevant consideration, the weight of which will vary according to the facts of each case. In the present case, it is an important factor. No one would wish to deprive a Jewish child of her right to her Jewish heritage. If she had remained with a Jewish family it would be almost unthinkable, other than in an emergency, to remove her from it. ... But in the unusual circumstances of this case her parents were not able to accommodate her within her community. The combination of the family illness and difficulties together with N's real medical problems as a young child made it impossible for her to be cared for within her family circle and it was then, not now, that she was deprived of her opportunity to grow up within the Jewish community. ...

The undoubted importance for an Orthodox Jew of his religion which provides in itself a way of life which permeates all activities, is a factor to be put in the balancing exercise, particularly in considering the welfare of the daughter of a

---

[160] [1991] 2 FLR 340.
[161] [1999] 2 FLR 573. See also *C v Salford CC and others* [1994] 2 FLR 926, an earlier decision in the case.

rabbi. But N's religious and cultural heritage cannot be the overwhelming factor in this case for the reasons set out by the judge nor can it displace other weighty welfare factors.'[162]

Re M (Child's Upbringing)[163]

6.151 The Court of Appeal upheld a decision that a 10-year-old Zulu, South African, boy who had lived in A's household in South Africa since birth and in England with A for 6 years, his parents remaining in South Africa, should return to his mother rather than be adopted by A.

What constitutes an appropriate family?

6.152 In some cases the answer may be obvious. For example, West African, Christian adopters are likely to provide a culturally appropriate home for a child born to West African Christian parents and raised in a West African, Christian culture. Many cases will pose questions more difficult to answer. In *Re C (Adoption; Religious Observance)*[164] the court had to consider the proposed adoption of a 2-year-old child whose background had Jewish, Irish Roman Catholic and Turkish-Cypriot Muslim elements, the mother describing herself as Church of England. The local authority who were applying for a care order, intended to place C with Mr and Mrs A, a couple who lived at 'a significant, though not high, level of Jewish cultural observance. The guardian objected on the basis that the proposed home was 'too Jewish'. Wilson J did not accept this.

> 'I do not agree with [the guardian's argument]. It is inflexible and doctrinaire; in one sense it has the anemic appearance of a search only for the lowest common denominator; and in my view the guardian's suggested type of placement is far from the only type indicated by the guidance in respect of a child such as C. Where a child's heritage is very mixed, it will rarely be possible for it all to be reflected in the identity of the adoptive home. ... I consider that it may well be in a child's interests to choose an adoptive home where only one strand of her heritage is reflected – provided that the adopters are sufficiently sensitive to help her (in the words of para 17 of the circular[165]) 'to understand and take pride in all elements in [her] racial heritage and feel comfortable about [her] origins'. ... Nor do I agree with the guardian that the secularity of C's home with her parents and latterly with the foster-parents is of major importance in this case. I acknowledge that, in assessing a child's ability to settle into an adoptive home, any substantial difference of practice in the proposed home from that in the home or homes to which the child has become accustomed will need carefully to be addressed; but I do not consider that, in the present case, the differences are so substantial as to be likely to cause C, particularly at her age, any extra difficulty. I also consider that, in circumstances where the need to find a permanent alternative home for C has been

---

[162] Per Butler-Sloss LJ at 585.
[163] [1996] 2 FLR 441. A planned to petition the European Court of Human Rights (see *Re M (Petition to European Commission of Human Rights* [1997] 1 FLR 755) but the boy did not settle in South Africa and was later returned voluntarily to the care of A.
[164] [2002] 1 FLR 1119.
[165] *Adoption – Achieving the Right Balance* op cit; see Appendix 3.

precipitated by the poverty, physical but in particular intellectual and emotional, of the home which the parents could offer to her, it is paradoxical to seek to replicate in the adoptive home the religious void in their home, even where she has a religious heritage; and that, subject to the point already acknowledged, the secularity of the family chosen to be her 'short-term' foster-parents is of no consequence'.[166]

Availability of a culturally appropriate family

6.153 In *Adoption: A New Approach*[167] the Government discussed examples of situations where special guardianship might be more appropriate for a child than adoption and commented that 'Some ethnic minority communities have religious and cultural difficulties with adoption as is set out in law'. Whether this was merely indicating that appropriate adoptive families might not be readily available within the child's community whereas carers willing to be special guardians could more easily be found, or whether something more fundamental was being suggested is not clear. If an adopted child is likely to be stigmatised in the community in which he was to grow up because he was adopted, that might be relevant when considering whether an order should be made.[168] However, the fact that the natural parents objected to adoption on the ground that adoption was alien to their culture may have little weight if the welfare of the child requires that he be adopted.

6.154 Courts are likely to require evidence as to the true situation rather than mere assertion that adoption was not accepted by their community. It is dangerous to rely on reported cases to provide the basis for 'judicial knowledge'. The factual situation may have changed.

6.155 In *Re R (Placement Order)*[169] counsel submitted that adoption rarely occurs in the Muslim community because of the attachment attached to the extensive and strong family network. Although Sumner J concluded that it would not be easy to place the children for adoption, it could not be ruled out. He made a placement order dispensing with the parents' consent. The children's welfare required 'such a draconian step as adoption for Muslim children of Muslim parents.'[170]

6.156 In *Re JK (Adoption: Transracial Placement)*[171] the court considered the difficulties of finding Sikh adopters and received evidence from an adoption worker about the difficulties in relation to the Sikh community. It was decided that the child should be adopted by his white foster parents (see **6.149**).

---

[166] [2002] 1 FLR 1119 at [37]–[38].
[167] op cit at para 5.8.
[168] In *Re S (Change of Names: Cultural Factors)* [2001] 2 FLR 1005 a Muslim mother was granted permission to have her son, born to a Sikh father, circumcised and to change his name to a Muslim one because of the difficulties he and she would otherwise have in being integrated into their community.
[169] [2007] EWHC 2742 (Fam), [2008] 1 FLR 1259.
[170] Ibid at [118].
[171] [1991] 2 FLR 340.

Islam and adoption

6.157 The issue of the availability of appropriate adopters commonly occurs in regard to Islam and it is often asserted that adoption is not recognised by the Islamic community. However this appears to oversimplify the situation although by and large there is no law of adoption in the Islamic world.

'Traditional Muslim law does not appear to allow formal adoption because it refuses to accept the legal fiction which adoption creates, namely that the adopted child can become equal to a blood relative of the adopting father. On the other hand, in view of social facts and circumstances, various devices have been used in Muslim law to take account of the welfare of orphans or otherwise destitute children and the interests of childless couples who may seek such a child as their own ... Some Muslim scholars argue that [adoption] ... is not actually prohibited but merely classify it in the category of acts known as *mubah-* acts towards which religion is indifferent ...'[172]

6.158 Pearl and Menski noted that not much could be said about Muslims and adoption in Britain in 1998 and commented that research is needed to ascertain details.

6.159 The approach of Islam to adoption was also considered by Charles J in 2002 in *Re J (Adoption: Consent of Foreign Public Authority)*[173] and by Munby J in *Re S; Newcastle City Council v Z*.[174]

'There is no adoption in our sense of the word in Islam but Kafala [long-term fostering of a child without the right to kinship] is well established in Islam as a means of providing care to children, allowing a child to benefit from a good home whilst at the same time losing neither his family name nor the rights in his birth family ... Under Kafala the 'adoptive family' never takes the place of the birth family whose ties to the child are never severed: the 'adoptive' family are trustees and caretakers of someone else's child.'

6.160 This does not mean however that there are no practising Muslims who are willing to adopt children. In *Re S: Newcastle City Council v Z*, for example, the local authority found Muslim adopters of Pakistani origin who were prepared to adopt a child who shared their national and religious background.

Adoption or a residence order?

Does the court have jurisdiction to make the decision?

6.161 In many cases the court will be considering these issues in the context of care proceedings or applications for placement or adoption orders in which it undoubtedly has the jurisdiction to decide the issue. In other cases, decisions by the adoption agency may be challenged in proceedings for judicial review where

---

[172] Pearl and Menski *Muslim Family Law* (3rd edn, 1998) p 410.
[173] [2002] EWHC 766 (Fam), [2002] 2 FLR 618 at [23].
[174] [2005] EWHC 1490 (Fam), [2007] 1 FLR 861 at [46].

the primary issue is not what is in the child's best interests but whether the agency, as the decision-maker, has reached a proper decision, the matter being decided by applying the *Wednesbury*[175] principles. In *R v Lancashire CC ex p M*[176] the Court of Appeal refused to overturn a decision by an authority to remove a child of mixed heritage parents from his short term foster carers although he had been with them from his birth, a period of nearly two years.

OTHER CONSIDERATIONS

6.162 Although s 1 in both the 1989 and 2002 Acts requires that the court and the agency must have regard to the matters discussed above, the checklist does not exclude other matters and the court will have regard to all relevant circumstances. The 2002 checklist does not, for example, mention the capability of the adopters in meeting the needs of the child but this will be a very important consideration. It may have been omitted from the list because most applicants will already have been approved by the authority or agency. However, when the court is considering making an order, it is for the court to be satisfied that the order will best meet the child's needs and it cannot rely totally on the views of the agency.[177] In addition, not all adoption applications will be sponsored by an authority or agency and although there will be a report filed by the applicant's authority under r 29 of the Family Procedure (Adoption) Rules 2005 the applicant will not have been assessed under Part 4 of the Adoption Agencies Regulations 2005. Assessing the capability of the applicants is considered in Chapter 8.

PUBLIC POLICY

6.163 The most common type of case where the court will consider matters of public policy is when granting the order will result in the acquisition by a non-British child of British nationality and the right of abode in the UK. The court cannot ignore such benefits provided the application is a genuine one (albeit tainted by deception), intended to create the psychological relationship of parent and child, and not a sham whose purpose is solely designed to achieve immigration benefits.[178] In the case of a genuine application, any benefit which will accrue to the child as a result of the adoption, during childhood or afterwards, is a relevant consideration. In *Re B (Adoption Order: Nationality)*[179] the House of Lords held that in such cases where it appears to the judge that adoption would confer real benefits to the child during its childhood, it is very unlikely that general considerations of immigration policy could justify refusal of an adoption order. However, as the purpose of an

---

[175] *Associated Provincial Picture Houses Ltd v Wednesbury Corporation* [1948] 1 KB 223.
[176] [1992] 1 FLR 109.
[177] And see *Re U (Application to Free for Adoption)* [1993] 2 FLR 992 at 1001H.
[178] *Re J (Adoption: Non-Patrial)* [1998] 1 FLR 225.
[179] *Re B (Adoption Order: Nationality)* [1999] 2 AC 136, [1999] 1 FLR 907 and *Re S and J (Adoption: Non-Patrials)* [2004] 2 FLR 111.

adoption is to give parental responsibility for the child to the adopters, an adoption order will not be made when the prospective adopters did not intend to exercise any parental responsibility but merely wish to assist the child to acquire a right of abode.[180] Lord Hoffman said that:

> 'Benefits which will accrue only after the end of childhood are not welfare benefits during childhood to which first consideration must be given. And if a right of abode will be of benefit only when the child becomes an adult, that benefit will ordinarily have to give way to the public policy of not usurping the Home Secretary's discretion.'[181]

6.164 It should be noted that his lordship was considering s 6 of the Adoption Act 1976 which required the court to promote the welfare of the child throughout his childhood whereas s 1 of the ACA 2002 refers to the child's welfare throughout his life. It is uncertain therefore whether his lordship's dicta will still apply. If it does, then any benefits to the child which accrue so close to the child's majority that they have no practical effect during what remained of his childhood or after his majority will have to be balanced against the public policy considerations and normally the adoption will be refused. In *Re K (A Minor) (Adoption Order: Nationality)*,[182] for example, the Court of Appeal set aside an adoption order made 8 days before the child reached her majority. The issue is discussed further at **2.86**.

Illegality

6.165 The placement of children is strictly controlled (see Chapter 7) and breaches of the regulations can constitute a criminal offence. Any illegality in the arrangements for adoption gives rise to important considerations of public policy. The issue of the impact of breaches on the welfare test regulation is discussed in Chapter 7.

ARTICLE 8 OF THE EUROPEAN CONVENTION FOR THE PROTECTION OF HUMAN RIGHTS AND FUNDAMENTAL FREEDOMS 1950

6.166 The provisions of the Human Rights Act 1998 mean that courts are now required to interpret and apply primary and secondary legislation in a way which is compatible with rights under the European Convention for the Protection of Human Rights and Fundamental Freedoms 1950.[183]

---

[180] *Re B (Adoption Order: Nationality)* [1999] 2 AC 136, [1999] 1 FLR 907.
[181] Ibid.
[182] [1994] 2 FLR 557, approved on this point by the House of Lords in *Re B (Adoption Order: Nationality)*.
[183] Human Rights Act 1998, s 3. For a useful description of Art 8, see Prest 'The Right to Respect for Family Life: Obligations of the State in Private Law Children Cases' [2005] Fam Law 124.

Article 8

6.167   Article 8 provides that:

'1   Everyone has the right to respect for his private and family life, his home and his correspondence.

2   There shall be no interference by a public authority with the exercise of this right except such as is in accordance with the law and is necessary in a democratic society in the interests of national security, public safety or the economic well-being of the country, for the prevention of disorder or crime, for the protection of health or morals, or for the protection of the rights and freedoms of others.'

WHEN DOES FAMILY LIFE EXIST?

6.168   That there is a broad approach to family life is illustrated by the leading European case of *Keegan v Ireland*.[184]

'In the present case, the relationship between the applicant and the child's mother lasted for two years during one of which they co-habited. Moreover, the conception of their child was the result of a deliberate decision and they had also planned to get married (see paragraph 6 above). Their relationship at this time had thus the hallmark of family life for the purposes of Article 8 (art. 8). The fact that it subsequently broke down does not alter this conclusion any more than it would for a couple who were lawfully married and in a similar situation. It follows that from the moment of the child's birth there existed between the applicant and his daughter a bond amounting to family life.'

6.169   Both the European Court of Human Rights in Strasbourg and domestic courts have recognised that family life can exist in a wide variety of circumstances. In *X, Y and Z v United Kingdom*[185] the ECtHR held that there was family life between a woman (Y) living with a female-to-male transsexual (X) and also between X and a child (Z) born to Y by donor insemination.

'[The] notion of family life in Article 8 is not confined solely to families based on marriage and may encompass other de facto relationships. When deciding whether a relationship can be said to amount to "family life", a number of factors may be relevant, including whether the couple was living together, the length of their relationship and whether they have demonstrated their commitment to each other by having children together or by any other means.'[186]

6.170   Likewise in *Ghaidan v Godin-Mendoza*[187] where the House of Lords held that the defendant who had a longstanding, monogamous homosexual relationship with a tenant, protected under the Rent Act 1977, could succeed to

---

[184]   (1994) 18 EHRR 342, ECtHR.
[185]   (1997) 24 EHRR 143, [1997] 2 FLR 892.
[186]   Ibid, at [36].
[187]   [2004] UKHL 30, [2004] 2 FLR 600.

the tenancy on his partner's death on the ground that they had been living together as 'husband or wife', Baroness Hale of Richmond said at [141]:

> '[The] presence of children is a relevant factor in deciding whether a relationship is marriage-like but if the couple are bringing up children together, it is unlikely to matter whether or not they are the biological children of both parties. Both married and unmarried couples, both homosexual and heterosexual, may bring up children together. One or both may have children from another relationship: this is not at all uncommon in lesbian relationships and the court may grant them a shared residence order so that they may share parental responsibility. A lesbian couple may have children by donor insemination who are brought up as the children of them both: it is not uncommon for each of them to bear a child in this way. A gay or lesbian couple may foster other people's children. When the relevant sections of the Adoption and Children Act 2002 are brought into force, they will be able to adopt: this means that they will indeed have a child together in the eyes of the law.'[188]

6.171   Whether or not there is family life is essentially a question of fact 'depending upon the real existence in practice of close personal ties'.[189] However, both the European Court of Human Rights and domestic courts have recognised a number of situations in which it can usually be said that family life exists. A mother shares a family life with her child even if they are separated at the moment of birth: 'The carrying and giving birth to a child brings with it a relationship between them both which is entitled to respect'.[190] The fact that parents are not married carries little weight. There is a bond amounting to family life between a child and its parents who have previously cohabited even if at the time of the birth their relationship has ended.[191] In addition, a child born to a couple who have not cohabited but who have other children in common is part of the family unit from the moment of birth 'and by the very fact of it'.[192] The mutual enjoyment of contact without cohabitation, for example, creates family life.

6.172   The question of whether a father, not married to the mother, enjoys a right to family life with his child from birth, because of their biological relationship, and independent of any actual enjoyment of family life is more difficult. In *Re H; Re G (Adoption: Consultation of Unmarried Fathers)*,[193] the President, relying on *McMichael v United Kingdom*,[194] held that in the absence of marriage, cohabitation or siblings there is no family life between the father

---

[188]   See also *Pawandeep Singh v Entry Clearance Officer, New Delhi* [2004] EWCA Civ 1075, [2005] QB 608 per Munby J at paras [57]–[88] and Munby 'Families old and new – the family and Article 8' [2005] CFLQ 487.

[189]   *Lebbink v The Netherlands* (App. No. 45582/99, judgment of 1 June 2004) at para 36, *Pawandeep Singh v Entry Clearance Officer, New Delhi* (above) per Dyson LJ at [20].

[190]   *Re B (Adoption by One Natural Parent to Exclusion of Other)* [2001] 1 FLR 589, per Hale LJ at 599.

[191]   *Keegan v Ireland* (1994) 18 EHRR 342.

[192]   *Kroon v Netherlands* (1995) EHRR 263.

[193]   [2001] 1 FLR 646.

[194]   (1995) 20 EHRR 205.

and the child at birth. Likewise in *Re J (Adoption: Contacting Father)*[195] Bennet J held that there was no family life between a father of a child, unmarried to the mother, and his child where the parents did not have a strong commitment to each other, had never cohabited and who had not seen each other since the child was born. Hale LJ in *Re B (Adoption by One Natural Parent to Exclusion of Other)*[196] seemed to disagree: 'The child is in any event, and independently of parental responsibility, a full member of his family'. In *Z County Council v R*,[197] Holman J appeared to agree with Hale LJ because he was prepared to assume that a mother's brothers and sisters with whom she was not living were part of her child's family.

6.173 Family life can also exist between siblings and near relatives[198] although the relationship between the child and near relatives, such as grandparents, is different in nature and degree from that between a child and its parents.[199] This is discussed further in Chapter 12.

PRIVATE LIFE

6.174 Most of the consideration of Art 8 in family proceedings in England and Wales has focused on the right to respect for family life. However as the European Court of Human Rights held in *Mikulic v Croatia*,[200] Art 8, protects not only 'family' but also 'private' life.

> 'Private life, in the court's view, includes a person's physical and psychological integrity and can sometimes embrace aspects of an individual's physical and social identity. Respect for "private life" must also comprise to a certain degree the right to establish relationships with other human beings (see, mutatis mutandis, *Niemietz v Germany*).'[201]

6.175 In *Bensaid v United Kingdom*[202] the ECtHR commented:

> 'Private life is a broad term not susceptible to exhaustive definition. The court has already held that elements such as gender identification, name and sexual orientation and sexual life are important elements in the personal sphere protected by Article 8. Mental health must also be regarded as a crucial part of private life associated with the aspect of moral integrity. Article 8 protects a right to identity and personal development and the right to establish and develop relationships

---

[195] [2003] EWHC 199 (Fam), [2003] 1 FLR 933.
[196] [2001] 1 FLR 589 at 593.
[197] [2001] 1 FLR 365.
[198] *Marckx v Belgium* (1979–80) 2 EHRR 330.
[199] *Price v UK* (1988) 55 DR 199, ECHR.
[200] [2002] 1 FCR 720.
[201] (1992) 16 EHRR 97 at 111 at [29].
[202] (2001) 33 EHRR 10 at [47].

with other human beings and the outside world. The preservation of mental stability is in that context an indispensable precondition to effective enjoyment of the respect for private life.'[203]

6.176 This raises two important aspects of application. First, it is a right to positive respect, to the promotion of what is entailed in a private life, not merely a protection from interference with one's privacy. The state – and this of course includes the court – may be under a duty to do something rather than merely refrain from action. Second, it can apply in family situations even where there is at present no family life. A child may have no family life with a father who is not married to his mother and has had no contact with him. However, the right to personal development may include the right to come to know one's father or one's child.[204] It is clearly engaged when the court is considering the establishment of paternity and whether there should be contact.

6.177 In *Rose v Secretary of State for Health*[205] Scott Baker J held that Art 8 was engaged when a child, born by artificial insemination by an anonymous donor, sought identifying information from the Secretary of State or the establishing of a contact register.

> 'Respect for family life has been interpreted by the European court to incorporate the concept of personal identity (see *Gaskin*[206]). Everyone should be able to establish details of his identity as a human being (*Johnston v Ireland*[207]). That, to my mind, plainly includes information about a biological parent who will inevitably have contributed to the identity of his child.'[208]

ARTICLE 8 AND THE EUROPEAN COURT OF HUMAN RIGHTS

6.178 The European Court of Human Rights has declined to interpret Art 8 as incorporating the principle that the interests of a child are paramount. Indeed, given the wording of Art 8, it is difficult to see how it could have done, Art 8 clearly providing that where the interests or rights of individuals conflict, a proper balance has to be struck. This was emphasised in *Johansen v Norway*[209] (a case which concerned a child being taken into care) in which the Court said that: 'a fair balance has to be struck between the interests of the child in remaining in public care and those of the parent in being reunited with the child'. However, the Court has indicated that the best interests of the child

---

[203] See also Munby 'Families old and new' (2005) 17 CFLQ 487 at 504–508.
[204] See also **6.9**.
[205] [2002] EWHC 1593 (Admin), [2002] 2 FLR 962.
[206] (1990) 12 EHRR 36, ECtHR.
[207] (1986) 9 EHRR 303 at [55].
[208] [2002] EWHC 1593 (Admin), [2002] 2 FLR 962 at [41] and [48].
[209] (1997) 23 EHRR 33.

have 'particularly' to be taken into account[210] and 'consideration of what is in the best interests of the child is in every case of crucial importance'.[211]

6.179 Strasbourg's approach can be illustrated by *Hendriks v Netherlands*,[212] a case in which the Commission had to examine a claim by a father that domestic courts had denied him contact with his child in breach of his Art 8 rights:

> 'Feelings of distress and frustration because of the absence of one's child may cause considerable suffering to the non-custodial parent. However, where … there is a serious conflict between the interests of the child and one of its parents which can only be resolved to the disadvantage of one of them, the interests of the child must, under Article 8(2), prevail.'

ARTICLE 8 AND ENGLISH COURTS

6.180 The question has been raised whether the paramountcy principle of s 1 of the CA 1989 (and, by extension, of s 1 of the ACA 2002) is compatible with the Convention. Jonathan Herring, for example has pointed out that there are fundamental differences between the approach of the Act and the Convention. Under the Convention, a case concerned with denying a parent contact with a child starts with the parent's right to contact and clear and convincing evidence is required to justify the interference with this right. Under the Act, the approach may start with a factual presumption that the child's welfare is generally promoted but this can be rebutted in a particular case on less evidence than is necessary to rebut the Art 8 right.[213] Others have expressed a concern lest a rights based approach will 'constitute a damaging step back from a world in which the welfare of the child is the focus of decision making to a world in which parental rights are privileged and prioritised'.[214] Sir James Munby has written extrajudicially that:

> 'We need, before it is too late, to examine whether the principle that the child's rights are paramount is really compatible with the Convention. This is something too readily assumed, on occasions asserted, but rarely subjected to very convincing analysis.'[215]

6.181 Before the advent of the Human Rights Act 1998, the House of Lords twice expressed the view that s 1 and Art 8 were not in conflict. In *Re KD (A*

---

[210] *Hokkanen v Finland* (1995) 19 EHRR 139 and see also *Olsson v Sweden (No 2)* (1994) 17 EHRR 134.

[211] *L v Finland* [2000] 2 FLR 118 at 138.

[212] (1983) 5 EHRR 223, ECtHR.

[213] Herring 'The Human Rights Act and the Welfare Principle in Family Law: Conflicting or Complementary?' in Butler (ed) *Human Rights for the New Millennium* (Kluwer Law International, 2000).

[214] Harris-Short 'Family Law and the Human Rights Act 1998: judicial restraint or revolution?' [2005] CFLQ 329 at 350.

[215] Munby 'Families old and new – the family and Article 8' [2005] CFLQ 487.

Minor) (Access: Principles),[216] for example, Lord Oliver of Aylmerton had said that if there was any conflict (which he doubted):

> '[It] is, I think, semantic only and lies only in differing ways of giving expression to the single common concept that the natural bond and relationship between parent and child gives rise to universally recognised norms which ought not to be gratuitously interfered with and which, if interfered with at all, ought to be so only if the welfare of the child dictates it.'

6.182 Post implementation however, judges at first instance and in the Court of Appeal, were more willing to consider Art 8 rights alongside the welfare test and so too, in recent years, has the House of Lords.[217] There is overwhelming agreement though that when the rights of adults conflict with the best interests of the child, those of the child must prevail, not just because of s 1, but also under Art 8.[218] This has produced a conscious and conscientious examination, more detailed than hitherto, of the interests of the adults involved as well as those of the child and in a re-examination of the way the courts should approach classes of case. Take, for example, *Payne v Payne*,[219] when the Court of Appeal dealt with a mother's application for permission to take her daughter to live in New Zealand:

> 'All those immediately affected by the proceedings, that is to say the mother, the father and the child have rights under Art 8(1). Those rights inevitably in a case such as the present appeal are in conflict and, under Art 8(2) have to be balanced against the rights of the others. In addition and of the greatest significance is the welfare of the child which, according to European jurisprudence, is of crucial importance, and where in conflict with a parent is overriding (see *Johansen v Norway*[220]). Article 8(2) recognises that a public authority, in this case the court, may interfere with the right to family life where it does so in accordance with the law, and where it is necessary in a democratic society for, inter alia, the protection of the rights and freedoms of others and the decision is proportionate to the need demonstrated. That position appears to me to be similar to that which arises in all child-based family disputes and the European case-law on children is in line with the principles set out in the Children Act 1989. I do not, for my part, consider that the Convention has affected the principles the courts should apply in dealing with these difficult cases. Its implementation into English law does however give us the opportunity to take another look at the way the principles [governing leave-to-remove cases] have been expressed in the past and whether there should now be a reformulation of those principles.'

---

[216] [1988] 2 FLR 139 at 153.

[217] But only to some extent. See *Re B (Adoption By One Natural Parent To Exclusion of Other)* [2001] UKHL 70, [2002] 1 FLR 196 per Lord Nicholls at [30].

[218] See *Re L (Contact: Domestic Violence)*; *Re V (Contact: Domestic Violence)*; *Re M (Contact: Domestic Violence)*; *Re H (Contact: Domestic Violence)* [2000] 2 FLR 334, per Dame Elizabeth Butler-Sloss P at 345.

[219] [2001] EWCA Civ 166, [2001] 1 FLR 1052, per Dame Elizabeth Butler-Sloss P at [B2].

[220] (1996) 23 EHRR 33 at [67] and [72].

CONSIDERING ARTICLE 8

6.183 When an Art 8 point is being put forward, the following questions need to be asked:

- Is there 'family life' shared by the relevant adult and the child?

- Does the proposed order interfere with a right to that life?

- Is the interference in accordance with the law?
  - Does it have a basis in law?
  - Does it enable the parties to foresee with a reasonable degree of certainty the circumstances in which and the conditions on which the court will act?[221]

- Is the interference necessary for the protection of the rights and freedoms of others?

    'Whilst the adjective "necessary" ... is not synonymous with "indispensable" neither has it the flexibility of such expressions as "admissible", "ordinary", "useful", "reasonable" or "desirable".'[222]

- Is the interference proportionate? Is there a reasonable relationship between the goal pursued and the means used?[223]

    'The intervention must be "necessary in a democratic society", that is, it must meet a pressing social need and be proportionate to that need. The more drastic the interference, the greater must be the need to do it.'[224]

ADOPTION AND ARTICLE 8

6.184 Strasbourg jurisprudence makes it clear that adoption proceedings constitute an interference with family life and require justification.[225]

'The adoption order... amounted to an interference with the applicant's right to respect for family life under Art 8, para 1 (see the *Keegan v Ireland* judgment of 26 May 1994, Series A no 290, pp 19–20, § 51). Such interference constitutes a

---

[221] *Malone v United Kingdom* (1985) 7 EHRR 14.

[222] *Handyside v United Kingdom* (1979–80) 1 EHRR 737.

[223] *Ashingdane v United Kingdom* (1985) 7 EHRR 528.

[224] *Re B (Adoption by One Natural Parent to Exclusion of Other)* [2001] 1 FLR 589, per Hale LJ at 599. See also *The Queen on the Application of Mahmood v Secretary of State for the Home Department* [2001] 1 FLR 756, per Lord Phillips of Worth Maltravers MR at 772.

[225] *Johansen v Norway* (1997) 23 EHRR 33; *Söderbäck v Sweden* (1998) EHRR 342, [1999] 1 FLR 250; *Kuijper v Netherlands* (application No 64848/01) (unreported but noted in *Eski*) and *Eski v Austria* (Application No 21949/03), [2007] 1 FLR 1650.

violation of this Article unless it is 'in accordance with the law', pursues an aim or aims that are legitimate under Art 8, para 2 and can be regarded as 'necessary in a democratic society.'[226]

6.185   This was also affirmed by the Court of Appeal in *Re B (Adoption By One Natural Parent To Exclusion of Other)*:[227]

'An adoption order is undoubtedly an interference by a public authority, in the shape of the court which makes it, with the exercise of the right to respect for family life, whether by the child herself or by anyone else with whom she enjoys 'family life'. Indeed, it is the most drastic interference with that right which is permitted by the law. In the right circumstances it is a most valuable way of supplying a child with the 'family for life' to which everyone ought to be entitled and of which some children are so tragically deprived.'[228]

6.186   However, in the House of Lords,[229] Lord Nicholls, while agreeing that making an adoption order was a very serious step, said that there was no need to go beyond the Adoption Act 1976 which complied with Art 8.

'On its face this permanent exclusion of the child's mother from the life of the child is a drastic and detrimental consequence of adoption so far as the child is concerned. How serious this loss is likely to be depends on the circumstances of the case. In deciding whether to make an order having this consequence the court must always be satisfied that this course is in the best interests of the child. There must be some reason justifying the exclusion of the other natural parent. The reason must be sufficient to outweigh the adverse consequences such an order may have by reason of the exclusion of one parent from the child's life. Consent of the excluded parent is not of itself a sufficient reason, but it is a factor to be taken into account. Its weight will depend on the circumstances ...

I do not see how an adoption order made in this way can infringe the child's rights under article 8. Under article 8 the adoption order must meet a pressing social need and be a proportionate response to that need: see, for example, *Silver v United Kingdom*[230]. Inherent in both these Convention concepts is a balancing exercise, weighing the advantages and the disadvantages. But this balancing exercise, required by article 8, does not differ in substance from the like balancing exercise undertaken by a court when deciding whether, in the conventional phraseology of English law, adoption would be in the best interests of the child. The like considerations fall to be taken into account. Although the phraseology is different, the criteria to be applied in deciding whether an adoption order is justified under article 8(2) lead to the same result as the conventional tests applied by English law. Thus, unless the court misdirected itself in some material respect when balancing the competing factors, its conclusion that an adoption order is in the best interests of the child, even though this would exclude the mother from the child's life, identifies the pressing social need for adoption (the need to safeguard

---

[226]   *Söderbäck* at [24].
[227]   [2001] 1 FLR 589. The Court of Appeal set aside an adoption order made in favour of a natural father but the decision was reversed by the House of Lords.
[228]   Ibid, per Hale LJ at 599.
[229]   *Re B (Adoption: Natural Parent)* [2001] UKHL 70, [2002] 1 FLR 196 at [30].
[230]   (1983) 5 EHRR 347, 376–377, at [97(c)].

and promote the child's welfare) and represents the court's considered view on proportionality. ... Article 8(2) does not call for more.'

6.187 This view has been the subject of academic criticism, Harris-Short calling it a conservative approach to the Convention which does not stand up to scrutiny.[231] She and others, for example, Herring,[232] argue that under Art 8 the rights of parents have to be balanced against the traditional welfare considerations: 'it becomes a balance between rights and welfare'.

6.188 In *Re S (Adoption Order or Special Guardianship Order)*[233] Wall LJ, agreed that in most cases there was little or no difference between s 1 and Art 8 but emphasised the importance of proportionality.

'The court will need to bear Art 8 of the European Convention for the Protection of Human Rights and Fundamental Freedoms 1950 in mind, and to be satisfied that its order is a proportionate response to the problem, having regard to the interference with family life which is involved. In choosing between adoption and special guardianship, in most cases Art 8 is unlikely to add anything to the considerations contained in the respective welfare checklists. Under both statutes the welfare of the child is the court's paramount consideration, and the balancing exercise required by the statutes will be no different to that required by Art 8. However, in some cases, the fact that the welfare objective can be achieved with less disruption of existing family relationships can properly be regarded as helping to tip the balance.'

Continuance of family life when a child is not living with birth parents

6.189 The natural family relationship is not terminated by reason of the fact that the child has been taken into public care and Art 8 continues to apply.[234] Moreover, it appears from *Söderback v Sweden*[235] that Art 8 continues to apply after adoption although the adoptive parent's right to respect for his family life will also have to be taken into account.

Is there a right to adopt?

6.190 Article 8 presupposes the existence of a family and just as it does not safeguard the mere desire to found a family,[236] it does not, of itself, guarantee

---

[231] 'Putting the child at the heart of adoption?' [2002] CFLQ 325 at 336. See also Harris-Short 'Family Law and the Human Rights Act 1998: judicial restraint or revolution?' [2005] CFLQ 329.

[232] See, for example, 'The Human Rights Act and the Welfare Principle in Family Law: Conflicting or Complementary?' in Butler (ed) *Human Rights for the New Millennium* (Martinus Nijhoff, 2000) and [1999] CFLQ 223 and Choudhry 'The Adoption and Children Act 2002 – the welfare principle and the Human Rights Act 1998 – a missed opportunity?' [2003 CFLQ 119.

[233] [2007] EWCA Civ 54, [2007] 1 FLR 819 at [49].

[234] *Eriksson v Sweden* [1989] 12 EHRR 183, ECtHR.

[235] Ibid

[236] *Marx v Belgium* (1979–80) 2 EHRR 330.

the right to adopt.[237] However, where the domestic law permits single people to adopt, a refusal to authorise adoption on the sole grounds of the applicant's sexual orientation is in breach both of Arts 8 and 14.[238]

6.191 Nevertheless where the applicant already shares family life with the child, Art 8 issues will arise. In *Re P (Adoption: Unmarried Couple)*[239] the House of Lords held that Northern Irish regulations which permitted single people to adopt but which prevented an unmarried couple (one being the mother of the child in question) being considered as potential adopters breached Arts 8 and 14.

6.192 The issues raised by the sexual orientation or married status of adopters is considered further at **8.41**.

Dispensing with consent

6.193 In *Scott v UK*[240] the ECtHR found that a decision to dispense with the consent of a mother to the freeing of her child for adoption on the ground that consent was being withheld unreasonably did not violate Art 8. In determining whether a measure was necessary in a democratic society the Court had to consider whether, in the light of the case as a whole, the reasons adduced to justify it were sufficient for the purposes of Art 8(2). The margin of appreciation to be accorded to the competent national authorities varied in the light of the nature of the issues at stake and while the Court recognised that the authorities enjoyed a wide margin of appreciation in assessing the necessity of taking a child into care, stricter security is required for any further limitations on parental rights and access. It had not been established that the decision-making process had been unfair or that it had failed to involve the mother to a degree sufficient to protect her interests. As regards the merits, the domestic Court could not be criticised for deciding to free the applicant's daughter for adoption. The interference with the mother's right to respect for her family life was necessary and the case did not disclose any violation of Art 8.

6.194 The matter is considered in more detail at **3.137**.

Fathers as parties

6.195 Courts have taken account of Arts 8 and 6 when considering whether fathers without parental responsibility should be joined as parties to proceedings freeing children for adoption.[241] In *Keegan v Ireland*[242] the

---

[237] *Fretté v France* [2003] 2 FLR 9.
[238] Ibid and *EB v France* (Application No 43546/02), [2008] 1 FLR 850.
[239] [2008] UKHL 38.
[240] (Case 34745/97), [2000] 1 FLR 958.
[241] See, for example, *Z County Council v R* [2001] 1 FLR 365 and *Re H; Re G (Adoption: Consultation of Unmarried Fathers)* [2001] 1 FLR 646. They are not always joined: see *Re J (Adoption: Contracting Father)* [2003] EWHC 199 Fam, [2003] 1 FLR 933.

European Court of Human Rights held that the making of an adoption order without allowing the natural parent to participate albeit that he was not married to the mother and had never lived with his child breached his Art 8 rights.

> 'The fact that Irish law permitted the secret placement of the child for adoption without the applicant's knowledge or consent, leading to the bonding of the child with the proposed adopters and to the subsequent making of an adoption order, amounted to an interference with his right to respect for family life. Such interference is permissible only if the conditions set out in paragraph 2 of Article 8 (art. 8-2) are satisfied.'

This matter is considered in more detail at **17.64**.

Family life post-adoption

6.196 Family life between an adopted child and his adoptive parent enjoys the same protection as if the adopter was the child's natural parent.[243] See also **6.189**.

PRACTICE

6.197 When the Human Rights Act 1998 is relied on, the court must be provided with a list of authorities it is intended to cite and copies of the reports, either as part of the bundle in cases to which the *Practice Direction (Family Proceedings: Court Bundles) (10 March 2000)*[244] applies or no less than 2 clear days before the hearing. Any authority which is to be cited must be an authoritative and complete report. Reports obtained from the European Court of Human Rights database (HUDOC) may be used.[245]

---

[242] (1994) 18 EHRR 342, ECtHR.
[243] *X v France* [1982] 31 DR 241 ECtHR.
[244] [2000] 1 FLR 536.
[245] *Practice Direction Human Rights Act (24 July 2000)* [2000] 2 FLR 429.

Chapter 7

REGULATION OF ADOPTION

INTRODUCTION

7.1   After the introduction of legal adoption in 1926 regulation of adoption developed only slowly. Initially adoption was largely a matter of private negotiation, the state becoming involved only at the court stage. But after the Adoption Act 1976 came into force, it could properly be said that that the process was largely state controlled by means of local authorities (and some state registered adoption societies) selecting children for whom adoption was thought appropriate, choosing and assessing prospective adopters as being suitable to adopt and 'matching' the two. Even where privately arranged adoptions remain possible – usually between relatives or involving step-parents – the local authority is involved in supervising the placement and preparing reports for the court. The most recent, if not the last, stage in development came with the provisions in the Adoption and Children Act 2002 (ACA 2002) designed to create national standards of good practice in all adoption agencies, whether local authorities or registered societies.

7.2   The distinction between privately arranged adoption placements and agency placements, however, remains one of real importance. Actions of private individuals in relation to adoption, for example, advertising for prospective adopters, are constrained by statute backed by penal provisions. Different provisions relate to the removal of children from private placements with prospective adopters and those whose placements were arranged by agencies.

Note. The chapter describes the procedure agencies have to follow before placing a child for adoption, including referring the child, the prospective adoptees and the 'match' to its adoption panel. Assessment of the child etc is covered in Chapter 8.

BACKGROUND

7.3   The Adoption Act 1926 left adoption 'almost entirely uncontrolled' by the State.[1] Newspaper advertisements freely offered children for adoption. It was alleged that voluntary adoption societies were lax when deciding whether and where to place children for adoption. There were concerns that children

---

[1]   Cretney *Family Law in the Twentieth Century* (Oxford University Press, 2003) at pp 606–607.

were being exported to countries whose laws did not provide for adoption and that, despite s 9 of the 1926 Act prohibiting payments to the adoptive or birth parent, money changed hands.

7.4 In 1937 the *Report of the Departmental Committee on Adoption Societies and Agencies*[2] ('The Horsburgh Committee') argued that while adoption societies in general performed a useful function, there were many instances of poor practice aggravated by the fact that while many voluntary societies arranged large numbers of adoption, many did so only occasionally. It recommended that all societies should be registered by local authorities and regulated by the Secretary of State. These recommendations were enacted in the Adoption of Children (Regulation) Act 1936 – 'an important landmark in the move towards state control of the adoption process'[3] – but, as Cretney observed, the approach remained cautious and adoption remained essentially a private contract between individuals, ratified by a court.

7.5 *The Report of the Departmental Committee on the Adoption of Children*[4] ('the Hurst Report') in 1954 noted the risks inherent in private placements of children for adoption and recommended that local authorities should be specifically empowered to arrange adoptions. At the same time, it expressly declined to recommend that restrictions be imposed on societies. It was left to the Houghton Committee[5] in 1972 to propose a proper adoption service.

7.6 The Houghton Committee noted much concern about private placements. Sometimes they were arranged through a friend of the mother, her family doctor, solicitors, individuals who made a regular practice of arranging adoptions or even a casual acquaintance such as someone met in a launderette. In the view of the Committee:

> 'The decision to place a child with a particular couple is the most important stage in the adoption process. Adoption law must give assurance of adequate safeguards for the child at this stage otherwise it is ineffective. This assurance rests mainly on the skilled work of the adoption services ... An independent adoption is one in which this assurance is lacking.'[6]

7.7 When the Houghton Committee reported, there were 63 voluntary adoption societies in England and Wales but geographically the spread of societies was uneven. Some offered just a local service; others, a national one. Some offered a range of services whilst others dealt only with the selection of prospective adopters. In some, a lack of trained social work staff imposed restrictions on the service offered.

---

[2]   Cmd 5499 (1937).
[3]   *Family Law in the Twentieth Century* op cit at p 608.
[4]   Cmnd 9248 (1954).
[5]   *The Report of the Departmental Committee on the Adoption of Children* Cmnd 5107 (1972).
[6]   Ibid, at para 84. See also *Re Adoption Application (Non-Patrial: Breach of Procedures)* [1993] 1 FLR 947 at 950–951.

'These factors influence considerably the kind of people, whether children, natural parents or prospective adopters to whom a service is available and the quality of the service which is offered. What is needed is a service which is comprehensive in scope and available throughout the country.'[7]

7.8 As Cretney has commented:

'The Committee's Report … is an impressive document, not least because it marked (for the first time …) an awareness that adoption could not sensibly be kept in isolation. In reality, adoption was merely one legal technique for dealing with the future of children whose birth parents were not going to provide their homes throughout their childhood.'[8]

7.9 The Committee recommended that a statutory duty should be placed on local authorities to provide, in co-operation with voluntary societies, a comprehensive adoption service as part of their general child care and family casework provision.

- The responsibility for registering voluntary societies should pass to the Secretary of State.

- Private placements of a child for adoption, other than to a relative of the child, should be prohibited.

- All agencies should have established machinery for making decisions about placement.

- The authority or agency which placed the child should be responsible for supervising the placement and for helping and advising the prospective adopters during the period between placement and the adoption order.

7.10 These recommendations were enacted in the Adoption Act 1976.[9] In Lowe's words: 'It was, at [this moment] that one might say that the process of "professionalisation of adoption work" was completed'.[10]

7.11 The framework which the Act laid down remains essentially unchanged by the Adoption and Children Act 2002. The *Prime Minister's Review: Adoption*[11] in 2002 criticised delay, caution and in some cases, poor practice, in operating the regulatory system but not the system itself. However, the 2002 Act gave the opportunity for new Regulations and Guidance to be issued to try to ensure uniform national standards of good practice. In addition, prohibitions on illegally arranging adoptions and advertising a child for

---

[7] op cit para 34.
[8] *Family Law in the Twentieth Century* op cit at p 624.
[9] Adoption Act 1976, s 11(1).
[10] Lowe 'The Changing Face of Adoption – The Gift/Donation Model Versus the Contract/Services Model' [1997] CFLQ 371 at p 373.
[11] (2000) Performance and Innovation Unit Report.

adoption were extended and express restrictions on the preparation and submission of reports concerning adoption by private individuals introduced.

PRIVATE ADOPTIONS AND AGENCY ADOPTIONS

7.12 In the system of regulation, a clear distinction is drawn between acts (including placements) performed by individuals and those carried out by registered societies and local authorities.

ADVERTISING

7.13 Under ACA 2002, s 124 it is illegal for a person other than by or on behalf of an adoption agency[12] to publish or distribute or cause to be published or distributed an advertisement indicating that:

- the parent or guardian of a child wants the child to be adopted;

- a person wants to adopt a child;

- a person other than an adoption agency is willing to take any step relating to the arrangement of adoptions which are set out in s 92(2) (see **7.22**);

- a person other than an adoption agency is willing to receive a child handed over to him with a view to the child's adoption by him or another; or

- a person is willing to remove a child from the UK for the purposes of adoption.[13]

7.14 It is also illegal for a person other than on behalf of an adoption agency to publish or distribute or cause to be published or distributed information about:

- anything which constitutes an offence under ACA 2002, s 85 (removing a child from the UK for the purpose of adoption – see **4.12**) or s 93 (offence relating to arrangements for adoption – see **7.22**) or various sections of the Adoption (Scotland) Act 1978 or arts 11 or 58 of the Adoption (Northern Ireland) Order 1987;

- a particular child as a child available for adoption.[14]

---

[12] ACA 2002, s 123(5).
[13] Ibid, s 124, 123(1), (2).
[14] Ibid, s 124, 123(1), (3).

7.15 A person guilty of an offence under this section is liable on summary conviction to imprisonment for a term not exceeding 3 months, or a fine not exceeding level 5 on the standard scale, or both.[15]

7.16 If sufficient evidence is adduced to raise an issue as to whether the person had the knowledge or reason mentioned it has to be proved that he knew or had reason to suspect that s 123 applied to the advertisement or information.[16]

7.17 'Publishing or distributing an advertisement or information' means publishing it or distributing it to the public and includes doing so by electronic means (for example, by means of the internet).[17] The Secretary of State can amend this subsection to take into account advances in publishing technology.[18]

7.18 'The public' includes selected members of the public as well as the public generally or any section of the public.[19]

7.19 References to 'adoption' are to the adoption of persons, wherever they may be habitually resident, effected under the law of any country or territory, whether within or outside the British Islands.[20]

7.20 References to 'an adoption agency' include a person prescribed by Regulations outside the UK exercising functions corresponding to those of an adoption agency, if the functions are being exercised in prescribed circumstances, as well as a Scottish or Northern Irish adoption agency.[21]

7.21 For placement for adoption by agencies, see **7.180**.

ARRANGING ADOPTIONS

7.22 Under s 93 it is illegal for a person who is neither an adoption agency nor acting in pursuance of an order of the High Court to take any of the following steps:

(a) asking a person other than an adoption agency to provide a child for adoption;

(b) asking a person other than an adoption agency to provide prospective adopters for a child;

---

[15] ACA 2002, s 124(3).
[16] Ibid, s 124(2).
[17] Ibid, s 123(4)(a).
[18] Ibid, s 123(6).
[19] Ibid, s 123 (4)(b).
[20] Ibid, s 123(9).
[21] Ibid, s 123(7) and (9).

(c)   offering to find a child for adoption;

(d)   offering a child for adoption to a person other than an adoption agency;

(e)   handing over a child to any person other than an adoption agency with a view to the child's adoption by that or another person;

(f)   receiving a child handed over to him in contravention of paragraph (e);

(g)   entering into an agreement with any person for the adoption of a child, or for the purpose of facilitating the adoption of a child, where no adoption agency is acting on behalf of the child in the adoption;

(h)   initiating or taking part in negotiations of which the purpose is the conclusion of an agreement within paragraph (g);

(i)   causing another person to take any of the steps mentioned in paragraphs (a) to (h).[22]

7.23   However, an offence is not committed under paragraphs (d), (e), (g), (h) and (i) if:

(a)   the prospective adopters are parents, relatives or guardians of the child (or one of them is); or

(b)   the prospective adopter is the partner of a parent of the child.[23]

7.24   A person guilty of an offence under this section is liable on summary conviction to imprisonment for a term not exceeding 6 months, or a fine not exceeding £10,000, or both.[24]

7.25   If sufficient evidence is adduced to raise an issue as to whether the person had the necessary knowledge or reason, it has to be proved that he knew or had reason to suspect that the step taken under paragraphs (a) to (h) would contravene the paragraph in question and in relation to paragraph (f) that he knew or had reason to suspect that the child was handed over to him in contravention of paragraph (e).[25]

7.26   'An agreement' includes an arrangement whether or not enforceable.[26]

7.27   References to 'an adoption agency' include a person prescribed by regulations outside the UK exercising functions corresponding to those of an

---

[22]   ACA 2002, ss 93(1), 92(1), (2).
[23]   Ibid, s 92(3), (4).
[24]   Ibid, s 9(5).
[25]   Ibid, s 93(2)–(4).
[26]   Ibid, s 92(7).

adoption agency, if the functions are being exercised in prescribed circumstances, as well as a Scottish or Northern Irish adoption agency.[27]

7.28 References to 'adoption' are to the adoption of persons, wherever they may be habitually resident, effected under the law of any country or territory, whether within or outside the British Islands.[28]

7.29 In *Re Adoption Application (Non-Patrial: Breach of Procedures)*[29] a couple resident in England made arrangements to adopt a child from El Salvador. The female applicant collected the child from El Salvador and returned to England. It was held that by handing the child over to her husband with the intention that they should both adopt she was acting in breach of the prohibition regarding placement other than by an agency.

7.30 The High Court can make orders under ACA 2002, s 92(1) which authorise arrangements retrospectively.[30] In a decision[31] under the Adoption Act 1976, Latey J held that in exercising its discretion the court has to balance all the circumstances of the case, with the welfare of the child being the first consideration against the degree of taint of the transaction. In a case involving illegal payments in relation to surrogacy[32] Wall J adopted the approach of Latey J including the welfare of the child being the first and not the paramount consideration and examined the reason the payment was made (for genuine expenses which were not disproportionate). Both Latey J and Wall J were applying the then welfare test under the Adoption Act 1976, Latey J because that was the Act then governing adoption and Wall J because the same test was applied to surrogacy by s 30 of the Human Fertilisation and Embryology Act 1990. If the approach is valid – and it has been applied on a number of occasions at first instance[33] – then the welfare of the child will now have to be treated as paramount under s 1 of the 2002 Act.

PROHIBITION OF CERTAIN PAYMENTS

7.31 Under s 95 it is illegal for a person:

- to make any payment as defined;

---

[27] ACA 2002, ss 92(5), 97(1).

[28] Ibid, s 97(c).

[29] [1993] 1 FLR 947.

[30] *Re Adoption Application AA212/86 (Adoption: Payment)* [1987] 2 FLR 291, *Re Adoption Application (Non-Patrial: Breach of Procedures)* [1993] 1 FLR 947.

[31] *Re Adoption Application AA212/86 (Adoption: Payment)* [1987] 2 FLR 291.

[32] *Re C: Application By Mr and Mrs X under Section 30 of the Human Fertilisation And Embryology Act* [2002] EWHC 157 (Fam), [2002] 1 FLR 909.

[33] See *Re Q (Parental Order)* [1996] 1 FLR 369, *Re A (Placement of Child in Contravention of Adoption Act 1976, s 11)* [2005] 2 FLR 727 and *Re X and another (Foreign Surrogacy)* [2008] EWHC 3030 (Fam), [2009] 1 FLR 733 surrogacy cases and *Re MW (Adoption: Surrogacy)* [1995] 2 FLR 759 which involved both adoption and surrogacy.

- to agree or offer to make any such payment; or

- to receive or agree to receive or attempt to obtain any such payment.

7.32 A person guilty of an offence under this section is liable on summary conviction to imprisonment for a term not exceeding 6 months, or a fine not exceeding £10,000, or both.[34]

7.33 'Any payment' (other than an excepted payment) means one which is made for or in consideration of:

- the adoption of a child;

- giving any consent required in connection with the adoption of a child;

- removing from the UK a child who is a Commonwealth citizen, or is habitually resident in the UK to a place outside the British Islands for the purpose of adoption;

- a person (who is neither an adoption agency nor acting in pursuance of an order of the High Court) taking any step mentioned in s 92(2) (see **7.22**);

- preparing, causing to be prepared or submitting a report the preparation of which contravenes s 94(1) (see **7.41**).[35]

7.34 A payment (which includes a 'reward'[36]) is an excepted payment if it is made:

- in accordance with the 2002 Act, the Adoption (Scotland) Act 1978 or the Adoption (Northern Ireland) Order 1987:[37]

- to a registered adoption society by:
    - a parent or guardian of a child, or
    - a person who adopts or proposes to adopt a child,
    in respect of expenses reasonably incurred by the society in connection with the adoption or proposed adoption of the child;[38]

- in respect of any legal or medical expenses incurred or to be incurred by any person in connection with an application to a court which he has made or proposes to make for an adoption order, a placement order, or an order under s 26 (contact) or s 84 (giving parental responsibility prior to adoption abroad – see **4.132**);[39]

---

[34] ACA 2002, s 95(4).
[35] Ibid, s 95(1), (3).
[36] Ibid, s 97(b).
[37] Ibid, s 96(1).
[38] Ibid, s 96(2).
[39] Ibid, s 96(3).

- in respect of s 95(1)(c) (removal from the UK for the purpose of adoption) provided:
  - the prospective adopters have parental responsibility for the child by virtue of an order under s 84 (giving parental responsibility prior to adoption abroad – see **4.102**); or
  - the child is removed under the authority of an order under s 49 of the Adoption (Scotland) Act 1978 or art 57 of the Adoption (Northern Ireland) Order 1987; and
  - the payment is made in respect of the travel and accommodation expenses reasonably incurred in removing the child from the UK for the purpose of adoption.[40]

7.35 'Removing a child from the United Kingdom' includes arranging to do so; and the circumstances in which a person arranges to remove a child from the UK include those where he:

- enters into an arrangement for the purpose of facilitating such a removal of the child;

- initiates or takes part in any negotiations of which the purpose is the conclusion of an arrangement within the above paragraph; or

- causes another person to take any step mentioned in either of the above paragraphs.[41]

7.36 'An arrangement' includes an agreement (whether or not enforceable).[42]

7.37 'An agency' includes a Scottish or Northern Irish adoption agency.[43]

7.38 References to 'adoption' are to the adoption of persons, wherever they may be habitually resident, effected under the law of any country or territory, whether within or outside the British Islands.[44]

7.39 The High Court can make orders under s 95(1)(d) which authorise payments and such a power can probably be made retrospectively.[45]

7.40 In *Re AW (Adoption Application)*[46] a couple were held to have breached a similar requirement in the Adoption Act 1976 by paying a pregnant woman £1,000 for her expenses in England in order that she could give birth in Germany and hand the child to them for adoption in England. It did not matter whether or not there was a commercial or profit motive. The nature of

---

[40] ACA 2002, s 96(4).
[41] Ibid, ss 95(2), 85(3).
[42] Ibid.
[43] Ibid, s 97(a).
[44] Ibid, s 97(c).
[45] *Re AW (Adoption Application)* [1993] 1 FLR 62.
[46] Ibid.

the payment was relevant only to the question whether the court should exercise its power to retrospectively authorise the payment.

RESTRICTIONS ON PREPARING REPORTS

7.41 Under s 94 it is illegal for a person who is not within a description prescribed by regulations, in any prescribed circumstances, to prepare a report for any person, to cause a person to prepare a report, or to submit to any person a report which has been prepared about the suitability of a child for adoption or of a person to adopt a child or about the adoption, or placement for adoption, of a child.[47]

7.42 A person guilty of an offence under this section is liable on summary conviction to imprisonment for a term not exceeding 6 months, or a fine not exceeding level 5 on the standard scale, or both.[48]

7.43 If sufficient evidence is adduced to raise an issue as to whether the person had the necessary knowledge or reason, it has to be proved that he knew or had reason to suspect that the report would be, or had been, by a person who is not within a prescribed description in any prescribed circumstances.[49]

7.44 Persons of a 'prescribed description' include a social worker with 3 years post qualification in child care or who is supervised by such a person employed by a local authority or registered adoption society.[50]

7.45 'Prescribed circumstances' include reports about whether a child should be placed for adoption generally or with a specific person and on the suitability of a prospective adopter.[51]

7.46 In *Re M (Adoption: International Adoption Trade)*[52] Munby J criticised in trenchant terms reports prepared by an independent social worker in breach of similar provision in the Adoption Act 1976.[53] They were 'deeply flawed and inadequate documents ... [which were] positively and dangerously misleading'. Any local authority faced with a situation in which a foreign adoption was proceeding on the basis of an illegal home study report should not hesitate to inform the foreign court and other agencies involved that the provision of home study reports other than by an agency or its agents were illegal. They should also inform them of any matters within their knowledge which

---

[47]   ACA 2002, s 94(1), (5). See also *In Re C (Adoption: Legality)* [1999] 1 FLR 370.

[48]   Ibid, s 94(5).

[49]   Ibid, s 94(4).

[50]   Ibid, s 94(1); Restriction on the Preparation of Adoption Reports Regulations 2005, SI 2005/1711, reg 3.

[51]   Ibid, reg 4.

[52]   [2003] EWHC 219 (Fam), [2003] 1 FLR 1111.

[53]   Reports by the same independent social worker, Jay Carter, had been criticised in *Re C (Adoption: Legality)* [1999] 1 FLR 370, *Re J-S (Private International Adoption)* [2000] 2 FLR 638 and *Flintshire CC v K* [2001] 2 FLR 476.

suggested that the prospective adopters were not suitable to adopt either in general or the particular child. 'All such concerns should be voiced, clearly, loudly and explicitly.'

EXTRA-TERRITORIALITY

7.47 In *Re Adoption Application (Non-Patrial: Breach of Procedures)*[54] Douglas Brown J held that prohibitions under the Adoption Act 1976 similar to the above gave rise to offences only when the acts took place in the UK. There was an established presumption that in the absence of clear and specific words to the contrary, a statute does not make conduct outside the jurisdiction a criminal offence.[55] Moreover although certain sections of the Act referred to 'adoption in Great Britain or elsewhere', no such wording was inserted in the criminal provisions.

7.48 The same arguments apply equally to offences created by the 2002 Act and it is likely that where the act wholly takes place outside the UK no offence will be committed.

7.49 There are two *caveats* though. Certain offences, for example, advertising under s 123 can be committed in relation to adoptions abroad[56] provided the act takes place in the UK. Second it can be argued[57] that a statute may have extra-territorial effect either under a traditional common law approach ('Does the essence or the gist of the act occur within the jurisdiction?')[58] or under the approach in *Treacy v DPP*[59] namely that where the definition of an offence contains a requirement that the conduct should be followed by specified consequences, it is sufficient that either the conduct or the consequences arise within the jurisdiction.[60]

ILLEGALITY AND THE WELFARE TEST

7.50 Breaches of the above prohibitions cause difficulty when the court is considering making an adoption order. If the prospective adopter is the guilty person, debarring him from adopting the child may prejudice the child's welfare.

---

[54] [1993] 1 FLR 947.
[55] *Air India v Wiggins* 71 Cr App R 213 HL per Lord Diplock at 217. See also, for example, *Re A (Adoption Placement)* [1988] 2 FLR 133.
[56] See ACA 2002, s 123(9)(b).
[57] See, for example, Bridge and Swindells *Adoption: The Modern Law* (Family Law, 2003) at pp 352–353.
[58] *R v Haren* [1963] 1 QB 8.
[59] [1971] AC 537.
[60] See also *Archbold: Criminal Pleading, Evidence and Practice* 2009 Edition paras 2.33–2.34.

7.51   Prior to the 2002 Act the Court would first ask whether the plain words of the section creating the illegality necessarily prevented the making of an adoption order. If it did, that was the end of the matter. Section 24(2) of the Adoption Act 1976, for example, forbade the making of an order where illegal payments had been made. However, breaches of other sections did not necessarily create such a bar. In *Re G (Adoption: Illegal Placement)*,[61] the Court of Appeal held that although the High Court was unable to authorise retrospectively an unlawful placement, it might nevertheless make an adoption order.

7.52   None of the restrictions in Chapter 7 of the ACA 2002 impose a veto on the making of an adoption order because of a breach, but the Court continues to have a discretion to refuse an adoption on grounds of public policy (see **6.163**) including when there has been illegality. The pre-Act decisions remain authority on the exercise of this discretion.

7.53   In *Re Adoption Application (Non-Patrial: Breach of Procedures)*[62] Douglas Brown J held that:

> 'Whereas the first consideration must be given to the welfare question, the circumstances include considerations of public policy. The question for the court, bearing in mind [the welfare test] is: does public policy require that the applicants should be refused the order they seek because of their criminal conduct? The court, still bearing in mind the guidance contained in s 6, must conduct a balancing exercise.'

7.54   Despite their reluctance to make orders where important statutory provisions designed to protect children had been breached, courts prior to the 2002 Act were reluctant to refuse orders where adoption was otherwise in the child's best interests. *In Re C (Adoption: Legality)*,[63] for example, Johnson J, despite serious misgivings about the applicant's ability to meet the child's needs, made an adoption order in relation to a child adopted in Guatemala by an English woman who later sought an adoption order in England having made illegal payments to facilitate the adoption.[64]

> 'Except for the very unusual case where there is a claim for a return of the child to the natural family, in all the reported cases the welfare considerations seem to have led the court to authorise or waive whatever breaches have occurred in the particular case and that is what I have decided to do in respect of this application. On reflection it seems to me that the situation and the difficulty that arises in these cases is one that was foreseen by Parliament ... It is a matter of speculation but it may be that Parliament recognised that breaches of these prohibitions could not in

---

[61]   [1995] 1 FLR 403.
[62]   [1993] 1 FLR 947 approved by the Court of Appeal in *Re G (Adoption: Illegal Placement)* [1995] 1 FLR 403 as setting out 'the jurisprudential position admirably and accurately. I cannot improve upon his words' – per Balcombe LJ at 409.
[63]   [1999] 1 FLR 370.
[64]   She had previously been rejected as a potential adopter by two local authorities and an independent agency.

reality lead the court to a decision contrary to the welfare of a child. Perhaps, and I speculate, Parliament provided the criminal remedy so that whilst a breach of the due process might itself not constitute a bar to the adoption, then at least those involved would have exposed themselves to criminal prosecution.'[65]

7.55 Now that the welfare of the child is the paramount and not just the 'first' consideration,[66] this reluctance to punish illegality by refusing an adoption contrary to the interests of the child is likely to be the greater.

7.56 Given the seriousness of the issues and the High Court's power to authorise some acts retrosectively (see **7.22** and **7.39**), cases involving illegality should be transferred to the High Court.[67]

7.57 The concern for the welfare of the child may result in the local authority instituting public law proceedings in order to remove the child. In the notorious case of a North Wales couple who made illegal payments relating to the adoption of twins born to a mother who lived in California and then obtained adoption orders in Arkansas, the adopters' local authority commenced care proceedings after the couple returned to Wales. The High Court later refused to make a residence order in favour of the couple and placed the children in the care of the authority, who planned to return the children to the United States.[68]

Examples

Re Adoption Application (Non-Patrial: Breach of Procedures)[69]

7.58 A couple resident in England made arrangements to adopt a child from El Salvador. The female applicant collected the child from El Salvador and returned to England. It was held that by handing the child over to her husband with the intention that they should both adopt she was acting in breach of the prohibition regarding placement other than by an agency. However, there had been no deception of the immigration authorities and full disclosure to the local authority and guardian. It was clearly in the child's interests for an adoption order to be made.

Re AW (Adoption Application)[70]

7.59 A couple paid a pregnant woman £1,000 for her expenses in England and Germany in order that she could give birth in Germany and then hand the child to them for adoption in England. After receiving the child the couple embarked on a course of 'devious and evasive conduct' concealing the true facts from

---

[65] [1999] 1 FLR 370 at 382. See also *Re A (Placement of Child In Contravention of Adoption Act 1976 s 11)* [2005] 2 FLR 727 and **7.30**.

[66] ACA 2002, s 1(2).

[67] *Re G (Adoption: Illegal Placement)* [1995] 1 FLR 403.

[68] *Flintshire County Council v K* [2001] 2 FLR 476. See also *Re M (Adoption: International Adoption Trade)* [2003] EWHC 219 (Fam), [2003] 1 FLR 1111.

[69] [1993] 1 FLR 947.

[70] [1993] 1 FLR 62.

their local authority in order to delay matters for so long that no one would contemplate removing the child. The options open to the court 2½ years later were limited and unsatisfactory. In the light of the fact that the child had to remain with them, her welfare required the making on an interim order under s 25 of the Adoption Act 1976 vesting legal authority in them for 2 years.[71]

Re ZHH (Adoption Application)[72]

7.60 A mother directly placed her baby with the applicant intending that she should adopt her. Notwithstanding the breach of the provisions of the 1976 Act, the fact that the applicant had looked after the child extremely well justified making an adoption order.

Re C (A Minor) (Adoption Application)[73]

7.61 A couple agreed with a pregnant woman that the male applicant would pretend to be the child's father and paid her various sums with the intention that they would adopt the child. The adoption application was heard when the child was 1¾ years old. During the hearing the application was withdrawn. Booth J held that the very grave concern raised by the deception and the payments meant that adoption would not have been in the best interests of the child. The child was made a ward so that an attempt could be made to rehabilitate him to his mother.

ADOPTION AGENCIES

Adoption agency

7.62 In the 2002 Act, 'adoption agency' means a local authority or a registered adoption society.[74]

Local authorities

7.63 Each local authority has to maintain within their area a service designed to meet the needs, in relation to adoption, of:

- children who may be adopted, their parents and guardians;

- persons wishing to adopt a child; and

- adopted persons, their parents, natural parents and former guardians.[75]

---

[71] Such an order can no longer be made.
[72] [1993] 1 FLR 83.
[73] [1993] 1 FLR 87.
[74] ACA 2002, s 2(1).
[75] Ibid, s 3(1).

7.64 As part of the service the authority must provide the requisite facilities including facilities not just for the adoption of children but also for the provision of adoption support services, defined as 'counselling, advice and information', and any other services prescribed by regulations.[76] The authority may provide these facilities by securing their provision by registered adoption societies, or by other persons who are within a description prescribed by regulations.[77]

7.65 The facilities of the service must be provided in conjunction with the local authority's other social services and with registered adoption societies in their area, so that help may be given in a coordinated manner without duplication, omission or avoidable delay.[78]

Registered adoption society

7.66 A 'registered adoption society' means a voluntary organisation which is registered under Part 2 of the Care Standards Act 2000 and whose function consists of or includes making arrangements for the adoption of children.[79]

Legal structure

Regulations

7.67 The legal structure for the provision of adoption services by adoption agencies is contained in the 2002 Act and in the Adoption Agencies Regulations 2005[80] (AAR 2005).

Guidance

7.68 Statutory guidance is provided by *Adoption Guidance*[81] ('Guidance') which is issued under s 7 of the Local Authority Social Services Act 1970.

> '[This] does not have the binding effect which a statutory provision or statutory instrument would have. It is what it purports to be, guidance and not instruction. But ... the guidance should be given great weight. It is not instruction but it is much more than mere advice which the addressee is free to follow or not as it chooses. It is guidance which [any authority] should consider with great care and from which it should depart only if it has cogent reasons for so doing.'[82]

---

[76] ACA 2002, ss 3(2), 2(6).
[77] Ibid, s 3(4).
[78] Ibid, s 3(5).
[79] Ibid, s 2(2), (5).
[80] SI 2005/389.
[81] (Department for Education and Skills, 2006).
[82] *Munjaz v Ashworth Hospital* [2005] UKHL 58, [2006] 4 All ER 736 per Lord Bingham at [21]. See also *B v Lewisham London Borough Council* [2008] EWHC 738 (Admin), [2008] 2 FLR 523 and also *R v Islington LBC ex p Rixon* [1996] 32 BMLR 136 at 140.

7.69 Additional Regulations and guidance are provided for the assessment of children and prospective adopters (see **8.19**) and the provision of adoption support (see **9.18**).

Adoption panel

7.70 Each agency must have at least one adoption panel[83] but two or more local authorities may establish a joint one.[84] The duty of the panel is to provide recommendations to the agency on whether a child should be paced for adoption, whether prospective adopters are suitable to adopt a child and whether a particular child should be placed with a particular couple (see **7.97**).

7.71 AAR 2005 provide detailed regulation specifying the constitution and independence of the panels.[85] In addition, the Guidance states that the agency should ensure that the membership of the panel should be gender balanced as far as possible and reflect the composition of the community that the agency serves.[86]

The agency adviser

7.72 Agencies are required to appoint as the 'agency adviser' to the panel a senior member of staff with at least 5 years post-qualification experience and relevant management experience as an adoption team leader or a person with more senior management experience.[87]

7.73 The functions of the agency adviser are to:

- assist the agency with the appointment, termination and review of members of the panel;

- be responsible for the induction and training of members of the panel;

- be responsible for liaison between the agency and the panel, monitoring the performance of panel members and the administration of the panel;

- give such advice to the panel as it may request in relation to any case or generally.[88]

---

[83] AAR 2005, reg 3(1).
[84] Ibid, reg 3(5).
[85] Ibid, reg 31.
[86] Op cit at para 1.15.
[87] AAR 2005, reg 8, Guidance op cit at paras 1.35–1.41.
[88] AAR 2005, reg 8.

7.74 The agency adviser is not a panel member but should attend panel meetings as its adviser. He or she should be able to contribute to panel meetings by raising issues and providing advice, for example about the agency's procedures and practices.[89]

7.75 The Guidance recommends that the agency adviser should maintain an overview of the quality of the agency's reports to the panel and liaise with team managers to quality assure the child's permanence report, the prospective adopter's report and the adoption placement report. Where there are concerns about a report, the agency adviser and the panel chair should consider whether it is adequate for submission to the panel. It also recommends that the agency adviser also update the panel on the general progress of the cases it has considered.[90]

Medical adviser

7.76 Each agency is required to appoint at least one registered medical practitioner to be the agency's medical adviser.[91] The medical adviser is to be consulted about the arrangements for accessing and disclosing health information, as required or permitted by AAR 2005.[92]

7.77 The medical adviser should be consulted where the agency:

- arranges for the child to be examined and obtains a report or reports on the child's health;[93]

- arranges for health information to be obtained about the child's parents and siblings;[94]

- prepares the child's permanence report for the adoption panel, which is to include a summary written by the medical adviser on the child's health;[95]

- obtains a report about the health of the prospective adopter;[96]

- prepares the prospective adopter's report for the adoption panel, which is to include a summary written by the medical adviser on the prospective adopter's health;[97]

- prepares the adoption placement report for the adoption panel;[98]

---

[89] Guidance op cit at para 1.39.
[90] Ibid at paras 1.40–1.41.
[91] AAR 2005, reg 9(1).
[92] Ibid, reg 9(2).
[93] Under ibid, reg 15 and Sch 1, Pt 2.
[94] Under ibid, reg 16 and Sch 1, Pt 4.
[95] Under ibid, reg 17.
[96] Under ibid, reg 25 and Sch 4, Pt 2.
[97] Under ibid, reg 25.
[98] Under ibid, reg 31.

- prepares a report to the court where there has been an application for a placement order, as the agency is required to provide a summary written by the medical adviser on the health of the child;

- reviews the child's case, including reviewing the arrangements for assessing and meeting the child's health care needs;[99]

- prepares a report to the court where there has been an application for an adoption order or section 84 order, as the agency is required to provide summaries written by the medical adviser on the health of the child and the prospective adopter.[100]

FINDING ADOPTERS

7.78 The *Prime Minister's Review: Adoption*[101] reported that a shortfall of suitable adopters was one of the two key problems for its proposal to increase the number of adoptions, the other being delays in assessing prospective adopters and matching them with children. In 1999, for example, 2,200 children were adopted from care but over 2,400 children were still waiting to find adoptive parents.

7.79 The Review discovered that almost all agencies used general recruitment campaigns to recruit adopters but the degree of activity varied. Local authorities recruited adopters using a variety of methods. They advertised in the press and on the radio, in specialist magazines, Yellow Pages and in GP surgeries. Many had internet sites listing adoption services and information leaflets on adoption, but few had translated them into other languages. Some societies tended to recruit 'hand-to-mouth' by targeting and assessing adopters for a particular child, sometimes adopting a saturation approach, whilst others tried to maintain a rolling list of people interested.

> 'These differences reflect both the differing scales of the recruitment function carried out by agencies, the agency culture and profile given to adoption. There is currently no guidance or criteria on recruitment methods nor requirements to attain a certain level of recruitment.'

7.80 In 2002 the Adoption and Children Act Register was established nationally to help find prospective adopters for children and vice versa. See **7.85**.

Advertising

7.81 The prohibition on advertising in relation to adoption imposed by ACA 2002, s 123 (see **7.13**) does not apply to adoption agencies. However because

---

[99]   Under AAR 2005, reg 36.
[100] Guidance op cit at para 43.
[101] Op cit at 3.70.

s 97(2) of the Children Act 1989 prohibits the publication of any material which is intended or is likely to identify a child as being involved in any proceedings under that Act or the 2002 Act, a child cannot be identified in an adoption advertisement while proceedings are pending unless a court is satisfied that the child welfare requires it and, under s 97(4) directs otherwise.[102]

7.82 No formal guidance on advertising has been given by the Department for Education and Skills but 'informal advice' has been offered[103] which states that an adoption agency may advertise a child for adoption where it has authority to place the child for adoption. Where it does not have such authority, it may advertise the child for adoption provided the following apply:

- there is a care order in respect of the child which was obtained on the basis of a care plan which set out the plan for adoption;

- the agency decision maker has endorsed the adoption panel's recommendation that the child should be placed for adoption;

- the agency has notified the child's parents/guardian in writing of the decision maker's decision and of its intention to advertise the child for adoption;

- the following are informed of the agency's intention to advertise the child for adoption:
  - the agency's legal adviser;
  - in cases where court proceedings are ongoing, the child's CAFCASS guardian;
  - the advertisement makes clear:
    - (a) that the agency intends to place the child for adoption and has informed the child's parents/guardian of this in writing; and
    - (b) that this is subject to obtaining parental consent or a placement order under adoption legislation.

It adds that 'some courts *may prefer* to be made aware of the intention to advertise the child for adoption where there is no authority to place the child for adoption'. However, in *Re K (Adoption: Permission to Advertise)*[104] MacFarlane J made it clear that consent under s 97(4) would be required where proceedings were pending.

7.83 He offered guidance which he recognised might have to be revisited or fine-tuned to meet the needs of individual cases, in particular after representations from national adoption bodies.

---

[102] *Re K (Adoption: Permission to Advertise)* [2007] EWHC 544 Fam, [2007] 2 FLR 326 at [9].
[103] http://www.everychildmatters.gov.uk/socialcare/childrenincare/adoption/materials/faqs, accessed on 16 April 2009.
[104] [2007] EWHC 544 (Fam), [2007] 2 FLR 326 at [36].

- It is not open to a local authority to place an advertisement advertising a particular child as being available for adoption, or to apply to a court for permission to do so, until the authority has obtained the necessary recommendation from its adoption panel and has decided that the child ought to be placed for adoption in compliance with the 2005 Regulations. A court faced with a premature application made prior to the approved officer deciding in favour of adoption in the light of a recommendation from the adoption panel should refuse permission to advertise.

- Where an application for permission to advertise is made in a case where the court has yet to hold a final hearing in care proceedings and has yet to endorse the local authority's care plan for adoption, the court is unlikely to give permission to advertise for adoption unless the adoption plan is unopposed or there is some exceptional feature of the case that justifies advertising notwithstanding the fact that the court has yet to form its own view on the merits of any adoption care plan (for example where the mother has died or cannot be traced, or the adoption plan is supported by all parties).

- In considering such an application the court is likely to bear in mind the fact that a local authority is at liberty to begin a search for potential adopters by looking at its own list of adopters, accessing any local group or consortium list of adopters, and accessing the Adoption Register without having to advertise and without having to obtain the court's permission. If an application to advertise is made at this comparatively early stage consideration should also be given to what the advertisement will actually say as to the child's status. Prior to the local authority having legal authority to place the child for adoption (either by consent or by a placement order) any advertisement cannot boldly state that the child is available for adoption.

- Where a final care order has been made and the court has expressly approved the local authority's plan for adoption, but a placement order has not yet been made, it is more likely that the court will look favourably on an application to advertise the child for adoption, without having to look for unusual or exceptional circumstances.

- In any case where the court has yet to approve the adoption plan the court is likely to require sight of the precise words that are to be used in the advertisement to describe the child's status at that time.

- An application generally 'to publicise' the child as available for adoption is likely to be seen as too widely drawn. Where the local authority wishes to advertise other than in other specialist adoption publications, the court is likely to require clarity as to the identity or type of other publications that are to be approached. Where publication is proposed in the ordinary national or local media, the organs of which are much less likely to apply the strict criteria described by *Be My Parent* (see **7.84**), the court should be shown the precise terms of the full advertisement that is proposed.

- As a matter of common sense, and based upon the submissions made in this case, an advertisement which is anonymous and/or does not contain a photograph of the child, is much less likely to attract a positive response. In most cases the court should consider either granting permission for a full advertisement which identifies the child and carries a photograph, or refusing to give permission at all rather than sanctioning an anonymous advertisement.

7.84 In *Royal Borough of Kensington and Chelsea v K and Q*[105] Hollings J gave guidance in cases where leave to advertise through the medium of television was being sought. The court should have regard to whether the maker of the programme is retaining an advisor who is experienced in finding adoptive and foster homes. If leave is granted, the agency will continue to have the responsibility to ensure that it remains in the best interests of the child to appear in the programme and should normally ensure that the agency is to withdraw permission for the child to appear at any time prior to transmission.

The Adoption Register

7.85 The Adoption and Children Act Register for England and Wales[106] is currently operated under contract by the British Association for Adoption and Fostering (BAAF) and comprises a computer-based database holding information of children awaiting adoption and prospective adopters awaiting a match.

7.86 In line with statutory guidance,[107] authorities refer approved prospective adopters to the Register 3 months after they have been approved as being suitable to adopt. They should also refer those children who have a plan for adoption but where there is not already a link identified locally which is being actively pursued. The children should be referred at the latest by 3 months after the agency has formally decided that adoption is in the child's best interest and either a full care order with a plan for adoption has been made, or there is an interim care order and all required consents, including that of the Court, have been obtained, or the child is accommodated and the consent of those with parental responsibility has been obtained.

7.87 The statutory guidance does not extend to voluntary societies who voluntarily refer prospective adopters immediately upon approval.

7.88 As soon as a new child is referred, a search is conducted and a list of potential links is compiled. The system searches on the basis of a number of pre-defined characteristics which the child has against which adopters would

---

[105] [1989] 1 FLR 399.
[106] Established under ACA 2002, s 125.
[107] LAC(2004)27.

'accept' or 'consider'. Once the list has been compiled, the computer operators will look at the family case records and will select the five best links to send on to the child's social worker for consideration. The process is then handled by that social worker.[108]

Be My Parent

7.89 *Be My Parent* is a family-finding service for children in the UK, provided by BAAF. It has a family-finding website and a monthly full-colour newspaper which feature children of all ages and backgrounds, from babies to teenagers – all looking for a family to adopt or foster them. Families and agencies can look at some of the children's profiles without having to subscribe. In order to read more, search all the children and make enquiries, families need to register their details online and subscribe.[109]

7.90 In *Re R (Identification: Restriction on Publication)*[110] the parents of four children who were subject to placement orders operated two websites containing the names and photographs of the children, warning that the children had been taken from them wrongly and that no one should attempt to adopt them. Sumner J granted an injunction preventing them publishing the names, addresses, photographs or video recordings of their children who were subject to placement orders or any other information which would lead to their identification or establishing they were in care.

PREPARATION AND COUNSELLING

The child

7.91 Where an adoption agency is considering adoption for a child it must set up a case record ('the child's case record') containing the information specified in AAR 2005, reg 12(1).[111]

7.92 It must also, unless it is satisfied that that this has been carried out by another adoption agency, so far as is reasonably practicable:

- provide a counselling service for the child;

- explain to the child in an appropriate manner the procedure in relation to, and the legal implications of, adoption for the child and provide him with appropriate written information about these matters; and

---

[108] *A Review of the Independent Review Mechanism and Adoption Register* DfES Research Report DCSF-RW044 (2008) at paras 119–206. The Report contains a review of the first 5 years of the operation of the Register. See also *Adoption Register for England and Wales: Guidance for Social Workers* BAAF http://www.adoptionregister.org.uk/files/agencies/guidance_sw.pdf.

[109] http://www.bemyparent.org.uk. See also *Re K (Adoption: Permission to Advertise)* [2007] EWHC 544 Fam, [2007] 2 FLR 326 at [12]–[15].

[110] [2007] EWHC 2742 (Fam), [2008] 1 FLR 1252.

[111] AAR 2005, reg 12(1).

- ascertain the child's wishes and feelings regarding:
  - the possibility of placement for adoption with a new family and his adoption;
  - his religious and cultural upbringing; and
  - contact with his parent or guardian or other relative or with any other person the agency considers relevant.[112]

7.93   The Guidance[113] provides that:

> 'Counselling should help a child – subject to age, background and development – to understand over time what adoption would mean for him or her now and in the longer term. The child should be helped to understand why the agency considers they should not stay with their own family or short term current carer and why adoption is the preferred option for their permanence. He or she also needs to know about the implications adoption may have for contact with their parent, other family members and others.'

The child's parents or guardian

7.94   Where an adoption agency is considering adoption for a child it must, unless it is satisfied that this has been carried out by another adoption agency, so far as is reasonably practicable:

(a)   provide a counselling service for the parent or guardian of the child;

(b)   explain to him:
  (i)   the procedure in relation to both placement for adoption and adoption;
  (ii)   the legal implications of:
    (aa) giving consent to placement for adoption under s 19 of the Act;
    (bb) giving consent to the making of a future adoption order under s 20 of the Act; and
    (cc) a placement order; and
  (iii)   the legal implications of adoption,
    and provide him with written information about these matters; and

(c)   ascertain the wishes and feelings of the parent or guardian of the child and, of any other person the agency considers relevant, regarding:
  (i)   the child;
  (ii)   the placement of the child for adoption and his adoption, including any wishes and feelings about the child's religious and cultural upbringing; and
  (iii)   contact with the child if the child is authorised to be placed for adoption or the child is adopted.[114]

---

[112]   AAR 2005, reg 13.
[113]   op cit at 2.13.
[114]   AAR 2005, reg 14(1).

7.95 If the father of the child does not have parental responsibility for the child and his identity is known to the adoption agency, the agency must, unless it is satisfied that this has been carried out by another adoption agency, if is satisfied it is appropriate to do so:

- carry out in respect of the father the requirements of paras (1)(a), (b)(i) and (iii) of AAR 2005, reg 14; and

- ascertain so far as possible whether the father:
    – wishes to acquire parental responsibility for the child under s 4 of the 1989 Act; or
    – intends to apply for a residence order or contact order with respect to the child under s 8 of that Act or, where the child is subject to a care order, a contact order under s 34 of the 1989 Act.[115]

7.96 For the Guidance on these provisions, see **3.77**.

Potential adopters

7.97 Where an adoption agency is considering a person's suitability to adopt a child, the agency must, unless it is satisfied that the requirements set out below have been carried out by another adoption agency:

(a) provide a counselling service for the prospective adopter;

(b) in a s 83 case, explain to the prospective adopter the procedure in relation to, and the legal implications of, adopting a child from the country from which the prospective adopter wishes to adopt;

(c) in any other case, explain to him the procedure in relation to, and the legal implications of, placement for adoption and adoption; and

(d) provide him with written information about the matters referred to in para (b) or, as the case may be, (c).[116]

7.98 Where the adoption agency receives an application in writing in the form provided by the agency from a prospective adopter for an assessment of his suitability to adopt a child, the agency must set up a case record[117] in respect of that prospective adopter ('the prospective adopter's case record') and consider his suitability to adopt a child.[118]

7.99 The Guidance[119] provides detailed advice on what information and counselling should be provided including enabling potential adopters to

---

[115] AAR 2005, reg 14(3), (4).
[116] Ibid, reg 21.
[117] Containing the information specified in ibid, reg 22(3).
[118] Ibid, reg 22.
[119] op cit at paras 3.6–3.16.

consider whether they would wish to adopt a child and to reflect on the parenting needs of children the agency has placed for adoption or of children who need adoption, their own expectations of adoption and the consequences for them and their family of caring for and adopting a child who will probably have a range of complex needs.

ASSESSMENT OF THE CHILD AND POTENTIAL ADOPTERS

7.100 The assessment of the child and potential adopters is considered in Chapter 8. Detailed information must be obtained about the child[120] and the proposed adopters[121] and police checks must be carried out on the prospective adopters and members of their household.[122]

THE ADOPTION PANEL

7.101 An agency can place a child for adoption only if the conditions set out in s 18 or 19 are satisfied (see **3.1**).

7.102 In addition, the agency must be satisfied about three matters:

- that the agency is satisfied that the child ought to be placed for adoption;[123]

- that the prospective adopter is suitable to adopt a child;[124] and

- that the child should be placed with the particular prospective adopter.[125]

7.103 Before it can be satisfied about any of these three matters, the suitability of the child, the adopter and the placement must be considered by an adoption panel and the agency must consider the panel's recommendation before reaching a decision (see **7.113**, **7.127** and **7.155**).[126] However, where an adoption agency ('agency A') intends to refer a proposed placement to its adoption panel and another agency ('agency B') has already decided that the child should be placed for adoption or the prospective adopter is suitable to be an adoptive parent, agency A may refer the proposed placement to the adoption panel if it has consulted agency B about the proposed placement.[127]

---

[120] AAR 2005, reg 15. See **8.9**.
[121] Ibid, reg 22. See **8.97**.
[122] Ibid, reg 23. See **8.93**.
[123] ACA 2002, s 18(2).
[124] Ibid, ss 19(1), 21(1), AAR 2005, reg 27(1).
[125] AAR 2005, reg 33(1).
[126] Ibid, reg 19(1) (child), reg 27(7) (prospective adopter), reg 33(1) (placement).
[127] Ibid, reg 31(7).

SHOULD THE CHILD BE PLACED FOR ADOPTION?

7.104   The adoption panel must consider the case of every child referred to it by the adoption agency and make a recommendation to the agency as to whether the child should be placed for adoption.[128]

Documents for the panel

7.105   The adoption agency must send:

- the child's permanence report;[129]

- if the agency's medical adviser advises it should do so, the child's health report and any other reports referred to in AAR 2005, reg 15;[130] and

- the information relating to the health of each of the child's natural parents,

to the adoption panel.[131]

7.106   The adoption agency must also obtain and send to the panel, so far as is reasonably practicable, any other relevant information which may be requested by the panel.[132]

7.107   In addition to the documents prescribed by the Regulations, the panel must also be supplied with all relevant information including expert reports or an accurate summary of such reports[133] and the views of the child's guardian in any proceedings.[134] In *Re B (Placement Order)*[135] Wall LJ described the following suggestions as 'eminently sensible'.

- Expert reports which have been filed and served in care proceedings and which address the present and future needs of the subject child (including, but not exclusively, dealing with placement issues) should be provided to members of an adoption panel in advance of the relevant meeting and to decision makers for pre-reading.

---

[128]   AAR 2005, reg 18(1).
[129]   See ibid, reg 17(1) and **8.91**.
[130]   See **8.88**.
[131]   Ibid, reg 17(2).
[132]   Ibid, reg 17(4).
[133]   *Re B (Placement Order)* [2008] EWCA Civ 835, [2008] 2 FLR 1404 at [81].
[134]   *R v North Yorkshire CC ex p M (No 2)* [1989] 2 FLR 79 at 81; *Re R (Adoption: Disclosure)* [1999] 2 FLR 1123.
[135]   [2008] EWCA Civ 835, [2008] 2 FLR 1404 at [81].

- Where such reports are voluminous, as a minimum those sections of the reports setting out the experts' opinion, conclusions and/or recommendations should be provided in advance to the members of the panel and to the decision maker.

- A summary of the expert(s)' opinions should only be provided to the panel members and the decision maker in substitution for the reports if:
  - the summary is in writing;
  - all parties to the care proceedings agree in writing that the summary is fair and accurate and should be provided to the panel and the decision maker in substitution for the reports; and
  - copies of the reports are available at the meeting for the members of the panel and the decision maker to consult if desired.

- A clear, full and accurate minute of the panel meeting should be made during the meeting with particular attention given to:
  - recording the documentation considered by the members of the panel; and
  - the questions asked by members of the panel and the answers given by the social worker(s) present; and
  - the social workers who attend the panel meeting to present the child's case should be invited to approve the record of the note of the questions asked of and answers given by them during the meeting.

7.108 In *R v Wokingham DC ex p J*[136] the High Court held that while it is desirable that an adoption panel should allow short written representations from parents, such an approach was not essential to the fairness of the entire adoption proceedings. Under the current regulations, the reports to the panel will include the views of the parents[137] but this does preclude the parents being allowed to make their views known in their own words.

7.109 In *Re B (Placement Order)*[138] the authority failed to provide the panel with paediatric, child psychiatric and psychological reports, one of which had indicated that the children had responded well to foster care and stated that it was not possible to be prescriptive about contact arrangements. The summary of the reports which was given to the panel mistakenly misrepresented that adoption had been recommended. Despite misgivings because of the delay which would result, the order was set aside and the application adjourned for the matter to be considered properly by the panel.

7.110 Although the views of the guardian should be made to the panel, the guardian is not entitled to insist on attending the panel meeting.[139]

---

[136] [1999] 2 FLR 1136.

[137] AAR 2005, reg 17(1)(d).

[138] *Re B (Placement Order)* [2008] EWCA Civ 835, [2008] 2 FLR 1404.

[139] *R v North Yorkshire CC ex p M (No 2)* [1989] 2 FLR 79, *Re R (Adoption: Disclosure)* [1999] 2 FLR 1123.

The recommendation

7.111 In considering what recommendation to make the panel must have regard to the duties imposed on the agency under s 1(2), (4), (5) and (6) of the Act (see **6.6**) and:

- must consider and take into account the reports and any other information passed to it in accordance with reg 17 (see **7.105**);

- may request the agency to obtain any other relevant information which the panel considers necessary; and

- must obtain legal advice in relation to the case.[140]

7.112 Where the panel makes a recommendation to the agency that the child should be placed for adoption, it must consider and may at the same time give advice to the agency about:

- the arrangements which the agency proposes to make for allowing any person contact with the child; and

- where the agency is a local authority, whether an application should be made by the authority for a placement order in respect of the child.[141]

Taking the decision

7.113 The adoption agency must take into account the recommendation of the adoption panel in coming to a decision about whether the child should be placed for adoption.[142] In *Re P-B (Placement Order)*[143] Arden LJ said that reg 19 clearly imposes a substantive duty to take account of the recommendation of the adoption panel.

> 'It is not enough to pay lip service to the recommendation of the adoption panel. On the other hand the duty is only one to take account. Thus it must be open in theory at least for an adoption agency to reach a different view from the recommendation of the adoption panel, but I anticipate that the local authority would have to have strong grounds for doing so.'[144]

7.114 In *R (AT, TT and S) v Newham LBC*[145] the Administrative Court considered the matter further in relation to prospective adopters:

> '[If] an independent review panel [see **7.160**] rationally concludes that e.g. it is reassured relating to corporal punishment, it seems to me that a decision-maker is

---

[140] AAR 2005, reg 18(2).
[141] Ibid, reg 18(3).
[142] Ibid, reg 19(1).
[143] [2006] EWCA Civ 1016, [2007] 1 FLR 1106.
[144] Ibid at [38].
[145] [2008] EWHC 2640 (Admin), [2009] 1 FLR 311.

in dangerous territory if she later concludes that the answers given by the [prospective adopters to the Panel were] "not sufficiently robust" ... she simply has not met the weight of the IRM panel's reasoning head on and dealt with it by giving clear and cogent reasons for rejecting it.'[146]

7.115 Additional guidance was given by the Court of Appeal in *Re B (Placement Order)*:[147]

'It is imperative that the decision to ratify the [Panel's] decision ... must never be a simple rubber stamp. The circumstances in which the decision is taken should be transparent, and the decision itself minuted. In my judgment, the manner in which the decision was taken in the instant case was unsatisfactory: it was a rubber stamp imposed by the Director of Social Services, who had no real knowledge of the case and who made the decision on the basis of the inaccurate information provided to the Panel. Whilst it may well be that in practice the decision to take proceedings for a placement order will be made by an individual rather than a group, the source and substance of the information given to the decision maker must be clear, and both the decision itself and the reasons for it minuted.'

7.116 Where the decision maker or the court detects a procedural error in the panel's recommendation, for example, their not being provided with all the relevant information, the matter should be re-referred to the panel for reconsideration.[148]

7.117 The agency must, notify its decision in writing to the parent or guardian if their whereabouts are known to the agency, and, where reg 14(3) applies (see **7.90**) and the agency considers it is appropriate, the father of the child.[149]

7.118 Where the parent or guardian of the child resides in England and Wales and is prepared to consent to the placement of the child for adoption under ACA 2002, s 19 and, as the case may be, give advanced consent to the making of a future adoption order under s 20 (see **3.91**), the agency must request CAFCASS to appoint an officer of the Service or the National Assembly for Wales to appoint a Welsh family proceedings officer for the purposes of the signification by that officer of the consent to placement or to adoption by that parent or guardian[150] and send with that request the information specified in Sch 2 to the Regulations.[151]

---

[146] Per Bennett J at [69] and [71].
[147] [2008] EWCA Civ 835, [2008] 2 FLR 1404 per Wall LJ at [82].
[148] Ibid, at [69], [73]–[74], [99].
[149] AAR 2005, reg 19(3).
[150] Ibid, reg 20(1).
[151] Ibid, reg 20(2).

APPROVING THE PROSPECTIVE ADOPTER

7.119 The adoption panel must consider the case of the prospective adopter referred to it by the adoption agency and make a recommendation to the agency as to whether the prospective adopter is suitable to adopt a child.[152]

Documents for the panel

7.120 The agency must send to the panel:

- the prospective adopter's report and the prospective adopter's observations;[153]

- a written report from a registered medical practitioner about the health of the prospective adopter following a full examination which must include matters specified in Part 2 of Sch 4 to the Regulations unless the agency has received advice from its medical adviser that such an examination and report is unnecessary;

- a written report of each of the interviews with the persons nominated by the prospective adopter to provide personal references for him; and

- any other relevant information obtained by the agency.

7.121 The agency must obtain and send to the panel, so far as is reasonably practicable, any other relevant information which may be required by the panel and send that information to the panel.[154]

The recommendation

7.122 In considering what recommendation to make, the panel:

- must consider and take into account all the information and reports passed to it in accordance with AAR 2005, reg 25;

- may request the adoption agency to obtain any other relevant information which the panel considers necessary; and

- may obtain legal advice as it considers necessary in relation to the case.[155]

7.123 The panel does not have to apply the s 1 welfare test.[156]

---

[152] AAR 2005, reg 26(1).
[153] See ibid, reg 25 and **8.102**.
[154] Ibid, reg 25(10).
[155] Ibid, reg 26(2).
[156] *R (AT, TT and S) v Newham LBC* [2008] EWHC 2640 (Admin), [2009] 1 FLR 311 at [39].

7.124 Before making any recommendation, the panel must invite the prospective adopters to attend a meeting of the panel.[157] The Guidance[158] recommends that the panel should make it clear that the purpose of the meeting is to provide an opportunity for both the panel and the prospective adopter to discuss and clarify the prospective adopter's reasons for wishing to adopt, and any other matter that either party considers relevant to the application. The invitation should also make it clear that the prospective adopters are under no obligation to meet the panel. If they decline the invitation this in itself should never be considered as a reason for recommending that they are unsuitable to adopt. The agency should also provide the prospective adopter with advice, as appropriate, about the meeting, including information about how it will be conducted.

7.125 Where the agency has not received all the information required under AAR 2005, reg 25 but is of the opinion that the prospective adopter is unlikely to be considered suitable to adopt a child and makes a report to that effect,[159] the panel must either request the agency to obtain further information or recommend that the prospective adopter is not suitable to adopt a child.[160]

7.126 Where the panel recommends to the adoption agency that the prospective adopter is suitable to adopt a child, the panel may consider and give advice to the agency about the number of children the prospective adopter may be suitable to adopt, their age range, sex, likely needs and background.

Taking the decision

7.127 The agency must make a decision about whether the prospective adopter is suitable to adopt a child.[161] Presumably the agency has to take into account the views expressed by the panel.

7.128 The Guidance[162] recommends that before reaching a decision on the panel's recommendation the agency decision maker should consider the minutes of the panel meeting and the reports submitted to the panel that considered the prospective adopter's application and made the recommendation. In reading the minutes of the meeting, he or she should have particular regard to the panel's reasons for making the recommendation and any particular concerns that are recorded in the minutes. See also **7.113**.

7.129 Where the agency decides to approve the prospective adopter as suitable to adopt a child, it must notify him in writing of its decision.[163]

---

[157] AAR 2005, reg 26(4).
[158] Op cit at paras 3.61–3.62.
[159] Under AAR 2005, reg 25(7).
[160] Ibid, reg 26(2A).
[161] Ibid, reg 27(1).
[162] Op cit at para 3.67.
[163] AAR 2005, reg 27(2).

7.130   Where the agency considers that the prospective adopter is not suitable to adopt a child, it must:

- notify the prospective adopter in writing that it proposes not to approve him as suitable to adopt a child ('qualifying determination');

- send with that notification its reasons together with a copy of the recommendation of the panel if that recommendation is different;

- advise the prospective adopter that within 40 working days beginning with the date on which the notification was sent he may:
    - submit any representations he wishes to make to the agency; or
    - apply to the Secretary of State for a review by an independent review panel of the qualifying determination.

7.131   For the procedure if the prospective adopter seeks a review, see **7.158**.

7.132   If, within the period of 40 working days of the notification the prospective adopter has not made any representations or applied to the Secretary of State for a review under the Independent Review Mechanism ('IRM') (see **7.160**), the agency must proceed to make its decision and has to notify the prospective adopter in writing of its decision together with the reasons for that decision.[164]

7.133   If the prospective adopter seeks a review, after any review has concluded the agency must make its decision having taken into account the further views of the agency panel or, as it may be, the views of the review panel under the IRM.[165] As soon as possible after making this decision, the agency must notify the prospective adopter in writing of its decision stating its reasons for that decision if they do not consider the prospective adopter suitable to adopt a child, and of the adoption panel's further recommendation if this is different from the agency's decision.[166] If the review was conducted under the IRM, a copy of the decision has also to be sent to the Secretary of State.[167]

Reviewing/terminating the decision

7.134   Where the prospective adopter has been approved as suitable to adopt a child, the agency will be trying to match them with a child and the adoption social worker should maintain contact with the prospective adopter and keep them informed of progress. However, the agency may not always be aware that the circumstances of the prospective adopter are changing or have changed. This could arise where:

- a couple separates;

---

[164]   AAR 2005, reg 27(6).
[165]   Ibid, reg 27(8).
[166]   Ibid, reg 27(9).
[167]   Ibid, reg 27(10).

- the prospective adopter becomes pregnant or has given birth to a child;

- there are substantive changes in their health or their economic circumstances;

- concerns are raised about child welfare and safety;

- any other matters arise which may affect their suitability to adopt.[168]

7.135 The Regulations therefore provide that the agency must review the approval of each prospective adopter whenever the agency considers it necessary but otherwise not more than 1 year after approval and thereafter at intervals of not more than a year[169] unless:

- in a case where a child is being brought into the country for the purpose of being adopted here (see **4.46** and **4.75**), the prospective adopter has visited the child in the country in which the child is habitually resident and has confirmed in writing that he wishes to proceed with the adoption; and

- in any other case, a child is placed for adoption with the prospective adopter or the agency is considering placing a child with him.[170]

7.136 When undertaking such a review the agency must:

- make such enquiries and obtain such information as it considers necessary in order to review whether the prospective adopter continues to be suitable to adopt a child; and

- seek and take into account the views of the prospective adopter.[171]

7.137 If at the conclusion of the review, the agency considers that the prospective adopter may no longer be suitable to adopt a child, it must:

- prepare a written report ('the prospective adopter's review report') which shall include the agency's reasons;

- notify the prospective adopter that his case is to be referred to the adoption panel; and

- give him a copy of the report inviting him to send any observations to the agency within 10 working days beginning with the date on which that report is given to him.[172]

---

[168] Guidance op cit at para 3.80.
[169] AAR 2005, reg 29(2).
[170] Ibid, reg 29(1).
[171] Ibid, reg 29(3).
[172] Ibid, reg 29(4).

7.138 At the end of the 10-day period (or earlier if the prospective adopter's comments are received before that period has expired), the agency must send the prospective adopter's review report together with the prospective adopter's observations to the panel.

7.139 The agency must obtain, so far as is reasonably practicable, any other relevant information which may be required by the panel and send that information to the panel. The panel must consider the prospective adopter's review report, the prospective adopter's observations and any other information passed to it by the agency and make a recommendation to the agency as to whether the prospective adopter continues to be suitable to adopt a child.[173]

7.140 The agency must make a decision as to whether the prospective adopter continues to be suitable to adopt a child and AAR 2005, reg 27(2)–(10) (see **7.129**) applies in relation to that decision by the agency.[174] This includes the right of the prospective adopter to request a review of any proposed decision to terminate his approval (see **7.158**).

MATCHING

Background

7.141 When attempting to match a child with prospective adopters, an agency will usually look first to its own pool of approved adopters but those which cover a small geographical area may wish to place a child outside its own area in order to avoid accidental meetings with the child's birth family.[175] If they have to go outside their own area or have no suitable matches of their own, they will look to other authorities or societies. 'To resist doing so could risk subsequent placement breakdown because ... corners are cut, the needs of the child minimized and the adopters' skills may not be appropriate.'[176] They may also seek unapproved prospective adopters (see **7.73**).

7.142 When possibly suitable adopters are identified ('linked') usually the *prospective adopters'* social worker will contact them about a child, giving only a general description. If on the strength of that they are interested, the *child's* social worker will visit them and provide more information to help them decide if they wish to proceed further. If they do, a plan for an introduction to the child will be made. The prospective adopters will become more involved with the child's social worker and carer and may meet other professionals. However, as Lowe and Murch[177] note, there are many variations in this process which will

---

[173] AAR 2005, reg 29(7).
[174] Ibid, reg 29(8).
[175] Lowe and Murch *Supporting Adoption: Reframing the Approach* (BAAF, 1999) at p 161.
[176] Ibid.
[177] Ibid, at p 169.

be influenced by a number of factors including the age and needs of the child. More than one set of prospective adopters may be being considered.

7.143 Matching a child with prospective adopters – at its most basic, matching the needs of the child with the ability of the prospective adopters to meet those needs – is one of the most difficult tasks for agencies but it is surprising that, other than for trans-racial placements (see **6.137**), there is no statutory or Departmental guidance other than:

> 'Where the agency is considering the placement of a child for adoption it may identify a number of possible prospective adopters. It needs to compare their potential to provide a stable and permanent family for the child, based on the child's permanence report, the prospective adopter's report and other information it has collected and assessed.'[178]

7.144 Based on their study of a number of local authorities and societies,[179] Lowe and Murch offer a number of recommendations including the following.

- Agencies should not be bound by rigid views about, for example, the age and marital status of those they recruit which might preclude consideration of those with much to offer.

- Agencies should be prepared to look outside their own pool of approved adopters in order to reduce the time the child waits for a permanent home. The longer the child waits, the stronger the attachment to the short-term carer may become and the more difficult the separation.

- The views of the child about what they want should be listened to. If they have become attached to their carers, they may wish to remain. However *Adoption Now: Messages from Research*[180] comments that if the needs of the child are to be met as closely as possible, the views of the child cannot be divorced from the capacities and expectations of prospective adopters.

- Before looking elsewhere, agencies should explore carers' views about the child moving. Are they interested in providing long term care and if so, might they be suitable?

- While 'same race' placements might be the ideal, consideration of a trans-racial placement should not be ruled out especially if the child has been waiting a long time. This is discussed in more detail at **6.103**.

- Foster carers may have the power to make or break the transition to an adoptive home. Their support means they will be more likely to prepare the child well and assist the prospective adopters. Prospective adopters will need support if they have to deal with obstructive carers.

---

[178] Guidance op cit at para 4.5.
[179] *Supporting Adoption: Reframing the Approach* op cit at ch 10.
[180] (Department of Health, 1999) at p 44.

- Adopters should be given all the available information about the child in order to help them make a considered decision. 'Agencies expect prospective adopters to be open and honest when they are assessed. They should be likewise with the adopters.'[181]

- Agencies should respect what adopters consider to be their limitations regarding the child in terms of age, gender, number and special needs. 'They should resist the temptation to bend and extend what the adopters can manage in order to place a child'.[182] Prospective adopters should know that not agreeing to be matched with a particular child does not preclude them from being considered for another child. *Adoption Now: Messages from Research*[183] adds that 'Placements that are made under a measure of duress and against the better judgment of adopters are best avoided.'

- Involving birth parents in selecting adopters can have both short and long-term benefits. It may help them come to terms with their loss, the adopters in the care of the child and the child in later life, knowing that they were involved. A meeting between the parents and the prospective adopters may be beneficial. See also **13.78**.

Pre-panel requirements of the agency

7.145 Where an agency is considering placing a child for adoption with a particular prospective adopter ('the proposed placement') the agency must:

- provide the prospective adopter with a copy of the child's permanence report and any other information the agency considers relevant;

- meet with the prospective adopter to discuss the proposed placement;

- ascertain the views of the prospective adopter about:
  - the proposed placement; and
  - the arrangements the agency proposes to make for allowing any person contact with the child; and

- provide a counselling service for, and any further information to, the prospective adopter as may be required.[184]

7.146 Where the agency considers that the proposed placement should proceed, the agency must:

---

[181]   Lowe and Murch op cit at p 190.
[182]   Ibid at p 189.
[183]   op cit at p 44.
[184]   AAR 2005, reg 31(1).

- where the agency is a local authority, carry out an assessment of the needs of the child and the prospective adopter and any children of the prospective adopter ('the adoptive family') for adoption support services (see Chapter 9);

- where the agency is a registered adoption society, notify the prospective adopter that he may request the local authority in whose area he has his home ('the relevant authority') to carry out an assessment of his needs for adoption support services and pass to the relevant authority, at their request, a copy of the child's permanence report and a copy of the prospective adopter's report;

- consider the arrangements for allowing any person contact with the child; and

- prepare a written report ('the adoption placement report') which shall include:
  (i)   the agency's reasons for proposing the placement;
  (ii)   the relevant information obtained by the agency;
  (iii) where the agency is a local authority, their proposals for the provision of adoption support services for the adoptive family;
  (iv)   the arrangements the agency proposes to make for allowing any person contact with the child; and
  (v)   any other relevant information.[185]

7.147 Where the agency remains of the view that the proposed placement should proceed it must notify the prospective adopter that the proposed placement is to be referred to the adoption panel and give him a copy of the adoption placement report, inviting him to send any observations in writing to the agency within 10 working days, beginning with the date on which the notification is sent.[186]

The panel

7.148 The adoption panel must consider the proposed placement referred to it by the adoption agency and make a recommendation to the agency as to whether the child should be placed for adoption with that particular prospective adopter.[187] The panel has to apply the s 1 welfare test.[188]

Documents for the panel

7.149 At the end of the period of 10 working days referred to in **7.147** (or earlier if observations are received before the 10 working days have expired) the agency must send to the panel:

---

[185] AAR 2005, reg 31(2).
[186] Ibid, reg 31(3).
[187] Ibid, reg 32(1).
[188] *R (AT, TT and S) v Newham LBC* [2008] EWHC 2640 (Admin), [2009] 1 FLR 311 at [39].

- the adoption placement report;

- the child's permanence report; and

- the prospective adopter's report and his observations.[189]

7.150   The agency must obtain so far as is reasonably practicable and send to the panel any other relevant information which may be requested by the adoption panel in connection with the proposed placement.[190]

The recommendation

7.151   In considering what recommendation to make, the panel has to have regard to the duties imposed on the agency under s 1(2), (4) and (5) of the Act (see **6.6**) and:

- must consider and take into account all information and the reports passed to it in accordance with AAR 2005, reg 31;

- may request the agency to obtain any other relevant information which the panel considers necessary; and

- may obtain legal advice as it considers necessary in relation to the case.[191]

7.152   The panel must consider:

- in a case where the agency is a local authority, the authority's proposals for the provision of adoption support services for the adoptive family;

- the arrangements the agency proposes to make for allowing any person contact with the child; and

- whether the parental responsibility of any parent or guardian or the prospective adopter should be restricted and if so the extent of any such restriction.[192]

7.153   Where the panel makes a recommendation to the agency that the child should be placed for adoption with the particular prospective adopter, the panel may at the same time give advice to the agency about any of the matters set out in AAR 2005, reg 32(3), for example, the need for support services, contact and whether parental responsibility post-placement should be restricted (see **7.195**).

---

[189]   AAR 2005, reg 31(4).
[190]   Ibid, reg 31(5).
[191]   Ibid, reg 32(2).
[192]   Ibid, reg 32(3).

7.154 A panel may only make the recommendation if:

- it is to be made at the same meeting of the panel at which a recommendation has been made that the child should be placed for adoption; or

- the agency, or another agency, has already made a decision that the child should be placed for adoption,

and in either case the recommendation is to be made at the same meeting of the panel at which a recommendation has been made that the prospective adopter is suitable to adopt a child or the agency, or another agency, has made a recommendation that the prospective adopter is suitable to adopt a child.[193]

Taking the decision

7.155 The agency must take into account the recommendation of the panel in coming to a decision about whether the child should be placed for adoption with the particular prospective adopter.[194] See also **7.113**.

7.156 As soon as possible after making its decision the agency must notify in writing the fact that the child is to be placed for adoption to:

- the prospective adopter of its decision; and

- if their whereabouts are known to the agency, the parent or guardian; and

- where AAR 2005, reg 14(3) applies (see **7.90**) and the agency considers it is appropriate, the father of the child.[195]

If the agency decides that the proposed placement should proceed, it must, in an appropriate manner and having regard to the child's age and understanding, explain its decision to the child.[196]

7.157 The agency must place on the child's case record:

- the prospective adopter's report;

- the adoption placement report and the prospective adopter's observations on that report;

- the written record of the proceedings of the adoption panel under AAR 2005, reg 32, its recommendation, the reasons for its recommendation and

---

[193] AAR 2005, reg 32(5).
[194] Ibid, reg 33(1).
[195] Ibid, reg 33(3). Presumably this applies only if the decision is taken to place the child with the prospective adopters.
[196] Ibid, reg 33(4).

any advice given by the panel to the agency; and the record and notification of the agency's decision under this regulation.[197]

CHALLENGING THE DECISIONS

Request for review

7.158 A prospective adopter may request a review of a proposed decision not to approve him as suitable to adopt a child (see **7.105**) or to terminate any approval under AAR 2005, reg 29(8). The request should be made within 40 working days of being notified.

7.159 If, within the period of 40 working days of the notification, the agency receives further representations from the prospective adopter, it may refer the case together with all the relevant information to the panel for further consideration.[198] The panel must then consider the case and make a fresh recommendation to the agency as to whether the prospective adopter is suitable to adopt a child.[199]

7.160 Alternatively the prospective adopter may apply under the IRM to the Secretary of State for a review by an independent panel.[200]

7.161 For a review of the operation of the IRM, see *A Review of the Independent Review Mechanism and Adoption Register*.[201]

7.162 For an illustration of the operation of the IRM, and how its recommendations should be treated by the decision maker, see *Guidance*[202] and *R (AT, TT and S) v Newham LBC*.[203]

Judicial review

7.163 A claim for judicial review may be brought in the Administrative Court to challenge the lawfulness of a decision, action or failure to act in relation to the exercise of 'a public function'.[204] There is no longer a requirement that the failure must be by a public body so long as the matter relates to a 'public function' which, given the public nature of adoption regulation, will cover decisions relating to adoption not only by a local authority but also a registered society.

---

[197] AAR 2005, reg 33(5). This is important not just for bureaucratic reasons but also to provide a record for the child when an adult.

[198] Ibid, reg 27(6).

[199] Ibid, reg 27(7).

[200] Ibid, reg 27.

[201] DfES Research Report DCSF-RW044 (2008).

[202] op cit Annex D and see **7.114**.

[203] [2008] EWHC 2640 (Admin), [2009] 1 FLR 311.

[204] Civil Procedure Rules 1998, Pt 54.1(2)(a)(ii).

7.164 The relief which may be granted includes:

- a mandatory order ie an order compelling the agency to act;

- a prohibiting order ie an order stopping the agency acting, for example, preventing a child being placed for adoption before the panel has considered the proposed placement;

- a quashing order ie an order nullifying the action, for example, stating that the child was not in law placed for adoption because the decision to place was invalid.

7.165 The grounds for challenging the decision include:

- Illegality.
  A decision is illegal if it:
  - contravenes the terms of the power which authorises the making of the power;
  - pursues an objective other than that for which the power was conferred;
  - is not authorised by any power;
  - contravenes or fails to implement a public duty.[205]

- It is procedurally unfair.
  This covers a broad variety of circumstances which vary according to the context in which the function is exercised. They can include a failure to give notice or refusal to receive representations and the right to be given reasons for the decision.[206]

- The manner of its exercise was unreasonable.[207]
  The well known *Wednesbury*[208] test ('so unreasonable that no reasonable decision maker could come to it') has been recast over the years, one suggested form of words being: 'My goodness, that is certainly wrong!'.[209] *De Smith's Judicial Review*[210] suggests that while the suggested tests give a flavour of the conduct which qualifies as being unreasonable, they are no more helpful than the *Wednesbury* test as a guide to its precise parameters. It is, however, conduct which the unbiased observer would recognise, if not at once, at least after a little thought.

---

[205] Woolf, Jowell and Le Sueur *De Smith's Judicial Review* (Sweet & Maxwell, 6th edn, 2007) at para 5-001 and chapter 5.

[206] Ibid, at para 7-001 and chapter 7.

[207] Ibid, at chapter 11.

[208] *Associated Provincial Picture Houses v Wednesbury Corporation* [1948] 1 KB 223.

[209] *Neale v Hereford and Worcester CC* [1986] ICR 471 per May LJ at 483, *R v Devon CC ex George* [1998] 3 WLR 49.

[210] op cit at p 554.

7.166 Applying these tests, judicial review might lie in relation to a decision by an agency to placing a child for adoption without the panel providing a recommendation (illegality), reaching a decision based on the advice of the medical adviser concerning the health of a prospective adopter without giving the person concerned an opportunity of commenting (unfairness) or refusing to place the child because of political intervention by a councillor (unreasonableness and possibly, illegality).

7.167 An application for permission to seek judicial review must be made 'promptly and in any event not more than 3 months after the claim arose'.[211] Parties may not extend the time by agreement.[212] Indeed, if anyone seeks to challenge the impropriety of any decision of the agency, whether in proceedings for judicial review or in some other way, they should do so immediately.[213]

7.168 It is well established that permission to bring a claim for judicial review will not be given unless the claimant has exhausted other possible remedies.[214] A prospective adopter who has not been approved is therefore unlikely to be granted permission if he has not sought a review under AAR 2005, reg 27 (see **7.158**).

7.169 In *Re C (Adoption, Religious Observance)*[215] a guardian was criticised for issuing proceedings for judicial review in order to challenge a decision by a local authority, contained in the child's care plan, to place a child of mixed background with Jewish, Irish Roman Catholic and Turkish-Cypriot Muslim elements with Jewish prospective adopters. The proper forum for the challenge was the care proceedings and the issue of judicial review proceedings had delayed the decision for over 6 months. 'I hope that no court is again required so painstakingly to consider the lawfulness of a decision when the real issue is as to whether it best serves the child's interests.'[216]

7.170 In *R (AT, TT and S) v Newham LBC*[217] the Administrative Court quashed a decision by a local authority not to approve a couple as suitable for adoption notwithstanding the recommendation of the IRM panel. The facts of the case show that a decision maker needs to have regard to the recommendations of the Panel and give them proper weight – see **7.114**.

> '[If] an independent review panel rationally concludes that e.g. it is reassured relating to corporal punishment, it seems to me that a decision-maker is in dangerous territory if she later concludes that the answers given by the [prospective adopters to the Panel were] "not sufficiently robust" ... she simply has

---

[211] CPR, r 54.5(1).
[212] CPR, Pt 55.4.
[213] *Re P (Adoption: Breach of Care Plan)* [2004] EWCA Civ 355 per Thorpe LJ at [20].
[214] *De Smith's Judicial Review* op cit para 3-041.
[215] [2002] 1 FLR 1119.
[216] Ibid, per Wilson J at [55].
[217] [2008] EWHC 2640 (Admin), [2009] 1 FLR 311.

not met the weight of the IRM panel's reasoning head on and dealt with it by giving clear and cogent reasons for rejecting it.'[218]

7.171 In *Re F (Placement Order)*[219] (see **3.51**) Wall LJ indicated that a decision to place a child for adoption while an application for leave to apply to revoke a placement order was pending would be susceptible to judicial review.

The Commission for Local Administration

7.172 The Commission for Local Administration ('the local ombudsman'), established by the Local Government Act 1974, can investigate actions of local authorities (not voluntary societies) relating to adoption.[220] Where an injustice has been caused by maladministration, it will seek a remedy that would, so far as possible, put the complainant back into the position he or she would have been in but for the fault. However, there will be many circumstances where this cannot be achieved because of the passage of time or of events which have occurred. In such cases financial compensation may be the only available approach. Remedies can include a recommendation that the local authority should apologise, make a payment in recognition of adverse effect, take action that should have been taken before, reconsider a decision that was not taken properly and improve procedures.[221] It cannot, however, compel a local authority to do any of these things.

7.173 In 2004, for example, the Commission found that there had been maladministration causing injustice when a local authority failed to inform Mr and Mrs B, who lived in Germany, that they had to be domiciled in the UK in order to become adoptive parents. It recommended that the authority reimburse the costs of £1,470 that the Bs incurred in attending preparation sessions for prospective adopters and pay them £3,500 compensation for the 'frustration, worry, outrage and the very considerable time and trouble' taken in pursuing their complaint. It further recommended that the authority review the way it handled social services complaints.[222]

Wardship

7.174 Wardship cannot be used to review the decisions of agencies, whether registered societies[223] or local authorities.[224]

---

[218] Per Bennett J at [69] and [71].
[219] [2008] EWCA Civ 439, [2008] 2 FLR 550 at [36].
[220] *Re A, Subpoena (Adoption: Commissioner for Local Administration)* [1996] 2 FLR 629.
[221] *Remedies: Guidance on Good Practice 6* (2005) The Commission for Local Administration http://www.lgo.org.uk.
[222] *London Borough of Lambeth* Complaint 04B08875.
[223] *Re W (A Minor)(Adoption Agency: Wardship)* [1990] 2 FLR 470.
[224] *A v Liverpool City Council* [1982] AC 363, (1981) 2 FLR 222, *Re C (Adoption: Notice)* [1999] 1 FLR 384.

AGENCY LIABILITY

7.175 There is no general duty of care owed by an agency or the staff whom it employs in relation to deciding what information is conveyed to prospective adopters. However, a negligent failure to comply with a specific duty of care, voluntarily accepted, is actionable.[225]

7.176 For example, if the agency has decided in general or in particular that certain information should be provided to the adopters, there is a duty to take reasonable care to ensure that the information is both given and received.[226] In *A v Essex County Council*[227] adoptive parents were awarded damages to be assessed for such injury, loss and damage they proved they suffered during the 14 months between a seriously disturbed child being placed with them for adoption and the adoption order being made. The authority had decided that the boy's Form E (giving his particulars) and a letter from their medical adviser describing the problems should be sent to the proposed adopters but these were not received. The adopters claimed that had they been given this information they would not have taken him on. As a result of his behaviour they alleged that they had suffered physical damage to their home and each had been physically assaulted on many occasions and suffered psychiatric injury. The court held, however, that they were not entitled to damages for the period post-adoption because they had proceeded to adopt him knowing about the problems.

7.177 A duty of care can also arise if the agency provides the prospective adopters with an undertaking requested by them, for example, not to disclose personal information to the birth family, and they negligently fail to honour the undertaking.[228]

'If the local authority fears that it may not be able to maintain that confidentiality; or reaches a stage where there may be good reasons for revealing the identity of the adopters; then the course that it should take is to discuss the implications of that with the potential adopters before the latter commit themselves ... And similarly, if the authority thinks that such an assurance on its part may not be of much use to the adopters because their names may become known from other sources ... then the implications of that must also be discussed with the potential adopters before any assurance is given. These considerations do not place an unreasonable burden on adoption agencies, because they do no more than hold the agency to what ought to be good practice. In the specific circumstances of this case, to hold the defendant liable when an express undertaking was asked for and given will not undermine the general system of adoption; and certainly should not have a chilling effect on the important activities of adoption agencies. If an agency is in the future asked to give such an undertaking it will have to decide whether it can prudently do so, balancing the possible liability accruing to it from a future

---

[225]   *A v Essex County Council* [2003] EWCA Civ 1848, [2004] 1 FLR 749 per Hale LJ at [47].
[226]   Ibid, at [59].
[227]   Ibid and [2002] EWHC 2707(QB), [2003] 1 FLR 615 at first instance.
[228]   *B and B v A County Council* [2006] EWCA Civ 1388, [2007] 1 FLR 1189 per Buxton LJ at [25] and [26].

breach of the undertaking against its interest in securing the adoption. It will also have to assess how certain it can be that its own agents will not carelessly breach the undertaking.'

7.178 In *B and B v A County Council*[229] such an undertaking was requested by the prospective adopters and given but the agency disclosed their name to the birth grandmother. One of its workers phoned her from the prospective adopters' home without taking precautions to prevent the call being traced and their surname was used in the presence of the birth mother. The trial judge found that there had been a breach of the local authority's general duty of care but dismissed the claim on the basis that there was no proof that the adopters had been the victims of a campaign of aggression and interference by the birth family. His findings were upheld by the Court of Appeal.

7.179 In *TCD v Harrow Council, Worcestershire County Council and Birmingham County Council*[230] a claim was brought by an adult who had been adopted against the first local authority on the ground that they had allowed a known sex offender to adopt her. He then abused her for 7 years. However, her claim was struck out under the Limitation Act 1980 on the ground that it had been commenced out of the time, the court declining to disapply the limitation period under s 33 because the claimant had been fixed with knowledge of the relevant acts or at least from the time she had achieved her majority, 19 years earlier. Because this was an interlocutory application, no decision was made as to whether or not a duty of care arose.[231]

PLACING THE CHILD

7.180 Where the agency has decided to place a child for adoption with a particular prospective adopter, it must hold a placement planning meeting with the prospective adopters to plan the proposed arrangements for the placement.[232] The Guidance[233] recommends that the agency should arrange for the child's social worker, the prospective adopter's social worker, the child's current carer and any relevant child specialists to attend the meeting with the prospective adopter. It may be helpful to involve the foster carer's social worker, if appropriate.

---

[229] [2006] EWCA Civ 1388, [2007] 1 FLR 1189.
[230] [2008] EWHC 3048 (QB), [2009] 1 FLR 719.
[231] See ibid, at [48]–[51].
[232] AAR 2005, reg 35(1)(b).
[233] Op cit at para 5.2.

The adoption placement plan

7.181 The agency must then, as soon as possible, prepare and send the prospective adopter and place on the child's case record an adoption placement plan in respect of the child which covers the matters specified in AAR 2005, Sch 5.[234]

7.182 These specified matters are:

- whether the child is placed under a placement order or with the consent of the parent or guardian;

- the arrangements for preparing the child and the prospective adopter for the placement;

- the date on which it is proposed to place the child for adoption with the prospective adopter. Where the child already has his home with the prospective adopter, the adoption agency must notify the prospective adopter in writing of the date on which the child is placed for adoption with him by that agency;[235]

- the arrangements for review of the placement;

- whether parental responsibility of the prospective adopter for the child is to be restricted, and if so, the extent to which it is to be restricted (see **7.195**);

- where the local authority has decided to provide adoption support services for the adoptive family, how these will be provided and by whom;

- the arrangements which the agency has made for allowing any person contact with the child, the form of contact, the arrangements for supporting contact and the name and contact details of the person responsible for facilitating the contact arrangements (if applicable);

- the dates on which the child's life story book and later life letter are to be passed by the adoption agency to the prospective adopter;

- details of any other arrangements that need to be made;

- details of how to contact the child's social worker, the prospective adopter's social worker and who to contact out of hours.

7.183 The agency must notify the prospective adopter in writing of any change to the adoption placement plan.[236]

---

[234] AAR 2005, reg 35(1), (2) and (8).
[235] Ibid, reg 35(5).
[236] Ibid, reg 35(7).

Requirements before the child can be placed

7.184   The agency may place the child for adoption – in the words of s 18(6), 'is authorised to place the child for adoption' – if:

- it has, following the decision of the panel, decided to do so;

- the adoption placement plan has been prepared and sent to the prospective adopters (see **7.181**);

- the requisite notifications under reg 35(6) have been sent (see **7.185**);

- if the child is over the age of 6 weeks it has the consent of all parents with parental responsibility and guardians (including special guardians[237]) and the consent has not been withdrawn[238] (see (**3.89**); or

- being a local authority, a placement order has been made in respect of the child and no application which has not been disposed of has been made to revoke the order.[239] If an application for leave to make such an application is pending it is normally good practice for a local authority either to agree not to place the child pending the application or at least give notice, say of 14 days, of the intended placement to the applicant so that he can either take steps to challenge the decision to place by way of judicial review or, probably more easily, to seek to expedite the hearing of the application for leave[240] (see **3.51**).

7.185   Before the child is placed for adoption the agency must:

- notify the prospective adopter's general practitioner and send with that notification a written report of the child's health history and current state of health;

- send to the local authority in whose area the prospective adopter has his home, written notification of the proposed placement; and

- where the child is of compulsory school age, send to the local education authority, in whose area the prospective adopter has his home, written notification of the proposed placement and information about the child's educational history and whether he has been or is likely to be assessed for special educational needs under the Education Act 1996.[241]

---

[237]   ACA 2002, s 144(1).
[238]   Ibid, ss 18(1), 19, 31(2).
[239]   Ibid, s 24(5).
[240]   *M v Warwickshire CC* [2007] EWCA Civ 1084 at [14].
[241]   AAR 2005, reg 35(6).

RIGHTS AND RESPONSIBILITIES IN RESPECT OF THE CHILD POST-PLACEMENT

7.186   There are two types of placement:

- Those made privately by handing the child to prospective adopters who are the child's parents, relatives or guardians of the child (or one of them is), or where the prospective adopter is the partner of a parent of the child or with the leave of the High Court[242] ('private placements') (see **7.23**).

- Those made by local authorities or registered societies ('agency placements').

7.187   The type of placement affects the rights and responsibilities in respect of the child until such time as an adoption order is granted or refused.

Private placements

7.188   The 2002 Act does not contain any provisions which change the child's status. The status of the child prior to the placement remains unchanged.

Parental responsibility

7.189   This remains with the parent(s) and any guardian.

Orders ceasing to have effect

7.190   All orders made under the Children Act 1989 continue to have effect.

Restrictions on orders which may be made

7.191   Applications under the Children Act 1989, for example, for a residence order, can continue to be made.

Supervision by the appropriate local authority

7.192   The prospective adopters must give notice of their intention to apply for an order to the appropriate authority, such notice to be given not more than 2 years or less than 3 months before the application is made.[243] The 'appropriate local authority' means the local authority for the area in which, at the time of

---

[242]   ACA 2002, s 92(3), (4).
[243]   Ibid, s 44.

giving notice of intention to adopt, they have their home[244] or, where they no longer have a home in England and Wales, the authority for the area in which they last had such a home.[245] See **2.75**.

7.193 On receipt of the notice of intention, the local authority must arrange for the investigation of the matter and submit a report of the investigation to the court.[246] See **8.62**.

Agency placements

7.194 In contrast, once an agency is authorised to place the child (see **3.1**) the rights and responsibilities change even if the child is not placed with prospective adopters.

Parental responsibility

7.195

- Parental responsibility is given to the agency[247] which may decide that the parental responsibility of a parent, guardian, special guardian or prospective adopter is restricted to the extent it may specify.[248]

- While the child is placed with prospective adopters, parental responsibility is given to them which is shared with the agency to the extent that it is not limited by the agency.[249]

- A guardian may not remove the child from the UK.[250]

See also **3.12**.

Orders ceasing to have effect

7.196

- All orders made under s 8 or 34(2) (contact order in respect of a child in care) or a supervision order under the 1989 Act cease to have effect.[251]

- Any care order ceases to have effect while the placement order is in force.[252]

---

[244] ACA 2002, s 44(9)(b).
[245] Ibid, s 44(9)(a), Local Authority (Adoption) (Miscellaneous Provisions) Regulations 2005, SI 2005/3390 reg 3.
[246] ACA 2002, s 44(5).
[247] Ibid, s 25(1)(b).
[248] Ibid, ss 25(4), 29(6).
[249] Ibid, s 25(3).
[250] Ibid, s 29(7)(b).
[251] Ibid, s 29 (1), (2).
[252] Ibid, s 29(1).

See also **3.13**.

Restrictions on orders which may be made

7.197

- No prohibited steps, specific issue, supervision or child assessment order may be made.[253]

- A residence order may be made only if an adoption application has been made and the application is made by a parent or guardian who has obtained leave to oppose an adoption order under ACA 2002, s 47(3) or (5) or by anyone who has obtained leave under s 29(5).[254]

- A special guardianship order may only be made if an application has been made for an adoption order and the person applying for the special guardianship order has obtained the leave of the court under s 29(5) or, if a guardian, has obtained leave under s 47(5).[255]

See also **3.14**.

Contact

7.198

- Any order for contact made under s 8[256] or 34(2)[257] of the Children Act 1989 ceases to have effect.

- The requirement imposed under s 34 of the 1989 Act on a local authority to allow parents, guardians and specified others reasonable contact with a child subject to a care order ceases to have effect.[258]

- No application for a section 8 contact order may be made.[259]

- Only specified persons people may apply for a contact order under s 26(3) of the 2002 Act.[260]

See **3.13**.

---

[253] ACA 2002, s 29(3).
[254] Ibid, s 29(5).
[255] Ibid, s 29(5). The applicant has to give notice of an intention to apply under s 14A(7) of the 1989 Act but not 3 months' notice – ACA 2002, s 29(6).
[256] Ibid, s 29(2).
[257] Ibid, s 26(1).
[258] Ibid, s 29(1).
[259] Ibid, s 26(2).
[260] Ibid, s 26(4).

7.199 Where an adoption agency decides that a child should be placed for adoption there is no statutory requirement to allow contact between the child and his birth family akin to that provided by s 34(1) of the 1989 Act. However the agency must consider what arrangements it should make for allowing any person contact with the child once the agency is authorised to place the child for adoption ('the contact arrangements').[261]

7.200 In doing this the agency must:

- take into account the wishes and feelings of the parent or guardian of the child and, where AAR 2005, reg 14(3) applies (see **7.95**) and the agency considers it is appropriate, the father of the child who does not have parental responsibility;

- take into account any advice given by the adoption panel in accordance with r 18(3) (see **7.53**); and

- have regard to the considerations set out in the welfare test and the checklist in ACA 2002, s 1.[262]

7.201 The agency must notify the following of the contact arrangements:

- the child, if the agency considers he is of sufficient age and understanding;

- if their whereabouts are known to the agency, the parent or guardian, and, where AAR 2005, reg 14(3) applies and the agency considers it is appropriate, the father of the child;

- any person in whose favour there was a provision for contact under the 1989 Act which ceased to have effect by virtue of s 26(1) of the Act; and

- any other person the agency considers relevant.[263]

7.202 Where the agency decides that the child should be placed for adoption with a particular prospective adopter, it must review the contact arrangements in light of the views of the prospective adopter and any advice given by the adoption panel in accordance with AAR 2005, reg 32(3).[264] If the agency proposes to make any change to the contact arrangements which affects any person mentioned in **7.201** it must seek the views of that person and take those views into account in deciding what arrangements it should make for allowing any person contact with the child while he is placed for adoption with the prospective adopter.[265]

---

[261] AAR 2005, reg 46(2).
[262] Ibid, reg 46(3).
[263] Ibid, reg 46(4).
[264] Ibid, reg 46(5).
[265] Ibid, reg 46(6).

7.203 The agency must set out the contact arrangements in the placement plan (see **7.81**) and keep the contact arrangements under review (see **7.202**).[266]

7.204 For a detailed discussion of contact and adoption, see Chapter 13.

The role of the agency

7.205 The child is treated as being 'looked after' by the agency[267] and Part 6 of AAR 2005 place certain requirements on the agency.

Review

7.206 Where the child is not placed for adoption the agency must carry out a review of the child's case:

- not more than 3 months after the date on which the agency first has authority to place; and

- thereafter not more than 6 months after the date of the previous review ('6 months review'), until the child is placed for adoption.[268]

7.207 Where the child is placed for adoption the agency must carry out a review of the child's case:

- not more than 4 weeks after the date on which the child is placed for adoption ('the first review');

- not more than 3 months after the first review; and

- thereafter not more than 6 months after the date of the previous review.

7.208 This obligation lasts until the child is returned to the agency by the prospective adopter or an adoption order is made.[269]

7.209 When carrying out a review the agency must consider each of the following matters:

- whether the agency remains satisfied that the child should be placed for adoption;

- the child's needs, welfare and development, and whether any changes need to be made to meet his needs or assist his development;

---

[266] AAR 2005, reg 46(7).
[267] ACA 2002, s 18(3).
[268] AAR 2005, reg 36(1).
[269] Ibid, reg 36(3).

- the existing arrangements for contact, and whether they should continue or be altered;

- where the child is placed for adoption, the arrangements in relation to the exercise of parental responsibility for the child, and whether they should continue or be altered;

- the arrangements for the provision of adoption support services for the adoptive family and whether there should be any re-assessment of the need for those services;

- in consultation with the appropriate agencies, the arrangements for assessing and meeting the child's health care and educational needs;

- the frequency of the reviews subject to the minimum requirements at **7.206**.[270]

7.210 The agency must also, so far as is reasonably practicable, ascertain the views of the following in relation to such of the matters set out at **7.209** as the agency considers appropriate:

- the child, having regard to his age and understanding;

- if the child is placed for adoption, the prospective adopter; and

- any other person the agency considers relevant.[271]

7.211 Where the child is subject to a placement order and has not been placed for adoption at the time of the first 6 months review, the local authority must at that review:

- establish why the child has not been placed for adoption and consider what further steps the authority should take in relation to the placement of the child for adoption; and

- consider whether it remains satisfied that the child should be placed for adoption.[272]

7.212 The agency must, so far as is reasonably practicable, notify:

- the child, where the agency considers he is of sufficient age and understanding;

- the prospective adopter; and

---

[270] AAR 2005, reg 36(5), (6).
[271] Ibid.
[272] Ibid, reg 36(7).

- any other person whom the agency considers relevant,

of the outcome of a review and of any decision taken by the agency in consequence of that review and ensure that details of the review are placed on the child's case record.[273]

Independent reviewing officer

7.213   An agency must appoint an independent reviewing officer[274] (IRO) to carry out the functions similar to those which an IRO would carry out if the child was being looked after (see **15.59**).[275]

7.214   The agency must inform the IRO of any significant failure to make the arrangements agreed at a review and any significant change in the child's circumstances after a review.[276]

Supervision by the agency

7.215   Where the child is placed for adoption the agency must:

- ensure that the child and the prospective adopter are visited within 1 week of the placement and thereafter at least once a week until the first review and thereafter at such frequency as the agency decides at each review;

- ensure that written reports are made of such visits; and

- provide such advice and assistance to the prospective adopter as the agency considers necessary.[277]

7.216   As Hale LJ pointed out in *A v Essex County Council*:[278]

'The purpose of the probationary period is for all concerned to test out the arrangement. Each side is free to withdraw at any time. It is just as important that prospective adopters are frank and forthcoming with the agency as it is that the agency is frank and forthcoming with them.'

7.217   The Guidance[279] notes that a placement is most likely to disrupt during the first few weeks so the agency should ensure that the child and the prospective adopter are visited within 1 week of the placement and at least once a week until the first review. The frequency of following visits is then to be decided by the agency at the first and each subsequent placement review.

---

[273]   AAR 2005, reg 36(8) and (9).
[274]   Ibid, reg 37(1).
[275]   Ibid, reg 37(1). The qualifications required of an IRO and his/her duties are set out in reg 37.
[276]   Ibid, reg 37(8).
[277]   Ibid, reg 36(4).
[278]   [2003] EWCA Civ 1848, [2004] 1 FLR 749 per Hale LJ at [69].
[279]   Op cit at para 5.15.

7.218 Visits should be shared wherever possible between the child's social worker and the prospective adopter's social worker and there should be clarity from the outset about which social worker will conduct each visit. Where the child is being placed outside the area of the placing agency and if the placing agency's social worker cannot visit the placement, the placing agency should make arrangements with another agency to ensure a child and family social worker visits the placement.[280]

7.219 As part of a visit, the visiting social worker should see the child without the prospective adopter being present, unless the child is of sufficient age and understanding and refuses to see the social worker alone.[281]

7.220 The social workers should write reports of their visits and share these with any other visiting social worker.[282]

7.221 The agency should provide such advice and assistance to the prospective adopter as the agency considers necessary.

Return of the child by the prospective adopters

7.222 Where a child is placed for adoption by an agency and the prospective adopters give notice to the agency of their wish to return the child, the agency must:

- receive the child from the prospective adopters before the end of the period of 7 days beginning with the giving of the notice; and

- give notice to any parent or guardian of the child of the prospective adopters' wish to return the child.[283]

7.223 When the child is returned, the agency must conduct a review of the child's case no earlier than 28 days, or later than 42 days, after the date on which the child is returned to the agency and when carrying out that review the agency must consider:

- whether it remains satisfied that the child should be placed for adoption;

- the child's needs, welfare and development, and whether any changes need to be made to meet his needs or assist his development;

- the existing arrangements for contact, and whether they should continue or be altered;

---

[280] Guidance, op cit, at paras 5.16–5.17.
[281] Ibid, at para 5.18.
[282] Ibid, at paras 5.15 and 5.16.
[283] ACA 2002, s 35(1).

- in consultation with the appropriate agencies, the arrangements for assessing and meeting the child's health care and educational needs.[284]

7.224 The Guidance[285] recommends that where a placement is disrupted the agency should provide support and counselling for the child and the prospective adopter before formally reviewing the case within the specified period. In addition, at the Review, it should also consider its own decisions and actions in the case.

REMOVING THE CHILD

7.225 The restrictions on the removal of a child from a home where he has been placed for adoption vary depending on whether the placement is a private or agency placement.

Private placement

7.226 Section 36 imposes restrictions which apply at any time when a child's home, whether or not the child in question is in England and Wales,[286] is with any persons ('the people concerned') with whom the child is not placed by an adoption agency[287] who:

- have applied for an adoption order in respect of the child and the application has not been disposed of;

- have given notice of intention to adopt unless the period of 4 months beginning with the giving of the notice has expired without the people concerned applying for an adoption order, or the notice is a second or subsequent notice of intention to adopt and was given during the period of 5 months beginning with the giving of the preceding notice;[288] or

- have applied for leave to apply for an adoption order under ACA 2002, s 42(6) and the application has not been disposed of.[289] If leave is granted, the application for leave is not to be treated as disposed of until the period of 3 days beginning with the granting of the leave has expired.[290]

---

[284] AAR 2005, reg 36(10).
[285] op cit at paras 5.26 and 5.28.
[286] ACA 2002, s 36(7).
[287] Including a child placed by a Scottish or Northern Irish adoption agency.
[288] ACA 2002, s 36(2).
[289] Ibid, s 36(1).
[290] Ibid, s 36(3).

7.227 A person may remove such child only in accordance with the following provisions contained in ACA 2002, ss 36–40.[291] However, this does not prevent the removal of a child who is arrested.[292]

7.228 If the persons concerned have applied for an adoption order in respect of the child and the application has not been disposed of, the child may be removed by:

- a person who has the court's leave;

- a local authority or other person in the exercise of a power conferred by any enactment, other than s 20(8) of the 1989 Act (removal by a person with parental responsibility from accommodation provided by a local authority).[293]

7.229 If the people concerned are not the child's local authority foster parents or a partner of the child's parent[294] and have given notice of intention to adopt, or have applied for leave to apply for adoption notwithstanding that the child has not lived with them for the prescribed period under ACA 2002, s 42(6) and the application has not been disposed of, the child may be removed by:

- a person who has the court's leave;

- a local authority or other person in the exercise of a power conferred by any enactment, other than s 20(8) of the 1989 Act.[295]

7.230 If the child's home is with local authority foster parents and he has his home with them at all times during the period of 5 years ending with the removal and the foster parents have given notice of intention to adopt, or an application has been made for leave to adopt under ACA 2002, s 42(6) and has not been disposed of, the child may be removed by the following persons:

- a person who has the court's leave;

- a local authority or other person in the exercise of a power conferred by any enactment, other than s 20(8) of the 1989 Act.[296]

7.231 If the five year period in **7.230** does not apply but the child has had his home with the local authority foster parents at all times during the period of 1 year ending with the removal, and the foster parents have given notice of intention to adopt, the child may be removed by:

---

[291] ACA 2002, s 36(1).
[292] Ibid, s 36(4).
[293] Ibid, s 37.
[294] Ibid.
[295] Ibid, s 40(1).
[296] Ibid, s 38(2).

- a person with parental responsibility for the child who is exercising the power in s 20(8) of the 1989 Act;

- a person who has the court's leave;

- a local authority or other person in the exercise of a power conferred by any enactment, other than s 20(8) of the 1989 Act.[297]

7.232   If the child's home is with a partner of his parent and has been for not less than 3 years (whether continuous or not) during the period of 5 years ending with the removal and the partner has given notice of intention to adopt, the child may be removed by:

- a person who has the court's leave;

- a local authority or other person in the exercise of a power conferred by any enactment, other than s 20(8) of the 1989 Act.[298]

7.233   If the 3-year period in **7.232** does not apply, the child may be removed from the partner by:

- a parent or guardian;

- a person who has the court's leave;

- a local authority or other person in the exercise of a power conferred by any enactment, other than s 20(8) of the 1989 Act.[299]

7.234   A person is the 'partner' of a child's parent if the person and the parent are a couple but the person is not the child's parent.[300]

Obligation to return

7.235   Where a parent or guardian may remove a child from the people concerned in accordance with the provisions of ACA 2002, ss 36–40, the people concerned must at the request of the parent or guardian return the child to the parent or guardian at once.[301]

Offence

7.236   A person who fails to return the child or who removes a child in contravention of ACA 2002, s 36 is guilty of an offence and liable on summary

---

[297]   ACA 2002, s 38(4).

[298]   Ibid, s 38(2).

[299]   Ibid, s 38(3).

[300]   Ibid, s 144(7).

[301]   Ibid, s 36(5).

conviction to imprisonment for a term not exceeding 3 months, or a fine not exceeding level 5 on the standard scale, or both.[302]

Agency placement

7.237 The restrictions on the removal of a child from a home vary depending on a number of circumstances including whether he has been placed for adoption and, if so, whether this is with the consent of his parents or guardian under ACA 2002, s 19 or under a placement order.

Removal where no placement order is in force

7.238 ACA 2002, s 30 imposes restrictions which apply at any time whether or not the child in question is in England and Wales[303] but they do not apply so as to prevent the removal:

- of a child who is arrested;[304]

- under a power conferred by any enactment other than s 20(8) of the 1989 Act.[305]

The child may therefore be removed under the authority of, an emergency protection order under CA 1989, s 44 or removal by the police under CA 1989, s 46.

7.239 Where a child who is not subject to a care order[306] and who is not for the time being placed for adoption is being provided with accommodation by a local authority, and the authority have applied to the court for a placement order and the application has not been disposed of, only a person who has the court's leave (or the authority) may remove the child from the accommodation.[307]

7.240 Where a child who is not for the time being placed for adoption is being provided with accommodation by an agency, and the agency is authorised to place the child for adoption under ACA 2002, s 19 or would be so authorised if any consent to placement under that section had not been withdrawn, a person (other than the agency) must not remove the child from the accommodation.[308]

7.241 Where a child is placed for adoption by an agency under ACA 2002, s 19, or is placed for adoption by an agency and either the child is less than 6

---

[302] ACA 2002, s 36(6).
[303] Ibid, s 30(5).
[304] Ibid, s 30(7).
[305] Ibid, s 30(6).
[306] Ibid, s 30(4).
[307] Ibid, s 30(2).
[308] Ibid, s 30(3).

weeks old or the agency has at no time been authorised to place the child for adoption, a person (other than the agency) must not remove the child from the prospective adopters.[309]

Offence

7.242 A person who removes a child in contravention of ACA 2002, s 30 is guilty of an offence and liable on summary conviction to imprisonment for a term not exceeding 3 months, or a fine not exceeding level 5 on the standard scale, or both.[310]

Removal where a placement order is in force

7.243 ACA 2002, s 34 imposes restrictions which apply at any time where a placement order in respect of a child is in force, or has been revoked, whether or not the child in question is in England and Wales[311] but they do not apply so as to prevent the removal of a child who is arrested.[312] Nor do they affect the exercise by any local authority or other person of a power conferred by any enactment, other than s 20(8) of the 1989 Act (see **7.238**).[313]

7.244 Where a placement order in respect of a child is in force, or has been revoked, but the child has not been returned by the prospective adopters or remains in any accommodation provided by the local authority, a person (other than the local authority) may not remove the child from the prospective adopters or from accommodation provided by the authority.[314]

7.245 Where a court revoking a placement order determines that the child is not to remain with any former prospective adopters with whom the child is placed, they must return the child to the local authority within the period determined by the court for the purpose.[315] The authority must return the child to the parent or guardian as soon as the child is returned to the authority or, where the child is in accommodation provided by the authority, at once.[316]

Offence

7.246 A person who removes a child in contravention of ACA 2002, s 34(1) under **7.244** or who fails to return a child under **7.245** is guilty of an offence and liable on summary conviction to imprisonment for a term not exceeding 3 months, or a fine not exceeding level 5 on the standard scale, or both.[317]

---

[309]   ACA 2002, s 31(1).
[310]   Ibid, s 30(8).
[311]   Ibid, s 34(8).
[312]   Ibid, s 34(7).
[313]   Ibid, s 34(6).
[314]   Ibid, s 34(1).
[315]   Ibid, s 34(3).
[316]   Ibid, s 34(4).
[317]   Ibid, s 34(2), (3), (5).

Recovery by parent where child not placed or is a baby

7.247 Where a child:

- who is not for the time being placed for adoption;

- is being provided with accommodation by an agency;

- the agency would be authorised to place him for adoption under ACA 2002, s 19 if consent to placement under that section had not been withdrawn; and

- any parent or guardian of the child informs the agency that he wishes the child to be returned to him,

the agency must return the child to him within the period of 7 days beginning with the request unless an application is, or has been, made for a placement order and the application has not been disposed of.[318]

7.248 Where:

- a child is placed for adoption by an agency; and

- either the child is less than 6 weeks old or the agency has at no time been authorised to place the child for adoption; and

- any parent or guardian of the child informs the agency that he wishes the child to be returned to him,

then, unless an application for a placement order is or has been made and it has not been disposed of, the agency must give notice of the parent's or guardian's wish to the prospective adopters who must return the child to the agency within the period of 7 days beginning with the day on which the notice is given.[319] As soon as a child is returned to the agency, the agency must return the child to the parent or guardian in question.[320]

Offence

7.249 A prospective adopter who fails to return the child is guilty of an offence and liable on summary conviction to imprisonment for a term not exceeding 3 months, or a fine not exceeding level 5 on the standard scale, or both.[321]

---

[318] ACA 2002, s 31(2).
[319] Ibid, s 31(4).
[320] Ibid, s 31(6).
[321] Ibid, s 31(5).

Recovery by parent where child placed and consent withdrawn

7.250 Where:

- a child is placed for adoption by an agency under ACA 2002, s 19;

- consent to placement under that section has been withdrawn; and

- a parent or guardian of the child informs the agency that he wishes the child to be returned to him,

then, unless an application for a placement order is or has been made and has not been disposed of, the agency must give notice of the parent's or guardian's wish to the prospective adopters, and the prospective adopters must return the child to the agency within the period of 14 days beginning with the day on which the notice is given.[322] However:

- if before the notice was given, an application for an adoption order,[323] special guardianship order or residence order, or for leave to apply for a special guardianship order or residence order, was made in respect of the child, and

- the application (and, in a case where leave is given on an application to apply for a special guardianship order or residence order, the application for the order) has not been disposed of,

the prospective adopters are not required by virtue of the notice to return the child to the agency unless the court so orders.[324]

7.251 As soon as a child is returned to an adoption agency under this section, the agency must return the child to the parent or guardian in question.[325]

Offence

7.252 A prospective adopter who fails to return the child is guilty of an offence and liable on summary conviction to imprisonment for a term not exceeding 3 months, or a fine not exceeding level 5 on the standard scale, or both.[326]

---

[322] ACA 2002, s 32(1)–(2).
[323] Including a Scottish or Northern Irish adoption order.
[324] ACA 2002, s 31(5).
[325] Ibid, s 32(4).
[326] Ibid, s 32(3).

Recovery by parent where child placed and placement order refused

7.253 Where:

- a child is placed for adoption by a local authority under ACA 2002, s 19;

- the authority have applied for a placement order;

- the application has been refused; and

- any parent or guardian of the child informs the authority that he wishes the child to be returned to him,

the prospective adopters must return the child to the authority on a date determined by the court.[327] As soon as a child is returned to the authority, they must return the child to the parent or guardian in question.[328]

Offence

7.254 A prospective adopter who fails to return the child is guilty of an offence and liable on summary conviction to imprisonment for a term not exceeding 3 months, or a fine not exceeding level 5 on the standard scale, or both.[329]

Removal by the agency

7.255 Where:

- a child is placed for adoption by an agency, whether or not the child in question is in England and Wales,[330]

- the agency is of the opinion that the child should not remain with the prospective adopters, and gives notice to them of its opinion;

the prospective adopters must, not later than the end of the period of 7 days beginning with the giving of the notice, return the child to the agency.[331] However:

- if before the notice was given, an application for an adoption order,[332] special guardianship order or residence order, or for leave to apply for a special guardianship order or residence order, was made in respect of the child, and

---

[327] ACA 2002, s 33(2).
[328] Ibid, s 33(4).
[329] Ibid, s 33(3).
[330] Ibid, s 35(6).
[331] Ibid, s 35(2).
[332] Including a Scottish or Northern Irish adoption order.

- the application (and, in a case where leave is given on an application to apply for a special guardianship order or residence order, the application for the order) has not been disposed of,

the prospective adopters are not required by virtue of the notice to return the child to the agency unless the court so orders.[333] The agency must also give notice to any parent or guardian of the child of the obligation of the prospective adopters to return the child.[334]

Offence

7.256 A prospective adopter who fails to return the child is guilty of an offence and liable on summary conviction to imprisonment for a term not exceeding 3 months, or a fine not exceeding level 5 on the standard scale, or both.[335]

Procedure

7.257 An application for permission to remove a child is made under Part 9 of the Family Procedure (Adoption) Rules 2005 (FP(A)R 2005) using form FP2.

7.258 If there are existing proceedings the parties to the application are the parties to those proceedings. If there are no existing proceedings, the parties are the local authority to whom notice of intention to adopt has been given and any other person as the court may direct.[336]

Recovery orders

7.259 Where it appears to the court that a child has been removed in contravention of any of the preceding provisions or that there are reasonable grounds for believing that a person intends to remove a child in contravention of those provisions, or that a person has failed to comply with ACA 2002, ss 31(4) (**7.248**), 32(2) (**7.250**), 33(2) (**7.253**), 34(3) (**7.245**) or 35(2) (**7.255**) it may, on the application of any person:

- direct any person who is in a position to do so to produce the child on request to any person named by the court, any constable or any person who, after the order is made under that subsection, is authorised to exercise any power under the order by an agency which is authorised to place the child for adoption;[337]

- authorise the removal of the child by any person mentioned above;

---

[333] ACA 2002, s 35(5).
[334] Ibid, s 35(3).
[335] Ibid, s 35(1), (4).
[336] FP(A)R 2005, r 86(4).
[337] ACA 2002, s 41(4).

- require any person who has information as to the child's whereabouts to disclose that information on request to any constable or officer of the court;

- authorise a constable to enter any premises specified in the order if it appears to the court that there are reasonable grounds for believing the child to be in them[338] and search for the child, using reasonable force if necessary.[339]

Offence

7.260 A person who intentionally obstructs a person exercising a power of removal conferred by the order is guilty of an offence and liable on summary conviction to a fine not exceeding level 3 on the standard scale.[340]

7.261 A person must comply with a request to disclose information as required by the order even if the information sought might constitute evidence that he had committed an offence.[341] But in criminal proceedings in which the person is charged with an offence (other than an offence under s 2 or 5 of the Perjury Act 1911 (false statements made on oath otherwise than in judicial proceedings or made otherwise than on oath) or an offence under s 44(1) or (2) of the Criminal Law (Consolidation) (Scotland) Act 1995 (false statements made on oath or otherwise than on oath[342]) no evidence relating to the information provided may be adduced, and no question relating to the information may be asked, by or on behalf of the prosecution, unless evidence relating to it is adduced, or a question relating to it is asked in the proceedings by or on behalf of the person.[343]

Procedure

7.262 Applications for recovery orders are made under Rule 107 of FP(A)R 2005 using form A57.

7.263 The parties are:

- if there are existing proceedings for placement orders or adoption orders or an order under ACA 2002, s 84 (for parental responsibility prior to adoption abroad) those who are parties to those proceedings;

- any agency authorised to place the child for adoption;

- any local authority to whom notice of intention to adopt has been given;

---

[338] ACA 2002, s 41(3).
[339] Ibid, s 41(2).
[340] Ibid, s 41(5).
[341] Ibid, s 41(6).
[342] Ibid, s 41(8).
[343] Ibid, s 41(7).

- any person who has parental responsibility for the child;

- any person in whose favour there is provision for contact;

- any person caring for the child immediately before the making of the application;

- any person whom the applicant alleges to have effected or to have been or to be responsible for taking or keeping the child.[344]

7.264 The application may be made without notice, in the High Court or county court, without permission being required or in a magistrates' court, with permission.[345]

---

[344] FP(A)R 2005, r 107(3).
[345] Ibid, r 107(1).

Chapter 8

ASSESSMENT – ADOPTION

INTRODUCTION

8.1 Detailed assessment of the needs and characteristics of the child being considered for adoption and of the capabilities and characteristics of adoption applicants is now central to the adoption process. The Adoption Agencies Regulations 2005 and Departmental Guidance endeavour to ensure that a high standard of uniform practice is adhered to nationally. Local authorities and adoption agencies take a leading role in carrying out assessments prior to placement and local authorities, supplemented by reports from guardians and occasionally expert reports and reports from CAFCASS, take a similar lead when reporting to courts on applications for placement orders and adoption orders. Assessment for adoption support services is dealt with at **9.51**.

BACKGROUND

8.2 The assessment of the suitability of those with whom children were placed for informal adoption prior to the Adoption of Children Act 1926 varied from the non-existent to the barely adequate. Baby farming with its high mortality rates was notorious for many years prior to a Committee Report in 1871.

> '[The] infant is ... moved [from the lying in establishment], generally immediately after birth to the worst class of baby farming houses ... Improper and insufficient food, opiates, drugs, crowded rooms, and air, want of cleanliness and wilful neglect are sure to be followed in a few months by diarrhoea, convulsions and wasting away.'[1]

8.3 After the First World War, assessments of prospective 'adopters' even by reputable Societies were still, by current standards, superficial. For example, the National Children's Home and Orphanage required applicants to complete a single page questionnaire asking, whether they abstained from alcohol and kept a domestic servant. They had to supply three references, one of which had to be provided by a church minister.[2]

---

[1] (1871) Protection of Infant Life Select Committee (372).
[2] Cretney *Family Law in the Twentieth Century* (Oxford University Press, 2003) at p 598.

8.4   Matters did not improve after the Adoption of Children Act 1926 created the concept of legal adoption. Most placements were arranged privately,[3] sometimes through advertisements. When adoption societies were involved, their work was unsupervised and uncontrolled and standards were extremely variable and sometimes haphazard.[4] The Adoption of Children (Regulation) Act 1939, based on the recommendations of the Horsburgh Committee[5] in 1937, gave the Secretary of State power to regulate societies and required placements for adoption made by 'third parties', ie not by parents or by local authorities to be notified to the relevant local authority. However, the Act did not come into force until 1943. In 1946 the Curtis Committee[6] drew attention to the need for careful assessment and supervision of prospective adopters. The Hurst Committee in 1954[7] repeated their advice, accepting evidence that adoptions arranged by trained and experienced social workers were much more likely to succeed than others. It noted that placement of the child was the crucial stage in the adoption process because once the child has been placed, much harm and unhappiness might result if a change has to be made. It also reported that there were cases where, on discovering that the child had serious physical or mental defects, the adopters wanted the adoption order revoked.[8]

8.5   The gradual development of good practice predated legislation. The Standing Conference of Societies Registered for Adoption, (now The British Association for Fostering and Adoption (BAAF)) was founded in 1951 and published its influential journal, *Child Adoption* (now, *Adoption and Fostering*) in the same year. Its Medical Group, formed in 1963, lead the way in focusing on the needs of the individual child. Legislation in the form of the Adoption Act 1975 caught up to some extent, resulting in the increasing involvement of social services departments and a decline in the number of voluntary societies, but it was not until the Adoption Agencies Regulations 1983 that a compulsory, detailed structure for assessment could be said to have been created.

The Prime Minister's Review

8.6   The Prime Minister's Review[9] in 2000 outlined a number of problems in the process of assessment, all of which resulted in delay (for which see **6.26**). Local authorities lacked 'grip' on the process. 'There is a very mixed picture as

---

3   In 1946 only 25% were arranged by Societies, the rest privately or by local authorities: *The Report on the Care of Children Committee ('The Curtis Report')*, Cmd 6922 (1946), para 449.
4   Heywood *Children in Care: The Development of the Service for the Deprived Child* (Routledge & Paul, 1978) at p 150.
5   *Departmental Committee on Adoption Societies and Agencies*, Cmd 5499 (1937).
6   Op cit, paras 448–459.
7   *Report of the Departmental Committee on the Adoption of Children*, Cmd 9248 (1954).
8   Ibid, paras 20, 43, 52, 139 summarised by Cretney, op cit, at pp 617, 620.
9   *Adoption* (PIU, 2000).

to whether Local Authorities track and manage the progress of their children through the process of matching, placement and adoption.'[10] There was an uneven quality of social work.

> 'Failure by social services to plan and assess properly and to explore fully and competently all the appropriate options to the child can often lead to [guardians] recommending to courts that additional work (eg. assessments and further attempts at rehabilitation) be carried out before Orders are granted.'[11]

8.7 A shortfall of suitable adopters was exacerbated by delays in assessing prospective adopters and matching them with children.[12]

8.8 The assessment process was a difficult one.

> '[Assessment] is a potentially difficult and sensitive area for all involved where trust on both sides is an important factor. Potential adopters, many of whom may have never come into contact with social workers, can feel a sense of powerlessness – being judged as to whether or not they meet an ideal of 'perfect parents'. Social workers, for their part, need to ensure that they have taken account of all the possible factors needed to inform the decision for approval.'[13]

8.9 The Prime Minister's Review found that there was very little information about how many applications failed before they reach the Adoption Panel stage, or for what reasons. Applicants might be rejected as a result of police checks, medicals or references. They might decide not to proceed, to pursue fertility treatment or they may become pregnant. They might drop out, as a result of the assessment process itself being perceived as being too intrusive or be 'counselled out' by social workers.[14] Of those that stayed the course, perhaps more than nine in ten (94%) would be recommended by the Adoption Panel for approval as adopters. Successful applicants were:

- predominately white couples;

- likely to be married – only 6% were single;

- early middle age – an average age at application of 37 when they applied;

- likely to be childless (74% unlikely to have children).[15]

---

[10] Prime Miniter's Review, op cit, para 3.51.
[11] Ibid, para 3.58.
[12] Ibid, para 3.70. In 1999, 2,200 children were adopted from care but over 2,400 were waiting for adopters.
[13] Ibid, para 3.89.
[14] Ibid, para 3.99.
[15] Not the experience of Lowe and Murch in their survey, *Supporting Adoption: Reframing the Approach* (1999) at p 111: 'A striking finding was just how many were already experienced parents.'

8.10 According to the Report there was some evidence that single applicants and older applicants are more likely to be turned down. A study of applications to voluntary adoption agencies revealed that of rejected applicants, 18% were single whilst single applicants accounted for only 6% of all successful applicants.[16]

8.11 The Report noted that, despite extensive media interest sparked by a relatively small number of cases, it was difficult to find consistent evidence about the degree to which unjustified discrimination, for example on the weight or smoking habits of applicants, applied. However, 'the lack of clarity and transparency in both the criteria and their application contributes to creating a climate of suspicion and mistrust which deters prospective adopters'.[17]

8.12 The Report made a number of recommendations.[18]

- New National Standards should be created to provide a more open, transparent and consistent system for recruitment and assessment which would encourage potential adopters to come forward and give them confidence in a fair assessment process. These should include appropriate evidence-based criteria for assessment of adopters.

- The assessment process should be reviewed to promote best practice and innovative approaches including those from recruitment processes in other fields, for example, employment.

- The assessment for 'second time round' adopters and foster carers should be streamlined with some accompanying safeguards regarding significant changes in circumstances and the length of time since the first assessment.

- An appeal mechanism for potential adopters should be required for all local authorities.

THE ASSESSMENT FRAMEWORK

8.13 The assessment framework for non-agency adoption cases remains the same as previously. The prospective adopter's local authority will prepare a report for the court (see **8.62**).

8.14 As regards adoptions of children placed by a local authority or agency, the Adoption Agencies Regulations 2005 make detailed provision for the assessment of the child and prospective adopters and their 'matching'. The procedure is discussed in Chapter 7 and the nature of the assessment in this

---

[16] Prime Minister's Review, paras 3.99–3.102.
[17] Ibid, para 3.106. See also Lowe, Murch et al *Supporting Adoption: Reframing the Approach* (1999), section 7.1.
[18] Prime Minister's Review, paras 5.5–5.9.

chapter. Where the child is being 'looked after'[19] by a local authority, the Arrangement for Placement of Children (General) Regulations 1991 and the Review of Children's Cases Regulations 1991 may also have to be considered.

8.15 In both categories of adoption, a report from the child's guardian will be filed in proceedings for a placement order or if the adoption is opposed (see **17.107**).

National Adoptions Standards for England

8.16 The following Standards under the National Adoptions Standards for England[20] are relevant.

'A1 Children whose birth family cannot provide them with a secure, stable and permanent home are entitled to have adoption considered for them ...

A2 Whenever plans for permanence are being considered, they will be made on the basis of the needs of each looked after child.

A3 The timescales below will be followed, taking account of the individual child's needs:

a) A match with suitable adoptive parents will be identified and approved by panel within 6 months of the agency agreeing that adoption is in the child's best interest;

b) In care proceedings, where the plan is adoption, a match with suitable adoptive parents will be identified and approved by panel within 6 months of the court's decision;

c) Where a parent has requested that a child aged under 6 months be placed for adoption, a match with suitable adoptive parents will be identified and approved by panel within 3 months of the agency agreeing that adoption is in the child's best interest.

A 4 Every child will have his or her wishes and feelings listened to, recorded and taken into account. Where they are not acted upon, the reasons for not doing so will be explained to the child and properly recorded.

A5 All children will have a named social worker who will be responsible for them throughout the adoption process.

A6 Children will be given clear explanations and information about adoption, covering what happens at each stage (including at court), and how long each stage is likely to take in their individual case.

A8 Children will be matched with families who can best meet their needs. They will not be left waiting indefinitely for a 'perfect family'.

A9 Every effort will be made to recruit sufficient adopters from diverse backgrounds, so that each child can be found an adoptive family within the timescales in 3) above, which best meets their needs, and in particular:

a) which reflects their ethnic origin, cultural background, religion and language;

b) which allows them to live with brothers and sisters unless this will not meet their individually assessed needs. Where this is the case, a clear explanation will be given to them and recorded.

---

[19] As defined in CA 1989, s 22(1).
[20] (Department of Health, 2002).

B 3   Written eligibility criteria and details of the assessment and approval process will be provided [to those interested in becoming adoptors].

    a)   Applicants will be considered in terms of their capacity to look after children in a safe and responsible way that meets their developmental needs. Where agencies have specific eligibility criteria e.g. because the agency has particular religious beliefs, applicants will be told what these are and, if necessary, be referred to another agency. People will not be automatically excluded on the grounds of age, health or other factors, except in the case of certain criminal convictions.

    b)   The assessment and approval process will be comprehensive, thorough and fair. An explanation will be given of the need for status checks and enquiries to be made about prospective adopters and members of their household.

B5   Foster carers who make a formal application to adopt children in their care will be entitled to the same information and preparation as other adopters and be assessed within four months.

B6   Applicants will be kept informed of progress throughout. They will receive a copy of the assessment report at least 28 days before an adoption panel and have the opportunity to comment on the report, and, if they wish, to attend the adoption panel and be heard.

B7   Prospective adopters will be informed of their right to make representations and complaints.'

8.17 Although some of the Standards are required either by primary legislation, regulation or statutory guidance, the rest do not have binding force. The following are requirements under s 7 of the Local Authority Social Services Act 1970:[21]

- A plan for permanence must be produced for all looked after children at the 4 month statutory review.

- Agencies must put in place systems to monitor their performance against the timescales set out in the Standards for matching children with adoptive families and taking a decision on prospective adopters.

The remaining Standards should be considered as good practice guidance. They are 'ambitious, and significant improvements in the adoption service will be needed over the coming years to meet them'.[22]

GUIDANCE ON ASSESSMENT

8.18 *Adoption Guidance*[23] ('Guidance') provides guidance on the process of assessing the child and the prospective adopters but not on the assessment itself.

---

[21]   See **12.22**.
[22]   National Adoption Standards for England, Introduction at p 5.
[23]   (Department for Education and Skills, 2006).

8.19 Guidance on the assessment of children is contained in *The Framework for the Assessment of Children In Need and their Families*[24] ('the Framework') which provides guidance on all assessments of children in need. In addition, *The Children Act 1989 Guidance and Regulations Volume 3 Family Placements*[25] ('the Children Act Guidance') deals specifically with the Arrangement for Placement of Children (General Regulations) and the other Regulations governing the care of 'looked after' children.

8.20 Guidance on the assessment of prospective adopters is provided by Departmental practice guidance, *Preparing and Assessing Prospective Adopters*[26] ('*Preparing and Assessing*').

8.21 Both the *Framework* and *Preparing and Assessing* will inform the preparation of the report to the court under s 44(5) (non-agency adoptions), s 43 (agency adoptions) and any report ordered under Family Procedure (Adoption) Rules 2005 (FP(A)R 2005),[27] r 24(3) (placement order).

8.22 *Preparing and Assessing*[28] points out that significant differences exist between assessing the capacity of birth parents and others to care for children already living with them and assessing the capacity of prospective adopters to care for children who, in most cases, may come to live with them in the future. Therefore the Framework should be applied to an adoption assessment as modified by *Preparing and Assessing*.

8.23 The Guidance and the Children Act Guidance are issued under s 7 of the Local Authority Services Act 1970.[29]

THE PROCESS OF ASSESSMENT

8.24 As the Prime Minister's Review noted,[30] the assessment process is a balance between exercising a judgement based on working closely with the families involved and operating criteria which are fair and objective.

Assessment of the child and the birth family

8.25 The Framework[31] discusses important principles which underpin the approach to assessments.

---

24 (Department of Health, Department for Education and Employment and the Home Office, 2000).

25 (Department of Health, 1991).

26 (Department for Education and Skills, 2006).

27 SI 2005/2795.

28 op cit at para 4.16.

29 For the statutory effect of such Guidance see **11.22**.

30 op cit at para 5.4.

31 op cit at para 1.33.

8.26 Assessments should

- be child centred;

- be rooted in child development;

- be ecological in their approach;

- ensure equality of opportunity;

- involve working with children and their family;

- build on strengths as well as identifying difficulties;

- be inter-agency in their approach to assessment and the provision of services;

- be a continuing process and not a single event;

- be carried out in parallel with other action and providing services;

- be grounded in evidence-based knowledge.

8.27 These principles are discussed in more detail at **10.37**.

Assessment of prospective adopters

What makes a good adopter?

8.28 The Prime Minister's Review[32] noted that there is little research available which informs the debate on what makes good adopters, the specific skills needed and whether these are significantly different from generally recognised parenting skills. Some factors have, however, been identified from studies as being important for successful placements:

- the new family has a child close in age to the child to be placed;

- adopters enjoy a challenge and enjoy spending time with children;

- the ability to understand and empathise with the child's early history.

8.29 Some studies showed that experienced and older parents are more successful; others show high success rates with younger childless couples. Some studies also showed that a very wide range of people – either single or couples – who have experienced difficulties or disabilities in their early lives, can be successful adopters.

---

[32] op cit at paras 103–105.

'Whilst the study evidence is not extensive, it does not suggest that there are any overriding factors which should exclude any particular group of people.'

8.30 A small sample survey of local authorities, specially commissioned for the Review, found a number of common criteria being used by authorities.

- Applicants should be fit and able to care for the child throughout their childhood.[33]

- Any marital or cohabiting relationship was of sufficient length to demonstrate stability and a minimum of 2–4 years was often given as a requirement.

- Children of less than 2/3 years of age or children with respiratory problems, would not be placed with people who smoke.

- Applicants should not be undergoing fertility treatment at the same time as applying to adopt a child.

- Applicants should live within the authority unless the application was for a particular child or children. The Report comments that this illustrates current local focus on recruitment, and the lack of perception of recruiting to provide a national pool of resources.

Assessing prospective adopters

8.31 The aims of the assessment are to:

- understand the **strengths and weaknesses** of the prospective adopter and to form a view of their capacity to adopt a child;

- identify areas where the prospective adopter will need **further development**, including the provision of **adoption support**, if they are approved;

- where the application concerns a couple, assess the **stability and permanence of their relationship**;

- **support and guide** the prospective adopter towards becoming an adoptive parent;

- prepare the prospective adopter's **report**, considering the information gathered during the assessment process, including evidence from enhanced CRB and other checks, references, reports, and from their preparation;

---

[33] For health and smokers, see Adoption Circular LAC(98)20 paras 46–47 – see Appendix 3.

- enable the practitioner to **recommend** to the adoption panel whether the prospective adopter is suitable to adopt.[34]

8.32 Information is central to informing the agency's decisions about the welfare of a child and the capacity of a prospective adopter. The assessment should be evidence based and requires the collection and consideration of information through careful discussion, listening, observation and exploration.[35]

8.33 Poor, incomplete or inaccurate information will lead to flawed decisions that could have serious consequences. Information and facts should be checked to establish the veracity of the prospective adopter and the information they provide. Their written and oral statements should be tested against documentary evidence where possible.[36]

8.34 Information should be analysed by the practitioner, not merely described. Assertions should be substantiated with supporting evidence.[37]

8.35 Personality testing is unlikely to receive judicial support.[38]

8.36 *Preparing and Assessing* states that research[39] into adoptive placements suggests a set of key criteria for assessing prospective adopters:

- ability to make and sustain close relationships;

- capacity for emotional openness;

- capacity for reflectiveness or 'psychological mindedness';

- successful resolution of earlier losses or traumatic experiences;

- for couples, the quality, stability and permanence of their relationship;

- support networks;

- tolerant social attitudes.[40]

Specific issues

8.37 *Preparing and Assessing* gives advice on how a number of commonly occurring issues should be approached.

---

[34]   *Preparing and Assessing* op cit at para 4.2.
[35]   Ibid, para 4.6.
[36]   Ibid, para 4.7.
[37]   Ibid, para 4.8.
[38]   *Re S (Care: Parenting Skills: Personality Tests)* [2004] EWCA Civ 1029, [2005] 2 FLR 658.
[39]   J Kaniuk et al *Adoption and Fostering* (BAAF, 2004) 28:2, at pp 61–67.
[40]   *Preparing and Assessing* at para 4.16.

Single people[41]

8.38 If the single prospective adopter does not have a relationship with a partner living elsewhere, the practitioner should explore their previous significant relationships to understand why they ended. To ensure that a prospective adopter is not seeking to meet their own needs purely through adoption, the practitioner should explore how they fulfil their need for companionship and emotional support.

8.39 The impact on the child of a future relationship should be explored as well as any significant relationship which the prospective adopter may have with a partner living elsewhere.

8.40 For adoption by single applicants, see also **2.50**.

Couples[42]

8.41 The assessment of the relationship of couples who live together should be the same whether they are married, civil partners or unmarried. The practitioner needs to establish whether their relationship is stable and permanent enough to withstand the stresses of adopting a child. The quality and strength of the relationship is more significant than its duration and agencies should avoid requiring couples to have lived together for a particular number of years before being able to apply. Setting a specific period of time may well be open to challenge and it is very difficult to define when a relationship starts.

Unmarried couples

8.42 In *Re P (Adoption: Unmarried Couple)*[43] the House of Lords discussed adoption by unmarried couples in the context of Northern Ireland legislation which forbade it.

'It is one thing to say that, in general terms, married couples are more likely to be suitable adoptive parents than unmarried ones. It is altogether another to say that one may rationally assume that no unmarried couple can be suitable adoptive parents. Such an irrebuttable presumption defies everyday experience ...'[44]

8.43 Such an irrebuttable presumption was in breach of Art 8 of the European Convention on Human Rights and Freedoms.

'There is clearly such a difference in treatment here. The unmarried couple are unable to gain legal recognition for the family life which they both enjoy with this child. The question is whether the difference in treatment can be justified ... If one

---

41   *Preparing and Assessing* at paras 5.43–5.44.
42   Ibid, at paras 5.45–50.
43   [2008] UKHL 38.
44   Per Lord Hoffmann at [18] and [20].

were only looking at this case from the point of view of a couple who could marry but chose not to do so, I would be inclined to say that the difference in treatment was not disproportionate ... But if one looks at this from the point of view of a child, whose best interests would be served by being adopted by this couple even if they remain unmarried, then the difference in treatment does indeed become disproportionate. At bottom the issue is whether the child should be deprived of the opportunity of having two legal parents. Whether in fact the would-be adopters prove suitable to adopt her is another matter. In my view, therefore, there is no longer an objective and reasonable justification for the "blanket ban" on joint adoption by unmarried couples.'[45]

8.44   *Preparing and Assessing* notes that while the core of the assessment of couples is the same there also need to be some differences. Unmarried couples, unless they are civil partners, have a different legal status in relation to each other for property and inheritance.[46] The implications of this need to be considered.

8.45   For adoption by unmarried couples, see also **2.49**.

Adoption by homosexual applicant/same-sex couples

8.46   Families comprising children and gay/lesbian parents/step-parents are no longer unusual[47] but adoption by a homosexual parent or couple remains a sensitive and delicate matter.[48] However, courts have long held that the sexual orientation of the applicant is not a bar to adoption.

'[An adoption application may be made] by a single applicant whether he or she at that time lives alone or cohabits in a heterosexual, homosexual or even an asexual relationship who it is proposed should fulfil a quasi-parental role towards a child. Any other conclusion would be illogical, arbitrary and inappropriately discriminatory in a context where the court's duty is to give first consideration [now, the paramount consideration] to the need to safeguard and promote the welfare of the child throughout his childhood.'[49]

8.47   Thus in *Re W (Adoption: Homosexual Adopter)*[50] an order freeing a girl for adoption with the intention that she should be adopted by her single, lesbian foster carer was made despite the objections of her mother.

---

[45]   Per Baroness Hale of Richmond at [108] and [112].

[46]   op cit at para 5.50.

[47]   *Ghaidan v Godin-Meddoza* [2004] UKHL 30, [2004] 2 FLR 600 per Baroness Hale at [158]. See also Smith 'Is Three a Crowd? Lesbian Mothers' Perspectives on Parental Status in Law' [2006] CFLQ 231.

[48]   Tasker and Bellamy 'Reviewing Lesbian and Gay Adoption and Foster Care: The Development Outcomes for Children' [2007] Fam Law 524 at p 529.

[49]   *Re W (Adoption: Homosexual Adopter)* [1997] 2 FLR 406 per Singer J at 413. *Re E (Adoption: Freeing Order)* [1995] 1 FLR 382 was a similar case where the Court of Appeal refused to overturn a freeing order.

[50]   Ibid.

8.48 States have a broad margin of appreciation when deciding whether to permit a child to be adopted by a homosexual applicant[51] but undue focusing on an applicant's sexual orientation to the exclusion of other relevant factors can amount to unlawful discrimination under Art 14 of the European Convention on Human Rights.[52]

8.49 The authors of a recent small study[53] suggests that the adoption process in England and Wales remains discriminatory and generally problematic for same-sex adopters with certain issues demonstrating a misalignment between theory and practice.

> 'By placing same-sex couples at the bottom of the pile when it comes to placement, the older/very damaged/severely disabled children may be placed with them and thus the likelihood of disruption is increased.'

8.50 A number of studies[54] have revealed no reason to suppose that making residence orders in favour of lesbian mothers will disadvantage children, by adversely affecting their mental state or by influencing their sex-role behaviour. Children of lesbian mothers were no more likely to be teased or bullied by their peers; they may be more likely to recall having been teased about being gay or lesbian themselves. There appears to be less academic comment or research concerning gay male adoptions and families.

8.51 *Fairness in Courts and Tribunals: A Summary of the Equal Treatment Bench Book,*[55] issued by the Judicial Studies Board, makes the following points.

- Lesbians or gay men still often experience unequal treatment in their daily lives.

- When dealing with apparent lack of candour, courts and tribunals should remember that being a lesbian or gay man is an individual experience that may have led to fear and concealment.

- Sexual orientation is just one of the many facets of a person's identity. Being a lesbian or gay man is sometimes described as being as much an emotional orientation as a sexual one.

---

[51] *Fretté v France* ECHR [2003] 2 FLR 9.

[52] *EB v France* ECHR [2008] 1 FLR 850.

[53] Hitchings and Sagar 'The Adoption and Children Act 2002: A Level Playing field for Same Sex Adopters?' [2007] CFLQ 60 at p 79.

[54] A summary of research is found in Tasker and Golombok 'Children Raised by Lesbian Mothers' [1991] Fam Law 184, Golombok 'Lesbian Mother Families' in Bainham, Sclater and Richards (ed) *What is a Parent?* (Murray, 1999), Murray 'Same-sex Families: Outcomes for Children and Parents' [2004] Fam Law 136, Tarker and Bellamy 'Reviewing Lesbian and Gay Adoption and Foster Care: The Development Outcomes for Children' [2007] Fam Law 524. See also Sifris 'The legal recognition of lesbian-led families: justifications for change' [2009] CFLQ 197.

[55] (2007) p 42.

- Nearly all lesbians and gay men were brought up in a heterosexual home.

- Objective mainstream research shows that children brought up by lesbian or gay parents do equally well as those brought up by heterosexual parents.

- Most lesbians and gay men feel that their sexual orientation was there from birth and is unalterable – just as most heterosexuals do.

- Some scientific research claims a genetic determinant for sexual orientation, suggesting that sexuality is not chosen.

- Parliament has now recognised that a same-sex couple can, as a matter of law, constitute an enduring family relationship.

- Gay couples are not the same as straight couples. Courts and tribunals should be careful not to judge same-sex relationships according to the principles of heterosexual married life. Families that do not conform to the traditional model are an increasingly common social reality.

8.52 *Preparing and Assessing*[56] comments that some types of couples may experience discrimination in their local community. The practitioner may need to help them understand how this could affect a child placed with them. For example, same sex couples should consider how they will explain their sexuality and their relationship to a child placed for adoption with them. They should be able to help the child feel at ease with their own sexuality as they grow through childhood and into adolescence.

8.53 For adoption by same-sex couples, see also **2.43**.

Local authority foster carers[57]

8.54 Where the local authority has previously assessed and approved foster carers, it will know much about them. However, they were assessed for a different caring role and their adoption assessment should consider anew their parenting capacities and skills for meeting the child's needs throughout their childhood and beyond. It may be necessary to arrange for a new medical report and if 2 years have elapsed since the foster carers had enhanced CRB checks, these will need to be renewed. New references will be needed as they are now being assessed as proposed adopters for a particular child.[58]

---

[56] op cit at para 5.50.

[57] *Preparing and Assessing* at paras 5.51–5.53.

[58] For an illustration of difficulties which have been faced by former foster-carers/second time adopters, see *R (AT, TT and S) v Newham LBC* [2008] EWHC 2640 (Admin), [2009] 1 FLR 311.

Infertility[59]

8.55 According to *Adoption Now, Messages from Research*[60] infertility is an important motive to adopt although less so than in the past. The process of being questioned about it is experienced as being particularly unwelcome.

8.56 *Preparing and Assessing* notes that a significant proportion of prospective adopters are infertile or make enquiries about adoption while they are still trying to conceive naturally or still undergoing treatment for assisted conception. Where prospective adopters are being assessed for infertility or receiving treatment, this should be disclosed and discussed fully. Experience suggests that following investigations and treatment that is unsuccessful, people need time to address their sense of loss before they are ready for adoption. Where treatment is successful, they may decide not to pursue adoption or to wait until their family life has adjusted to the new baby.

'It is widely recognised in adoption that applicants should not begin the process of being assessed as prospective adopters until any fertility treatment is complete and, if unsuccessful, they have come to terms with it.'

8.57 Individuals who wish to pursue fertility treatment at the same time as an application to adopt, should not be rejected out of hand on the basis of a blanket ban. However, the agency should explain to them why this is not in the interests of children and should be advised to wait until such time as their treatment is complete.

Diversity[61]

8.58 For a detailed discussion of the importance of ethnic and racial background, see **6.103**.

8.59 *Preparing and Assessing* advises that prospective adopters who are considering adopting children from a different ethnic or racial background to their own need to consider the effect on the child and demonstrate an awareness of the value of promoting self-esteem, providing knowledge and understanding of the child's background and proactively challenging discrimination. Living in a multi-racial and multi-ethnic community, where the intake of the local schools reflects this diversity may also help a child to feel more accepted in the community.

'While there are clearly benefits for a child placed with prospective adopters from the same ethnic or cultural group, this is not always possible and could lead to a prolonged delay in placing the child for adoption. The agency should strike a

---

[59] *Preparing and Assessing* at para 1.12.
[60] (Department of Health, 1999) at pp 36–37.
[61] *Preparing and Assessing*, at paras 7.12–7.15.

balance. Although the agency should consider the child's religious persuasion, racial origin and cultural and linguistic background, it should avoid undue delays that could harm the child's welfare.'

See also Adoption Circular LAC(98)20, paras 11–18 (Appendix 3).

Contact

8.60   For the importance of contact, see Chapter 13.

8.61   The views of prospective adopters concerning contact are an essential part of their assessment and should be explored. According to *Preparing and Assessing*,[62] many prospective adopters are uncertain and ambivalent about contact and find it difficult, especially if they associate the child's neglect or harm with the child's birth family. They should be made aware that the child's adoption plan will specify the proposed contact arrangements and that these are based on the child's assessed needs. Their anxieties about contact and reluctance to support it could motivate them to deny the significance of the child's past. The practitioner should decide whether such views might change with the help of further preparation. It needs to be borne in mind that for the first-time prospective adopter this is a theoretical discussion: their feelings and views will not be tested until a child is placed with them.

LOCAL AUTHORITY/AGENCY COURT REPORT

Adoption

8.62   An adoption order may not be made unless the court is satisfied that sufficient opportunities to see the child with the applicant, or, in the case of an application by a couple, both of them together, in the home environment has been given:

- where the child was placed with the applicants by an adoption agency, to that agency;

- in any other case, to the local authority in whose area the home is[63] (see **17.17**).

Child not placed for adoption by an agency

8.63   An adoption order cannot be made in respect of a child who was not placed for adoption with the applicants by an adoption agency unless the applicants have given notice of their intention to apply for an order to the appropriate authority, such notice to be given not more than 2 years or less

---

[62]   *Preparing and Assessing* at paras 5.31–5.40.
[63]   ACA 2002, s 42(7).

than 3 months before the application is made.[64] The 'appropriate local authority' means the local authority for the area in which, at the time of giving notice of intention to adopt, they have their home[65] or, where they no longer have a home in England and Wales, the authority for the area in which they last had such a home.[66] See **17.77**.

8.64 On receipt of the notice of intention, the local authority must arrange for the investigation of the matter and submit a report of the investigation to the court.[67]

Child placed for adoption by an agency

8.65 Where an application for an adoption order relates to a child placed for adoption by an adoption agency, the agency must:

- submit to the court a report on the suitability of the applicants and any other matter relevant to the operation of ACA 2002, s 1; and

- assist the court in any manner the court directs.[68]

Placement order

8.66 The court may direct an authority to file a report on the placement of a child for adoption.[69]

Other reports

8.67 The court may at any stage request a further report or ask the local authority or agency to assist the court in any other manner.[70]

Filing the reports

8.68 The adoption agency or local authority must file the report, which is confidential,[71] within the timetable fixed by the court.[72]

---

[64] ACA 2002, s 44.
[65] Ibid, s 44(9)(b).
[66] Ibid, s 44(9)(a); Local Authority (Adoption) (Miscellaneous Provisions) Regulations 2005, SI 2005/3390, reg 3.
[67] ACA 2002, s 44(5).
[68] Ibid, s 43.
[69] FP(A)R 2005, r 24(3).
[70] Ibid, r 29(4).
[71] Ibid, r 29(6).
[72] Ibid, r 2(1) and (2).

Content of the adoption report

8.69 The reports must cover the matters specified in Practice Direction Part 5C.[73]

Section A Part 2 Matters for the proceedings

- Who should be made a party in addition to the existing respondents.

- Whether any respondent is under the age of 18.

- Whether any respondent lacks capacity to take part in the proceedings and, if so, attaching medical evidence in particular in relation to the incapacity.

Section B Part 1 i) The child

- Specified information about matters including:
    - nationality, racial origin, cultural and linguistic background and religious persuasion;
    - personality and social development including emotional and behaviour needs;
    - health and any known learning difficulties or health factors likely to have or which may have genetic implications;
    - any special needs including educational needs;
    - history;
    - likes and dislikes;
    - inheritance rights and any claim under the fatal accidents act 1976 which the child stands to retain or lose if adopted;
    - any other relevant information which may assist the court.

Section B Part 1 ii) Information about birth parents

- Specified information about matters including:
    - photograph and physical description;
    - nationality, racial origin and cultural and linguistic background;
    - marriage/civil partnership history including whether they were married to each other at the time of the child's birth or subsequently;
    - if the parents were/are not married, whether the father has parental responsibility;
    - if the whereabouts or identity of the father are unknown, information about him and the steps that have been taken to establish paternity;
    - information about the parents' health and factors which may have genetic implications;
    - religious persuasion, educational and employment history, personality and interests;

---

[73]   FP(A)R 2005, r 29(3).

    –   any other relevant information which may assist the court.

Section B Part 2 Relationships, contact and the child's wishes and feelings

- Specified information about the child's wishes and feelings (if appropriate having regard to his age and understanding) about:
  - adoption, religious and cultural upbringing;
  - contact;

  and as recorded in any other proceedings and the date when the above wishes were last ascertained.

- Details of his past homes including foster homes.

- Specified information about the wishes and feelings of the birth parents about:
  - the placement, adoption and the child's religious and cultural upbringing;
  - contact;

  and the date when the above wishes were last ascertained.

- Arrangements and court proceedings concerning siblings, half-siblings and step-siblings.

- Extent of contact between the child and his parents and the nature of the relationship enjoyed.

- The relationship the child has with relatives and any other person considered relevant including the likelihood of such relationship continuing and the value to the child of its doing so.

- The ability and willingness of any of the child's relatives and any other person considered relevant to provide the child with a secure environment in which the child can develop or otherwise meet the child's needs.

- The wishes and feelings of the child's relatives and any other person considered relevant regarding the child.

- Whether the parents or members of the child's family have met or are likely to meet the proposed adopters and if they have met, the effect on all involved.

- Dates when the views of the wider family and any other person considered relevant were last ascertained.

Section B Part 3 A summary of the actions of the adoption agency in relation to the child and the birth parents

- Specified information about matters including:

- details of any consents to adoption;
- whether either parent has made a statement under s 20 that they do not wish to be informed of any application for adoption;
- details of the support and advice given to the parents;
- if the father does not have parental responsibility, details of the steps taken to inform him of the adoption application;
- brief details of the assessments of the child's needs;
- reasons for considering that adoption would be in the child's best interests.

Section C Part 1 Information about the prospective adopters including suitability to adopt

- Specified information about matters including:
  - photograph and physical description;
  - nationality, racial origin and cultural and linguistic background;
  - marriage/civil partnership history and status;
  - relationship if any to the child;
  - if married or civil partner is applying alone, the reasons for this;
  - previous experience of caring for children;
  - health;
  - assessment of ability and suitability to bring up the child;
  - income and living standards;
  - others in the household;
  - religious persuasion, educational and employment history, personality and interests;
  - confirmation that there are no convictions within the meaning of reg 23(3) of the Adoption Agencies Regulations 2005;
  - confirmation that the applicant is still approved;
  - confirmation that the referees have been interviewed with a report on their views and opinion of the weight to be placed on them;
  - details of other family court proceedings in which the prospective adopter has been involved.

Section C Part 2 The prospective adopter's wishes, views and contact arrangements

- Specified information about matters including:
  - whether the prospective adopter is willing to follow any wishes of the child or his parents regarding the child's religious and cultural upbringing;
  - the views of the prospective adopter's household and wider family about the adoption;
  - reasons for the prospective adopter wanting to adopt;
  - any hopes and expectations the proposed adopter has for the child's future;
  - the prospective adopter's wishes and feelings in relation to contact.

Section C Part 3 A summary of the actions of the adoption agency in relation to the proposed adopter

- Specified information about matters including:
    - the agency's proposals for contact;
    - the agency's opinion on the likely effect on the prospective adopter and the security of the placement of any proposed contact;
    - where the prospective adopter has been approved by an agency, the agency's reasons for considering that the proposed adopter is suitable to be the adoptive parent for the child.

Section D The Placement

- Specified information about matters including:
    - adoption support to be offered if any and, if not, the reasons for this;
    - summary of information gained from visits to the prospective adopter's home;
    - assessment of the child's integration within the adopter's family;
    - any other relevant information which may assist the court.

Section E Recommendations

- The agency's/authority's recommendations about:
    - the relative merits of adoption and other orders such as a residence or special guardianship order;
    - as to whether the order should be made and, if not, alternative proposals;
    - future contact arrangements, if any.

Content of the report in an application for a placement order

8.70 The report must cover the matters specified in Practice Direction Part 5C.[74]

8.71 These are the same as for an adoption order with the exception of Sections C, D and E.

8.72 In addition the report has to cover the following matters.

Section C Recommendations

- The agency's/authority's recommendations about:
    - the relative merits of a placement order and other orders such as a residence or special guardianship order;

---

[74]   FP(A)R 2005, r 29(3).

- an assessment of why the child's long term interests are likely to be best met by a placement order rather than any other order;
- future contact arrangements, if any, including whether a section 26 contact order should be made.

MEDICAL REPORTS

8.73 In the case of adoption, health reports on the child and the applicants must be attached to the application unless:

- the child was place for adoption by an agency;

- the applicant or one of the applicants is the child's parent;

- the applicant is a partner of the child's parent.[75]

8.74 The reports must contain prescribed information set out in Practice Direction 5D.[76]

8.75 The reports are confidential.[77]

GUARDIAN'S REPORT

8.76 The guardian in an application for an adoption or placement order must, unless the court directs otherwise, file a written report advising on the interests of the child.[78]

8.77 There are no prescribed contents.

8.78 The report is confidential.[79]

REPORTING OFFICER

8.79 In adoption or placement order proceedings, when a reporting officer has been appointed (see **17.112**), the officer must make a report to the court, in accordance with the timetable set by the court, on his investigations into the giving of the various consents or refusal to consent, drawing attention to any matter which in his opinion may be of assistance to the court.[80]

---

[75]   FP(A)R 2005, r 30(1).
[76]   Ibid, r 30(2).
[77]   Ibid, r 30(3).
[78]   Ibid, r 65(4).
[79]   Ibid, r 65(5).
[80]   Ibid, r 72(1).

8.80   The report is confidential.[81]

CHILDREN AND FAMILY REPORTER

8.81   In adoption or placement order proceedings the court may ask a children and family reporter to prepare a report on matters relating to the welfare of the child.

8.82   The report is confidential.[82]

8.83   Because the court will have detailed reports from the local authority or agency and, if the proceedings are opposed, from the guardian, such reports are rare.

EXPERT EVIDENCE

8.84   This is covered in detail at **10.53**.

LOCAL AUTHORITY/AGENCY ASSESSMENTS FOR THE PANEL

Assessment of the child

Information about the child

8.85   The agency must obtain so far as is reasonably practicable, the information about the child which is specified in Part 1 of Schedule 1 of the Adoption Agencies Regulations 2005.[83]

8.86   This information includes:

- a photograph and physical **description**;

- nationality, racial origin and cultural and linguistic background, religious persuasion (including details of baptism, confirmation or equivalent ceremonies);

- details of the child's **status** with a local authority and court orders;

- whether the child has any **rights** to, or interest in, property or any claim to damages under the Fatal Accidents Act 1976 or otherwise which he stands to retain or lose if he is adopted;

---

[81]   FP(A)R 2005, r 65(5).
[82]   Ibid, r 73(3).
[83]   Adoption Agencies Regulations 2005, SI 2005/389 (AAR 2005), reg 15(1).

- a **chronology** of the child's care since birth;

- a description of the child's **personality**, his social, emotional and behavioural **development;**

- whether the child has any difficulties with his personal care;

- the **educational history** of the child including whether he is subject to a statement of special educational **needs** under the Education Act 1996 and any special needs and where he is looked after, details of his personal education plan prepared by the local authority;

- information about:
  - the child's **relationship** with his parent or guardian, any siblings and any other person the agency considers relevant;
  - the likelihood of any such relationship continuing and the value to the child of its doing so;

- the **ability** and willingness of the child's **parent** or guardian or any other person the agency considers relevant, to **provide the child with a secure environment** in which he can develop, and otherwise to meet his needs;

- the current arrangements for **contact** between the child's parent or guardian or other person with parental responsibility for him, his father, and any relative, friend or other person;

- a description of the child's **interests, likes and dislikes**;

- any **other relevant information** which might assist the adoption panel and the adoption agency.

8.87 'Parent' includes the child's father whether or not he has parental responsibility for the child.[84]

Information about the child's health

8.88 The agency must arrange for the child to be examined by a medical practitioner, and obtain a report ('the child's health report') on the state of the child's health which shall include any treatment which the child is receiving, any need for health care and the matters specified in Part 2 of Schedule 1, unless the agency has received advice from the medical adviser that such an examination and report is unnecessary.[85] The agency must also make arrangements:

---

[84]   AAR 2005, Sch 1, Part 1, para 17.
[85]   Ibid, reg 15(2)(b).

- for such other medical and psychiatric examinations of, and other tests on, the child to be carried out as are recommended by the agency's medical adviser; and

- for written reports of such examinations and tests to be obtained,

unless the child is of sufficient understanding to make an informed decision and refuses to submit to the examinations or other tests.[86]

Information about the child's family

8.89 The agency must obtain, so far as is reasonably practicable, the information about the child's family which is specified in Part 3 of Sch 1.[87] 'Family' includes both parents, whether or not the father has parental responsibility,[88] siblings, other relatives and any other person the agency considers relevant.

- a photograph and physical **description**;

- nationality, racial origin and cultural and linguistic background, religious persuasion;

- a description of their **personality and interests**;

- if siblings are under the age of 18, details of where they are living, **local authority status**, **court orders** and whether they are considered **suitable for adoption**;

- **marital status and history** of the parents and whether the father has **parental responsibility** for the child;

- if the identity or whereabouts of the **child's father** are not known, the information about him that has been ascertained and from whom, and the steps that have been taken to establish paternity;

- so far as is possible, a **family tree** with details of the child's grandparents, parents and aunts and uncles with their age (or ages at death);

- where it is reasonably practicable, a **chronology of each parent** from birth;

- observations of the child's parents about their **own experiences of being parented** and how this has influenced them;

- the **past and present relationship** of the child's parents;

---

[86]   AAR 2005, reg 15(3), (4).
[87]   Ibid, reg 16(1).
[88]   Ibid, Sch 1, Part 3, para 29.

- details of the **wider family** and their role and importance to the parents, and siblings;

- information about their **home and neighbourhood**;

- details of the parents' educational and employment history;

- information about the parents' **parenting capacity** particularly their ability and willingness to parent the child;

- any **other relevant information** which might assist the adoption panel and the adoption agency.

Medical history of parents and siblings

8.90 The agency must obtain, so far as is reasonably practicable, the information about the health of each of the child's natural parents and his brothers and sisters (of the full blood or half-blood) which is specified in Part 4 of Sch 1.[89]

Permanence report

8.91 The adoption agency must prepare a written report ('the child's permanence report') which shall include:

- the information about the child and his family as specified above;

- a summary, written by the agency's medical adviser, of the state of the child's health, his health history and any need for health care which might arise in the future;

- the wishes and feelings of the child regarding:
    - the possibility of placement for adoption with a new family and his adoption;
    - his religious and cultural upbringing; and
    - contact with his parent or guardian or other relative or with any other person the agency considers relevant;[90]

- the wishes and feelings of the child's parent[91] or guardian regarding:
    - the child;
    - the placement of the child for adoption and his adoption, including any wishes and feelings about the child's religious and cultural upbringing; and

---

89   AAR 2005, reg 16(2).
90   ie matters covered in ibid, reg 13(1)(c).
91   Including the father who does not have parental responsibility if his identity is known to the adoption agency and the adoption agency is satisfied it is appropriate to do so – ibid, reg 14(3), (4).

- contact with the child if the child is authorised to be placed for adoption or adopted;

- the views of the agency about the child's need for contact with his parent or guardian or other relative or with any other person the agency considers relevant and the arrangements the agency proposes to make for allowing any person contact with the child;

- an assessment of the child's emotional and behavioural development and any related needs;

- an assessment of the parenting capacity of the child's parent or guardian and, where AAR, reg 14(4)(a) applies (see **7.90**), his father;

- a chronology of the decisions and actions taken by the agency with respect to the child;

- an analysis of the options for the future care of the child which have been considered by the agency and why placement for adoption is considered the preferred option; and

- any other information which the agency considers relevant.[92]

8.92 The Permanence Report, a report on the health of the birth parents and (so far as is reasonably practicable) any other information which may be requested by the adoption panel must be provided to the adoption panel.[93]

Assessment of the prospective adopters

Police checks

8.93 The agency must[94] take steps to obtain in respect of the prospective adopter and any other member of his household aged 18 or over an enhanced criminal record certificate.[95]

8.94 An agency may not consider a person suitable to adopt a child if he or any member of his household aged 18 or over:

- has been convicted of a specified offence committed at the age of 18 or over; or

- has been cautioned by a constable in respect of any such offence which, at the time the caution was given, he admitted.[96]

---

[92] AAR 2005, reg 17(1).
[93] Ibid, reg 18(2), (3).
[94] Ibid, reg 23(1) and (2).
[95] As defined by s 115 of the Police Act 1997 including the matters specified in subsection (6A).
[96] AAR 2005, reg 23(2).

8.95 'Specified offence' means:

- an offence against a child;[97]

- an offence specified in Part 1 of Sch 3 to AAR 2005;

- an offence contrary to s 170 of the Customs and Excise Management Act 1979 in relation to goods prohibited to be imported under s 42 of the Customs Consolidation Act 1876 (prohibitions and restrictions relating to pornography) (where the prohibited goods included indecent photographs of children under the age of 16);

- any other offence involving bodily injury to a child, other than an offence of common assault or battery.

8.96 In addition an agency may not consider a person suitable to adopt a child if he or any member of his household aged 18 or over:

- has been convicted of an offence specified in para 1 of Part 2 of Sch 3 to AAR 2005 committed at the age of 18 or over or has been cautioned by a constable in respect of any such offence which, at the time the caution was given, was admitted; or

- falls within para 2 or 3 of Part 2 of Sch 3,

notwithstanding that the statutory offences specified in Part 2 of Sch 3 have been repealed.[98]

Information

8.97 Where the agency, having provided the prospective adopter with information under reg 24, considers he may be suitable to adopt a child, it must obtain the information about the prospective adopter which is specified in Part 1 of Sch 4 to AAR 2005.

8.98 The specified information includes:

- A photograph and **physical description**.

- Whether the prospective adopter is **domiciled or habitually resident** (and if so, for how long) in a part of the British Islands and if habitually resident for how long he has been habitually resident.

---

[97] As defined by s 26(1) of Criminal Justice and Court Services Act 2000 except that it does not include an offence contrary to s 9 of the Sexual Offences Act 2003 (sexual activity with a child) in a case where the offender was under the age of 20 and the child was aged 13 or over at the time the offence was committed.

[98] AAR 2005, reg 25(4).

- Racial origin, cultural and linguistic background and religious persuasion.

- Relationship (if any) to the child.

- Description of his personality and interests.

- **Reasons for applying alone** for an assessment of his suitability to adopt if the prospective adopter is married or has formed a civil partnership.

- Details of any **previous family court proceedings** in which the prospective adopter has been involved.

- Past and present **marriage/civil partnership** status and other relationships.

- A **family tree** with details of the prospective adopter, his siblings and any children of the prospective adopter, with their ages (or ages at death).

- A **chronology** of the prospective adopter from birth.

- The observations of the prospective adopter about his **own experience of being parented** and how this has influenced him.

- Details of any **experience of caring for children** the prospective adopter has had and an assessment of his ability in this respect.

- Any other information which indicates how the prospective adopter and anybody else living in his household is likely to relate to a child placed for adoption with the prospective adopter.

- A description of the **wider family** of the prospective adopter and their role and importance to the prospective adopter and their likely role and importance to a child placed for adoption with the prospective adopter.

- Information about the prospective adopter's **home, neighbourhood and his integration** into the local community and social networks.

- Details of other members of the prospective adopter's **household** (including any children of the prospective adopter whether or not resident in the household).

- Details of the prospective adopter's **educational and employment history** and attainments.

- The **current employment** of the prospective adopter and his views about achieving a balance between employment and child care.

- Details of the prospective adopter's **income and expenditure**.

- Information about the prospective adopter's **capacity** to:
    - **provide for a child's needs**, particularly emotional and behavioural development needs;
    - **share a child's history** and associated emotional issues; and
    - **understand and support** a child through possible feelings of loss and trauma;

- The prospective adopter's:
    - **reasons** for wishing to adopt a child;
    - **views and feelings** about:
        - adoption and its significance;
        - his parenting capacity;
        - parental responsibility and what it means;
        - a suitable home environment for a child;
        - the importance and value of education;
        - the importance of a child's religious and cultural upbringing;
        - contact.

- The views of other members of the prospective adopter's household and wider family in relation to adoption.

- Any other relevant information which might assist the adoption panel or the agency.

Medical history

8.99 The agency must obtain a written report from a registered medical practitioner about the health of the prospective adopter following a full examination which must include matters specified in Part 2 of Sch 4 to AAR 2005 unless the agency has received advice from its medical adviser that such an examination and report is unnecessary.[99]

References

8.100 The agency must obtain a written report of each of the interviews with the persons nominated by the prospective adopter to provide personal references for him.[100]

8.101 The agency must ascertain whether the local authority in whose area the prospective adopter has his home have any information about the prospective adopter which may be relevant to the assessment and if so obtain from that authority a written report setting out that information.[101]

---

[99] AAR 2005, reg 25(3)(a).
[100] Ibid, reg 25(3)(b). Three referees must be provided – ibid, Sch 4, Part 1, para 10.
[101] Ibid, reg 25(4).

The prospective adopter's report

8.102 The agency must prepare a written report ('the prospective adopter's report') which shall include:

- the information about the prospective adopter and his family which is specified in **8.108**;

- a summary, written by the agency's medical adviser, of the state of health of the prospective adopter;

- any relevant information the agency obtains from the referees or other local authority;

- any observations of the agency on the matters referred to in the police checks;

- the agency's assessment of the prospective adopter's suitability to adopt a child; and

- any other information which the agency considers to be relevant.[102]

MATCHING

8.103 The process of matching the child with prospective adopters is described at **7.141**.

---

[102] AAR 2005, reg 25(5).

Chapter 9

SUPPORT – ADOPTION

INTRODUCTION

9.1   The promotion of adoption as a service for children in care who need permanent substitute families requires that adopters should receive such support and assistance as is necessary to enable them to meet the extraordinary needs of those children as well as assistance in adopting children with ordinary needs if the financial and other circumstances of the proposed adopters would otherwise preclude adoption.[1] The Adoption and Children Act 2002 (ACA 2002), the various Regulations and statutory guidance contain a detailed scheme for assessing needs and providing the necessary services both before and after the making of an adoption order. Some of the services, for example, financial support, are limited to adoptive parents of a child adopted through a local authority or voluntary adoption agency.

9.2   The Act also extends the ways in which an adopted adult person, his birth parents and other relatives can be given information about each other, perhaps with the aim of making contact.

BACKGROUND

9.3   The idea that support for the adopted child and the adopters can properly – and in some cases should – be provided has slowly taken root, developing in tandem with the changing nature of adoption. When the child being adopted was more likely than not a healthy baby, being adopted with the consent of his or her single mother, there was little need and great reluctance for financial and other support from the agency. The *Report of the Care of Children Committee* in 1946 ('the Curtis Committee')[2] contained no suggestion that adopters should receive any support. Although the numbers of children being adopted were increasing, according to one local authority there were many more would-be adopters than children. In addition there may have been an unspoken fear that payment to the adopters could mark a return to 'baby

---

[1]   See, for example Lowe 'The changing face of adoption – the gift/donation model versus the contract/services model' [1997] CFLQ 371 at p 383. See also **9.15**.

[2]   Cmd 6922.

farming'. In parallel with the reluctance to permit allowances, there was a view that upon the adoption order being made, the work of the authority or the agency ceased.[3]

9.4   By the time of the *Report of the Departmental Committee on the Adoption of Children* ('the Houghton Committee')[4] in 1972 the issue of financial support was being discussed but still met with opposition.

> 'We suggested in our working paper that consideration should be given to the possibility of guardians and adopters being paid regular subsidies in appropriate cases ... While there was considerable support for allowances for guardians ... many witnesses saw a clear distinction between adoption and guardianship and opposed the idea of any payments to adopters. Some took the view that adoption should put the child in precisely the same position as a child born to the adopters. While some agreed with our suggestion that, if allowances were payable, more homes might be found for children with special needs, others said that it would be unfair to the parents of handicapped children if the adopters of these children could get an allowance which was not available to their natural parents.'[5]

9.5   However, while the Committee did not advocate payments for adopters generally, it was of the view there was a case for allowances in some circumstances, for example where suitable adopters were available for a family of children who needed to be kept together but, for financial reasons, adoption was not possible if an allowance could not be paid. It recommended therefore that there should be pilot schemes of allowances.[6]

9.6   1972 also marked the publication of *Children Who Wait*[7] which argued that there were large numbers of children in care and likely to remain so until adulthood unless substitute parents could be found. Nearly half of the children studied had one or more of a number of physical, mental or behavioural problems. Successful placements would not be achieved 'without a great deal of effort and a certain amount of expense' as well as specialist help from social services, remedial teachers, doctors, psychologists and perhaps psychiatrists. 'Enlightened self-interest was required in spending money to save both money and suffering'.[8]

9.7   Despite some parliamentary opposition, local authorities were allowed to submit voluntary schemes of support to the Secretary of State for approval. As the ideas of *Children Who Wait* took hold, virtually all local authorities with social service functions and many voluntary agencies applied for approval

---

[3]   See Lowe 'English Adoption Law: Past, Present and Future' in Katz, Eekelaar and Maclean (eds) *Cross Currents: Family Law and Policy in the United States and England* (Oxford University Press, 2000) at p 329.
[4]   Cmd 5107.
[5]   Ibid, at para 93.
[6]   Ibid, paras 94 and 95.
[7]   Rowe and Lambert (Association of British Adoption Societies, 1972).
[8]   Ibid at p 114.

and eventually the Children Act 1989 amended the Adoption Act 1976 to allow all agencies to pay adoption allowances in accordance with the Adoption Allowances Regulations 1991.[9]

9.8 However as the Department of Health recognised, there remained:

'a lack of clarity about what post-adoption services adoption agencies are required to provide ... Services are patchy and often more likely to be available from voluntary resources'.[10]

Research

9.9 A number of studies in the 1990s examined the needs of the families who had adopted older children.

9.10 Quinton, Rushton and others[11] looked at the needs of a cohort of children between the ages of 5 and 9 during their first year in adoptive homes. It was clear that the adjustments required by adopters and the children – more than two-thirds of whom had had four or more placements – were difficult to make and the families needed 'skilled and continuing support'. One month after placement the children demonstrated considerably more problems at school than their peers – both within the classroom, for example, poor concentration, and with other pupils. There was little change over the year. The rate of clinical disorder was almost five times greater than that found in the general population and around twice that found in groups of 'looked after' children. Many adoptive parents felt they needed substantial support in securing the educational provision their child needed. Although original problems might be resolved within about a year, new problems arose for two-thirds of the children. Some adopters pointed out that informal support from family and friends began to diminish once they embarked on adoption. Two in five did not think that social workers had sufficiently taken into account the needs of their birth children.

9.11 In 1994 Owen examined adoptions by single people.[12] About half of the children in the sample had a history of physical and/or sexual abuse. Typically the adoptive family received informal support from family and friends but help from the mental health services was infrequent. The problems of combining work and child care were often resolved by reason of the nature of their work (many were business or professional workers with a good deal of autonomy) or

---

[9] For further details, see Lowe 'The changing face of adoption – the gift/donation model versus the contract/services model' (1997) CFLQ 371 at p 379, and Lowe, Murch et al *Supporting Adoption* (BAAF, 1999) at pp 26–27.

[10] *Inter-Departmental Review of Adoption Law Discussion Paper Number 3: The Adoption Process* (Department of Health, 1991) at para 88.

[11] Quinton, Rushton, Dance and Mays *Joining New Families: A Study of Adoption and Fostering in Middle Childhood* (Wiley, 1998), summarised in *Adoption Now: Messages From Research* (Wiley, 1999).

[12] *Single-Person Adoption: For and Against* (1994); *Children and Society 8.151* summarised in *Adoption Now: Messages From Research* op cit.

by changing their work, for example, working from home. Virtually all of them said that the extra financial costs were greater than they expected. Where allowances were paid, there was criticism that, contrary to the requirements of the regulations, they were not reviewed annually.

9.12 Lowe and Murch's wide ranging review, *Supporting Adoption: Reframing the Approach*,[13] examined the whole adoption process based on a sample of 226 families who had adopted children over the age of 5. Three in five of the families received financial support but only half of these said that the allowances were reviewed annually. Two-fifths received financial support with the initial caring costs but only one in eight, special needs allowances, for example, disability living allowances.

9.13 The researchers found that the families experienced difficulties in obtaining information about the practical support they needed. It was also clear that there were considerable variations among agencies concerning the provision of both financial and practical support. Many adopters pointed out the differences in support, particularly financial support, depending on whether or not the child had been previously fostered. Another cause of concern was that some families assumed that financial support would continue indefinitely, only to find that they were severely reduced or terminated without much notice.

9.14 The authors of the Department of Health publication, *Adoption Now: Messages from Research*,[14] drew a number of conclusions from these and other studies.

- Many children placed for adoption will have experienced numerous disruptions which will make them wary of placing too much reliance on new attachments. They and the adopters will need support.

- Informal networks are an important source of support but these may change as a result of the placement and social workers need to consider how informal support can be strengthened.

- Challenging and difficult behaviour is likely to occur and will cause new parents considerable stress. Sexualised behaviour gives cause for special concern and where it is known to have occurred, children should receive appropriate counselling or therapy and special preparation.

- Children can display behaviour of sufficient severity which warrants specialised support and treatment not least from the mental health services.

- Relationships between adoptive and birth families are liable to be complicated and support is likely to be needed for all concerned.

---

[13]   Lowe, Murch and others (BAAF, 1999) ch 14 summarised in *Adoption Now: Messages From Research* op cit, ch 7.

[14]   Ibid.

- Relationships at school are likely to be difficult. Both adopters and social workers assume that it is the adopters who are responsible for sorting out issues with schools but additional help should be offered, perhaps by educational advisers.

- Practical and financial needs should not be underestimated. Domestic help, child care or respite care may be needed but there is little evidence of it having been provided.

- Financial help whether by way of allowances or one-off payments was inconsistent. Many adopters do not know what they might reasonably expect, when and under what conditions. The nature of support should be made clear at the outset and for financial help should be made less discretionary.

- When emergencies and crises occur, a swift and well-informed response should be readily available.

- Little support is available from professions other than social work.

- There is no evidence from the studies that the level of formal support affected outcomes but less than satisfactory support may mean that the 'costs' to the children and their new parents are unnecessarily heavy.

Proposals for reform

9.15 Professor Lowe[15] has argued that adoption should not be regarded as the end of the process and the state has a duty to continue its support of needy and vulnerable children and their adopters after an order is made.

> '[The contract/services model of adoption][16] poses awkward questions: for the State it means having to come to terms with the fact that adoption is not a cheap option for bringing up children currently languishing in care; for adoption agencies it means having to make agreements with the adopters *inter alia*, undertaking to give full and up-to-date information both about the child's circumstances and about the risks to adopters and their family …; for the adopters, it may mean their having to accept that they are not in complete control of their adoptive child's upbringing.'

9.16 The *Prime Minister's Review of Adoption*[17] recognised that there were problems with adoption support, in particular, a lack of consistency, unfavourable rates of adoption financial support compared with those for foster families, means testing, health and educational services not being focused on the needs of families and the need for an allowance to be agreed before an

---

[15] 'The changing face of adoption – the gift/donation model versus the contract/services model' [1997] CFLQ 371 at p 385.
[16] See **1.57**.
[17] (PIU, 2000), paras 3.118–3.122.

adoption order was made, thereby ruling out help if unforeseen problems developed later. It made detailed suggestions of what was needed.[18]

9.17 The White Paper, *Adoption: A New Approach*[19] promised that 'Better, more comprehensive post-placement support will help improve the success of adoptive placements.' All families adopting children would have the right to be assessed for support and there would be:

> '... a clear duty on authorities to provide post-adoption support, including financial support, planned jointly with local education authorities and the NHS and any other relevant agencies. This support will be available from the time a placement is made, for as long as it is needed.'

THE STATUTORY FRAMEWORK

9.18 The framework for the assessment and provision of adoption support services is provided by s 3 of the ACA 2002, and the Adoption Support Services Regulations 2005 (ASSR 2005).[20] Guidance on the Regulations is provided by Chapter 9 of *The Adoption Guidance*[21] which is issued under s 7 of the Local Authority Social Services Act 1970 ('the Guidance').

9.19 In *Munjaz v Ashworth Hospital*[22] Lord Bingham said of similar guidance:

> 'The Code does not have the binding effect which a statutory provision or statutory instrument would have. It is what it purports to be, guidance and not instruction. But ... the guidance should be given great weight. It is not instruction but it is much more than mere advice which the addressee is free to follow or not as it chooses. It is guidance which [any authority] should consider with great care and from which it should depart only if it has cogent reasons for so doing.'[23]

In *B v Lewisham London Borough Council*[24] Black J said that 'whilst the document does not have the full force of statute, it should be complied with unless local circumstances indicate exceptional reasons which justify a variation'.[25]

---

[18] Prime Minister's Review, paras 5.21–5.39.
[19] Cm 5017 (2000) at paras 6.26–6.40.
[20] SI 2005/691.
[21] Department for Education and Skills (2002).
[22] [2005] UKHL 58, [2006] 4 All ER 736.
[23] Ibid at [21]. See also *R v Islington LBC ex p Rixon* [1996] 32 BMLR 136 at 140.
[24] [2008] EWHC 738 (Admin).
[25] Ibid at [20].

Adoption services

9.20 Under s 3(1) of the ACA 2002 local authorities must continue to maintain within their area a service designed to meet the needs, in relation to adoption, of:

- children who may be adopted, their parents and guardians;

- persons wishing to adopt a child; and

- adopted persons, their parents, natural parents and former guardians.

9.21 As part of the service, the authority must provide the requisite facilities. These must include making and participating in arrangements for:

- the adoption of children; and

- the provision of adoption support services.[26]

9.22 The latter are defined as:

- counselling, advice and information; and

- other services prescribed by regulation.[27]

9.23 Regulation 3 prescribes the following services:

- financial support payable under Part 3 of the Regulations;

- services to enable groups of adoptive children,[28] adoptive parents[29] and natural parents or former guardians of adoptive children to discuss matters relating to adoption;

- assistance, including mediation services, in relation to arrangements for contact between an adoptive child and a natural parent, natural sibling, former guardian or a related person[30] of an adoptive child;

---

[26] ACA 2002, s 3(2).

[27] Ibid, s 2(6).

[28] 'A child who has been adopted or in respect of whom a person has given notice of an intention to adopt under section 44 or a child whom an agency has matched with a prospective adopter or placed for adoption': ASSR 2005, reg 2(1).

[29] 'A person who has adopted a child or who has given notice under section 44 or a person an agency has matched with a child or with whom it has placed a child for adoption': ibid.

[30] Defined by ASSR 2005, reg 2 as: (a) a relative within the meaning of s 144(1) of the Act (ie grandparent, brother, sister, uncle or aunt whether of the full blood or half blood or by marriage) or (b) any person with whom the adoptive child has a relationship which appears to the local authority to be beneficial having regard to the matters referred to in ACA 2002, s 1(4)(f)(i), (ii) and (iii).

- services in relation to the therapeutic needs of an adoptive child;

- assistance for the purpose of ensuring the continuance of a relationship between an adoptive child and his adoptive parent including:
  - training for adoptive parents for the purpose of meeting any special needs of the child; and
  - respite care;

- assistance where disruption of an adoptive placement, or of an adoption arrangement following the making of an adoption order, has occurred or is in danger of occurring, including:
  - making arrangements for the provision of mediation services; and
  - organising and running meetings to discuss disruptions in such placements or arrangements.

9.24 By virtue of ACA 2002, s 3(4) the authority may provide any of the facilities by securing their provision by registered adoption societies or other persons within the description prescribed by regulations.[31] These currently are:

- another local authority;

- a registered adoption support agency;

- a Local Health Board or Primary Care Trust; and

- a local education authority.[32]

The Guidance envisages that this may be appropriate, for example, if there is a low demand in a particular area or to avoid duplication.[33]

ADOPTION SUPPORT SERVICES ADVISOR

9.25 Regulation 3(3) allows the services prescribed in reg 3(1)(b)–(f) (ie all the services excluding counselling, advice and information) to include giving assistance in cash. The Guidance provides the illustrations of giving an adoptive parent cash to pay a babysitter or for petrol where contact has been arranged. 'When cash is provided in this way it should **not** be means tested as it is being provided as part of a service rather than financial support.'[34]

9.26 All authorities are required to appoint an adoption support services adviser (ASSA) whose role is to:

---

[31]   See ASSR 2005, reg 5.
[32]   Ibid, reg 5.
[33]   Guidance, Chapter 9, para 30.
[34]   Guidance, Chapter 9, para 3. Emphasis in the original text.

- give advice and information to persons who may be affected by the adoption or proposed adoption of a child, including as to:
  - services that may be appropriate to those persons; and
  - how those services may be made available to them;

- give advice, information and assistance to the local authority including as to:
  - the assessment of needs for adoption support services;
  - the availability of adoption support services;
  - the preparation of support plans.[35]

- consult with and give advice, information and assistance to another local authority when appropriate.[36]

9.27 The Guidance states that the appointment of the ASSA:

'provides clarity for adoptive parents about who in the authority to approach for advice and identifies a first port of call for questions about adoption support services, the process for assessing support and queries in relation to existing support services. It is important that contact details for the ASA – a phone number and postal and/or email address – are appropriately publicised ...'[37]

Services for whom?

9.28 Regulation 4 prescribes that the following services must be extended to the following people.

- *Agency adoptive child*[38]
  - Services to enable discussion of matters relating to adoption
  - Assistance in relation to arrangements for contact
  - Therapeutic services
  - Services to enable the continuation of adoptive relationship
  - Services to assist in the case of disruption
  - Counselling, advice and information

- *Adoptive parent of an agency adopted child*
  - Services to enable discussion of matters relating to adoption
  - Assistance in relation to arrangements for contact
  - Services to enable the continuation of adoptive relationship
  - Services to assist in the case of disruption
  - Counselling, advice and information
  - Financial support

---

[35] See **9.62**.
[36] ASSR 2005, reg 6.
[37] Guidance, Chapter 9, para 11.
[38] Defined by ASSR 2005, reg 2 as (a) a child who has been adopted after having been placed for adoption by an adoption agency or (b) a child whom an adoption agency has matched with a prospective adopter or placed for adoption or (c) a child whose adoptive parent has been a local authority foster child in relation to him (unless the authority opposes the adoption).

- *Child of adoptive parents*
  - Services to enable the continuation of adoptive relationship
  - Services to assist in the case of disruption
  - Counselling, advice and information

- *Natural parents or guardians of an agency adoptive child*
  - Services to enable discussion of matters relating to adoption
  - Assistance in relation to arrangements for contact
  - Counselling, advice and information

- *A related person*[39]
  - Assistance in relation to arrangements for contact
  - Counselling, advice and information

- *Adoptive child in the case of a Convention*[40] *adoption*
  - Therapeutic services
  - Services to enable the continuation of adoptive relationship
  - Services to assist in the case of disruption
  - Counselling, advice and information

- *Adoptive parent in the case of a Convention adoption*
  - Services to enable the continuation of adoptive relationship
  - Services to assist in the case of disruption
  - Counselling, advice and information

- *Natural sibling of an adoptive child*
  - Assistance in relation to arrangements for contact
  - Counselling, advice and information

- *Non agency adoptive children, their parents and guardians*
  - Counselling, advice and information

- *Prospective adopters*
  - Counselling, advice and information

- *A related person of a non-agency adoptive child*
  - Counselling, advice and information

9.29 An important exclusion relates to adoption by the child's natural parent or the partner of a natural parent. By virtue of ASSR 2005, reg 3(2) the services which are prescribed for such people are limited to counselling, advice and support.

---

[39] See above, ASSR 2005, reg 2.
[40] See ACA 2002, s 66(1)(c).

9.30 The authority is also under a duty to assess for support certain categories of people who live outside their area.[41] This is considered at **9.74**. In addition an authority is not prevented from supplying adoption support services to persons outside their area where they consider it appropriate to do so.[42]

Financial support

9.31 By virtue of ASSR 2005, reg 8(1) financial support is payable to an adoptive parent for the purpose of supporting the placement of an adoptive child or the continuation of adoption arrangements after an order is made only in the following circumstances:

(a) where it is necessary to ensure the adoptive parent can look after the child;

(b) where the child needs special care which requires greater expenditure of resources by reason of illness, disability, emotional or behavioural difficulties or the continuing consequences of past abuse or neglect;

Support under this ground is intended where the child's condition is 'serious and long term'. The Guidance gives examples of a child needing a special diet or items such as shoes, clothing or bedding needing to be replaced at a higher rate than would normally be the case with a child of similar age who was unaffected by the particular condition.[43]

(c) where it is necessary for the local authority to make any special arrangements to facilitate the placement or adoption by reason of:
   (i)   the age or ethnic origin of the child; or
   (ii) the desirability of the child being placed with the same adoptive parent as his brother or sister (whether of full or half blood) or with a child with whom he has previously shared a home;

Support under this ground is payable so that the authority can facilitate the placement of a child for whom it may be difficult to find prospective adopters able to meet the child's needs.[44]

(d) where such support is to meet recurring costs in respect of travel for the purpose of visits between the child and a related person;[45]

(e) where the local authority considers it appropriate to make a contribution to meet the following kinds of expenditure:
   (i)   expenditure on legal costs, including fees payable to a court in respect of adoption (see also **9.50**);
   (ii) expenditure for the purpose of introducing an adoptive child to his adoptive parent (see also **9.44**);

---

41 ASSR 2005, reg 7(1).
42 Ibid, reg 7(3)
43 Guidance, Chapter 9, para 28.
44 Ibid, Chapter 9, para 29.
45 See **9.28**.

(iii) expenditure necessary for the purpose of accommodating and maintaining the child, including the provision of furniture and domestic equipment, alterations to and adaptations of the home, provision of means of transport and provision of clothing, toys and other items necessary for the purpose of looking after the child.

9.32 Financial support may be paid periodically if it is provided to meet a need which is likely to give rise to recurring expenditure or by a single payment which can, with the consent of the recipient, be paid by instalments.[46]

9.33 As with support for Special Guardianship (see **11.25**) there is a general principle that Adoption Support Services should not be seen in isolation from mainstream services. Regulation 15(2) provides that in determining the amount of financial support, the local authority must take into account any other grant, benefit, allowance or source which is available to the person in respect of his needs as a result of the adoption of the child.' One of the functions of the ASSA is to signpost adopters to information about other forms of support which may be available, for example, tax credits and benefits.[47]

9.34 It is for each authority to decide its own scheme of payments. The Guidance states that:

> 'In determining the amount of any ongoing financial support, the local authority should have regard to the amount of fostering allowance which would have been payable if the child were instead to be adopted. The local authority's core allowance together with any enhancement that would be payable in respect of the particular child will make up the maximum payment that a local authority could consider paying the family.'[48]

9.35 For consideration of similar Guidance in relation to Special Guardianship, see *B v Lewisham London Borough Council*,[49] in relation to payments to short-term kinship carers, *The Queen on the Application of L and Others v Manchester City Council*[50] and **11.35**.

9.36 Murch and Lowe commented in relation to earlier Regulations that 'Given the wide discretion vested in agencies, it is hardly surprising that our research has revealed a general lack of consistency, both as to the policy of whether to make payments at all and as to the level of any payment'.[51] The same complaint may be expected under current Regulations.

---

[46]   ASSR 2005, reg 10.
[47]   Guidance, Chapter 9, para 12.
[48]   Ibid, para 9.52.
[49]   [2008] EWHC 738(Admin).
[50]   [2002] EWHC (Admin) 707, [2002] 1 FLR 43.
[51]   Op cit at p 257.

Former foster carers

9.37 Many foster carers receive an element of remuneration in their fostering allowance. As a general rule, post-adoption financial support cannot include such an element.[52] However under reg 9 it can be paid but only if the decision to pay it is taken before the adoption order is made, the authority considers it necessary in order to facilitate the adoption and an element of remuneration was formerly included in the fostering allowance. The element of remuneration ceases at the end of 2 years commencing with the date of the order unless the authority considers it necessary having regard to the exceptional needs of the child or exceptional circumstances.[53]

9.38 The purpose of the Regulation is to enable authorities to maintain payments to foster parents who go on to adopt for a transitional period '*at the same rate*' [italics inserted] as formerly paid.[54]

State benefits

9.39 One of the functions of the adoption support services adviser is to signpost information about tax credits and benefits (see **9.26**).

9.40 Adoption allowances are disregarded in full (with some minor exceptions) for Income Support and income based Job Seeker's Allowances.[55] They are taken into account for housing benefit and council tax benefit but only to the level of the child's personal allowance and any disabled child premium. Conversely, when a carer's means are assessed for the purpose of most but not all adoption financial support, welfare benefits are taken into account.[56]

9.41 In addition to the usual state benefits and subject to various conditions, if the adopter's average weekly earnings are £87 or more (before tax), Statutory Adoption Pay is paid for a maximum of 39 weeks at £127.06 or 90% of the average weekly earnings if this is less.[57] The earliest date on which the pay period can normally begin is 14 days before the recipient expects the child to be placed and the latest, the date of placement.

9.42 A Guide to other adoption pay and leave entitlements is available at http://www.direct.gov.uk/en/Parents/Moneyandworkentitlements.

---

[52] Guidance, Chapter 9, para 30.
[53] ASSR 2005, reg 9(2).
[54] Guidance, Chapter 9, para 31.
[55] Income Support (General) Regulations 1987, SI 1987/1967, Sch 9, para 25(1)(a) and (1A); Jobseeker's (Allowance) Regulations 1996, SI 1996/206, Sch 7, para 26(1)(a) and (1A).
[56] ASSR 2005, reg 15(1) and (5).
[57] Statutory Paternity Pay and Statutory Adoption Pay (General) Regulations 2002, SI 2002/2822 as amended by the Statutory Paternity Pay and Statutory Adoption Pay (General) and the Statutory Paternity Pay and Statutory Adoption Pay (Weekly Rates) (Amendment) Regulations 2006 (SI 2006/2236).

Assessing resources

9.43 When deciding the amount of financial support to be paid the local authority has to assess and take into account:

- any other grant, benefit, allowance or resource which is available to the person in respect of his needs as a result of the adoption of the child;

- the person's financial resources including any tax credit or benefit which would be available if the child lived with him;

- the amount required by the person in respect of his reasonable outgoings and commitments (excluding outgoings in respect of the child); and

- the financial resources and needs of the child.[58]

9.44 There are two exceptions to this general rule. When the authority is considering whether to provide financial support in respect of legal costs in respect of an application for an adoption order in respect of an agency adoptive child or expenditure for the purpose of introducing an agency adoptive child to his adoptive parents it *must* disregard reg 15(3).[59] Local authorities are not required to meet the legal costs of an adoption which they oppose.[60]

9.45 In addition, the authority *may* also disregard means when considering:

- initial costs of accommodating an agency adoptive child;

- recurring travel costs for the purpose of contact between the child and a related person;

- any special care referred to in reg 8(2)(b) or (c)[61] which requires a greater expenditure of resources than would otherwise be the case;[62] or

- any remuneration element.[63]

The Guidance suggests that it is not expected that the initial costs of accommodating an agency adoptive child ('a settling-in grant') will be means tested 'but local authorities might, for example, want to means test any contribution to an adaptation to the home'.[64]

---

[58]   ASSR 2005, reg 15(3).
[59]   Ibid, reg 15(4).
[60]   Guidance, Chapter 9, para 57.
[61]   See **9.31**.
[62]   ASSR 2005, reg 15(5).
[63]   Ibid, reg 15(6).
[64]   Guidance, Chapter 9, para 55.

9.46   There is a suggested means test and notes on its use on the Department's website but authorities are not required to use it.[65]

Conditions

9.47   Where financial support is to be paid periodically, it cannot be paid until the adoptive parent (or if the adopters are a couple, each of them) agrees:

- to inform the authority immediately if:
  - he changes address;
  - the child dies;
  - changes occur which are mentioned in reg 11 and which have the effect of automatically terminating financial support; or
  - there is a change in his or the child's financial services; and

- to supply the authority with an annual statement of his and the child's financial circumstances, his address and whether the child still has a home with him.[66]

The authority may also provide financial support subject to any condition it considers appropriate including the timescale within which and the purposes for which financial support is to be utilised.[67]

Respite care

9.48   Respite care is part of the prescribed services[68] but if it is met by the provision of accommodation, it must be by way of s 23 of the Children Act 1989 (accommodation for looked after children) or by a voluntary organisation under s 59.[69]

> 'This requires that appropriate safeguards are in place ... and that any foster parent providing respite care has been approved under the Fostering Services Regulations 2002.'[70]

Contact

9.49   The support which the authority can provide includes:

- counselling, advice and information;[71]

---

[65]   Guidance, Chapter 9, para 53.
[66]   ASSR 2005, reg 12(1).
[67]   Ibid, reg 12(2).
[68]   Ibid, reg 3(1)(e)(ii).
[69]   Ibid, reg 3(4).
[70]   Guidance, Chapter 9, para 4.
[71]   ASSR 2005, reg 3(1).

- assistance including mediation.[72] This could presumably include facilitating family group conferences (as recommended by Hunt) and supervision;

- travel costs in cash[73] or by way of financial support payments when on a recurring basis;[74]

Where the costs are of a recurring kind, the authority may disregard the financial circumstances of the adopters.[75] Unlike cases of special guardianship, (see **11.48**) financial assistance for the purpose of assisting with legal costs in relation to opposing an application for contact is not payable.

Assistance with legal services

9.50 Local authorities frequently fund legal advice and representation for prospective adopters of an agency adoptive child in relation to the adoption. Under reg 8(2)(e)(i) the authority can provide assistance if it thinks it appropriate towards legal costs (including court fees) associated with an adoption. The costs of applying for an SGO are not subject to financial assessment provided that the child is an agency adoptive child.[76]

ASSESSMENT

9.51 Local authorities are required to undertake an assessment of adoption support service needs at the request of:

- children who may be adopted, their parents and guardians;[77]

- persons wishing to adopt a child;[78]

- adopted persons, their parents, natural parents and former guardians;[79]

- children of adoptive parents (whether or not they are adopted);[80]

- natural siblings of adoptive children;[81]

---

[72] ASSR 2005, reg 3(1)(c).
[73] Ibid, reg 3(3); Guidance, Chapter 9, para 3.
[74] ASSR 2005, reg 8(2)(d).
[75] ASSR 2005, reg 15(5)(a)(ii).
[76] Ibid, reg 15(4)(a).
[77] ACA 2002, s 4(1).
[78] Ibid.
[79] Ibid.
[80] ASSR 2005, reg 13.
[81] Ibid.

- relatives of the adoptive child or other persons with whom the child has a beneficial relationship.[82]

9.52 In addition, where an authority has 'decided to proceed' with a proposed placement[83] of a particular child with a particular adoptive parent, it must undertake an assessment (whether it has been requested or not) of adoption support service needs of:

- the child;

- the proposed adopters;

- any child of the adoptive parent.[84]

9.53 In addition the authority is not required to but may undertake assessments at the request of any person.[85]

9.54 The requirement to carry out an assessment applies only to an assessment of the need for the type of service which has, under reg 4 of the ASSR 2005 (see **9.28**), to be extended to the person being assessed.[86] The assessor is not however prevented from considering other services which may be appropriate.

9.55 If the authority has decided to provide counselling advice and information, it will not always be necessary for an assessment to be undertaken. However, when additional needs are being considered, an assessment should be carried out in order that an informed decision can be made.[87]

Procedure for assessment

9.56 The authority carrying out the assessment must have regard to such of the following considerations as are relevant:

(a) the needs of the person being assessed and how these might be met;

(b) the needs of the adoptive family and how these might be met;

(c) the needs, including developmental needs, of the adoptive child and how these might be met;

---

[82] ASSR 2005, reg 13.
[83] In the context of the rest of reg 31 of the Adoptions Agencies Regulations 2005, SI 2005/389, this seems to mean that the authority has decided to refer a proposed placement to the Panel rather than that the recommendation of the Panel has been accepted.
[84] Ibid, reg 31. This applies only to local authorities and not to other adoption agencies.
[85] ACA 2002, s 4(2).
[86] ASSR 2005, reg 13(3).
[87] Guidance, Chapter 9, para 42.

(d)   the parenting capacity of the adoptive parent;

(e)   wider family and environmental factors;

(f)   in the case of a child who is, or was, placed for adoption or matched for adoption, the circumstances that led to the child being so placed or matched; and

(g)   any previous assessment of needs for adoption support services undertaken in relation to the person in question.[88]

9.57   The Guidance states that these factors reflect those to be considered under the *Framework for the Assessment of Children in Need and Their Families*.[89] There is also Practice Guidance on *Assessing the Support Needs of Adoptive Families*[90] which is intended as a tool for the assessment of adoptive children in the context of the adoptive family. When assessing persons other than the immediate adoptive family, authorities will need to use whichever of their existing assessment tools is the most appropriate, bearing in mind the adoption context.[91]

9.58   The assessment will not always be a 'paper' exercise. The local authority must, if it considers it appropriate, interview the person whose needs are to be assessed and where that person is the child, the adoptive parents.[92]

9.59   Where it appears to the authority that the person may have a need for services from a Local Health Board, Primary Care Trust or local education authority, they must consult that body.[93]

9.60   For an assessment for financial support, see **9.43**.

9.61   After undertaking the assessment the authority must prepare a written report.[94] Details of the assessment must be provided to the person making the request for services once a draft plan has been prepared or the authority decides that a plan is not necessary.[95]

The plan

9.62   If following the assessment the authority proposes to provide support services to a person on more than one occasion and those services are not limited to the provision of advice or information it must prepare a plan unless

---

[88]   ASSR 2005, reg 14.
[89]   Department of Health (2000) and see **8.25**.
[90]   The latest version is published by the Department for Children, Schools and Families (2008).
[91]   Guidance, Chapter 9, para 45.
[92]   ASSR 2005, reg 14(3).
[93]   Ibid, reg 14(4).
[94]   Ibid, reg 14(3).
[95]   Ibid, reg 17(1) and (3)(a); see **9.65**.

the services are limited to providing advice or information.[96] Where it appears to the authority that the person may have a need for services from a Local Health Board, Primary Care Trust or Local Education Authority, they must consult that body before preparing the plan.[97]

9.63 The plan should set out:

- the services to be provided;

- the objectives and criteria for evaluating success;

- timescales for provision;

- procedures for review;

- the name of the person nominated to monitor the provision of the services in accordance with the plan.[98]

9.64 Before making a final decision on whether to provide services and, if so, what services the authority must allow the person making the request an opportunity of making representations by giving notice of the proposed decision and the time allowed for making representations.[99] The notice must contain the following information:

- a statement of the person's needs for support services;

- where the assessment relates to a need for financial support, the basis upon which the support is determined;

- whether the authority proposes to provide support services;

- the services (if any) it is proposed to supply;

- if financial support is to be provided, the amount payable; and

- any proposed conditions under reg 12(2).[100]

In addition, if a plan is required, the authority must supply a copy of the plan.[101]

---

[96] ASSR 2005, reg 16(2).
[97] Ibid, reg 16(3).
[98] Guidance, Chapter 9, para 60.
[99] ASSR 2005, reg 17(1). No minimum time for making representations is specified but the Guidance suggests a period of 28 days (Chapter 9, para 63).
[100] ASSR 2005, reg 17(3).
[101] Ibid, reg 17(4).

9.65 After considering any representations, the authority decides whether or not to provide services, and has to give the person applying for the services notice of its decision and the reasons for it.[102]

9.66 If the authority decides that financial support is to be provided, the notice must include the following information:

- the method of determination of the amount of financial support;

- where it is to be provided in instalments or periodically:
  - the amount of the support;
  - the frequency with which it will be paid;
  - the period for which it will be paid;
  - when payment will commence;

- where financial support is to be paid as a single payment, when it will be made;

- where financial support is to be subject to any conditions under reg 12 the conditions, the date by which they are to be met and the consequences of failing to meet them;

- the arrangements and procedure for review, variation and termination of financial support;

- the responsibilities of:
  - the local authority under Part 5 of the Regulations (Reviews); and
  - the adoptive parent pursuant to an agreement under reg 12 (notifying change of circumstances).

Where service providers other than the social services have been involved in the assessment, the authority should try wherever possible to ensure that decisions made by those providers follow the same timetable. They should be covered in a single notification and plan to provide wherever possible a whole service package.[103]

9.67 Where the assessment is carried out before the authority prepares its report for the court under s 43 or 44(5) (see Chapter 8) the authority must include in the report a summary of the special guardianship support services provided by the authority including the plan provided by the authority, the period of time for which they are to be provided or, if they are not to be provided, the reasons for this.[104]

---

[102] ASSR 2005, reg 18(1).

[103] Guidance, Chapter 9, para 69.

[104] Family Procedure (Adoption) Rules 2005, SI 2005/2795 (FP(A)R 2005), r 29(3); Practice Direction 5C Section B, Part 3(e) (support to natural parents) and Section D(c) (support to others).

REVIEW

9.68

'Regular reviews enable the local authority and the service user to review the effectiveness of any services provided and consider whether it is appropriate to continue that service or change the provision in some way.'[105]

The authority providing the support must review its plan:

- if any change in the recipient's circumstances which may affect the provision of the services comes to their attention;

- at such stage of implementation as they consider appropriate; and

- at least annually.[106]

9.69 Financial support must be reviewed:

- on receipt of the annual statement (see **9.47**);

- if any relevant change of circumstances or breach of condition comes to the attention of the authority; and

- at such stage of implementation as they consider appropriate.[107]

Regulations 19(3) and 20(4) make provision for the review similar to that for assessment.

9.70 The Guidance suggests that the format and content of the review will vary according to the circumstances of the individual case.

'Where the change of circumstances is relatively minor [or at the annual review of financial support] the review might be limited to an exchange of correspondence ... However where the change of circumstance is substantial, for example a major change in the behaviour of the child, it will normally be appropriate to conduct a new assessment of needs.'[108]

APPLYING FOR SERVICES AFTER AN ADOPTION ORDER HAS BEEN MADE

9.71 The need for support services may become apparent only after an adoption has been granted. Two matters should be noted.

---

[105] Guidance, Chapter 9, para 70.
[106] ASSR 2005, reg 19(1).
[107] Ibid, reg 20(2).
[108] Guidance, Chapter 9, para 76.

9.72   Given the frequent changes in social services personnel, the social worker with whom the adopters or natural parents may have had contact may have left the authority by the time support is needed and, in any event, may not be the best person to give advice. Therefore advisers should ensure that their clients (whether adopters or natural parents) are provided with the name and address of the adoption support services adviser (see **9.29**).

9.73   Secondly, the adopters may move to the area of another authority. If this happens, see **9.74**.

WHICH AUTHORITY?

9.74   The authority tasked with carrying out the assessment will be the authority where the person applying for services is living[109] unless the child was an adoption agency child whom an authority has placed for adoption or who has been adopted after being placed for adoption by the authority, in which case for 3 years from the adoption order the placing authority is also under a duty to assess the child or the adoptive parent.[110] However, where that authority is providing financial support agreed before the order as made, the authority's responsibility continues so long as the financial support is provided.[111]

9.75   Any plan will remain in force (and the originating authority will be under a duty to continue to supply the support under the plan) until it is varied or terminated. Such termination could be for the reason that the move constituted a relevant change of circumstances under regs 19 and 20. The Guidance states that:

> 'Adoption Support Services Advisers should also aim to secure smooth transition for families in receipt of services who are moving between areas. The ASA should liaise with the appropriate authority before the family moves to ensure continuity of support.'[112]

9.76   An authority is not prevented from providing adoption support services to people outside their area where they consider it appropriate.[113] For example, the authority might make transitional arrangements to allow the new authority time to review the existing plan without a break in service provision. It may also be appropriate for an authority which has had previous contact with a family to provide ongoing support that is practicable to deliver across a distance in cases where a family has had no contact with the authority in whose area they now live.[114]

---

[109]   ACA 2002, s 4, ASSR 2005, reg 4 and Guidance, Chapter 9, para 20.
[110]   ASSR 2005, reg 7(1).
[111]   Ibid, reg 7(2).
[112]   Guidance, Chapter 9, para 15.
[113]   ASSR 2005, reg 7(3).
[114]   Guidance, Chapter 9, para 26.

ACCESS TO INFORMATION ABOUT BIRTH FAMILIES AND THE ADOPTED PERSON

Background

9.77 In 1992 the *Review of Adoption Law: Report to Ministers* commented that 'It is generally undisputed that many adopted people experience a need to know about their origins.'[115] It pointed out that for some people, the information on their birth record is sufficient. Others might wish to trace their birth family. Sometimes this could lead to the establishment of mutually satisfying relationships but others would be content with 'filling in the blanks' in their personal history not only for their own account but for the benefit of their children.

9.78 The Review also recognised that it was apparent that many birth parents felt a need to know what has happened to their child who has been adopted. On the other hand some suffered anxiety at being traced.

Difficulties

9.79 Without statutory provision adopters and their natural family, would face legal, as well as practical, problems in obtaining the information they seek. The basic information contained on the Adopted Children's Register, linking the adoption to the child's original birth certificate, and in court and adoption agency records have always been treated as confidential. Until 1972 the confidentiality was strictly maintained and until 1989, as two commentators have said, 'Other than tiny cracks, the shutters on access to information remained tightly shut'.[116] Absent the new scheme, the current restrictions are as follows.

- the adoption certificate contains only the name given on adoption and no details of the birth parents;

- the Adopted Children's Register[117] is not open to public inspection or search;[118]

- the contents of agency[119] adoption records are generally to be treated as confidential;[120]

- the general rule is that court records are withheld from inspection by any person;[121]

---

[115] Department of Health (1992) paras 31.3–31.8.
[116] Bridge and Swindells *Adoption: The Modern Law* (Family Law, 2003) at 12.3.
[117] See ACA 2002, s 125.
[118] Ibid, s 77.
[119] Defined as including local authorities exercising their adoption functions: ibid, s 2(1).
[120] Adoption Agencies Regulations 2005, reg 41and ACA 2002, s 57.
[121] FP(A)R 2005, r 83.

- the Data Protection Act 1984 restricts disclosure of information relating to people other than the person requesting disclosure.

9.80 There are also practical difficulties. Birth parents may have moved from any addresses held for them and the adoption agency which may have been involved may have amalgamated or ceased to operate.

9.81 Legislators have also had to consider the privacy of other people involved, notably that of the birth parents and the adopted child, who may not want contact to be made.

Article 8

9.82 The importance placed on the right to be aware of one's origins by Art 8 of the European Convention for the Protection of Human Rights and Fundamental Freedoms 1950 is considered in Chapter 12. The legislature has had to consider how to implement a system which recognises not just the Art 8 rights of the adopted person but also similar rights held by others.

9.83 In *Gaskin*[122] the European Court of Human Rights (ECtHR) considered a case brought by an adult who had spent nearly 14 years of his childhood in care (but had not been adopted) who wished to have access to his social services case file. It held that:

> 'persons in the situation of the applicant have a vital interest, protected by the Convention, in receiving the information necessary to know and to understand their childhood and early development.'[123]

9.84 The ECtHR noted that confidentiality of public records served an important purpose and a system which made access to records dependent on the consent of the contributor of the information, could in principle be considered to be compatible with the obligations under Art 8, taking into account the State's margin of appreciation. However, under such a system the interests of the individual seeking access to records relating to his private and family life must be secured when a contributor to the records either is not available or improperly refuses consent.

> 'Such a system is only in conformity with the principle of proportionality if it provides that an independent authority finally decides whether access has to be granted in cases where a contributor fails to answer or withholds consent. No such procedure was available to Mr Gaskell and accordingly, the procedures followed failed to secure respect for his private and family life as required by art. 8.'

9.85 In 2001 in *Gunn-Russo v Nugent Care Society and Secretary of State for Health*[124] Scott Baker J recognised the tension between the competing rights of

---

[122] *Gaskin v United Kingdom* Case No 10454/83, [1990] 1 FLR 167.

[123] Ibid, para 49.

[124] [2001] EWHC Admin 566, [2002] 1 FLR 1.

the adults. He was considering an application for judicial review of a decision by an adoption agency under reg 15 of the Adoption Agencies Regulations 1983 to refuse an adoptive adult access to that part of her adoption file which related to the adopters and the birth parents.

> '[Since the *Houghton Report*[125]] the balance has continued to shift towards greater freedom of information to adopted people. It is now recognised that many adopted people wish to have information about their history and background including the reasons for their adoption. Many find it important to have a complete personal history in order to develop a positive sense of identity. The issue will often be how to resolve the tension between on the one hand maintaining the confidentiality under which the information was originally supplied and on the other providing the information that the adopted person has a real desire, and often need, to have.'[126]

9.86 In resolving the tension in the individual case it was incumbent on the agency to have regard to all the circumstances including the background of the legislation and the public interest element in maintaining the confidentiality of adoption records. 'Clearly it would be unsatisfactory were public confidence in the integrity of confidential information supplied during the adoption process to be undermined.'[127]

9.87 Scott Baker J found that a very important, perhaps crucial, consideration in the instant case was that 54 years had elapsed since the adoption order was made and none of the relevant people other than the claimant was still alive. He concluded that there is little if any purpose in maintaining confidentiality from their viewpoint and therefore withholding the information had not been justified.

9.88 Although the Regulations and the statutory regime have changed, this approach remains valid, not just in emphasising the importance of knowledge about one's background, and informing the drafting of the Scheme but also in indicating the approach which agencies and courts should take when exercising their discretionary powers.

Previous legislation

9.89 In 1972 the *Report of the Departmental Committee on the Adoption of Children*[128] (the 'Houghton Report') concluded that the weight of the evidence it had considered was in favour of greater access to background information. It recommended that all adopted adults in England and Wales, whenever adopted, should in future have the right to obtain a copy of their original birth certificate. It did not favour an automatic right to access court records but

---

[125] See **9.89** and **12.13**.
[126] *Gunn-Russo v Nugent Care Society and Secretary of State for Health* at [46]–[47].
[127] Ibid, at [54].
[128] Cmnd 5107. See also **12.13**.

instead proposed that adults should be able to apply for disclosure of information, the court having a discretion to grant or refuse the application.[129]

9.90   Section 26 of the Adoption Act 1976 gave all adult adopted children the right to obtain their original birth certificate regardless of when they had been adopted. Children under the age of 18 could apply only if they intended to marry.[130] In addition s 50(5) allowed an adopted adult to apply to the court for the name of the agency which arranged the placement.

9.91   This right received a great deal of publicity both at the time it was introduced and subsequently. Between 1977 and 2001 over 70,000 people adopted in out-of family adoptions received their original birth certificates. In 2001 it was calculated that 25% of adopted men and 40% of women would be likely to receive the certificates in their lifetime. This was wholly unexpected when the right was introduced.[131]

9.92   John Triseliotis who studied early applicants for certificates in Scotland suggested there were two groups of applicants – those who applied following a 'trigger event' and those who did so as a result of 'intolerable internal strain'. The triggers for the first group were: adolescent crisis; marriage; giving birth; separation; divorce; middle life crisis; death of adoptive parent.[132] However, Rushbrooke[133] argues that statistics for England and Wales do not fully support this. The main factors which determined applications were the age of the applicants and their gender.

> 'The event which precipitates full consciousness or at least sufficient consciousness to apply for one's records may well be one of [these] major life-events, or it may be some other life event or it may be something seemingly inconsequential.'

See also *Adoption, Search and Reunion: The Long Term Experiences of Adopted Adults.*[134]

9.93   The Children Act 1989 amended the Adoption Act 1976[135] by creating an Adoption Contact Register to provide a confidential way for birth parents and other relatives to inform an adopted adult who consulted the Register that contact would be welcome and to give a contact address.[136] As at 30 June 2001

---

[129]   Cmnd 5107, paras 303–305.

[130]   Adoption Act 1976, s 51(2).

[131]   Rushbrooke *The proportion of adoptees who have received their birth records in England and Wales* Population Trends 104 Summer 2001, p 26.

[132]   *In Search of Origins: The Experiences of Adopted People* (1973).

[133]   *The proportion of adoptees who have received their birth records in England and Wales* op cit at p 32.

[134]   Feast and Howe, The Children's Society, noted at [2000] Fam Law 371.

[135]   CA 1989, s 26 amending the 1976 Act by inserting s 51A.

[136]   *The Children Act 1989 Guidance and Regulations*, vol 9 *Adoption Issues* (Department of Health, 1991).

there were details of 19,683 adopted people and 8,492 relatives on the Register. Since 1991, 539 successful matches had been made.[137]

Proposals for reform

9.94 In 2000 the Prime Minister's Review[138] noted that while the Adoption Act 1976 reflected an increased understanding of the wishes and needs of adopted people, local authorities generally gave low priority to providing counselling to those who wanted access to their records. There was also concern about the way courts had exercised their discretion about giving access to records. 'The difficulty for courts is that files sometimes contain very sensitive information – for example, where adoption as followed a rape – and they are reluctant to release them without counselling and support in place'.

9.95 The White Paper, *Adoption – A New Approach*[139] stated that 'All adopted people should be able to find out about their family history if and when they wish to do so.' There would be legislation to set out what should be in agency files and how they were to have access both to those and court files. Other approved bodies in addition to agencies would be allowed to provide birth record counselling.

The Scheme

9.96 The new scheme is contained in:

- ACA 2002, ss 56–65 and 98 and Sch 2;

- Regulations:
    - Adopted Children and Adoption Contact Registers Regulations 2005 (ACCR 2005);[140]
    - Disclosure of Adoption Information (Post-Commencement Adoptions) Regulations 2005 (AIR 2005);[141] and
    - Adoption Information and Intermediary Services (Pre-Commencement Adoptions) Regulations 2005 (ISR 2005).[142]

- *Adoption Guidance*[143] chapters 10, 11 and 12.

9.97 Importantly, the Scheme is divided into two parts: that which applies to adoptions made before the commencement of the 2002 Act on 30 December 2005 and that which applies to adoptions post-commencement. The distinction is justified on the basis that the Act both provides a relaxation of current rules

---

[137] *Summary statistics* (BAAF, 2009) www.baaf.org.uk/info/stats
[138] Op cit at 3.137–3.138.
[139] Op cit, at 6.44–6.45.
[140] SI 2005/924.
[141] SI 2005/888.
[142] SI 2005/890.
[143] Op cit.

to enable greater access to information whilst at the same time imposing greater regulation on how rather than if the information is obtained. It was necessary therefore to protect the existing rights of adopted people and, to some extent, the expectation of birth families and adopted people that the normal rule was that access was restricted. For adoptions after 30 December 2005 the main duty of supervising the provision of information is placed on the adoption agency. For adoptions before that date, the duty is shared with intermediary agencies (see **9.108**) provided the person seeking information chooses to use such an agency.

9.98   The Scheme also regulates more closely than previously the information to be kept post-implementation. As well as 'identifying any background information' (see **9.101**) it includes the case record established under Part 3 of the Adoption Agencies Regulations 2005. In addition, under AIR 2005, reg 4, the agency must keep:

• information supplied by a natural parent, birth relative or other significant person in the adopted person's life with the intention that he may, should he wish, have access to it;

• information supplied by the adoptive parents or other persons which is relevant to matters arising after the making of the order;

• any information the adopted person has requested should be kept;

• any information given to the adopted person by the agency about an entry related to the adopted person on the Adoption Contact Register;

• any information required to be kept by AIR 2005, regs 10, 11, 14 or 18 which relate to the disclosure of information.

9.99   The Scheme is much more complex and prescriptive[144] than the previous one and has not met with universal approval.

'While the statutory scheme endeavours to provide clarity, and fairness to all concerned many of those who are experienced in post-adoption work are concerned that the legislative scheme will be too prescriptive and will not allow for the exercise of appropriate discretion in dealing with a very varied and complex area.'[145]

9.100   A useful website offering guidance for those seeking to trace members of their birth family, which is run by the British Association for Adoption and Fostering can be found at www.adoptionsearchreunion.org.uk.

---

[144]   Bridge and Swindells *Adoption: The Modern Law* op cit at 12.55.
[145]   Cullen 'Adoption – a (fairly) new approach' [2005] CFLQ 475 at p 480.

Information

9.101 Common to both parts are the concepts of 'section 57 information', 'identifying information', 'background information' and 'protected information'.

9.102 Section 56 defines **'information'** as being any information kept by an agency pursuant to Regulations and seemingly this covers information kept pursuant to previous Regulations as well as the 2005 Regulations. It includes both 'identifying information' and 'background information'.

9.103 **'Identifying information'** is defined as 'information which, whether taken on its own or together with other information disclosed by an adoption agency, identifies the person or enables the person to be identified',[146] ISR 2005, reg 7(4) adding for the purpose of those Regulations, 'or traced'. According to the Guidance[147] it is wide ranging and includes information about the adopted person, natural parents, other birth relatives and the adoptive parents as well as information about others in the adoption process such as former carers, professionals involved in assessment and social workers. Identifying information may comprise names, residential, educational or employment addresses, legal and medical information and photographs.

9.104 **'Background information'** is section 56 information which is not 'identifying information'.

> 'It is information which the adoption agency should disclose to the adoptive parents to help them care effectively for the child and address any specific needs. It could also be information which the agency may disclose to the natural parents, or other birth relatives, to inform them about the adopted child's progress in the adoptive family without revealing the child's new identity or whereabouts or the identity or whereabouts of the family.'[148]

9.105 **'Protected information'** is defined by ACA 2002, s 57(1) as 'information kept by an adoption agency about an adopted person or any other person which is or includes identifying information about the person in question.' Section 57(1) provides that it may only be disclosed by an agency pursuant to the provisions of the Act and breach of the section constitutes an offence under s 59.

Adoptions before 30 December 2005

9.106 The Act has preserved the same rights of adopted people to seek information about their birth families as they enjoyed before 30 December 2005. However, it has provided additional assistance by creating registered adoption support ('intermediary') agencies who may assist adopted adults.

---

[146] ACA 2002, s 57(4); ISR 2005, reg 7(4).
[147] Guidance, Chapter 11, paras 27, 28.
[148] Ibid, Chapter 11, para 30.

Help may include, for example, approaching the Registrar General, adoption agencies or courts on their behalf. In addition, adult birth families can also be assisted by intermediary agencies but they will continue to have no right to information which the adopted person may access.

> 'Most birth relatives, including natural parents, will have little or no information which enables them to seek to trace a person from whom they have been separated by adoption and establish if they wish to have contact. This framework enables an intermediary agency to seek information from a range of sources which it may use to establish the current identity of an adopted adult, to trace them and – subject to obtaining their informed consent – disclose identifying information about them to the birth relative and facilitate contact. The intermediary agency will have an important role to play in providing specialist support and advice to all parties throughout this process.'[149]

9.107 The use of the agency in obtaining information from the Registrar General, the adoption agency or the court which made the adoption order is not compulsory. Intermediary agencies may charge a reasonable fee.[150]

Intermediary services and agencies

9.108 Under ACA 2002, s 98(7) and reg 4 of the ISR 2005, 'A registered adoption support agency' means an agency registered under Part 2 of the Care Standards Act or an adoption agency that provides an intermediary service. An adoption agency may chose to provide an intermediary service but there is no statutory requirement for them to do so.

9.109 An 'intermediary service' is defined by reg 4 as

'a service provided for the purposes of –

(a) assisting adopted persons aged 18 or over, who were adopted before 30th December 2005, to obtain information in relation to their adoption; and
(b) facilitating contact between such persons and their relatives.'

The function of the adoption agency in providing access to its records is not an intermediary service.[151]

9.110 ISR 2005, reg 5 makes it clear that adult birth relatives may apply for assistance in contacting an adult adopted person. If the agency discovers that the subject of the application is over 18, it must not proceed further.[152]

9.111 Where the intermediary agency has limited capacity to deal with applications, it must give priority to applications in respect of adoptions before

---

149 Guidance, Chapter 10, para 2.
150 ISR 2005, reg 18.
151 Guidance, Chapter 10, para 22.
152 ISR 2005, reg 6(4).

12 November 1975[153] so that elderly birth relatives who relinquished a child for adoption many years ago, will benefit from having early access to services. In relation to adoptions on or after 12 November 1975, where the intermediary agency has limited capacity it may only accept applications where it is satisfied that the circumstances are sufficiently exceptional, such as where the applicant is terminally ill.[154]

9.112 The services provided include:

- undertaking preparatory work with the applicant;

- obtaining information from a range of sources (ie adoption agencies, the Registrar General and the courts);

- using that information to trace and contact individuals;

- acting as intermediary between the applicant and the subject and facilitating contact between them; and

- providing counselling, support and advice.[155]

9.113 The Guidance expects that adopted persons who are only seeking information about their adoption should continue to apply to the adoption agency which holds their records.[156]

9.114 The Regulations provide detailed provision, supplemented by the Guidance about how these functions are to be performed.

9.115 The intermediary agency has a general discretion not to proceed or continue proceeding with an application unless it considers it appropriate to do so.[157] In exercising this discretion the intermediary agency has to have regard to all the circumstances including the welfare of the applicant, the subject of the application and any other person who may be identified or otherwise affected by the application with particular regard to anyone under the age of 18 and any information obtained from the Adoption Contact Register (see **9.150**).[158]

9.116 If the adopted person is over 18 and has notified the adoption agency in writing that he does not want to be contacted by an intermediary agency, the intermediary agency must not proceed unless the notification has said that the adopted person only wishes to be contacted in specified circumstances and those circumstances apply.[159]

---

[153] ISR 2005, reg 5(2).
[154] Guidance, Chapter 10, para 9.
[155] Ibid, Chapter 10, para 15.
[156] Ibid, Chapter 10, para 21.
[157] ISR 2005, reg 6.1.
[158] Ibid, reg 6(2)(a) and (3).
[159] Ibid, reg 8(3).

9.117   The intermediary agency may not disclose identifying information (see **9.103**) about a person without that person's consent unless the subject of the information has died or is incapable of giving consent and the intermediary agency considers that disclosure is appropriate.[160] 'Each case will be different but the intermediary agency should, as a minimum, take steps to seek the views of the deceased person's next of kin before deciding whether it is appropriate to disclose the identifying information.[161] However where the subject of the application refuses consent or has died or is incapable of giving consent or a veto under reg 8 applies, the intermediary agency may provide the applicant with any information which is not identifying information if it considers it appropriate.[162]

Disclosure of information by Registrar General

9.118   The Registrar General is under a duty to maintain an Adopted Children's Register which includes prescribed information including the child's date of birth and the name under which the birth was registered.[163] The High Court does not have the power to limit or edit the information to be included on the Register[164] even though there have been a number of cases in which children have been traced by using the information.[165] However under its inherent jurisdiction the High Court can direct that during the minority of the child in question, the Registrar General should not disclose the details of the adoption including the adoption certificate, to any person without leave of the Court.[166] Such an order was made in *Re X (A Minor) (Adoption Details: Disclosure)*[167] when the Court of Appeal was satisfied that there was a real risk that the adopted child's birth mother might seek to trace her and disrupt the placement. A similar order was made in *Re W (Adoption Details: Disclosure)*[168] when the adopters had to move house after being traced by the birth grandparents. In county court proceedings the application for the order should be transferred to the High Court. If the adoption application is pending, that too should be transferred.[169]

9.119   The Register is not open to public inspection[170] but there are four exceptions to this general rule.

---

[160]   ISR 2005, reg 7(1) and (2).
[161]   Guidance, Chapter 10, para 48.
[162]   ISR 2005, reg 9.
[163]   Adoption Act 1976, s 50(3) and ACA 2002, s 77(1).
[164]   *Re X (A Minor) (Adoption Details: Disclosure)* [1994] 2 FLR 450.
[165]   *Re W (Adoption Details: Disclosure)* [1998] 2 FLR 625 per Wall J at 627.
[166]   *Re X (A Minor) (Adoption Details: Disclosure)* [1994] 2 FLR 450.
[167]   Ibid.
[168]   [1998] 2 FLR 625. It is unclear from the report what extra protection this afforded because the birth family already knew the name of the adopters.
[169]   *President's Direction. Adopted Children Register: Restriction on Disclosure* 17 December 1998 [1999] 1 FLR 315.
[170]   ACA 2002, s 77(2).

- Save where the High Court has made an order prohibiting this (see **9.118**), anyone may obtain a copy of the adoption certificate.

- On an application made by an adopted person over the age of 18, the Registrar General must give the applicant any information necessary to obtain a certified copy of the record of his birth.[171] The application does not have to be made through an intermediary agency and there is no statutory exception to the duty imposed on the Registrar General save that where the applicant was adopted before 12 November 1975, the Registrar General may not provide the information until the applicant has attended an interview with a counsellor from one of a number of specified[172] bodies.[173] However where the request comes from an intermediary agency, the Registrar General must take reasonable steps to comply with it.[174]

- The court[175] may, in exceptional circumstances, order the Registrar General to give the information 'to a person'.[176] The 'person' need not be an adult and, apparently need not be the adopted person. There is no requirement that the discretion should be exercised sparingly and only in exceptional circumstances. The burden on the applicant is no heavier than one of establishing a case of sufficient weight and justification.[177] In *Re H (Adoption: Disclosure of Information)*,[178] for example, the Court directed the Registrar General to disclose information on the Adopted Children Register about an adopted adult to his adult sister who was suffering from a genetically transmitted disease. On the evidence it appeared advisable that other members of the sister's family should be screened. In *D v Registrar General*[179] the Court of Appeal, approving *Re H*, refused to direct the Registrar General to disclose information to the birth mother of an adopted child who was now an adult. Disclosure should be ordered only in 'truly exceptional circumstances' justifying an 'exceptional "need to know"'.

- On an application made by an adopted person who is under the age of 18 and intends to marry, the Registrar General must inform the applicant whether or not it appears from information in the registers of live births or other records that the applicant and the person the applicant intends to marry may be within the prohibited degrees of relationship for the purposes of the Marriage Act 1949.[180]

---

[171] ACA 2002, Sch 2, para 1.
[172] Ibid, Sch 2, para 2(1)(a).
[173] Ibid, Sch 2, para 4.
[174] ISR 2005, reg 14(1).
[175] Apparently, the court which made the adoption order.
[176] ACA 2002, s 79(4).
[177] *Re H (Adoption: Disclosure of Information)* [1995] 1 FLR 236.
[178] Ibid.
[179] [1996] 1 FLR 707 and, on appeal, [1997] 1 FLR 715.
[180] ACA 2002, s 79(7).

9.120 Instead of approaching the Registrar General direct, the adopted person may use the services of an intermediary agency (se **9.108**). The Registrar General must take reasonable steps to comply with the request.[181] However, once the intermediary agency has the information it has a duty to consider the various matters set out in ISR 2005, reg 6 (see **9.15**) before disclosing it to the applicant.

9.121 Notwithstanding the terms of the statute and Regulations the right to obtain information is not an absolute one.

9.122 In *R v Registrar General ex p Smith*[182] the Divisional Court refused an application for judicial review of the Registrar General's refusal to provide the applicant with this information. Having been adopted as a baby, the applicant had a disturbed childhood and as a teenager was convicted of murder. Some years later he applied for such information as was necessary to obtain access to his birth records. After obtaining two psychiatric reports which indicated that the applicant's birth mother might be at risk if her identity was disclosed, the Registrar General refused to supply the information. The Court of Appeal dismissed the applicant's appeal. Although the justification given was the general one of public policy, on the facts of the case two of the three Lords Justice confined the justification of the refusal to circumstances where 'there is current and justified apprehension of a significant risk that the [applicant] might, in the future, use the information to commit a serious crime.'[183] However, Staughton LJ indicated that while that statement sufficed in the instant case, other cases might require further elucidation.

9.123 In *Re X (A Minor) (Adoption Details: Disclosure)*[184] the Court of Appeal (see **9.118**) held that there was a fear of 'an attack' by the birth mother and this would therefore bring the facts within the ambit of *Smith*. The order made in that case merely prevented information being provided without the leave of the court. When such an application is heard the court will be better placed to assess the actual risk.

9.124 It is uncertain whether the risk required to justify a refusal is restricted to risk of a serious crime. The general tenor of *Re X* and *Re W* which were based on risks of serious disruption to the placements seems to indicate that a less restrictive approach will be adopted.

Disclosure of information by the adoption agency

9.125 Prior to the commencement of the Adoption Agencies Regulations 2005 on 30 December 2005, agencies were under a duty to ensure that the adopted child's case record and all indices to its records had to be preserved for

---

[181]   ISR 2005, reg 14(1).
[182]   [1991] 1 FLR 255.
[183]   Ibid, per McCowan LJ at 263D and see also Staughton LJ at 262D.
[184]   [1994] 2 FLR 450.

at least 75 years and other records for 'so long as it considers appropriate'.[185] Broadly speaking the 'case record' had to contain all the information gathered in respect of the proposed adoption.[186] According to Departmental Guidance:

'The intention is to provide the adopted person with as much information as possible about his social and personal history and the reason for the adoption. Painful or unpleasant information should not necessarily be "glossed over". The identification of such material may, indeed, prove to be the basis for future post adoption support and service contingencies. Care must nevertheless be taken to anonymise the material and exceptionally exclude confidential information about third parties or information provided "in confidence and not for wider dissemination". There follows a check list of most of the documents which should be included in the case records. Among these are:

- record of social work with child about his adoption;
- adoption panel minutes and recommendations;
- summary of steps taken to find suitable adopters for the child and a copy of the child's profile records used for this purpose;
- adoption panel minutes and recommendation in respect of matching the child with prospective adopters;
- placement agreement with adopters.
- open letter from social worker describing how and why adoption plans became the plan for the child.'[187]

9.126 In *Gunn-Russo v Nugent Care Society and the Secretary of State for Health*[188] Scott Baker J commented that 'the significance [of this Guidance] is that such information is now placed on the file routinely with a view to the disclosure of the child'.

9.127 The contents of the child's care record and the adopter's case record are to be treated as confidential[189] but there is mandatory access in certain circumstances.[190] In addition the agency 'may provide such access to its records and disclose such information in its possession as it thinks fit'[191] for the purpose of its functions as an adoption agency. This includes access to the adopted person.[192] In *Re An Adoption*[193] a girl's father was appealing his conviction for raping his daughter who had alleged but then denied that he was the father of her child who had been adopted through an agency some years earlier. In the criminal proceedings the Court of Appeal gave the appellant permission to apply for the child's blood to be tested. The agency discovered in

---

[185] ISR 2005, reg 14(3).
[186] See ibid, reg 14(2).
[187] Local Authority Circular (97) 13, para 58.
[188] [2001] EWHC Admin 566, [2002] 1 FLR 1 at [28].
[189] Adoption Agencies Regulations 2005, SI 2005/389, reg 41.
[190] Ibid, reg 42(1). For example, to the Commissioner for Local Administration – see *Re A Subpoena (Adoption: Commissioner for Local Administration)* [1996] 2 FLR 629.
[191] Ibid, reg 42(2).
[192] *Gunn-Russo v Nugent Care Society and the Secretary of State for Health* [2001] EWHC Admin 566, [2002] 1 FLR 1.
[193] [1990] 1 FLR 412.

its adoption records an account by the mother dealing with the circumstances of the child's conception. The agency sought directions from the High Court on whether the information should be disclosed and to whom. Ewbank J directed that it should be disclosed to the Attorney General. See also **9.133**.

9.128   In *Gunn-Russo* Scott Baker J held that the wide discretion possessed by the agencies had to be exercised against the background of the adoption legislation and in the light of all the circumstances of the case. In the instant case where the adoption order had been made 53 years earlier, all the birth and adoptive parents had died and the adopted person had a genuine interest in disclosure, there was little if any purpose in maintaining confidentiality.

> 'Most reasonable people would not, I feel, think that after half a century disclosure would be likely to impair public confidence in the integrity of the confidentiality of the system. After all, a great many public records are now disclosed after a lapse of thirty years.'[194]

9.129   The adopted person seeking information can approach the agency themselves or may use the services of an intermediary agency (see **9.108**). It may prove easier to obtain information through the intermediary agency because the adoption agency must take reasonable steps to provide the information to that agency unless a veto under reg 8 (see **9.116**) exists.[195] However, once the intermediary agency has the information it has a duty to consider the various matters set out in reg 6 (see **9.115**) before disclosing it to the applicant.

Disclosure of records by the Court

9.130   The current rules governing the protection of documents relating to court proceedings are contained in Part 8 of the Family Procedure (Adoption) Rules 2005. All documents are to be kept in a place of special security[196] and, save as provided by the Rules or any practice direction 'or any direction of the Court' are open to inspection.[197]

9.131   An adoptive person over the age of 18 'has the right' to receive from the court, after the removal of any protected information,[198] a copy of:

- The application for an adoption order (but not the documents attached to it).

- The adoption order.

- Any orders relating to the adoption proceedings.

---

[194]   [1990] 1 FLR 412 at [54]–[55].
[195]   ISR 2005, reg 12(4).
[196]   FP(A)R 2005, r 82.
[197]   Ibid, r 83.
[198]   FP(A)R 2005, r 84. See also ACA 2002, s 57(3).

- Orders allowing any person contact with the child after the order was made.

- Any transcript or written reasons for the court's decision.[199]

- A report made to the court by the child's guardian, reporting officer, children and family reporter, a local authority or adoption agency.[200]

In addition the Court has to disclose any information identifying the adoption agency which has been requested in writing by an intermediary agency.[201]

9.132 The rules[202] also make provision for disclosure of documents to specified persons, including 'a professional acting in furtherance of the protection of children' (defined as including the NSPCC and a police officer serving in a child protection unit[203]) and to others in the exercise of its general powers. There is no *right* of disclosure save under r 84. Even then, following *R v Registrar General ex p Smith*,[204] the court probably has the right to refuse disclosure, if required in the public interest.

9.133 Cases have arisen where disclosure is sought for the purpose of criminal proceedings.[205] The court is likely to adopt the same approach as that for any application for access of confidential documents relating to proceedings involving children. This was described by Sir Thomas Bingham MR in *Re L (Police Investigation: Privilege)*[206] thus:

> 'I doubt whether the discretion to order or refuse disclosure is properly described as unfettered, since every judicial discretion must be exercised judicially. The authorities[207] show that many factors are potentially relevant, depending on the facts, to the exercise of the discretion. ... [It] is plain that consideration of the welfare of the child will be a major factor in the exercise of the discretion: if disclosure will promote the welfare of the child, it will readily be ordered; if disclosure will not affect the welfare of the child, other considerations are likely to carry the day one way or the other; if disclosure will prejudice the welfare of the child, disclosure may nevertheless be ordered if there are potent arguments for disclosure, but the court will be much more reluctant to make the order. It is plain that the public interest in the fair administration of justice, and the right of a criminal defendant to defend himself, are accepted as potent reasons for disclosure. If, on the other hand, it could be shown that disclosure would for some

---

[199] Practice Direction: Disclosing Information to an Adopted Adult. Available at www.justice.gov. uk/family/procrules/practice_directions/pd_part08b.htm.

[200] Ibid.

[201] ISR 2005, regs 12(2(c) and 15.

[202] FP(A)R 2005, r 79.

[203] Ibid, r 78(2)(d).

[204] [1991] 1 FLR 255.

[205] eg *Re H (Criminal Proceedings)* [1995] 1 FLR 964. See also *Re An Adoption* [1990] 1 FLR 412 and **9.127**.

[206] [1995] 1 FLR 999 at 1019, approved by the House of Lords on appeal at [1996] 1 FLR 731 at 741.

[207] eg *Re Manda (Wardship: Disclosure of Evidence)* [1993] 1 FLR 205.

reason be unfair or oppressive to a party to the ... [children] proceedings, that would weigh against an order for disclosure.'

Adoptions after 30 December 2005

Intermediary agencies

9.134 Intermediary agencies have no function where the adoption order pre-dated 30 December 2005.

Disclosure of information by Registrar General

9.135 A request for disclosure is no longer made directly to the Registrar General but to the agency. In addition, the right of the High Court to prohibit disclosure is given a statutory basis.

9.136 On attaining the age of 18 an adopted person has the right to receive from the appropriate adoption agency any information which will allow him to obtain a copy of his birth certificate.[208]

9.137 If the agency does not hold the information, it must apply to the Registrar General for the information on behalf of the adopted person.[209] The Registrar General is required to disclose the information to the agency[210] which by implication must pass it to the adopted person.[211]

9.138 Where any person wishes to apply to the adoption agency for disclosure of information but does not know which agency to approach, they can apply to the Registrar General for information which will enable them to contact the agency and the Registrar General must supply it.[212]

9.139 The High Court may prohibit disclosure.[213] This statutory power given to the High Court is likely to be exercised in the same way as the Court exercised its inherent power under *R v Registrar General ex p Smith.*[214]

> '[AIR r 19] provides for cases where the agency has grounds for believing that disclosing birth record information to the adopted person could place others at risk of harm. This might arise where, for example, a child was placed for adoption as a result of sexual abuse by a member of their birth family and the agency had grounds to believe that disclosing birth record information to the adopted adult could place members of the birth family at risk of serious harm.'[215]

---

[208] ACCA 2002, s 60(2).
[209] AIR 2005, reg 19(1).
[210] ACA 2002, s 79(5).
[211] Guidance, Chapter 11, para 99.
[212] AIR 2005, reg 20(1)(b).
[213] ACCA 2002, s 60(2) and AIR 2005, reg 19.
[214] [1991] 1 FLR 255.
[215] Guidance, Chapter 11, para 4.

Disclosure of information by the adoption agency

9.140 The agency has to keep prescribed information ('section 56 information')[216] which includes:

- The information on the adopted person's case record as required by Part 3 of the Adoption Agencies Regulations 2005 which will include information about the adopted person, their natural parents and other birth relatives, the adoptive parents and other persons involved in the adoption such as former carers or social workers.

- Information prescribed by AIR 2005, reg 4(3) including information given to the agency by a natural parent or birth relative (or other significant people in the adopted person's life and any information about a relevant entry on the Adoption Contact Register.

This information may include 'protected information' (see **9.105**).

9.141 Subject to the requirements of specific rules, any adult may apply to the agency for disclosure and not just the adopted person.

9.142 The agency may disclose section 56 information which is not protected information as it thinks fit for the purposes of carrying out its functions as an agency.[217] See **9.127**.

9.143 Where the information is protected the agency is not required to proceed with the application unless it considers it is appropriate to do so.[218]

9.144 In deciding whether to disclose it the agency must take all reasonable steps to obtain the views of any adult to whom the information relates.[219] It must also consider all the circumstances including:

- the welfare of the adopted person;

- any views obtained from the subject of the information; and

- any other prescribed matters.[220]

9.145 Where the protected information relates to a child (note, not necessarily the adopted child) the agency must take all reasonable steps to obtain the views of the child's parent or guardian and the views of the child if the agency

---

[216] ACA 2002, s 56(1) and AIR 2005, reg 4.
[217] AIR 2005, reg 8(1).
[218] ACA 2002, ss 61(2) and 62(2).
[219] Ibid, s 61(3).
[220] Ibid, s 61(5). As yet, there is no additional prescribed matter.

considers it appropriate having regard to his age, understanding and all the circumstances of the case.[221] It must consider all the circumstances including:

- the welfare of the adopted person;

- any views obtained from the subject of the information and if a child, the parent, guardian and where appropriate, the child; and

- any other prescribed matters.[222]

9.146 Where a relevant person is an adopted child (note, not necessarily *the* adopted child), his welfare is the paramount consideration.[223] Where the information relates to a child who is not an adopted child the agency must have particular regard to that child's welfare.[224]

9.147 As regards the exercise of the discretion to disclose, the Guidance notes that the agency may withhold protected information, contrary to the views expressed by the person the information is about.

'It could, for example, decide to withhold the disclosure of protected information on the grounds that it was in the interests of the adopted person's welfare – even though the person the information was about had agreed to its disclosure. This discretion may come into play where, for example, one of the natural parents agreed to the disclosure of protected information but the other did not.'[225]

9.148 Where the agency decides to disclose or withhold protected information contrary to the view expressed by the subject of the information, that person may seek an independent review of the agency's determination.[226]

9.149 In order to assist in the disclosure of information, an adult may enter into an agreement with the agency as regards disclosure of protected information about himself.[227] The adoptive parent or, in the case of adoption by a couple, the adoptive parents or a birth parent who had parental responsibility before the adoption order was made, may also enter into a similar agreement. However, where an agreement is being contemplated, the agency must be satisfied that all parties are fully aware of the implications of entering into such an agreement and its effect.[228]

9.150 The information recorded in the agreement will include the reason for making it, the information which may be disclosed and any restrictions on the circumstances in which it may be disclosed. Where an agreement is in place, the

---

[221] ACA 2002, s 62(3) and (4).
[222] Ibid, s 62(7). As yet, there is no additional prescribed matter.
[223] Ibid, s 62(6)(a).
[224] Ibid, s 62(6)(b).
[225] Guidance, Chapter 11, para 16.
[226] AIR 2005, reg 15.
[227] ACA 2002, s 57(5) and AIR 2005, reg 11.
[228] Guidance, Chapter 11, para 63.

agency may disclose protected information within the terms of the agreement without, for example, having to seek[229] the views of the adult making the agreement. However, it seems that the agency will still retain a discretion on whether or not to disclose.

9.151 The Guidance notes that

> 'Formal agreements for the sharing of protected information between the agency, the adoptive parents and the natural parents are likely to be rare. The majority of children being placed for adoption will have been the subject of care proceedings and it is not uncommon for one or both of the natural parents to be hostile to the plan for adoption and where the need to maintain the confidentiality of the adoptive placement is important.'[230]

Disclosure of records by the Court

9.152 Part 8 of the Family Procedure (Adoption) Rules 2005 applies with the exception that an intermediary agency will not be involved. See **9.130**.

Adoption Contact Register

9.153 Since 1989 the Adoption Contact Register has provided a confidential way for birth parents and other relatives to inform an adopted adult that contact would be welcome and to give a contact address.[231]

9.154 The Register which is maintained by the Registrar General contains prescribed information about:

- adopted persons over the age of 18 who have given notice expressing their wishes as to making contact with their relatives,[232] registered under Part 1 of the Register;

- relatives of an adopted person who have given notice expressing their wishes as to making contact with that person,[233] registered under Part 2 of the Register.

9.155 The prescribed information in relation to an adopted person consists of:

- his full name, address and date of birth;

- named relatives they wish to contact and not contact;

---

[229] Under ACA 2002, ss 61 and 62.

[230] Guidance, Chapter 11, para 27.

[231] *The Children Act 1989 Guidance and Regulations* vol 9 *Adoption Issues* (Department of Health, 1991).

[232] Defined as 'any person who (but for his adoption) would be related to him by blood (including half-blood), marriage or civil partnership: ACA 2005, s 81(2).

[233] ACA 2005, s 80 and the Adopted Children and Adoption Contact Registers Regulations 2005, SI 2005/924 (ACCR 2005), reg 6.

- an indication that they are aware of the possibility of withdrawing the registration at any time.[234]

9.156 The prescribed information in relation to a relative of an adopted person consists of:

- their full name, address and date of birth;

- the name of the adopted person with whom they desire contact or the fact that they do not desire contact with the named adopted person.[235]

9.157 The Registrar General is under a duty to give an adopted person whose name is in Part 1 of the Register, the name, in writing, of any relative of his whose name is in Part 2 and who has asked for contact with that adopted person, together with the address at or through which the relative may be contacted.[236] The Guidance notes that under these new Regulations, the onus of taking the first steps with regards to actual contact continues to be placed on the adopted person.[237] The requirements for the adopted person to be registered under Part 1 and that he can be registered only if an adult means that an adopted person under the age of 18 cannot apply for the information on the Register.

---

[234] ACCR 2005, Sch 3.
[235] Ibid, Sch 4.
[236] Ibid, reg 8.
[237] Guidance, Chapter 12, para 26.

Chapter 10

ASSESSMENT – SPECIAL GUARDIANSHIP

INTRODUCTION

10.1 The status of special guardianship and the growing recognition that children who are the subjects of applications for special guardianship orders and their carers may have needs different from or greater than others in the general population make it important that all applicants and subjects of special guardianship applications receive a detailed assessment. Section 14A(8) of the Children Act 1989 requires the relevant local authority to carry out such an assessment in every case and not only in those cases where the child is being 'looked after'. If the circumstances of an individual case require it, further assessments can be obtained by way of a report under s 7, from an expert witness or by appointing a guardian for the child.

BACKGROUND

10.2 Most applicants for special guardianship orders are likely to be members of the child's extended families and children who are the subject of applications for special guardianship are more likely to be currently 'looked after'[1] by a local authority than to be living with the applicants as a result of private arrangements. Research by Hall[2] found that of the 372 orders made in England and Wales in 2006 (excluding orders made in Family Proceedings Courts) nearly nine in ten (87%) of applicants were kinship carers rather than local authority foster parents (12%). Nearly three quarters (74%) of orders were made in care proceedings and 26% in private law proceedings. An analysis of a sample of 70 cases found that a quarter of the special guardians had not previously cared for the child.

10.3 A literature review by Hunt[3] found that a high proportion of children in kinship care outside the foster care system were likely to have needs very similar to those within it. 'Probably, the majority of children in kinship care will have needs greater than children in the general population.'[4] Research indicates that kinship carers too had high levels of needs which were not being met.

---

[1]   Ie the subject of final or interim care orders or being accommodated under s 20 of the Children Act 1989 (see s 22(1)).
[2]   *Special Guardianship: A Missed Opportunity – Findings From Research* [2008] Fam Law 148.
[3]   *Family and Friends Carers* (Department of Health, 2001).
[4]   Ibid at p 44.

'One American study has also shown that kinship care giving is more stressful than any other form of care. [However] it is not clear from the UK research whether kinship carers are experiencing the levels of poverty, ill-health and psychological distress which are such a feature of the American literature.'[5]

A more detailed account of the problems encountered by kinship carers is given at **11.7**.

10.4 There is little information about which characteristics possessed by carers are predictive of a successful placement. Hunt makes the point that the scarcity of research evidence highlights the importance of high quality assessments in each case. However:

'One of the important questions is whether placements made by a welfare agency after full assessment are likely to be more or less successful than placements where the child is already in situ. The only study[6] to comment on this found there to be little difference.'[7]

10.5 One theme in the research literature, both in the United Kingdom and internationally is that many of the problems presented by kinship care 'are the result of trying to force a traditional, private form of care into a mould designed by professionalized child welfare systems for care provided by strangers'.[8]

The role of the local authority

10.6 The legislature in developing special guardianship attempted to bridge the gap by partially adopting the model of adoption. Although applications for both types of order are private applications, the quasi-permanent nature of the orders makes it important that in all cases an independent assessment of the applicant is carried out by social services.

10.7 Where local authority is in a position of responsibility by reason that it is 'looking after' the child, it not only has to assess the couple but also has to consider whether to approve the placement. An absence of approval is a barrier, admittedly not insurmountable, to the application. A child cannot be placed for adoption by the authority unless the case has been considered by the adoption panel and the authority as an adoption agency approves the placement. Likewise, if the authority does not approve the guardianship application, it may be more difficult for an applicant who requires leave from the court to bring the application (for example a foster carer with whom the child has not been living for at least a year or a relative with whom a child has

---

[5] *Family and Friends Carers* at p 44.
[6] Rowe et al *Longterm Foster Care* (Batsford, 1984).
[7] Hunt op cit at p 37.
[8] Ibid, at p 46.

not lived for at least a year)[9] to obtain leave especially as the court will need to consider the authority's plans for the child's future.[10]

10.8 The role played by the authority may create tension between the perspectives of the prospective kinship carers who see themselves as family members and social workers who see them as part of the child care system.[11]

10.9 In summary:

- The assessment of the application needs to include not just an assessment directed at the suitability of the order but also a consideration of how the needs of the applicant and child can be met whether by special guardianship support services or otherwise (for which see Chapter 11).[12]

- The assessment needs to be carried out especially sensitively where the applicant is a member of the child's family.

How accurate are the assessments?

10.10 A positive or negative assessment is not a guarantee of success or failure. Hunt and others examined a cohort of 133 children removed from their parents' care by the courts and placed with kinship carers.[13] They found that in general predictions were rarely accurate. Most of the specific concerns identified in the care proceedings did not materialise and most of the issues which arose in placement had not been forecast. However, practitioners were more accurate at predicting the future parenting capacity of carers. 'Assessments should therefore keep a clear focus on this core task.'[14]

SECTION 14A(8) REPORT

10.11 No special guardianship order can be made without the court considering a report from the relevant local authority whether the order is sought by way of an application or the court is considering making the order of its own initiative under s 14A(6).[15] The importance of a detailed assessment of the child and the prospective special guardians is underlined by the words of Wall LJ in *Re S (Adoption Order or Special Guardianship Order)*:[16]

---

9   See **5.21**.

10   CA 1989, s 10(9)(d).

11   Hunt op cit at p 47.

12   See also Talbot and Kidd 'Special Guardianship Orders – Issues in Respect of Family Assessment' [2004] Fam Law 273.

13   Hunt, Waterhouse and Lutman *Keeping them in the family* (2008, BAAF) summarised in [2008] Fam Law 435.

14   Ibid at p 161.

15   CA 1989, s 14A(11) *Re S (Adoption Order Or Special Guardianship) (No 2)* [2007] EWCA Civ 90, [2007] 1 FLR 855 at [4].

16   [2007] EWCA Civ 54, [2007] 1 FLR 819 at [47].

'The carefully constructed statutory regime (notice to the local authority, leave requirements in certain cases, the role of the court and the report from the local authority-even where the order is made by the court of its own motion) demonstrates the care which is required before making a special guardianship order, and that it is only appropriate if, in the particular circumstances of the particular case, it is best fitted to met the needs of the child or children concerned.'

Which authority?

10.12   The authority preparing the report is the authority to whom the prospective special guardian has given notice under s 14(7), that is, where the child is being looked after, that authority or otherwise, the local authority in whose area the individual making the application is ordinarily resident (for which see **18.13**).

Contents of the report

10.13   The information to be sought includes not only information relevant for assessing the suitability of the special guardian but also information about the natural family which may be helpful to the child and special guardian in the future.

10.14   The Schedule to the Special Guardianship Regulations 2005[17] prescribes a number of matters with which the report has to deal. They are divided into ten parts.

1 The child

10.15   The matters under this part include the child's immigration status, racial origin and background and religious persuasion. Details of siblings must be given and the extent of the child's contact with his relatives and any other person the authority considers relevant must be considered. The report must describe the child's personality, development (including educational attainment) and health and educational history and address his needs. Details of any orders made under the Children Act 1989 must be given.

2 The child's family

10.16   The required details include basic information about the family – parents and siblings – and the health history (including any hereditary disease, disorder or disability), religious persuasion, educational and employment history and personality and interests as well as a photograph of the parents. If the identity and whereabouts of the father is not known, the report must contain the information which has been ascertained and from whom and the steps which have been taken to establish paternity.

---

[17]   SI 2005/1109.

3 The wishes and feelings of the child and others

10.17 This includes the wishes and feelings of the child and each parent regarding special guardianship, his religious and cultural upbringing and contact between the child, his parents, relatives and any other person the local authority considers relevant as well as the wishes and feelings of any of the child's relatives or any other person the local authority considers relevant.

4 The prospective special guardians

10.18 The required information includes the basic details of the prospective special guardian – nationality, immigration status (where appropriate) racial origin and cultural and linguistic background), parents and siblings, health, educational and employment history, personality and interests and details of other members of the prospective guardian's household, home and neighbourhood. Details must be given of any past or present, marriages, civil partnerships or current relationships and, where there is to be a joint application the nature of the applicants' relationship and its stability must be assessed. If there is to be a sole application by someone who is a member of a couple, the reason for this must be given.

10.19 The authority has to enquire into the prospective special guardian's previous experience of caring for children, any past assessments as a prospective adopter, foster parent or special guardian, any involvement in any previous family court proceedings, and provide a description of how he relates to children in general.

10.20 The authority must report on whether the prospective guardian is willing to follow any wishes of the child or his parents in relation to religious or cultural upbringing and the prospective special guardians' views in relation to contact between the child and his relatives and any other person the authority considers relevant.

10.21 The hopes and expectations the prospective special guardian holds for the child and his reasons for applying for and the extent of his understanding of the nature and effect of special guardianship must be ascertained.

10.22 The prospective special guardian has to nominate three personal referees and the report has to include details of the interviews carried out by the referees.

10.23 An assessment has to be carried out of the prospective special guardian's and his family's relationship with the child and his ability or suitability to bring up the child.

5 The local authority

10.24 The authority must report on the prospective special guardian's past involvement with the authority and, where the reporting authority is looking after the child and the prospective special guardian lives in an area of another authority,[18] details of the enquiries made of that other authority.

10.25 The authority must provide a summary of the special guardianship support services (see Chapter 11) provided by the authority, the period of time for which they are to be provided or, if they are not to be provided, the reasons for this.

6 Medical information

10.26 A summary must be prepared by the medical professional who provided the medical information relating to the child and the prospective special guardian.

7 The implications of the making of a special guardianship order

10.27 The report must assess the implications of the making of a special guardianship order for the child, his parents, the prospective special guardian and his family and any other person the authority considers relevant.

8 Relative merits of a special guardianship order and other orders which may be made

10.28 The report must consider the relative merits of a special guardianship order and other orders which may be made under the CA 1989 or the Adoption and Children Act 2002 together with an assessment of whether the child's long-term interests would best be met by a special guardianship order.

9 Recommendation

10.29 The report must contain a recommendation of whether or not the special guardianship order should be made and, if not, any alternative proposal in respect of the child.

10 Contact

10.30 The report must contain a recommendation as to what arrangements there should be for contact between the child and his relatives or any person the authority considers relevant.

---

[18]   CA 1989, s 14A(7).

Comparison with the report provided for an adoption application

10.31 The report provided under the Regulations is similar but not identical to the report required under the Family Procedure (Adoption) Rules 2005[19] in relation to adoption applications. Notable differences are the exclusion of a recommendation as to whether or not the local authority should be made a party, whether a respondent is incapable of managing his own affairs, inheritance rights, arrangements concerning siblings and the ability and willingness of any of the child's relatives to 'provide the child with a secure environment in which the child can develop and otherwise to meet the child's needs'.[20] Also missing is the requirement for confirmation that the applicant has not been convicted of or cautioned for a specified offence.[21] Where such matters are relevant to an application for Special Guardianship, they should, of course, be included in the report.

ASSESSMENT WHEN THE CHILD IS LOOKED AFTER

10.32 Where a child is being 'looked after'[22] whether under a voluntary arrangement with those with parental authority or under a care order, the local authority has various duties under the Arrangement for Placement of Children (General) Regulations 1991 (APC(G)R 1991)[23] and the Review of Children's Cases Regulations 1991 (RCCR 1991)[24] which may apply when the authority is considering whether to approve an application for a special guardianship order or whether to place the child with the prospective adopters.

10.33 Before a child is placed the authority has, so far as is reasonably practicable, to make immediate and long-term arrangements for the placement and for promoting the welfare of the child.[25] Children's cases have to be reviewed within 4 weeks from the date they are looked after, not more than 3 months after the first review and thereafter not more than 6 months after the previous review.[26] The duty of the authority is to safeguard and promote the child's welfare[27] including a duty to promote his educational achievement[28] and it must, unless it is not reasonably practicable or consistent with his welfare, endeavour to promote contact between the child, any other person who has parental responsibility for him and any relative (including by marriage or civil partnership), friend or other person connected with him.[29]

---

[19] Practice Direction 5C, Annex A. See also Chapter 8.
[20] SI 2005/2795, Annex A, Section, B Part 2, para (f)(ii).
[21] Under reg 23(3) of the Adoption Agencies Regulations 2005, SI 2005/389. See Annex A, Section C, Part 1, para (r).
[22] As defined in CA 1989 s 22(1)
[23] SI 1991/890.
[24] SI 1991/895.
[25] APC(G)R 1991, reg 3.
[26] RCCR 1991, reg 3.
[27] CA 1989, s 22(3).
[28] Ibid, s 22(3A).
[29] PC(G)R 1991, reg 6.

10.34   Before making any decision, the authority must, so far as is reasonably practicable, ascertain the wishes and feelings of the child, his parents, any other person who has parental responsibility for him and any other person whose wishes and feelings the authority considers relevant.[30] In addition it has to give 'due consideration' to these wishes and feelings, to the child's religious persuasion, racial origin and cultural and linguistic background.[31] Both sets of regulations require the authority to have regard to specified health considerations[32] and educational considerations.[33]

10.35   For a further discussion, see **15.49**.

10.36   The considerations are therefore similar to those under the Schedule to the Special Guardianship Regulations 2005[34] but cannot be ignored. An additional requirement is that if the authority is of the view that communication between the child and his parents or person with parental responsibility for him has been infrequent or he has not been visited or lived with such a person for 12 months, it has to consider whether to appoint a visitor to visit, advise and befriend him.[35]

GUIDANCE ON ASSESSMENT

10.37   Save in relation to the assessment of the need for special guardianship support services (for which see Chapter 11) the Special Guardianship Guidance[36] contains no specific guidance on preparing the section 14A(8) report. However *The Framework for the Assessment of Children in Need and their Families*[37] provides guidance on all assessments of children in need. In addition, *The Children Act 1989 Guidance and Regulations Vol 3 Family Placements*[38] deals specifically with the Arrangement for Placement of Children (General Regulations) and the other Regulations governing the care of 'looked after' children. Both are issued under s 7 of the Local Authority Services Act 1970.[39]

The principles

10.38   Important principles underpin the approach to assessing children recommended in *The Framework*.[40] Assessments:

---

30   CA 1989, s 22(4).
31   Ibid, s 22(5).
32   PC(G)R 1991, Sch 2, RCCR 1991, Sch 2.
33   PC(G)R 1991, Sch 3, RCCR 1991, Sch 3.
34   SI 2005/1109.
35   CA 1989, Sch 2, para 17(1) and (2).
36   DFES (2005).
37   Department of Health, Department for Education and Science and the Home Office (2000).
38   Department of Health (1991).
39   For the statutory effect of such Guidance see **11.22**.
40   Op cit, para 1.33.

- are child centred;

- are rooted in child development;

- are ecological in their approach;

- ensure equality of opportunity;

- involve working with children and their family;

- build on strengths as well as identifying difficulties;

- are inter-agency in their approach to assessment and the provision of services;

- are a continuing process and not a single event;

- are carried out in parallel with other action and providing services;

- are grounded in evidence based knowledge.

10.39 A **child centred** approach means that the child is seen and kept in focus throughout the assessment. Account is always taken of the child's perspective irrespective of other issues the family may be facing.[41]

10.40 The *Framework* notes that children have a range of different and complex **developmental needs** which must be met at different stages of childhood if optimal outcomes are to be achieved.[42] The **ecological approach** recognises that an understanding of the child must be located within the context of the child's family (parents or carers and the wider family) and of the community and culture in which he or she is growing up.[43]

'Assessment therefore should take account of three domains:

- The child's developmental needs;
- The parents' or caregivers' capacities to respond appropriately;
- The wider family and environmental factors'[44]

10.41 Ensuring **equality of opportunity** does not mean that all children are created the same. It means understanding and working sensitively and knowledgeably to identify the particular issues for the child and his family.[45] As for **working with children and their families**, 'the concept of partnership between the State and the family in situations where families are in need of assistance

---

[41] *The Children Act 1989 Guidance and Regulations Vol 3 Family Placements*, para 1.34.
[42] Ibid, para 1.36.
[43] Ibid, para 1.39.
[44] Ibid, para 1.40.
[45] Ibid, para 1.43.

lies at the heart of childcare legislation'.[46] It requires sensitivity towards the particular circumstances of the family, for example, where English is not the parent's first language. 'Parents value taking part in discussions about how and where the assessment will be carried out, as well as what they hope it will achieve.'[47]

10.42   The assessment must **build on strengths as well as identifying difficulties** which will vary for each child. It is important that the assessments not only identifies deficits but also makes a 'realistic and informed appraisal of the strengths and resources in the family'.

> 'Nothing can be assumed ... What is working well or what may be acting as positive factors for the child and family may be overlooked. For example a single mother, in crisis over health, financial and housing problems may still be managing to get her child up in time in the mornings, washed, dressed, breakfasted and off to school each day'[48]

10.43   Assessment is a **continuous process** and must necessarily be a process of gathering information from a variety of sources and making sense of it with the family and any other professionals who may be involved.[49] If **action and services** are required, where necessary they should not await completion of the assessment.[50] Practice is expected to be **evidence based**, by which the Framework means that the assessors should use up-to-date knowledge gained critically from research and practice and the outcomes of services and interventions.[51] The Framework contains details of an appropriate knowledge base.

10.44   Chapter 2 of the *Framework* is particularly valuable and contains a discussion of the dimensions of a child's developmental needs and dimensions of parenting capacity. These are discussed further at **6.5** and **6.67**.

Guidance on 'looked after' children

10.45   *The Children Act 1989 Guidance* deals in general with the various Regulations and makes useful points about the **need to consult** the child and the family.

> 'The more mature the child the more fully he will be able to enter into a discussion about plans and proposals and participate in the decision making process. When older children are involved ... there may well be a different perception of the child's needs and interests as seen by the child and his parents.'[52]

---

[46]   *The Children Act 1989 Guidance and Regulations Vol 3 Family Placements*, para 1.44.
[47]   Ibid, para 1.46.
[48]   Ibid, para 1.48.
[49]   Ibid, para 1.51.
[50]   Ibid, para 1.56.
[51]   Ibid, para 1.58.
[52]   *The Children Act 1989 Guidance and Regulations Vol 3 Family Placements* para 2.47.

10.46 Chapter 2 of the Guidance considers arrangements for the placement of children. All factors relevant to the welfare of the individual child must be taken into account.

'None of the separate factors involved should be abstracted and converted into a general pre-condition which overrides the others or causes any of them to be less than fully considered ...'.[53]

10.47 Authorities should act as 'good parents' in relation to the **health** of children looked after.

'Health care implies a positive approach to the child's health and should be taken to include general surveillance and care for health and developmental progress as well as treatment for illness and accidents'.[54]

10.48 In addition authorities need to be alert to the health care needs of children from ethnic minority groups.[55]

10.49 Further specific guidance is given on the need to consider the child's **race, culture, religion and linguistic background**. See **6.103**.

SECTION 7 REPORT

10.50 In many and probably most applications, the section 14A(8) report, coupled with the internal planning process where the child is looked after will provide sufficient assessment of the child and the prospective adopters. Where the application is made alongside public law proceedings, there will be the added safeguard of a report from the child's guardian. There may be some purely private law proceedings where the court might wish to direct that a report is prepared by the Children and Family Court Advisory and Support Service ('CAFCASS') under s 7 of the CA 1989. Such a report could be directed on the application generally but it is good practice to specify any particular matter about which the court is concerned and doing so may reduce the delay in the report being prepared.

'The CAFCASS practitioner's contribution is unique and we would wish to see an emphasis in reports on the key issues at stake with professional analysis and judgment designed to assist the court reach the best decision. Judges should, where appropriate, direct focussed reports and should be clear about the precise points of information, analysis and judgment they are looking for.'[56]

---

[53] *The Children Act 1989 Guidance and Regulations Vol 3 Family Placements*, para 2.22.
[54] Ibid, para 2.23.
[55] Ibid, para 2.26.
[56] *Memorandum from the President of the Family Division and the Chief Executive of CAFCASS*, 9 March 2005.

10.51   Section 7 reports are discussed more fully in *Children Act Private Law Proceedings: A Handbook*.[57]

10.52   It is possible for a guardian to be appointed for the child – see **18.70**. The duties of the guardian are set out in FPR 1981, rr 4.11 and 4.11A.

EXPERT EVIDENCE

10.53   As in all private law and public law applications, the court may permit expert evidence to be called. Without permission, no information or documents relating to the proceedings may be disclosed to a potential expert without risking being in contempt of court. Furthermore, without the permission of the court nobody may cause the child to be medically or psychiatrically examined or otherwise assessed for the purpose of preparing an expert report.[58] These two restrictions make it impossible for any useful report to be obtained without the permission of the court. Furthermore it is 'contrary to both the spirit and the letter of the approach to expert evidence' for one party, without notice to the other party or the court to commission a report.[59]

10.54   Courts are expected to scrutinise critically any application for permission to adduce expert evidence. Instructing experts may cause delay and is expensive. Permission should be given only when it is necessary to resolve a relevant issue. Where possible, the expert should be instructed jointly by the parties.[60] Where a non-medical report from a jointly instructed expert is adverse to one party who wishes to obtain a second report, the first question for the court is whether the joint report appears to be fundamentally flawed, biased, wrong, unbalanced or unfair. If the answer is yes, then that may be sufficient grounds for giving leave to adduce further evidence. If the answer is no, the next questions are whether the report is pivotal and whether it can be challenged without the need for a further report. The answers to these questions may be determinative. Finally, the impact of a further report on the trial timetable needs to be considered.[61] In civil procedure, it is common practice to consider whether, as a first step, the aggrieved party should be expected to put written questions to the single joint expert as a means of attempting to solve the difficulties. If a further report is necessary, permission to adduce it in evidence can be withheld until the original and the new experts have discussed their reports.[62]

---

[57]   Mitchell (2nd edn, 2006) ch 18.
[58]   Family Proceedings Rules 1991, r 4.18, Family Proceedings Court (Children Act 1989) Rules 1991, r 18.
[59]   *Re A (Family Proceedings: Expert Witnesses)* [2001] 1 FLR 723 per Wall J at 730.
[60]   *Re B (Sexual Abuse: Expert's Report)* [2000] 1 FLR 871.
[61]   *Re SK (Local Authority: Expert Evidence)* [2007] EWHC 3289 (Fam), [2008] 2 FLR 707, *W v Oldham Metropolitan Borough Council* [2005] EWCA Civ 1247, [2006] 1 FLR 543.
[62]   See, for example, *Daniels v Walker* [2000] 1 WLR 1382, *Cosgrove v Patisson* [2000] All ER (D) 2007.

10.55 Issues on which it may be appropriate for an expert to report on special guardianship cases may include the child's physical, mental or emotional needs or educational or general development, the health of the proposed special guardian and the importance to the child of maintaining or limiting contact with a parent or family member.

10.56 The procedure for obtaining expert reports in private law proceedings is governed by the Practice Direction *Experts in Family Proceedings Relating to Children.*[63] This covers:

- the need to obtain **information about the expert** which will enable the court to decide whether or not to give permission for the expert;[64]

- the need to **raise as quickly as possible,** by or at the First Hearing Dispute Resolution hearing (in private law proceedings) or the Case Management Conference (public law) the issue of whether expert evidence should be permitted;[65]

- the overriding duty to the court of the expert which takes precedence over any instructing party and the expert's particular duties including the duties to provide advice which accords with the best practice of the expert's profession and to provide an opinion which is independent of the parties;[66]

- the **content** of the report;[67]

- the **preliminary information** which should be provided to the proposed expert and the enquiries which need to be made including whether or not permission has been granted or sought for the examination of the child, whether it will be necessary for the expert to conduct interviews and, if so, of whom, and the response to these enquiries including confirmation that the work can be carried out within the suggested timescale, dates to avoid for giving evidence and the fee to be charged;[68]

- the **information which the court will require** when considering whether or not to give permission including the name and qualifications of the expert, his availability, the relevance of the evidence sought to be adduced and the specific questions to be asked; the timetable, the responsibility for the instruction, whether the evidence can properly be obtained by joint instruction of two or more of the parties, why the evidence cannot be

---

[63] 1 April 2008. See *The Family Court Practice 2009.*
[64] Ibid, para 1.7.
[65] Ibid, para 1.9.
[66] Ibid, paras 3.1 and 3.2.
[67] Ibid, para 3.3.
[68] Ibid, paras 4.1 and 4.2.

given by social services or the guardian and the likely cost and how it is to be apportioned between the parties;[69]

- drafting the letter of instruction;[70]

- putting **questions to the expert** for the purpose of clarifying the report;[71]

- the **experts' meeting** to identify and narrow the issues, to attempt to reach agreement on expert issues and to identify the reasons for disagreement and what, if any, action needs to be taken to resolve any outstanding disagreement, to explain or add other evidence in order to assist the court and to limit, where possible the need of the experts to attend court;[72]

- what should be done **when a party refuses to be bound by an agreement** reached at the experts' meeting;[73]

- **arrangements** for the experts to give evidence including experts of a like discipline giving evidence on the same day and the need to consider whether evidence can be given by telephone or video link;[74]

- the steps to be taken to notify the experts of the **outcome** of the case including providing a copy of the transcript of the judgment if one is prepared.[75]

---

[69]   *The Family Court Practice 2009*, para 4.3.
[70]   Ibid, para 5.1.
[71]   Ibid, para 6.1.
[72]   Ibid, paras 6.2 and 6.3.
[73]   Ibid, para 7.
[74]   Ibid, paras 8.1 and 8.2.
[75]   Ibid, para 9.

Chapter 11

SUPPORT – SPECIAL GUARDIANSHIP

INTRODUCTION

11.1   There is a growing recognition that children who are the subjects of applications for special guardianship orders and their carers may need support because they have needs different from or greater than others in the general population. There is little doubt that more support than formerly offered to kinship carers is needed. One recent study[1] suggests that better service provision might have prevented half of the premature terminations of care and reduced the risk of termination in half of the vulnerable placements which were still continuing.

11.2   Research suggests that applicants who have not already had contact with social services as carers may underestimate the support that will be required and the difficulties they may experience in obtaining it. It is important that legal advisers and the court are alert to any need for support and that the scheme for support is not regarded as merely ancillary to the making of a special guardianship order.

11.3   The Act and Regulations make provision for wide-ranging support both at the time an order is made and thereafter. Before a special guardianship order is granted advisers must ensure that the local authority preparing the report to the court under s 14A(8) or (9) has carried out a proper assessment of the support which may be required and that a clear and specific commitment to meeting any identified needs has been made.

BACKGROUND

11.4   The difficulties experienced by some kinship carers have been recognised for some time. In 2001 the late Alison Richards conducted a Home Office-funded survey of 180 grandparent carers.[2] The majority of carers were aged between 55 and 65 and just under half had long term health problems or disabilities that impaired their ability to look after the children. Approximately one-third were lone grandparents. Three-quarters said that that their social life

---

[1]   Hunt, Waterhouse and Lutman *Keeping Them In The Family: Outcomes for Abused and Neglected Children Placed With Family or Friends Carers Through Care Proceedings* (BAAF, 2008) summarised in [2008] Fam Law 435.

[2]   *Second Time Around – A Survey of Grandparents Raising Their Grandchildren* (Family Rights Group 2001) [2003] Fam Law 749.

had altered significantly. They received little assistance in caring for children with special needs and seven in ten found it hard to adapt to the physical and emotional demands of young children. Several spoke of the strain which was placed on their relationship with their partners and the child's parents.

11.5 Some of these difficulties might be expected because Richards' carers were exclusively grandparents but in a later study[3] Hunt and others found similar problems in a non-exclusive sample.

> 'Carers highlighted how taking on care affected them in many dimensions, including life plans and expectations, freedom to pursue outside interest/maintain peer group relationships and the loss of the expected 'grandparent' relationship with the child.

Just over one-third of the placements were problem free, just under half had some problems and one in five, 'major problems'. Half of the carers had felt like giving up at some point.

Types of need

11.6 The types of needs can be analysed on a number of matrices:

- One off needs/ongoing needs.

- Needs at the outset of the placement/needs occurring later.

- Needs apparent at the outset of the placement/unforeseen needs.

- Needs associated with the personal circumstances of the carer, the child, the parents.

- Financial/non financial needs.

- Specific needs/need for general support and advice.

Research has highlighted commonly occurring problems.

Financial difficulties

11.7 An 'overwhelming' majority of Richards' respondents reported financial difficulties including paying for school uniforms and meals. Seven in ten said they had made financial sacrifices and two in five (from a sample not all of whom had been employed) had had to stop working or reduce their working hours. It was unusual for parents to contribute towards the costs of raising

---

[3]   Op cit.

their children in cases where the child had moved to grandparents following a crisis such as bereavement, relationship breakdown or where there were child protection concerns.

11.8 Hunt too found that finance was an issue for many carers. Only just over one-third managed without difficulty and several suffered financial strain. Support was inconsistent. Some received grants for start-up costs, extensions and special expenses as well as a regular allowance while others received very little.

Emotional difficulties

11.9 In Hunt's survey one-third of the children had abnormal scores on a standardised test of 'well being' compared with 10% of the general population. Over one-third of the children were receiving specialised help, usually from mental health services, but there was evidence of unmet need in a few cases. Forty five per cent of the carers had an abnormal or borderline score on a standardised test of wellbeing, more than twice that expected in the general population.

Respite care

11.10 In Hunt's study respite care was rarely given and practical help from the extended family was less frequent than emotional support. Although most enjoyed some support from their family 'this was typically emotional rather than practical and occasional rather than regular'.[4]

Contact

11.11 Richards found that grandparents caring for children following a family crisis repeatedly stressed the impact of children of poor quality contact with their birth-parents and said they had not known who to contact for help.

11.12 In Hunt's study, most children were in touch with at last one parent, usually the mother, but contact, particularly paternal contact, diminished over time. Problems with contact were common and in a substantial minority of cases contact appeared to be entirely negative for the child. Families seemed to have assistance in less than half of cases. The authors cautioned that:

> 'It should not be assumed that the family can make contact arrangements [work] smoothly themselves. There needs to be more focus on contact planning at the assessment stage and perhaps more use of formal written agreements'.[5]

---

4   Op cit at p 173.
5   [2008] Fam Law 435 at 439.

11.13 In 2007 Ananda Hall studied a sample of 70 of 372 of the special guardianship orders which had been made in the first year of the implementation of s 14A.[6]

11.14 Of the 60% or more of parents having contact in her survey only 5% of visits were unsupervised. This reflected the high proportion of parents with personal problems. Over one-half of parents had substance misuse problems, one-third involved a history of domestic violence, one-third of the parents had mental health problems and one-fifth involved a history of sexual or physical abuse of the child.

Assistance with legal services

11.15 In Richards' sample nearly all (86%) of the carers who had been involved in proceedings had been legally represented but only 54% had been eligible for legal aid. Two-fifths of all who were involved in proceedings reported that this had caused financial hardship with many saying that they had to use all their savings. Overall, one-third of all carers – whether involved in proceedings or not – had not been able to obtain information on their legal rights and responsibilities.

11.16 In *Re L (Special Guardianship: Surname)*[7] the Court of Appeal noted that the litigation had placed grandparents who were applying for special guardianship:

> 'under considerable stress and had taken its toll on their resilience. They are not far short of breaking point. Their financial position is such that they are not eligible for legal aid. By contrast, of course the parents are.'[8]

Assistance from social services

11.17 In the past, support by social services has been perceived to be patchy. In Richards' sample, although just under half were having or had had some contact with social services, there was a general criticism of the lack of support. Hunt's findings were more positive but not overwhelmingly so. In those cases still 'open', one-third were judged to be well supported, just under one-half to have some support and one-fifth, little or no support. A few carers in closed cases needed more sustained support but had mixed experiences when seeking it. Overall one-quarter of carers had nothing positive to say about social services.

---

[6] Hall 'Special Guardianship: A Missed Opportunity – Findings From Research' [2008] Fam Law 148, 'Special Guardianship – Themes Emerging From Case Law' [2008] Fam Law 244 and 'Special guardianship and permanency planning: unforeseen circumstances and missed opportunities' [2008] CFLQ 359.

[7] [2007] EWCA Civ 196, [2007] 2 FLR 50.

[8] Per Ward LJ at [22].

The effect on outcome

11.18 It is clear from these three surveys that special guardians are likely to need assistance at some stage during the life of the order. This is echoed by the experience of a large number of organisations. In *The Role of the State in Supporting Relatives Raising Children Who Cannot Live With Their Parents*[9] the Family Policy Alliance, formed of 14 organisations such as Barnados, the British Association for Adoption and Fostering (BAAF) and the Grandparents Association submitted that:

> 'It is crucial that the support needs of family and friends are addressed if these children [who could be placed with their extended family rather than state care] are to reach their full potential. The overwhelming evidence from the advice work of our respective organisations is that the more informal the arrangement, the less likely the family member who takes on care is to receive support. This lack of support is likely to have a detrimental effect on the child and sometimes causes the placement to break down and the children to end up in state care after all.'

11.19 Hunt considered that the research provided some grounds for thinking that better service provision might have improved outcomes. About half of the premature terminations of placement might have been prevented and the risk might have been reduced in half of the placements which were continuing but were vulnerable.

Provision of assistance

11.20 The quality and range of the assistance required to meet the needs is important.

> 'The literature suggests that service provision needs to meet a number of cross-cutting requirements. It should, for example, be customised – tailored not only to the unique needs of kinship families in general but to the needs of the individual family in particular: kinship carers are a heterogeneous group and needs will change over time. It needs to be holistic, addressing the needs of the whole family, not just the child or the carers. The aim should be to develop 'wrap-around' services which address the whole range of need. It should be culturally attuned, recognising the specific needs of different ethnic minority groups. Finally, it should be enabling, building on the family's strengths.'[10]

Assessment

11.21 Hunt's sample reported that it was rare for a full assessment to be made before children were placed. There is a risk that when it is offered, it may be thought intrusive. Prior to the implementation of s 14A Richards and Lindley questioned varied groups of family carers to see whether their views about

---

[9] A response to the Green Paper *Care Matters* co-ordinated by the Family Rights Group (2007).
[10] Hunt 'Substitute Care of Children by Members of Their Extended Families and Social Networks: An Overview' in Ebtehaj, Lindley and Richards (eds) *Kinship Matters* (Hart Publishing, 2006) at p 127.

special guardianship coincided with those of the Government and found them ambivalent.[11] While many carers were sceptical as to the extent of support on offer and said that they would not apply for guardianship if residence orders were adequately supported in terms of financial and practical help, most said the intrusive nature of the proposed assessment and the lack of certainty over ongoing support would militate against their applying for SGOs.

THE STATUTORY FRAMEWORK

11.22   The framework for the assessment and provision of adoption support services is provided by s 14F of the CA 1989 and the Special Guardianship Regulations 2005 (SGR 2005).[12] Guidance on the regulations is provided by the *Special Guardianship Guidance* (Guidance)[13] which is issued under s 7 of the Local Authority Social Services Act 1970; as Black J pointed out in *B v Lewisham London Borough Council*[14] 'whilst the document does not have the full force of statute, it should be complied with unless local circumstances indicate exceptional reasons which justify a variation'.[15] In *Munjaz v Ashworth Hospital*[16] Lord Bingham said of similar guidance:

> 'The Code does not have the binding effect which a statutory provision or statutory instrument would have. It is what it purports to be, guidance and not instruction. But ... the guidance should be given great weight. It is not instruction but it is much more than mere advice which the addressee is free to follow or not as it chooses. It is guidance which [any authority] should consider with great care and from which it should depart only if it has cogent reasons for so doing.'[17]

Duty to provide services

11.23   Each local authority must 'make arrangements for the provision within their area of special guardianship support services which means a) counselling, advice and information and b) such other services as are prescribed'.[18] 'Prescribed services' consist of:

(a)   financial support;

(b)   services to enable children, parents, special guardians (SGs) and prospective special guardians (PSGs) to discuss matters relating to special guardianship;

---

[11]   Jordan and Lindley (eds) *Special Guardianship: A Family View* in *Special Guardianship: What Does It Offer Children Who Cannot Live With Their Parents?* (Family Rights Group, 2006).
[12]   SI 2005/1109.
[13]   DCFS (2005).
[14]   [2008] EWHC 738 (Admin).
[15]   Ibid at [20].
[16]   [2005] UKHL 58, [2006] 4 All ER 736.
[17]   Ibid at [21]. See also *R v Islington LBC ex p Rixon* [1996] 32 BMLR 136 at 140.
[18]   CA 1989, s 14F(1).

(c)   assistance including mediation services in relation to contact;

(d)   services relating to the therapeutic needs of the child;

(e)   assistance to ensure the continuance of the relationship between the children, the SG or PSG including training, respite care and mediation.[19]

11.24 The services can be provided either by the local authority or through other organisations of a specified nature and except as regards counselling, advice and information, can be provided by a cash payment to enable the recipient to purchase the services.[20] The Guidance provides the illustrations of giving an SG cash to pay a baby sitter or for petrol to travel to contact. 'When cash is provided in this way it should **not** be means tested as it is being provided as part of a service rather than financial support.'[21]

11.25 The Guidance states that special guardianship support services should not be seen in isolation from mainstream services. 'It is vital to ensure that children and families involved in special guardianship arrangements are assisted in accessing mainstream services and are aware of their entitlement to social services benefits and tax credits as appropriate.'[22]

11.26 Other than for 'out of area' support when the s 14F duty ceases after 3 years, there is no limit on the time when support is provided other than, normally, that the child must be under the age of 18 (but see **11.80**).

11.27 An authority is not prevented from providing special guardianship support services to people outside their area where they consider it appropriate.[23] For example, the authority might make transitional arrangements to allow the new authority time to review the existing plan without a break in service provision.[24]

11.28 Section 14F(9)(b) allows an authority to supply support through another authority and SGR 2005, reg 4 extends this provision to registered adoption societies, Primary Care Trusts and certain other bodies. The Guidance envisages that this may be appropriate, for example, if there is a low demand in a particular area or to avoid duplication.[25]

---

[19]   SGR 2005, reg 3.
[20]   Ibid, reg 4.
[21]   Guidance, para 27. Emphasis as in the original.
[22]   Ibid, para 26. See also reg 12(3) for the duty when relevant to consult health organisations and local education authorities when assessing needs.
[23]   SGA 2005, reg 5(3).
[24]   Guidance, para 36.
[25]   Ibid, para 30.

TYPES OF SUPPORT

Financial support

11.29 Financial support is to be given to the SG or PSG:

(a) to facilitate arrangements for a person to become an SG where the local authority consider such arrangements to be beneficial to the child's welfare; or

(b) to support the continuation of such arrangements after a special guardianship order (SGO).[26]

11.30 However, it is payable only if the local authority considers:

(a) it is necessary to ensure that the SG or PSG can look after the child; or

(b) that the child needs special care which requires a greater expenditure of resources than would otherwise be the case because of his illness, disability, emotional or behavioural difficulties or the consequences of past abuse and neglect; or

(c) it is appropriate to help meet legal expenses (see below); or

(d) it is appropriate to contribute to expenditure necessary for accommodating or maintaining the child including the provision of furniture and domestic equipment, alterations to and adaptations for the home, provision of means of transport and provision of clothing, toys and other items necessary for the purpose of looking after the child.[27]

11.31 These provisions give the authority a wide discretion by using words such as 'considers it necessary' or 'considers it appropriate'. Sometimes an objective test is combined with a subjective one, for example reg 6(2)(d): 'where the local authority considers it appropriate to contribute [subjective] to the expenditure necessary [objective] …'.

11.32 Financial support can be paid periodically if there is likely to be a recurring need or by a single payment which can, with the consent of the recipient, be paid by instalments.[28] This ability to make 'one off' payments is important. A grandmother in *B v Lewisham London Borough Council*,[29] for example, was given £839 so that she could buy essential equipment and furniture.

---

[26] SGR 2005, reg 6(1).
[27] Ibid, reg 6(2).
[28] Ibid, reg 8.
[29] [2008] EWHC 738 (Admin).

11.33   There can be no doubt that the provision of financial support is a major part of the Services. The Guidance stipulates that 'Financial issues should not be the sole reason for a special guardianship arrangement failing to survive'.[30] However, following the principle that SG support should not be seen in isolation from mainstream services, regard must be had to welfare benefits available to the population at large. The Guidance also states that it is important that local authorities help special guardians to take advantage of all benefits and tax credits available (see **11.39**).

'Financial support under [The Special Guardianship] Regulations cannot duplicate any other payment available.'[31]

11.34   Each local authority is able to decide its own scheme of payments after having regard to the Guidance, paragraph 63 of which states:

'The local authority should have regard to the amount of fostering allowance which could have been payable if the child were fostered. The local authority's core allowance plus any enhancement that would be payable in respect of the particular child, will make up the maximum payment the local authority could consider paying the family.'

11.35   There are no nationally prescribed fostering rates but the National Foster Care Association annually publishes foster-parent rates paid by all local authorities. Current rates can be found in the annual publication, *At a Glance*.[32] The NFA *recommended* rates contain no element of reward but measures the average costs of caring for a child living in his own home.[33]

11.36   In *B v Lewisham London Borough Council*[34] Black J interpreted the amount of fostering allowance as 'a ranging shot for the local authority's consideration of what their SG provision should be or at least be held firmly in mind when fixing that provision'.[35] In *The Queen on the Application of L and Others v Manchester City Council*[36] Munby J held that it was unlawful for a local authority to pay short-term kinship foster carers at a much lower rate than that paid to other foster carers.

11.37   The lack of a national rate of fostering allowances and the discretion vested in individual authorities currently creates difficulties for carers. If they are in receipt of allowances in Area A but then move to Area B they will not necessarily receive the same financial support. It also means a period when authorities are uncertain about whether they face judicial review. In *B v*

---

[30]   Guidance, para 37.

[31]   Ibid, para 63.

[32]   Family Law Bar Association.

[33]   See *The Queen on the Application of L and Others v Manchester City Council* [2002] EWHC Admin 707, [2002] 1 FLR 43 at [19].

[34]   [2008] EWHC 738 (Admin).

[35]   Ibid at [47].

[36]   [2002] EWHC Admin 707, [2002] 1 FLR 43.

Lewisham London Borough Council[37] the respondent local authority's scheme fixed the maximum allowances in the mid-range of the authorities which had agreed rates but these were very significantly below the national minimum allowance prescribed by the DfES for foster carers. Black J sitting in the Administrative Court quashed the scheme on the basis that Lewisham had failed to have proper regard to paragraph 65.

11.38 Some foster carers receive an element of remuneration in their allowances. The Regulations provide that financial support may include such an element but only where the decision is taken before the SGO is granted, the local authority considers it necessary and the recipient had been a local authority foster carer for the child and in receipt of remuneration.[38] This element can be paid only for 2 years from the making of the SGO unless the local authority considers it necessary having regard to the exceptional needs of the child or any other exceptional circumstances.[39] It remains to be seen whether this will dissuade foster carers who may have no employment other than being carer from applying for SGOs.

> 'For former foster carers the possibility of receiving financial support similar to that which they received while the child was fostered could make an important difference – provided they really believe it will continue as long as they and the child need it.'[40]

State benefits

11.39 Unlike local authority foster parents, SGs are entitled to child benefit so long as the child is living with them. This should overcome the difficulties encountered by one-fifth of Richards' grandparents who said that parents refused to surrender the child benefit book.[41] Like adoption allowances, special guardianship allowances are disregarded in full (with some minor exceptions) for Income Support and income based Job Seeker's Allowances.[42] It is taken into account for housing benefit and council tax benefit but only to the level of the child's personal allowance and any disabled child premium. Conversely, when a carer's means are assessed for the purpose of SG financial support, welfare benefits are taken into account.[43]

Assessing resources

11.40 When deciding the amount of financial support to be paid the local authority has to assess and take into account:

---

[37]   [2008] EWHC 738 (Admin).
[38]   SGR 2005, reg 7(1).
[39]   Ibid, reg 7(2).
[40]   Cullen 'Adoption – a (fairly) new approach' [2005] CFLQ 475 at p 478.
[41]   Op cit at p 753.
[42]   Income Support (General) Regulations 1987, SI 1987/1967, Sch 9, para 25(1)(a) and (1A); Jobseeker's (Allowance) Regulations 1996, SI 1996/206, Sch 7, para 26(1)(a) and (1A).
[43]   SGR 2005, reg 13(2) and (3).

- any other grant, benefit, allowance or resource which is available to the person in respect of his needs as a result of becoming the special guardian of the child;[44]

- the SGs' financial resources including any tax credit or benefit which would be available if the child lived with the SG or PSG;[45]

- the amount required by them in respect of their reasonable outgoings and commitments (excluding outgoings in respect of the child);[46] and

- the financial resources and needs of the child.[47]

11.41 There are two exceptions to this general rule.

- When the authority is considering whether to provide financial support in respect of legal costs in respect of an application for an SGO when the child is being looked after by the authority when, subject to certain conditions (see **11.48**) it *must* disregard reg 13(3).[48]

- In addition, the authority *may* also disregard means when considering initial costs of accommodating the child, recurring travel costs for the purpose of contact, any special care referred to in reg 6(2)(b) which requires a greater expenditure of resources than would otherwise be the case and any remuneration element.[49]

11.42 There is a suggested means test and notes on its use on the DCSF website[50] but authorities are not required to use it.

Conditions

11.43 Where financial support is to be paid periodically, it cannot be paid until the SG or prospective SG agrees:

- to inform the authority immediately if he changes address, the child dies, changes occur which are mentioned in reg 9 and which have the effect of automatically terminating financial support or there is a change in his or the child's financial services; and

---

[44] SGR 2005, reg 13(2).
[45] Ibid, reg 13(3).
[46] Ibid.
[47] Ibid.
[48] Ibid, reg 13(4).
[49] Ibid, reg 13(5).
[50] www.dcsf.goc.uk/everychildmatters/resources-and-practice/ig00027.

- to supply the authority with an annual statement of his and the child's financial circumstances, his address and whether the child still has a home with him.[51]

The authority may impose any condition it considers appropriate including the timescale within which and the purposes for which financial support is to be utilised.[52]

How is it working?

11.44   Ananda Hall[53] examined 70 out of the 372 SGOs granted in the first 2 years to both kinship carers and foster parents. Seventy per cent had been granted financial support. However the chance of obtaining support was greater for former foster parents who were also considered to be 'much more difficult', engaging in lengthy negotiations for acceptable financial packages.

Respite care

11.45   Respite care is part of the 'prescribed services'[54] but if it is met by the provision of accommodation, it must be by way of s 23 of the CA 1989 (accommodation for looked after children) or by a voluntary organisation under s 59.[55]

> 'This requires that appropriate safeguards are in place ... and that any foster parent providing respite care has been approved under the Fostering Services Regulations 2002'.[56]

11.46   Carers will therefore be unable to make their own arrangements if they need financial assistance to obtain the care. As one of the argued benefits of special guardianship is the autonomy of the carer,[57] this may not be attractive for special guardians.

Contact

11.47   The support which the authority can provide includes:

- counselling, advice and information;[58]

---

[51]   SGR 2005, reg 10(1).
[52]   Ibid, reg 10(2).
[53]   Op cit.
[54]   SGR 2005, reg 3(1)(e)(ii).
[55]   Ibid, reg 3(3).
[56]   Guidance, para 28.
[57]   *Adoption – A New Approach* Cm 5017 (2000), para 5.10.
[58]   CA 1989, s 14F(1)(a); SGR 2005, reg 3(1)(b).

- assistance including mediation.[59] This could presumably include facilitating family group conferences as recommended by Hunt, and supervision;

- travel costs in cash[60] or when on a recurring basis;[61]

- legal costs in relation to a section 8 application.[62]

Assistance with legal services

11.48 Given the possible difficulties in obtaining and sustaining SGOs, including negotiating support services, it is obviously desirable that applicants have access to legal advice. Richards drew attention to the financial and other difficulties encountered by grandparents who were unrepresented or had to meet their own costs. If legal aid is available, it is unlikely that local authority assistance will be provided bearing in mind reg 13(2) which requires the authority to take account of any other resource available. However, where it is not available (and in Hunt's sample although 86% of carers had been involved in legal proceedings, only 54% were eligible) the authority can provide assistance under reg 6(2)(c) if it thinks it appropriate towards legal costs associated with:

- obtaining an SGO;

- an application to vary or discharge an SGO;

- an application under section 8;

- an order for financial provision to be made to or for the benefit of the child.

11.49 The costs of applying for an SGO are not subject to financial assessment provided that either the child is being looked after by the authority and the authority supports the making of the order[63] or an application is made to vary or discharge an SGO in respect of 'such a child'.[64] This last phrase may be intended to refer to a child who *has* been looked after by the authority.

11.50 In *Re L (Special Guardianship: Surname)*[65] the local authority 'recognised the inequality of arms'[66] between the parents who had the benefit

---

[59] SGR 2005, reg 3(1)(c).
[60] Ibid, reg 3(1)(b) and reg 3(2); Guidance, para 41.
[61] SGR 2005, reg 6(2)(b); Guidance, para 41.
[62] SGR 2005, reg 6(2)(c).
[63] And see Guidance, para 70: authorities are not expected to meet legal costs of an application for an SGO when they oppose the application.
[64] SGR 2005, reg 13(4).
[65] [2007] EWCA Civ 196, [2007] 2 FLR 50.
[66] Ibid, per Ward LJ at [22].

of legal aid and the grandparents who were applying for an SGO and provided some financial help with their legal costs in the court of first instance but not in the (largely unsuccessful) appeal.

ASSESSMENT

11.51   The key to the provision of services is a proper assessment of the needs of the special guardian, natural parents and the child. Section 14F(3)–(8) of the Act and SGR 2005, regs 11–16 make detailed provision for:

- an assessment of a person's need for special guardianship support services as defined in s 14(1);

- a plan of the services to be provided.

Needs for services must be assessed at the time the section 14A report is being prepared but an assessment may also be requested before or after the report and the making of the order.

11.52   The report made to the Court under s 14A(8) must include a 'summary' of any SG support services provided, the period for which they are to be provided and where the authority has decided not to provide support, the reasons for this.[67]

11.53   However, there is no requirement for an assessment to take place before an order is made. Therefore, where there is a possibility that services will be required in the foreseeable future, the prospective special guardian should request an assessment under s 14F(4).

11.54   The Guidance states that it is important that the assessment process does not delay the provision of services where there is an urgent need.[68] Regulation 19 therefore provides that where any requirements in relation to assessment, preparing a plan or giving notice would delay provision in the case of emergency, those requirements do not apply. In such a case the authority will need to review the provision as soon as possible after the support has been provided.

Request for assessment

11.55   When the child is looked after or was looked after by the authority immediately before the making of an SGO, the authority *must* carry out an assessment if requested by a special guardian, prospective special guardian, the child or a parent.[69]

---

[67]   SGR 2005, Sch, paras 5(d) and (e).
[68]   Guidance, para 93.
[69]   CA 1989, s14F(3) and SGR 2005, reg 11(1)(b).

11.56 Where the child is not being looked after and was not looked after by the authority to whom the request is made by those listed above, the authority *may* carry out an assessment.[70] The Guidance advises that:

> 'It is important that children who are not (or were not) looked after are not unfairly disadvantaged by this approach. In many cases the only reason the child is not looked after is that a relative stepped in quickly to take over the responsibility for the child when a parent could no longer do so.'[71]

11.57 If the authority decides not to carry out an assessment it must give written notice and reasons to the person making the request and that person must be allowed at least 28 days in which to make representations.[72]

Request after a special guardianship order has been made

11.58 The need for support services may become apparent only after an SGO has been granted. Two matters should be noted.

11.59 First, given the frequent changes in social services personnel, the social worker preparing the section 14A(8) report may have left the authority by the time support is needed. Therefore advisers should ensure that SGs are provided with the name of the section in the department responsible for carrying out assessments and the title of the head of the section.[73]

11.60 Secondly, the authority tasked with carrying out the assessment will be the authority where the person applying for services is living[74] unless the child is or was, immediately before the making of the SGO, being looked after by another authority, in which case that authority is also under a duty to assess but only for the first 3 years of the order.[75]

Procedure for assessment

11.61 The authority carrying out the assessment must have regard to such of the following considerations as are relevant:

- the developmental needs of the child;

- the parenting capacity of the special guardian or prospective special guardian;

---

[70] CA 1989, s 14F(3).
[71] Guidance, para 51.
[72] SGR 2005, reg 11(3).
[73] There is no statutory requirement to have an equivalent of the Adoption Support Services Advisor (see **9.26**).
[74] SGR 2005, reg 5.
[75] Ibid, reg 5(1).

- the family and environmental circumstances that have shaped the life of the child;

- what the life of the child might be like with the special or prospective special guardian;

- any previous assessments of the child or the special or prospective special guardian;

- the needs of the special or prospective special guardian and of that person's family;

- where it appears to the authority that there is a pre-existing relationship between the special or prospective special guardian and the parent of a child, the likely impact of the SGO on the relationship between the special or prospective special guardian, the child and that parent.[76]

According to the Guidance these factors reflect those which are considered under the *Framework for the Assessment of Children in Need and their Families*.[77]

11.62 There is a surprising gap in this list. The persons seeking support are not necessarily special or prospective special guardians or the child.[78] They can include parents and yet the reg 12(1) list makes no specific reference to the parents other than at the last consideration and only then in relation to the special guardian or any siblings. It might be argued that the list is not an exhaustive one and that any reasonable authority would consider all the relevant circumstances.

11.63 The assessment will not always be a 'paper' exercise. The local authority must, if it considers it appropriate, interview the person whose needs are to be assessed, where that person is the child, the special or prospective special guardian and any adult the authority may consider it appropriate to interview.[79]

11.64 Where it appears to the authority that the person may have a need for services from a local health board, primary care trust or local education authority, they must consult that body.[80]

11.65 Assessment of needs is discussed in detail at **10.15**. For an assessment for financial support, see **11.40**.

---

[76] SGR 2005, reg 12(1).
[77] Department of Health (2000).
[78] SGR 2005, reg 6(2)(b).
[79] Ibid, reg 12(2).
[80] Ibid, reg 12(3).

11.66 After undertaking the assessment the authority must prepare a written report.[81] Details of the assessment must be provided to the person making the request for services once a draft plan has been prepared or the authority decides that a plan is not necessary.[82]

THE PLAN

11.67 If following the assessment the authority proposes to provide support services on more than one occasion and those services are not limited to the provision of advice or information it must prepare a plan unless the services are limited to providing advice or information.[83] Where it appears to the authority that the person may have a need for services from a local health board, primary care trust or local education authority, they must consult that body before preparing the plan.[84]

11.68 The plan should set out:

• the services to be provided;

• the objectives and criteria for evaluating success;

• timescales for provision;

• procedures for review;

• the name of the person nominated to monitor the provision of the services in accordance with the plan.[85]

> 'The result of this process of preparation and consultation should be that social workers, other professionals and the recipient of the services (or [in the case of a child] the appropriate adult)[86] is clear what the support services plan is. The plan should be set out in writing in a way which everyone affected can understand.'[87]

11.69 Before making a final decision on whether to provide services and, if so, what services the authority must allow the person making the request an opportunity of making representations by giving notice of the proposed decision and the time allowed for making representations.[88] The notice must contain the following information:

---

[81]   SGR 2005, reg 12(4).
[82]   Ibid, reg 15(1) and (3)(a). See **11.70**.
[83]   Ibid, reg 14(2).
[84]   Ibid, reg 12(3).
[85]   Guidance, para 71.
[86]   Defined in SGR 2005, reg 20 as the special or prospective special guardian (where applicable) or otherwise to the adult the authority considers most appropriate.
[87]   Guidance, para 72.
[88]   SGR 2005, reg 15(2). No minimum time for making representations is specified but the Guidance suggests a period of 28 days (para 77).

- a statement of the person's needs for support services;

- where the assessment relates to a need for financial support, the basis upon which the support is determined;

- whether the authority proposes to provide support services;

- the services (if any) it is proposed to supply;

- if financial support is to be provided, the amount payable; and

- any proposed conditions under reg 10(2).[89]

In addition, if a plan is required, the authority must supply a copy of the plan.[90]

11.70   After considering any representations, the authority decides whether or not to provide services. It has to give the person applying for the services notice of its decision and the reasons for it.[91]

11.71   If the authority decides that financial support is to be provided the notice must include the following information:

- the method of determination of the amount of financial support;

- where it is to be provided in instalments or periodically:
  - the amount of the support;
  - the frequency with which it will be paid;
  - the period for which it will be paid;
  - when payment will commence;

- where financial support is to be paid as a single payment, when it will be made;

- where financial support is to be subject to any conditions under reg 10(2), the conditions, the date by which they are to be met and the consequences of failing to meet them;

- the arrangements and procedure for review, variation and termination of financial support;

- the responsibilities of:
  - the local authority under regs 17 and 18 (reviews); and

---

[89] SGR 2005, reg 15(3).
[90] Ibid, reg 15(4).
[91] Ibid, reg 16(1).

–   the special or prospective special guardian pursuant to an agreement under reg 10 (notifying change of circumstances).[92]

11.72 Where service providers other than the social services have been involved in the assessment, the authority should try wherever possible to ensure that decisions made by those providers follow the same timetable. They should be covered in a single notification and plan to provide, wherever possible, a whole service package.[93]

11.73 Where the assessment is carried out before the authority prepares its report for the court under s 14A(8) or (9), the authority must provide in the report a summary of the special guardianship support services provided by the authority, the period of time for which they are to be provided or, if they are not to be provided, the reasons for this.[94]

REVIEW

11.74

'Regular reviews enable the local authority and the service user to review the effectiveness of any services provided and consider whether it is appropriate to continue that service or change the provision in some way.'[95]

The authority providing the support must review its plan:

- if any change in the recipient's circumstances which may affect the provision of the services comes to their attention;

- at such stage of implementation as they consider appropriate; and

- at least annually.[96]

11.75 Financial support must be reviewed:

- on receipt of the annual statement (see **11.43**);

- If any relevant change of circumstances or breach of condition comes to the attention of the authority; and

- at such stage of implementation as they consider appropriate.[97]

---

[92]   SGR 2005, reg 16(3).
[93]   Guidance, para 81.
[94]   SGR 2005, Sch, para 5.
[95]   Guidance, para 82.
[96]   SGR 2005, reg 17(2).
[97]   Ibid, reg 18(2).

Regulations 17 and 18(4) make provision for the review similar to that for assessment.

11.76   The Guidance suggests that the format and content of the review will vary according to the circumstances of the individual case.

> 'Where the change of circumstances is relatively minor [or at the annual review of financial support] the review might be limited to an exchange of correspondence ... However where the change of circumstance is substantial, for example a serious change in the behaviour of the child, it will normally be appropriate to conduct a new assessment of needs.'[98]

Recipients moving out of area

11.77   The scheme makes a number of provisions for recipients of support who may move to another authority area.

11.78   For a period of 3 years from the making of an order in respect of a child who was previously looked after by an authority, that authority has a responsibility to assessing and, if necessary or appropriate providing support.[99] Moreover where that authority is providing financial support agreed before the order as made, the authority's responsibility continues so long as the financial support is provided.[100]

11.79   Any plan will remain in force (and the originating authority will be under a duty to continue to supply the support under the plan) until it is varied or terminated. Such termination could be for the reason that the move constituted a relevant change of circumstances under regs 17(2) and 18(2).

SUPPORT FOR THE OLDER CHILD OR YOUNG PERSON

11.80   Without special provision, the duty to assess the need for and provide support would end when the young person reached the age of 18. This would have left a difference between children looked after by an authority and children who had been looked after but in respect of whom an SGO had been made because a local authority is under a duty to provide advice and assistance[101] to a young person over the age of 16 and under 21 who was, while over 16, looked after, accommodated or fostered by the authority.[102] In order to rectify this, s 24(1A) extends this duty to such a child in respect of whom an SGO is in force (or if the person is over 18, was in force when he reached that

---

[98]   Guidance, para 87.
[99]   SGR 2005, reg 5(1).
[100]   Ibid, reg 5(2).
[101]   Defined in CA 1989, s 24A.
[102]   Ibid, s 24(4). See **15.91**.

age) provided he was looked after by an authority immediately before the order was made. In the case of special guardianship the authority is the authority which last looked after him.[103]

---

[103] CA 1989, s 24(5)(za) and SGR 2005, reg 22.

Chapter 12

THE IMPORTANCE OF THE BIRTH FAMILY

INTRODUCTION

12.1 The importance of a child's biological and social relationship with his birth family always has to be considered whenever an alternative permanent placement is being considered. This importance is underlined by Art 8 of the European Convention for the Protection of Human Rights and Fundamental Freedoms 1950 ('ECHR') and informs decisions about paternity testing, obtaining information about his paternity and family, both in childhood and later life, placement and contact. It is also reflected in the growing recognition that if a child cannot live with at least one of his birth parents, his wider family should be considered and may be able to offer him a home which is as least as satisfactory if not better than living with strangers. Although much of the discourse is about the child's relationship with adults in his birth family, his relationship with his siblings must not be ignored, not least because it may outlive any relationship with the older generation.

ARTICLE 8

12.2 Although the importance of family life has long been recognised by the family courts, it finds its fundamental expression in Art 8 of the ECHR.

'1   Everyone has the right to respect for his private and family life, his home and his correspondence.
2   There shall be no interference by a public authority with the exercise of this right except such as is in accordance with the law and is necessary in a democratic society in the interests of national security, public safety or the economic well-being of the country, for the prevention of disorder or crime, for the protection of health or morals, or for the protection of the rights and freedoms of others.'

12.3 As is discussed at **6.176** much of the consideration of Art 8 in family proceedings in England and Wales has focused on the right to respect for family life. However, the right to respect for a private life is of similar, considerable relevance and is much wider than what might loosely be termed a right to privacy.

12.4 In *Bensaid v United Kingdom*[1] the European Court of Human Rights (ECtHR) commented:

'Private life is a broad term not susceptible to exhaustive definition. The court has already held that elements such as gender identification, name and sexual orientation and sexual life are important elements in the personal sphere protected by Article 8. Mental health must also be regarded as a crucial part of private life associated with the aspect of moral integrity. Article 8 protects a right to identity and personal development and the right to establish and develop relationships with other human beings and the outside world. The preservation of mental stability is in that context an indispensable precondition to effective enjoyment of the respect for private life.'[2]

12.5 This is a right to positive respect and the promotion of what is entailed in a private life. The State – and this includes courts – may be under a duty to do something rather than merely refrain from action. Secondly, it can apply in family situations even where there is at present no family life. A child may have no family life with a father who is not married to his mother and has had no contact with him. However, the right to personal development may include the right to come to know one's father or one's child.[3]

The right to know the truth about one's parentage

12.6 Article 8 runs through most of the topics which are involved in the legal search for a permanent home for a child.

12.7 In *Milkulic v Croatia* the ECtHR held that:[4]

'[Respect] for private life requires that everyone should be able to establish details of their identity as individual human beings and that an individual's entitlement to such information is of importance because of its formative implications for his or her personality (see the *Gaskin v United Kingdom* judgment).'[5]

12.8 In domestic law, in *Re G (Parentage: Blood Sample)*,[6] Ward LJ said that it was 'the entitlement' of the child to know who her father was.

12.9 The right finds its expression, for example, in the determination of parentage through DNA tests and orders that a child should be told the truth about his paternity. These topics are discussed in detail at **14.41**.

---

[1]   (2001) 33 EHRR 10 at [47].
[2]   See also Munby 'Families old and new' [2005] 17 CFLQ 487 at 504–508.
[3]   See also **14.56**.
[4]   [1990] 1 FLR 167.
[5]   [2002] 1 FCR 720. See also *M v W (Declaration of Parentage)* [2006] EWHC 2341 (Fam), [2007] 2 FLR 270 and **12.12**.
[6]   [1997] 1 FLR 360.

12.10 The right also includes the right to have one's paternity acknowledged. In *M v W (Declaration of Parentage)*[7] in an unopposed application, the High Court granted an adult, adopted, man a declaration as to his parentage, the Court accepting his argument that it was a matter of great importance to his self-perception and identity and that he wanted to pass on to his children and grandchildren an accurate and recognised account of his ancestry. This 'well-known and universally acknowledged principle'[8] has been challenged. Ayesha Hasan,[9] for example, has argued that the right may conflict with a competing right of the child to have the current stability of his family life protected. It may be difficult to strike a balance in favour of 'telling' where the value and culture of the community in which the child lives regards illegitimacy as a stigma.[10]

The right to know about one's background

12.11 Article 8 extends beyond the right to know who one's parents are to the right to be able to receive information about them, one's birth family and the facts about one's early life.

12.12 In *Gaskin*[11] the ECtHR, when considering a case brought by an adult who had spent nearly 14 years of his childhood in care, who wished to have access to his social services case file held that:

'Persons in the situation of the applicant have a vital interest, protected by the Convention, in receiving the information necessary to know and to understand their childhood and early development.'[12]

12.13 In 1972, the Houghton Committee on Adoption[13] observed that:

'The importance of telling a child that it has been adopted has long been recognised and there is a growing recognition that the child should be told early and helped to understand it more fully as he grows older. It is also increasingly recognised that at some stage the child will need to know about his origins – the positive factors about his parents, such as any special qualities, gifts or interests; their appearance; their reasons for giving him up and any medical background which may be relevant. This kind of information helps the proper development of a sense of identity and gives the child ... a fuller understanding of him as an individual with his own unique combination of characteristics, both inherited and acquired from his upbringing and environment.'

---

[7] [2006] EWHC 2341 (Fam), [2007] 2 FLR 270.

[8] Hasan 'To Tell or Not To Tell' [2007] Fam Law 458.

[9] Ibid.

[10] Or where one parent is of a different religion; see *Re S (Change of Names: Cultural Factors)* [2001] 2 FLR 1005.

[11] *The Gaskin Case* Case No 2/188/146/200, [1990] 1 FLR 167.

[12] Ibid, at para 49.

[13] Report of the Departmental Committee on the Adoption of Children Cmnd 5107 (1972).

12.14   In 2001 in the domestic case of *Gunn-Russo v Nugent Care Society and Secretary of State for Health*[14] Scott Baker J recognised this right.

> '[Since the *Houghton Report*] the balance has continued to shift towards greater freedom of information to adopted people. It is now recognised that many adopted people wish to have information about their history and background including the reasons for their adoption. Many find it important to have a complete personal history in order to develop a positive sense of identity. The issue will often be how to resolve the tension between on the one hand maintaining the confidentiality under which the information was originally supplied and on the other providing the information that the adopted person has a real desire, and often need, to have.'[15]

12.15   The right finds its expression in the right (subject to certain safeguards) to see any social work case records and the ability of an adopted person to obtain a copy of his birth certificate and obtain information from the adoption agency and court records.

12.16   These topics are discussed in detail at **14.41** (paternity testing and knowledge about paternity), **8.28** (ability of adopters to raise the child knowing about his history)[16] and **8.108** (obtaining information in adult life).

The right to live with and have a relationship with one's family

12.17   The right to live with one's family[17] has to be protected from state interference and can be justified only where it is necessary for the protection of the rights and freedoms of others.

> 'The intervention must be "necessary in a democratic society", that is, it must meet a pressing social need and be proportionate to that need. The more drastic the interference, the greater must be the need to do it.'[18]

12.18   In *Johansen v Norway*[19] the ECtHR said that:

> 'The [European Court of Human Rights] recognises that the authorities enjoy a wide margin of appreciation in assessing the necessity of taking a child into care. However, a stricter scrutiny is called for both of any further limitations, such as restrictions placed by those authorities on parental rights and access, and of any legal safeguards designed to secure an effective protection of the right of parents

---

[14]   [2001] EWHC Admin 566, [2002] 1 FLR 1.
[15]   Ibid at [46]–[47].
[16]   See also *Re S (A Minor) (Adoption by Step-parents)* [1988] 1 FLR 418 and **2.113**.
[17]   In *Re C (Family Placement)* [2009] EWCA Civ 72, [2009] 1 FLR 1425 (see **12.70**) Wilson LJ at [19] referred to the right as 'the law's bias in favour of placement within the family'.
[18]   *Re B (Adoption by One Natural Parent to Exclusion of Other)* [2001] 1 FLR 589, per Hale LJ at 599. See also *The Queen on the Application of Mahmood v Secretary of State for the Home Department* [2001] 1 FLR 756, per Lord Phillips of Worth Maltravers MR at 772.
[19]   [1996] 23 EHRR 33.

and children to respect for their family life. Such further limitations entail the danger that the family relations between the parents and a young child are effectively curtailed ...

The Court considers that taking a child into care should normally be regarded as a temporary measure to be discontinued as soon as circumstances permit and that any measures of implementation of temporary care should be consistent with the ultimate aim of reuniting the natural parent and the child ...'

Particular importance has to be given to the welfare of the child (see **12.30**).

Adoption checklist

12.19   The right to have a relationship with one's family finds expression in the adoption checklist (see **6.90** and **6.98**). Section 1(4)(c) of the Adoption and Children Act 2002 (ACA 2002) provides that when a court or adoption agency is coming to a decision relating to the adoption of a child it must have regard amongst other matters to 'the likely effect on the child (throughout his life) of having ceased to be a member of the original family and become an adopted person'.

12.20   The effect on the child of losing these relationships may not be immediate. The *Review of Adoption Law*[20] said that:

'One of the special features of adoption is that it has a significant effect on a person's identity and family relationships not just during childhood but after the age of 18. It is known that some adopted people who have had no great difficulties during childhood coming to terms with the fact they are adopted and have enjoyed having a close relationship with their adoptive parents subsequently experience difficulties in the area of personal identity.'

12.21   In addition s 1(4)(f) provides that the court and agency must have regard to the relationship which the child has with relatives and with any other person in relation to whom the court or agency considers the relationship to be relevant, including:

- the likelihood of any such relationship continuing and the value to the child of its so doing;

- the ability and willingness of any of the child's relatives or of any such person to provide the child with a secure environment in which the child can develop, and otherwise to meet the child's needs;

- the wishes and feelings of any of the child's relatives or of any such person, regarding the child.

---

[20]   Report to Ministers of an Interdepartmental Working Group (Dept of Health, 1992) at para 7.2.

Local authority duty

12.22 Section 17(1) of the Children Act 1989 imposes a general duty on local authorities:

- to safeguard and promote the welfare of children within their area who are in need; and

- so far as is consistent with that duty, to promote the upbringing of such children *by their families*,

by providing a range and level of services appropriate to those children's needs.

12.23 In addition, when the authority is making arrangements for the accommodation of children who are being looked after[21] one of the options it currently has to consider is 'a relative'.[22]

12.24 This current requirement has been amended by the Children and Young Person's Act 2008 from a date to be fixed. The new CA 1989 s 22C provides that if it is not consistent with the child's welfare or it would not be reasonably practicable to place him with a parent or someone with parental responsibility or a person in whose favour a residence order was in force immediately before the care order was made,[23] the authority must place him in the most appropriate placement available, preference being given to an individual who is the child's relative, friend or other person connected with the child who also a local authority foster parent.[24]

12.25 These duties are discussed in detail at **15.68**.

The right to continue and develop a relationship with one's family by way of contact

12.26 The right to family life continues even when the child cannot live with members of his family.

12.27 Article 9(3) of the UN Convention on the Rights of the Child declares that:

> 'States Parties shall respect the right of the child who is separated from one or both parents to maintain personal relations and direct contact with both parents on a regular basis, except if it is contrary to the child's best interests.'

---

[21] Either in the care of the authority under a care order or being provided with accommodation with the agreement of those with parental responsibility or because there is no one with parental responsibility: CA 1989, ss 22(1) and 20(1).

[22] CA 1989, s 23(2).

[23] Ibid, s 23C(2) and (3).

[24] Ibid, s 22C(7)(a).

12.28 In *Hendriks v Netherlands*[25] the ECtHR held that:

'The natural link between a parent and a child is of fundamental importance and ... where the actual "family life" in the sense of "living together" has come to an end, continued contact between them is desirable and should in principle remain possible. Respect for family life within the meaning of Article 8 thus implies that this contact should not be denied unless there are strong reasons ... which justify such an interference ... However, where there is a serious conflict between the interests of the child and one of its parents which can only be resolved to the disadvantage of one of them, the interests of the child must, under Article 8(2) prevail.'

12.29 The topic of contact when the child is in a permanent, alternative home is discussed in detail in Chapter 13.

Welfare of the child

12.30 The above rights are not absolute and can be overridden by the welfare of the child assessed in the light of all the circumstances.

'Art 8 requires that the domestic authorities should strike a fair balance between the interests of the child and those of the parents and that, in the balancing process, particular importance should be attached to the best interests of the child which, depending on their nature and seriousness, may override those of the parents. In particular, a parent cannot be entitled under Art 8 of the Convention to have such measures taken as would harm the child's health and development (*Scozzari and Giunta v Italy* (2002) 35 EHRR 12, sub nom *S and G v Italy*[26] at para 169, and *P, C and S v United Kingdom*.[27,28]

KINSHIP CARE – BACKGROUND

12.31 The provisions of the Children Act 1989 which emphasised the importance of the child's wider family as potential carers (see **12.65**) marked the rediscovery of the extended family after a lengthy period in which such placements had tended to be regarded with suspicion and had come to constitute a decreasing proportion of foster care placements.[29] Volume 3 of the Guidance on the Children Act 1989, *Family Placements*,[30] states that:

'Possibilities for a child to be cared for within the extended family should have been investigated and considered as an alternative to the provision of accommodation ... Even when it has become necessary for the ... authority to

---

[25] (1983) 5 EHRR 233, ECtHR.
[26] [2000] 2 FLR 771.
[27] (2002) 35 EHRR 31, [2002] 2 FLR 631 at para 117.
[28] *Görgülü v Germany* (ECtHR) [2004] 1 FLR 894 at [43].
[29] Hunt *Family and Friends Carers: A Scoping Paper* (Department of Health, 2002) at p 1.
[30] (Department of Health, 1991) at para 3.33.

arrange provision of accommodation, placement with a relative will often provide the best opportunities for promoting and maintaining family links in a familiar setting.'

12.32 Hunt[31] suggests that there are a number of reasons for this growing interest in kinship care.

- a rising demand for out of home placements particularly for minority ethnic or hard to place children;

- poor outcomes for children in public care;

- a change from theories about trans-generational transmission of abuse to ones which were ecological and strengths-based;

- increased sensitivity of the needs of ethnic minority children and their community;

- political philosophies aimed at reducing the role of the State.

For a more jaundiced approach, see **1.30**.

12.33 In the White Paper *Care Matters: Time for Change*[32] in 2007 the Government underlined this new approach.

'Family and friends carers play a key role in enabling children to remain with people they know and trust if they cannot live with their parents and these arrangements happen both within and outside the care system. We know that many family and friends carers are often older carers with health and financial difficulties of their own yet they provide a stable, safe and nurturing home during a short term family crisis or until the child reaches adulthood and beyond ... We will put in place a "gateway approach" to family and friends care to make sure that it is considered as an option at the first and every subsequent stage of decision-making by introducing a requirement that relatives and friends are, as far as possible, considered in all cases as potential carers as part of the care plan lodged with the court at the outset of care proceedings.'

Research

12.34 Although there is international research into kinship care, there is very little research for the United Kingdom[33] and comparisons between practice in

---

[31]　Hunt 'Substitute Care of Children by Members of their Extended Families and Social Networks: An Overview' in Ebtehaj, Lindley and Richards (eds) *Kinship Matters* (Hart Publishing, 2006) at p 113.

[32]　Cm 7137 (DES, 2007) at paras 2.34 and 2.38.

[33]　Farmer and Moyes *Children Placed with Family and Friends: Placement Patterns and Outcomes: Executive Summary* (DES, 2005) at p 1.

different countries should be treated cautiously.[34] However, there are at least three important recent studies. In 2001, Broad, Hayes and Rushforth[35] examined 50 kinship placements of children aged from 11 to 25 in a London Borough. In 2005 Farmer and Moyes[36] based their research on 270 children from four local authorities. One hundred and forty two of the children lived with family or friends and the rest with unrelated foster carers. The third was conducted by Hunt, Waterhouse and Lutman[37] who studied a cohort of 113 children in two local authorities who had either been placed with family and friends following care proceedings between 1995 and 1999 or in the period 1999 and 2001 together with a comparison group of 31 children who had been placed in non-kincare.

12.35 In addition, useful literature reviews have been prepared by Joan Hunt[38] and by Sellick, Thoburn and Philpot.[39]

How much kinship care?

12.36 UK statistical data about kinship care is very limited, in part because there are two groups of kinship carers: those looking after children with the approval and involvement of social services (for which there are statistics) and those looking after children on an informal basis for whom there are no reliable statistics. As at 31 March 2001, 6,600 children were 'looked after' in foster placements with family and friends. As a percentage of the total number of children in local authority foster care, this has increased from 14% in 1996 to 17% in 2001.[40]

Who are the carers?

12.37 Carers tend to be considerably older than foster carers, largely because grandparents predominate, nearly half (42%) of Broad's carers, 45% of Farmer's and 62% of Hunt's. The next largest group are aunts. Placements with the maternal side of the family predominate. In Hunt's sample, it was three times more likely than with the paternal side.[41]

---

[34] Sellick, Thoburn and Philpot *What works in adoption and foster care?* (2004) at p 66 and Hunt *Family and Friends Carers: A Scoping Paper* at p 3.

[35] *Kith and Kin: Kinship Care for Vulnerable Young People* (Joseph Rowntree Foundation,2001) summarised in Findings D11, JRF.

[36] *Kinship Care: Fostering Effective Family and Friends Placements* (2007) summarised in *Children Placed with Family and Friends: Placement Patterns and Outcomes: Executive Summary* (DES, 2005).

[37] *Keeping them in the family* (BAAF, 2008). Summarised in Waterhouse, Hunt and Lutman 'Children Placed with Kinship Carers through Care Proceedings' [2008] Fam Law 435.

[38] *Family and Friends Carers: A Scoping Paper* (Department of Health, 2002). Hunt is also the author of a valuable paper on kinship care, 'Substitute Care of Children by Members of their Extended Families and Social Networks: An Overview' in Ebtehaj, Lindley and Richards (eds) *Kinship Matters* (Hart Publishing, 2006).

[39] *What works in adoption and foster care?* (2004).

[40] *Friends and Family Care: Discussion Paper* (DCFS, 2002).

[41] This accords with research by Cardiff University which found that when parents separate, grandparents on the maternal side of the family were more likely to be involved with the

12.38 The family and friends carers are likely to be significantly more disadvantaged than unrelated foster carers, being more likely to be lone carers, living at least initially in overcrowded conditions, being nearly twice as likely (31% compared to 17%) to have a disability or a chronic illness and six times more likely (71% as against 13%) to experience financial hardship.[42]

Who is looked after?

12.39 Children living with kinship carers are significantly more likely to be placed with carers who had the same ethnic background. In contrast, Farmer found that significantly more black and minority ethnic children were placed with unrelated carers.

12.40 It may be that children are more likely to be the only child in the household.[43]

12.41 Children are likely to have suffered some kind of adversity prior to placement and are also likely to have some difficulty themselves.[44] In Hunt's sample 70% had difficulties such as ill health, physical or learning difficulties, emotional or behavioural problems. In this they are similar to non-kin placed children.[45] Farmer commented that 'Many kinship carers struggled valiantly to bring order to these children's fragmented lives.'[46]

Contact

12.42 Children placed with kinship carers have high levels of contact with relatives including parents than those living with non-kinship foster carers. In Farmer's sample, nearly two in five (37%) of children placed with non-relatives had no contact with either parent, twice the rate (17%) of those placed with relatives. However, this may typically be only with the side of the family with whom they were living. Hunt found that very few children had contact with both parents.[47]

12.43 The evidence about whether contact causes difficulties is unclear. Farmer found that there was cause for concern in only 6% of cases. 'In most cases relatives managed the tricky business of putting the children's needs first very well.'[48] In comparison Hunt found that there were no problems in less than a third of cases. 'Problematic contact, however, was common and in a

---

children, most of whom would be living with the mother. Douglas and Ferguson 'Grandparents After Divorce' [2003] Fam Law 653.

[42]   Farmer op cit.
[43]   Farmer op cit.
[44]   *Keeping them in the family* op cit at p 68; Farmer op cit.
[45]   Ibid.
[46]   op cit at p 5.
[47]   *Keeping them in the family* op cit at p 285.
[48]   op cit at p 4.

substantial majority of cases, contact appeared to be entirely negative for the child.'[49] Even where there were difficulties, contact, especially with mothers, continued.

The views of children

12.44 Broad found that many of the young people in his sample expressed a sense of 'emotional permanence' – feeling safe and secure because of the love they received. Hunt reported a similar finding. The children recounted 'a sense of ordinariness'. Where a sense of difference to other children existed, this related more to the existence of a care order/social services involvement rather than to the fact that they did not live with a parent. All the children interviewed showed 'an overwhelming sense of safety in the placement and reliance and trust in the kinship carer'.[50]

Local authority role

12.45 There are significant differences between local authorities. Farmer and Moyes found that among four authorities in 1 month, family and friends placements accounted for 14, 19, 26 and 41% of all placements.

12.46 Hunt found[51] that in a third of cases where children had been placed with non-kinship carers, there was no evidence that a kinship placement had been considered while in another quarter of cases, although relatives had been identified, they were not fully assessed.

12.47 Where the care is informal, neither the placement nor the needs of the carers will have been assessed, at least at the commencement of the placement.[52]

Support

12.48 There is universal agreement that kinship carers require both financial and non-financial support. Hitherto, the amount of support across the country has been inconsistent and, in many instances, lacking.

12.49 The issue of support is discussed in detail in Chapter 11.

Outcomes

12.50 In her paper, *Substitute Care of Children by Members of their Extended Families and Social Networks: An Overview*,[53] Hunt comments that one can almost guarantee that at every conference on kinship care someone will claim

---

[49] *Keeping them in the family* op cit at p 285.
[50] Ibid, at pp 250–251.
[51] *Keeping them in the family* op cit at p 288.
[52] Farmer op cit.
[53] op cit at p 121.

that research shows that kinship care is better for children than stranger care. 'In fact, research does not yet give a definitive answer.'

12.51   In Broad's study, the placements appeared to be relatively stable, nearly half having continued for between 1 and 5 years and a third for over 5 years. Farmer found that placements with kin lasted on average longer than non-kin placements perhaps because there were planned moves from the latter. Breakdown rates between the two groups were similar although family and friends carers showed a considerably higher commitment to the children than local authority carers.[54] Hunt[55] found that 56% of placements were stable or had lasted as long as needed.

12.52   Stability, though, is only part of the picture. What of the standard of care? Farmer reported that 'in most cases, family and carers, like unrelated foster carers, provide excellent care for the children'.[56]

12.53   Hunt found that over a third (36%) were problem free and only a fifth had major problems.[57] She suggests that factors associated with a positive outcome were:

- younger children;

- previous full-time care by the carer;

- grandparent care;

- single carer;

- pre-placement assessment;

- positive assessment of parenting capacity;

- child's acceptance of care;

- no other children in the household other than siblings;

- disagreement about placement during proceedings;

- placement instigated by carer;

- low level of child difficulties pre-placement.[58]

12.54   Hunt commented that:

---

[54]   op cit at p 6.
[55]   *Keeping them in the family* op cit at p 65.
[56]   op cit at p 6.
[57]   *Keeping them in the family* op cit at p 68.
[58]   Ibid, at p 99.

'The majority of our poor outcome children would struggle in any care situation. In contrast, the children who had good outcomes ... would probably have done well in any placement, being typically young and presenting few problems from the start.'[59]

12.55 In their literature review, Sellick and Thoburn concluded that:

'Kinship care or care by relatives and friends with the agreement of local authorities has been found to be more successful for the full range of children than placement with "stranger" carers.'[60]

Conclusions

12.56 The studies discussed above all offer a positive but cautious view of kinship care.

12.57 Farmer suggests that:

'Kinship care occupies an uneasy position on the boundary between public and private spheres of caring and this leads to a situation where some kin carers struggle to care for needy children with low levels of support and financial help ... At present [their] commitment and willingness to continue against the odds benefits the children they look after but the good outcomes for these children are sometimes achieved at the expense of the kin carers themselves.'[61]

12.58 Hunt reached the conclusion that kinship care can be a positive option for many children but it is not straightforward and requires careful assessment and adequate support.[62]

12.59 Nevertheless,

'However wide the net may be cast, in many families there does not appear to be a "bottomless pit" of willing and able relatives to care.'[63]

'We need to be realistic ... about the extent to which kinship care can be extended. It is fanciful to assume that there are potential relative carers for every child. The successful expansion of kinship care may depend more on encouraging and supporting those relatives who have already shown some interest in and potential to care for the child than on recruiting extended family members who have had little or no involvement.'[64]

12.60 Notwithstanding her caution, in her paper Hunt concludes that:

---

[59] *Keeping them in the family* op cit at p 100.
[60] op cit at p 65 *per* Hunt above at **12.50**.
[61] op cit at p 7.
[62] *Keeping them in the family* op cit at p 296.
[63] Ibid, at p 159.
[64] Ibid, at p 289.

'It clearly cannot be said ... that research has demonstrated that kinship care is *better* for children than non-related foster care. Nonetheless the evidence is broadly positive: children appear to do as least as well and possibly better and there is little to suggest they do worse.'[65]

LEGAL APPROACH TO KINSHIP CARE

Leave to issue proceedings

12.61 By virtue of ss 10(1) and 14A(3) of the Children Act 1989 family members need the permission of the court to apply for a residence or special guardianship order unless the child has lived with them for a period of at least 3 years or has the consent of everyone in whose favour a residence order is in force, or the local authority if the child is subject to a care order or, in any other case the consent of everyone who holds parental responsibility.[66] For the grant of leave, see **5.21**.

12.62 It is unlikely this requirement would be held to breach Art 8. In *Price v UK*,[67] the Commission drew a distinction between the relationship between a child and its parents and between a child and its wider relatives:

> 'In normal circumstances the relationship between grandparents and grandchildren is different in nature and degree from the relationship between parent and child ... When a parent is denied access to a child taken into public care this would constitute in most cases an interference with the parent's rights to respect for family life as protected by Article 8(1), but this would not necessarily be the case where grandparents are concerned ... there may be interference by the local authority if it diminishes contacts by refusing to grandparents what is in all the circumstances the reasonable access necessary to preserve a normal grandparent–grandchild relationship.'

12.63 However, when an application for leave is considered, Art 8 will be engaged.[68]

12.64 The Court of Appeal has emphasised that in many cases it is in the best interests of the child that grandparents should be given leave more readily than in the past. In *Re J (Leave to Issue Applications for a Residence Order)*,[69] Thorpe LJ said that:

> 'I am particularly anxious at the development of a practice that seems to substitute the test, "has the applicant satisfied the court that he or she has a good arguable case" for the test that Parliament applied in s 10(9). That anxiety is

---

[65] op cit at p 121 and see also *Family and Friends Carers: A Scoping Paper* op cit at 14.
[66] CA 1989, s 10(5).
[67] (1988) 55 DR 224, ECHR.
[68] *Re J (Leave to Issue Applications for a Residence Order)* [2003] 1 FLR 114 at [18].
[69] Ibid, at [18].

heightened in modern times where applicants under s 10(9) manifestly enjoy Art 6 rights to a fair trial and, in the nature of things, are also likely to enjoy Art 8 rights.

Whilst the decision in *Re M (Care: Contact: Grandmother's Application for Leave)*[70] no doubt served a valuable purpose in its day and in relation to s 34(3) applications [for contact with children in care], it is important that trial judges should recognise the greater appreciation that has developed of the value of what grandparents have to offer, particularly to children of disabled parents. Judges should be careful not to dismiss such opportunities without full inquiry. That seems to me to be the minimum essential protection of Arts 6 and 8 rights that Mrs J enjoys, given the very sad circumstances of the family.'

Importance of considering family members as potential carers

12.65 In many cases courts at first instance will make orders placing children with family members, whether under a residence or special guardianship order and no authority is required for the proposition that if it is not possible for children to be brought up by a parent, family carers should be considered as the first option.

12.66 Courts are also alert to the need to investigate kinship carers at an early stage of care proceedings. At the First Appointment[71] one of the steps which the court must take is to consider 'the identification of family and friends as proposed carers'.[72] In *G and B (Children)*[73] the President said that:

'The moral of this case, yet again, is that the available options for a child should be teased out as early as possible, and if a family member wishes to be considered to care for a child, he or she should come forward at the earliest possible opportunity.'

12.67 Often, family members are slow in coming forward (or, despite s 17(1) (see **12.22**), may not be approached by the local authority (see **12.45**)) but, if it is in the child's interests, even a late approach needs to be considered notwithstanding the delay to the final proceedings.

12.68 In *Re A (A Child) (Care Order)*[74] a local authority sought a care order in respect of a child, with a view to placing him for adoption. The father was a Turkish national and late in the proceedings proposed that the child be cared for by his paternal family in Turkey. The judge adjourned the hearing to allow the guardian to travel to Turkey to assess the situation. After a brief but unsatisfactory assessment of the family the guardian concluded that the child should not be placed with the family. A care order was made. The Court of Appeal allowed the father's appeal and directed a report from international

---

[70] [1995] 2 FLR 86.
[71] See *The Public Law Outline* (2008).
[72] Ibid, at para 12.3(6)(d).
[73] [2007] EWCA Civ 358, [2007] 2 FLR 140 at [42].
[74] [2006] All ER (D) 247 (Oct).

social services. The judge had exceeded the bounds of his wide discretion in dismissing the possibility of the child residing with his Turkish family on the basis of the guardian's report (which had only been available to the father on the eve of the trial, and with which his legal team had had no opportunity to deal). No doubt the child was highly adoptable, but that was a poor substitute for being brought up in his own family, not only with the father, but with uncles, aunts and the grandmother.[75]

12.69 A different conclusion was reached in *G and B (Children)*[76] when the Court upheld a refusal of a judge to adjourn an application for a placement order so as to enable the children's half-sister to be assessed as a carer. The application had been made late and the judge had ample evidence to show that the aunt was unsuitable and that delay would disadvantage the children.

12.70 Even where family members are identified, local authorities and, in some cases even guardians, may be slow to recognise their worth. In *Re C (Family Placement)*,[77] for example, the local authority 'severely curtailed' contact between a 3-year-old child and his 70-year-old grandmother who had 'a significant relationship' with him and then unsuccessfully opposed her being given party status in care proceedings. Despite the objections of the local authority and the guardian, the trial judge (upheld by the Court of Appeal who recognised that he was faced with a 'particularly difficult decision') placed the boy with his grandmother under a residence order and dismissed the application for a placement order.

SIBLINGS

Background

12.71 In their 2000 study of local authority permanency decision making, Lowe and Murch[78] found it was unclear whether being part of a sibling group influenced the decision. Despite expressed preferences to keep siblings together it was not unusual for the plan for the youngest sibling to be adoption with an older child to have long-term fostering as his plan. Some authorities found it as hard to find a foster home for three or four siblings as to find an adoptive home.

12.72 *The Prime Minister's Review: Adoption*[79] recorded that children who were adopted were likely to be part of sibling groups, but placed apart. A fifth of children adopted from care in 1998–1999 had no birth siblings; nearly a quarter (24%) had one and more than half had two or more. However, nearly

---

[75]   See also *Re M-H (Assessment: Father of Half-Brother)* [2006] EWCA Civ 1864, [2007] 1 FLR 1715.
[76]   op cit.
[77]   [2009] EWCA Civ 72, [2009] 1 FLR 1425.
[78]   *The Plan for the Child: Adoption or Long-term Fostering* (BAAF, 2001) at p 66.
[79]   (2000) PIU Report at para 2.10.

two-thirds (64%) of placements for adoption were single child placements, 30% were placements of sibling groups of two and 7% were of 3 or more.

The legal approach

12.73   Section 23(7) of the Children Act 1989 provides that when an authority is providing accommodation for a 'looked after' child and providing accommodation for his sibling, it shall 'so far as is reasonably practicable and consistent with his welfare secure that they are accommodated together'.

12.74   Courts consider that it is normally in the interests of all siblings to remain together. In *C v C (Minors: Custody)*[80] Purchas LJ said that:

> 'It is really beyond argument that unless there are strong features indicating a contrary arrangement that brothers and sisters should, wherever possible, be brought up together, so that they are an emotional support to each other in the stormy weathers of the destruction of their family.'

12.75   In *B v B (Residence Order: Restricting Applications)*,[81] Butler-Sloss LJ agreed.

> '... In the normal course of events it is clearly in the interests of children that they should live together. Where parents are in dispute, children give each other enormous moral support and emotional support. It is only in the unusual case that one has to separate children, and any judge who separates children does so with a heavy heart.'

She added that it is an error to confuse frequent contact with living together so as to lessen the weight to be given to the importance of living together.

12.76   Neither Purchas LJ nor Butler-Sloss LJ were saying that siblings should never be separated. In some cases, children may already be living apart and the benefit of living together may be outweighed by the disruption of a move. In others, the age difference may mean that the relationships are less strong than in cases where they are close in age. In cases where alternative plans for permanent places are being considered, placement together may not be in the best interests of all the children.

Whose interests are paramount?

12.77   Where two or more children are involved in the same proceedings, for example an application by child A for contact with child B, it is only the interests of the one who is the subject of the proceedings (ie child B) which are paramount, although the interests of the other child fall to be considered as

---

[80]   [1988] 2 FLR 291 at 302.

[81]   *B v B (Residence Order: Restricting Applications)* [1997] 1 FLR 139 at 144. See also Edwards, Hadfield and Mauthner *Children's Understanding of Their Sibling Relationships* (National Children's Bureau) summarised in *Findings* 0245 (Joseph Rowntree Foundation).

part of all the circumstances of the case.[82] Where they are each the subject of concurrent proceedings, the interests of each are paramount in the proceedings in which they are the subject. Thus, where A and B were subject to care orders and there was no opposition to A being freed for adoption but the father applied for a residence order in respect of B, the order was granted notwithstanding that it was in A's best interests to be adopted with B.[83] The Law Commission had recommended that the welfare test be amended to provide that the interests of the child whose future was being decided by the court should not in principle prevail over those of other children likely to be affected by the decision but this was not accepted by the legislature.[84]

12.78 Where, however, two or more children are the subject of the same proceedings, the interests of each are paramount and the court has to carry out a balancing exercise:[85]

'While the welfare of [the two children], taken together, is to be considered as paramount to the interests of any adults concerned in their lives, as between themselves the court must approach the question of their welfare without giving one priority over the other. You start with an evenly balanced pair of scales. Of course, when you start to put into the scales the matters relevant to each child – and in particular those listed in s 1(3) – the result may come down in favour of the one rather than the other, but that is a balancing exercise which the court is well used to conducting in cases concerning children.'[86]

'But the welfare of the two individuals cannot both be "paramount" in the ordinary and natural meaning of that word. If that is the requirement of s 1(1) in the circumstances, then the Act presents the court with an impossible task. For this reason, I agree with Balcombe LJ that the requirement must be regarded as qualified, in the cases where the welfare of more than one child is involved, by the need to have regard to the potential detriment for one in the light of potential benefit for the other. Only in this way, it seems to me, can the subsection be applied and the manifest objects of the Act achieved.'[87]

[82] *Birmingham City Council v H (No 3)* [1994] 1 FLR 224.
[83] *Re T and E (Proceedings: Conflicting Interests)* [1995] 1 FLR 581.
[84] *Family Law Review of Child Law: Guardianship and Custody* (1988) Law Com No 172, para 3.13.
[85] *Birmingham City Council v H (No 2)* [1993] 1 FLR 883.
[86] Ibid, per Balcombe LJ at 891.
[87] *Birmingham City Council v H (No 2)* [1993] 1 FLR 883, per Evans LJ at 899.

Chapter 13

CONTACT

INTRODUCTION

13.1 The importance of contact between children and parents with whom they do not live is widely recognised. However, the problems, benefits and practicalities of contact vary according to the child's situation. A common approach for frequent contact following parental separation is well established – although not without its problems – and the same applies when the child is in care. An approach for contact for children who are subject to special guardianship orders, when their special guardian has enhanced parental responsibility, is developing.

13.2 Contact between adopted children and their birth parents and family is perhaps the most contentious issue in adoption. While there is general agreement that both direct and indirect contact has the potential for benefiting the child, extensive research, while generating fierce academic debate is far from satisfying neutral commentators that as a general rule, there should be more contact than hitherto. Bridge[1] has pointed out that the conflicting opinions of Masson[2] who has argued for maintaining a reduction in regulation and court involvement and of Ryburn[3] who contends that courts should apply the same 'robust stand' as is shown in contact disputes between separated parents, are more than simply contrary views on how post-adoption contact should be handled. 'They illustrate a fundamental dilemma ... can and should the law attempt to offer problems which are primarily human and social rather than legal?'[4]

13.3 There has been a change in approach during recent decades and it has become accepted that 'open' adoption can bring benefits to some children. Currently however, courts remain reluctant, to some extent at least, to force contact on unwilling adopters, preferring to rely on negotiation, aided by preparation and counselling by the adoption agency.

---

[1] In Herring (ed) *Adoption law: a balance of interests* in *Family Law: Issues, Debates, Policy* (Willan Publishing, 2001), Chapter 6 at p 232.
[2] 'Thinking about Contact – a social or a legal problem?' [2000] CFLQ 28.
[3] For example, 'Welfare and Justice in Post-Adoption Contact' [1997] Fam Law 28 at 29 and 'In whose best interests? – post-adoption contact with the birth family' [1998] CFLQ 53.
[4] See also Smith and Logan 'Adoptive parenthood as a "legal fiction" – its consequences for direct post-adoption contact' [2002] CFLQ 281.

THE GENERAL IMPORTANCE OF CONTACT

13.4 The importance of contact between parents and children is recognised widely, internationally through Conventions, in domestic case law and by parents and children themselves. There is a common theme that contact should be the norm but that the interests of a child in the circumstances of a particular case may dictate that there should not be contact.

Article 8

13.5 The issue of contact engages the right to respect for family life and a private life under Art 8 of the European Convention for the Protection of Human Rights and Fundamental Freedoms 1950.

> 'The natural link between a parent and a child is of fundamental importance and ... where the actual "family life" in the sense of "living together" has come to an end, continued contact between them is desirable and should in principle remain possible. Respect for family life within the meaning of Article 8 thus implies that this contact should not be denied unless there are strong reasons ... which justify such an interference.
>
> Feelings of distress and frustration because of the absence of one's child may cause considerable suffering to the non-custodial parent. However, where there is a serious conflict between the interests of the child and one of its parents which can only be resolved to the disadvantage of one of them, the interests of the child must, under Article 8(2) prevail.'[5]

Denying contact not only needs to be justified as necessary for one of a variety of reasons, including the protection of the rights and freedoms of others, but also has to be proportionate to the aim which it is sought to achieve. A fair balance has to be struck between the interests of the child and those of the parents and particular importance should be attached to the best interests of the child which, depending on their nature and seriousness may override those of the parents. In particular, a parent is not entitled to contact under Art 8 which would harm the child's health or development.[6]

The approach of the courts

13.6 Domestic case-law contains many similar statements. In *Re K (A Minor) (Access Order: Breach)*,[7] Latey J said:

> 'Save in comparatively rare and exceptional cases, where a marriage has broken down it really is of the first importance in the interests of the children that they should have, and know that they have, the love and support of both parents; and

---

[5]   *Hendriks v Netherlands* (1983) 5 EHRR 233, ECtHR.
[6]   *Sahin v Germany, Sommerfield v Germany* Applications Nos 30943/96 and 31871/96 [2003] 2 FLR 671 at [66].
[7]   [1977] 2 All ER 737.

that they can only know that, especially if they are very young, if they have real and regular contact with the non-custodial parent.'

The views of the children

13.7 Children in a number of studies indicate that they want continuing contact, especially if conflict between their parents is absent or contained. 'Children are distressed and saddened by their parents' divorce and want to remain in contact with their non-residential parent.'[8] In 2000, a team from Kings College London interviewed over 400 children aged between 5 and 16 living in a variety of family situations.[9] Many children who were not living with both parents said that they missed their non-resident parent very much and wanted to see more of him, making practical suggestions as to how this might be achieved.

Benefits of contact

13.8 In 2000, a psychiatric review[10] of the issues involved in contact in private law cases in circumstances where there has been or is a risk of domestic violence was commissioned by the Official Solicitor when he was instructed in the appeals of *Re L (Contact: Domestic Violence)*; *Re V (Contact: Domestic Violence)*; *Re M (Contact: Domestic Violence)*; *Re H (Contact: Domestic Violence)*.[11] Sturge and Glaser prepared a list of the purposes of contact from the point of view of the child.

13.9 Benefits to the child include:

- sharing information and knowledge about the child's roots;

- maintaining meaningful and beneficial relationships or forming and building relationships which have the potential for benefiting the child;

- providing experiences which can be the foundations for healthy emotional growth and development;

- providing role models;

- repairing broken or problematic relationships;

- providing opportunities for testing fantasy and idealisation against reality;

---

[8] Rodgers and Pryor *Divorce and Separation: The Outcomes for Children* (Joseph Rowntree Foundation, 1998). See also Chapter 1.

[9] Dunn and Deater-Deckard *Children's Views of their Changing Families* (Joseph Rowntree Foundation, 2001) summarised in *Findings* 931.

[10] *Contact and Domestic Violence: the Experts' Court Report* [2000] Fam Law 615.

[11] [2000] 2 FLR 334.

- facilitating the assessment of the quality of the relationship or contact when a return to the care of that parent is being considered;

- helping to sever relationships when contact is to cease in the long term.

13.10 A list of the benefits of contact from the adult's view (not discussed in the review) include:

- providing the benefits for the child set out above or (to put it colloquially) 'being there' for the child;

- sharing information and knowledge about the child;

- maintaining meaningful and beneficial relationships or forming and building relationships which have the potential for benefiting the adult;

- providing the means for the adult to maintain a sense of his or her role as a parent;

- providing some continuity after a separation.

Risks of contact

13.11 Sturge and Glaser list the risks of contact as follows:

- escalating the climate of conflict around the child thereby undermining a sense of stability and well-being, causing tugs of loyalty and a sense of responsibility for the conflict and affecting the relationships between the child and both parents;

- direct experiences of physical, sexual or emotional abuse, neglect and being placed in a situation of danger, emotional abuse by way of the child or his or her carer being denigrated;

- continuing unhealthy relationships including situations where the child is aware of the carer's fear of contact;

- undermining the child's sense of security by deliberately or inadvertently setting different moral standards or standards of behaviour;

- experiences lacking in endorsement of the child as a valued individual, for example, where little or no interest is shown in the child;

- unstimulating experiences;

- continuing unresolved situations, for example if the child has a memory or belief about a negative aspect of the non-resident parent where this is denied or the parent refuses to acknowledge the memory or to apologise or help the child;

- unreliable contact in which the child is frequently let down or feels rejected;

- contact which the child does not want to attend;

- significantly difficult contact situations where there is little potential for or prospect of change;

- contact which causes stress to the child and/or his carer:

  'Proceedings often mean a standstill in the child's overall life and development while his or her carer's emotional energies are taken up with the case and the child is only too aware that he or she is the centre of attention and somehow responsible for this and the resulting distress.'

13.12 A literature review carried out by Kelly in 2000[12] concluded that after parental separation, contact with the non-resident parent has a 'buffering' effect. Large-scale studies have found no relationship between frequency of contact and child adjustment. What is important is the quality of the relationship between the child and the non-resident parent. The extent of any benefit appears to be linked to the degree of conflict, the type of paternal involvement, maternal acceptance and the regular payment of child support. Visiting schedules that permit both school-week and leisure-time involvement with the non-resident parent may enable 'real parenting'.

CARE ORDERS

13.13 Making a care order – but not the accommodation of a child under s 20 – automatically discharges any order for contact made under s 8 of the Children Act 1989 (CA 1989).[13]

13.14 When a child is in care, the local authority is under a duty to allow the child reasonable contact with his parents, any guardian or special guardian, any person who has parental responsibility by virtue of CA 1989 s 4A (see **14.71**) and, where a residence order or an order for care under the inherent

---

[12] Kelly 'Children's Adjustment in Conflicted Marriage and Divorce: a Decade Review of Research' (2000) *Journal of the American Academy of Child and Adolescent Psychiatry* vol 39, no 39, pp 963–973, summarised in Buchanan and Others *Families in Conflict* (The Policy Press, 2001).
[13] CA 1989, s 91(2).

jurisdiction of the High Court was in force immediately before the care order was made, the person in whose favour the order was made.[14]

13.15 This duty can be terminated by an order under CA 1989, s 34(4). However the court cannot fetter the authority's discretion to allow certain types of contact, for example overnight contact or to permit contact with a particular individual.[15]

13.16 Although the court cannot make a contact order under CA 1989, s 8 when a child is in the care of a local authority[16] it can make a contact order under CA 1989, s 34(2) in favour of anyone mentioned above or who has leave or, in family proceedings[17] or when making a care order, even without an application being made.[18] The order may be subject to conditions.[19]

13.17 The duty under the order to permit contact is placed only on the authority. It cannot oblige a person (including the child) to have contact, nor can it force anyone to permit contact (for example, the foster carer or, in the case of siblings, the parents with whom the siblings live).[20] However, a penal notice can be placed on the order rendering the local authority liable to be fined for contempt of court if the order is disobeyed.[21]

13.18 The authority may depart from the terms of the order with the agreement of the person in whose favour the order is made and that of the child (if he is of sufficient understanding) provided written notification is sent within 7 days to specified persons.[22] The authority may, as a matter of urgency, refuse contact for a period of not more than 7 days if it considers it necessary in order to safeguard or promote the child's welfare.[23]

13.19 An order for contact under CA 1989, s 34(2) or an order terminating contact under s 34(4) can be varied or discharged under s 34(9).

13.20 In appropriate cases an order can be made under CA 1989, s 91(14) prohibiting a parent from making a further application for an order, in exceptional cases without limit of time.[24]

---

[14]   CA 1989, s 34(1).
[15]   *Re W (Section 34(2) Orders)* [2000] 1 FLR 502. In *SB and County Council: P (a child)* [2008] EWCA Civ 535; sub nom *P (a child)* [2008] 2 FCR 185 the Court of Appeal criticised a local authority for terminating contact unilaterally.
[16]   CA 1989, s 9(1).
[17]   As defined in ibid, s 8(3).
[18]   Ibid, s 34(5).
[19]   Ibid, s 34(7).
[20]   *Re F (Contact: Child in Care)* [1995] 1 FLR 510.
[21]   *Re P-B Children* [2009] EWCA Civ 143 [2009] 2 FLR 66.
[22]   Contact with Children Regulations 1991 (SI 1991/891), reg 3. See also *Kent CC v C* [1993] 1 FLR 308 and *Re W (Section 34(2) Orders)* [2000] 1 FLR 502.
[23]   CA 1989, s 34(6). See also Contact with Children Regulations 1991 (SI 1991/891).
[24]   See, for example, *Re J (A Child) (Restriction on Applications)* [2007] EWCA Civ 906, [2008] 1 FLR 369, per Ward LJ.

Guidance

13.21 Guidance is provided by volume 3 of the Children Act Guidance – *Family Placements* (the Guidance).[25]

> 'For the majority of children there will be no doubt that their interests will best be served by efforts to sustain or create links with their natural families. Contact in the sense of personal meetings and visits will generally be the most common and, for both families and children, the most satisfactory way of maintaining their relationship. But other means which can help to keep family links alive should be borne in mind: letters, telephone calls, exchange of photographs. Contacts, however occasional, may continue to have value for the child even when there is no question of returning to his family. These contacts can keep alive for a child sense of his origins and may keep open options for family relationship in later life.'[26]

The contact arrangements should include all those people with whom contact should be preserved including relatives, siblings, grandparents and unmarried fathers. In some cases it may be appropriate to identify relatives with whom contact has lapsed and to follow up the prospects of establishing contact.[27]

Care Plans and reviews

13.22 The child's care plan[28] (see **15.42**) must contain details of the arrangements and purpose of contact which it is proposed to make. Contact must be considered at the regular Looked After Care ('LAC') Reviews[29] (see **15.51**).

Contact in practice

13.23 The European Court of Human Rights in *Johansen v Norway*[30] considered that taking a child into care should (subject to a fair balance being struck between the interests of the child in remaining in public care and those of the parent in being reunited with the child, particular importance being attached to the best interests of the child), normally be regarded as a temporary measure to be discontinued as soon as circumstances permit. Any measures of implementation of temporary care should be consistent with the ultimate aim of reuniting the natural parent and the child, particular importance being given to the best interests of the child.[31]

---

[25] (Department of Health, 1991) chapter 6. This is statutory guidance issued under the Local Authority Social Services Act 1970, s 7 and as such should be complied with unless local circumstances indicate exceptional reasons which justify a variation (see **11.22**).
[26] Ibid, para 6.9.
[27] Ibid, 6.15.
[28] CA 1989, s 31A and Circular LAC (99) 29 *Care Plans and Care Proceedings under the Children Act 1989*.
[29] Review of Children's Cases Regulations 1991 (SI 1991/891), reg 5 and Sch 2, para 3.
[30] (17383/90) (1997) 23 EHRR 33.
[31] And see also *Olson v Sweden No 1* (10465/83) [1988] ECHR 2 at [81].

13.24 However Biehal[32] found no evidence that it is contact *per se* which leads to reunification although regular contact together with other factors are probably linked to a return.

> 'There is some evidence that frequent parental visiting indicates the presence of a number of other factors which may predict reunion, including a positive relationship and strong attachment between parent and child, parental motivation, placement for reasons such as parental ill health or other crises rather than serious and persistent parenting problems, support to parents from social workers and purposeful, planned social work activity.'

13.25 In 2004 Sellick and Thoburn reviewed the literature on contact and permanent placements[33] and concluded that continued contact with birth parents, relatives or siblings can provide continuity for children in forming attachments to new families. Having contact is also found in some, but not all, studies to be associated with a reduced risk of the placement breaking down.

13.26 A number of possible problems have been identified.[34]

Practical problems

13.27

- **Distance** between the child's home and the parents' home. The prospective replacement of CA 1989, s 23 by s 22A now places a stronger duty on the authority to ensure that, unless it is not reasonably practical, the child's home, if not with his extended family, must be within the authority's area (see **15.69**). In addition the authority has power to assist in visiting costs.[35]

- **Logistical difficulties** when siblings are placed separately.

- **Timing and frequency** of visits may be perceived as being arranged more at the convenience of carers rather than the visitors and may not be synchronized with important dates such as birthdays.

- The **location** of contact may pose difficulties. Although the Guidance[36] states that visits to the child in his foster home, residential home or at the family home 'are the most usual forms of contact', contact in the family

---

[32] *Reuniting looked after children with their families* (2006). This literature review is summarised at www.jrf.org.uk/publications. The author warns that most of the research is from the US and the extent to which this can be extrapolated to the UK is unclear.

[33] *What works in adoption and foster care?* (Barnados, 2004) at 109.

[34] Miles and Lindley 'Contact for Children Subject to State Intervention' in Bainham, Lindley, Richards and Rinder (eds) *Children and Their Families* (Hart Publishing,, 2003), Chapter 12.

[35] CA 1989, Sch 2, para 16 and see the Guidance op cit at 6.23.

[36] Op cit at paras 6.18–6.20.

home occurs in only a minority of cases. The Guidance notes that contact in the foster home can be a source of severe distress especially where there has been insufficient preparation.[37]

Psychological problems

13.28

- Parents may be suffering from **depression**.

- Parents may feel **inadequate** and **uncertain** of their current role.

- Parents may feel **disempowered** by the social worker or a foster carer.

- **Foster carers** may not support contact if there are problems associated with contact which disturb the child and threaten the placement.

- **Children may be reluctant** to have contact for a variety of reasons: negative attitudes to parents, loyalty to or fear of rejection by carers.

- Some children may want **more contact** than their resilience can sustain.

- The **venue** may carry a strong message to the child about the perceived value of the relationship. **Supervision** can cause a lack of spontaneity.

Professional problems

13.29

- **Discontinuity** of social worker or a social worker ceasing to be actively involved in monitoring the child's welfare.

- Foster **carers not being involved** in planning contact.

- Insufficient encouragement of contact.

- **Signals** from the parents or child being **misconstrued** and interpreted as the parents being uninterested in contact.

The approach of the courts

13.30 The 'presumption'[38] of contact always has to be balanced against the long-term welfare of the child and particularly, the stability of his permanent home.

---

[37] Guidance op cit at 6.20.
[38] See *Re B (Minors) (Care: Contact: Local Authority's Plans)* [1993] 1 FLR 543 per Butler-Sloss LJ at 551.

'Contact must not be allowed to destabilise or endanger the arrangements for the child and in many cases the plans for the child will be decisive of the contact application.'[39]

13.31 However, although the grounds set out in CA 1989, s 31 have been proved and parents may be inadequate, contact may still be fundamentally important to the long-term welfare of the child by providing the security of knowing that his parents love him and are interested in his welfare, by avoiding any damaging sense of loss to the child, by enabling the child to commit to the substitute family with the seal of approval of the natural parents and by giving the child the necessary sense of family and personal identity.

'Contact, if maintained, is capable of reinforcing and increasing the chances of success of a permanent placement, whether on a long-term fostering basis or by adoption'.[40]

13.32 As Hale J pointed out in *Berkshire CC v B*,[41] cases range from one situation where a child clearly needs a new family and contact with his birth family is likely to impede this with little or no benefit, to others where the child is likely to return home in the short or medium term and contact is essential for this to take place. Many cases are in the middle: the child needs a permanent long-term home but his relationship with his birth family is so important that it must be maintained. In cases where adoption is not likely to succeed, 'a child must not be deprived of his existing relationships which matter to him for the sake of putative ones which may never be found'.

'In these very difficult cases the court has to balance these various advantages against the difficulties that contact is likely to cause in finding and sustaining an appropriate placement for the child. Obviously contact, however important, cannot be pursued to a level which makes a successful placement impossible to find because the child needs a home and to be properly looked after, and that must be the first priority.'

13.33 The proposals of the local authority, must command 'the greatest respect' from the court but the duty of deciding on contact when an application is made under CA 1989, s 34 rests on the court which may require the authority to justify their proposals.[42] Where the local authority is complying with its duty to promote contact (see **13.14**) and is positive about it, an order under s 34 may be unnecessary.[43]

13.34 An order terminating contact under CA 1989, s 34(4) should not be made while there remains a realistic possibility of rehabilitation of the child with the person in question or merely against the possibility that circumstances

---

[39] [1993] 1 FLR 543 per Butler-Sloss LJ at 551.
[40] *Re E (A Minor) (Care Order: Contact)* [1994] 1 FLR 146 per Simon Brown LJ at 154.
[41] [1997] 1 FLR 171 at 176.
[42] *Re B (Minors) (Care: Contact: Local Authority's Plans)* [1993] 1 FLR 543 per Butler-Sloss LJ at 551 and *Berkshire CC v B* [1997] 1 FLR 171 per Hale J at 176.
[43] *Re F (Contact: Child in Care)* [1995] 1 FLR 510.

may change in such a way as to make termination of contact desirable. For the order to be justified, a probable need to terminate contact must be foreseeable and not too remote.[44] Courts must be astute to see that the application to discharge is bona fide and not a disguised attempt to appeal the original order.[45]

13.35 If on an application to discharge a section 34(4) order the court exceptionally concludes that the factors are so evenly balanced as not to come down on one side or the other, then the order should be discharged. If an order under s 34(4) cannot be justified, it should not remain in force.[46]

SPECIAL GUARDIANSHIP

13.36 Before making a special guardianship order (SGO), the court has to consider:

(a)   whether a section 8 contact order, which may contain conditions[47] should also be made;

(b)   whether any section 8 order, including a contact order, should be discharged;

(c)   where a contact order is not discharged, whether any enforcement order[48] should be revoked;

(d)   whether any contact activity direction[49] should be discharged.[50]

The report to the court made by the applicant's local authority under s 14A(8) or (9) must contain a recommendation as to what arrangements there should be for contact between the child and his relatives or any person the authority considers relevant.[51]

13.37 When a court is considering making, varying or discharging a contact order it may make a contact activity direction requiring a party to take part in an activity that promotes contact with the child.[52] The activity may include programmes, classes, counselling or guidance sessions which may assist a

---

[44]   See also *Re H (Children) (Termination of Contact)* [2005] EWCA Civ 318, [2005] 2 FLR 408.
[45]   *Re T (Termination of Contact: Discharge of Order)* [1997] 1 FLR 517.
[46]   Ibid, per Holman J at 529.
[47]   CA 1989, s 11(c).
[48]   See ibid, s 11J.
[49]   See ibid, s 11A.
[50]   Ibid, s 14B(1).
[51]   The Special Guardianship Regulations 2005 (SI 2005/1109) (SGR 2005), Sch, para 10.
[52]   CA 1989, s 11A(2).

person to establish, maintain or improve contact with a child or may, by addressing a person's violent behaviour, enable or facilitate contact.[53]

13.38 The purpose of such a direction is both to facilitate contact and to provide a court with information as to whether a contact order should be made and the form it should take. Therefore CA 1989, s 11A(7) provides that a court cannot, on the same occasion, make a contact activity direction and dispose finally of the proceedings.[54]

13.39 Special guardianship support services which local authorities must provide in their area[55] include support for contact.[56] The support which the authority can provide includes:

- counselling, advice and information;[57]

- assistance including mediation[58] which presumably can include facilitating family group conferences;[59]

- travel costs in cash[60] or when on a recurring basis;[61]

- legal costs in relation to a section 8 application.[62]

The provision of services is discussed in detail in Chapter 11.

Contact in practice

13.40 Special guardianship is such a recent innovation that there is no research on how contact generally works. However, there are studies of contact where the child is living with a relative. Children placed with kin-carers have higher levels of contact with other relatives, including parents, than those living with non-kin foster carers. This may only typically be with the side of the family with whom they are living.

13.41 Evidence about whether contact causes difficulties for the child and the extent of the difficulties is unclear. It frequently appears to cause difficulties for the carer. This is likely to be more common where local authorities have been the instigators of the placement. A study of a sample of SGOs made in the first year that s 14A[63] was implemented found that a high proportion of parents had

---

[53] CA 1989, s 11A(5).
[54] Ibid, s 11A(7).
[55] Under ibid, s 14F(1).
[56] SGR 2005, reg 3(1)(c).
[57] CA 1989, s 14F(1)(a), SGR 2005, reg 3(1)(b).
[58] SGR 2005, reg 3(1)(c).
[59] See **18.7**.
[60] SGR 2005, reg 3(1)(b), 3(2), Special Guardianship Guidance (DfES, 2005), para 41.
[61] SGA 2005, reg 6(2)(b), Special Guardianship Guidance op cit, para 41.
[62] SGA 2005, reg 6(2)(c).
[63] Hall 'Special Guardianship: A Missed Opportunity – Findings From Research' [2008] Fam

personal problems. Over half had problems with substance misuse; a third had been involved in a history of domestic violence; a third had mental health problems and in a fifth of families there was a history of sexual or physical abuse of the child. Only 5% of visits were unsupervised.

13.42 Support is often needed for contact arrangements and kinship carers but hitherto has not been provided.

13.43 The nature of contact in kinship placements is discussed in more detail at **11.11**.

The approach of the courts

13.44 There is, at present, little guidance on how issues of contact should be approached when an SGO is in place or is intended. When contact orders are made when parents separate, the parent with whom the child lives cannot veto contact although the effect contact may have on the parent's care of the child may be a factor to be considered. In comparison, courts have historically been reluctant to impose contact on unwilling adopters (see **13.57**).

13.45 There are arguments that contact applications where an SGO is in force should be treated more like other applications for contact under s 8 rather than those involving an adopted child. One of the purposes behind the introduction of SGOs was to enable the relationship between the child and his parents and siblings to continue.[64] Moreover, only adopters have parental responsibility, whereas the making of an SGO does not remove a parent's parental responsibility even though special guardians may exercise their parental responsibility to the exclusion of any other person.[65] It will be difficult for parental responsibility to be exercised if there is no contact. However, at the same time, special guardianship is intended to provide the child with a permanent home. The child may have a greater need for stability than the ordinary child[66] and caution will have to be exercised to avoid a risk of the home being destabilised.

13.46 In *Re L (Special Guardianship: Surname)*,[67] an appeal was brought by grandparents who had been granted an SGO. They objected to the grant of contact orders to the children's parents which required the continued involvement of social workers, who would arrange and supervise contact which would take place away from their home and in their absence. The Court of Appeal pointed out that links with the birth parents, in SGO cases are not severed as in adoption but undoubtedly the purpose was to give the special

---

Law 148, 'Special Guardianship – Themes Emerging From Case Law' [2008] Fam Law 244 and 'Special Guardianship and Permanency Planning: Unforeseen Circumstances and Missed Opportunities' [2008] CFLQ 359.

[64] *Adoption – A New Approach* (Cm 5017) para 5.8. See also Chapter 11.
[65] CA 1989, s 14C(1).
[66] See **13.11**.
[67] [2007] EWCA Civ 196, [2007] 2 FLR 50 at [66].

guardians freedom to exercise parental responsibility in the best interests of the child. 'That however does not mean that the special guardians are free from the exercise of judicial oversight.' The trial judge clearly had the jurisdiction to make the contact orders she did and in the circumstances of the case, the exercise of her discretion was unobjectionable. However, the orders would be varied so that the supervision of contact would last for only one year.

ADOPTION

Background

13.47 In the early decades after the Adoption of Children Act 1926, the law was primarily concerned with the adoption of babies who had no existing social relationship with their birth parents and for whom it was intended that the adopters should become their parents in every sense except the biological. It is not surprising therefore that the Curtis Committee in 1946,[68] whose recommendations led to the Adoption of Children Act 1949, did not discuss post-adoption contact.

13.48 The Hurst Committee[69] in 1958 was troubled by adopters 'all too commonly' concealing the fact of adoption from the child as well as from the community and recommended that before granting the order the court should be satisfied that the adopters intended to tell the child about his adoption. This was not enacted in the Children Act 1958 which amended the adoption legislation. However, the Act gave courts an unrestricted power to impose terms and conditions on an adoption order and although this may have been intended to be used solely for the purpose of deciding issues relating to religion,[70] it inadvertently laid the foundation for courts to be able to consider post-adoption contact.

13.49 By 1972 there had been a decline in the number of 'baby' adoptions but it was increasingly recognised that adoption might be appropriate for children with disabilities who needed an alternative permanent home, most of whom would know their parents. Although the Houghton Committee[71] welcomed this trend and noted a growing acceptance that children should know about their adoption and have information about their background (see **12.13**), there was no overt consideration of post-adoption contact.

---

[68]   *Report of the Care of Children Committee* Cmd 6922 (1946).
[69]   *Report of the Departmental Committee on the Adoption of Children* (1958) Cmnd 9248, para 22. See also **2.109**.
[70]   Maidment 'Access and Family Adoptions' [1977] MLR 293.
[71]   *Report on the Departmental Committee on the Adoption of Children* Cmnd 5107 (1972) at para 24.

13.50 Social work practice was however changing. Not only was adoption being seen as a way of providing permanence for children with disabilities, it was also being considered for other children – not babies – whose parents could not or would not look after them.[72]

> 'These adoptions could bring great benefits for the child but they also brought a new set of challenges for social work and for the law. The children were older. They had a history. This might well include damaging experiences from their past. But it might also include significant relationships with members of their birth family. The use of compulsory adoption, dispensing with the need for parental agreement, was increasing. But the fact that these children had a history also meant that their best interests might require that any significant links with the birth family be preserved in a more 'open' form of adoption.[73]

13.51 The courts cautiously recognised the change. In *Re G (D M) An Infant*[74] in 1962, for example, Pennycuick J referred to 'adoption societies and local authorities regard[ing] ... [complete severance of the child from his natural parents] as a primary consideration' in adoption. In the early 1970s Rees J at first instance in *Re J (A Minor) (Adoption Order: Conditions)*[75] and the Court of Appeal in *Re S (A Minor) (Adoption Order: Access)*,[76] while not encouraging a practice of contact, stated that 'the general rule which *forbids* [emphasis added] contact between an adopted child and his natural parent may be disregarded in an exceptional case where the court is satisfied that by so doing the welfare of the child may be best promoted'.[77] Neither case involved an adoption agency.

13.52 Notwithstanding *Re J (A Minor) (Adoption Order: Conditions)* and *Re S (A Minor) (Adoption Order: Access)* courts were reluctant to impose contact conditions on unwilling adopters. In 1989 the House of Lords addressed the issue in the leading case of *Re C (A Minor) (Adoption Order: Conditions)*.

> 'It seems to me essential that, in order to safeguard and promote the welfare of the child throughout his childhood, the court should retain the maximum flexibility given to it by the Act and that unnecessary fetters should not be placed upon the exercise of the discretion entrusted to it by Parliament. The cases to which I have referred illustrate circumstances in which it was clearly in the best interests of the child to allow access to a member of the child's natural family. The cases rightly stress that in normal circumstances it is desirable that there should be a complete break, but that each case has to be considered on its own particular facts. No doubt the court will not, except in the most exceptional case, impose terms or conditions as to access to members of the child's natural family to which the adopting parents do not agree. To do so would be to create a potentially frictional

---

[72] See, for example, Tizard *Adoption: A Second Chance* (Open Books, 1977).
[73] *Down Lisburn Health and Social Services Trust v H* [2006] UKHL 36, [2007] 1 FLR 121 per Baroness Hale of Richmond at [7]–[8].
[74] [1962] 2 All ER 546. See also, for example, *Re B (M F) (An Infant)* [1972] 1 All ER 898 per Salmon J at 900.
[75] [1973] 2 All ER 410.
[76] [1975] 1 All ER 109.
[77] *Re J (A Minor) (Adoption Order: Conditions)* [1973] 2 All ER 410 at 417.

situation which would be hardly likely to safeguard or promote the welfare of the child. Where no agreement is forthcoming the court will, with very rare exceptions, have to choose between making an adoption order without terms or conditions as to access, or to refuse to make such an order and seek to safeguard access through some other machinery, such as wardship. To do otherwise would be merely inviting future and almost immediate litigation.'[78]

13.53   By the early 1990s the term 'open adoption'[79] was in common use and some agencies, especially in New Zealand, had taken the stance that prospective adopters should not be accepted unless they were able to see the value of some degree of contact with the birth parents, if only by letter.[80] In 1992, the *Departmental Review of Adoption Law: Report to Ministers*,[81] addressed the issue of contact directly and in detail. Openness in adoptions was encouraged.

'Adoption has traditionally been a somewhat closed and secretive process in which many children have been shielded from knowledge about and contact with their birth families. In practice, for many years now, there has been an increasing recognition that a child's knowledge about his or her background is crucial to the formation of positive self-identity and that adoptive families should be encouraged to be open about the child's adoptive status and the special nature of the adoptive relationship.'[82]

Noting the range of contact possibilities available, it said that:

'Although adoption involves the severance of all legal ties with one's birth family, there is no inherent reason why this should preclude the possibility of some contact being maintained nor should it preclude the possibility that there is no contact at all'.[83]

13.54   The appropriateness of a particular form of contact was likely to depend on a number of factors, most importantly the wishes, feelings and welfare of the child, the willingness of the adoptive parents and the ability of those with whom the child is to have contact to recognise and respond to the child's needs. However: 'Contact should normally take place only with the prior agreement of all those concerned.'[84] Nor should legislation prescribe the circumstances under which contact should or should not take place. The agency should be left to work this out with all concerned.[85]

---

[78]   [1973] 2 All ER 410 per Lord Ackner at 167.

[79]   'A continuum of possibilities ranging from an initial exchange of non-identifying information via the agency to ongoing contact in some form negotiated directly' as opposed to 'closed contact', the traditional model: Fratter *Adoption with Contact* (BAAF, 1996), p 5.

[80]   Thoburn *Review of Research Relating to Adoption*, Appendix C, *Review of Adoption Law: Report to Ministers* (Department of Health, 1992), para 49.

[81]   *Review of Adoption Law: Report to Ministers*, op cit.

[82]   Ibid, para 4.1.

[83]   Ibid, para 5.1.

[84]   Ibid, para 5.2.

[85]   Ibid, para 5.3.

13.55 The Children Act 1989 had created a regime whereby birth parents – albeit with leave – could apply for an order (as opposed to a condition) to secure post adoption contact and the Review considered that decisions on contact would best be taken by this route rather than by imposing conditions on adoption orders.

13.56 Following the Report courts were more ready to recognise the benefits to the child that post-adoption contact might bring. In *Re E (A Minor) (Care Order: Contact)*[86] Simon Brown LJ said that:

'Contact, if maintained, is capable of reinforcing and increasing the chances of success of a permanent placement, whether on a long-term fostering basis or by adoption. There is, I appreciate, an ongoing debate regarding the merits of open or closed adoption and it is not one that I propose to enter. But whatever be the arguments, there will undoubtedly be cases, and this I believe to be one, in which some continuing face-to-face contact is clearly desirable and which call, accordingly, at the very least for some positive efforts on the local authority's part to find, if at all possible, prospective open adopters; here, it seems to me, there have been none.'

13.57 However, the courts remained reluctant to imposing contact by way of an order on reluctant adopters. In *Re T (Adoption Contact)*[87] Butler-Sloss LJ commented that she knew of no case where a contact order had been imposed on objecting adopters 'and I would hesitate to make an order imposing upon adopters that which they are prepared to do in any event'. In that case the Court of Appeal allowed the appeal against a post-adoption contact order, holding that in the circumstances of the case the mother should trust the adopters who if circumstances changed, should have the flexibility to be able to change the arrangements rather than be tied to an order.

13.58 In 2002 *The Prime Minister's Review: Adoption*[88] came to the conclusion that the organisation, but not necessarily the principle, of post-adoption contact was far from satisfactory.

- The prospect of direct contact could adversely impact on whether a child can be adopted at all.

- In some cases there was an unfounded belief that the birth relative could work with the adoptive family despite a history of not being able to work with statutory agencies.

- In some cases social workers seemed over-influenced by the interests of the birth family rather than of the child.

---

[86] [1994] 1 FLR 146 at 154.
[87] [1995] 2 FLR 251 per Butler Sloss LJ at 257.
[88] op cit, paras 3.140–3.147.

- Contact was being used as a negotiating tool in the hope of avoiding a contested hearing.

- Support for both birth and adoptive parents was needed to make even letter box contact work properly.

- Most social workers did not have sufficient skills or knowledge to be able to provide guidance to birth parents about the best way to communicate with the child.

- Few agencies had systems for reviewing contact.

13.59   It recommended that

- consideration should be given to providing guidance about post-adoption contact;

- provision for contact should form part of the local authority's duty to provide post-adoption support;

- training for social workers, guardians and the judiciary should be provided.

13.60   Government and both professional and legal opinion now recognise that contact between an adopted child and members of his birth family is not incompatible with an adoption order and is capable of benefiting a child. However, the historical background highlights the issues which still have to be resolved both generally and in the circumstances of each case.

- When is contact appropriate?

- Is the agreement of the adopters necessary?

- Should matters be left to the adoption agency to try to arrange or should orders be made and, if so, at what stage in the proceedings?

- If orders are made, should they be enforced and if so, how?

Research

13.61   There is much research both in the United Kingdom and internationally about post-adoption contact but, as was noted at **13.2**, the issue remains highly controversial.

13.62   In 1987 Fratter[89] examined a small sample of 17 adoptive families where there was some contact after adoption and followed it up in 1991. Lowe

---

[89]   Fratter *Adoption with Contact* (BAAF, 1996).

and Murch[90] conducted a large-scale study of how agencies approach post-adoption contact in practice. They sent a questionnaire to all (then, 160) statutory and voluntary agencies in England and Wales, interviewed representatives from 48 agencies, sent questionnaires to 515 adoptive families and interviewed 48 families. A third study which provides insights into the feelings of children, and birth and adopting parents was conducted by Neil and others from the University of East Anglia[91] who studied a group of 41 children who had been placed for adoption under the age of 4, following them up 7 years later. All children had initially had contact with some members of their birth family although this had ceased in some cases at follow up.

13.63 These studies are not necessarily representative. Three informative literature reviews are *Adoption Now: Messages from Research*,[92] *What Works in Adoption and Foster Care?*[93] and *Adoption and Contact: A Research Review*.[94]

How much contact is there?

Contact

13.64 Three-quarters of the children in Lowe and Murch's sample had some form of ongoing contact with a birth family. Nearly half had contact with their mothers and just under a quarter with fathers. In 16% of cases, children had contact with both birth parents. Sibling contact was as common as that with mothers and was most common when the sibling was living with other adopters or foster carers, although 18% had contact with siblings living with birth relatives. Nearly a quarter of adopted children had contact with grandparents, more commonly with maternal grandparents (18%) than paternal (11%). Only 3% of children had contact with both sets of grandparents.

Direct contact

13.65 Brocklesby[95] found that about one in five adopted children are likely to have direct contact with birth parents or siblings and 15% with other birth relatives. About half of children were estimated to have indirect contact.

13.66 More than two families in five in Lowe and Murch's sample had direct contact with at least one birth relative.[96] It was more common than indirect contact except for birth parents. One in five children had direct contact with

---

[90]   *Supporting Adoption: Reframing the Approach* (BAAF, 1999).
[91]   The results of the study have been published in a number of papers. They are summarised in Neil and Young Centre for Research on the Child and Family *The Contact after Adoption Study: Key Findings* (2007).
[92]   Ridgeway and Others (Department of Health, 1999), Chapter 5.
[93]   Sellick, Thoburn and Philpot (Barnados, 2004), Chapter 3.
[94]   Neil, in Bainham and others (eds) *Children and Their Families: Contact, Rights and Welfare* (Hart Publishing, 2003), Chapter 14.
[95]   Unpublished research cited in *The Prime Minister's Review: Adoption* (PIU, 2002), paras 3.142 and 3.145.
[96]   Ibid, p 295.

mothers, one in twelve with fathers, 16% with siblings and 8% with grandparents. Direct contact for the immediate birth family was less common for families approved by voluntary as opposed to statutory agencies.

Indirect contact

13.67 Neil found that in many families indirect contact had not lived up to people's hopes. Fewer than half the children where indirect contact had been planned were receiving any information and many relatives were not responding to letters and photographs from the adopters.

Persistence of contact

13.68 Contact may diminish over time but continues in most cases. Parental contact is most likely to cease and that is because birth parents do not keep in touch with the adoptive families. Fratter found that after 4 years contact ceased in five of the twelve cases where there had been face to face contact. Neil found that 7 years after first interviewing the families in her sample, direct contact was still taking place in 86% of cases where it was with a non-birth parent but only in half of cases involving birth parents. She made the point that it is hard for birth parents to sustain contact because of practical and emotional difficulties. Contact can be of poor quality because of poor child/parent relationships and unresolved feelings of deprivation, guilt and anger.

Agreement or order?

13.69 There was a formal agreement for contact in less than two-fifths of Lowe and Murch's families, agreements being more common where a voluntary adoption agency was involved.[97] Some agencies though preferred to have court orders or contact conditions imposed because, as some agencies made clear to families, ultimately agreements are not legally binding. However, Lowe and Murch point out that the 'goodwill' element of agreements conveys a positive message of trust as opposed to a contact order which implies the adopters cannot be trusted.[98]

13.70 In some cases, as noted in the *The Prime Minister's Review: Adoption*, adopters argued that contact was used as a bargaining tool to secure the birth parents' consent to the adoption.[99] Agencies varied in the steps they were willing to take if agreements were broken.[100]

---

[97] *Supporting Adoption* op cit, p 319. Unsurprisingly given the date when the children were placed, all contact in Fratter's study was by voluntary agreement: *Adoption with Contact* op cit, p 251.

[98] Ibid, pp 320–321.

[99] Ibid, p 316.

[100] *Supporting Adoption* op cit p 320.

The experience of children

13.71 The children in Neil's sample were on average less than 2 years old when placed with their adoptive families. She found they took contact with birth relatives for granted and in most cases contact was positive. Any negative feelings were most commonly about contact they wanted to happen but which did not. Most children who had direct contact said they enjoyed the meetings and, for most, it was not a big emotional event. There was no evidence that direct contact improved or hindered the child's emotional or behavioural development.[101]

13.72 The children in Fratter's sample were older. For about half of them, contact was a significant part of their life. They had maintained a sense of loyalty towards their birth mother, become attached to their adoptive parents and most saw other birth relatives as well. Contact with siblings was particularly valued. For the rest, contact had ceased altogether or was very infrequent. Yet they were able to identify ways in which they had benefited from the contact which had taken place.

The experience of adopters

13.73 According to Neil, adopters can fear contact, the main worry being that it will interfere with their relationship with the child but contact rarely proves these fears well-founded. However, in her sample, most adoptive parents were very positive about contact.

13.74 Most of Fratter's adopters continued to feel positive about adoption after 4 years and those who had previously expressed concern were able to describe ways in which contact had benefited the children. Some said that contact had increased their own satisfaction. Only one couple was entirely negative.

13.75 However, Lowe and Murch found some adopters for whom the experience of direct contact was very difficult. Parents were known to pass improper information to the child or make destructive comments about the placement.[102]

13.76 Both Fratter[103] and Neil[104] comment that the significance of contact for the child will vary according to the child's age and development. In Fratter's sample contact was not thought to have adversely affected the attachment of any children placed under the age of 7 nor to have given rise to divided loyalties, whereas some of the older children took several years to form an attachment. Neil suggests that the reasons for this are that most children did not have an established relationship before placement; birth parents generally

---

[101] *The Contact After Adoption Study: Key Findings* op cit, at pp 4–5.
[102] *Supporting Adoption* op cit, p 298.
[103] *Adoption with Contact* op cit, p 234.
[104] *The Contact After Adoption Study: Key Findings* op cit, at p 5.

showed a high level of support for the adoption and contact meetings were generally set up as 'whole family' events with the adoptive parents in control, something Fratter's adopters also felt important.

The potential benefits of contact

13.77 A number of possible benefits for the child have been identified.

- It can be important for the child's sense of identity and knowledge of his or her family background. This does not necessarily mean contact with close relatives.[105]

- It can reduce any feelings the child has of being rejected.[106] *Messages from Research*[107] notes that a recurring theme in studies was the child's sense of loss at having to leave the birth family, the person most missed being the mother, then siblings and then the father.

- It can help the child settle in with the adopting family.[108]

- It can relieve any anxiety the child has about the well being of birth relatives.[109]

What needs to be in place?

13.78 The studies suggest that several conditions need to be in place for adopters to feel comfortable with contact and to be able to see the benefits for the child.

- The **birth relatives need to approve the adoption** and not make disruptive comments to the children. Contact is likely to be adversely affected although not necessarily reduced if adoption was opposed by the birth family and they continue to be antagonistic towards it.[110] About half of Neil's birth relatives showed positive acceptance of the adoption; about a third were resigned but often positive about the adopters; about a fifth were angry and resistant. Grandparents were more likely than birth parents to accept the adoption positively.

- **Meeting the adopters** is likely to have a major impact on how the birth parents and relatives view the adopters. Virtually all birth relatives in Neil's sample who had met the adopters spoke of how they liked them,

---

[105] *Supporting Adoption* op cit, p 324; *Adoption with Contact* op cit, p 114.

[106] *Supporting Adoption* op cit, p 324.

[107] *Adoption Now: Messages from Research* op cit, p 45.

[108] *Supporting Adoption* op cit, p 324.

[109] *Supporting Adoption* op cit, p 324; *Adoption with Contact* op cit.

[110] *Supporting Contact* and *Messages from Research* p 50.

using only positive terms. In contrast, relatives who had not met them said that they had 'no idea' what they were like and very few expressed positive feelings.[111]

- **Adopters need to be positive about contact**. They must accept that the child has birth relatives and may need to see them and to some extent accept them into the adoptive family.[112]

- It must be recognised that **needs for contact may change** as the child's understanding develops or the circumstances of the relatives change.[113]

- **Social work support** prior to the placement makes a significant impact.[114]

Support

Direct contact

13.79 Although adopters can be sympathetic to the idea of direct contact with birth parents, the practical and emotional realities of direct contact may reduce their support for such contact. Regulation can be difficult; meetings at contact centres and supervision, while helping to ensure that agreed limits are adhered to, are likely to be uneasy and artificial.[115] They are a considerable strain on the resources of local authorities. However many adopters valued contact being supervised.[116]

13.80 Some families need feedback and others, more intensive support.[117] Neil found that where direct contact continued, it had tended to broaden out to include more birth relatives and in quite a few cases, adoptive parents had started to manage contact themselves rather than through the agency.[118]

Indirect contact

13.81 Both adopters and birth families need practical help in writing appropriate letters.[119] Many adopters found it very difficult to communicate by letter with a complete or virtual stranger about an emotional subject, not knowing what to say and when and whether to include children in letter contacts. Working through third parties, such as the agency, sometimes caused delay and miscommunications. Lowe and Murch suggested that good

---

[111] *The Contact After Adoption Study: Key Findings* op cit, pp 9, 11.
[112] Lowe and Murch; Fratter p 229.
[113] Lowe and Murch; Neil p 292.
[114] Fratter p 230. Neil p 292.
[115] *Messages from Research* op cit, p 54.
[116] *Supporting Contact*, p 325.
[117] Ibid.
[118] *The Contact After Adoption Study: Key Findings* op cit, p 5.
[119] *Supporting Adoption* op cit, p 325 and *Adoption Now: Messages from Research* op cit, p 56.

preparation may lessen the necessity of agencies to vet correspondence between families and Neil commented that direct contact made indirect contact easier. For 'letter box' contact, see **13.159**.

Conclusions

13.82　Lowe and Murch were cautious in their conclusions. Contact can be threatening in situations where there are any insecurities about the adoption but it can work well in cases where the birth parent consents to the adoption, believing it to be in the best interests of the child.[120]

> 'However, we should make it absolutely clear that we are by no means committed to the view that any form of contact between the child and birth family is always in the child's interest. On the contrary, we take the view that the issue of contact has to be governed by the welfare of the particular child (taking into account the child's own wishes and feelings) in his or her circumstances which may change from time to time. What has to be avoided is the imposition of inflexible rules based on doctrinaire policies.'[121]

13.83　Neil was equally cautious. Benefits for all participants flow from sensitively managed contact but research findings do not support a blanket policy. By its nature, the quality of contact will be constantly evolving: what works at one time may not necessarily work at another.

> 'The question "is post-adoption contact a good thing?" is not really the best question to be asking. The better starting point is to give detailed thought to what a child needs or is likely to need, both now and later in his or her life, to deal with maturing issues of loss and identity. Once an idea of the child's needs has been reasonably clarified, it should be possible to develop more sensitive and effective strategies for contact.'[122]

13.84　*Messages from Research*[123] drew the conclusion that the varieties of contact in the different studies are so great it is difficult to judge consequences in general.[124]

> 'Although the assessment of these consequences should focus primarily upon the needs of the child, it has to go further and include the possible repercussions for others who are involved.'

---

[120]　Op cit, p 324.
[121]　Op cit, p 323.
[122]　*Adoption and Contact: A Research Review* op cit, p 292.
[123]　*Adoption Now: Messages from Research* op cit, p 58.
[124]　*What works in adoption and foster Care?* op cit, p 79 is similarly non-committal.

Policy

White Paper

13.85 The White Paper, *Adoption – a New Approach*[125] said little expressly about post-adoption contact other than that a child's need to maintain links with the birth family should always be considered.[126] Some of the concerns of the Prime Minister's Review (see **13.58**) were met by the general proposals for post-adoption support and better social work training.

National Adoption Standards

13.86 There are four relevant *National Adoption Standards*[127] which concern post-adoption contact:

- The child's needs, wishes and feelings, and their welfare and safety are the most important concerns when considering links or contact with birth parents, wider birth family members and other people who are significant to them.[128]

- Adoption plans will include details of the arrangements for maintaining links (including contact) with birth parents, wider birth family members and other people who are significant to the child and how and when these arrangements will be reviewed.[129]

- Adoptive parents will be involved in discussions as to how they can best maintain any links, including contact, with birth relatives and significant others identified in the adoption plan.[130]

- Where it is in the child's best interest for there to be ongoing links, including contact, with birth parents and families (including siblings separated by adoption), birth families will be involved in discussions about how best to achieve this and helped to fulfil agreed plans, eg through practical or financial support.[131]

Adoption Guidance

13.87 Departmental guidance is given in *Adoption Guidance*.[132] After noting that one of the key principles of the Children Act 1989 is the presumption that

---

[125] Cm 5017 (2000).
[126] Ibid, at para 6.43.
[127] (Department of Health, 2001). Those which concern contact were not issued under s 7 of the Local Authority Social Services Act 1970 but are to be considered as 'good practice guidance' (see p 6).
[128] Standard A10.
[129] Standard A11.
[130] Standard C4.
[131] Standard D7.
[132] (Department for Education and Skills, 2002). This is statutory guidance issued under section 7

there should be continued contact between the child and his or her family while the child is in the care of the local authority, it points out that:

> 'The purpose of an adoptive placement is fundamentally different, as the intention is that the child should become part of another family. Therefore – where the agency is authorised to place the child for adoption – there should be no general presumption for or against contact. This is why Adoption Agencies Regulations removes the general duty in the 1989 Act to promote contact. Contact arrangements should be focused on and shaped around the child's needs. The child's welfare should at all times be the paramount consideration and each child's needs for contact should be individually considered. Contact arrangements may need to be varied as the child's relationships and needs for contact change over time.'[133]

Article 8

13.88 An order allowing a child to be placed for adoption will inevitably interfere with the rights of the child under Art 8 of the European Convention on Human Rights and Fundamental Freedoms 1950 to a family life. Such interference will therefore need to be justified. However, while there is Convention jurisprudence on contact between a child and his parents (see **13.5**) and in relation to adoption (see **2.85**), the European Court of Human Rights has assumed that adoption means a cessation of adoption and there is no jurisprudence on contact within adoption.

13.89 Article 9(3) of the UN Convention on the Rights of the Child declares that:

> 'States Parties shall respect the right of the child who is separated from one or both parents to maintain personal relations and direct contact with both parents on a regular basis, except if it is contrary to the child's best interests.'

13.90 This is sometimes used to support a claim that adopted children have a right to contact with their birth parents.[134] Fortin suggests that such an argument is implausible, the provisions being intended to cover a very different situation, namely the removal of children from their parents by the state except where there has been abuse and neglect.[135] However in *Re R (A Minor) (Contact)*[136] Butler-Sloss LJ said (in relation to a paternity dispute) that the right of a child to have a relationship with both parents wherever possible is 'underlined' in the UN Convention.

---

of The Local Authority Social Services Act 1970 and as such should be complied with unless local circumstances indicate exceptional reasons which justify a variation (see **11.22**).

[133] Ibid, paras 7.19–7.20.

[134] See, for example, Ryburn 'Welfare and Justice in Post-Adoption Contact' [1997] Fam Law 28 at 29.

[135] Fortin *Children's Rights and the Developing Law* (2nd edn, Butterworths, 2003), at p 389.

[136] [1993] 2 FLR 762 at 767.

The duties of the local authority

13.91 Section 26 of the Adoption and Children Act 2006 (ACA 2006) and the Adoption Agencies Regulations 2005[137] (AAR 2005) contain a number of provisions which either modify statutory duties when a child is being looked after or create new ones. Other than the duty to make general provision for support, the duties will continue for so long as the placement order is in force.

13.92 When the authority is authorised to place the child for adoption or a child less than 6 weeks old has been placed for adoption, any provision for contact under the Children Act 1989 (ie any order or duty placed on the authority under CA 1989, s 34 – see **13.14**) ceases to have effect[138] and, absent an order (see **13.16**) the authority has a discretion whether or not to permit contact. Although parental responsibility is shared, s 25(9) enables the authority to restrict the exercise of any responsibility by the parent, for example, deciding that there should be contact.

13.93 Two duties imposed by the CA 1989 in relation to children being looked after are modified by the regulations when the authority is authorised to place the child for adoption (see **13.1**) or a child less than 6 weeks old has been placed for adoption. Similar amendments are made to the duties owed by voluntary adoption agencies under CA 1989, s 61.

- The duty[139] of an authority to ascertain the wishes and feelings of the child's parents before making any decision in relation to the child is replaced by a similar duty owed to the prospective adopters.[140] However, there remains a duty to ascertain the wishes and feelings of 'any other person' and this may include the parents.[141]

- The general duty[142] to promote contact with the birth family (see **13.14**) is removed.[143]

Planning for placement

13.94 The agency, when considering whether to place a child for adoption, has, as far as is reasonably practicable, to ascertain the wishes and feelings regarding contact of the child,[144] and of the parent, guardian or any other person the agency considers relevant.[145]

---

[137] SI 2005/389.
[138] ACA 2002, s 26(1).
[139] Under ACA 2002, s 22(4)(b).
[140] AAR 2005, reg 45(2).
[141] *Adoption Guidance* op cit, para 3.
[142] ACA 2002, Sch 2, para 15.
[143] AAR 2005, reg 45(2).
[144] Ibid, reg 13.
[145] Ibid, reg 14.

13.95 The Guidance states that any counselling[146] should include the consequences of the adoption process for contact and how this will change.[147]

Prospective adopters

13.96 The preparation of prospective adopters[148] must include the provision of information about contact.[149]

13.97 When the authority is considering placing the child with identified prospective adopters, it has to ascertain the views of the adopters about any contact arrangements the agency propose to make.[150]

Planning and decision making

13.98 When the child is referred to the adoption panel, the permanency report must include:

- the wishes and feelings of the child regarding contact with his or her parent or guardian or other relative or with any other person the agency considers relevant;

- the wishes and feelings of the child's parent or guardian, and any other person the agency considers relevant;

- the agency's views about the child's need for contact with his or her parent or guardian or other relative or with any other person the agency considers relevant and the arrangements the agency proposes to make for allowing any person contact.[151]

13.99 Where the panel makes a recommendation to the agency that the child should be placed for adoption, it is required to consider and may at the same time give advice to the agency about the proposed contact arrangements.[152]

13.100 When an agency has been authorised to place a child who has not been placed, the reviews under AAR 2005, reg 36 must include a review of contact.[153]

---

[146] Provided under AAR 2005, reg 14.
[147] *Adoption Guidance* op cit, para 7.8.
[148] Under AAR 2005, reg 24.
[149] Ibid, reg 31.
[150] Ibid, reg 31(2).
[151] Ibid, reg 17.
[152] Ibid, reg 18(3).
[153] Ibid, reg 36(6).

13.101 Where the proposed placement is referred to the 'matching' panel, the adoption placement report must include the arrangements the agency proposes to make for contact.[154]

13.102 The matching panel must consider the proposals and may give advice about contact arrangements.[155] This advice must be considered by the agency.[156]

13.103 Where the authority decides to place the child for adoption, it has to consider the contact arrangements,[157] discuss them with the proposed adopters and the adoption placement plan given to the proposed adopters under reg 35(2) and notified to parents and any other person under reg 46(4) must include any arrangements for adoption.

Post placement

13.104 Plans for contact must be kept under review so long as the child is placed for adoption.[158]

Adoption support

13.105 The agency's duty, both before and after the making of a placement or adoption order, to assess the support that may be needed in relation to contact and to provide support is considered in Chapter 9 and at **13.159**.

Court reports

Placement application

13.106 The local authority's report filed under r 29 of the Family Procedure (Adoption) Rules 2005[159] (FP(A)R 2005) must include details of:

- the wishes and feelings of the child, parents or guardian about contact;

- the extent of the child's contact with the parents;

- recommendations as to whether or not there should be future contact arrangements including whether a contact order under ACA 2002, s 26 should be made.[160]

---

[154] AAR 2005, reg 31(2).
[155] Ibid, reg 32.
[156] Ibid, reg 46(5).
[157] Ibid, reg 46.
[158] Ibid, reg 46(7).
[159] SI 2005/2795.
[160] AAR 2005, reg 29(3); Practice Direction 5C, Annex B.

13.107 The guardian's report filed under FP(A)R 2005, r 65 should, as a matter of practice, although not a legal requirement, contain a discussion of the issue of contact. The court can direct that the issue is considered.[161]

Adoption application

13.108   The agency's report filed under FP(A)R 2005, r 29 must include details of:

- the wishes and feelings of the child, parents or guardian about contact;

- the extent of the child's contact with the parents;

- whether the parents or members of the child's family have met or are likely to meet the prospective adopters and, if they have met, the effect on all involved;

- recommendations as to future contact or not;

- the prospective adopter's wishes and feelings in relation to contact;

- the agency's proposals for contact;

- the agency's opinion on the likely effect on the prospective adopter and on the security of the placement of any proposed contact.[162]

13.109 Any guardian's report filed under FP(A)R 2005, r 65 should, as a matter of practice although not a legal requirement, contain a discussion of the issue of contact. The court can direct that the issue is considered.[163]

Orders

Placement applications

13.110 Any existing order for contact under CA 1989, s 8 or s 34 ceases to have effect on the making of a placement order[164] or an adoption order.[165]

13.111 When the court is considering whether to make a placement or adoption order it has to consider the child's relationship with his family and any other relevant person, the likelihood of the relationship continuing and its value to the child as well as the full range of its powers both under the CA 1989 and the ACA 2002.[166]

---

[161] AAR 2005, reg 65(2)(f).
[162] Ibid, reg 29(3); Practice Direction 5C, Annex A.
[163] AAR 2005, reg 65(2)(f).
[164] ACA 2002, s 26(1).
[165] Ibid, s 46(2)(b).
[166] ACA 2002, s 1(4)(f) and (6). See **6.98** and **6.82, 6.85**.

13.112 Before making a placement order, the court must consider the arrangements which the agency has made or proposes to make for any person to have contact and invite the parties to comment on them.[167]

13.113 When a placement order is made, absent an order, the agency has a discretion whether or not to permit contact (see **13.93**).

13.114 When making a placement order or at any time thereafter until an adoption order is made, the court may make an order for contact, if required, with conditions,[168] under ACA 2002, s 26(2) (but not CA 1989, s 8). The order requires an application unless the court is making a placement order in which case, the contact order can be made on the court's own initiative.[169]

13.115 The application can be made by:

- the child or the agency;

- any parent, guardian or relative;[170]

- any person in whose favour a section 8 contact order was in force when the authority was authorised to place the child (ie the making of a placement order or the receipt of consent under ACA 2002, s 19);

- any person in whose favour a residence order was in force or who had the care of the child under the inherent jurisdiction of the High Court when the authority was authorised to place the child;

- any person who has the leave of the court.[171]

13.116 An order made under ACA 2002, s 26 has effect for so long as the agency is authorised to place the child for adoption or the child is so placed. It can be varied or revoked on an application by the child, the agency or a person named in the order.[172] It will cease on the making of an adoption order.[173]

13.117 The agency may refuse to allow contact under the order if it is satisfied that it is necessary to do so in order to safeguard or promote the child's welfare, the refusal is decided upon as a matter of urgency and does not last for more than 7 days.[174]

---

[167] ACA 2002, s 27(4).
[168] Ibid, s 27(5).
[169] Ibid, s 26(4).
[170] Defined by ibid, s 144(1) as a grandparent, brother, sister, uncle or aunt whether of the full or half blood or by marriage.
[171] ACA 2002, s 26(3). Unlike CA 1989, s 10(9), there is no provision expressly concerning leave and the section 1 welfare test and checklist do not apply (CA 1989, s 1(7)).
[172] ACA 2002, s 27(1).
[173] Ibid.
[174] Ibid, s 27(2).

Adoption application

13.118 Before making a placement order, the court must consider the arrangements which the agency has made or proposes to make for any person to have contact and invite the parties to comment on them.[175]

13.119 When making an adoption order[176] or at any time thereafter the court may make an order for contact, if required, with conditions,[177] under CA 1989, s 10(1). The order requires an application unless the court is hearing family proceedings,[178] in which case the contact order can be made on the court's own initiative.[179]

The approach of the court

13.120 Since the ACA 2002 came into force, the House of Lords has examined the issue of post-adoption contact. In *Down Lisburn Health and Social Services Trust v H*[180] Baroness Hale of Richmond reviewed the change in approach from exclusively 'closed' to some acceptance of 'open' adoptions (see **13.53**) and commented that:

> '[Preserving] some limited contact between an adopted child and her birth family ... might serve two rather different functions. One, which can often be accomplished by life story books and occasional letters and cards, is to help the adopted child develop her sense of identity and self as she grows up. Another, which may indicate the occasional face to face meeting, is to preserve significant attachments, prevent the feelings of loss and rejection which the child who remembers her birth family may feel if she is completely cut off from her past and help her not to worry about the family she has left behind, including siblings (see Department of Health, *Adoption Now. Messages from Research,* 1999). This form of contact requires the birth parents to be able to put their own feelings of grief and anger aside so that they do not use their contact to undermine the adoptive placement. But if they can do this it can be a great help to the child in making the transition to her new "family for life". Hence the case for some form of post adoption contact may be strongest when the adoption itself is particularly contentious. The parents may rightly feel that they have something to offer the child even if she can no longer live with them. The problem for the court is to enable all the competing issues to be properly tried and resolved.'

13.121 Contact where a child is in care is different from when a child is adopted even though the functions of contact are not entirely dissimilar. The child may return to his family, if not before he is 18, then after. Moreover he legally remains a member of his birth family.

---

[175] ACA 2002, s 46(6).
[176] CA 1989, ss10(1) and 8(4).
[177] Ibid, s 11(7).
[178] Ibid, ss 10(1) and 8(4).
[179] Ibid, s 10(1).
[180] [2006] UKHL 36, [2007] 1 FLR 121 at [6]–[7]. See also *Re G (Adoption: Contact)* [2002] EWCA Civ 761, [2003] 1 FLR 270 per Ward LJ at [14].

'The goal of long-term fostering is to maintain and develop the relationship between the parent and the child, and the child is put into long-term fostering because the parent is unable properly to look after him or her. Whereas, in adoption, the purpose of adoption is for the child to develop in a quite different family and adoptive parents in law become his or her parents and the purpose of contact is, as Mr Metexas put it, for identity purposes, not to develop a relationship between the natural parent and the child who is adopted.'[181]

Placement applications

13.122 In many cases prospective adopters will not have been identified – much less 'matched' with – the child before a placement order application is heard. This creates a number of problems for the court when deciding whether a placement order or a contact order under ACA 2002, s 26 should be made:

- The views of the prospective adopters regarding contact may be unknown.[182]

- The existence of an order or the prospect of an order under section 8 post-adoption may hinder the search for prospective adopters.[183]

- The prospect of finding adopters and the time this will take will be uncertain. A reduction or termination of contact may affect the child's relationship with his parents and family thereby causing problems if difficulties in finding adopters result in the care plan being changed to long term foster or kinship care.

- If a placement order is made, the birth parents or anyone else in relation to whom contact may be relevant will not automatically be parties to the adoption application (see **17.58**).

An additional difficulty is that an order for contact under ACA 2002, s 26(2) cannot extend beyond the making of an adoption order.[184]

13.123 In *Down Lisburn Health and Social Services Trust v H*[185] Baroness Hale of Richmond said that:

'The court has to take into account the child's need for contact with the birth parents in deciding whether adoption is in the best interests of the child. These days, as already indicated, adoption can take many different forms. In many cases,

---

[181] *Re C (Contact)* [2008] 1 FLR 1151 per Bennett J at [36]. His Lordship was quoting submissions of counsel which he appeared to accept. *Down Lisburn Health and Social Services Trust v H* was not cited. The agency's proposal for contact four times a year if the children were fostered but once a year if adopted was accepted by the trial judge and upheld by Bennett J on appeal.

[182] See *Down Lisburn Health and Social Services Trust v H* [2006] UKHL 36, [2007] 1 FLR 121 at [8].

[183] See, for example, *Re P (Adoption: Freeing Order)* [1994] 2 FLR 1000 at 1003B.

[184] ACA 2002, s 27(1).

[185] [2006] UKHL 36, [2007] 1 FLR 121 at [27].

particularly those where the child has a significant history, it is not enough for the court to decide in a vacuum whether 'adoption' is in the best interests of the child. It must decide what sort of adoption will best serve her interests. If the court takes the view that some form of open adoption will be best, then it will have to take that into account in deciding whether it will accord with its most important consideration, the welfare of the child, to make an order freeing the child for adoption before there is any evidence available of the efforts made to secure the right sort of adoptive placement and to prepare both families for it. The court may, of course, take the view that the need to free the child for adoption is so pressing that this should be done even if it is not yet known whether an open adoption will be possible. But the need to free the child for adoption is different from the need for the child to be adopted. It may be premature to free a child for adoption even though it would not be premature to make an adoption order.'

13.124 There is no single solution to these difficulties other than that an approach specific to the needs of the individual child should be adopted rather than a standardised approach. In some cases the needs of the child for continuing contact are so clear that a placement order should not be made until the views of prospective adopters have been ascertained. In others, the child's need for a permanent home is so urgent that nothing should be done which would hinder a search.

13.125 Where a child is in care and enjoying beneficial contact with a parent, who has made an application for contact and has consistently shown a keen interest in continuing contact, a placement order cannot be made in the long-term and best interests of the child without first deciding the issue of contact.[186]

13.126 Where prospective adopters have been identified, some applications will require direct evidence from the prospective adopters as to their attitude to contact. In the absence of such direct evidence, crucial to the issue of contact, the court would be deprived of material vital to a proper decision. The prospective adopters may need to be joined as parties to the proceedings.[187]

13.127 Courts may be reluctant to rely on general evidence from the agency about its policy regarding contact. Where contact is a live issue, clear evidence should be adduced about how many adoption orders in the last few years have been made where there is to be continuing contact. How many current prospective adopters are willing to have contact? What specifically is done to inform prospective adopters about the potential benefits of contact? Often, these matters lie outside the experience of the child's social worker and evidence from the agency worker responsible for the child will be required.

13.128 In the past when the issue of contact could not be resolved because prospective adopters have not been identified, the Court of Appeal said that

---

[186] See *Re C (Minors) (Adoption)* [1992] 1 FLR 115. It was intended that the children should be adopted by their current foster carers. See also *Re G (A Minor) (Adoption and Access Applications* [1992] 1 FLR 642.

[187] *Re C (Minors) (Adoption)* [1992] 1 FLR 115.

the trial judge should consider being robust, refusing the placement application and saying '[Parental consent] is a matter to be dealt with on adoption' or making the order on the basis that 'Adoption is more important than contact'.[188] However, it seems that this may no longer be possible because the agency cannot place a child under the age of 6 weeks for adoption without either parental consent or a placement order.[189]

13.129 If there is doubt about whether a suitable adoption home will be found, the court can make a section 26 contact order to last 'until the agency accepts the Panel's recommendation that the child should be placed with a named prospective adopter'.

13.130 Where the court considers that although it is in the child's best interests to be adopted but only if there is to be some contact, one option is for the court to give a judgment explaining in detail why contact is necessary, give permission for the judgment to be disclosed to prospective adopters and make a section 26 order unlimited in time. This will therefore continue until an adoption order is made, allowing the matter to be reconsidered. If difficulties are encountered the agency can apply to discharge the order under s 27(1).

13.131 It may be uncertain whether a court granting a placement order is able to direct who should be made parties to any adoption application. However, directions can be given reserving the application to a named judge.[190] Alternatively, the placement order could recite the court's view that if there is no written agreement between the prospective adopters, the birth parents and the agency about contact, the parents should be made parties to any adoption proceedings for the sole purpose of applying for a contact order under CA 1989, s 8. This will serve to bring the issue to the attention of the judge giving case management directions on the adoption application.

13.132 If a placement order is refused on the basis that contact needs to be considered, it will usually be inappropriate to make an order under CA 1989, s 34(4) permitting the authority to refuse contact.[191]

Examples

Re R (Placement Order)[192]

13.133 Placement orders were made for five children aged 7 years to 18 months born to Muslim parents who were going to be placed with two separate adoptive families. Section 26 contact orders for parent/child and inter-sibling contact were refused. The parents' total failure to accept the findings of abuse made against them and the poor contact experienced to date meant that direct

---

[188] *Re P (Adoption: Freeing Order)* [1994] 2 FLR 1000 per Butler-Sloss LJ at 1004.
[189] ACA 2002, s 18(1).
[190] *SB and County Council: P (A Child)* [2008] EWCA Civ 535; sub nom *P (a child)* [2008] 2 FCR 185.
[191] See *Re G (Adoption: Contact)* [2003] 1 FLR 270.
[192] [2007] EWHC 3031 (Fam), [2008] 1 FLR 1259.

contact post-adoption with the parents or extended family was not in the children's best interests. There was a greater need for ongoing contact between the siblings and the authority hoped that there would be twice yearly contact between them. However, the dynamics of the siblings, changing relationship and the possible restriction on placement with a family otherwise suited to adopt them ruled against the making of an order. The potential difficulties surrounding any placement of Muslim children demanded that as few restrictions were placed upon the prospective adopters as possible.

SB and County Council: P (A Child)[193]

13.134 Placement orders were made in respect of five children aged between nearly 6 and 2, the trial judge having dispensed with their mother's (M's) consent. The elder two children, D and S, were seriously damaged children and it was likely that they would be placed separately. S had a positive relationship with M and contact between D and M might be required once she had settled into a permanent placement. However, the local authority had unilaterally terminated contact between D and M. It was agreed that the relationship between D and S needed to be preserved. The children's social worker did not think it a high risk that there would not be post-adoption contact. The trial judge made a section 26 order, unlimited in time, for contact between both children, seven times a year.

13.135 The Court of Appeal approved the section 26 order but considered that in the circumstances, more protection was needed. It directed that all further applications, including adoption applications, should be reserved to the judge who had heard the applications for placement orders. It also indicated that if the prospective adopters were unwilling to facilitate contact between the two children, that would provide a proper basis for the mother to be granted leave to apply for the placement orders to be revoked under ACA 2002, s 24(2) (see **3.47**) or to oppose the making of the adoption orders under s 47)(5) (see **3.142**).

A Local Authority v J[194]

13.136 Three half-siblings, D1, aged 12, D2, aged 9 and L, aged 15 months, were removed from the care of their mother, M. D1 and D2 went to live with their respective fathers. M remained emotionally involved with one of the fathers and had contact with D1 and D2 in breach of court orders. The local authority sought a care order and placement order in respect of L which was granted by Hogg J who refused to make an order for contact between L and her siblings. D1 and D2 were fond of L and would miss and worry about her. This was a significant problem. However the issue of confidentiality of the adoptive placement in the long term was also difficult. Contact should be discussed with

---

[193] [2008] EWCA Civ 535; sub nom *P (A Child)* [2008] 2 FCR 185.
[194] [2008] EWHC 1484 (Fam), [2008] 2 FLR 1389.

prospective carers, but a placement should not be put in jeopardy by ongoing direct contact to the older children. L's security and stability in the new home had to be the prime motivator.

Adoption applications

13.137 Before the ACA 2002 came into force, the approach of the courts could be summarised in three propositions.

- Courts are more willing than hitherto to consider post-adoption contact and there are cases where some continuing face-to-face contact is clearly desirable.[195]

- If contact is to take place, it should normally be by way of agreement.

- Only in the most exceptional cases will a contact order be made without the agreement of the adopters.[196]

13.138 Post-implementation, the first proposition has been strengthened by dicta of Baroness Hale of Richmond in *Down Lisburn Health and Social Services Trust v H*.[197]

13.139 As to the second proposition, Wall LJ in *SB and County Council: P (A Child)*[198] expressed the view that, at least in some cases, the court should comply with its duty under ACA 2002, s 46(6) to consider contact (see **13.111**) by taking a more active role than hitherto.

> 'In [the circumstances of this case] it is not, in our judgment, a proper exercise of the judicial powers given to the court under the 2002 Act to leave contact between the children themselves, or between the children and their natural parents to the discretion of the local authority and/or the prospective carers of D and S, be they adoptive parents or foster carers. It is the court which must make the necessary decisions if contact between the siblings is in dispute, or if it is argued that it should cease for any reason.
>
> We do not know if our views on contact on the facts of this particular case presage a more general sea change in post adoption contact overall. It seems to us, however, that the stakes in the present case are sufficiently high to make it appropriate for the court to retain control over the question of the children's welfare throughout their respective lives under sections 1, 26, 27 and 46(6) of the 2002 Act; and, if necessary, to make orders for contact post adoption in accordance with section 26 of the 2002 Act, under section 8 of the 1989 Act. This is what Parliament has enacted. In section 46(6) of the 2002 Act Parliament has specifically directed the court to consider post adoption contact, and in

---

[195] *Re E (A Minor) (Care Order: Contact)* [1994] 1 FLR 146.
[196] *Re C (A Minor) (Adoption Order: Conditions)* [1988] 2 FLR 159 and *Re T (Adoption Contact)* [1995] 2 FLR 251.
[197] [2006] UKHL 36, [2007] 1 FLR 121 and see **13.123**.
[198] [2008] EWCA Civ 535; sub nom *P (A Child)* [2008] 2 FCR 185 at [153]–[154].

section 26(5) Parliament has specifically envisaged an application for contact being heard at the same time as an adoption order is applied for. All this leads us to the view that the 2002 Act envisages the court exercising its powers to make contact orders post adoption, where such orders are in the interests of the child concerned.'

13.140 Whether or not the views of the senior judiciary on the third proposition has or will change remains to be seen. Where adopters do not agree, one issue may be whether they merely take a different view about contact or whether their views are strongly held that they are likely to refuse to obey a contact order. As Lord Ackner said in *Re C (A Minor)*[199] to direct contact in the face of opposition:

> 'would be likely to create a potentially frictional situation which would be hardly likely to safeguard or promote the welfare of the child. Where no agreement is forthcoming, the court with very rare exceptions, have to choose between making an adoption order without [contact] or refuse to make such an order and seek to safeguard access in some other way.'

13.141 Wall LJ seemed to take a similar view in *SB and County Council: P (A Child)*[200] when he indicated that a failure by the prospective adopters to agree to contact would provide a proper basis for the mother to be granted leave to oppose the making of the adoption orders.

13.142 A post-adoption contact order can be monitored[201] or enforced[202] in the same way as any other section 8 contact order. However, the difficulties of enforcing the latter orders have exercised the courts for years and there would be great reluctance to make any order where the need for enforcement was a real possibility.

Agreements

13.143 There is nothing in *SB and County Council: P (A Child)* which suggests that it is not desirable, if at all possible, for matters to proceed by way of agreement as appears to happen in practice. Care needs to be taken, however, that the agreement is genuine and not merely used as a bargaining tool to obtain the adoption (see **13.70**). If there are irreconcilable differences, these should be resolved at the time of the adoption and not postponed.[203]

13.144 The process of negotiating an agreement can be a long one with critical points around the time when the adopters are approved and leading up to the placement.[204]

---

[199] [1988] 2 FLR 159.
[200] [2008] EWCA Civ 535; sub nom *P (A Child)* [2008] 2 FCR 185.
[201] Under CA 1989, s 11H.
[202] For example, enforcement orders under CA 1989, ss 11J–11O, or, as a last resort, by committal.
[203] *Re T (Adopted Children: Contact)* [1995] 2 FLR 792 per Balcome LJ at 798.
[204] *Supporting Adoption: Reframing the Approach* Lowe and Murch op cit p 318.

'[Without] a doubt ... the process of negotiation leading to the preparation of written contact agreements and the agreements themselves proved invaluable in reducing conflict, establishing a clear understanding of the expectations of all parties and forming a basis for subsequent review.'[205]

13.145 It appears that in the mid-1990s written agreements were not the norm,[206] although by 2000 almost all social services departments reported that their contact arrangements were always written and, wherever possible, were mutually agreed. However, only half regularly reviewed contact arrangements, many ceasing to do so at the point the adoption order was made.[207]

13.146 As a matter of good practice and in order to avoid later misunderstanding, the agreement should be in writing and should contain detail of what has been agreed. How often will the adopters provide reports? How often can the parents write or send letters and photographs?

13.147 If the adopters later want to resile from their agreement, they should inform the other party to the agreement, giving their reasons clearly. A simple explanation of their reasons in non-legal terms is all that is required and adopters should not fear that the reasons will be subjected to critical legal analysis. If they do not provide reasons or the reasons turn out to be inadequate, wrong or unjust, the adopters should know that the other party will be able to seek leave to apply for leave to apply for a contact order.[208]

Consent orders

13.148 Example of contact orders being made by consent are *Re W (A Minor) (Adoption: Custodianship: Access)*[209] when an adoption order was made in favour of grandparents and *Re O (Transracial Adoption: Contact)*[210] where the benefits to a 10-year-old Nigerian girl of developing a relationship with her parents were advocated by a child psychiatrist. In both cases, the court had dispensed with the parents' consent to adoption.

13.149 In *Re T (Adoption: Contact)*[211] (see **13.57**) the Court of Appeal allowed an appeal against a contact order made without the consent of the adopters, Butler-Sloss LJ indicating that if the adopters unreasonably failed to honour their statement that they were willing to facilitate contact, the birth mother could apply for leave to apply for a contact order.

---

[205] Social Services Inspectorate *Moving Goalposts: A Study of Post Adoption Contact in the North of England* (Department of Health, 1995) p 33.

[206] *For Children's Sake: An SSI Inspection of Local Authority Adoption Services* (Department of Health, 1996) p 47; *Supporting Adoption: Reframing the Approach* op cit at p 318.

[207] Social Services Inspectorate *Response to issues arising from SSI survey of local authority social service departments' implementation of the Circular LAC(98)20* (2000).

[208] *Re T (Adoption: Contact)* [1995] 2 FLR 251 per Butler-Sloss LJ at 256 and *Re T (Adopted Children: Contact)* [1995] 2 FLR 792 per Balcome LJ at 798.

[209] [1988] 1 FLR 175.

[210] [1995] 2 FLR 597.

[211] [1995] 2 FLR 251.

Orders after an adoption order is made

13.150 Once an adoption order is made, the birth family, including the parents, will no longer be treated in law as parents or relatives and will require leave under CA 1989, s 10(1) to make an application for contact.

13.151 When considering whether to grant leave, the court has to have particular regard to:

(a) the nature of the proposed application;

(b) the applicant's connection with the child;[212]

(c) any risk there might be of the proposed application[213] disrupting the child's life to such an extent that he would be harmed by it.[214]

See also **5.22**.

13.152 At the leave stage, the court can carry out a broad assessment of the prospects of success but the application could not be decided on the basis that there was no reasonable prospect of success.[215]

13.153 It is undesirable for applications for leave to be advanced without a preliminary consideration by the court.[216] The local authority or agency should be given notice of the application but notice should only be given to the adopters if the court was satisfied that the applicant had a prima facie case for leave. The court should have as much relevant information as possible at the preliminary hearing but the application for leave should not be treated as if it were the substantive application.[217] Although Thorpe J said in *Re C (A Minor) (Adopted Child: Contact)*[218] that the Official Solicitor should also be made a party and that he, and not the court, should be responsible for notifying the adopters after the preliminary hearing if the court considered that there was a prima facie case, the Court of Appeal in *Re T (Adopted Children: Contact)*[219] expressed the view that this was not required in every case. Presumably, with the subsequent change in the Official Solicitor's responsibility, CAFCASS or CAFCASS Legal should be involved if necessary but not be made parties.

---

[212] What weight should be given to the applicant being the child's birth parent is a moot point.

[213] The harm is limited to that which might be caused by the substantive application, not the order sought – that is a matter to be decided at the hearing if leave is granted. See *Re M (Care: Contact: Grandmother's Application for Leave)* [1995] 2 FLR at 96.

[214] CA 1989, s 10(9).

[215] *Re J (Leave to Issue application for Residence Order)* [2002] EWCA Civ 1364, [2003] 1 FLR 114; *Re R (Adoption: Contact)* [2005] EWCA Civ 1128, [2006] 1 FLR 373.

[216] *Re C (A Minor) (Adopted Child: Contact)* [1993] 2 FLR 431. Approved by the Court of Appeal in *Re T (Adopted Children: Contact)* [1995] 2 FLR 792.

[217] *Re T (Adopted Children: Contact)* [1995] 2 FLR 792.

[218] [1993] 2 FLR 431.

[219] [1995] 2 FLR 792.

13.154 There is no general rule that all such applications should be transferred to the High Court.[220] The criteria for transfer set out in the Allocation and Transfer of Proceedings Order 2008,[221] supplemented by the Practice Direction – Allocation and Transfer of Proceedings[222] (see **18.33**) should be applied.

Examples

Re C (A Minor) (Adopted Child: Contact)[223]

13.155 A mother applied for leave to apply for contact to her 5-year-old son who had been removed from her care 1 month after he was born and whom she had last seen 4 years earlier, before his adoption. Leave was refused. A fundamental matter such as contact, albeit indirect, should not be reopened unless there was a fundamental change in circumstances of which there was none in the present case.

Re T (Adopted Children: Contact)[224]

13.156 A young woman was given permission to apply for a contact order in respect of her half siblings who had been adopted, the adopters having failed to provide annual reports as agreed. The Court of Appeal allowed her appeal against the dismissal of her application at the preliminary stage. The application was limited to the production of an annual report; no explanation had been given for the refusal to provide the report as agreed and there was no evidence that the proposed application might disrupt the children's life to such an extent that they might be harmed by it.

Re S (Contact: Application by Sibling)[225]

13.157 A 9-year-old girl, Y, applied, by her next friend and adoptive mother and supported by psychiatric evidence, for leave to apply for contact with her 7-year-old half-brother, S, who had been taken into care at the age of 1, adopted at the age of 3 and who had cystic fibrosis. Y was very distressed by her separation from S. S's adoptive mother said she did not intend to inform S of his adoptive status until he was much older and vehemently opposed contact. The application was dismissed on the basis that it was S's welfare which was paramount, not Y's and that there would be a real risk of disruption to his life to the extent that he would be harmed if the application proceeded. Because S was adopted, the court had to be satisfied that the adopter's decision was sufficiently contrary to the child's best interests or sufficiently unreasonable to warrant the court overriding the adopter's discretion.

---

[220] [1995] 2 FLR 792 per Balcombe LJ at 799.
[221] SI 2008/2836.
[222] 3 November 2008.
[223] [1993] 2 FLR 431.
[224] [1995] 2 FLR 792.
[225] [1998] 2 FLR 897.

Re R (Adoption: Contact)[226]

13.158   K, aged 17, applied for leave to seek, at the hearing of the adoption application, contact with her half sister, L, aged nearly 7, in respect of whom she had been the main carer until L was taken into care at the age of 4. The Adoption Panel recommended that there should be direct contact three times a year. Post-placement K sought an increase in contact but the local authority and the proposed adopters then proposed reducing direct contact to once a year. The Court of Appeal upheld the dismissal of the application. Although post-adoption contact had become more common, the imposition of contact orders without the agreement of the adopters was extremely unusual. The prospective adopters had not resiled completely from their agreement: had they done so, leave would have been granted.

'Letter box' contact

13.159   Most local authorities and agencies operate a 'letter box' scheme whereby information can be exchanged via the agency. However practice varies. Some do not read or even open the letters before forwarding them; in some cases, forwarding the letters was treated as an administrative task, not performed by social workers. Lowe and Murch recommended that it should be made clear to the adults whether or not such communications will be vetted.[227] Nor can it be assumed that any social worker who reads the correspondence will have up to date, detailed information about the child.

13.160   Although the Prime Minister's Review[228] recommended that criteria are developed for the management and review of 'letter box' arrangements, none have been published.

13.161   There are also difficulties experienced by both birth relatives and adopters in knowing how to conduct indirect contact. See **13.81**.

13.162   The additional support which the authority can provide is discussed at **9.49**.

---

[226]   [2005] EWCA Civ 1128, [2006] 1 FLR 373.
[227]   Lowe and Murch *Supporting Adoption: Reframing the Approach* op cit, pp 301–307.
[228]   op cit, at para 5.42 and see Adoption Standard A11.

Chapter 14

PERMANENCY AND STEP-PARENTS

INTRODUCTION

14.1 Many children are likely to live in a stepfamily at some time in their life. However, there are many kinds of stepfamilies. The step-parent may be married or in a civil partnership with one of their birth parents or not. He or she may bring their own children to the stepfamily. Children may be born to the birth parent and the step-parent may be of the opposite sex to that of the birth parent with whom they are living or of the same sex. The other parent may be fully involved in the life of the child or may be permanently absent. The child may believe the step-parent to be her birth parent. The step-parent may be fully engaged with the child or no more than the birth parent's cohabitee.

14.2 These features mean there is no single answer to the legal role which a step-parent should be granted. Three matters are clear, however. First, the biological parentage of the child, if in doubt, will probably need to be ascertained. Secondly, save in exceptional circumstances, the child will need to be told the truth about his parentage. Thirdly, courts are very reluctant to authorise the removal of an involved, non-resident birth parent from his or her role in the child's life

BACKGROUND

14.3 Legal issues surrounding step-parenthood have troubled lawyers for over 1,500 years. Justinian's Digests of the sixth century, for example, warned that parents who disinherit their children in their wills do so 'for the most part corrupted by inducement and instigations of stepmothers'.[1]

14.4 Currently around a quarter of children are growing up in lone parent households[2] whereas one in 10 families with dependent children are now stepfamilies.[3]

---

[1] Digest 5.2.4. And see also Boswell *The Kindness of Strangers* (Pantheon Books, 1988) at p128, n140. Similar allegations are still made today.

[2] *Social Trends 37* 2007. The exact figure is 24%.

[3] Ibid.

Formation of stepfamilies

14.5   The late twentieth century increase in the rates of divorce and separation has changed the ways in which stepfamilies are created and their structure. Until the second half of the twentieth century, stepfamilies were created by the marriage of widowers – and sometimes but less frequently, widows. The mortality rates associated with childbirth meant that the widower more often than not had dependent children, the remarriage often following soon after the death of their mother.[4] Now, because children tend to stay with their mothers following separation, most (84%)[5] stepfamilies in Great Britain consist of a stepfather and a natural mother compared with 10% of families with a stepmother and a natural father. The proportion of children living with their natural mother and a stepfather remained fairly stable (between 83 and 88%) over the last 10 years. However, there has been an increase (albeit with fluctuations) in the proportion of children living with their natural father and a stepmother from 6% in 1991 to 10% in 2006.[6]

Structure of stepfamilies

14.6   Stepfamilies can well be described as 'complex and heterogeneous structures'.[7]

14.7   During the last 25 years, increases in cohabitation, births outside marriage and an increase in the levels of separation and divorce, with an associated increase in lone parent households and stepfamilies – changes which can be summarised as an increasing separation of sex, marriage and parenthood – have highlighted the imprecise boundaries around the concept of 'family'.[8] There are variations in the way stepfamilies are formed. A man may join a mother and her children. He may come alone or with his own children. The same is true for the woman. In 6% of cases, the family will contain children from both partner's previous marriage/cohabitation[9] and in this case, both the man and the woman will be in a step-parent role.[10] In addition further children may be born to the couple.[11]

14.8   There are also variations in the role played by the non-resident birth parent. Two models of the role have been suggested: the 'substitute model' in

---

4   See, for example, Macfarlane *Marriage and Love in England 1300–1840* (Blackwell, 1987) at pp 231–239. In Earls Colne, for example, in the period 1580–1740 nearly three in 20 (13.5%) of all women who married were widows and nearly one in five (19%) of men, widowers. Of those who remarried, three out of five men remarried within a year compared with nearly three in 20 (14%) women. However, having children made little difference for men in the speed of remarriage.

5   Figures for 2006.

6   *Social Trends 38* 2008.

7   Smith 'New stepfamilies – a descriptive study of a largely unseen group' [2003] CFLQ 185.

8   Allan and Crow *Families, Households and Society* (Palgrave, 2001) at p 2.

9   *Social Trends 38* 2008.

10   Ibid.

11   Over half (56%) in the study, Ferri and Smith *Step-parenting in the 1990s* (1998) summarised in *Findings* 658 (Joseph Rowntree Foundation).

which the birth parent is replaced by the step-parent and the 'accumulation model' in which children add a parent to their lives by gaining a step-parent.[12]

14.9 The step-parent may also have the same gender as the biological parent. A quarter of women and one in 10 men forming a civil partnership in the UK in 2006 had previously been in a legal partnership, the large majority having previously been married.[13] At least some of these will have children from their former relationship.

14.10 If the non-resident parent has also formed a new relationship, the child will belong to two stepfamilies – mother/stepfather and father/stepmother. Step-parents may also introduce the children into their extended families, perhaps including other nuclear stepfamilies at the same or different generational levels (for example step-grandparents).

Legal consequences

14.11 The nature of the family structure – informal cohabitation or formal marriage – may have legal consequences. For example, within marriage the step-parent will acquire some financial responsibility for the child whom he treats as 'a child of the family'.[14]

Social consequences

14.12 The high rates of divorce and separation mean that there is an increasing chance that children will live in different types of family during their childhood. In 1998 it was estimated that 7.5% of children would experience their parents' divorce by the age of 5 and about 19% by the age of 10.[15] The percentages are now likely to be higher. A lack of clarity about what 'cohabiting' means and how it can be identified as having ended makes it difficult to obtain statistics about the proportion of cohabitations which end other than in marriage but there is no reason to suppose that children born of cohabiting parents will experience a lesser rate of separation. Separation is commonly followed by a period of the child living in a single parent household but that is often a temporary state, the parent remarrying or cohabiting. This re-marriage or cohabitation is likely to be no more, and probably less permanent that the first relationship. In 2000, for example, the General Household Survey found that 44% of first cohabitations lasted for less than 2 years compared with 56% of second cohabitations.

---

[12] White and Gilbreth 'When Children Have Two Fathers' (2001) 63 *Journal of Marriage and the Family* 155, Pryor 'Children and their Changing Families' in Ebtehaj, Lindley and Richards (eds) *Kinship Matters* (Hart Publishing, 2006) at p 102.

[13] *Social Trends 38* 2008.

[14] Matrimonial Causes Act 1973, ss 23, 52(1).

[15] Rodgers and Prior 'Divorce and Separation: The Outcomes for Children' (Joseph Rowntree Foundation, 1998) summarised in *Foundations* 6108 (Joseph Rowntree Foundation).

14.13 In the words of Rodgers and Prior, the consequences of these phenomena are that:

> 'The birth of a child into a two-parent family is no guarantee of future parental stability. Rates of divorce indicate that a sizeable minority of children in de jure marriages will experience the separation and divorce of their parents and the likelihood of family dissolution is even higher for cohabiting parents. Moreover the separation of parents is likely to be followed by new partnerships. In turn, the chances that a second union will dissolve are higher than for first marriages or cohabitation.'[16]

Relationships within the stepfamily

14.14 A number of studies have examined relationships in stepfamilies both between the adults and the children. For example, in the 1990s Ferri and Smith[17] studied a group of 878 adults who were raising children in stepfamilies. At the end of the decade, Dunn and Deater-Deckard[18] examined the views of 457 children about their current family relationships. A study by Smith in 2003 examined a group of 200 stepfamilies that had been in existence for at least 1 and no more than 4 years.[19] In addition Rodgers and Pryor conducted a literature review, *Divorce and Separation: The Outcomes for Children*,[20] in 1998.

Are stepfamilies different?

14.15 In some areas, stepfamilies are very much like birth families. The majority of adults indicated they were happy in their partnership but the proportion reporting unhappiness were higher than partners in first families. Likewise there was a higher proportion of those who said they disagreed about the way children should be brought up.[21]

How do children view stepfamilies?

14.16 Most parents, step-parents and children did not identify themselves as being in a 'stepfamily'. An identification as a stepfamily did not appear to be associated with the length of time the family had been in existence nor with marital status.[22] Just over half of the children studied by Smith denied that their family was a stepfamily even when the definition was explained to them.

---

[16] Rodgers and Prior 'Divorce and Separation: The Outcomes for Children' op cit.
[17] Ferri and Smith 'Step-parenting in the 1990s' op cit.
[18] Dunn and Deater-Deckard 'Children's Views of their Changing Families' (2001) summarised in *Findings* 931 (Joseph Rowntree Foundation).
[19] 'New stepfamilies – a descriptive study of a largely unseen group' op cit.
[20] Rodgers and Pryor *Divorce and Separation: The Outcomes for Children* op cit.
[21] Ferri and Smith op cit.
[22] Smith op cit.

The non-resident birth parent

14.17 Children tended to have inclusive views about their family. Nearly two-thirds of the children in Smith's sample included their non-residential parent as part of the family and where there had been contact within the last year, this proportion was as high as 85%.[23] Many children greatly missed their other birth parent and wanted to see him/her more.[24] Smith found no association between contact and child well-being but there was some evidence that the nature of the children's relationship with the non-resident parent was important. Those children who viewed it as 'the same as before' showed significantly better scores when their 'well-being' was assessed.[25]

The step-parent

14.18 According to Dunn and Deater-Deckard, feelings of warmth, closeness, companionship and confiding were less common between children and their step-parents than with their birth parents. However they varied in the way they saw the role of step-parents. Some stressed that the step-parent should be a friend; others said, a parent. Many found it difficult to accept discipline from a step-parent.[26] In Smith's sample, three-quarters called their step-parent by his/her first name.

The presence of other children

14.19 The studies found that the existence of children in the family born to the birth parent and the step-parent or previously born to the step-parent made a real difference. Children in Smith's sample where the step-parent had no biological children were more likely and those with shared biological children were less likely to describe their family as a 'stepfamily'. Higher levels of conflict were more common in stepfamilies in which children had been born to the couple.[27] Half the children studied by Dunn and Deckard felt they took second place to children born jointly to their parent and step-parent and three in 10 felt displaced by the step-parent's own children. 'This suggests that far from "cementing" the new family unit there are stresses associated with the more complex relationships created by its expansion.'[28]

Legal relationships

14.20 Smith also examined the legal relationship between children and step-parents. Only one child of the 233 in the study had been adopted by his step-parent. Five per cent of adults did not know that adoption was a possibility while just over half said they had not considered it. A quarter of

---

[23] Smith op cit.
[24] Dunn and Deater-Deckard op cit.
[25] Smith op cit.
[26] Dunn and Deater-Deckard op cit.
[27] Ferri and Smith op cit.
[28] Ibid.

families had considered it but had rejected it while 13% were still considering it. Decisions on changing the child's name were only slightly more common. Most adults had not thought about it. The children's names had been legally changed in 4% of families and informally in a further 9%.

The children's well-being

14.21   Smith found few variables concerning the children's well-being related to the structure of the stepfamily. There was a strong association though with the quality of relationships within the household, particularly between the child and his biological parent and between the adults and to some extent (but less so) between the child and step-parent.

14.22   Rogers and Pryor's literature review found that studies suggest that, in a number of ways, children in stepfamilies fare less well than those in intact families and in some instances those in single-parent families. They are, for example, likely to have lower self-esteem and high levels of distress at 16. They are more likely than children from single-parent families to leave school without qualifications. They are more likely to leave home by the age of 18 and to form early partnerships. Young children, however, seem to fare better, possibly because it is easier to adapt to a new family structure at an early age.

Conclusions

14.23   Ferri and Smith concluded that:

> 'In areas of parenting investigated – employment, domestic roles and family life, stepfamilies are very similar to first marriages. However, they also differ in important ways. Their economic disadvantage means that many will find it difficult to meet the material needs of their relatively large numbers of dependent children. The complexity of relationships within stepfamilies creates pressures on the adult partnership which appear to be exacerbated, rather than relieved, by the birth of children to the couple. It is against this background of economic and emotional difficulties facing stepfamilies that the greater propensity for second partnerships to breakdown can be understood.'

14.24   Smith reached a similar conclusion:

> 'Although the majority of parents in stepfamilies and their children do not identify as stepfamilies, it remains the case that they face a number of issues and potential problems either directly or indirectly because of their stepfamily status. These can be summarised as due to the presence in the household of an adult who does not have parental responsibility and, in most cases, the absence from the household of another adult who does.'

What are the issues?

14.25   As a result of her study Smith posed a number of questions which lie at the root of a proper legal approach to stepfamilies.

- What sort of a relationship is it appropriate for a stepfather to develop with his stepchild?

- Should this relationship be the same as a parental relationship or how should it differ?

- What sort of contact arrangements and financial arrangements should be agreed with non-resident parents?

These questions apply generally as an aid to policy making and specifically in relation to legal proceedings concerning an individual child. There are some who doubt. Professor Judith Mason,[29] however, sounds a warning that very few step-parents are likely to obtain a formally recognised relationship with their stepchildren.

'Despite the growth in numbers of step-families and their recognition in social law, family law remains unsure whether and how to recognise them ... [The restrictions on the grant of parental responsibility] reflects uncertainty about whether parental responsibility for step-parents really matters at all.'

POLICY

Background

14.26 Although the Adoption of Children Act 1926 had not made specific provision for the adoption of children by their step-parents, such applications were regularly made from the start and the Adoption of Children Act 1949 expressly allowed adoption by birth parents and their spouses. By 1951, nearly a third of adoptions of legitimate children and nearly a half of illegitimate children were step-parent adoptions.[30]

14.27 In the period from 1951–1968 the proportion of step-parent adoptions continued to rise albeit slowly from nearly a third (32%) of all adoptions in 1951 to just over a third (34%) in 1968. The increase in numbers is reflected in an increase in the numbers of legitimate children adopted, rising from less than 1,000 in 1950 to 4,038 in 1968. According to Professor Lowe, it is generally accepted that this reflects the growing number of divorces.[31] Most applicants saw adoption of the new partner's children as a formality to change the child's name and birth certificate and to confer on the stepfather full legal rights – 'a logical step to take following marriage'.[32]

---

[29] 'Caring for our Future Generations' in Douglas and Lowe (eds) *The Continuing Evolution of Family Law* (Family Law, 2009) at p 230.

[30] Masson, Norbury, Chatterton *Mine, Yours or Ours?* (HMSO, 1983) at pp 1–2.

[31] Lowe 'English Adoption Law: Past, Present and Future' in Katz, Eekelaar and Maclean (eds) *Cross Currents: Family Law and Policy in the USA and England* (Oxford University Press, 2000) at p 317.

[32] *A Guide to Adoption Practice* (Advisory Council on Child Care, HMSO, 1970) at p 96.

14.28 By 1970, step-parent adoptions were causing concern amongst professionals. The matrimonial relationship and parental roles might be complicated; the mother may have married to provide a home for her child while the husband may accept the child in order to win the mother. The child might be the odd-man-out when children were born to the couple. Both the mother and her husband might have conflicting feelings towards the birth father. Telling the child of his adoption and background could cause particular problems.[33]

14.29 In 1972 the Houghton Committee[34] reported that:

> 'Adoptions of legitimate children on the remarriage of a parent are increasing and the circumstances in these cases may be varied.'

14.30 It asked the question: should adoption by step-parents still be allowed?

> 'The step-father might feel that guardianship [recommended by the Committee and introduced by the Children Act 1975 as custodianship – see **5.3**] was not quite the same as being recognised in law as the child's parent. Adoption confers such a recognition and would achieve the aims in view by one step instead of a number of separate steps.[35] However, the disadvantages of severing a child from one half of his family are such that we considered there as less justification for permitting the adoption by a step-parent of a legitimate child of his spouse ... [However] the evidence we received was overwhelmingly opposed to our suggestion ... We have come to the conclusion that it would be wrong to distinguish between legitimate and illegitimate children and that the law should not prohibit adoption by step-parents in either case. But we remain of the opinion that guardianship will be more appropriate in most cases. We recommend that whenever a step-parent applies to adopt a child of his spouse, the court should first consider whether guardianship would be more appropriate in all the circumstances of the case, first consideration being given to the long-term welfare of the child.'[36]

14.31 The latter recommendation was enacted as s 10(3) of the Children Act 1975 and re-enacted by s 14(3) of the Adoption Act 1976. Notwithstanding the delay in introducing custodianship the number of step-parent adoptions fell to 4,545 by 1977 and to 2,872 by 1983. However, the overall fall in adoption numbers meant that in that year, step-parent adoptions accounted for half of all adoptions. It may be thought surprising that numbers had not fallen further. One reason may by that such adoptions were usually unopposed and reports by

---

[33]   *A Guide to Adoption Practice* op cit.
[34]   Report of the Departmental Committee on the Adoption of Children Cmnd 5107 (HMSO, 1972) at para 106.
[35]   For example, guardianship, change of name, step-parent making a will.
[36]   Op cit at paras 107–110.

local authorities to the court were often inadequate.[37] In addition, it is generally agreed that custodianship, when it was eventually introduced in 1985 was not a success.[38]

14.32 In 1992 the authors of the *Review of Adoption Law: Report to Ministers of an Interdepartmental Working Group*,[39] like the Houghton Committee, were concerned that some applications for adoption were made without a full consideration of the needs of the child. They recognised that step-parents might wish to seek some kind of legal recognition of their role and there were circumstances where this could appropriately be achieved by adoption but where the child had a relationship with his other parent or relatives, it was unlikely to be in the child's interests for that relationship to be extinguished.

> 'Where the prime motivation behind an adoption application is the wish to cement the family unit and put away the past, this may be confusing and lead to identity problems for the child especially (as is statistically not unlikely) the new marriage breaks down. As divorce becomes more common, it is less necessary for families to pursue step-parent adoption in order to avoid embarrassment and difficult explanations ... It is likely that in many circumstances a residence order would be a better way of confirming a step-parent's responsibility for a child because it does not alter a child's legal relationship with his or her parents and family.'[40]

14.33 Its proposals that there should be a new type of adoption order for step-parents which could be revoked on divorce or death and for step-parents to be granted parental responsibility were not enacted.

14.34 The proportion of step-parent adoptions fell to 23% by 2004,[41] possibly because of an increase in the number of children being adopted from care.

14.35 The programme for the reform of adoption law in 2002 was primarily concerned with looked after children and neither the *Prime Minster's Review*[42] nor the White Paper *Adoption: A New Approach*[43] commented on step-parent adoptions. However, the reforms affected step-parent adoptions in a number of ways.

- Step-parents married to a birth parent became able to acquire parental responsibility.

- Special guardianship was introduced.

---

[37] See Thoburn 'Review of Research Relating to Adoption' (1990) Appendix C to *Review of Adoption Law: Report to Ministers of an Interdepartmental Working Group* (Department of Health and Welsh Office, 1992) at p 154.
[38] See **5.3**.
[39] op cit.
[40] Ibid, at paras 19.1–19.2.
[41] *Judicial Statistics 2004*.
[42] *Adoption* (PIU, 2000).
[43] Cm 5017 (HMSO, December 2000).

- Couples who adopted no longer needed to be married to each other.

- An adoption order can be granted solely to a 'partner' of a birth parent without affecting the parental responsibility of that birth parent.

The rationale for distinguishing between married/civil partnership couples and cohabitees for the purpose of parental responsibility orders and not for adoption orders is unclear.

PSYCHOLOGICAL PARENTS

14.36 The step-parent role in a particular family is likely to be placed somewhere on a continuum running from the biological parent's recent partner who currently plays and is likely to play no part in the child's upbringing and about whom the child (if a baby) may be ignorant to that of a psychological parent whom the child has always known and whom he believes to be his biological parent.

14.37 The phrase 'psychological parent' was, if not coined, at least placed in circulation by Goldstein, Freud and Solnit,[44] who defined it as:

> '… one based on a day-to-day interaction, companionship, shared experiences. The role can be fulfilled either by a biological parent or an adoptive parent or by any other caring adult – but never by an absent, inactive adult, whatever his biological or legal relationship to the child may be.'[45]

14.38 The direct cause of this emotional relationship is not the biological relationship.

> 'This attachment results from day-to-day attention to his needs for physical care, nourishment, comfort, affection and stimulation. Only a parent who provides for these needs will build a psychological relationship to the child … and will become his "psychological parent" in whose care the child can feel valued and "wanted".'[46]

14.39 In *Re G (Children)*[47] Baroness Hale of Richmond, referring to *Beyond the Best Interests of the Child*, described the relationship in this way.

> 'There are at least three ways in which a person may be or become a natural parent of a child, each of which may be a very significant factor in the child's welfare, depending upon the circumstances of the particular case. The first is genetic parenthood: the provision of the gametes which produce the child. This can be of deep significance on many levels. For the parent, perhaps particularly for a father, the knowledge that this is "his" child can bring a very special sense of love for and commitment to that child which will be of great benefit to the child (see, for

---

44   *Beyond the Best Interests of the Child* (The Free Press, 1973).
45   Ibid, at p 19.
46   Ibid at p 17.
47   [2006] UKHL 43, [2006] 2 FLR 629 at [33]–[37].

example, the psychiatric evidence in *Re C (MA) (An Infant)*.[48] For the child, he reaps the benefit not only of that love and commitment, but also of knowing his own origins and lineage, which is an important component in finding an individual sense of self as one grows up. The knowledge of that genetic link may also be an important (although certainly not an essential) component in the love and commitment felt by the wider family, perhaps especially grandparents, from which the child has so much to gain.

The second is gestational parenthood: the conceiving and bearing of the child. The mother who bears the child is legally the child's mother, whereas the mother who provided the egg is not: 1990 Act, s 27. While this may be partly for reasons of certainty and convenience, it also recognises a deeper truth: that the process of carrying a child and giving him birth (which may well be followed by breast-feeding for some months) brings with it, in the vast majority of cases, a very special relationship between mother and child, a relationship which is different from any other.

The third is social and psychological parenthood: the relationship which develops through the child demanding and the parent providing for the child's needs, initially at the most basic level of feeding, nurturing, comforting and loving, and later at the more sophisticated level of guiding, socialising, educating and protecting.

Of course, in the great majority of cases, the natural mother combines all three. She is the genetic, gestational and psychological parent. Her contribution to the welfare of the child is unique. The natural father combines genetic and psychological parenthood. His contribution is also unique. In these days when more parents share the tasks of child rearing and breadwinning, his contribution is often much closer to that of the mother than it used to be; but there are still families which divide their tasks on more traditional lines, in which case his contribution will be different and its importance will often increase with the age of the child.

But there are also parents who are neither genetic nor gestational, but who have become the psychological parents of the child and thus have an important contribution to make to their welfare. Adoptive parents are the most obvious example, but there are many others.'

14.40 Resolving a dispute about the status to be given to a particular step-parent will depend to some extent on his psychological relationship with the child but the child's psychological relationship with the non-resident parent also has to be considered. Unlike biological parentage, children can have more than two psychological parents.

---

[48]   [1966] 1 WLR 646.

TRUTH ABOUT PATERNITY

The child's right to knowledge about his paternity

14.41 Professionals have long held the view that it is important for a child to have knowledge of his or her origins. In 1972, the Houghton Committee on Adoption[49] observed that:

> 'The importance of telling a child that it has been adopted has long been recognised and there is a growing recognition that the child should be told early and helped to understand it more fully as he grows older. It is also increasingly recognised that at some stage the child will need to know about his origins – the positive factors about his parents, such as any special qualities, gifts or interests; their appearance; their reasons for giving him up and any medical background which may be relevant. This kind of information helps the proper development of a sense of identity and gives the child ... a fuller understanding of him as an individual with his own unique combination of characteristics, both inherited and acquired from his upbringing and environment.'

14.42 By 1992, the *Interdepartmental Review of Adoption Law*[50] expressed the view that 'For many years now there has been increasing recognition that a child's knowledge of his or her background is crucial to the formation of positive self-identity'. It continued by saying that:

> 'It is essential that an adopted child of sufficient age and understanding is told that he or she is adopted and what this means ... Some adopted people experienced considerable trauma to discover by chance – and sometimes at quite a late age – that they were adopted.'

14.43 This 'right to know' has been recognised by the European Court of Human Rights as being an Art 8 right.

> '[Respect] for private life requires that everyone should be able to establish details of their identity as individual human beings and that an individual's entitlement to such information is of importance because of its formative implications for his or her personality (see the *Gaskin v United Kingdom* judgment [1990] 1 FLR 167).'[51]

14.44 This was also recognised by the domestic court in *Rose v Secretary of State for Health*[52] when Scott Baker J ruled that Art 8 was engaged when two claimants who had been born as a result of artificial insemination sought information about the anonymous donors.

> 'Respect for family life ... plainly includes the right to obtain information about a biological parent who will inevitably have contributed to the identity of his child.'

---

[49]   op cit.
[50]   (Department of Health) at paras 4.1 and 27.4.
[51]   *Milkulic v Croatia* [2002] 1 FCR 720. See also *M v W (Declaration of Parentage)* [2006] EWHC 2341 (Fam), [2007] 2 FLR 270 and **12.11**.
[52]   [2002] EWHC 1593 (Admin), [2002] 2 FLR 962.

14.45 Conversely a child has the right not to have the identity of the person assumed to be her father changed unilaterally. In *Re L (Family Proceedings Court) (Appeal: Jurisdiction)*[53] the court set aside a declaration of non-paternity which had been made in the Family Proceedings Court, without the knowledge or participation of the child or her mother, on an appeal by the mother's husband against a decision by the Child Support Agency (CSA) that he was the child's father.

> 'The order made [by the FPC] has brought into question the issue of her parentage ... [The decision] is an affront to justice. L has been the victim ... of a miscarriage of justice in a matter going ... to the very heart of her identity as a human being. Her human rights have been infringed.'[54]

14.46 There are, however, competing rights including the right of the child, the mother and her partner that their life and privacy should not be intruded upon or interfered with.[55] A balance therefore has to be struck and in striking the balance the court has to consider the welfare of the child.[56]

14.47 In *Re D (Paternity)*[57] D grew up with someone he believed to be his paternal grandmother. When he was 10, X (not the grandmother's son) was introduced to him as his birth father. There were reasonable grounds for believing that X might be his father. X applied for parental responsibility and a residence order. DNA tests were sought but the boy, who had a number of educational and behavioural difficulties refused to provide a sample. Headley J found that D understood what testing meant and what its conclusions might be. The applications challenged the only emotional security D had ever known at a highly emotive stage of his life. The judge held that although the court could exercise its compulsive powers under s 21 of the Act to override his lack of consent to the tests and it was in D's best interests to know the truth about his paternity, sooner rather than later, it was not in his best interest to press the issue at the present time. He directed that the applicant provide samples to be stored. He also ordered that a sample be taken from D but stayed this order with liberty to restore. D's Rule 9(5) guardian was directed to explain to D that the issue of paternity should not be indefinitely put off, and that, in the end, truth was easier to live with than doubt.

Serological/DNA tests

14.48 Family Law Reform Act 1969, s 20 provides that in any civil proceedings in which the paternity of a person falls to be determined, a court has power to direct the use of bodily tests to ascertain whether such tests show

---

[53] [2003] EWHC 1682 (Fam), [2005] 1 FLR 210.
[54] Per Munby J at [23]–[24].
[55] *Re T (Paternity: Ordering Blood Tests)* [2001] 2 FLR 1190 and *Yousef v The Netherlands* (Application No 33711/96) [2003] 1 FLR 210.
[56] *Re L (Contact: Domestic Violence); Re V (Contact: Domestic Violence); Re M (Contact: Domestic Violence); Re H (Contact: Domestic Violence)* [2000] 2 FLR 334 and *Hendriks v Netherlands* (1983) 5 EHRR 223.
[57] [2006] EWHC 3545 (Fam), [2007] 2 FLR 26.

that a party to the proceedings is or is not excluded from being the father.[58] Part III of the Act provides a code for the formal aspects of the carrying out of the tests. The report of the tester is received by the court as evidence in the proceedings. Within 14 days of receiving the report, a party may serve notice on the other parties that he wishes to call the tester to give oral evidence. Originally, the testing envisaged by the legislature was serological testing but the wording of the section is wide enough to encompass DNA testing of samples,[59] which provides a higher degree of reliability and is now the most commonly used mode of testing.

14.49 For guidance on the directions to be given, see *Re F (Children) (DNA Evidence)*.[60]

14.50 As amended by the Child Support, Pensions and Social Security Act 2000, the section provides that where the person having control of the child does not consent, the court may authorise a taking of the sample if it considers that it is in the best interests of the child.[61]

Should a test be ordered?

14.51 The court has a discretion to refuse to direct blood testing and indeed may refuse to allow an issue of paternity to be tried at all. It will rarely do this nowadays if paternity is a real issue, because of the weight given to the child's right to know the true facts about his paternity.

14.52 When the court is considering how to exercise its discretion, the s 1 paramountcy test does not apply, because the issue is not one concerning the upbringing of the child[62] but the welfare of the child still has to be considered. Since the decision of the House of Lords in *S (an Infant, by her Guardian ad Litem the Official Solicitor to the Supreme Court) v S; W v Official Solicitor (acting as Guardian ad Litem for a Male Infant Named PHW)*[63] most courts which have considered the issue of directing blood tests have regarded a child knowing who his genetic father is as normally being in his best interests.

14.53 A number of factors are generally considered.

The interests of justice

14.54 Courts have been unanimous in holding that the interests of justice almost always require that the truth be established by the most reliable means possible:

---

[58]   Samples other than blood may now be taken (Blood Tests (Evidence of Paternity) (Amendment) Regulations 2001, SI 2001/773).
[59]   See *Re H (Paternity: Blood Test)* [1996] 2 FLR 65.
[60]   [2007] EWHC 3235 (Fam), [2008] 1 FLR 348.
[61]   Child Support, Pensions and Social Security Act 2000, s 21(3).
[62]   *S v S* [1972] AC 24.
[63]   [1972] AC 24.

'The interests of justice in the abstract are best served by the ascertainment of the truth and there must be few cases where the interests of children can be shown to be best served by the suppression of truth ... Failure to submit the child to a blood test may eventually lead the child to unnecessary doubt as to his paternity and the chance of removing that doubt may be lost in the passing of time. There may be genetic consequences in some cases which could have been avoided if the blood test had been taken.'[64]

14.55 This argument has grown even stronger with the availability of DNA testing. As Waite LJ said in *Re A (A Minor) (Paternity: Refusal of Blood Test)*:[65]

'Genetic testing, already advanced to a high degree of probability through the negative techniques of exclusion, has now moved on to the point where it has become possible to achieve positive certainty.'

The interests of the child in knowing the true identity of its father

14.56 As discussed above, most courts which have considered the issue of directing blood tests have regarded it as normally being in the best interests of a child to know who its father is. In *S v S*,[66] Lord Morris of Borth-y-Gest considered that in most cases the interests of the child are best served if the truth is known and courts considering the issue since then have usually expressed the same view. For example, in *Re G (Parentage: Blood Sample)*,[67] Ward LJ said that it was 'the entitlement' of the child to know who her father was.

The interests of the child in not having a settled life disturbed

14.57 The possibility of the loss of a status of being legitimate was not considered sufficient justification by their lordships in *S v S*, nor is the possibility that the person whom the child believes to be his father will be shown not to be. If no purpose is to be achieved by the tests, this is a reason for not allowing the issue of paternity to be tried at all. *Re JS (A Minor) (Declaration of Paternity)*[68] is a rare example of the Court of Appeal stating that tests should not be taken. At the time of conception, the mother was having a sexual relationship with her partner but also had a very brief relationship with J, a work colleague. She became pregnant and gave birth to a child who was brought up by her and her partner, R, as though he was the child of both of them. J became obsessed with the thought of the child, insisted on seeing him and applied for a declaration that he was the father and for contact. Informal blood tests did not preclude him from being the father, R refusing to undergo tests. The trial judge dismissed J's applications. The Court of Appeal dismissed J's appeal, holding that even if there was jurisdiction to grant a

---

[64] [1972] AC 24, per Lord Hodson at 57–58.
[65] [1994] 2 FLR 463 at 472.
[66] [1972] AC 24.
[67] [1997] 1 FLR 360.
[68] [1980] 3 WLR 984 and also *K v M (Paternity: Contact)* [1996] 1 FLR 312.

declaration (and at that time the Family Law Act 1996 was not in force), it was wrong to entertain the application on two grounds. The first was that it would bind only the parties and not R, the second that a declaration would 'transmute a mathematical probability into a forensic certainty' when there was no need to:

> 'With hindsight it is now clear that it was unnecessary to consider the biological parentage of this child in order to reach a conclusion about access, which was the only live issue. The child is securely based in a two-parent family with the mother and Mr R, who fully accepts his role as de facto father, with the knowledge of the doubt of his being the biological father; [J] is, to all intents and purposes, a stranger to the child. To allow the paternity issue to disturb this settled relationship was, in our view, an undoubted mistake ...'[69]

14.58   Given the emphasis now placed on the importance of a child knowing the truth about its origins and the certainty of DNA testing, it is doubtful whether *Re JS* would be decided in the same way today.

14.59   The court will need to balance all these factors, but given the decision of the House of Lords in *S v S*, a test will normally be ordered unless it can be clearly demonstrated that there is a likelihood of harm being caused to the child. In *Re T (Paternity: Ordering Blood Tests)*,[70] blood tests were ordered in an application for contact and parental responsibility, even though it was far from certain that such orders would be made:

> 'The applicant's application ... cannot, simply, be "wished away". Those applications are going to have to be heard, whether or not blood tests are ordered. In that event, how much more satisfactory must it be in principle for the evidence to be the best that science can provide (probably certainty) as compared to the unsatisfactory situation of the court being left with presumptions and inferences.'

See also *Re D (Paternity)*[71] where the court ordered that a sample be taken but stayed the order because of the child's objection.

Inferences to be drawn from a refusal to undergo a blood test

14.60   The Child Support, Pensions and Social Security Act 2000, s 21 states that samples may not be taken from anyone other than the child, except with his or her consent. However, when a direction has been given for tests, the court may draw such inferences, if any, as appear proper from any failure to take the test or to consent to the test being taken by a person named in the direction.[72] Where there is a presumption of legitimacy in favour of the person who fails to take any step required of him in the direction, the court may adjourn the proceedings and may, if at the end of the period of adjournment the person has still refused without reasonable cause to comply, dismiss his claim for relief

---

[69]   [1980] 3 WLR 984, per Ormrod LJ at 152.
[70]   [2001] 2 FLR 1190, per Bodey J at 1196.
[71]   [2006] EWHC 3545 (Fam), [2007] 2 FLR 26; see **14.47**.
[72]   Child Support, Pensions and Social Security Act 2000, s 23(1).

notwithstanding the absence of evidence to rebut the presumption.[73] The Court of Appeal has held that an indication by a party that he or she will refuse, made in advance of a direction, also permits an adverse inference to be drawn.[74]

14.61 In *Re G (Parentage: Blood Sample)*[75] Thorpe LJ said:

> 'The court must be astute to discern what are the real motivations behind the refusal. It should look critically at any proffered explanation or justification. It should only uphold an explanation that is objectively valid, demonstrating rationality, logicality and consistency. Anything less will usually lead to an adverse inference.'

Giving effect to paternity

14.62 The issue of whether a child should be told the truth about his biological parentage may be a discrete issue[76] or may arise in the course of proceedings, for example, an order for contact. In both cases the court has power under CA 1989, s 8 to determine the issue of whether, when and how a child should be told the truth of his paternity.[77]

14.63 The issue is more difficult than the one of deciding whether to order paternity testing. In these cases, unlike the issue of deciding whether or not to order tests, the welfare of the child is, of course, paramount. The attitude of the parent with care is crucial. When the parent is so opposed to the relationship that telling the child will cause him serious upset, the court has to balance the advantage to the child in knowing the truth against the impact that the process was likely to have on the carer and the family.[78] The perceived importance of knowledge of the truth is such that courts rarely accept an argument opposing 'telling'.

14.64 Where the court has decided that it is in the best interests of the child to be told the truth, it can grant a specific issue order and, if the parent with care threatens to ignore the order, it will put in place an alternative mechanism for telling the child,[79] for example a child psychiatrist or Rule 9(5) guardian.[80]

---

[73] Child Support, Pensions and Social Security Act 2000, s 23(2).
[74] *Re H (Paternity: Blood Test)* [1996] 2 FLR 65, per Ward LJ at 76. and see *Re A (A Minor) (Paternity: Refusal of a Blood Test)* [1994] 2 FLR 463 per Waite LJ at 473.
[75] [1997] 1 FLR 360 at 367.
[76] For example, *Re J (Paternity: Welfare of Child)* [2006] EWHC 2837(Fam), [2007] 1 FLR 1064.
[77] *Re F (Paternity: Jurisdiction)* [2007] EWCA Civ 873, [2008] 1 FLR 225.
[78] *Re J (Paternity: Welfare of Child)* [2006] EWHC 2837(Fam), [2007] 1 FLR 1064. See also *Re L (Identity of Birth Father)* [2008] EWCA Civ 1388, [2009] 1 FLR 1152.
[79] *Re F (Paternity: Jurisdiction)* [2007] EWCA Civ 873, [2008] 1 FLR 225.
[80] See *Re R (A Minor) (Contact)* [1993] 2 FLR 762.

The general approach

14.65

- In the majority of cases, the best interests of the child require him to be told the truth.

- The decision as to whether to tell the child should not be delayed.

- Once the decision is made, telling the child should not generally be postponed beyond any careful preparation which may be needed.

- If the parent with care refuses or is unable to tell the child, arrangements should be made for this to be performed by someone else.

However, the circumstances of each individual child need to be considered and the general approach may be less appropriate for an older child.

Examples

Re R (A Minor) (Contact)[81]

14.66   Married parents separated when their daughter was 1 year old. Contact between father and child ceased soon afterwards, when the mother formed a relationship with a new partner, the child being brought up to believe that the partner was her father. When the child was 5, the father applied for contact which the mother opposed. Contact was ordered but when the mother was unable or unwilling to co-operate in preparing the child for the first period of contact, the order was revoked. The Court of Appeal held that the trial judge had been wrong to do so. Butler-Sloss LJ said:

> 'It is the right of a child to have a relationship with both parents wherever possible. This principle has been stated again and again in the appellate courts. It is underlined in the United Nations Convention on the Rights of the Child and endorsed in the Children Act 1989 ...
>
> ... I agree with the judge that the child and her father cannot meet at this moment. But I differ from the judge in leaving the long-term decision in limbo. I believe the child has not only the right to see her father; if this can eventually be realised without causing her damage, she also has a right ... to know the truth.'[82]

The Court of Appeal invited the Official Solicitor to represent the child and to instruct a child psychiatrist to assist the mother to inform the child of her true parentage or, if that proved impossible, to do so himself if considered appropriate.

---

[81]   [1993] 2 FLR 762.
[82]   [1993] 2 FLR 762, at 767.

A v L (Contact)[83]

14.67 The parents were unmarried. There had been no contact for some time and the mother had a partner (D) whom the 3-year-old boy thought was his father. The father (LA), who was serving a long prison sentence, applied for indirect contact, accepting that the boy should not be told his true parentage until older. The justices dismissed the application. On appeal, Holman J held they were wrong to do so:

'It is precisely because J is still young and has no understanding of the facts of life that it is more appropriate and better to introduce him, very gently, and in age-appropriate ways, at this stage, to the fact that he in fact has two fathers. That is not to say that he should be given any encouragement not to regard and address D as "Daddy" or that he needs to think LA is "Daddy". But he needs to know now, whilst he is still sufficiently young that it is in no way threatening to him, that there is another father so that, in due course, as he begins to learn the biological facts of life he can gently assimilate this truth about his parentage. To do and say nothing now is in truth storing up a potential bombshell for the future, which might be very damaging for J to learn and might indeed seriously undermine his sense of trust in his mother and D who are otherwise parenting him so well.'[84]

An order was made for indirect contact by letters, cards and modest presents and the judge directed that the mother must ensure that the child opened them and had the messages read to him. The applicant was not, however, to refer to himself as the child's father.

Re K (Specific Issue Order)[85]

14.68 The parents, who were unmarried, separated soon after the child was born. There was no contact and the mother brought the child up to believe that his father was dead. When the boy was 12, the father applied for contact and a specific issue order that his son be told that his father was alive and who he was. The mother adamantly opposed this and the Official Solicitor recommended that if the mother co-operated, it was in the child's best interests to be told, but not otherwise. The deputy High Court judge refused to make the order on the grounds that, because of the mother's obsessional hatred of the father, informing the child about his father would cause an emotional upset in the child's life which would be seriously detrimental. The Court of Appeal invited the Official Solicitor to instruct a child psychiatrist to assist the mother to inform the child of her true parentage or, if that proved impossible, to do so himself if considered appropriate.

---

[83] [1998] 1 FLR 361.
[84] Ibid, at 366.
[85] [1999] 2 FLR 280.

Re J (Paternity: Welfare of Child)[86]

14.69   J, aged 10, believed that his mother's long-term partner, Mr O, was his birth father and that his two half-siblings were in fact his full siblings. His father applied for contact but then failed to pursue the application. On his own initiative Sumner J raised the issue of whether J should be told the truth, but having heard argument from the mother and after reading a psychiatric report which said that the mother was a vulnerable person and having to tell J might precipitate a mental illness, he decided that it was not in J's best interests to order that he must be told but commended that his mother and Mr O seek advice.

> 'The ... longer J remains in ignorance, the greater the chance that he will learn the truth from some other source.[87] That could be potentially very damaging for him. Secondly, by 16 [the age by which his mother proposed to tell him the truth] he will have been through puberty. Given the turmoil that this can cause, the impact of then learning that his mother has kept from him the truth about his paternity could well cause him even greater upset than had he learned earlier. There may well be reasons for not telling him now. Provided the mother and Mr O progress in the strength of their relationship, and the mother can cope with it, for J to know sooner rather than later may well be to his advantage.'[88]

PARENTAL RESPONSIBILITY

14.70   The introduction of the concept of parental responsibility by s 3 of CA 1989 prepared a way to avoid step-parent adoptions in many cases. A step-parent with parental responsibility has virtually the same legal status as a birth parent or adopter during the child's childhood but, unlike the latter, not in adulthood. There are, however, other differences[89] between mere parental responsibility and adoption which include the following:

• Parental responsibility can be revoked.

• Parental responsibility is more likely to be shared with others and in some cases, for example, changing the child's name, removing the child from the jurisdiction or immunisation[90] can be exercised only with the consent of all others with parental responsibility.

---

[86]   [2006] EWHC 2837(Fam), [2007] 1 FLR 1064.
[87]   'Some man at a banquet who had drunk too much shouted out ... that I am not my father's son ... I questioned my father and mother closely and they were enraged ... but still this thing kept gnawing at me.' Sophocles *Oedipus The King* trans Fagles (Viking Press, 1982) ll 858–866.
[88]   Ibid, at [14]–[15].
[89]   For a schedule of differences see *Re AJ (Adoption Order or Special Guardianship Order)* [2007] EWCA Civ 55, [2007] 1 FLR 507. See also **16.34**.
[90]   *See Re C (Welfare of Child: Immunisation)* [2003] EWCA Civ 1148, [2003] 2 FLR 1095.

- Adoptive parents do not require leave to issue applications under s 8 of the CA 1989 for residence, contact, specific issue and prohibited steps orders. However this difference exists only when parental responsibility is not granted under s 4A.

- The child will not benefit under intestacy rules if the person with parental responsibility dies intestate.

However, although the courts refer to parental responsibility as giving a status[91] it is by no means certain that this is how a non-lawyer would see it.

Grant of parental responsibility under CA 1989, s 4A

14.71 The White Paper *Adoption: A New Approach*[92] did not comment on step-parent adoptions but it is likely that this thinking lay behind the introduction of s 4A in the same form as a clause in an Adoption Bill introduced in 1996. The consultative document which accompanied it, *Adoption – A Service for Children*,[93] stated that it was intended to provide new alternatives to adoption.

14.72 Section 4A of the CA 1989 introduced by s 112 of the Adoption and Children Act 2002[94] provides that:

'(1) Where a child's parent ("parent A") who has parental responsibility for the child is married to, or a civil partner of, a person who is not the child's parent ("the step-parent")

(a) Parent A or, if the other parent of the child, both parents may by agreement with the step-parent provide for the step-parent to have parental responsibility for the child; or

(b) the court may, on the application of the step-parent, order that the step-parent shall have parental responsibility for the child.'

Grant by agreement

14.73 An agreement under s 4A(1)(a) is termed a 'parental responsibility agreement' and, like an agreement under s 4(1)(b) between the mother and the birth father which grants the birth father parental responsibility, is subject to formalities.[95] The agreement must be recorded on a form (C(PRA)2) prescribed by the Parental Responsibility Agreement Regulations 1991[96] and must be filed in the Principal Registry.

---

91 See, for example, *Re H (Shared Residence: Parental Responsibility)* [1995] 2 FLR 883 per Ward LJ at 888.
92 (HMSO, December 2000).
93 (Department of Health and Welsh Office, 1996).
94 As amended by the Civil Partnership Act 2004, s 75(1), (2).
95 CA 1989, s 4A(2), s 4(2).
96 SI 1991/1478 as amended by the Parental Responsibility Agreement (Amendment) Regulations 2005 (SI 2005/2808).

14.74 Parents can agree to the acquisition of parental responsibility even when the child is subject to a care order and even when the local authority, which also has parental responsibility by virtue of s 33, disagrees.[97]

Grant by order

14.75 Like the grant of parental responsibility orders to birth parents, applications under s 4A(1)(b) are governed by CA 1989, s 1 and the welfare checklist applies.[98]

14.76 In 1991, Balcombe LJ in *Re H (Illegitimate Children: Father: Parental Rights)*[99] created a three-pronged approach, consistently followed by the Court of Appeal, for granting parental responsibility to a father:

> 'In considering whether to make an order … the court will have to take into account a number of factors, of which the following will undoubtedly be material (although there may well be others, as the list is not meant to be exhaustive):
>
> (1)   the degree of commitment which the father has shown towards the child;
> (2)   the degree of attachment which exists between the father and the child;
> (3)   the reasons of the father for applying for the order.'

14.77 As was made clear by Butler-Sloss LJ in *Re H (Parental Responsibility)*,[100] this approach is only the starting point and cannot replace s 1. In some cases, it might be right to make an order even though the test is not satisfied and in other cases the welfare of the child may require that the order is not made, even though it was.

14.78 Commitment has to be viewed in the round and an order will not be refused solely, for example, because the father fails to provide maintenance[101] or has been convicted of possessing obscene literature[102] or is a transsexual.[103] In *Re P (Parental Responsibility)*,[104] Hirst LJ commented that the order will not be refused where a father has shown commitment and has sound and genuine reasons for wanting it simply because, through hostility towards the mother or an excess of zeal, the father might seek to exercise his responsibility inappropriately. In such a case, any inappropriate exercise of parental responsibility can be controlled by prohibited steps orders or orders for supervised contact. A parental responsibility order will not be refused merely because the father will be unable to exercise responsibility in the immediate future, for example, because the child is subject to a care order and in foster

---

[97]   *Re X (Parental Responsibility Agreement: Children in Care)* [2000] 1 FLR 517.
[98]   *Re H (Parental Responsibility)* [1998] 1 FLR 855.
[99]   [1991] 1 FLR 214 at 218.
[100]   [1998] 1 FLR 855.
[101]   *Re H (Parental Responsibility: Maintenance)* [1996] 1 FLR 867.
[102]   *Re S (Parental Responsibility)* [1995] 2 FLR 648.
[103]   *Re L (Contact; Transsexual Applicant)* [1995] 2 FLR 438.
[104]   [1997] 2 FLR 722.

care.[105] Even if there is little prospect of parental responsibility being exercised, it may still be appropriate to grant it to enable a father to oppose the making of an order freeing the child for adoption. He would still have the right to receive progress reports and to apply to revoke the freeing order.[106] As Waite LJ neatly put it in *Re C (Minors) (Parental Rights)*,[107] he has 'rights in waiting'.

14.79 The granting of a parental responsibility order is a different matter from granting contact and it may be appropriate to grant parental responsibility even though a contact application is dismissed. Because it grants status and responsibilities which may not immediately be exercisable or the exercise of which may be controlled by a prohibited steps order, the hostility of the parent with care and hostility without good grounds, is less of an obstacle than when contact is being considered. In *Re J-S (Contact: Parental Responsibility)*[108] the Court of Appeal criticised a judge who had refused to grant a father parental responsibility on the ground that he had harassed the 4-year-old child's mother by referrals to social services but had failed to take into account important aspects of the case including the father's genuinely held concerns for the child and the fact that the mother had not been affected by the referrals.

> 'Here we have a father who has played an important part in the life of this young child, certainly during his first 2 years ... The parents then had a shared care regime. The father is clearly devoted to him and the boy responds in turn ... In my judgement the case is overwhelming that he should be granted parental responsibility.'[109]

14.80 In *B v A (Parental Responsibility)*[110] the father of a child born to a lesbian couple was granted parental responsibility upon giving undertakings not to exercise it in certain areas without the consent of the couple.

14.81 Normally, therefore, an application for parental responsibility should not be deferred. Exceptionally, this was done in *Re D (Parental Responsibility: IVF Baby)*[111] to allow a man who had undergone treatment with the mother under the Human Fertilisation Act 1990 and who was accordingly to be treated as the child's father under s 28(3) to demonstrate commitment through maintaining indirect contact. Likewise, it should not be made and then immediately suspended.[112]

---

[105] *D v Hereford and Worcester County Council* [1991] 1 FLR 205, *Re CB (A Minor) (Parental Responsibility Order)* [1993] 1 FLR 920 and *Re G (A Minor) (Parental Responsibility Order)* [1994] 1 FLR 504.

[106] *Re H (Illegitimate Children: Father: Parental Rights) (No 2)* [1991] 1 FLR 214. A decision to the opposite effect was made by *W v Ealing London Borough Council* [1993] 2 FLR 788.

[107] [1992] 1 FLR 1.

[108] [2002] EWCA Civ 1028, [2003] 1 FLR 399.

[109] Per Ward LJ at [53].

[110] [2006] EWHC 0002 (Fam).

[111] [2001] EWCA Civ 230, [2001] 1 FLR 972 and see also *Re G (Parental Responsibility Order)* [2006] EWCA Civ 745, [2006] 2 FLR 1092.

[112] *Re G (A Minor) (Parental Responsibility Order)* [1994] 1 FLR 504.

14.82 It is unlikely that courts will impose an easier test for step-parents than the tripartite test. Requiring the step-parent to demonstrate commitment and attachment may normally mean that the applicant will have had to live with the child, whether before or after marriage/civil partnership to the child's parent for some time. The extent to which courts will have regard to the fact that second marriages, on average, last a shorter period than first marriages is uncertain.

14.83 Unlike section 4 orders, there may be another birth parent who has parental responsibility. It is uncertain how far this will affect the court's approach. When the absent parent plays little or no part in the child's life, an order is likely to be more readily granted to a committed applicant in order to ensure that there are at least two people who are able and willing to exercise parental responsibility. Where the absent parent plays a full part in the child's life, emphasis may be placed on the requirement imposed by s 1(5) that the court must be satisfied that granting the order is better for the child than not granting it, thereby requiring the applicant to show that an order is needed.

Revoking the order

14.84 A parental responsibility agreement or section 4A order can be revoked by the court on an application made by any person who has parental responsibility or, with leave of the court, by the child himself.[113] The court may grant leave for the child to make an application only if it is satisfied that the child has sufficient understanding to make the application.[114]

14.85 The test to be applied is the s 1 welfare test.

14.86 The Court Service does not provide statistics for the number of orders which are discharged or agreements terminated each year, but they are likely to be very low indeed because, since 1991, only two cases of a revocation of a section 4 order have been reported. In *Re P (Terminating Parental Responsibility)*,[115] Singer J terminated a parental responsibility agreement in circumstances in which a father had been convicted of causing serious injury to his 9-week-old daughter. The agreement had been entered into after the injuries had been caused, at a time when, according to the mother, she believed the father to be innocent. Singer J held that parental responsibility, once obtained, should not be terminated on less than solid grounds, with a presumption for continuance rather than termination. Nor should the ability of the mother to apply for an order be allowed to become a weapon in her hands:

> '[Termination] should be used by the court as an appropriate step in the regulation of the child's life where the circumstances really do warrant it and not otherwise.'

14.87 In the instant case, the father's lack of commitment, the difficulties which continuation would have caused the child's foster parents and the local

---

[113] CA 1989, s 4A(3).
[114] Ibid, s 4A(4).
[115] [1995] 1 FLR 1048.

authority in whose care she had been placed and the absence of any prospect that the father would be able to exercise responsibility in a way which would be beneficial to the child justified terminating the agreement.

14.88 In *Re F (Indirect Contact)*[116] a parental responsibility order was revoked because of a persistent campaign of harassment against the mother by the father who was twice committed to prison for numerous breaches of a non-molestation order. The relationship between the parents was at an end and the father's anger towards the mother and propensity to violence were such that the mother would be seriously at risk if he discovered where she and the child were living. The Court of Appeal commented that 'In these circumstances the revocation of the order giving the father parental responsibility naturally followed.'[117]

What effect did the amendment have?

14.89 The extent to which s 4A is used is uncertain. No statistics are available for the number of step-parent parental responsibility agreements and the annual Judicial Statistics does not distinguish between parental responsibility orders granted to birth fathers and those to step-parents. There is, as yet, an absence of case-law to illustrate the approach of the courts. Are step-parents going to be concerned enough, even if they know about the amendment, to seek parental responsibility when all is going well with their spouse? If there are problems with the absent parent, how will the grant of parental responsibility add anything of benefit? Masson has argued that although s 4A(1)(a) appears to allow status to step-parents though 'private ordering' the wish to extend parental responsibility is more likely to lead to further litigation.[118] In any event parental responsibility can be granted under s 4A only if the applicant is married to or in a civil partnership with, rather than just living with, one of the child's parents and many stepfamilies will therefore be excluded.

Grant of parental responsibility by way of a residence order

14.90 The grant of a residence order under CA 1989, s 8 automatically confers parental responsibility on the person in whose favour the order has been made for the duration of the order.[119] A step-parent who is unable to obtain an order under s 4A, perhaps because s/he is not married to a birth parent, can, with leave if necessary, therefore obtain parental responsibility by applying for a joint residence order if living with the child's parent or a shared residence order, if not. In addition the step-parent may apply for a residence order solely in his favour. If the order is made in favour of a person who is not the parent or guardian of the child, the court may, at his request, direct that the

[116] [2006] EWCA Civ 1426, [2007] 1 FLR 1015.
[117] Per Phillips LCJ at [16].
[118] Masson 'The Impact of the Adoption and Children Act 2002 Part 1' [2003] Fam Law 580 at 582.
[119] CA 1989, s 12(2).

order continues until the child reaches the age of 18 rather than 16.[120] It is uncertain whether the court can give this direction if the order is made in favour of the parent as well as the step-parent.

14.91   The test is the s 1 welfare test.

14.92   Courts have become increasingly willing to grant birth parents shared residence orders and exceptional circumstances no longer need to be shown.[121] Decisions of the Court of Appeal have shown that objections to shared residence, distance between the homes, unresolved issues or lack of agreement or even co-operation between parents are not absolute bars to the making of an order. 'Indeed, the presence of [an] ... harmonious relationship is a contraindication of a shared residence order since such parents would fall within the no order principle emphasised by s 1(5) of the Act'.[122] Nor does an order for shared residence mean that time will be shared equally.[123] However, it must be intended that residence will be shared. In *Re A (Children) (Shared Residence)*[124] the Court of Appeal overturned a shared residence order. The child was going to live with the father and did not want even contact with his mother. The court's order had to reflect the true position and in the circumstances of the case was inappropriate.

Examples

Re H (Shared Residence: Parental Responsibility)[125]

14.93   The mother's husband was not the father of her elder son (now 14) but treated the boy as his own throughout the child's life. Indeed, the boy learned the truth about his paternity only after the mother and stepfather separated. After the separation, a residence order was made by consent with the intention that the children should spend alternate weeks with the mother and stepfather/father. This arrangement was never implemented and the mother applied for a sole residence order. Her application was dismissed, as was her appeal:

> 'The essential element of the judge's decision was to alleviate the confusion that would arise in the children's minds if they did not have the comfort and security of knowing not only that the [step]father wished to treat the boy as if he was his father, but that the law would give some stamp of approval to that de facto situation.

This was a case where a shared residence order was not artificial but of important practical therapeutic importance. It reflected the reality of the

---

[120]   CA 1989, s 12(5).
[121]   *D v D (Shared Residence Order)* [2001] 1 FLR 495.
[122]   Ibid.
[123]   *Re F (Shared Residence Order)* [2003] EWCA Civ 592.
[124]   [2001] EWCA Civ 1795, [2002] 1 FCR 177.
[125]   [1995] 2 FLR 883.

stepfather's involvement and reflected the need for him to be given some status with the school to continue to play his part as both parties wished to do.[126]

G v F (Contact and Shared Residence: Applications for Leave)[127]

14.94 A child was born to a lesbian couple, the mother being artificially inseminated. After the couple separated, the mother's former partner applied for leave to apply for a shared residence order. Bracewell J granted the partner leave, despite the mother indicating that she would object to the final order being made. There appeared to be very genuine reasons for the application which was not a device in order to obtain parental responsibility. It was conceded by the mother that the applicant had undertaken the role of parent even after the separation, had supported the child financially and had a good and close relationship with the child. There was nothing which suggested that the making of the order would disrupt, confuse or harm the child.

Re G (Residence: Same-Sex Partner)[128]

14.95 The Court of Appeal allowed an appeal from a refusal to grant the mother's former same-sex partner a shared residence order in relation to two children born by artificial insemination during their relationship. The order was necessary to prevent the mother marginalising the importance of her former partner in the lives of the children.

Re WB (Residence Orders)[129]

14.96 The children (aged 11 and 8) had been born during the marriage and the husband treated them as his own, the fact that he was not the father being established only during proceedings. Thorpe J refused his appeal against the justices' refusal to make a shared residence order. In the circumstances of that case, the children were confused and their welfare required that their primary home with their mother should be established and confirmed. It would have been quite wrong for the justices to grant a shared residence order 'for no other reason than to arrive at a finding of parental responsibility in the appellant'. *Note:* It may be that parental responsibility would have been granted had s 4A been available.

SPECIAL GUARDIANSHIP

14.97 Anyone who is or has been married to or in a civil partnership with a birth parent may apply for a residence or contact order without leave[130] and

[126] [1995] 2 FLR 883, per Ward LJ at 888.
[127] [1998] 2 FLR 799.
[128] [2005] EWCA Civ 462, [2005] 2 FLR 957. The mother continued to try to exclude her former partner from the children's lives – see *Re G (Children)* [2006] UKHL 43, [2006] 2 FLR 629.
[129] [1995] 2 FLR 1023.
[130] CA 1989, s 10(5).

any person who has parental responsibility under s 4A may apply for any section 8 order.[131] In comparison, s 14A makes no special provision for step-parents. Unless the step-parent has lived with the child for at least 3 years or has a residence order or has the consent of all with parental responsibility, the leave of the court is required, save where the general exceptions of s 14A(6) apply.[132]

14.98   When making a special guardianship order, the court may give leave for the child to be known by a new surname[133] (see **5.38**).

14.99   A step-parent who makes a sole application for guardianship rather than a joint one with the birth parent, will be able to exercise parental responsibility to the exclusion of the birth parent[134] (see **5.29**). It is not possible to avoid this by making a joint application because a birth parent cannot apply for special guardianship.[135]

ADOPTION

14.100   There are a number of variations to the normal rules governing adoption when the applicant is a step-parent of the child.

Adoption by one person

14.101   Notwithstanding the general rule that an order cannot, save exceptionally, be made on the application of one person who is married,[136] it can be made if the court is satisfied that the single adopter is not the child's parent but the partner of a parent of the person to be adopted.[137] The applicant is a 'partner' if he and the parent are a couple.[138] 'A couple' means a married couple, a couple in a civil partnership or two people (whether of different sexes or the same sex) living as a partner in an enduring family relationship.[139] However, this does not include two people one of whom is the other's parent, grandparent, sister, brother, aunt or uncle whether of the full or half blood or, in the case of parents, by adoption.[140]

---

[131]   CA 1989, s 10(5).
[132]   Ibid, s 4A(5).
[133]   Ibid, s 14B(2)(a).
[134]   Ibid, s 14C(1)(b).
[135]   Ibid, s 14A(2).
[136]   ACA 2002, s 51(1), (3).
[137]   Ibid, s 51(2), s 144(7).
[138]   Ibid, s 144(7).
[139]   Ibid, s 144(4).
[140]   Ibid, s 144(5), (6).

Child to live with the adopter before the application

14.102 The normal rule is that the child must have his home with the applicant at all times during a period of 10 weeks preceding the application (if the child is placed by an adoption agency or with leave of the High Court or the applicant is the child's parent),[141] for 1 year if the applicants are local authority foster-parents[142] or for not less than 3 years during a period of 5 years.[143] However if the applicant or one of the applicants is the partner of the child, the period is 6 months.[144]

Effect of adoption order

14.103 Where the child is adopted as a result of a sole application by the parent's partner, the child is to be treated as the child of the relationship of the parent and the partner[145] and as not being the child of any other person.[146] That parent will not therefore lose parental responsibility.

The approach of the courts to step-parent adoptions

Article 8

14.104 Adoption of a child by a step-parent is an interference with the birth parent's respect for family life and needs to be justified under Art 8(2) as being necessary in a democratic society and proportionate.[147] In *Söderbäck v Sweden*[148] the ECtHR declined to find that such an adoption was not justified on the facts of the case. The 7-year-old child's stepfather was married to her mother and had lived with the child since she was 8 months old. She regarded him as her father. Her birth father had never lived with her and had seen her only once, albeit in part because of her mother's opposition. The Court held that *de facto* family ties existed between the child and stepfather. The domestic court had considered the child's welfare, had balanced the interests of all parties and its decision fell within the margin of appreciation. See also *Eski v Austria*[149] and *Chepelev v Russia*.[150]

Domestic courts

14.105 Until the ACA 2002 came into effect, courts considering the questions raised by step-parent adoption did so against the obstacles created by s 10(3) of the Children Act 1975 and then s 14(3) of the Adoption Act 1976 (see **14.30**).

---

[141] ACA 2002, s 42(2).
[142] Ibid, s 42(4).
[143] Ibid, s 42(5).
[144] Ibid, s 42(3).
[145] Ibid, s 67(2).
[146] Ibid, s 67(3)(a).
[147] *Söderbäck v Sweden* [1999] 1 FLR 250.
[148] Ibid.
[149] [2007] 1 FLR 1650.
[150] [2007] Fam Law 956.

In addition, where the birth parent refused to consent, no order could be made unless the court was satisfied that it should dispense with his consent on the ground that it was withheld unreasonably. These factors no longer apply but earlier decisions demonstrate that even without these obstacles the higher courts did not readily consider such applications to be appropriate.

14.106   In *Re B (A Minor) (Adoption: Jurisdiction)*[151] Cumming-Bruce J said:

'Where there has been a divorce and the parent with custody and care and control of the child has married again, and seeks with her new husband by adoption to extinguish the relationship between the children and their father, against the will of the father who honestly wishes to preserve his relationship, and who is not said to be culpable, it is likely to be difficult to discover any benefit to the child from the adoption commensurate with the probable long-term disadvantages.'

Bagnall J added:[152]

'There is a body of opinion that where there is a divorce followed by remarriage and a very young child, the best course for the child is to make a complete break and allow the child to be brought up exclusively as a member of the new family established by a parent and a step-parent. That this view has not found favour in these courts is clear from recent decisions of the Court of Appeal to which I need not refer. Nevertheless it may well be that where all parties are in agreement and the relevant parent consents, it can be established that adoption by a parent and the step-parent is for the welfare of the child. In such a case the other parent agrees, so to say, to disappear wholly from the child's life and to accept a change of the child's legal status. Even there I think that parents should hesitate long and think carefully before taking such an irrevocable step.'

14.107   In 1998, Thorpe LJ in *Re PJ (Adoption: Practice On Appeal)*[153] rejected the argument that the revocation of s 14(3) had altered the approach.

'In my judgment cautionary dicta are still apt since applications in step-parent adoptions may be driven or complicated by motives or emotions derived from conflict within the triangle of adult relationships. They may also be buoyed up by quite unrealistic hopes and assumptions as to the quality of the marriage replacing that into which the children were born.'

14.108   In *Re G (Adoption Order)*[154] the Court of Appeal allowed an appeal against the making of an adoption order in respect of a 5-year-old who had been seeing her birth father on a weekly basis for 3 years until the mother unilaterally terminated contact 2 years after she started living with the step-father, whom she later married. The Court of Appeal found that the trial judge had erred in preferring the evidence of the guardian to that of a child psychiatrist but in addition, Thorpe LJ added:

---

[151]   [1975] 2 All ER 449 at 451i.
[152]   Ibid, at 464f.
[153]   [1998] 2 FLR 252 at 260.
[154]   [1999] 1 FLR 400 at 404.

'For my part I am very doubtful as to whether the judge was right to elevate the mother's anxiety [about contact] to the level of key factor. This was an extremely complex case and it is, in my opinion, impossible to simplify it in that way. All sorts of factors were fairly to be described as key. One was the extent of the father's involvement and commitment, another was the absolutely fundamental and immutable character of the adoption order that was sought. To make the adoption order involved an investment on the child's behalf in a new family unit that was relatively recent in origin and relatively untried. Whether the judge had that factor in mind sufficiently I have to question. Certainly there is nothing within the judgment that gives that consideration the emphasis that I believe it deserved.'

14.109   However, on occasions adoption is seen as being in the best interests of a child. In *Re B (Adoption: Father's Objections)*[155] the Court of Appeal dismissed an appeal against the making of an adoption order in respect of a 12-year-old child and which refused contact to the birth father. He had not seen the child for nearly the first 2 years of his life. He then twice abducted him and there had subsequently been no direct contact for the last 9 years. The child's clear wishes were that he wanted to be adopted by his mother and step-father.

WHICH ORDER?

14.110   A general approach to deciding between adoption, special guardianship and other orders is discussed in detail in Chapter 17.

14.111   There is nothing in either the CA1989 or the ACA 2002 which limits the grant of special guardianship or adoption to any given set of circumstances. There is no presumption within the statute that special guardianship is preferable to adoption although it is a material feature of special guardianship that it is less intrusive than adoption and therefore involves less fundamental interference with existing relationships. 'In some cases ... [that] can properly be regarded as helping to tip the balance.'[156] The welfare of the individual child is the court's paramount consideration and each case must be decided on its particular facts.

14.112   This approach applies just as much to applications by step-parents for parental responsibility, special guardianship or adoption. The variety in step-parent families (see **14.6**) emphasises the need to consider the welfare and circumstances of the particular child.

14.113   There is an aspect in step-parent applications, however, which features more prominently than in other applications: the child will remain living with a birth parent who is deemed to be at least a 'good enough' carer. That parent will already have parental responsibility which will not be supplanted by the order.

---

[155]   [1999] 2 FLR 215.
[156]   *Re S (Adoption Order or Special Guardianship Order)* [2007] EWCA Civ 54, [2007] 1 FLR 819 per Wall LJ at [47]–[49].

14.114 A key element to be considered will therefore be the issue of parental responsibility and the main factor in the checklist is likely to be the needs of the child. Does the child need another person to have parental responsibility? If the non-resident birth parent has parental responsibility and is exercising it appropriately, is there a case for a third person having it? On the other hand, if the non-resident birth parent plays no part in the child's life and the step-parent is a psychological parent to the child, there would seem to be some justification for him to be granted parental responsibility, either under s 4A or by way of a shared/joint residence order, even if he was separated from the resident birth parent.

14.115 If the grant of parental responsibility is needed, does the child also need a special guardianship order or the extinguishing of the non-resident birth parent's parental responsibility by way of adoption? There may be difficulties in granting a sole special guardianship order to a step-parent because he or she will have greater freedom to exercise parental guardianship than the resident birth parent: why is this required?

14.116 Where the non-resident parent is playing a role in the child's life, adoption is seldom likely to be seen as being appropriate. Even if he is not, any role in the child's life played by members of the non-resident parent's birth family will also have to be considered. What is the justification for terminating at least their legal relationship with the child?

14.117 Whatever the answers to the above questions, given the greater risk of separation for couples in a second relationship, another important matter which will need to be investigated is the duration and stability of the relationship between the birth parent and the step-parent.[157] It may be in the child's best interests for there to be another person with parental interest but the question is: should it be granted to *this* step-parent at *this* time?

---

[157] And see *Re G (Adoption Order)* [1999] 1 FLR 400 per Thorpe LJ at 404.

Chapter 15

THE CHILD IN CARE

INTRODUCTION

15.1 It is difficult for the state to look after children whether by accommodating them under s 22(2) of the Children Act 1989 or under a care order. Despite regulation and efforts to reform the system, renewed over many years, for many children, State care has been far from satisfactory. According to one author:[1]

> 'Children who have spent time in care are the most disadvantaged of the child population. They are prone to psychiatric disorders, they suffer in terms of education and health and they often "graduate" from care lacking the most basic life-skills. Deprived of the kin-support systems which reaffirm and sustain most young adults, they are more likely to become homeless, unemployed or in prison. The problems are intergenerational: graduates of "care" often see their own children absorbed into the same system.'

15.2 This view is shared to some extent by central government:[2]

> 'For too many children the care system does not provide the chance for a long-term family life in which they can thrive.'[3]

However, the picture is more complicated than this might suggest. Many children are severely disadvantaged before they come into care perhaps because of years of neglect and abuse. They will not be the easiest of children to place with alternative families nor, when they are placed, is success guaranteed. In some cases, because of the circumstances and wishes of the individual child, being in care may be the only or the least detrimental possibility. At the same time it has to be recognised that care by an authority, even with parental responsibility, is vulnerable to organisational failure and for many children is likely to be second best to an alternative, permanent home if one can be found.

---

[1] Morgan *Adoption and the Care of Children* (Institute of Economic Affairs, 1998) at p 115.
[2] See, for example, *Adoption: A New Approach*, Cm 5017 (2000) chapter 2.
[3] *Adoption: A New Approach* at para 2.2.

BACKGROUND

Development of social services care

15.3   Although there had been centuries of some support for children who were orphaned or abandoned both by charitable societies and by local bodies at the parish level, the foundation of the present system of social services was laid by the recommendations of the *Report of the Care of Children Committee*[4] ('the Curtis Committee') in 1946.

15.4   The aims of the Report were high.

> 'We wish to emphasise once more the extreme seriousness of taking a child away from even an indifferent home. Every effort should be made to keep the child in its home or with its mother if it is illegitimate provided that the home is or can be made reasonably satisfactory. The aim of the authority must be to find something better – indeed much better – if it takes the responsibility of providing a substitute home.'[5]

This would be done in one of three ways. Adoption was seen as especially appropriate for a child who had finally lost his own parents by death, desertion or their misconduct and for an illegitimate child whose mother was unable or unwilling to maintain him. Boarding out (foster care) was on the whole the best method short of adoption of providing the child with a substitute for his own home. Although 'it must be remembered that a considerable proportion of children are unsuited by habits, age or physical or mental condition to be placed in a private house', 'it remains true that more children could be boarded out if there were suitable homes for them'. Finally, the difficulties in the way of boarding out or arranging adoption for all children for whom a family life must be provided were obviously very great. For some there was a need for institutional care 'with the aim of making it as good a substitute for the private home as it can possibly be'.[6]

15.5   The history of the way in which, following the Curtis Report, social services developed and the associated legislation is a complicated one.[7] Adoption gradually came to be seen in practice as being a viable option which was not restricted to 'healthy white babies'. Foster care rather than living in children's homes became the norm for children who were not teenagers. However by 2000, it was 'all too clear that the confident expectations inspired by the Curtis Report 50 years earlier that the State could act as a good parent to the country's deprived and needy children were unrealistic'.[8] It was

---

[4]   Cmd 6922 (1946). A detailed description of the report which contained 62 recommendations can be found in Cretney *Family Law in the Twentieth Century: A History* (Oxford University Press, 2003) at pp 672–680.

[5]   The Curtis Committee, at para 447.

[6]   Ibid, paras 448, 460, 476.

[7]   See Cretney op cit chs 19 and 20.

[8]   Ibid, p 735.

recognised in the last decade of the twentieth century that children in some residential homes were at risk of physical abuse[9] and sexual abuse.[10]

15.6 In 1997 the Government commissioned the report *People Like Us: The Report of the Review of Safeguards for Children Living Away from Home*[11] which made 20 principal recommendations for protecting the welfare and safety of children living away from home. The Secretary of State accepted that 'the whole system had failed' and promised reform of the regulations governing children in care, better health and education for children in care homes, more help for children leaving care and systems for improving quality across the care system.

15.7 A review of these actions in 2004[12] concluded that legislation, policy and procedures had been much improved but effective implementation had been more problematic. The welfare of the main groups of children living away from home seemed to be better safeguarded.

> 'There has been a welcome recognition that the needs of children should be looked at holistically. It is not enough for them to be securely attached to their parents/carers – they also need to have their health, educational and other needs met. Local authorities do now seem to recognise their responsibilities as "corporate parents" for the children they look after.'[13]

15.8 The improvement of life for children in care remained on the political agenda. The Care Standards Act 2000 created the National Care Standards Commission whose functions include the regulation of voluntary children's homes and registered children's homes and made provision for the inspection of local authority fostering and adoption services.

15.9 In 2006 the Secretary of State for Education and Skills published a Green Paper, *Care Matters: Transforming the Lives of Children and Young People in Care*[14] which stated that although outcomes for children in care have improved in recent years, there remained a significant and widening gap between those and the outcomes for all children. 'This situation is unacceptable and needs to be addressed urgently'.[15] In 2007 the White Paper, *Care Matters: Time for Change*[16] promised that over the next 4 years over £300 million more would be spent to ensure that children in care had a better start in life.

---

[9]   For example, the Report of the Staffordshire Child Care Inquiry, *The Pindown Experience and the Protection of Children* (1991).

[10]   Most notoriously, *Lost in care: report of the tribunal of inquiry into the abuse of children in care in Gwynedd and Clwyd since 1974* (HC 201, 1999–2000).

[11]   (HMSO, 1997) ('The Utting Report'). See also 'Children – Whose responsibility?' [1998] Fam Law 48 based on a lecture by Sir William Utting.

[12]   Stuart and Baines 'Progress on safeguards for children living away from home', summarised in *Findings Ref N54* (Joseph Rowntree Foundation, 2004).

[13]   Ibid, p 3.

[14]   Cm 6932 (2006). See Arnold 'Care Matters' [2007] Fam Law 622.

[15]   *Care Matters: Transforming the Lives of Children and Young People in Care* Executive Summary, at p 5.

[16]   Cm 7137 (2007). See Arnold 'Care Matters' op cit.

'We will clarify the responsibilities of social workers and enable them to devote more one to one time to children in their care. We will ensure that care placements are stable with better training and support for carers who may be facing multiple difficulties ...'[17]

The Children and Young Person Act 2008 was passed on 13 November 2008. It placed a general duty on the Secretary of State to promote the well-being of children in England,[18] amended s 23 of the Children Act 1989 (which governed the provision of accommodation for children who are being looked after by giving priority to placement with a parent or someone with parental responsibility, unless to do so would be impracticable or not in the child's interests) and created other duties in relation to looked after children. These are discussed at **15.45**.

Who is being looked after?

15.10   The number of children in care at any one time is decreasing. Nor are all the children in care living away from home. One in five are living with family and friends.

15.11   As at 31 March 2008, 59,500 children in England were being looked after, a 3% decrease from 2004.[19] The number of children who started being looked after in 2007–2008 had decreased by 4% from 2006–2007 and 8% from 2003–2004.

Gender/age

15.12   More than half (56%) of the children were male. One in 20 were under the age of 1 year, three in 20, aged 1 to 4, slightly more (17%), aged 5 to 9, just over two in five (42%) aged 10 to 15 and just over a fifth (21%) aged 16 and over.

Ethnic background

15.13   Just over three-quarters (78%) of children were of white British/white Irish or other white origin, 8% were of mixed background, 8% black/black British, 5% of Asian/Asian British background and 2% from other ethnic groups. Children from mixed black and mixed ethnic backgrounds are over-represented among children who are looked after and Asian children tend to be under-represented. However, all ethnic groups cease to be looked after at the same rate so it seems that disproportionalities in the care population are because of differences in the rates of starting to be looked after.[20]

---

[17]   *Care Matters: Time for Change*, Foreword.
[18]   Section 7(1) in force from the date of Royal Assent (s 44(1)).
[19]   *Children Looked After in England Year Ending 31 March 2008 Statistical First Release* (Department for Children, Schools and Families).
[20]   Owen and Statham *Disproportionality in Child Welfare* (DCSF, 2009) summarised in Research Brief DCSF-RB124 www.dcsf.gov.uk/research.

Orders

15.14 Just under two-thirds of children (63%, 37,200) were subject to a care order, a decrease of 6% from 2004. Six per cent were subject to a placement order. The main reason why social services were involved was because of abuse or neglect (62%), little changed from 2004.

Placement

15.15 Seven children in 10 (71%) were in a foster placement, a decrease of 3% from 2004. Eight per cent of children were placed with parents and 11% with friends or relatives. A similar percentage lived in children's homes, secure units or hostels. Of the children living with foster carers just under two-thirds were living within their local authority boundary. Just over two-thirds (67%) of children under the age of 16 who had been looked after continuously for at least 2½ years were in the same placement for at least 2 years or were placed for adoption.

Adoption from care

15.16 Three thousand two hundred children who were looked after were adopted in 2007–2008. Four per cent were under the age of 1; 70%, aged 1 to 4; 22%, aged 5 to 9, 4%, aged 10 to 15 and 1%, aged 16 and over. On average children were in their final period of care for 2 years and 7 months before being adopted, little changed since 2002–2003.

Leaving care

15.17 In 2007, 824,100 children that is, two-fifths of all children being looked after, left care. Just over one in 20 (6%) were under the age of 1 (45% of the children of that age being looked after); just under a quarter (23%), aged 1 to 4 (61%); just over one in eight (13%), aged 5 to 9 (31%); nearly a quarter (24%), aged 10 to 15 (23%).

15.18 Of these children over one-eighth (13%) were adopted and just under two in five (39%) returned home to live with parents and relatives. Three percent were made subject to special guardianship orders in favour of former foster carers and 2% in favour of others.

15.19 No statistical information is available to link the children returning to the care of their parents by their age or whether they were subject to care orders. However at the time children aged 16 and over left care, 6% were already living with their parents (compared to two in five in foster homes and three in ten in residential settings) and one in eight left to live with parents or relatives compared to two in five who lived independently.

15.20   Overall, 12% of looked after children are adopted, and 18% cease being looked after by returning to their parents.[21] Return to parents varies much more by ethnic group than does being adopted. Children from the Pakistani, Indian and Bangladeshi ethnic groups are much more likely to be returned to their parents than Chinese, black African, black Caribbean children or those categorised 'Other'. For children from the mixed ethnic groups, the rates of return to their parents were between these two patterns. It is not possible to tell just from the statistics why there were such big differences in the rates at which children looked after were returned to their parents. Mixed ethnicity and the white British children are the most likely to be adopted and black children and those of Pakistani and Bangladeshi origin are least likely to be adopted.[22]

Adoption or fostering?

Profile of children who are adopted rather than long-term fostered

15.21   The *Prime Minister's Review: Adoption*[23] compared children who were adopted with those who were looked after.

15.22   Children who are looked after were becoming younger and more challenging. The population was split between those experiencing a few weeks of care and those staying for much longer. Forty per cent of those leaving care in 1998–1999 had been looked after for 8 weeks or less. The children experienced a lower chance of successfully returning home the longer they remained in care. A child who had been in care for 6 months or more had a 60% chance of remaining in care for 4 years or more (and most likely until 16). By 15–18 months their chance of remaining in care had stabilised at around 80%.

15.23   Compared to the rest of children who were being looked after, children who were adopted were:

- more likely to be female
  There was little difference in the proportion of each gender being adopted (51% male and 49% female) but the proportion of boys in the looked after population was greater (55% and 45%).

- more likely to be white
  Nine in ten were white, 7% of mixed parentage, 2% were black and 1% were Asian. Non-whites were estimated to make up about 17% of the looked-after child population.

- were likely to be part of sibling groups, but placed apart

---

[21]   The difference between this figure and 38% cited above is not explained by Owen and Statham. It may reflect the fact that the higher figure includes children going to live with relatives or that it includes children ceasing to be looked after because of their age.

[22]   Owen and Statham *Disproportionality in Child Welfare* op cit.

[23]   (PIU, 2000) at para 2.10.

A fifth of children adopted from care in 1998–1999 had no birth siblings, just under a quarter (24%) had one and more than half had two or more. However, nearly two-thirds (64%) of placements for adoption were single child placements, 30% were placements of sibling groups of two and 7% were of three or more. Siblings were frequently placed apart.

- becoming younger and had an average age lower than that of the looked after population

    The average age had fallen from 5 years 9 months in 1995 to 4 years 4 months in 1999. Relatively few children over 10 were adopted from care.

- more likely to enter care at a younger age than the general looked after population

- more challenging than the rest of children being looked after.

    Statistics in 1996 suggested that 44% of children adopted from care had entered care because of abuse, neglect or risk, compared to 17% of the number of children ceasing to be looked after that year.

Why was the choice made?

15.24 The perceptions of social workers as to what is best or achievable for the child will influence both their recommendations to the court and the profile of children for whom the plan is long-term fostering.

15.25 In 2000 Lowe and Murch investigated the factors which determine a local authority's decision to pursue adoption rather than long-term fostering for children for whom returning to their birth families was no longer thought possible.[24] Their sample consisted of 113 children aged 12 or under who had been looked after by one of six authorities for at least a year.

15.26 The **age** of the child was the single most influential and statistically significant factor. Children aged 1–4 were twice as likely to be the subject of an adoption plan as for long-term fostering and conversely, for children aged 5–9, long-term fostering was four times more likely to be the plan than adoption. Practices however varied between authorities. Social workers generally considered the upper age limit for adoption as 9–11 years but some said 7–9.

15.27 **Gender** was not a conscious consideration but 57% of girls were found to be the subject of plans for adoption compared with 41% of boys. Four in five girls aged 1–4 years had adoption as their plan as against just over 53% of boys.

15.28 The third main factor, but with only marginal statistical significance, was the amount of **contact** retained with the children's mothers. The older the child, the more significant the relationship with their birth mother and the

---

[24] *The Plan for the Child: Adoption or Long-term Fostering* (BAAF, 2001).

greater the probability that long-term fostering would be the plan. Eighty-five per cent of children aged 5–9 with ongoing direct contact with their mother had long-term fostering as their plan compared with 69% of children with no or only indirect contact. Just under three in 10 children aged 1–4 with ongoing contact were subject to a plan for long-term fostering compared with a quarter with indirect or no contact.

15.29 Other less influential factors favouring long-term fostering included **ethnicity and culture**. Black and minority ethnic children were more likely (65%) than white children (47%) to have long-term fostering as their plan. The plan for children with **emotional or behavioural problems** was twice as likely to be long-term fostering than adoption.[25] The reasons for choosing long-term fostering were primarily related to the child's perceived inability to form attachments and the level of therapeutic and possibly financial support required by the carer. Children who had suffered **physical or sexual** abuse were nearly twice as likely to have a long-term fostering plan.

15.30 It was unclear whether being part of a **sibling group** influenced the decision. Despite expressed preferences to keep siblings together it was not unusual for the plan for the youngest sibling to be adoption, with an older child to have long-term fostering as his plan. Some authorities found it as hard to find a foster home for three or four siblings as to find an adoptive home.

15.31 The **child's wishes and feelings** were stated by social workers as being an important factor and were the third most frequently stated reason for long-term fostering and the fourth for adoption. However, the views of only one-third of children were taken into account. In just over two in five cases the child was said to be too young or unable because of a disability to express an opinion.

15.32 The authors comment that the issues surrounding children who are 'hard to place' are inextricably linked with the availability of resources and the degree of support that could be offered.

'It might also be added that the quite understandable reluctance to plan for adoption for "hard to place" children pays no heed to whether the alternative of long-term fostering offers a better or at least no worse an option for the child.'[26]

---

[25] The authors advise that this figure should be treated with caution because of a lack of consistency in the use of terms and it being unclear how severe the conditions were.
[26] Ibid, at p 143.

LOCAL AUTHORITY STATUS

15.33 A child is 'looked after' by a local authority if provided with accommodation under s 20 of the Children Act 1989 or is in their care pursuant to a care order.[27]

15.34 A local authority has a duty to provide accommodation for a child who appears to require accommodation as a result of:

- there being no person who has parental responsibility for him;

- his being lost or having been abandoned; or

- the person who has been caring for him being prevented (whether or not permanently and for whatever reason) from providing him with accommodation or care.[28]

15.35 The authority may not provide accommodation under s 20 if a person who has parental responsibility is willing and able to provide accommodation or arrange for it to be provided[29] and a person with parental responsibility may remove the child at any time from accommodation the authority provides.[30]

Parental responsibility

The accommodated child

15.36 Where a child is accommodated, the local authority does not have parental responsibility but is able to exercise its powers under s 22 having ascertained, so far as is reasonably practicable, amongst other matters the wishes and feelings of the parents and any other person who has parental responsibility.[31] A person with parental responsibility who disagrees, can remove the child.

The child subject to a care order

15.37 In contrast, where a child is subject to a care order, the authority has parental responsibility. This is shared with anyone else who has parental responsibility but the authority has the power to determine the extent to which any parent, special guardian, guardian or any one with parental responsibility can exercise parental responsibility if it is satisfied that it is necessary to do so in order to protect or safeguard the child's welfare.[32]

---

[27] CA 1989, s 22(1). In this chapter 'looked after' and 'in care' are used synonymously. Where children are subject to a care order, this is made clear in the text.
[28] CA 1989, s 20(1).
[29] Ibid, s 20(7).
[30] Ibid, s 20(8).
[31] Ibid, s 23(4).
[32] Ibid, s 33(3) and (4).

15.38   Before making any decision the authority has, so far as is reasonably practicable, to ascertain the wishes and feelings of:

- the child;

- his parents;

- any other person who has parental responsibility;

- any other person whose wishes and feelings it considers to be relevant.[33]

15.39   It is the local authority and, not, for example, the child's foster carer, who has parental responsibility although a foster carer may be someone whom the authority considers it appropriate to consult under s 22(4) before exercising responsibility.

THE ROLE OF THE COURT

15.40   Once a final care order is made, control of decisions about the child passes to the local authority. In some cases there may be a tension between this and the court's natural desire to influence certain decisions, for example whether the child should remain with his current foster carer. The key to resolving the tension is the 'care plan'.

15.41   In proceedings under s 31 of the Children Act 1989 in which a care order might be made, the authority has to prepare and then keep under review, revising as required, a care plan for the future care of the child, 'a document of key importance'.[34] It must contain prescribed information.[35]

15.42   The court has to consider the plan before making a care order.[36] In some cases the court will accept the plan. In others the plan may seem inchoate or there are uncertainties, for example, whether the current foster carer is willing to become the child's long-term foster carer, which may be resolved in a relatively brief period of time. In such cases, a limited period of 'planned and purposeful' delay before making a final order can be justified.[37]

> 'Despite all the inevitable uncertainties, when deciding whether to make a care order the court should normally have before it a care plan which is sufficiently firm and particularised for all concerned to have a reasonably clear picture of the

---

[33]   CA 1989, s 22(4).

[34]   *Re S (Minors) (Care Order: Implementation of Care Plan); Re W (Minors) (Care Order: Adequacy of Care Plan)* [2002] UKHL 10, [2002] 1 FLR 815 per Lord Nicholls of Birkenhead at [91].

[35]   Currently LAC (99)29 *Care Plans and Care Proceedings under the Children Act 1989.*

[36]   CA 1989, s 31(3A).

[37]   *Re S (Minors) (Care Order: Implementation of Care Plan); Re W (Minors) (Care Order: Adequacy of Care Plan)* [2002] UKHL 10, [2002] 1 FLR 815 at [95].

likely way ahead for the child for the foreseeable future. The degree of firmness to be expected, as well as the amount of detail in the plan, will vary from case to case depending on how far the local authority can foresee what will be best for the child at that time.'[38]

15.43 However, the making of an interim care order should not be used as a means by which the court may continue to exercise a supervisory role over the local authority in cases where it is in the best interests of a child that a final care order should be made. Once a final care order is made, the resolution of the remaining uncertainties will be a matter for the authority, not the court.[39]

15.44 Nor can the court impose conditions on a care order,[40] direct that a guardian should continue to be involved[41] or make a specific issue order or invoke the inherent jurisdiction of the High Court for the purpose of controlling a local authority's power to make decisions under Part III of the Act.[42]

'The Act delineated the boundary of responsibility with complete clarity. Where a care order is made the responsibility for the child's care is with the authority rather than the court. The court retains no supervisory role, monitoring the authority's discharge of its responsibilities. That was the intention of Parliament.'[43]

A study of how care plans were implemented[44] found that of 100 cases studied, 60 of the children had their placement plans met within 21 months. Kinship care (78%) had the highest proportion of fulfilled plans followed by foster care (68%) and adoption (58%). The lowest rate was for returning or maintaining children at home (41%). After 21 months, 11 of the 40 children whose plans had not been met moved twice and the rest, up to six times or more.

---

[38] [2002] UKHL 10, [2002] 1 FLR 815 at [99].

[39] Ibid, at [90].

[40] *Re T (A Minor) (Care Order: Conditions)* [1994] 2 FLR 423.

[41] *Kent CC v C* [1993] 1 FLR 308.

[42] CA 1989, s 9(5)(b), s 100(2); *Re S (Minors) (Care Order: Implementation of Care Plan); Re W (Minors) (Care Order: Adequacy of Care Plan)* [2002] UKHL 10, [2002] 1 FLR 815 at [25] per Lord Nicholls of Birkenhead and [109] per Lord Mackay of Clashfern. For academic criticism of this decision see Fortin *Children's Rights and the Developing Law* (Cambridge University Press, 2nd edn, 2003), at pp 491–494.

[43] *Re S (Minors) (Care Order: Implementation of Care Plan); Re W (Minors) (Care Order: Adequacy of Care Plan)* [2002] UKHL 10, [2002] 1 FLR 815 at [25].

[44] Harwin and Morag 'The implementation of care plans and its relationship to children's welfare' [2003] CFLQ 71. See also Harwin and Owen 'A Study of Care Plans and Their Implementation and Relevance for *Re W and B and W (Care Plan)*' in Thorpe and Cowton (eds) *Delight and Dole: The Children Act 10 Years On* (Family Law, 2002).

THE DUTY OF THE LOCAL AUTHORITY

15.45 It is the duty of the local authority looking after a child:

- to safeguard and promote his welfare, including in particular a duty to promote his educational achievement; and

- to make such use of services available for children cared for by their own parents as appears to the authority reasonable in his case.[45]

This duty is not an absolute one. An authority may exercise its powers in a manner not consistent with it if it appears to them necessary for the purpose of protecting members of the public.[46]

15.46 Before making a decision, the authority has to ascertain the wishes and feelings so far as is practicable of those persons listed in s 22(4), namely:

- the child;

- his parents;

- any person who is not a parent of his but who has parental responsibility for him; and

- any other person whose wishes and feelings the authority consider to be relevant,

and have regard to them and to the child's religious persuasion, racial origin and cultural and linguistic background (for which see **6.103**).

Article 8

15.47 The local authority is required to respect the right of the child and parents to family life even after the welfare of the child has required that the child is taken into care.

> 'The margin of appreciation so to be accorded to the competent national authorities will vary in the light of the nature of the issues and the seriousness of the interests at stake. Thus, the [European Court of Human Rights] recognises that the authorities enjoy a wide margin of appreciation in assessing the necessity of taking a child into care. However, a stricter scrutiny is called for both of any further limitations, such as restrictions placed by those authorities on parental rights and access, and of any legal safeguards designed to secure an effective protection of the right of parents and children to respect for their family life. Such

---

[45]   CA 1989, s 22(3) and (4) as amended by Children Act 2004, s 52.
[46]   CA 1989, s 22(6).

further limitations entail the danger that the family relations between the parents and a young child are effectively curtailed.'[47]

15.48 It is sometimes argued that the taking of a child in care should normally be regarded as a temporary measure but the European Court of Human Rights in *Johansen v Norway*[48] made it clear that this may give way to the welfare needs of the individual child.

'The Court considers that taking a child into care should normally be regarded as a temporary measure to be discontinued as soon as circumstances permit and that any measures of implementation of temporary care should be consistent with the ultimate aim of reuniting the natural parent and the child (see, in particular, *Olson v Sweden No 1*)[49]. In this regard, a fair balance has to be struck between the interests of the child in remaining in public care and those of the parent in being reunited with the child (see, for instance, *Olson v Sweden No 2*[50] and *Hokkanen v Finland*[51]). In carrying out this balancing exercise, the Court will attach particular importance to the best interests of the child, which, depending on their nature and seriousness, may override those of the parent. In particular, as suggested by the Government, the parent cannot be entitled under Article 8 of the Convention (art 8) to have such measures taken as would harm the child's health and development.'[52]

STATUTORY STRUCTURE

15.49 The scheme regulating the care of looked after children is contained in ss 22–30 and 34 of the Children Act 1989 and various statutory regulations, the most important of which for current purposes are the Review of Children's Cases Regulations 1991[53] as amended by the Review of Children's Cases (Amendment) (England) Regulations 2004,[54] Arrangements for Placement of Children (General) Regulations 1991,[55] Placement of Children with Parents etc Regulations 1991,[56] Children's Homes Regulations 2001,[57] Contact With Children Regulations 1991,[58] Children (Leaving Care) (England) Regulations 2001[59] and the Review of Children's Cases Regulations 1991.[60]

---

[47] *Johansen v Norway* [1996] 23 EHRR 33.
[48] Ibid.
[49] 10465/83 [1988] ECHR 2 at [81].
[50] 13441/87 [1992] ECHR 75.
[51] 19823/92 [1994] ECHR 32 at [55].
[52] Ibid.
[53] SI 1991/895.
[54] SI 2004/1419.
[55] SI 1991/1890.
[56] SI 1991/1893.
[57] SI 2001/3967.
[58] SI 1991/1891.
[59] SI 2001/2874.
[60] SI 1991/1895.

15.50 The scheme is subject to Departmental Guidance: *The Children Act 1989 Guidance and Regulations* Vol 3 *Family Placements* and Vol 4 *Residential Care*[61] and Independent Reviewing Officers Guidance.[62] This Guidance is issued under s 7 of the Local Authority Services Act 1970[63] and therefore there is a requirement that it must be complied with unless local circumstances indicate exceptional reasons which justify a variation.

Planning and monitoring

LAC Reviews

15.51 A child who is made subject to a final or interim care order will have a formal care plan by virtue of s 31A (see **15.40**). A child who is accommodated under s 20 will have one by virtue of reg 3 of the Arrangements for Placement of Children Regulations 1991. Either child's case must be reviewed ('Looked after Care Review' or 'LAC') within 4 weeks of the date when they begin to be looked after; the second review must be carried out no later than another 3 months and thereafter 6 monthly.[64]

15.52 The purpose of the LAC review is to ensure that the child's welfare is safeguarded and promoted in the most effective way throughout the period he is looked after or accommodated.[65] Schedule 1 of the Review of Children's Cases Regulations 1991 lists the elements to be included in each review and Sch 2 the considerations to which the authority must have regard. These include:

- the immediate and long-term arrangements for looking after the child;[66]

- whether plans need to be made for a permanent substitute family;[67]

- the need for any changes to contact;[68]

- the child's educational needs and progress[69] including any need for assessments in respect of special educational needs;[70]

- whether arrangements need to be made for the time when the child ceases to be looked after;[71] and

---

[61]   (HMSO, 1994).
[62]   (DES, 2004).
[63]   See **11.22**.
[64]   Review of Children's Cases Regulations 1991 (SI 1991/1895), reg 3.
[65]   *Guidance Family Placements* at para 8.1.
[66]   Review of Children's Cases Regulations 1991 (SI 1991/1895), Sch 1, para 1, Sch 2, para 5.
[67]   Ibid, Sch 2, para 9.
[68]   Ibid, Sch 2, para 3.
[69]   Ibid, Sch 2, para 7.
[70]   Ibid, Sch 2, para 4.
[71]   Ibid, Sch 2, para 8.

- considering whether to apply to discharge any care order.[72]

15.53 Schedule 3 lists the health considerations to which regard must be had.

15.54 One of the key principles of the Children Act 1989 is that authorities should work in partnership with parents and with the child himself where he is of sufficient understanding provided this approach will not prejudice his welfare.[73] When conducting a review the authority, unless it is not reasonably practical to do so, must seek and take into account the views of the child, his parents, anyone else with parental responsibility and any other person whose views the authority considers to be relevant.[74] Such a person must include the independent reviewing officer[75] (see **15.59**), should include the child's carer and may include, for example, the child's GP, health visitor, or school teacher.[76] They must also be told of the result of the review.[77]

15.55 Whenever serious decisions have to be taken about the child other than as part of the scheme of regular reviews, for example at a permanency planning meeting,[78] in order to comply with Art 8(1) of the European Convention on Human Rights and s 6(1) of the Human Rights Act 1998, the decision making progress must be such as to secure that the views and interests of the parents are made known and are taken into account and that parents are able to exercise any remedies available to them.[79]

Independent visitor

15.56 When it appears to a local authority that communication between a looked-after child and his parents or anyone else with parental responsibility has been infrequent or the child has not been visited in the last 12 months, it has a duty to consider whether it would be in the child's best interests for an independent person to be appointed his visitor.[80] The independent visitor has the duty of 'visiting, advising and befriending' the child.[81]

15.57 The independent visitor may be a person whose views should be considered by a review.[82]

---

[72]   Review of Children's Cases Regulations 1991 (SI 1991/1895), Sch 2, para 1.
[73]   *Guidance Family Placements* at para 2.10.
[74]   Review of Children's Cases Regulations 1991 (SI 1991/1895), reg 7(1).
[75]   Ibid, reg 2A.
[76]   *Guidance Family Placements* at para 8.17.
[77]   Review of Children's Cases Regulations 1991 (SI 1991/1895), reg 7(2).
[78]   See, for example, *Re M (Care: Challenging Decisions By Local Authority)* [2001] 2 FLR 1300, *Re G (Care: Challenge to Local Authority's Decision)* [2003] EWHC 551(Fam), [2003] 2 FLR 42.
[79]   *R v United Kingdom* (1991) 13 EHRR 457, ECHR, *Re M (Care: Challenging Decisions By Local Authority)* [2001] 2 FLR 1300.
[80]   CA 1989, Sch 2, para 17(1).
[81]   Ibid, Sch 2, para 17(2) and see *Guidance Family Placements* Chapter 7.
[82]   Ibid at para 8.17.

15.58 Children who have independent visitors consider them to be very important – 'someone who chooses to spend time with them rather than a paid professional'.[83]

Independent reviewing officers

15.59 Concern about the court having no power to keep care plans under review (see **15.44**) resulted in the Review of Children's Cases Regulations 1991 being amended by the Review of Children's Cases (Amendment) (England) Regulations 2004 to introduce a duty to appoint an independent reviewing officer (IRO) in each case to chair reviews, monitor the performance of the authority's functions in relation to the child and to refer the case to the Children and Family Court Advisory and Support Service (CAFCASS) if the reviewing officer considers it appropriate.[84] The authority must inform the IRO of any significant failure to make arrangements in accordance with the Regulations or significant change in circumstances.[85]

15.60 The independent visitor has no formal standing in relation to the child.[86]

15.61 Wherever possible, the IRO is supposed to attempt to resolve a problem concerning the child's care plan by negotiation, including contacting the team responsible for the child and expediting a solution. When a problem is identified, the IRO should make a decision about the timescale in which the problem should be resolved, and make this clear to the local authority at each stage of the resolution process. If resolution proves unsuccessful, the IRO has to take the case to senior management, to the Assistant Director, the Director and ultimately, if necessary, to the Chief Executive. If a satisfactory resolution is still not obtained and there is a danger of the child's human rights being breached, the IRO should consider whether to refer the case to CAFCASS, who will consider legal action.[87] However, referrals to CAFCASS should be only a matter of last resort.[88]

15.62 Referrals to CAFCASS are made to CAFCASS Legal who may assist parents, relatives or the guardian in the original institute legal proceedings such as further family proceedings (for example, for the discharge of a care order or for contact), a freestanding application under the Human Rights Act 1998 or an application for judicial review.[89]

---

[83]   *Care Matters: Transforming the Lives of Children and Young People in Care* op cit at para 3.35.

[84]   Review of Children's Cases Regulations 1991 (SI 1991/1985), reg 2A. See also Posner 'IROs: Starred Milestones by Any Other Name?' [2005] Fam Law 487 and Frank 'Children in Care – is the Legal Profession Doing Enough?' [2007] Fam Law 642.

[85]   Review of Children's Cases Regulations 1991 (SI 1991/1895), reg 8A.

[86]   Although she might be regarding as having sufficient interest to seek judicial review.

[87]   *Independent Reviewing Officers Guidance* op cit.

[88]   *CAFCASS Practice Note* [2005] Fam Law 60.

[89]   See, for example, *S (A Child Acting By the Official Solicitor) v Rochdale MBC and The Independent Reviewing Officer* [2008] EWHC 3283 (Fam), [2009] 1 FLR 1090.

15.63 CAFCASS Legal has issued a Practice Note[90] on how it approaches cases.

15.64 When IROs were introduced in 2004 there was concern that they might not prove effective.[91] The concerns were born out. In the first 12 months only seven queries were made by IROs to CAFCASS Legal ranging from a threat by an authority to withdraw a taxi service to take a child to school to a dispute with the Housing Department. There were no formal referrals.[92]

15.65 In 2007, the White Paper, *Care Matters: Time for Change*[93] stated that:

'There is widespread concern that the IRO role is not being carried out effectively across all local authorities and that they are not challenging decisions made by local authorities even in cases where professional practice is obviously poor and not in young people's interests.'[94]

It proposed that the role would be 'significantly' strengthened so that each IRO was expected to fulfill their role with 'credibility and independence'.

Criticism

15.66 The Green Paper, *Care Matters: Transforming the Lives of Children and Young People in Care*[95] stated that although the vast majority of children already had care plans, many do not know that their plan exists or what it contains.

'It is vital, especially for the many children who change placements or social workers, that there is a care plan which addresses all the aspects of their lives and which children have been genuinely involved in drawing up.'

The White Paper stated that a composite of Regulations and new Guidance will be issued.

ACCOMMODATION

15.67 The current regime for accommodating children has recently been amended. From a date to be determined, s 23 of the Children Act 1989 and the Placement of Children with Parents etc Regulations 1991 will be replaced by ss 22A–22D and new Regulations.

---

90 Op cit, amended in 2007.
91 See Posner 'IROs: Starred Milestones by Any Other Name?' op cit at p 490.
92 Hinchcliffe 'CAFCASS and the Work of The Independent Reviewing Officers' [2007] Fam Law 748.
93 op cit.
94 op cit at para 7.28. See also *S (A Child Acting By the Official Solicitor) v Rochdale MBC and The Independent Reviewing Officer* [2008] EWHC 3283 (Fam), [2009] 1 FLR 1090.
95 op cit at paras 3.40–3.41.

Current regime

15.68 By virtue of s 23(2) the authority looking after a child has to provide him with accommodation by:

- placing him with:
  - a family (known as a local authority foster parent unless the child's parent, someone else with parental responsibility or, where in care, a person in whose favour a residence order was in force immediately before the care order was made[96]);
  - a relative of his;
  - any other suitable person;

- placing him in an appropriate children's home;

- making such other arrangements as seem appropriate.

15.69 So far as is reasonably practicable and consistent with the child's welfare the authority must secure that:

- the accommodation is near his home; and

- if accommodation is also being provided for a sibling, that they are accommodated together.[97]

However, the authority may arrange for the child to live outside England and Wales with the permission of the court if the child is in care, or the consent of those with parental responsibility if the child is looked after.[98]

15.70 Where the child is disabled the authority shall so far as is reasonably practicable, secure that the accommodation 'is not unsuitable to his particular needs'.[99]

15.71 The Placement of Children with Parents etc Regulations 1991 require that the authority must satisfy themselves that the placement is the most suitable having regard to all the circumstances.[100] Before making the decision the authority has to make all necessary enquiries into the health of the child, the educational and social needs of the child, the suitability of the person with whom it is proposed to place the child[101] and all other members of the household over the age of 16 and the suitability of the accommodation.[102] Thereafter the authority has a continuous duty to satisfy themselves that the

---

[96]   CA 1989, s 23(4).

[97]   Ibid, s 23(7).

[98]   Ibid, Sch 2, para 19.

[99]   Ibid, s 23(8).

[100] Placement of Children with Parents etc Regulations 1991 (SI 1991/1893), reg 4.

[101] Taking into account so far as is practicable the matters set out in ibid, Sch 1 (reg 3(2)).

[102] Placement of Children with Parents etc Regulations 1991 (SI 1991/1893), reg 3.

welfare of the child is appropriately met by the placement.[103] If it appears to the authority the placement no longer accords with its duty towards the child under s 22(3) or would prejudice the child's safety, it must terminate the placement and remove the child.[104]

15.72 The authority has to provide such advice and assistance to the carer as is necessary and make arrangements for the child to be visited within 1 week of placement, at intervals of not less than 6 weeks for the first year and thereafter at intervals of not less than 3 months and whenever the child or carer reasonably requests.[105]

15.73 If the carer has parental responsibility that responsibility can continue to be exercised subject to the power of the authority to restrict it under s 33(3) if the child is subject to a care order (see **16.39**). However, a local authority foster carer has no such right and can take only such decisions as the authority permits under the placement agreement.[106]

Residential homes

15.74 Arrangements for residential homes are regulated by the Children's Homes Regulations 2001.

15.75 The registered person responsible for the home is under a duty to ensure that the home is so conducted as to 'promote and make proper provision for the welfare of the children' accommodated there and for their care, education, supervision and, where appropriate, treatment.[107]

15.76 Each child has to have a placement plan setting out on a day-to-day basis how he will be cared for and his welfare safeguarded and promoted, the arrangements for his health care, education and contact with his parents, relatives and friends.[108]

Criticism of the current regime

15.77 The Green Paper, *Care Matters: Transforming the Lives of Children and Young People in Care*[109] praised both foster carers and residential care workers who devoted 'huge energy and commitment' to the children in their care. In a recent report,[110] over half of the children in care who were asked said that their

---

[103] Ibid, reg 9.
[104] Ibid, reg 11.
[105] Ibid.
[106] See ibid, reg 7 and Sch 2.
[107] Children's Homes Regulations 2001 (SI 2001/3967), reg 11.
[108] Ibid, reg 12.
[109] op cit at paras 4.3–4.13.
[110] *Placements, Decisions and Reviews: A Child's View Report* (Children's Rights Director, 2006).

present placement was definitely the right one for them. 'However, [said the Green Paper] sadly this is not the case for all children in care.'[111]

15.78 Far too many found themselves in placements which do not meet their needs, resulting in a high level of instability. Around 1 in 10 of the children who ceased to be in care in 2005 had nine or more placements while in care, and only 65% of children who had been in care for over 2½ years had been in the same placement for 2 years or more. The White Paper, *Adoption a New Approach*[112] reported that 18% experience three or more placements a year.

15.79 The Green Paper reported that a lack of effective planning and 'market management' could lead to children being placed outside their home authority. Nearly a third of children in care were in placements outside the local authority area which cares for them. For some children, for example, with very complex needs who may need specialist therapeutic residential provision, being placed away from their home area may be appropriate. However, most children in care want to remain in the area which is most familiar to them. Children placed far away from home were less likely to succeed in education (though in some cases this will reflect the more complex needs of the child rather than being solely a consequence of the distance from home). Just over half (55%) of children placed out of authority fail to achieve any GCSEs compared to under half (48%) of those in their local authority.

15.80 It concluded that:

'It is vital that every child is given a choice of placements which meet their needs, create a good learning environment and offer value for money.'

Amended regime

15.81 As a result of the White Paper s 8 of the Children and Young Persons Act 2008 has, from a date to be appointed, revoked s 23 and substituted ss 22A–22D.

15.82 Unless to do so would not be consistent with the child's welfare or it would not be reasonably practicable,[113] the authority must make arrangements for the child to live with:

- a parent;

- someone who has parental responsibility for the child;

- where the child is in care, a person in whose favour a residence order was in force immediately before the care order was made.[114]

---

[111]   *Placements, Decisions and Reviews: A Child's View Report* op cit at para 4.4.
[112]   Cm 5017 (2000) at para 2.3.
[113]   CA 1989, s 22C(4).
[114]   Ibid, s 23C(2) and (3).

15.83 If the authority is unable to make such arrangements, they must place the child in the most appropriate placement available:

- with an individual who is the child's relative, friend or other person connected with the child who is also a local authority foster parent; or

- with a local authority foster parent who does not fall within the previous category; or

- in a registered children's home; or

- in accordance with other arrangements which must comply with regulations.[115]

15.84 When making the arrangements set out in s 22C(6) preference must be given to an individual who is the child's relative, friend or other person connected with the child who is also a local authority foster parent.[116] In addition such a placement must ensure that:

- it allows the child to live near his home;

- it does not disrupt his education or training;

- it enables the child to live with any sibling for whom the authority is also providing accommodation;

- if the child is disabled, the accommodation is suitable for the child's particular needs.[117]

15.85 Unless it is not reasonably practicable, the 'most appropriate accommodation' must be within the local authority's area.[118]

CONTACT

15.86 The making of a care order – but not the accommodation of a child under s 20 – automatically discharges any order for contact made under s 8 of the Children Act 1989.[119]

15.87 When a child is in care, the local authority has to allow the child reasonable contact with his parents, any guardian or special guardian, any person who has parental responsibility by virtue of s 4A (see **14.71**) and, where a residence order or an order for care under the inherent jurisdiction of the

---

[115] CA 1989, s 22C(6).
[116] Ibid, s 22C(7)(a).
[117] Ibid, s 23C(8).
[118] Ibid, s 23C(7) and (9).
[119] Ibid, s 91(2).

High Court was in force immediately before the care order was made, the person in whose favour the order was made.[120]

15.88   In addition the court may make a contact order in favour of anyone mentioned above or who has leave.[121]

15.89   Notwithstanding the above the authority may, as a matter of urgency, refuse contact for a period of not more than 7 days if it considers it necessary in order to safeguard or promote the child's welfare.[122]

15.90   Contact is discussed in more detail in Chapter 13.

DUTIES WHEN THE CHILD LEAVES CARE

15.91   The average age that young people leave home is 24 but a young person in care will usually leave at 18. Over a quarter (27%) leave at 16.[123]

15.92   Detailed provision is made for preparing young people for leaving care and for supporting them for a period thereafter.

15.93   Under para 19A of Sch 2 to the Children Act 1989 the local authority looking after a child has a duty to advise, assist and befriend him 'with a view to promoting his welfare when they have ceased to look after him'.

15.94   Departmental Guidance,[124] states that the principles underlying preparation for leaving care should reflect good child care practice generally, taking into account the principles of the Children Act 1989. Services must take into account the lengthy process of transition from childhood to adulthood and reflect the gradual transition from dependence to independence.

> 'The support provided should be, broadly, the support that a good parent might be expected to give. The young person should be fully involved and his parents, if not estranged from him, should be invited to help formulate the plan. Preparation for leaving care should help to develop a young person's capacity to make satisfactory relationships, develop his self-esteem and enable him to acquire the necessary practical skills for independent living.'

It should be planned in conjunction with all other interested agencies, for example, education and housing.

---

[120]   CA 1989, s 34(1).
[121]   Ibid, s 34(2).
[122]   Ibid, s 34(6). See also Contact with Children Regulations 1991 (SI 1991/1891).
[123]   White Paper, *Care Matters: Time for Change* op cit Ch 6.
[124]   The Children Act 1989 Guidance and Regulations Vol 3 Family Placements at para 9.18, and Vol 4 Residential Care at para 7.18.

15.95   Where the young person is aged 16 or 17 and has been looked after for at least 13 weeks between the ages of 14 and 16 (but excluding those looked after only for periods of short-term) ('an eligible child') the local authority has to carry out an assessment of his needs with a view to determining what advice, assistance and support it would be appropriate to provide both while they are looking after him and afterwards.[125] After the assessment, a 'Pathway Plan' has to be prepared and kept under review[126] which sets out the manner in which the authority proposes to meet the needs of the child.[127] In addition the authority has to ensure that the child has a personal adviser.

15.96   When an 'eligible child' leaves care and is 16 or 17 ('a relevant child') it is the duty of the local authority to take reasonable steps to keep in touch with him and, if he does not have one, to appoint a personal adviser and prepare a Pathway Plan.[128] The authority remains under a duty to safeguard and promote the child's welfare and, unless it is satisfied that his welfare does not require it, to support him by maintaining him, providing him with or maintaining him in suitable accommodation and support in relation to education, training and support.[129]

15.97   When a 'relevant child' reaches the age of 18, he becomes known as 'a former relevant child'.[130] The authority's duties to take reasonable steps or re-establish contact, and in relation to the Pathway plan and personal adviser, continue until he is 21.[131] In addition, to the extent that his welfare requires it, the authority is under a duty to give advice and assistance by either contributing to expenses incurred by living near the place where he will be employed or seeking employment, receiving education or training, or making a grant to enable him to meet expenses associated with education or training and other assistance.[132] If the young person's Pathway Plan sets out a programme of education beyond the age of 20 the duty to provide assistance with education or training will continue for so long as the education or training continues.[133]

15.98   Additional duties in relation to people who have left care are set out in ss 24–24C.

---

[125]   CA 1989, Sch 2, para 19B (2) and (4) and the Children (Leaving Care) (England) Regulations 2001 (SI 2001/2874), reg 3(1) and (3). For the nature of the assessment, see regs 5–7.
[126]   CA 1989, Sch 2, para 19B(4) and (5).
[127]   Children (Leaving Care) (England) Regulations 2001 (SI 2001/2874), reg 8.
[128]   CA 1989, s 23B.
[129]   Ibid, s 23B(8) and Children (Leaving Care) (England) Regulations 2001 (SI 2001/2874), reg 11.
[130]   CA 1989, s 23C.
[131]   Ibid, s 23C(2) and (3).
[132]   Ibid, ss 23C(4), 24B.
[133]   Ibid, s 23C(7).

Criticism

15.99   The Green Paper, *Care Matters: Transforming the Lives of Children and Young People in Care*[134] stated that:

> 'Too many young people in care are forced to enter adult life before they are ready. 28% still leave care at 16 at a time when most young people are focused on their education, not on having to learn to fend for themselves. Young people have told us clearly that they are not being given the kind of support they need at this age.'

15.100   A report[135] by the Children's Rights Director found that many young people believed that they were made to leave care at the wrong time, with poor planning made for their accommodation and little practical advice. For example, one said 'You are given a flat, given your money and left to get on with it.'

15.101   Data on the outcomes of young people after leaving care showed that only about three-fifths (59%) of care leavers are in education, employment or training compared to nearly nine-tenths (87%) of all young people at 18 to 19. National and local initiatives had led to an increase in participation in employment and training from under half (46%) in 2002 to three-fifths (59%) in 2005:

> 'but the fact remains that this leaves a vast gap between the participation rate of young people in care and that of all young people.'[136]

15.102   The Green Paper continued:

> 'It is enormously important to young people that they should enter adult life when they are ready. We know from research evidence both in this country and elsewhere that staying in a family environment for longer can make all the difference. Given the choice, many young people would want to remain with a family for longer, making the bridge to independent living easier for them.'[137]

Reform

15.103   The White Paper, *Care Matters: Time for Change*[138] states that the Government will create a pilot scheme to allow young people who have established familial relationships with their foster carers to stay with them until the age of 21. In addition young people will have greater involvement in deciding when they leave care and personal advisers will be provided until the age of 21 and, if requested up to 25.[139] Local authorities will be required to provide a minimum of £2,000 for all young people in care who go to university.

---

[134]   op cit at para 7.1.
[135]   *Young People's Views on Leaving Care* (Children's Rights Director, 2006).
[136]   *Care Matters: Transforming the Lives of Children and Young People in Care* op cit at para 7.7.
[137]   Ibid, at paras 7.8–7.9.
[138]   op cit at Chapter 6.
[139]   Now enacted: Children and Young Persons Act 2008, s 23 from a date to be appointed.

CHILDREN RETURNING HOME

15.104 As noted at **15.18** many children return home before the age of 18. Although the likelihood of returning home declines sharply after about 6 months of being looked after, Biehal states that it is a misconception to think that the length of time in care in itself reduces the chance of rehabilitation. 'Research evidence from the United States and the United Kingdom suggests that a variety of factors are related to the length of time that children remain looked after, including the characteristics and attitudes of parents and children, the reasons for placement and the characteristics of services. Variations in rates of discharge between local authorities may also be related to local thresholds for entry to care'.[140]

15.105 A review of research from the United States and the United Kingdom by Biehal[141] found that children who are looked after because of parental illness (a diminishing group) are most likely to be reunited with their families quickly followed by those with behavioural problems and then abused children. Children in care because of physical or sexual abuse are more likely to return to their families than those placed for neglect. Amongst these, children who have been sexually abused are likely to return home soonest, perhaps because the perpetrator is removed from the home.[142]

15.106 Biehal found no evidence that it is contact *per se* which leads to reunification although regular contact together with other factors are probably linked to a return.

> 'There is some evidence that frequent parental visiting indicates the presence of a number of other factors which may predict reunion, including a positive relationship and strong attachment between parent and child, parental motivation, placement for reasons such as parental ill health or other crises rather than serious and persistent parenting problems, support to parents from social workers and purposeful, planned social work activity.'

15.107 Only a few British studies have followed up children after returning home. Most found that between one-third and just over half of reunited children subsequently return to care. They found that some children who return home may be at considerable risk of re-abuse or neglect. These findings are supported by US research which also suggests that children were more likely to re-enter care as a result of further neglect than further abuse.[143]

---

[140] Biehal *Reuniting Looked After Children with their Families* (2006). This is a literature review and is summarised at www.jrf.org.uk/publications. The author warns that most of the research is from the US and the extent to which this can be extrapolated to the UK is unclear.
[141] Ibid.
[142] Ibid.
[143] Ibid.

THE EXPERIENCE OF BEING IN CARE

15.108   The White Paper *Care Matters: Time for Change*[144] looked at the experience of children in care. Those consulted said that it was crucial to them that they are not singled out in front of their peers as being in care. They told of numerous examples where children in placements were prevented from taking part in routine activities because of a series of rules and regulations – either perceived or real – which the carers and social workers were abiding by.

15.109   The White Paper concluded that, as stated in Local Authority Circular (2004) which provided guidance on overnight stays:

> 'Children should, as far as possible, be granted the same permissions to take part in normal and acceptable age-appropriate activities as would reasonably be granted by the parents of their peers, and we would expect carers to behave as any other parent would in such situations.'

The vulnerability of the individual child had to be considered but:

> 'We want to see such interventions delivered in as normal a way as possible to minimise the sense of difference which children in care often feel. For example, necessary health and safety requirements, particularly in children's homes, should not get in the way of children cooking and engaging in other activities which are essential for acquiring skills for life ... The expectation is that children in care should be allowed to stay overnight with friends as other children would. However, agreements as to who is responsible for such decisions should be made on the basis of the vulnerability of the individual child.'

PROBLEMS OF CORPORATE PARENTING

15.110   There is a fundamental problem with what has been called 'corporate parenting': the child does not have a single person (or a couple) who is personally and consistently responsible for his immediate and long-term care and who is able to take all the individual decisions which a parent would make. Although the child may have a carer in the role of a quasi-parent, this is far from being guaranteed and if he has, there is no assurance that this will be permanent. In any event, that person cannot act autonomously.

15.111   In addition, fluctuating budgetary restraints, predictable only in so far as there will never be enough money, affect the services that can be provided, the consistency and quality of social workers and the support given to carers.

---

[144]   op cit at paras 3.7–3.10.

Criticism

15.112 Commentators are in agreement. In 2002, for example, Lowe and Murch[145] commented that:

> 'Our over-riding impression remains that the strength of the system lies in the dedication and commitment of many of the staff to the children concerned, to their families and the ways in which the complex task of finding supportive stable placements are grappled with. But .... structural weaknesses in the system such as lengthy chains of command; inappropriate, mechanistic and inflexible management; excessive pressure of work (often resulting from competing responsibilities); inadequate child care training for front line staff; and an over-emphasis on bureaucratic "paper pushing" all too often mar the service.'

15.113 In the two London boroughs studied they were disturbed by the Directors' reports of the serious difficulties in staff recruitment and retention.

> 'We do not see how a good quality childcare service which aims to bring stability to children's lives can ever be achieved where, if the reports we received are correct, there is such chronic staff instability and where up to half the field workers move within six months.'

15.114 The Green Paper, *Care Matters: Transforming the Lives of Children and Young People in Care*[146] concluded that:

> 'For children in care the day to day responsibility of parenting is divided between carers and the social worker representing the local authority as corporate parent. However, there are high rates of turnover among social workers and staff in children's homes, and a lack of stability in children's placements means that many children lack a consistent adult in their lives. In addition, organisational structures in local authorities can result in responsibility for children being passed from one part of the organisation to another during their time in care. Whilst many children in care receive an excellent service, far too many do not ...
>
> The quality of support received in placements is ... fundamental to the outcomes of children in care. There are some excellent placements, and there is no doubt that both foster and residential carers are committed to the children they care for. However, despite this dedication, far too many placements are not meeting children's needs. Many placements are not meeting children's needs. Only around 25% of care homes are meeting 90% or more of the National Minimum Standards. Qualification levels of staff tend to be poor, and only 23% of residential care staff are qualified to the expected standard for these settings. Fostering services have similar problems. Over a third fail to meet National Minimum Standards on suitability to work with children and one in four fail to meet the standard on providing suitable carers. A high level of placement instability and frequent breakdowns suggest that many children are not in the right placement for them or are not receiving sufficient support.'

---

[145] op cit at p 155.
[146] op cit at paras 1.33, 1.35–1.37.

Reform

15.115   The White Paper, *Care Matters: Time for Change*[147] promises reform, an emphasis on improving the lives of children in care and a package of proposals. Such attempts have been made on a number of occasions since the Curtis Committee in 1946. It is difficult to see how changes to the system cannot overcome the fundamental problems defined above.

OUTCOMES

15.116   In the last 8 years, in part in pursuing its programme of reforming adoption law, the Government has provided evidence to demonstrate poor outcomes in a range of matters for children in care albeit with some recent improvement between 2000 and 2005, for example in education.[148]

15.117   The Prime Minister's Review: *Adoption*,[149] the White Paper, *Adoption: A New Approach*,[150] The Green Paper, *Care Matters: Transforming the Lives of Children and Young People in Care*[151] and the White Paper, *Care Matters: Time for Change*[152] all provide statistical evidence for a range of outcomes.

15.118   The fact that poor outcomes can be shown for children in care does not mean that these outcomes are the result of being in care. Outcomes are subject to complex and interacting factors and the more complex the placement circumstances, the more difficult it is to attribute success to any one factor or type of placement.[153] Children enter and leave care at different ages. Although all will enter care with some difficulties, the range of difficulties and the age at which they enter care will effect the outcome[154] as may the type of placement, whether fostering or residential care. The outcomes for a child of 5 who spends his time in care with the same foster family may be different than for a very disturbed teenager entering care at 14 and accommodated in a series of children's homes. Sellick and Thoburn have pointed out that 'it has become increasingly clear that good outcomes are harder to obtain for some children than others.'[155]

---

[147]   op cit at para 1.4.
[148]   Green Paper, *Care Matters: Transforming the Lives of Children and Young People in Care* op cit.
[149]   op cit.
[150]   op cit.
[151]   op cit.
[152]   op cit.
[153]   Sellick, Thoburn and Philpot *What Works in Adoption and Foster Care?* (Barnados, 2004) at p 25 and ch 3.
[154]   See **15.2**.
[155]   *What Works in Adoption and Foster Care?* op cit at p 59.

15.119 No large scale longitudinal study in the UK of a group of foster placements made with the intention that children will remain in care until at least 16 has yet been completed.[156]

Statistical outcomes

Education

15.120 An estimated third (30%) of looked after children in 2000 had statements of special educational needs compared to a quarter (23%) of children in the population at large. In the same year a quarter of looked after children aged 14–16 did not attend school regularly. Many have been excluded and have no regular educational placement. In 2005 70% left care without having gained any GCSE or GNVQ qualifications.[157] Although the proportion gaining 5 A*–C GCSEs had risen from 7% in 2000 to 11% in 2005, the proportion in the general population has also risen and the gap is widening slightly.[158]

> 'GCSE attainment for children in care is not only far behind that of all children, but also significantly lower than that of children entitled to free school meals and those from deprived communities. Even when compared against children with similar levels of SEN, deprivation, and mobility, children in care do significantly worse.'[159]

15.121 In 2006, at the age of 19, only one-fifth (19%) of care leavers were in further education and 6% in higher education compared to just under two-fifths (39%) of all young people.[160] The proportion of care leavers in university and other education rose between 2002 and 2005.

Health

15.122 In 2002, just over two-thirds (67%) of children who are looked after had an identifiable mental health problem.[161]

> 'The physical and mental health of children and young people in care is often too poor in comparison with their peers. Children in care have higher rates of substance misuse and pregnancy than those in the non-care population and a much greater prevalence of mental health problems.'[162]

---

[156] op cit at p 62. Scofield, Beek and others are currently carrying out such a study.

[157] White Paper *Adoption: A New Approach* at para 2.4.

[158] Green Paper, *Care Matters: Transforming the Lives of Children and Young People in Care* op cit at para 1.14 and Annex C 10.

[159] Ibid. See also Chapter 5 of the Paper.

[160] Ibid at para 1.16.

[161] White Paper *Adoption: A New Approach* op cit at para 2.4.

[162] White Paper, *Care Matters: Time for Change* op cit at para 5.1.

Employment

15.123   Compared to the general population, in 2000, children who grew up looked after were four times more likely to be unemployed.[163] In 2006, at the age of 19 over 30% were not in education, employment or training compared to 13% of all young people.[164]

Other problems

15.124   Compared to the general population, in 2000, children who grew up looked after were 60 times more likely to be homeless.[165]

15.125   They constituted a quarter of the prison population.[166] Just under two-fifths (39%) of male prisoners under 21 had been looked after.[167]

15.126   Between 14% and 25% of young women leaving care by 2000 were pregnant or had a child compared to 3% of 20-year-old women in the population at large.[168]

Other considerations

15.127   Despite the outcomes outlined above it appears that many children are satisfied with their arrangements. In a recent report,[169] over half of the children in care who were asked said that their present placement was definitely the right one for them. The Green Paper, *Care Matters: Transforming the Lives of Children and Young People in Care*[170] reported that given the choice, many young people would want to remain with a family for longer, making the bridge to independent living easier for them.

15.128   In 2004, Sellick and Thoburn in *What Works in Adoption and Foster Care?*[171] carried out a literature review of studies comparing the outcomes of long-term foster care with those of adoption. They reported that it was an area where researchers and commentators disagree. Some long-term foster children who were later adopted had come down firmly in favour of adoption when interviewed. Adoption might have a higher level of emotional security and a sense of belonging and general well being but was not an answer for every child.[172]

---

[163]   Prime Minister's Report op cit at para 2.14.
[164]   Green Paper, *Care Matters: Transforming the Lives of Children and Young People in Care* op cit at para 1.16.
[165]   Prime Minister's Report op cit at para 2.14.
[166]   Ibid, at para 2.14.
[167]   White Paper *Adoption: A New Approach* op cit at para 2.4.
[168]   Ibid.
[169]   *Placements, Decisions and Reviews: A Child's View Report* (Children's Rights Director, 2006).
[170]   Op cit.
[171]   Op cit at p 84.
[172]   Triseliotis 'Long-term foster care or adoption? The evidence examined' (2002) *Child and Family Social Work* vol 7 23.

15.129 According to Sellick and Thoburn, several writers believe that there is a group of mainly older children who would not allow themselves to be placed with substitute families if they could no longer have a relationship with their birth family, something noted by the Government in the White Paper, *Adoption: A New Approach*.[173]

15.130 In summary, Sellick and Thoburn conclude that:

'There is insufficient evidence on the desirability of adoption, permanent fostering or residence orders, from the child's point of view. There is, however, evidence that the generally negative view of long-term or "permanent" foster care is not supported by recent evidence. There appears to be no difference in break down rates [when other variables are held constant] and the evidence on well-being and satisfaction of children and new parents is inconclusive.'[174]

The comparative outcomes for adoption and long-term fostering are considered in more detail in Chapter 16.

THE ATTITUDE OF THE COURTS

15.131 Decisions of the Court of Appeal have showed a recognition of the advantages and disadvantages of foster care.

15.132 The Court has long recognised the problems with corporate parenting. In *Re H (Adoption: Parental Agreement)*[175] a boy of 8 had been in care for most of his life. The authority concluded that he could not be rehabilitated with his mother and placed him with long-term foster parents 'with a view to adoption'. The mother appealed the making of an adoption order, arguing that fostering would be better. Her counsel posed the question: what do the adoptive parents gain by adoption over what they already have as long-term foster parents? Ormrod LJ answered:

'The answer is always the same – and it is always a good one – adoption gives us total security and makes the child part of our family, and places us in parental control of the child; long-term fostering leaves us exposed to changes of view of the local authority, it leaves us exposed to applications and so on by the natural parent. That is a perfectly sensible and reasonable approach; it is far from being only an emotive one.'

15.133 Likewise in *Re B (Adoption Order)*[176] Hale LJ said that 'the continued support of the local authority [through a care order] comes at the price of continued monitoring and insecurity'.

---

[173] Op cit at 5.8. See **5.9**.

[174] Op cit at pp 86 and 63.

[175] (1982) 3 FLR 386 at 388 approved in *Re C (A Minor) (Adoption Order: Conditions)* [1988] 2 FLR 159 by Lord Ackner at 168.

[176] [2001] EWCA Civ 347, [2001] 2 FLR 26 at [28].

15.134 In *Re KD (A Minor) (Access: Principles)*[177] Lord Oliver of Aylmerton commented that:

> 'No judge called upon to exercise the court's jurisdiction in wardship can be unaware that cases do occasionally occur where a decision is taken by a local authority – sometimes effectively by a single social worker who is the only person with first hand knowledge of the case – which viewed by any reasonable objective standard is properly categorized as dictatorial, insensitive or prejudiced. To say that is to say no more than that local authorities are conducted and staffed by human beings and thus subject, as is the common lot, to human fallibility.'

15.135 However, the higher courts also recognise that foster care can enable valuable links with the birth family to be retained and relationships continue.

> '[In adoption] the child is treated in law as if she had been born a child of the marriage of the applicants. She ceases in law to be a child of her mother and the sister of her siblings. The old family link is destroyed and new family ties are created. The psychological effect is that the child loses one identity and gains another. Adoption is inconsistent with being a member of both old and new family at the same time. Long-term fostering does enable the child to have the best of both worlds by feeling she belongs to both families though she must reside with and will anyway usually choose to live with only one – the one who gives her the daily love and care.'[178]

15.136 Courts recognise that one cannot deal in general propositions. They have to give way to the welfare of the individual child viewed in the light of his circumstances. For example, in *Re F (Adoption: Welfare of Child: Financial Considerations)*[179] the court refused to approve adoption plans for three children aged between 7 and 4 and recommended the authority to consider funding the children's long-term placement with their foster parents to whom they were attached.

> 'It cannot be denied that long-term foster care lacks the quality of permanence that adoption has, at least ostensibly. There are a number of observations to make about this, however. ... We know that adoption is no guarantee of permanence. Adoptions break down, and the statistics for this are alarming, particularly where the children are placed at an age a bit older than B is now ... One must look at the individual case to determine the prospects for permanence of a long-term foster placement, and cannot rely wholly on research statistics which deal in generalities.
>
> The local authority also points to the continuing local authority involvement there has to be with any foster placement, which it says can be unsettling, to the stigma of being in care, and to all the uncertainties that attend a foster placement ... In view of the fact that S and R are to stay in long-term foster care, however, it is clear that the local authority is not wedded to adoption in each and every case, but recognises that it is not the best answer, or not perhaps an answer at all, for some children.'

---

[177] [1988] 2 FLR 139 at 142.
[178] *Re M (Adoption or Residence Order)* [1998] 1 FLR 570 per Ward LJ at 589.
[179] [2003] EWHC 3348 (Fam), [2004] 2 FLR 440 per Black J at [74]–[75].

15.137 The High Court either exercising its civil or administrative jurisdiction has considered the adverse effects of local care in a number of cases.[180]

---

[180] For example, *C v Flintshire County Council* [2001] EWCA Civ 347, [2001] 2 FLR 26, *Re F: F v Lambeth LBC* [2002] 1 FLR 217 and *S (A Child Acting by the Official Solicitor) v Rochdale MBC and The Independent Reviewing Officer* [2008] EWHC 3283 (Fam), [2009] 1 FLR 1090. See as well, Bailey-Harris and Harris 'Local authorities and child protection – the mosaic of accountability' [2002] CFLQ 117.

Chapter 16

MAKING THE CHOICE

INTRODUCTION

16.1 The question of which order should be made in respect of a child in need of permanent care which will not or cannot be provided by his parents falls into two halves:

- Where should the child live?

- Which of the four possible orders – adoption, special guardianship, residence or a care order – best meets his needs?

16.2 The four orders have their own features relating to the grant and control of parental responsibility, both that held by the carer and that held by others; whether or not the order is irrevocable; its duration; the court's approach to contact and the support which a local authority must or may provide.

16.3 One matter is unique to adoption. Unlike the other orders, it brings about a complete and irrevocable change in the child's status, the child being treated in law as the child of and only of the adopters (or, where the child is adopted by a parent's partner, that parent and the adopter).

16.4 As shown by the cases reported since the commencement of the Adoption and Children Act 2002, particularly difficult issues arise when the child is going to be placed within the family. Although this does not exclude adoption, caution needs to be exercised and adoption by grandparents, standing in direct line with the child, is not readily granted.

PARENTS

16.5 The fundamental issue in every case concerning the provision of permanent care for children is whether parents wish to continue to care for their child and, if so, whether the care which is being given or is likely to be given to the child by them is of such a standard as to justify the state interfering with the family life of the child and the parents. However, the examination of this question lies outside the scope of this Handbook, which starts from the premise that the parents have conceded or a court has decided that the answer is that a permanent removal of the child is both justified and in the child's best interests.

16.6   Where a court has reached this answer it will usually have been satisfied that the threshold for making a care order, set out in s 31(2) of the Children Act 1989 (CA 1989) has been met and that, bearing in mind the welfare checklist provided by s 1(3) of that Act and taking as its paramount consideration, the child's welfare,[1] the permanent displacement of the parents is justified.

16.7   In reaching its decision the court will have borne in mind the importance of what Lord Oliver of Aylmerton in *Re KD (A Minor) (Access: Principles)*[2] described as:

'the single common concept that the natural bond and relationship between parent and child gives rise to universally recognized norms which ought not to be gratuitously interfered with and which, if interfered with at all, ought to be so only if the welfare of the child dictates it ... Parenthood, in most civilised societies, is generally conceived as conferring upon parents the exclusive privilege of ordering within the family, the upbringing of children of tender age, with all that that entails.'

16.8   In the same case, Lord Templeman said:

'The best person to bring up a child is the natural parent. It matters not whether the parent is wise or foolish, rich or poor, educated or illiterate, provided the child's moral and physical health are not endangered. Public authorities cannot improve on nature. Public authorities exercise a supervisory role and interfere to rescue a child when the parental tie is broken ...'[3]

16.9   This reminder that it is not the function of the court to decide who is best able to look after a child unless parents are not able to do so can be illustrated by *Re K (A Minor) (Custody)*[4] which concerned a father's appeal against a refusal to make a residence order in his favour in respect of his 4½-year-old son who had been living with his maternal aunt for a year, his mother having died. In allowing the appeal Waite J said:

'The speeches in the House of Lords [in *Re KD (A Minor) (Access: Principles)*] make it plain that the term "parental right" is not there used in any proprietary sense, but rather as describing the right of every child, as part of its general welfare, to have the ties of nature maintained wherever possible with the parents who gave it life.

... [The trial] judge proceeded ... as though the question before him had been: which claimant will provide the better home? The question he ought of course to have been asking was: are there any compelling factors which require me to override the prima facie right of this child to an upbringing by its surviving natural parent?

---

[1]   CA 1989, s 1(1).
[2]   [1988] 2 FLR 139 at 153.
[3]   [1988] 2 FLR 139 at 141.
[4]   [1990] 2 FLR 64.

[His] approach led him to embark upon a careful and detailed assessment of the merits of the two competing households with a view to deciding in which of them R would have a better prospect of achieving a sense of security and stability, qualities, certainly, which he will badly need after his sufferings. That comparative exercise was conscientiously undertaken and involved the most careful weighing of minutiae such as the age differences between the parties, of imponderables such as the father's future marriage prospects, and even of wholly unknown quantities such as the emotional effect of a change of primary carer, which the judge undertook, in the absence of any medical or psychiatric evidence one way or the other. It was, despite its thoroughness, an exercise misconceived in law.'[5]

16.10 In parallel to this common law approach, the court will also have had regard to Art 8 of the European Convention for the Protection of Human Rights and Fundamental Freedoms and will also have decided that:

- the interference is necessary for the protection of the rights and freedoms of others, namely those of the child; and

- that the interference is proportionate, that is, that there was a reasonable relationship between the goal pursued and the means used.[6]

16.11 As discussed at **6.183**, 'necessary' is not synonymous with 'indispensable' but it does have the flexibility of such expressions as 'useful', 'reasonable' or 'desirable.'[7]

'The intervention must be "necessary in a democratic society", that is, it must meet a pressing social need and be proportionate to that need. The more drastic the interference, the greater must be the need to do it.'[8]

16.12 Proportionality requires that where there are no long standing problems which interfere with the capacity to provide even 'good enough' caring, such as serious mental illness, a serious personality disorder or intractable substance abuse, evidence of past chronic neglect or abuse or serious ill-treatment and physical harm, the aim of the local authority and the court, notwithstanding that some intervention may be required, should be to reunite the family when circumstances enable it. 'Cutting off all contact and the relationship between the child or children and their family is only justified by the overriding necessity of the interests of the child.'[9] In short, was this decision necessary at the time it was taken?

---

[5] [1990] 2 FLR 64 at 70.
[6] *Ashingdane v United Kingdom* (1985) 7 EHRR 528.
[7] *Handyside v United Kingdom* (1979–80) 1 EHRR 737.
[8] *Re B (Adoption by One Natural Parent to Exclusion of Other)* [2001] 1 FLR 589, per Hale LJ at 599. See also *The Queen on the Application of Mahmood v Secretary of State for the Home Department* [2001] 1 FLR 756, per Lord Phillips of Worth Maltravers MR at 772.
[9] *Re C and B (Care Order: Future Harm)* [2001] 1 FLR 611 per Hale LJ at [30] and [34].

16.13   The court when examining the care given or likely to be given by the parents adopts the standard of 'good enough' parenting, not requiring it to be anything more.

> 'Society must be willing to tolerate very diverse standard of parenting, including the eccentric, the barely adequate and the inconsistent. It follows too that children will inevitably have both very different experiences of parenting and very unequal consequences flowing from it. It means that some children will experience disadvantage and harm, while others flourish in an atmosphere of loving security and emotional stability. These are the consequences of our fallible humanity and it is not the provenance of the state to spare children all the consequences of defective parenting'.[10]

FAMILY

16.14   In the vast majority of cases the court will be seeking to identify the individuals who are best able to provide a family life for the child. 'All children need a "stable and harmonious home" in which to grow up'.[11]

> 'Families are the bedrock of our society, providing a wide range of functions. They nurture children, help to build strength, resilience and moral values in young people, and provide the love and encouragement that helps them lead fulfilling lives. Families are vital in ensuring all children have good life chances and the opportunities to get on in life.'[12]

16.15   It may be that the best option for some, probably older, teenage children will be residential care if their needs are such that they cannot be met in a family setting or they wish to be in residential care perhaps because it allows greater freedom for continuing contact with their birth family. For most children though, their needs throughout their childhood and beyond will best be met by belonging to a family even if they may need some residential care because of special physical or emotional needs.

16.16   It has been suggested that a perception of family life in the twenty-first century is that it is 'not like it used to be'. Whether this perception is accurate or based to some extent on myth, for some, its change is cause for concern but for others, for celebration.[13] Nevertheless, demographics, social change and an increase in pluralism has meant that the traditional concept of a family which includes children, namely a heterosexual couple married to each other and bringing up children born to them both, is no longer the only model.[14]

---

10   *Re L (Care: Threshhold Criterias)* [2007] 1 FLR 2050 per Hedley J at [50].
11   *Re P (Adoption; Unmarried Couple)* [2008] UKHL 38, [2008] 2 FLR 1084 per Baroness Hale of Richmond at [108].
12   *Families in Britain: An Evidence Paper* (Department for Schools and Families, 2008) at p 4. The Paper makes it clear that it is 'an analytical discussion paper and not a statement of government policy'.
13   Diduck *Law's Family* (Butterworths, 2003) at p 21.
14   For a discussion of the demographic data, see Douglas and Lowe (eds) *The Continuing*

'If the couple are bringing up children together, it is unlikely to matter whether or not they are the biological children of both parties. Both married and unmarried couples, both homosexual and heterosexual, may bring up children together. One or both may have children from another relationship: this is not at all uncommon in lesbian relationships and the court may grant them a shared residence order so that they may share parental responsibility. A lesbian couple may have children by donor insemination who are brought up as the children of them both: it is not uncommon for each of them to bear a child in this way. A gay or lesbian couple may foster other people's children.'[15]

16.17 These changes have resulted in much academic and political discussion about what, in law, does or should constitute a family.[16] However, what is of primary importance when deciding how to provide an alternative family life for a child is what the life will mean for the child and the other family members.

16.18 The Ministerial Foreword to *Families in Britain: An Evidence Paper*[17] states that:

'Extended family members provide one another with support throughout life, especially in difficult times and during critical moments, such as when a child is born, when a couple is separating or when relatives need caring for. It is within families that a sense of identity develops, and cultural and social values are passed on from one generation to the next ... The family has also shown itself able to endure, shape and adapt to changes in social and economic circumstances, and it continues to do so today. So we see an increasing range of family structures, to the extent that there is arguably no longer a one size fits all family in Britain today. But this is diversity and not decline. Warm, loving and stable relationships matter more for our happiness and wellbeing than the legal form of a relationship. And while marriage will remain of central importance, the reality in many people's everyday lives is that more and more families experience a range of family forms throughout their life time. There is no single family form that guarantees happiness or success. All types of family can, in the right circumstances, look after their family members, help them get on in life and, for their children, have high hopes and the wherewithal to put them on the path to success.'

16.19 However, this is not necessarily a description of what an individual family *is* rather than an expression of what it is thought it *should* be. Distinguishing between the two is especially important for legal and social work practitioners and the court when considering the future of children. A decision must be taken based on the family life as it is likely to be in fact and not on what the professionals optimistically assume it will be.

Evolution of Family Law (Family Law, 2009) at pp 3–10; Mitchell *Children Act Private Law Proceedings: A Handbook* (Family Law, 2nd edn, 2006) chapter 1 and *Families in Britain: An Evidence Paper* (2008) op cit.

[15] *Ghaidan v Godin-Mendoza* [2004] UKHL 30, [2004] 2 FLR 600 per Baroness Hale of Richmond at [141].

[16] See, for example, *Law's Family* op cit chapter 2; McGlynn *Families and the European Union: Law, Politics and Pluralism* (Cambridge University Press, 2006) chapter 4.

[17] op cit.

16.20 It is also important to try to understand how the child in question sees family life and what their hopes and expectations (not necessarily the same) about family life are.

16.21 One study by Morrow in 1998,[18] for example, of 183 children aged between 8 and 14 found that narrow definitions of 'the family' as nuclear obscured a wide diversity in family forms and family practices.

16.22 Children of different ages described 'family' differently, younger children tending to use more concrete examples and emphasising being cared for by 'parents'. Older children were less likely to see family as depending upon formal contractual relationships but were more likely to see the quality of the relationships between people as being the defining feature. Nevertheless there was wide variation and some 8- and 9-year-olds could generalise beyond their own experiences.

16.23 Overall, children had an accepting and inclusive view of what counted as family. For all children regardless of age, gender and ethnicity, 'family' was defined by caring, love and the quality of the relationships involved. In the words of one 13-year-old girl:

> 'A family is a group of people which all care about each other. They can all cry together, laugh together, argue together and go through all the emotions together. Some live together as well. Families are for helping each other through life.'

16.24 Their definitions did not centre around the nuclear norm or genetic ties. While some children used the terms 'related' and 'relations' in their definitions of family, they were not necessarily meaning genetic links. Some were clear that people can be connected in different ways, through marriage as well as blood ties. However, parents, especially mothers, emerged clearly as providers of physical and emotional care. Sibling relationships were also important, and while such relationships are rarely conflict-free, they were often underpinned by a good deal of mutual affection and support. Morrow commented that pets should not be overlooked as being of central importance, particularly for some rural children, offering companionship to supplement that from family, relatives and friends.

THE LEGAL ORDERS AVAILABLE

Aspects of the orders

16.25 The legal characteristics and effect of the four possible orders – adoption, special guardianship, a residence order or a care order with the intention that the child should be placed in a foster home or, less likely in contested cases, a residential home – require a careful examination in order to

---

[18] Morrow *Understanding families: Children's Perspectives* (National Children's Bureau, 1998), summarised in *Children's perspectives on families* Findings 798 (Joseph Rowntree Foundation).

see which best suit the welfare of the individual child. Adoption is examined in detail in Chapter 2, special guardianship in Chapter 5 and care orders in Chapter 15.

16.26 A useful schedule comparing the legal aspects of adoption and special guardianship is attached to the report of *Re A-J (Adoption Order or Special Guardianship Order)*.[19]

Duration of the order

Adoption

16.27 An adoption order lasts for life.

Other orders

16.28 All other orders end when the child is 18 (16 in the case of a residence order unless the court extends the period to 18[20]) or earlier by way of an order.

Revocation of the order

Adoption

16.29 An adoption order cannot be revoked (see **2.119**). All other orders can be discharged.[21] However, parents, the child and most other individuals except for the special guardian need the leave of the court before applying to discharge a special guardianship order[22] (see **5.100**).

Acquiring and extinguishing parental responsibility

16.30 An adoption order gives parental responsibility for a child to the adopters[23] and extinguishes the parental responsibility which any person other than the adopters or adopter has for the adopted child immediately before the making of the order[24] save where the adopter is the partner of one of the child's parents.[25]

---

[19] [2007] EWCA Civ 55, [2007] 1 FLR 507.
[20] CA 1989, s 12(5).
[21] Ibid, s 14D(1) – special guardianship; s 8(2) – residence order; s 39(1) – care order.
[22] Ibid, s 14D(3).
[23] ACA 2002, s 46(1).
[24] Ibid, s 46(2)(a).
[25] Ibid, s 46(3)(b). See **14.103**.

Special guardianship and residence orders

16.31 In contrast, although both special guardians[26] and those granted a residence order[27] have parental responsibility so long as the order remains in force, making the order does not remove the parental responsibility of the parents or anyone else save for anyone who has parental responsibility solely because of a previous residence order which is superseded by the new order.

Care order

16.32 A local authority only acquires parental responsibility on the making of a care order[28] (and a placement order). Foster carers do not acquire it as a result of the care order, no matter how long they have been looking after the child. All they have by way of legal right is that they may be someone whose wishes the authority may consider to be relevant and who therefore should be consulted before the local authority makes a decision concerning the child.[29]

16.33 Making a care order does not extinguish the parental responsibility of the parents or anyone else save for anyone who has parental responsibility solely by reason of a previous residence order which is superseded by the new order.

Exercising and controlling parental responsibility

16.34 The general rule on the exercise of parental responsibility is governed by s 2(7) of CA 1989 which provides that:

> 'Where more than one person has parental responsibility for a child, each of them may act alone and without the other (or others) in meeting that responsibility but nothing in this Part shall be taken to affect the operation of any enactment which requires the consent of more than one person in a matter affecting the child.'

However, there is some uncertainty as to whether this applies to the making of all decisions or whether there are some decisions which require the consent of all those with parental responsibility.[30]

---

[26] CA 1989, s 14C(1).

[27] Ibid, s 12(2).

[28] Ibid, s 33(3).

[29] Ibid, s 22(4), (5).

[30] See, for example, *Re PC (Change of Surname)* [1997] 2 FLR 730; *Re G (Parental Responsibility: Education)* [1994] 2 FLR 964; *Re J (Specific Issue Order: Child's Religious Upbringing and Circumcision)* [2000] 1 FLR 571; Eekelaar 'Do parents have a duty to consult?' (1998) 114 LQR 337; Maidment 'Parental Responsibility – Duty to Consult?' [2001] Fam Law 518 and Mitchell *Children Act Private Law Proceedings: Handbook* (Family Law, 2nd edn, 2006) at 6.7–6.11.

Adoption

16.35 The parental responsibility held by adopters is not subject to any restriction save in respect of anyone who has parental responsibility themselves. It can be controlled only by means of a prohibited steps or specific issue order under CA 1989, s 8 or by the court if the child is a ward. Birth parents no longer have parental responsibility and, like most others who do not have parental responsibility,[31] will require the leave of the court under s 10(9) before making an application.

Special guardianship

16.36 The general rule is restricted where there is a special guardianship order or a care order.

16.37 The special guardian is entitled to exercise parental responsibility to the exclusion of any other person with parental responsibility apart from another special guardian,[32] unless any enactment or rule of law requires the consent of more than one person with parental responsibility.[33] If there is a dispute in relation to any exercise of parental responsibility, the parent or special guardian or anyone with a residence order[34] (and others who have obtained leave under CA 1989, s 10(8)) may apply under s 10 for a specific issue or prohibited steps order.

16.38 In *Birmingham City Council v R*,[35] Wall LJ commented that special guardianship:

> 'is plainly not something to be embarked upon lightly or capriciously, not least because the status it gives the special guardian effectively prevents the exercise of parental power on the part of the child's natural parents ... In this respect it is substantially different from a residence order which ... does not confer on any person who holds the order the exclusivity in the exercise of parental responsibility which accompanies a special guardianship order.'

Care order

16.39 Where a care order is in force, the local authority's parental responsibility is shared with anyone else who has parental responsibility, but the authority has the power to determine the extent to which any parent, special guardian, guardian or any one with parental responsibility can exercise parental responsibility if it is satisfied that it is necessary to do so in order to protect or safeguard the child's welfare.[36] However, before making any decision the authority has, so far as is reasonably practicable, to ascertain the wishes and

---

[31] CA 1989, s 10(4)–(6).
[32] Ibid, s 14C(1)(b).
[33] Ibid, s 14C(2)(a).
[34] Ibid, s10(2)
[35] *Birmingham City Council v R* [2006] EWCA Civ 1748, [2007] 1 FLR 564 per Wall LJ at [78].
[36] CA 1989, s 33(3) and (4).

feelings of the child, his parents, any other person who has parental responsibility and any other person whose wishes and feelings it considers to be relevant.[37] See **15.37**.

16.40 When a child is subject to a care order, no specific issue order or a similar order in wardship can be made.[38]

General restrictions

16.41 There are other exceptions to the general rule.

16.42 While a special guardianship order is in force no one may cause the child to be known by a new surname or to remove him from the UK (save in the case of a special guardian, for less than 3 months[39]) without either the written consent of every person who has parental responsibility or the leave of the court.[40]

16.43 A similar but not identical provision applies in relation to a residence order.[41] No one may cause the child to be known by a new surname or remove him from the United Kingdom (except, in the case of the person in whose favour the residence order was made, for a period of less than 1 month) without the written consent of every person who has parental responsibility or the leave of the court.

Applying for orders under s 8 of the Children Act 1989

16.44 Subsections 19(4) and (5) of the 1989 Act govern who can apply for section 8 orders, regardless of whether an adoption order is in force. However as noted above, birth parents no longer have parental responsibility following an adoption order and will have to apply for leave.

Contact[42]

Adoption

16.45 An adoption order extinguishes any order for contact made under CA 1989, s 8.[43]

---

[37]   CA 1989, s 22(4).
[38]   Ibid, s 9(1), (5), s 100(2).
[39]   Compare ibid, s 13 where a person with a residence order may remove the child for less than one month.
[40]   Ibid, s 14C(3) and see below **5.31**.
[41]   Ibid, s 13(1).
[42]   See Chapter 13.
[43]   ACA 2002, s 46(2)(b).

16.46 When an adoption order is made, a section 8 contact order can be made of the court's own volition[44] or on an application (for which the birth parents and members of their family as well as others will require leave if a placement order has been made) at the time the adoption order is made. Before making an adoption order, the court must consider whether there should be arrangements for allowing any person contact with the child. In reaching its decision it must consider any existing or proposed arrangements and obtain any views of the parties to the proceedings.[45] After the proceedings, the court can make an order under the same section of the court's own volition in any family proceedings or on an application. The birth parents, members of the birth family and most others will require leave to make the application (see **5.21**).

16.47 Before the 2002 Act was enacted, courts were more willing than hitherto to consider post-adoption contact and considered there were cases where some continuing face-to-face contact was clearly desirable.[46] However, if contact was to take place, it was thought that should normally be by way of agreement. Only in the most exceptional cases was a contact order made without the agreement of the adopters.[47]

16.48 It is not yet clear whether the 2002 Act will create or support a greater willingness of courts to order post-adoption contact (see **13.120**) but in *SB and County Council: P (A Child)*[48] Wall LJ said that s 26(5) 'leads us to the view that the 2002 Act envisages the court exercising its powers to make contact orders post adoption, where such orders are in the interests of the child concerned'.

Special guardianship and residence orders

16.49 The making of a special guardianship or residence order does not revoke any section 8 contact order which is already in existence. The court can make a section 8 contact order at the same time or after it grants a special guardianship or residence order. When considering whether to make a guardianship order, the court must consider whether a contact order should also be made.[49]

16.50 As yet, there is no indication that the existence of a special guardianship order will inhibit the court in making a contact order.

---

[44] CA 1989, s 10(1)(b).
[45] ACA 2002, s 46(6).
[46] *Re E (A Minor) (Care Order: Contact)* [1994] 1 FLR 146.
[47] *Re C (A Minor) (Adoption Order: Conditions)* [1988] 2 FLR 159 and *Re T (Adoption Contact)* [1995] 2 FLR 251.
[48] [2008] EWCA Civ 535; sub nom *P (A Child)* [2008] 2 FCR 185 at [154].
[49] CA 1989, s 14B(1)(a).

Care order

16.51   Making a care order discharges any order for contact made under s 8.[50]

16.52   When a child is in care, the local authority is under a duty to allow him reasonable contact with his parents, any guardian or special guardian, any person who has parental responsibility by virtue of ACA 2002, s 4A and, where a residence order or an order for care under the inherent jurisdiction of the High Court was in force immediately before the care order was made, the person in whose favour the order was made.[51] This duty can be terminated by an order under CA 1989, s 34(4).

16.53   Although the court cannot make a contact order under s 8[52] it can make a contact order under s 34(2) of its own volition or upon an application.

Support

Adoption and special guardianship

16.54   There are detailed similar schemes placing a local authority under a duty to assess and provide support both before and after the making of an adoption or special guardianship order. See Chapter 9 for adoption and Chapter 11 for special guardianship.

Residence order

16.55   Often local authorities place children in need with members of their extended family or families of friends as an alternative to their being 'looked after' under ACA 2002, s 22 or being in care. Sometimes, the carers are encouraged to apply for residence orders as part of a permanent solution. However, the need for support is likely to be the same as when a special guardianship order is made to a family member. See also **11.4**.

16.56   This need for support is discussed in *Children Placed with Kinship Carers Through Care Proceedings*.[53] The authors conclude that:

> 'Kinship care can be a positive option for any children but it is not straight forward and requires careful assessment and support. If the full potential of kinship care is to be realised, there must be clear policies both at central and government level.'

---

[50]   CA 1989, s 91(2).
[51]   Ibid, s 34(1).
[52]   Ibid, s 9(1).
[53]   Waterhouse, Hunt, Lutman [2009] Fam Law 435.

16.57 There is no specific scheme where there is a residence order other than that available to everyone under ss 17–20 of and Sch 1 to the 1989 Act (see for example, *R (C) v Knowsley MBC*[54] and *R (JL) v Islington LBC*.[55]

16.58 Paragraph 15 of Sch 1 provides that where a child lives, or is to live, with a person (other than a parent of the child or the husband or wife of a parent of the child) as the result of a residence order, a local authority may make contributions to that person towards the cost of the accommodation and maintenance of the child. In *R (M) v Birmingham City Council*[56] where a child in need of accommodation because of her mother's drug abuse went to live with her uncle under a care order, Charles J held that the local authority had the discretion to provide financial and other assistance. However, unlike adoption and special guardian support, there was no statutory guidance, albeit that the authority was entitled to have a policy as to when and how to provide support and that the position was different from that relating to the provision of financial assistance in circumstances of adoption and special guardianship. Every application has to be assessed on its individual merits. Any local policy which requires an application for support to be made before a residence order is granted is unlawful. Policies which state that support will be given 'only in exceptional circumstances' may also encounter difficulties.[57]

16.59 There is a further source of local authority assistance when the child has been in care. Under para 19A of Sch 2 to the CA 1989 the local authority looking after a child has a duty to advise, assist and befriend him 'with a view to promoting his welfare when they have ceased to look after him'. This is discussed at **15.90**.

STATUS OF ADOPTION

16.60 The summary given above illustrates that the difference between the individual features of adoption and the other orders centres around the extent and control of parental responsibility. This flows from the fundamental difference between the two classes of order. From the date an adoption order is made, the child is irrevocably treated in law as if he was born as the legitimate child of the adopters or adopter[58] and, save where adopted under s 51(2) by his parent's partner, as the child of no one other than the adopter. See **2.96**. As such, he inherits under intestacy and may benefit under life policies and pension policies and settlements (see **2.104**). In comparison, every other order leaves the child in law as well as in fact as the child of his parents.

16.61 It is this distinction, above all others, which gives adoption its special character and distinction. And it is this distinction, that the child is fully and

---

[54] [2008] EWHC 2551 (Admin), [2009] 1 FLR 493.
[55] [2009] EWHC 458 (Admin), [2009] Fam Law 485.
[56] [2008] EWHC 1863 (Admin), [2009] 1 FLR 1068.
[57] *R (H) v Essex County Council* [2009] EWHC 353 (Admin), [2009] 2 FLR 91.
[58] ACA 2002, s 67(1), (2).

irrevocably a member of the adopters' family, which is the foundation for the special psychological impact which it has both on the child, the adopters, their family, the birth parents and their family and on the way it has historically been treated by the courts.

16.62   The approach of the *Review of Adoption Law: Report to Ministers of an Interdepartmental Working Group*[59] remains an accurate description of this fundamental difference.

'It has been suggested that adoption should not always entail the complete severance of existing familial relationships and a change of the child's identity. Adoption in its present form is an extremely important step in a child's life which determines his or her identity and family relationships throughout life. It is essential that adoption is regarded not as a means of determining with whom a child is to live but as a way of making the child legally part of a new family and severing any legal relationship with the birth family. It should stand apart from other orders, not in such a way that it is thought to be a superior option but so there are no doubts as to its special features.'

16.63   The White Paper, *Adoption – A New Approach*,[60] shared the same view of adoption.

'Adoption is not always appropriate for children who cannot return to their birth parents. Some older children may not wish to be legally separated from their birth families. Adoption may not be best for some children being cared for on a permanent basis by members of their wider birth family. Some minority ethnic communities have religious and cultural difficulties with adoption as it is set out in law. Unaccompanied asylum-seeking children may also need secure, permanent homes, but have strong attachments to their families abroad. All these children deserve the same chance as any other to enjoy the benefits of a legally secure, stable permanent placement that promotes a supportive, lifelong relationship with their carers, where the court decides that is in their best interests.

In order to meet the needs of these children where adoption is not appropriate, and to modernise the Government believes there is a case to develop a new legislative option to provide permanence short of the legal separation involved in adoption ...'

16.64   This 'new legislative option' was special guardianship whose key features were the provision of permanency, security and the preservation of the 'basic legal link' between the child and his birth family.[61] In this it took the same approach as *Review of Adoption Law: Report to Ministers of an Interdepartmental Working Group* which suggested that:

---

[59]   (Department of Health and the Welsh Office, 1992) at para 3.6.
[60]   Cm 5017 (2000) at paras 5.8–5.9.
[61]   Ibid, para 5.10

'Where a child is living away from his parents and it is unlikely he will be able to return home, he and his carers – be they relatives, foster-parents or people with a residence order – may wish to enhance the *security and stability* [italics inserted] of their relationship.'[62]

The approach of the courts

16.65 The above approach has been consistently endorsed by the courts. In 2008 in *Re P (Adoption: Unmarried Couple)*[63] Baroness Hale of Richmond said that 'adoption is the most serious and far-reaching order known to family law ... an adoption order [achieves] an almost "total legal transplant" of a child from one family to another.'

16.66 Ten years earlier in *Re M (Adoption or Residence Order)*[64] Ward LJ said:

'[Adoption] changes status. The child is treated in law as if she had been born a child of the marriage of the applicants. She ceases in law to be the child of her mother and the sister of her siblings. The old family link is destroyed and new family ties created. The psychological effect is that the child loses one identity and gains another. Adoption is inconsistent with being a member of both old and new family at the same time ... The disadvantage is that it is unlike any other decision made by adults during the child's minority because it is irrevocable.'

16.67 While it might be suggested that for the older, cognisant child, the sentence, 'the psychological effect is that the child loses one identity and gains another' might more appropriately read 'the *legal* effect is that the child loses one identity and gains another', it cannot be denied that the legal effect of the order, if one is properly required, will have a profound psychological effect both on the child and the adults.

16.68 However, there is an argument that the divide between the adopted child and the non-adopted child may be currently less clear cut in practice than hitherto asserted. In *Down Lisburn Health and Social Services Trust v H*[65] Baroness of Hale of Richmond considered the adoption of older children:

'These adoptions could bring great benefits for the child but they also brought a new set of challenges for social work and for the law. The children were older. They had a history. This might well include damaging experiences from their past. But it might also include significant relationships with members of their birth family. The use of compulsory adoption, dispensing with the need for parental agreement, was increasing. But the fact that these children had a history also meant that their best interests might require that any significant links with the birth family be preserved in a more "open" form of adoption. It was increasingly recognised that there could be more ways than one of achieving the desired

---

62   op cit para 6.1.
63   [2008] UKHL 38, [2008] 2 FLR 1084 at [85].
64   [1998] 1 FLR 570 at 589.
65   [2006] UKHL 36, [2007] 1 FLR 121 at [6].

permanency for the child. (The recent introduction of special guardianship in England and Wales is a further step in the same direction.)'

It is to be noted that Baroness Hale did not appear to suggest that special guardianship will necessarily replace adoption for older children.

RANKING THE ORDERS

16.69   In the case of *Re S (Adoption Order or Special Guardianship Order)*[66] the Court of Appeal examined the question of whether or not the various orders could or should be ranked in order so that, having regard to Art 8 of the European Convention on Human Rights and Fundamental Freedoms, the court could select the least intrusive order which was appropriate. Giving the judgment of the court,[67] Wall LJ said:

'There is nothing in the statutory provisions themselves which limits the making of a special guardianship order or an adoption order to any given set of circumstances. The statute itself is silent on the circumstances in which a special guardianship order is likely to be appropriate, and there is no presumption contained within the statute that a special guardianship order is preferable to an adoption order in any particular category of case. Each case must be decided on its particular facts; and each case will involve the careful application of a judicial discretion to those facts. The key question which the court will be obliged to ask itself in every case in which the question of adoption as opposed to special guardianship arises will be: which order will better serve the welfare of this particular child?'[68]

16.70   He added that although the 'no order' principle[69] as such is unlikely to be relevant, it is a material feature of the special guardianship regime that it is 'less intrusive' than adoption.

---

[66]   [2007] EWCA Civ 54, [2007] 1 FLR 819.
[67]   The case was heard in the same period as *Re AJ (Adoption Order or Special Guardianship Order)* [2007] EWCA Civ 55, [2007] 1 FLR 507 and *Re M-J (Adoption Order or Special Guardianship Order)* [2007] EWCA Civ 56, [2007] 1 FLR 691. Each of the three appeals was heard by a different constitution and on a different date. Only one member of the court (Wall LJ) sat in each constitution. Because it was the first time that the question of the relationship between adoption and special guardianship was considered by the Court of Appeal, all five members of the court involved in the three appeals took the opportunity to consider the underlying principles to be applied in making one or other of the two orders and to give guidance to courts of first instance. Each judgment was a judgment of the court. In addition, each member of each constitution read, contributed to and expressed agreement with the commentary on the statutory provisions and general considerations, which were set out in the judgment in *Re S* at [40]–[77] and which should be read as part of each of the other judgments. Given the importance and likely prevalence of the question in adoption, care and private law proceedings, the three judgments were shown to the President, who authorised the Court to say that he agreed with that commentary. Per Wall LJ at [3]–[4].
[68]   Ibid at [47].
[69]   ACA 2002, s 1(6).

'In other words, it involves a less fundamental interference with existing legal relationships. The court will need to bear Article 8 of ECHR in mind, and to be satisfied that its order is a proportionate response to the problem, having regard to the interference with family life which is involved. In choosing between adoption and special guardianship, in most cases Article 8 is unlikely to add anything to the considerations contained in the respective welfare checklists. Under both statutes the welfare of the child is the court's paramount consideration, and the balancing exercise required by the statutes will be no different to that required by Article 8. However, in some cases, the fact that the welfare objective can be achieved with less disruption of existing family relationships can properly be regarded as helping to tip the balance.'

16.71 In *Down Lisburn Health and Social Services Trust v H*[70] Baroness of Hale of Richmond also commented on the need for proportionality.

'There is, so far as the parties to this case are aware, no European jurisprudence questioning the principle of freeing for adoption, or indeed compulsory adoption generally. The United Kingdom is unusual amongst members of the Council of Europe in permitting the total severance of family ties without parental consent. … It is, of course, the most draconian interference with family life possible. That is not to say that it can never be justified in the interests of the child. The European Court has said that where the interests of the child and the interests of the adults conflict, the interests of the child must prevail: e g *Yousef v The Netherlands.*[71] But it can be expected that the European Court would scrutinise the relevance and sufficiency of the reasons given for such a drastic interference with the same intensity with which it has scrutinised severance decisions in other care cases: see, in particular, *P, C and S v United Kingdom.*[72] The margin of appreciation accorded to the national authorities is correspondingly reduced. In a freeing application, the question must be whether it is necessary and proportionate to sever the links with the family of birth if a new family has not yet been identified.'

16.72 However, in *Re M-J (Adoption Order or Special Guardianship Order)*[73] the Court of Appeal said that it goes too far to say that it is 'incumbent' on the court to adopt 'the least interventionist option'.

'It is true that section 1(5) of the 1989 Act (the terms of which we have set out in paragraph 26 of the judgment in *Re S*) requires the court to make an order under the Act only if it considers that doing so would be better for the child than making no order at all. However, in the instant case, an order is manifestly necessary. Indeed, MJ is already subject to a care order. The recorder was right to consider whether the order was a 'proportionate' response to the child's needs. In that context, it may be material for the court to be required to consider which order is less 'interventionist'. However, in so far as any such consideration is allowed to derogate from the welfare principle, it is plainly unacceptable. The danger of the recorder's formulation is that because a special guardianship order is less 'interventionist' than an adoption order, that is the order which the court will feel constrained to make. That would be wrong as a matter of law, because it would be

---

[70]   [2006] UKHL 36, [2007] 1 FLR 121 at [34].
[71]   [2003] 1 FLR 210 at para 73.
[72]   [2002] 2 FLR 631 at para 118.
[73]   [2007] EWCA Civ 56, [2007] 1 FLR 691 at [19].

a clear derogation from the paramountcy of the welfare principle. It is also not the decision which the recorder ultimately reached.'

PLACEMENT WITHIN THE FAMILY

16.73 There is no prohibition on a child being adopted by relatives but caution has long been advised especially where the relatives are the child's grandparents, not least because of their age. It has been argued that relatives may have their own particular motives such as a desire for secrecy or arising from feelings of guilt, the wish to make reparation or 'sheer possessiveness'. On the other hand there may be a genuine sense of responsibility and a wish to work out the problem within the family.[74] Such adoptions may pose acute problems of identity and 'skewed' relationships,[75] if, for example, his mother becomes his sister and his grandparents, his parents,[76] especially if, as was apparently going to be the case in *S v B and Newport City Council*[77] (see **16.125**) the child might not be told the true situation.

16.74 The *Review of Adoption Law: Report to Ministers of an Interdepartmental Working Group*[78] shared some of these concerns:

> 'We are particularly concerned that a number of adoption applications particularly by relatives and step-parents, are made without giving proper consideration to the needs of the child and the effect of being cut-off from his or her birth family. Adoption is too often regarded as the only way of securing permanence, in part, no doubt because it is more familiar than other orders and because its long term implications are not always understood. We therefore recommend that the court should have a duty[79] ... to consider the alternative orders available ... Of course, it is important that these alternatives are explored before the application is made and discussed fully with the child, his family, the applicants and other relevant persons. The knowledge that the court will expect to know why adoption is considered more appropriate for the child than other orders should encourage agencies and guardians ... to ask this type of question from a much earlier stage in the process.'

16.75 In *Re S (Adoption Order or Special Guardianship Order)*[80] Wall LJ commented that:

> 'A particular concern is that an adoption order has, as a matter of law, the effect of making the adopted child the child of the adopters for all purposes. Accordingly, where a child is adopted by a member of his wider family, the familial relationships are inevitably changed. This is frequently referred to as the

---

[74] *A Guide to Adoption Practice* (Advisory Council on Child Care, 1970) at para VIII.12.
[75] As submitted in *Re M-J (Adoption Order or Special Guardianship Order)* [2007] EWCA Civ 56, [2007] 1 FLR 691 at [29].
[76] *A Guide to Adoption Practice* op cit para VIII 13.
[77] [2007] 1 FLR 1116.
[78] (Department of Health and the Welsh Office, 1992) at para 6.3.
[79] Supplied by CA 1989, s 1(3)(g) and now, as regards adoption by ACA 2002, s 1(6).
[80] op cit at [51].

"skewing" or "distorting" effect of adoption, and is a factor which the court must take into account when considering whether or not to make an adoption order in such a case. This is not least because the checklist under section 1 of the 2002 Act requires it to do so – see section 1(4)(f) ("the relationship which the child has with relatives"). However, the weight to be given to this factor will inevitably depend on the facts of the particular case, and it will be only one factor in the overall welfare equation.[81] As will be seen, the three appeals before this court illustrate the different weight to be placed on this factor in different circumstances, and that in some it may be of only marginal importance. In particular, as the case of *Re AJ*[82] demonstrates, both children and adults are capable of penetrating legal forms and retaining hold of the reality.'

16.76 In the linked case of *Re AJ (Adoption Order or Special Guardianship Order)*[83] Wall LJ said that 'the question of the likely distortion of family relationships by an adoption order is very fact specific and should not be overplayed.' In that case, the boy, AJ, who was nearly 6 knew 'precisely who he is'.

'He knows that his birth parents are Mr and Mrs J and that they are unable to look after him. He knows he is living with his aunt and uncle. He is not confused, nor is he likely to be in the future. What matters for him is that he should be fully accepted and cared for by his aunt and uncle as a member of their household, and as a brother to W. The difference between brother and cousin on the facts of this case is readily understandable: what matters is the relationship between the two children. In our view it is not a major or negative distortion of family relationships in this case for cousins to grow up together as brothers.'[84]

16.77 The issue of familial adoption was also considered by Hedley J in *S v B and Newport City Council: Re K*[85] when he granted a special guardianship order in respect of a 6-year-old boy to his grandparents, with whom he had lived since he was 6 months old. After considering the risk of 'skewing',[86] he drew attention to the fact that adoption was formulated principally as the means by which a child could be given security in a home 'where otherwise he would be a stranger'.

'One purpose of adoption is ... to give lifelong status to carers where otherwise it would not exist. In a familial placement that is not necessary because family status exists for life in any event. That is not to say that a familial status may never be secured by adoption. One can imagine a case where the need for security against aggressive parents including forensic aggression, may be overwhelming or where the child has such disabilities that the need for carer to have parental status may last long into majority where adoption may still be right and necessary. No doubt there will be other cases too.'

---

[81] And see also *Re AJ (Adoption Order or Special Guardianship Order)* [2007] EWCA Civ 55, [2007] 1 FLR 507 at [44].

[82] [2007] EWCA Civ 55, [2007] 1 FLR 507 and see **16.123**.

[83] Ibid at [51].

[84] Per Wall LJ at [51].

[85] [2007] 1 FLR 1116 and see **16.125**.

[86] The case was decided before *Re AJ* and the other two cases were heard by the Court of Appeal.

16.78 In the reported cases since the Act came into force, there are no examples of grandparents being granted adoption orders, although examples do exist pre-2002 where there were special circumstances – see, for example *Re B (Adoption Order: Nationality)*[87] (discussed at **2.93**).

16.79 Adoption orders in favour or uncles and aunts have been made under the 2002 Act (see **16.122** and **16.123**).

RESEARCH

16.80 Research on the outcomes of different types of placements are discussed in detail throughout this Handbook.

Kinship placements

16.81 Research into kinship placements is discussed at **12.34**.

16.82 Children placed with family members are significantly more likely to be placed with carers who have the same ethnic background.

16.83 Kinship care is not without its difficulties, both because of the demographic profile of the carers and because of potential difficulties in their relationship with the child's parents. They are likely to be significantly more disadvantaged than unrelated foster carers, being more likely to be lone carers, living at least initially in overcrowded conditions, being nearly twice as likely to have a disability or a chronic illness and six times more likely to experience financial hardship. Children placed with kin-carers have high levels of contact with relatives including parents than those living with non-kin foster carers and despite the difficulties which are experienced – the frequency of which is unclear – contact persists.

16.84 According to Joan Hunt, research does not yet give a definitive answer on whether kinship care may be better than 'stranger' care.[88] Placements appear to be at least, and probably, as stable and to be at least as good as non-kinship placements.

16.85 Hunt[89] suggests that factors associated with a positive outcome were:

- younger children;

- previous full-time care by the carer;

---

[87]   [1999] 1 FLR 907.

[88]   Ebtehaj, Lindley and Richards (eds) *Substitute Care of Children by Members of their Extended Families and Social Networks: An Overview* in *Kinship Matters* (Hart Publishing, 2006) at p 121.

[89]   Hunt, Waterhouse and Lutman *Keeping them in the family* (BAAF, 2008) at p 99.

- grandparent care;

- single carer;

- pre-placement assessment;

- positive assessment of parenting capacity;

- child's acceptance of care;

- no other children in the household other than siblings;

- disagreement about placement during proceedings;

- placement instigated by carer;

- low level of child difficulties pre-placement.

16.86 Hunt reached the conclusion that kinship care can be a positive option for many children but it is not straightforward and requires careful assessment and adequate support.[90]

> 'It clearly cannot be said ... that research has demonstrated that kinship care is *better* for children than non-related foster care. Nonetheless the evidence is broadly positive: children appear to do as least as well and possibly better and there is little to suggest they do worse.'[91]

Adoption

16.87 Research into adoption is considered at **2.25**.

16.88 Although adoption is seen as having a low rate of breakdown, the authors of the two literature reviews cited in Chapter 2, *What Works in Adoption and Foster Care*[92] and *Adoption Now Messages from Research*,[93] point to 'disruption' of the placement as being only a crude measure of success.

16.89 Factors associated with whether placements are 'successful' or not appear to include:

- Age at placement which is generally reckoned to be an important factor in a 'successful' placement because it is a proxy for other variables.[94]

---

[90] *Keeping them in the family* op cit at p 296.
[91] *Substitute Care of Children by Members of their Extended Families and Social Networks: An Overview* op cit p 121 and see also *Family and Friends Carers: A Scoping Paper* op cit at p 14.
[92] Sellick and Thoburn *What Works in Adoption and Foster Care?* (Barnados, 2004) at pp 8–14.
[93] (Department of Health, 1999) at pp 10–11.
[94] Sellick and Thoburn op cit at p 57; *Adoption Now* op cit at p 15.

'Children who are older ... tend to have experienced more separations from people who were important to them, are more likely to have been maltreated and more likely to have emotional and behavioural problems.'[95]

- Predictors of high risk associated with the child's past experiences may include:
    - the longer children have been looked after;
    - the greater the number of moves;
    - early rejection by birth parents and other siblings or half-siblings remaining at home;
    - abuse or severe deprivation.[96]

- Behaviour problems associated with high risk include:
    - hyperactivity and restlessness;
    - aggressive or sexualised behaviour;
    - defiant behaviour.[97]

- The presence of the adopters' birth children increases the risk of poorer outcomes but this factor may be sensitive to whether the children are close in age.[98] However, the presence of other unrelated children or the adopted child's siblings is not related to poor outcomes.[99]

- The parenting style of the adopters appears to be related to outcome[100] and in particular, a responsive approach involving the expression of warmth, emotional involvement and sensitivity is a positive factor.

Foster care

16.90 Chapter 15 provides a volume of statistical information, which suggests that being in care ('having a corporate parent') provides most children with a poor quality of outcome. Much of the evidence is provided by the Government in support of its argument that there should be more adoption.

16.91 Lowe and Murch[101] have commented that:

'Our over-riding impression remains that the strength of the system lies in the dedication and commitment of many of the staff to the children concerned, to their families and the ways in which the complex task of finding supportive stable placements are grappled with. But ... structural weaknesses in the system such as lengthy chains of command; inappropriate, mechanistic and inflexible management; excessive pressure of work (often resulting from competing responsibilities);

---

[95]   Sellick and Thoburn op cit at p 59.
[96]   *Adoption Now* op cit at p 15; Sellick and Thoburn op cit at p 109.
[97]   *Adoption Now* op cit at p 16.
[98]   *Adoption Now* op cit at p16; Sellick and Thoburn op cit at pp 88, 109.
[99]   *Adoption Now* at p16; Sellick and Thoburn op cit at p 109.
[100] Sellick and Thoburn op cit at p 89.
[101] *The Plan for the Child: Adoption or Long-term Fostering* (BAAF, 2001) at 155.

inadequate child care training for front line staff; and an over-emphasis on bureaucratic "paper pushing" all too often mar the service.'

16.92 However, the fact that poor outcomes can be shown for children in care does not mean that these outcomes are the result of being in care. Outcomes are subject to complex and interacting factors, for example the age at which a child enters care and his previous experiences. The outcomes for a child of 5 who spends his time in care with the same foster family may be different than for a very disturbed teenager entering care at 14 and accommodated in a series of children's homes. Sellick and Thoburn point out that 'it has become increasingly clear that good outcomes are harder to obtain for some children than others.'[102]

16.93 Despite the difficulties it appears that many children are satisfied with their arrangements. In a recent report,[103] over half of the children in care who were asked said that their present placement was definitely the right one for them.

Comparing the outcomes

16.94 Sellick and Thoburn express the opinion that 'in summary, there is insufficient evidence on the desirability of adoption, permanent fostering or residence orders, from the child's point of view'.[104] On average one in five placements from care with adoptive parents or permanent foster carers not previously known to the child breaks down within 5 years.[105] They add:

'When age at placement and other variables are held constant, there are no differences in breakdown rates between adoptive placements and placements with permanent families.'[106]

16.95 The authors of *Adoption Now: Messages from Research*[107] call for more research and point out that:

'There are ... differences between the two forms of permanent substitute care that derives from ways in which they are interpreted, from the expectations they create and from the consequences to which they are believed to lead. Such differences are not simply reflections of their different legal status although they may well have been determined by it. Nevertheless there are also similarities between foster care and adoption not least in the problems that have to be faced, in the support that is needed ...'

---

[102] *What works in adoption and foster care?* op cit at p 59.
[103] *Placements, Decisions and Reviews: A Child's View Report* (Children's Rights Director, 2006).
[104] *What works in adoption and foster care?* op cit at p 86.
[105] Ibid at p 109.
[106] Ibid.
[107] op cit at p 125.

16.96 Sellick and Thoburn[108] identify factors which may be associated with a greater risk of breakdown in all permanent placements:

- Beyond the age of 6 months, vulnerability to emotional problems stemming from difficulties with attachment, separation and loss increase.

- Children who have been institutionalised, or who have behavioural or emotional difficulties or who have been abused or neglected are at greater risk of their placement breaking down. However, children with physical or learning difficulties generally do as well or better than other children.

- Children of mixed race may be at greater risk.

- Carers having a child close in age to the child who is placed appears to increase the risk of breakdown.

16.97 Sellick and Thoburn[109] also identify moderating factors:

- Being placed with siblings has been associated with a more successful outcome in some studies.

- Having continued contact with members of the birth family has been associated with a reduced risk of breakdown in some studies but not others.

16.98 Whatever the nature of the placement, careful preparation of the carers, the honest provision of accurate information about possible difficulties and support are needed to optimise the chances of the placement succeeding.[110]

16.99 *Adoption Now: Messages from Research* points out that none of these predictive or moderating factors should be viewed in isolation, not least because there is a considerable degree of interaction.

> 'Simply checking through such factors will not be enough to ensure a successful placement but if not sufficient, it is certainly necessary.'[111]

The authors add:

> 'The satisfactions accompanying adoption for both children and adults should not be underestimated. They may serve to offset the risks.'[112]

Nor can these be more than an indication of factors which *may* be relevant. They cannot be predictive of what will happen to a particular child.

---

[108] op cit at pp 108–109.
[109] Ibid.
[110] Ibid at p 109; *What works in adoption and foster care?* op cit at p 18.
[111] Ibid.
[112] Ibid.

MAKING THE CHOICE

16.100 There are three parts to any decision about a child's placement.

- Where should the child live?[113]

- What should be the status of the child?

- What order should be made?

All must be separately addressed especially when what is at stake is not just where the child should live 'for the next few years' but whether 'the legal ties that bind the child to his [parent]' should be permanently severed by adoption.[114]

16.101 When the final decision is taken, the three questions may merge. In *Re M (Adoption or Residence Order)*,[115] for example the court had to decide whether a child should remain with her foster carers who said that they would refuse to look after her unless they could adopt her. In other cases, for example, *Re F (Adoption: Welfare of Child: Financial Considerations)*,[116] it may be impossible for foster carers to adopt the child because of financial constraints. In both cases the children needed to remain in their current placements but to do so as an adopted child in the first instance or as a foster child in the second, would be to forgo other advantages.

Where should the child live?

16.102 The decision about where a child should live is governed by the welfare tests and the checklists (see Chapter 6). While the welfare test in the 2002 Act differs from the one for the 1989 Act in that the paramount consideration is the welfare of the child *throughout his life*, it is artificial when making a decision about where a child is to live permanently to disregard his welfare after the age of 18 merely because that is when the order will cease to have effect. One disadvantage of a child remaining in care and being fostered is the fact that at 18 foster parents would be under no obligation to continue to provide a home for the young person who might then be dependent for emotional and practical support on the local authority under the provisions of s 23A to 24 D of the 1989 Act (see Chapter 15).

---

[113] 'The fundamental question': *Birmingham City Council v R* [2006] EWCA Civ 1748, [2007] 1 FLR 564 per Wall LJ at [85].

[114] *Re M (Adoption or Residence Order)* [1998] 1 FLR 570, per Judge LJ at 601 and Ward LJ at 590 and *Re B (Adoption by One Natural Parent to Exclusion of Other)* [2001] 1 FLR 589 per Hale LJ at 596.

[115] [1998] 1 FLR 570. See **16.117**.

[116] [2003] EWHC 3448 (Fam), [2004] 2 FLR 440.

The child's wishes and needs

16.103 The first stage in deciding where the child should live must be to identify:

- his wishes and feelings considered in the light of his age and understanding[117] (see **6.51**); and

- his needs (see **6.5**), including his need for continuing any relationship with his parents, siblings and relatives and other significant people in his life[118] (see Chapters 12 and 13).

The assessment of these wishes and needs is covered in Chapters 8 and 10.

The child's current carers

16.104 The second stage is to assess whether his current carers are willing and able to meet his needs, including:

- their ability to provide a home beyond childhood;

- their willingness to encourage such contact with his natural family as is required.

When carrying out the assessment it is important to consider not just the primary adult carers but also their own children (and their wishes) and their wider family.

Possibly alternative carers

16.105 The third stage is to identify alternative carers and assess their ability to meet the needs of the child including their willingness to encourage such contact with his natural family and former carers as is required.

16.106 If carers have not yet been identified (see, for example *Re F (Adoption: Welfare of Child: Financial Considerations)*[119] the court will need to assess:

- the steps which have been and will be taken to identify suitable carers;

- the likelihood of suitable carers being found;

- the time which is likely to elapse before suitable carers are found and approved;

---

[117]   ACA 2002, s 1(4)(a); CA 1989, s 1(3)(a).
[118]   ACA 2002, s 1(4)(b) and (f); CA 1989, ss 1(3) (b), 14B(1)(a).
[119]   [2003] EWHC 3448 (Fam), [2004] 2 FLR 440.

- the likely effect on the child of having to wait including the likely strengthening of any psychological bond with his current carers.[120]

16.107 The agency should be able to provide statistics on the length of time children with similar characteristics to the instant child have to wait for a placement. When seeking both this information and information about the ability of the agency to find adopters who may accept some continuing contact, it may be useful for the advocates for the parents or guardian to send the agency a series of carefully drafted and specific questions some weeks in advance of the hearing of the application for a care or placement order so as to enable a considered and informed response to be given at final hearing if not before.

16.108 The Court of Appeal in *Re P (Placement Orders: Parental Consent)*[121] said that a local authority can be 'satisfied that the child ought to be placed for adoption'[122] even though it recognises the reality that a search for adoptive parents may be unsuccessful and that, if it is, the alternative plan will have to be for long-term fostering (see **3.42**). However uncertainty and delay in some cases may persuade a court to reject this as an alternative if another appropriate family is already available.[123]

The effect of a move

16.109 Where it is proposed that the child should leave his current carers, the court will need to assess:

- his wishes and feelings;[124]

- the likely effect on him of moving and the ability of his both his current and future carers to help him overcome it;[125]

- the likelihood that he will settle after the move;

- his need, if any, for a continuing relationship with his current carers and their family and how this will be met.[126]

What status should the child have?

16.110 This is the most important question when deciding which order should be made. Given that 'there is nothing in the statutory provisions themselves

---

[120] ACA 2002, s 1(3), (4)(e); CA 1989, s 1(2), (3)(e).
[121] Op cit per Wall LJ at [135]–[140].
[122] ACA 2002, s 22(1)(d).
[123] See, for example *Re F (Adoption: Welfare of Child: Financial Considerations)* [2003] EWHC 3448 (Fam), [2004] 2 FLR 440 and **16.101**.
[124] ACA 2002, s 1(4)(a); CA 1989, s 1(3)(a).
[125] ACA 2002, s 1 (4)(e); CA 1989, s 1(3)(e).
[126] ACA 2002, s 1(4)(b),(f), (8); CA 1989, s 1(3)(b).

which limits the making of a special guardianship order or an adoption order to any given set of circumstances'[127] any of the orders *can* be made. However the fundamental effect of adoption is such that it is suggested, *per Re M-J (Adoption Order or Special Guardianship Order)*[128] that no adoption order should be made unless the other possible orders have been considered and rejected as not meeting the child's needs.

What order should be made?

16.111   The difficulties in choosing between different orders is mirrored on a micro-scale by decisions relating to the grant of orders to step-parents (see **14.111**).

Making the choice

16.112   In some cases, the decision will be obvious. For example, the child's needs will overwhelmingly require that he stays in his current placement or, if the placement is only a temporary one, he is so young that adoption is the only appropriate status and suitable prospective adopters have been identified and approved.

16.113   Other cases, however, will be much more difficult. The child may need to maintain a relationship with his parents, siblings or relatives and although adoption would otherwise be thought appropriate, prospective adopters are yet to be identified and their willingness to facilitate contact, unassessed. General assertions by agencies that they support post-adoption contact and counsel prospective adopters about the importance of contact may need to be examined. What proportion of their placements include contact? What proposals if any do they have for the prospective adopters to meet the parents? Such meetings can be helpful in securing agreement to post-adoption contact (see **13.78**).

16.114   If a placement order is made but there is a need for continuing contact and it is uncertainty about the time which will be taken to find a suitable placement or whether prospective adopters can be found who will support adoption, the court will need to consider whether to make a contact order under s 26 of the 2002 Act and if so, whether this should continue only until, for example, prospective adopters have been approved or whether it should continue after placement until the making of an adoption order. The effect of making such an order on the ability of the agency to find prospective adopters will also have to be considered. This topic is discussed at **13.112** and **13.129**.

16.115   In some cases there will be both advantages and disadvantages about two or more possible placements, not just in relation to the needs of the child

---

[127]   *Re S (Adoption Order or Special Guardianship Order)* [2007] EWCA Civ 54, [2007] 1 FLR 819 per Wall LJ at [47] and see **16.69**.

[128]   [2007] EWCA Civ 56, [2007] 1 FLR 691, see **16.72**.

and the carers' ability to meet those needs but also about the status to be accorded the child. The decision can only be taken after the most careful analysis of all possibilities. The advantages and disadvantages might usefully be examined in the light of whether their effect is likely/merely possible and short, medium and long term. Can any of the difficulties be moderated in some way, for example by strengthening a special guardianship order by making an order under s 91(14) of the 1989 Act?[129]

16.116 Whether or not the child's mother and the father if he has parental responsibility consents to the making of the order or, if not, the court can dispense with their consent on the ground that the child's welfare requires it, may be decisive. However, given the change in the test for dispensing with consent, this may be a less weighty factor than under previous legislation (see **3.137**).

16.117 An excellent example of this process of careful analysis of the various advantages and disadvantages is provided by *Re F (Adoption: Welfare of Child: Financial Considerations)*.[130] Care orders had been made in respect of five siblings because of gross neglect. They were placed in two separate foster homes. B (7 years old), C (6) and D (4) had lived with Mr and Mrs O for 2 years by the time the local authority applied for freeing (placements) orders. A loving relationship grew between the Os and the boys who thrived under their care. The Os wanted to continue to look after the boys but were unable to adopt them because of their financial circumstances. The local authority stated that because of budgetary constraints they were unable to continue to pay them a fostering allowance at the current enhanced rate but during the hearing they indicated that if the court considered that the boys' welfare required that they remain with the Os, they would reconsider the issue of financial support. However, they were of the opinion that the boys would benefit from the permanence which adoption would afford. They planned to move the boys to a 'bridging' placement until prospective adopters were identified.

16.118 After a detailed analysis of the advantages and disadvantages of both of the boys remaining where they were and of the respective benefits of adoption and disadvantages of foster care, Black J decided that the boys should remain with the Os. As a general principle adoption had more to offer children and in particular younger children than long term foster care.

> 'It cannot be denied that long-term foster care lacks the quality of permanence that adoption has, at least ostensibly ... [but] adoption is no guarantee of permanence.'[131]

16.119 After criticising the local authority's planning as being too theoretical and disowning the views of those who had actually assessed the situation in the

---

[129] See, for example, *Re S (Adoption Order or Special Guardianship Order)* [2007] EWCA Civ 54, [2007] 1 FLR 819 at **16.124** and *S v B and Newport City Council* [2007] 1 FLR 1116 at **16.125**.
[130] [2003] EWHC 3448 (Fam), [2004] 2 FLR 440.
[131] Ibid, at [76].

instant case,[132] Black J held that it was not in the interests of these particular children 'to abandon the known and loving family they were living in and to step into the unknown in pursuit of the benefits of adoption with as yet unidentified adopters. The risks of that course are too great and too likely to materialise.'[133]

16.120   One thing is clear. The decision must be taken on the basis of what is best for the subject child rather than be applying generalisations about, for example, the perceived advantages of adoption and the disadvantages of long term care. This point has been powerfully made extra-juridically by Baroness Hale of Richmond:

> 'The message for us all ... must be that the legal status should follow from the answers to the key questions about the child's future rather than the other way around. The legal status is a means and not an end. The end is the successful upbringing of the child.'[134]

Examples

16.121   Since the ACA 2002 came into force on 30 December 2005 there has been a surprising shortage of reported cases concerning which orders should be made. It is probably not a coincidence that of the seven cases discussed below, none were concerned with placement orders. Five applications concerned members of the child's extended family and the other two involved carers who were known to the parents. It may be that the reason for this lack of reported cases is that the factors which lead local authorities to seek placement orders discussed at **15.24** still influence decisions, notwithstanding the stated intention of the Government that 'more can and should be done to promote the wider use of adoption for looked after children who cannot return to their birth parents'.[135] It was suggested prior to the Act that choices were likely to be influenced by the determination of parents to oppose adoption.[136] It may be that, sub-consciously, decision makers are still influenced by the difficulties formerly encountered when attempting to dispense with consent on the ground that it was being unreasonably withheld and have not yet adapted to the new ground – that the welfare of the child requires it to be dispensed with – referred to by the Court of Appeal in *Re S (Special Guardianship)*[137] as 'a major change' (see **3.141**).

---

[132]   [2003] EWHC 3448 (Fam), [2004] 2 FLR 440 at [78].
[133]   Ibid, at [99].
[134]   Jordan and Lindley (eds) *Special Guardianship: What Does It Offer Children Who Cannot Live With Their Parents?* (Family Rights Group, 2006) Foreword at p iv.
[135]   *Adoption: A New Approach* Cm 5017 (2000) at para 1.13.
[136]   See *Adoption: Messages from Research* op cit at p 126.
[137]   [2007] EWCA Civ 54, [2007] 1 FLR 819 per Wall LJ at [69]–[72].

Adoption

Re M-J (*Adoption Order or Special Guardianship*)[138]

16.122 M was placed with foster carers at the age of about 6 months because of his mother's drug and alcohol dependency as a result of which he had suffered foetal growth retardation. Following the making of a care order he was placed with his maternal aunt at the age of 2 with a view to adoption and contact apparently ceased. His mother completed a three stage detoxification programme and when her son was just over 3, applied for the care order to be discharged and for contact. At the hearing she withdrew her applications but unsuccessfully opposed the making an adoption order, arguing that special guardianship was more appropriate. The Court of Appeal dismissed her appeal. The trial judge, supported by expert evidence, had been entitled to conclude that although many of M's needs could be met by special guardianship, the fact that he was a vulnerable child because of his small stature, his emotional history of inadequate parenting and many changes of carer meant that adoption with its clarity and certainty was required.

Re AJ (*Adoption Order or Special Guardianship Order*)[139]

16.123 AJ's parents engaged in criminal activities and their relationship was violent and unstable. When he was 6 months old, AJ was removed from their care and placed with his paternal uncle and aunt, Mr and Mrs T. A care order was made on the basis that AJ would remain with them as a long term foster child having contact with his parents. However, when AJ was 5, after a threat from AJ's father and the parents ceasing to attend contact for a period, Mr and Mrs T applied to adopt him. His parents did not oppose AJ remaining with the Ts but argued, unsuccessfully, that a special guardianship order was more appropriate given their family connection. Dismissing the appeal, the Court of Appeal held that the existence of a family tie did not preclude the making of an adoption order. AJ had been with the Ts since the age of 6 months and needed the assurance that the security of the placement could not be disturbed. This could be provided only by adoption.

Special guardianship

Re S (*Adoption Order or Special Guardianship Order*)[140]

16.124 S was placed under a care order at the age of 3 because she suffered a non-accidental injury (the perpetrator not being identified) when living with her parents and because of violence and drug taking within the home. At the age of 4 she moved from her foster carer to live with members of her extended family, but this placement broke down after 6 months and she returned to her former foster carer, who applied to adopt her. It was agreed that S's mother, who had a good relationship with the carer, should continue to have frequent

---

[138] [2007] EWCA Civ 56, [2007] 1 FLR 691.
[139] [2007] EWCA Civ 55, [2007] 1 FLR 507.
[140] [2007] EWCA Civ 54, [2007] 1 FLR 819.

and regular contact with S and that her father should continue to have some contact. The trial judge dismissed the adoption application, instead making a special guardianship order of her own volition. The Court of Appeal dismissed the carer's appeal holding that the trial judge was entitled to find on the facts of the finely balanced case that special guardianship met both S's needs for stability and provided 'a legal expression for S's loyalty both to the appellant and her mother'. The carer would have the day-to-day management of the decisions relating to S's life and the parents would not be given leave to challenge them unless something major occurred such as indicated that the whole basis of the arrangement had been changed or undermined. Both parents had agreed to an order being made under s 91(14) of the 1989 Act and this would provide 'a further level of protection from the [carer] having her autonomy over S undermined'.

S v B and Newport City Council[141]

16.125   K had lived with his maternal grandparents under a care order since he was 6 months old because his father was a long-term drug abuser who suffered from a borderline personality disorder and was violent and unpredictable. Contact between K and his parents ended and when K was 6, his grandparents applied for an adoption order and, in the alternative a special guardianship order. The parents did not actively oppose the proceedings. Hedley J granted a special guardianship order, a prohibited steps order preventing the parents having contact with K without a court order, a s 91(14) order without limitation of time and an order giving leave for K to be known by his grandparents' surname. He held that the case was one of those for which special guardianship was specially designed. The order permitted familial carers to have all the practical authority and the standing of parents while leaving intact real and readily comprehensible relationships within the family and avoiding the child having to learn that the apparent relationship was not a 'real' one.

Re L (Special Guardianship: Surname)[142]

16.126   When E was 3 months old she was placed with her maternal grandparents under a residence order because of the highly volatile relationship between her parents, both of whom were drug takers. The grandmother and the mother had a particularly complex relationship and both grandparents suffered hostility from E's father. When E was nearly 3 her grandparents applied to adopt her. This was opposed by the local authority who were concerned about the grandparents' reluctance to clarify for E who her birth parents were. The grandparents 'under considerable pressure' did not pursue the application. Black J made a special guardianship order, refused permission for E's surname to be changed and ordered some direct contact for the mother and some indirect contact for the father. The Court of Appeal dismissed the

---

[141]   [2007] 1 FLR 1116.
[142]   [2007] EWCA Civ 196, [2007] 2 FLR 50.

grandparents' appeal against the last two orders. E's welfare was the litmus test and overwhelmingly justified the refusal to allow a change of name. Honesty was the best policy.

Foster care

Re F (Adoption: Welfare of Child: Financial Considerations)[143]

16.127   See **16.117**.

Residence order

Re C (Family Placement)[144]

A 5-year-old boy, J, was living with short-term foster carers with his 13-year-old half-sister, S, because both his parents were unable to look after him because of their drug use. In care proceedings it was agreed that S should live with her father. The local authority, supported by J's guardian recommended that he should be the subject of a placement order rather than go to live with his 70-year-old grandmother with whom he had a significant relationship. The trial judge rejected the application and made a residence order in favour of the grandmother. The Court of Appeal dismissed the guardian's appeal on the basis that the judge's decision was not plainly wrong[145] although a placement order, too, might not have been plainly wrong.

'There is no doubt that it is very unusual to consider it appropriate to commit a five year old child to the care of a seventy year old grandmother[146] ... [But] first, this was the candidacy of a member of J's wider family, with the result that the law's bias in favour of placement within the family was engaged. Second, and most importantly, it was the candidacy of a grandmother who had a substantial track-record of commitment to J, through contact, in very difficult circumstances and who had established a relationship with him which [the independent professionals], all of whom had observed periods of contact, described in very positive terms. Third, there was also no doubt that, notwithstanding the absence of any biological link on her part with S, the grandmother was sincere in expressing commitment to the idea of substantial continuing contact between J and S, particularly in [her home town]. The proposal of [the local authority] and of the guardian was not, after all, for the adoption of a baby but rather of a five year old child, who had built up important attachments with family members, in particular with the grandmother, and also with S with whom ... he has lived in effect throughout his life. The proposal for J's adoption involved gross curtailment, if not effective elimination, of those two relationships. Indeed, whatever the degree of care with which J's adopters would no doubt be chosen, it could not be guaranteed that the adoption of a five year old child would not itself fail as the years proceeded.'[147]

---

[143]   [2003] EWHC 3448 (Fam), [2004] 2 FLR 440.
[144]   [2009] EWCA Civ 72, [2009] 1 FLR 1425.
[145]   See *G v G (Minors: Custody Appeal)* [1985] FLR 894.
[146]   There were other problems as well as her age – see ibid, at [16].
[147]   Per Wilson LJ at [19].

The judgment contains no reference to whether special guardianship was considered.

Chapter 17

PROCEDURE: ADOPTION

INTRODUCTION

17.1 This chapter considers the rules which apply in general to proceedings under the Adoption and Children Act 2002 (ACA 2002).

THE FAMILY PROCEDURE (ADOPTION) RULES 2005[1]

17.2 Proceedings under the Adoption and Children Act 2002, other than criminal proceedings, are governed by the Family Procedure (Adoption) Rules 2005[2] (FP(A)R 2005), described as a 'new procedural code'.[3] The FP(A)R 2005 apply not just to adoption and placement proceedings, proceedings under ACA 2002, s 84 (giving parental responsibility prior to adoption abroad) and for the annulment of overseas or Hague Convention adoptions under s 89 but also to the making and revocation of contact orders under s 26.

17.3 The FP(A)R 2005, with one exception – costs in the High Court and county courts for which parts of the Civil Procedure Rules 1998 (CPR) apply[4] – are self-contained. The Family Proceedings Rules 1991 (FPR 1991) and the Family Proceedings Court (Children Act 1989) Rules 1991 (FPC(CA)R 1991) have no application in adoption proceedings[5] and there is no cross-referencing between the two sets of Rules.

17.4 For the first time in family proceedings, the Rules govern proceedings in all three types of court: the High Court, county courts and family proceedings courts (FPCs).[6]

---

[1]   SI 2005/2795.
[2]   FP(A)R 2005, r 22.
[3]   Ibid, r 1(1).
[4]   Ibid, r 5.
[5]   Part IV of FPR 1991 is confined to proceedings under the CA 1989 – FPR 1991, r 4.1(2) – and likewise the FPC(CA)R 1991 – CA 1989, s 93(1).
[6]   FP(A)R 2005, r 5(1).

Practice directions

17.5 Based on the model of the CPR, the FP(A)R 2005 are extensively supplemented by Practice Directions given by the President of the Family Division by reason of his powers under Part 1 of Sch 2 to the Constitutional Reform Act 2005.[7]

17.6 A judge is bound to recognise and has no power to vary or alter any Practice Direction whether made under the above power or by the President under his inherent power before the 2005 Act.[8]

The overriding objective

17.7 Like the CPR[9] and applications for ancillary relief,[10] FP(A)R 2005 contains an Overriding Objective which governs the exercise of the courts' case management powers. Its purpose, like that of the objective in other Rules, is to provide 'a compass to guide courts and litigants and legal advisers as to their general course'.[11] As Lord Woolf wrote in *Access to Justice Final Report*:[12]

> 'Rules of court are not like an instruction manual for operating a piece of machinery. Ultimately their purpose is to guide the court and the litigants towards the just resolution of the case. Although the rules can offer detailed directions for the technical steps to be taken, the effectiveness of those steps depends upon the spirit in which they are carried out. That in turn depends on an understanding of the fundamental purpose of the rules and the underlying system of procedure.'

17.8 Rule 1(1) defines the objective as 'enabling the court to deal with cases justly, having regard to the welfare issues involved'.

17.9 'Dealing with a case justly' includes, so far as is practicable:

- ensuring that it is dealt with expeditiously and fairly;

- dealing with the case in ways which are proportionate to the nature, importance and complexity of the issues;

- ensuring that the parties are on an equal footing;

- saving expense; and

---

[7]   *Bovale v Secretary of State for Communities and Local Government* [2009] EWCA Civ 171, [2009] 3 All ER 340 per Waller and Dyson LJJ at [18].
[8]   Ibid, per Waller and Dyson LJJ at [28].
[9]   CPR, Pt1.1.
[10] FPR 1991, r 2.51D.
[11] *Access to Justice Final Report* (HMSO, 1996) (Lord Woolf) at p 275.
[12] Ibid, at p 274.

- allotting to it an appropriate share of the court's resources, while taking into account the need to allot resources to other cases.[13]

17.10 In applying the objective, the court has to balance all the factors without giving undue weight to any of them.[14]

17.11 The court must seek to give effect to the overriding objective when it exercises any power given to it by the Rules or interprets any rule.[15]

17.12 The parties are required to help the court to further the overriding objective.[16]

Court's duty to manage cases

17.13 The court must further the overriding objective by actively managing cases.[17] This includes:[18]

- encouraging the parties to co-operate with each other in the conduct of the proceedings;

- identifying at an early stage:
  - the issues; and
  - who should be a party to the proceedings;

- deciding promptly:
  - which issues need full investigation and hearing and which do not; and
  - the procedure to be followed in the case;

- deciding the order in which issues are to be resolved;

- encouraging the parties to use an alternative dispute resolution procedure if the court considers that appropriate and facilitating the use of such procedure;

- helping the parties to settle the whole or part of the case;

- fixing timetables or otherwise controlling the progress of the case;

---

[13] FP(A)R 2005, r 1(2). For a detailed discussion of the difficulties in applying these goals 'which are capable of pointing in different directions', see *Zuckerman on Civil Procedure* (Sweet & Maxwell, 2nd edn, 2006) paras 1.7–1.38.

[14] *Holmes v SGB Services Plc* [2001] EWCA CIv 354 per Buxton LJ at [38].

[15] FP(A)R 2005, r 2.

[16] Ibid, r 3.

[17] Ibid, r 4(1).

[18] Ibid, r 4(2).

- considering whether the likely benefits of taking a particular step justify the cost of taking it;

- dealing with as many aspects of the case as it can on the same occasion;

- dealing with the case without the parties needing to attend at court;

- making use of technology;[19] and

- giving directions to ensure that the case proceeds quickly and efficiently.

COMMENCING PROCEEDINGS

Alternative dispute resolution

17.14 The possibility of resolving disputes by way of alternative dispute resolution (ADR), including mediation and family conferences, needs to be considered as much in adoption as in other litigation involving children although the unique issues in adoption, especially where prospective adopters wish to remain anonymous, may make ADR less appropriate and common.

17.15 ADR is considered in detail at **18.1**, mediation at **18.3** and family conferences at **18.7**.

Giving notice

Child placed for adoption by an adoption agency

17.16 No notice of an intention to adopt a child needs to be given to the proposed adopters' local authority when the child is placed for adoption by an agency.

Child not placed for adoption by an agency

17.17 An adoption order may not be made in respect of a child who was not placed for adoption with the applicants by an adoption agency[20] unless the applicants have given notice of their intention to apply for an order to the appropriate authority, such notice to be given not more than 2 years or less than 3 months before the application is made.[21] The 'appropriate local authority' means the local authority for the area in which, at the time of giving

---

[19] For example, by conducting case management conferences by telephone or taking evidence over a video link (FP(A)R 2005, r 125 and PD 15 Annex 3).
[20] Defined as including a Scottish or Northern Irish adoption agency.
[21] ACA 2002, s 44.

notice of intention to adopt, they have their home[22] or, where they no longer have a home in England and Wales, the authority for the area in which they last had such a home.[23]

17.18 Whether or not the applicant has a 'home' in the area of a local authority is a question of fact. The term 'home' is incapable of precise definition for the purposes of the Act. However, using common sense, it comprises the essential elements of regular occupation (whether past, present, intended for the future or intermittent) with some degree of permanency and based on a right of occupation.[24] However, the requirement does not involve the child and the applicant having to be actually living in the home for any particular length of time. What is required is that they should spend sufficient time there – the length of which will depend on the circumstances of the individual case – to enable the local authority to see the applicants and the child together.[25]

17.19 If the applicant has a home in England and Wales when the application is issued and the relevant authority has had sufficient opportunities to see the child with the applicant it does not matter that the applicant moves from the jurisdiction before the order is granted.[26]

Example

Re Y (Minors) (Adoption: Jurisdiction)[27]

17.20 The applicants wished to adopt the female applicant's two children by a previous marriage. The male, but not the female, applicant was domiciled in the UK. They resided in Hong Kong although the children attended boarding school in England, returning to Hong Kong for the holidays. During half term the children stayed in England at the home of the male applicant's daughter, a home which both applicants used as a base when visiting England. It was held that they did not have a 'home' in the jurisdiction.

Child to live with the proposed adopters before the application

17.21 Section 42 of the ACA 2002 requires that no application for an adoption order made be made unless:

- Where the child was placed for adoption with the applicant or applicants by an adoption agency or in pursuance of an order of the High Court, or

---

[22] ACA 2002, s 44(9)(b).
[23] Ibid, s 44(9)(a), Local Authority (Adoption) (Miscellaneous Provisions) Regulations 2005, SI 2005/3390, reg 3.
[24] *Re Y (Minors) (Adoption: Jurisdiction)* [1986] 1 FLR 152 followed in *Ecc v M* [2008] EWHC 332 (Fam).
[25] Ibid.
[26] *Re SL (Adoption: Home in the Jurisdiction)* [2004] EWHC 1283 (Fam), [2005] 1 FLR 118.
[27] [1986] 1 FLR 152.

the applicant is a parent of the child, the child must have had his home with the applicant or, in the case of an application by a couple, with one or both of them at all times during the period of 10 weeks preceding the application.[28]

- If the applicant or one of them is the partner of a parent of the child, the child must have had his home with the applicant at all times during the period of 6 months preceding the application.[29]

- If the applicants are local authority foster parents, the condition is that the child must have had his home with the applicants at all times during the period of 1 year preceding the application.[30]

- In any other case, the condition is that the child must have had his home with the applicant or, in the case of an application by a couple, with one or both of them for not less than 3 years (whether continuous or not) during the period of 5 years preceding the application.[31]

17.22   In the case of local authority foster parents or applicants under ACA 2002, s 41(5) ('any other case') the court can give leave to make the application if the condition is not satisfied.

17.23   The application for leave is made in Form FP2 and is governed by Part 9 of the Rules (see **17.136**). Parents who have parental responsibility, even though a placement order is in force, are proper respondents. The child probably does not have to be but may be joined as a respondent.[32]

17.24   The test for granting leave is the same as for granting leave to apply for the revocation of a placement order[33] (see **3.52**). The court's discretion to grant leave is not governed by the welfare test[34] but both the welfare of the child and the prospect of the application succeeding should be weighed. In the vast majority of cases the court may usefully apply the test applicable to permission to appeal: does the application have 'a real prospect of success?' However the required analysis of success might not always be carried out within an analysis of the prospects of success.[35]

---

28   ACA 2002, s 42(2).
29   Ibid, s 41(3).
30   Ibid, s 41(4).
31   Ibid, s 41(5).
32   *Re A: Coventry County Council v CC and A* [2007] EWCA Civ 1383, [2008] 1 FLR 959.
33   Ibid.
34   *M v Warwickshire CC* [2007] EWCA Civ 1084, [2008] 1 FLR 1093 at [22].
35   Ibid.

Example

Re A: Coventry County Council v CC and A[36]

17.25 A child was placed with a short term foster mother when 6 days old. Five months later she told the local authority that she wished to adopt the child. They rejected the proposal but delayed responding to the foster mother's response as to why she should be allowed to adopt. A placement order was obtained and a match with prospective adopters approved. The foster carer, supported by the guardian and the child's mother, applied for leave to apply for an adoption order. Leave was refused at first instance but granted on appeal. Suitability to foster a child could not be equated with either suitability or a lack of suitability to adopt. The trial judge should have asked whether there was a real prospect that the foster carer could persuade the court that her adopting the child was the optimum placement for the child.

Opportunity to see the child

17.26 Where the child was not placed by the agency, it may be that, as when the child is placed by an agency, the opportunity to see the applicants and the child does not have to be in England and Wales but can be elsewhere so long as there is a home within the area of the local authority to whom notice has been given.[37] However, it may be difficult to show that the authority 'had sufficient opportunity' to see the child if it meant, in a non-agency case, a social worker having to travel abroad.

17.27 In addition, an adoption order may not be made unless the court is satisfied that sufficient opportunities to see the child with the applicant or, in the case of an application by a couple, both of them together in the home environment, have been given

- where the child was placed for adoption with the applicant or applicants by an adoption agency,[38] to that agency;

- in any other case, to the local authority within whose area the home is.[39]

Obtaining leave

17.28 There is no equivalent rule such as that contained in s 10 of the Children Act 1989 (CA 1989) which requires any prospective applicants to have the leave of the court before making an adoption application. However, the court may not hear an application for an adoption order in relation to a child,

---

[36] [2007] EWCA Civ 1383, [2008] 1 FLR 959.
[37] See *Re A (A Child) (Adoption: Assessment Outside Jurisdiction)* [2009] EWCA Civ 41 per Wall LJ at [63]–[67] where the question was not answered.
[38] References to an adoption agency include a Scottish or Northern Irish adoption agency; ACA 2002, s 42(8).
[39] ACA 2002, s 42(7).

where a previous application for an adoption order made in relation to the child by the same persons was refused by any court in England and Wales, Scotland, Northern Ireland, the Isle of Man or any of the Channel Islands unless it appears to the court that, because of a change in circumstances or for any other reason, it is proper to hear the application.[40]

Do the courts have jurisdiction?

Placement order

17.29 In *Re M (Care Orders: Jurisdiction)*[41] Hale J held that it is sufficient to confer jurisdiction to hear public law cases that the child is physically present in England and Wales, or, possibly, even if not physically present, has his ordinary or habitual presence here. As the local authority will already have or be seeking a care order when applying for a placement order, the same approach might be adopted for those proceedings.

Adoption order

17.30 Where the application is made by a couple, at the time the application is issued either at least one of them must be domiciled in a part of the British Islands[42] or both of them must have been habitually resident in part of the British Islands for a period of not less than 1 year ending with the date of the application.[43]

17.31 Where the application is made by a single person, s/he must either be domiciled in a part of the British Islands or have been habitually resident in part of the British Islands for a period of not less than 1 year ending with the date of the application.[44] For habitual residence, see **18.18**.

17.32 In cases where the child was not placed for adoption by an agency, the proposed adopters must give notice of intention to adopt to the 'appropriate' local authority.[45] However, such an authority can include where they no longer have a home in England and Wales, the authority for the area in which they last had such a home.[46] Therefore, where they qualify by way of domicile they are not required to be resident in England and Wales or, indeed, in any part of the UK.

---

[40]   ACA 2002, s 48.
[41]   [1997] 1 FLR 456.
[42]   Ie the United Kingdom, the Channel Islands and the Isle of Man – the Interpretation Act 1978, Sch 1. For an example of an adoption application transferred from the High Court to the county court where the prospective adopters resided in the Isle of Man, see *Re J (Adoption Procedure: Isle of Man)* [2000] 2 FLR 633.
[43]   ACA 2002. s 49(1)–(3).
[44]   Ibid, s 49(1)–(3).
[45]   Ibid, s 44(2).
[46]   Ibid, s 44(9)(a), Local Authority (Adoption) (Miscellaneous Provisions) Regulations 2005, SI 2005/3390, reg 3.

Section 26 order

17.33 On the date the application is made ('the relevant date') the child concerned must be habitually resident in England and Wales, or be present in England and Wales and not habitually resident in any part of the UK and, in either case, matrimonial proceedings or civil partnership proceedings for divorce, nullity or judicial separation are not continuing in a court in Scotland or Northern Ireland in respect of the marriage of the parents of the child concerned.[47]

Which court?

17.34 Proceedings under the Act can be heard at and, subject to exceptions, commenced in any level of court. The exceptions are:

- Proceedings under ACA 2002, s 23 to vary a placement order by substituting one local authority for another must be commenced in a family proceedings court.[48]

- Proceedings for an adoption order must be commenced in a family proceedings court unless any local authority will be a party.[49]

- Proceedings which are commenced in a county court must be started in or, if commenced elsewhere and transferred, must be transferred to, an adoption centre.[50]

- Proceedings for a Convention adoption order or an adoption order under ACA 2002, s 83 (children brought into the UK for the purpose of adoption) must, subject to art 7 be started in, and if transferred to, a country court, transferred to an intercountry adoption centre.[51]

- Where proceedings for an adoption order are pending, proceedings concerning the same child under:
  - s 29(4)(b) (leave to apply for a residence order);
  - s 29(5)(b) (leave to apply for a special guardianship order);
  - s 8 of the 1989 Act where s 28(1)(a) or s 29(4)(b) of the 2002 Act applies (leave obtained to make application for a residence order);
  - s 14A of the 1989 Act where s 28(1)(b) or 29(5)(b) of the 2002 Act applies (leave obtained to make application for a special guardianship order);
  - s 37(a) (leave to remove the child); or
  - s 47(3) or (5) (leave to oppose the making of an adoption order);

---

[47] Family Law Act 1986, ss 2(2B), 3(1), (2), 7(aa), (b), (c).
[48] Allocation and Transfer of Proceedings Order 2008, SI 2008/2836 (L18), art 5(1)(d).
[49] Ibid, art 5(1)(e).
[50] Ibid, art 11(1), art 21(1).
[51] Ibid, arts 6(d), 11(2) and 21(2). An 'intercountry adoption centre' is defined in art 2 as one listed in column 4 of the Schedule to the Order.

must be started in the court in which the adoption proceedings are pending.[52]

- Where proceedings for a placement order are pending, proceedings under s 30(2)(b) (leave to remove a child from accommodation provided by the local authority) must be started in the court in which the placement proceedings are pending.[53]

- Where proceedings under s 42(6) (leave to apply for an adoption order) are pending, proceedings under s 38(3)(a) or s 40(2)(a) of that Act (leave to remove a child) must be started in the court in which those proceedings are pending.[54]

Transferring applications between courts

17.35 Part 3 of the Allocation and Transfer of Proceedings Order 2008 controls the transfer of proceedings between courts of the same kind or between courts of a different kind. This is supplemented by the Practice Direction: Allocation and Transfer of Proceedings.[55]

17.36 The Rules and Practice Direction are discussed in detail at **18.24**. There are, however, additions to the guidance relating to the transfer to the High Court of proceedings under the Act. In addition to the matters set out at **18.47**, when a court is considering transferring proceedings to the High Court it must consider the following matters:

- [Whether] an adoption order is sought in relation to a child who has been adopted abroad in a country whose adoption orders are not recognised in England and Wales;[56]

- [Whether] an adoption order is sought in relation to a child who has been brought into the UK in circumstances where s 83 (restrictions on bringing children into the United Kingdom) applies and:
  - (a) the person bringing the child, or causing the child to be brought:
    - (i) has not complied with any requirement imposed by regulations made under s 83(4); or
    - (ii) has not met any condition required to be met by regulations made under s 83(5) within the required time; or
  - (b) there are complicating features in relation to the application.[57]

17.37 In addition, because ACA 2002, s 95 (prohibitions of certain payments) enables the High Court to approve payments retrospectively, and because of the

---

[52]   Allocation and Transfer of Proceedings Order 2008, SI 2008/2836, art 8(1).
[53]   Ibid, art 8(2).
[54]   Ibid, art 8(3).
[55]   2 November 2008.
[56]   Ibid, para 5.1(3).
[57]   Ibid, 5.1(4).

need to consider issues of public policy (see **6.163**), it would seem appropriate for cases involving breaches of the prohibition – or indeed of any breaches of prohibitions in s 92 (restrictions on arranging adoptions), s 94 (reports) and s 123 (restrictions on advertisements) (see **7.50**) – to be transferred to the High Court.

Which judge?

17.38 In the High Court and the county court the following judges have jurisdiction to hear all proceedings under the Act:

- a judge of the Family Division of the High Court;[58]

- save for certain exceptions, a person acting as a judge of the Family Division under s 9(1) of the Supreme Court Act 1981;[59]

- a recorder authorised to sit as a judge of the Family Division under s 9(4) of that Act;[60]

- a person sitting as a recorder who is a District Judge (Magistrates' Courts) and is nominated for public family law proceedings;[61]

- a person sitting as a recorder who is a district judge of the Principal Registry;[62]

- a circuit judge, deputy circuit judge or recorder nominated for public family law proceedings.[63]

17.39 In the High Court and the county court the following judges have jurisdiction to hear interlocutory proceedings under the Act or under s 21 of the Adoption Act 1976 or for a residence order or special guardianship order where the child is placed for adoption or a placement order is in force:[64]

- a district judge of the Principal Registry;

- a district judge nominated for private family law proceedings.

17.40 For the Family Proceedings Court, see **18.77**.

17.41 A single justice may perform the functions listed in Practice Direction 2.

---

[58] Family Proceedings (Allocation to Judiciary) Directions 2008, para 7(a).
[59] Ibid, para 7(b).
[60] Ibid, para 7(c).
[61] Ibid, para 7(d).
[62] Ibid, para 7(e).
[63] Ibid, para 6.
[64] Ibid.

THE APPLICATION

17.42 The Forms to be used for various applications are listed in Practice Direction Forms.

17.43 The applications must be accompanied by any documents referred to in those Forms.

17.44 For the use of serial numbers in adoption applications, see **17.142**.

Commonly used Forms

17.45

Placement order	**Form A 50** This must be accompanied by:

- a certified copy of the child's birth certificate or, where the child has previously been adopted, a certified copy of the entry in the Adopted Children Register;
- any written consent of the parent or guardian to the child being placed for adoption and any notice of withdrawal of such consent;
- where the court is asked to dispense with the consent of a parent, a brief statement of the facts relied on;
- a copy of any final care order;
- if available, a copy of any order or agreement relating to the grant of parental responsibility;
- if the authority was a party to the proceedings, a copy of any final order relating to the child that has effect and, if available, any maintenance award or agreement;
- if the authority was a party, a copy of any final order that has effect relating to a full, half- or step-sibling of the child.

Variation of a placement order	**Form A 51**

This must be accompanied by:

- a copy of the placement order;
- if either authority was a party to the proceedings, a copy of any final order relating to the child that has effect;

- if either authority was a party, a copy of any final order that has effect relating to a full, half- or step-sibling of the child.

Revocation of a placement order

Form A 52

This must be accompanied by:

- a copy of the placement order;
- if the applicant was a party to the proceedings, a copy of any final order relating to the child that has effect;
- if the applicant was a party, a copy of any final order that has effect relating to a full, half- or step-sibling of the child;
- a copy of any order giving the applicant permission to apply for the order to be revoked.

Contact order

Form A 53

This must be accompanied by:

- A copy of any of the following orders which were in effect immediately before the agency was authorised to place the child for adoption or placed a child when s/he was less than 6 weeks old:
  - a contact order made under s 8 or 34 of the CA 1989 in favour of the applicant;
  - a residence order in favour of the applicant;
  - an order made under the jurisdiction of the High Court giving the applicant the care of the child;
- if the applicant was a party to the proceedings, a copy of any final order relating to the child that has effect;
- if the applicant was a party, a copy of any final order that has effect relating to a full, half- or step-sibling of the child;
- a copy of any order giving the applicant permission to apply for a contact order.

Variation or revocation of a contact order

Form A54

This must be accompanied by

- a copy of the contact order the applicant is asking the court to vary or revoke;

- if the applicant is a party to the proceedings, a copy of any other final order relating to the child that has effect;
- if the applicant is a party to the proceedings, a copy of any final order relating to a full, half- or step-sibling of the child that has effect.

Adoption order   **Form A 58**

This must be accompanied by:

- a certified copy of the child's birth certificate or, where the child has previously been adopted, a certified copy of the entry in the Adopted Children Register;
- where the court is asked to dispense with the consent of a parent, a brief statement of the facts relied on;
- a copy of any placement or freeing order relating to the child;
- if the applicant was a party to the proceedings, a copy of any final order relating to the child that has effect and, if available, any maintenance award or agreement;
- if the applicant was a party, a copy of any final order that has effect relating to a full, half- or step-sibling of the child;
- reports by a registered medical practitioner on the health of the child and the applicants covering the matters specified in the Practice Direction: Reports by a registered medical practitioner (health reports) unless:
  - the child was placed with the applicant by an agency;
  - the child is the child of the applicant or one of the applicants; or
  - the applicant is applying alone as the partner of a parent of the child;
- if a parent of the child has died, a certified copy of the entry in the Register of Deaths;
- if the applicant is submitting evidence of marriage or civil partnership, a certified copy of the entry in the Register of Marriage or the Register of Civil Partnerships;

- where the husband, wife or civil partner of the applicant has died, a certified copy of the entry in the Register of Deaths;

- a copy of any decree absolute of divorce or decree of nullity of the applicant's marriage;

- in relation to a civil partnership, a copy of any dissolution order or nullity order of the applicant's civil partnership;

- any documentary evidence supporting the reasons why the applicant is applying to adopt the child without their husband, wife or civil partner, such as a decree of judicial separation;

- if the applicant's name as entered on the application form is different from the name shown on any evidence of marriage or civil partnership sent with the application, any documentary evidence to explain the difference.

Giving parental responsibility prior to adoption abroad ('Section 84')

Form A61

This must be accompanied by:

- a certified copy of the child's birth certificate or, where the child has previously been adopted, a certified copy of the entry in the Adopted Children Register;

- where the court is asked to dispense with the consent of a parent, a brief statement of the facts relied on;

- a copy of any placement or freeing order relating to the child;

- if the applicant was a party to the proceedings, a copy of any final order relating to the child that has effect and, if available, any maintenance award or agreement;

- if the applicant was a party, a copy of any final order that has effect relating to a full, half- or step-sibling of the child;

- reports by a registered medical practitioner on the health of the child and the applicants covering the matters specified in the Practice Direction: Reports by a registered medical practitioner (health reports) unless:

- the child was placed with the applicant by an agency;
- the child is the child of the applicant or one of the applicants; or
- the applicant is applying alone as the partner of a parent of the child;

- if a parent of the child has died, a certified copy of the entry in the Register of Deaths;
- if the applicant is submitting evidence of marriage or civil partnership, a certified copy of the entry in the Register of Marriage or the Register of Civil Partnerships;
- where the husband, wife or civil partner of the applicant has died, a certified copy of the entry in the Register of Deaths;
- a copy of any decree absolute of divorce or decree of nullity of the applicant's marriage;
- in relation to a civil partnership, a copy of any dissolution order or nullity order of the applicant's civil partnership;
- any documentary evidence supporting the reasons why the applicant applying for parental responsibility prior to adopting the child abroad without their husband, wife or civil partner, such as a decree of judicial separation;
- if the applicant's name as entered on the application form is different from the name shown on any evidence of marriage or civil partnership sent with the application, any documentary evidence to explain the difference.

Annulment of overseas or Hague Convention adoptions (section 89)

Form A63

This must be accompanied by:

- a copy of the Convention adoption, Convention adoption order or other overseas adoption order the applicant is asking the court to annul;
- a copy of any other determinations under s 91;
- if the applicant was a party to the proceedings, a copy of any final order relating to the child that has effect;

- if the applicant was a party to the proceedings, a copy of any final order relating to a full, half- or step-sibling of the child that has effect;
- a copy of any court order giving the applicant permission to apply for the Convention adoption, Convention adoption order or other overseas order to be annulled.

THE RESPONDENTS

17.46 Part 5 of the Rules differentiate between respondents to an application[65] – who are parties – and those who are also to receive a copy of the application[66] – who may have a role to play, for example a local authority to whom notice of an intention to adopt has been given or a reporting officer who have an interest in the proceedings and who may wish to apply to be joined as a party.

17.47 Persons who are not parties but who are to receive a copy of the application will not receive the documents required to be filed with the application, except for the child's guardian, reporting officer and any local authority to whom notice of intention has been given. These will receive a copy of the birth or previous adoption certificate and any health report filed in support of an adoption application. In addition, where the court is being asked to dispense with the consent of a parent, the statement of facts will be sent to the parent or guardian, the child's guardian, reporting officer, local authority and any agency which has placed the child for adoption.[67]

Placement order

Respondents

17.48

- Each parent who has parental responsibility for the child or guardian of the child;

- any person in whose favour an order under the 1989 Act is in force in relation to the child;

- any adoption agency or voluntary organisation which has parental responsibility for, is looking after, or is caring for, the child;

- the child; and

---

[65] FP(A)R 2005, r 23, Table 2.
[66] Ibid, r 24(1)(b)(ii), Practice Direction Part 5.
[67] Ibid, r 24(1).

- the parties or any persons who are or have been parties to proceedings for a care order in respect of the child where those proceedings have led to the application for the placement order.

Persons who are to receive a copy of the application

17.49

- Each parent with parental responsibility for the child or guardian of the child;

- any appointed children's guardian, children and family reporter and reporting officer;

- any other person directed by the court to receive a copy.

Variation of a placement order

Respondents

17.50

- The parties to the proceedings leading to the placement order which it is sought to have varied except the child who was the subject of those proceedings; and

- any person in whose favour there is provision for contact.

Persons who are to receive a copy of the application

17.51

- Each parent with parental responsibility for the child or guardian of the child;

- any appointed children's guardian, children and family reporter and reporting officer;

- any other person directed by the court to receive a copy.

Revocation of a placement order

Respondents

17.52

- The parties to the proceedings leading to the placement order which it is sought to have revoked; and

- any person in whose favour there is provision for contact.

Persons who are to receive a copy of the application
17.53

- Each parent with parental responsibility for the child or guardian of the child;

- any appointed children's guardian and children and family reporter;

- the local authority authorised by the placement order to place the child for adoption;

- any other person directed by the court to receive a copy.

Contact order

Respondents
17.54

- The adoption agency authorised to place the child for adoption or which has placed the child for adoption;

- the person with whom the child lives or is to live;

- each parent with parental responsibility for the child or guardian of the child; and

- the child where:
  - the adoption agency authorised to place the child for adoption or which has placed the child for adoption or a parent with parental responsibility for the child opposes the making of the contact order under ACA 2006, s 26;
  - he opposes the making of the contact order under s 26;
  - existing provision for contact is to be revoked;
  - relatives of the child do not agree to the arrangements for allowing any person contact with the child, or a person not being allowed contact with the child; or
  - he is suffering or is at risk of suffering harm within the meaning of the 1989 Act.

Persons who are to receive a copy of the application
17.55

- All the parties;

- any appointed children's guardian and children and family reporter;

- any other person directed by the court to receive a copy.

Variation or revocation of a contact order

Respondents

17.56

- The parties to the proceedings leading to the contact order which it is sought to have varied or revoked; and

- revoking a contact order, any person named in the contact order.

Parties who are to receive a copy of the application

17.57

- All the parties;

- any appointed children's guardian and children and family reporter;

- any other person directed by the court to receive a copy.

Adoption order

Respondents

17.58

- Each parent who has parental responsibility for the child or guardian of the child unless he has given notice under ACA 2002, s 20(4)(a) (statement of wish not to be informed of any application for an adoption order) which has effect. This does not therefore include parents after a placement order has been made;

- any person in whose favour there is provision for contact;

- any adoption agency having parental responsibility for the child under s 25;

- any adoption agency which has taken part at any stage in the arrangements for adoption of the child;

- any local authority to whom notice under s 44 (notice of intention to adopt or apply for a s 84 order) has been given;

- any local authority or voluntary organisation which has parental responsibility for, is looking after, or is caring for, the child; and

- the child where:
  - permission has been granted to a parent or guardian to oppose the making of the adoption order under s 47(3) or 47(5);
  - he opposes the making of an adoption order;
  - a children and family reporter recommends that it is in the best interests of the child to be a party to the proceedings and that recommendation is accepted by the court;
  - he is already an adopted child;
  - any party to the proceedings or the child is opposed to the arrangements for allowing any person contact with the child, or a person not being allowed contact with the child after the making of the adoption order;
  - the application is for a Convention adoption order or a section 84 order;
  - he has been brought into the UK in the circumstances where s 83(1) applies (restriction on bringing children in);
  - the application is for an adoption order other than a Convention adoption order and the prospective adopters intend the child to live in a country or territory outside the British Islands after the making of the adoption order; or
  - the prospective adopters are relatives of the child.

Persons who are to receive a copy of the application

17.59

- Any appointed children's guardian, children and family reporter and reporting officer;

- the local authority to whom notice under s 44 (notice of intention to apply to adopt or apply for a section 84 order) has been given;

- the adoption agency which placed the child for adoption with the applicants;

- any other person directed by the court to receive a copy.

Giving parental responsibility prior to adoption abroad (s 84)

Respondents

17.60 As for an adoption order.

Persons who are to receive a copy of the application

17.61   As for an adoption order.

Annulment of overseas or Hague Convention Adoptions (s 89)

Respondents

17.62

- The adopters;

- the parents;

- the adoption agency; and

- the local authority to whom notice under s 44 (notice of intention to adopt or apply for a section 84 order) has been given.

Persons who are to receive a copy of the application

17.63

- All the parties;

- any appointed children's guardian and children and family reporter;

- any other person directed by the court to receive a copy.

The father without parental responsibility

Background

17.64   The consent to a child being adopted is required of the child's father if he has parental responsibility (see **3.6**). Likewise he is entitled to be a party to any proceedings for a placement order or adoption (see **17.48**). However, a father without parental responsibility has no such rights.

17.65   The circumstances of a father without parental responsibility vary enormously. Some are totally involved with the child, lacking parental responsibility only because they have not married the mother, the child was born before 1 December 2003[68] and he and the mother never thought there was a need to enter into a parental responsibility agreement. Such a father can easily acquire responsibility either by entering into an agreement under s 4(1) of the CA 1989 or obtain a parental responsibility order from the court (see **14.75**). At the other end of the spectrum are fathers of children born as a result of rape, transient or coercive relationships or fathers who are indifferent to

---

[68]   And therefore the provisions of s 4(1A) of the CA 1989 do not have effect.

their child's welfare or even existence. The European Court of Human Rights in the case of *B v UK*[69] held that this spectrum of situations provides an objective and reasonable justification for the difference in treatment between married fathers who automatically had parental responsibility and unmarried fathers who did not.

17.66 The difficulty faced by some fathers is that while they may be potentially suitable fathers, they may have had only a fleeting relationship with the mother and are unaware that she became pregnant and given birth. They may be unaware of the adoption proceedings. The birth mother may oppose them being informed. The issue for adoption agencies, reporting officers and guardians is whether, in these circumstances the father should be traced and told about the child and the proceedings.

17.67 In some cases, no benefit may accrue to the child from the father being informed. In other cases, he may be a suitable carer. In *Re B (Adoption: Natural Parent)*,[70] for example, the mother put her child up for adoption without informing the father of the pregnancy or the birth. Purely by chance the agency learned of the father's whereabouts. When he was contacted, he expressed the desire to look after the child. The child thrived in his care and he was later granted an adoption order. In most cases it will be of benefit to the child to have some knowledge of who his father was (see **12.6**). In the Court of Appeal Dame Elizabeth Butler-Sloss P expressed her concern about the position of the father in relation to the decisions made by the mother:

'In principle natural fathers should be joined as respondents ... I recognize, of course, that there will be cases where it would be entirely inappropriate to join the natural father such as possible violence to the mother or risk to her life if the father was informed.'[71]

There is an argument that any father has a right (albeit not under Art 8) to know that he has a child and to be at least consulted about his child's future.

17.68 Against these arguments, the mother may argue that she fears violence from the father if he is informed or she fears repercussions if her family were to find out about the birth. In other cases she may want her privacy to be respected. In France, for example mothers are allowed to register their child's birth anonymously.[72]

17.69 Mothers have always held these reasons for not wanting the putative father informed and until the belief developed that it was in the best interests of children to know about their origins, these provided few if any difficulties for

---

[69] [2000] 1 FLR 1.
[70] [2001] UKHL 70, [2002] 1 FLR 196.
[71] [2001] 1 FLR 589, at 600.
[72] See Steiner '*Odievre v France*: Desperately seeking Mother – Anonymous Births in the European Court of Human Rights' [2003] CFLQ 425; *Odievre v France* [2003] 1 FCR 621; *Kearns v France* [2008] 1 FLR 888 and *Re C (A Child) v XYZ County Council* [2007] EWCA Civ 1206, [2008] 1 FLR 1294 per Thorpe LJ at [61].

the legal process. However in 1972 the Houghton Committee[73] both emphasised the importance of knowing about one's origins (see **12.13**) and examined the position of putative fathers, although without linking the two topics.

> 'It is important that the putative father should be notified of the proceedings where he is known and can be found. If the putative father does not appear, the court will need to be satisfied that he does not wish to or that the agency has made reasonable efforts to trace him without success ... If he cannot be found after genuine enquiry ... this should not prevent the court proceeding ...'[74]

17.70 The increasing awareness of the implications of the European Convention for the Protection of Human Rights and Fundamental Freedoms 1950 following the passing of the Human Rights Act 1998 gave further impetus to a growing problem. As Dame Elizabeth Butler-Sloss P commented in 2001, 'the climate of opinion has changed over the last 10–15 years and the approach of the family courts to the position of the father without parental responsibility has reflected that change'.[75]

The duty of the agency, the guardian and the Court

17.71 The agency is under a number of duties, created by various statutory provisions, regulations and rules, to ascertain information about the putative father albeit that the duties are subject to such limitations as 'so far as is reasonably practicable'. For example:

- Where the child is being looked after by a local authority, the authority is under a duty to consult all parents 'so far as is reasonably practicable'.[76]

- Where the putative father does not have parental responsibility and his identity is known to the agency, the agency must so far as is reasonably practicable provide a counselling service for him, explain the implications of adoption, and ascertain his wishes and feelings regarding the child, the proposed placement of the child for adoption and the adoption as well as any wishes and feelings about the child's religious and cultural upbringing and contact with the child[77] (see **7.90**).

- The agency's report to its adoption panel must discuss the ability and willingness of the child's parent or guardian or any other person the agency considers relevant, to provide the child with a secure environment in which he can develop, and otherwise to meet his needs[78] (see **8.99** and **8.101**).

73　Report of the Departmental Committee on the Adoption of Children Cmnd 5107 (1972).
74　Ibid, at para 196.
75　*Re H: Re G (Adoption: Consultation of Unmarried Fathers)* [2001] 1 FLR 646 at 653.
76　CA 1989, s 22(4).
77　Adoption Agency Agencies Regulations 2005, reg 14(3), (4).
78　Part 1 of Schedule 1 of the Adoption Agency Agencies Regulations 2005.

- In the report to the court the agency must provided specified information about the putative father including if his whereabouts or identity are unknown, information about him and the steps that have been taken to establish paternity[79] (see **8.79**).

17.72 The guardian's investigatory and reporting duties (see **17.99** and **17.109**) are wide enough to cover investigating and reporting on putative fathers.

17.73 When making a decision about the adoption of a child, the court and the agency must have regard to the matters set out in ACA 2002, s 1, including the relationship which the child has with relatives; with any other person in relation to whom the court or agency considers the relationship to be relevant, including the likelihood of any such relationship continuing and the value to the child of its doing so; the ability and willingness of any of the child's relatives, or of any such person, to provide the child with a secure environment in which the child can develop; and otherwise to meet the child's needs and the wishes and feelings of any of the child's relatives, or of any such person, regarding the child.[80] However, the section does not provide any express machinery for ascertaining those matters which is left to the inherent powers of the court or statutory powers of the agency. 'The legislation is not prescriptive, and it has been left to the exercise of discretion as to whether any means available as a matter of inherent jurisdiction or under statutory powers is actually employed.'[81] Moreover the section does not establish any preference for any particular result or prescribe any particular conclusion and, importantly, does not express a preference for following the wishes of the birth family or placing a child with the child's birth family 'though this will often be in the best interests of the child'.[82]

Seeking directions

17.74 The agency or guardian may seek the directions from the court in which the matter is proceeding about contacting a putative father or joining him as a party. In addition the Rules also provide that where no proceedings have started an adoption agency or local authority may ask the High Court for directions on the need to give a father without parental responsibility notice of the intention to place a child for adoption.[83] Where the mother consents to the child being placed for adoption under ACA 2002, s 19, this route should be used rather than applying for a care order.[84]

---

[79] Practice Direction 5D.

[80] ACA 2002, s 1(4)(f).

[81] *Re C (A Child) v XYZ County Council* [2007] EWCA Civ 1206, [2008] 1 FLR 1294 per Arden LJ at [17].

[82] Ibid.

[83] FP(A)R 2005, r 108.

[84] *Re C (A Child) v XYZ County Council* [2007] EWCA Civ1206, [2008] 1 FLR 1294 at [68].

Article 8

17.75   A difficulty faced by the father in the circumstances being discussed is that at present he may have no family life with the child. The European Court of Human Rights has found that family life can be present:

- following some but limited contact between the child and his father;[85]

- because of a significant relationship between the parents which had ended prior to the birth;[86] or even

- because there is a potential relationship.[87]

However the Court is less flexible where the father was not aware of the birth and had only a brief relationship with the mother.[88] In *Keegan v Ireland*[89] the ECtHR held that the making of an adoption order without allowing the natural parent to participate albeit that he was not married to the mother and had never lived with his child breached his Art 8 rights.

> 'The fact that Irish law permitted the secret placement of the child for adoption without the applicant's knowledge or consent, leading to the bonding of the child with the proposed adopters and to the subsequent making of an adoption order, amounted to an interference with his right to respect for family life. Such interference is permissible only if the conditions set out in paragraph 2 of Article 8 (art. 8-2) are satisfied.'

The approach of the domestic courts

17.76   In some cases, nothing can be done because the mother refuses to identify the father and 'there is something deeply unattractive and unsettling in the idea that a woman in the mother's position should be cross-examined in order to compel her to reveal the name of her child's father'.[90]

17.77   Where a father or his family can be identified, the following guidance has been given.

- There is a 'general rule' that the father should be told about adoption proceedings 'however unpalatable this might be for the mother or problematic for the agency.'[91]

---

[85]   *Söderbäck v Sweden* [1999] 1 FLR 250.

[86]   *Görgülü v Germany* (2004) Application no. 74969/01.

[87]   *Pini v Romania* [2005] 2 FLR 596. See also *Re C (A Child) v XYZ County Council* [2007] EWCA Civ 1206, [2008] 1 FLR 1294 per Lawrence Collins LJ at [54].

[88]   Sloan '*Re C (A Child) (Adoption: Duty of A Local Authority)* – Welfare and the Rights of the Birth Family in 'Fast Track' Adoption Cases' [2009] CFLQ 87 at p 97.

[89]   (1994) 18 EHRR 342.

[90]   *Re L (Adoption: Contacting Natural Father)* [2007] EWHC 1771 Fam, [2008] 1 FLR 1079 per Munby J at [38].

[91]   *Re M (Adoption: Rights of Natural Father)* [2001] 1 FLR 745 per Bodey J at 755; *Re H: Re G (Adoption: Consultation of Unmarried Fathers)* [2001] 1 FLR 646.

- There will inevitably be a wide variety of cases where the question arises and every case has to be determined on its particular facts.[92]

- There are good social policy reasons for accepting the option of a private birth[93] but although a mother's desire for confidentiality might carry more weight in some cases than others, it ought not to deprive a father of his right to be informed and consulted in the majority of cases.[94]

- Where family life exists within the meaning of Art 8 'strong countervailing factors',[95] 'very compelling reasons indeed'[96] or 'cogent and compelling grounds'[97] are generally required in order to justify the exclusion of a putative father from the adoption process.[98]

- The fact that the father or a relative has no right to respect for family life in the particular case does not mean that their position should not be considered and s 1(4)(f) of the 2002 Act[99] applies irrespective of Art 8 rights. However, the position of a person commands more importance if they are entitled to that right.

- Although s 1(4)(f) includes a father or other relatives who do not know about a baby's birth, when a decision requires to be made about the long-term care of the child, whom a mother wishes to be adopted, there is no duty to make enquiries of an absolute kind. There is only a duty to make enquiries, if it is in the interests of the child to make those enquiries.[100] In particular:
  - the local authority is not under an obligation to approach the grandparents or seek out the father. Rather it has to decide whether to place the newborn baby on a fast track adoption under s 19 (see **3.1**) or explore a family placement;[101]
  - there is nothing in the Act or Regulations to suggest that it would be a proper use of the guardian's powers to pursue enquiries as to who the father might be in order to assist the child in establishing his identity later in life.[102]

---

[92] *Re C (A Child) v XYZ County Council* [2007] EWCA Civ 1206, [2008] 1 FLR 1294 per Arden LJ at [40]; *Re L (Adoption: Contacting Natural Father)* [2007] EWHC 1771 Fam, [2008] 1 FLR 1079 per Munby J at [25].
[93] *Re C (A Child) v XYZ County Council* [2007] EWCA Civ 1206, [2008] 1 FLR 1294 Thorpe LJ at [82].
[94] *Re H: Re G (Adoption: Consultation of Unmarried Fathers)* [2001] 1 FLR 646 per Butler-Sloss P at 655.
[95] Ibid, at [48].
[96] *Re C (Adoption: Disclosure to Father)* [2005] EWHC 3385 (Fam), [2006] 2 FLR 589 at [17].
[97] *Birmingham City Council v S, R and A* [2006] EWHC 3065 (Fam), [2007] 1 FLR 1223 at [73].
[98] *Re L (Adoption: Contacting Natural Father)* op cit per Munby J at [25].
[99] See **6.98**.
[100] *Re C (A Child) v XYZ County Council* [2007] EWCA Civ 1206, [2008] 1 FLR 1294 per Arden LJ at [21].
[101] Ibid, per Lawrence Collins LJ at [52].
[102] Ibid, per Arden LJ at [34].

- Potential harm to the mother's health or the child's health may be a reason for the withholding of information from relatives or the father of a child in an appropriate case.[103]

- The interests of the individual child in being adopted or kept within the extended family must be considered.

  'In some cases, the birth tie will be very important, especially where the child is of an age to understand what is happening or where there are ethnic or cultural or religious reasons for keeping the child in the birth family. Where a child has never lived with her birth family, and is too young to understand what is going on, that argument must be weaker.'[104]

- The delay which may be caused in investigating the circumstances of the father or family is relevant. In some cases, absent any successful application by a member of the family, '[the "birth tie"] is overtaken by the need to find the child a permanent home as soon as that can be done'.[105]

17.78 The perceived emphasis on the importance of 'fast tracking' baby adoptions at the expense of seeking to involve the putative father and extended family has been criticised as 'utilising an unnecessarily narrow concept of welfare and giving undue weight to the interests of the mother'.[106]

Examples

Re X (Care: Notice of Proceedings)[107]

17.79 M, an unmarried Bangladeshi 17-year-old girl, gave birth to C. The father, F, her brother-in-law, was unaware of the birth. The court heard evidence that if the liaison between M and F became known in the wider community, she would face ostracism and F's family would be placed under great strain. 'The overall effect could be catastrophic.' The court held that on balance it was in the best interests of C and the wider family that F should not be given notice of the proceedings.

Z County Council v R[108]

17.80 Before M gave birth to C she made arrangements for him to be adopted. She told the agency she knew who the father was and that he knew of

---

103 [2007] EWCA Civ 1206, [2008] 1 FLR 1294 per Arden LJ at [38] and see, for example, *Re X (Care: Notice of Proceedings)* [1996] 1 FLR 186. at **17.79**.
104 *Re C (A Child) v XYZ County Council* [2007] EWCA Civ 1206, [2008] 1 FLR 1294 per Arden LJ at [43].
105 Ibid, per Arden LJ at [43] and Thorpe LJ at [69].
106 Sloan '*Re C (A Child) (Adoption: Duty of A Local Authority)* – Welfare and the Rights of the Birth Family in 'Fast Track' Adoption Cases' op cit.
107 [1996] 1 FLR 186.
108 [2001] 1 FLR 365.

the birth but refused to name him, saying she wished to protect him from embarrassment and disruption to his family. Nor did she did want her family told, stating that they could not offer C a home. Holman J held that the balancing of the Art 8 rights of C, the mother, the father and her family came down in favour of preserving the confidentiality of what M had told the agency.

Re H: Re G (Adoption: Consultation of Unmarried Fathers)[109]

17.81 H's mother had cohabited with H's father, F1, for a period and had an older child X with whom the father had contact. She kept her pregnancy and the birth of H secret from him because she feared the information would damage their relationship. Dame Elizabeth Butler-Sloss P held that the local authority should take steps to identify F1 and inform him about the proceedings. The parents had had a relationship which had included cohabitation and had lasted for a number of years. He had shown commitment to X. Accordingly he had a family life with H and was entitled to be consulted about his future.

17.82 In comparison, G's mother had never lived with G's father (F2) although their relationship had lasted for 7 years. At one stage they had been engaged although their marriage plans had been vague. F2 now lived abroad and his immigration status was uncertain. The President held that the relationship between G's parents did not have enough constancy to demonstrate family life and it was not necessary for F2 to be given notice or joined as a party.

Re M (Adoption: Rights of Natural Father)[110]

17.83 M and F had been involved in a relationship for 2–3 years and had a child, X. When M became pregnant with the second child, C, she decided to place the child for adoption and told F that he had been stillborn. She told the agency and gave evidence to the court that F was a violent and dangerous man who had assaulted her in front of X. She feared for her safety and that of X if F was told about the deception. Her evidence was corroborated by F's convictions for violence including rape, drug offences and offences of dishonesty and by medical evidence. Bodey J held that it was only possible in exceptional circumstances to depart from 'the general rule' that the father should be told about adoption proceedings. However, this was an exceptional case with a serious conflict between the rights of C and F which must be resolved by favouring the interests of the child.

---

[109] [2001] 1 FLR 646.
[110] [2001] 1 FLR 745.

Re C (A Child) v XYZ County Council[111]

17.84   M became pregnant after a 'one night stand'. She wanted to keep the pregnancy a secret from her family, with whom she had had a difficult relationship, and left the child, C, now aged 4 months, in hospital after she was born. Her family discovered that C had been born and wrote to the authority offering to help but not specifying what form this could take or applying to take part in the proceedings. The Court of Appeal held that although the extended family could apply to be joined if they wished, the putative father, F, had no family life with C or M and there was no reason to suppose he could provide a home for C. It would not be right to delay placing C for adoption and the guardian and the local authority were directed to take no steps to identify F or inform him of C's birth or to introduce her to her grandparents.

Re C (Adoption: Disclosure to Father)[112]

17.85   M, the mother of C, had six other children, three of whom had been adopted. She wanted C placed for adoption. C's father (F) was serving a prison sentence of 3 years and 9 months for various offences of burglary and drugs. Although there was some history of domestic violence towards M she had never raised it as an issue. No member of the extended families knew of C's birth. Despite the objections of the mother Hedley J directed that F should be given notice of the proceedings. There had to be compelling reasons to justify not telling him and there were none. In addition, given the links between the parents, there was a real prospect that F would find out and this might result in real problems in terms of the placement.

17.86   For another example, see *Re J (Adoption: Contacting Father)*.[113]

Applications to be joined

Procedure

17.87   At the first directions hearing (see **17.120**) the court will consider whether the child or any other person should be a party to the proceedings.[114] In addition, the court may at any time direct that any other person or body be made a respondent to proceedings or that a respondent be removed.[115] Where adoption will result in a child acquiring British nationality (see **2.88**) and the circumstances are known to be contentious, it may be appropriate for the Secretary of State of the Home Office to be joined as an intervenor.[116]

---

[111]   Op cit.
[112]   [2005] EWHC 3385 (Fam), [2006] 2 FLR 589.
[113]   [2003] EWHC 199 (Fam), [2003] 1 FLR 933.
[114]   FP(A)R 2005, r 26(1)(c).
[115]   Ibid, r 23(3).
[116]   As in *Re H (Adoption: Non Patrial)* [1996] 1 FLR 717 and [1996] 2 FLR 187.

17.88   The guardian, if appointed, must where practicable, notify any person of the court's power to join that person as a party if he considers that that person being joined would be likely to safeguard the interests of the child. He must inform the court of any such notification and of anyone whom he attempted to notify under this paragraph but was unable to contact and of anyone whom he believes may wish to be joined to the proceedings.[117]

17.89   Any application to be joined as a party should be made using Form FP2, following the procedure set out in Part 9 of the Rules.[118]

17.90   The court may at any time direct that a child, who is not already a respondent to proceedings, be made a respondent to proceedings where the child wishes to make an application or has evidence to give to the court or a legal submission to make which has not been given or made by any other party or there are other special circumstances.[119]

Exercise of the court's discretion

17.91   Other than the overriding objective[120] and the principle that in general any delay in reaching a decision is likely to prejudice the child's welfare,[121] there is no statutory guidance[122] and none has been provided by authority on how the discretion should be exercised. The exercise should obviously include a consideration of the child's interests.

THE CHILDREN'S GUARDIAN AND THE REPORTING OFFICER

Who may be appointed?

17.92   The guardian and the reporting officer must be an officer of CAFCASS or a Welsh Family proceedings officer.[123]

17.93   The same person may be appointed to act as the children's guardian, the reporting officer and the children and family reporter (see **3.92**).[124] The same person may be appointed as the reporting officer for two or more parents or guardians of the child.[125]

---

[117]   FP(A)R 2005, r 65(4)(b).
[118]   Ibid, r 65(5).
[119]   Ibid, r 23(2).
[120]   Ibid, r 2.
[121]   ACA 2002, s 1(3).
[122]   As for example, CA 1989, s 10(9).
[123]   Ibid, s 102(1).
[124]   Ibid, r 76.
[125]   Ibid, r 70.

17.94 In adoption proceedings or proceedings for an order giving parental responsibility prior to adoption abroad[126] or an order revoking an overseas or Hague Convention adoption,[127] a person may not be appointed as a children's guardian, reporting officer or children and family reporter if he:

- is a member, officer or servant of a local authority which is a party to the proceedings;

- is, or has been, a member, officer or servant of a local authority or voluntary organisation who has been directly concerned in that capacity in arrangements relating to the care, accommodation or welfare of the child during the 5 years prior to the commencement of the proceedings; or

- is a serving probation officer who has, in that capacity, been previously concerned with the child or his family.[128]

17.95 In placement proceedings, a person may not be appointed as a children's guardian, reporting officer or children and family reporter if he:

- is, or has been, a member, officer or servant of a local authority or voluntary organisation who has been directly concerned in that capacity in arrangements relating to the care, accommodation or welfare of the child during the 5 years prior to the commencement of the proceedings; or

- is a serving probation officer who has, in that capacity, been previously concerned with the child or his family.[129]

The children's guardian

Appointment

17.96 As soon as an application has been issued, the court will appoint a guardian for the child where the child is a party to the proceedings unless it is satisfied that it is not necessary to do so to safeguard the interests of the child.[130]

17.97 In addition the court may at any stage, whether on an application or of its own initiative, appoint a guardian.[131] The court will grant any application for a guardian to be appointed application unless it considers that such an appointment is not necessary to safeguard the interests of the child.[132]

---

[126] ACA 2002, s 84.
[127] Ibid, s 89.
[128] FP(A)R 2005, r 75(1).
[129] Ibid, r 75(2).
[130] Ibid, rr 24(1)(a)(iii), 59(1).
[131] Ibid, r 59(2).
[132] Ibid, r 59(3).

17.98 When appointing a guardian the court will consider the appointment of anyone who has previously acted as the child's guardian.[133] In *Re J (Adoption: Appointment of Guardian ad Litem)*[134] the court refused an application by the child's mother to disqualify a guardian who had been the guardian in the previous care proceedings. Although her appointment had technically ceased, the guardian had continued to be involved in questions about the child's future. It was 'quite untenable' to assert that the expression of views adverse to a parent amounted to bias or the appearance of bias. The advantages of appointing a guardian with a high degree of familiarity with the case and the child were overwhelming.

Powers and duties

17.99 The child's guardian has to act on behalf of the child with the duty of safeguarding the child's interests. The guardian must also provide the court with such other assistance as it may require.[135]

Service

17.100 The children's guardian must serve and accept documents on behalf of the child.[136]

Appointing a solicitor

17.101 The guardian must:

- appoint a solicitor for the child unless a solicitor has already been appointed;

- give such advice to the child as is appropriate having regard to his understanding; and

- where appropriate instruct the solicitor representing the child on all matters relevant to the interests of the child, including possibilities for appeal, arising in the course of proceedings.[137]

17.102 However, he need not appoint a solicitor where he is authorised to conduct litigation or exercise a right of audience[138] and he intends to have conduct of the proceedings on behalf of the child, unless the child wishes to

---

[133] FP(A)R 2005, r 59(4).
[134] [1999] 2 FLR 86.
[135] FP(A)R 2005, r 62.
[136] Ibid, r 66(1).
[137] ACA 2002, s 63(2).
[138] In accordance with s 15(1) of the Criminal Justice and Court Services Act 2000 or s 37(1) of the Children Act 2004.

instruct a solicitor direct and the children's guardian or the court considers that he is of sufficient understanding to do so.[139]

17.103   Where it appears to the children's guardian that the child is instructing his solicitor direct or intends to conduct and is capable of conducting the proceedings on his own behalf he must inform the court.[140] When this happens, the guardian must still perform the duties otherwise required of him set out in rr 62–67, other than those in relation to appointing and instructing a solicitor. He must take such part in the proceedings as the court may direct and may, with the permission of the court, have legal representation.[141]

Attending direction hearings

17.104   The children's guardian or the solicitor who is appointed must attend all directions hearings unless the court directs otherwise.[142]

Investigations

17.105   The guardian must make such investigations as are necessary for him to carry out his duties and must, in particular:

• contact or seek to interview such persons as he thinks appropriate or as the court directs; and

• obtain such professional assistance as is available to him which he thinks appropriate or which the court directs him to obtain.[143]

17.106   Where the children's guardian inspects records under s 42 of the 1989 Act or s 103 of the 2002 Act he must bring all records and documents which may, in his opinion, assist in the proper determination of the proceedings to the attention of the court and (unless the court directs otherwise) the other parties.[144]

Report

17.107   The guardian must unless the court directs otherwise, file a written report advising on the interests of the child in accordance with the timetable set by the court.[145] There are no prescribed contents for the report.

17.108   Any report to the court under this rule will be confidential.[146]

---

[139]   FP(A)R 2005, r 63(3).
[140]   Ibid, r 64(1).
[141]   Ibid, r 64(2).
[142]   Ibid, r 65(1).
[143]   Ibid, r 63.
[144]   Ibid, r 66(2).
[145]   Ibid, r 65(4)(a).
[146]   Ibid, r 65(5).

Advising the court

17.109 The guardian must advise, orally or in writing, the court on the following matters:

- whether the child is of sufficient understanding for any purpose including the child's refusal to submit to a medical or psychiatric examination or other assessment that the court has the power to require, direct or order;

- the wishes of the child in respect of any matter relevant to the proceedings including his attendance at court;

- the appropriate forum for the proceedings;

- the appropriate timing of the proceedings or any part of them;

- the options available to it in respect of the child and the suitability of each such option including what order should be made in determining the application; and

- any other matter on which the court seeks his advice or on which he considers that the court should be informed.[147]

Advising the child

17.110 If the child has sufficient understanding the guardian must advise him of the contents of any document which has been served unless these have been served on the child.[148]

17.111 If the guardian considers it appropriate to the age and understanding of the child, he must ensure that the child is notified of a decision made by the court in the proceedings and that it is explained to him in an appropriate manner.[149]

The reporting officer

Appointment

17.112 As soon as an application has been issued, the court will appoint a reporting officer where it appears that a parent or guardian is willing to consent to the placing of the child, or adoption, or to the making of an adoption order and that parent or guardian is in England and Wales.[150]

---

[147] FP(A)R 2005, r 65(2).
[148] Ibid, r 66(1).
[149] Ibid, r 67.
[150] Ibid, rr 24(1)(a)(iv), 69.

Powers and duties

17.113 The reporting officer must witness the signature by a parent or guardian on the document in which consent is given to:

- the placing of the child for adoption;

- the making of an adoption order; or

- the making of an order[151] giving parental responsibility prior to adoption abroad.[152]

17.114 See **3.92**.

17.115 The reporting officer must:

- ensure so far as reasonably practicable that the parent or guardian is giving consent unconditionally and with full understanding of what is involved;[153]

- investigate all the circumstances relevant to a parent's or guardian's consent to the placing of the child for adoption or to the making of an adoption order or a section 84 order;[154] and

- on completing his investigations:
  - make a report in writing to the court in accordance with the timetable set by the court, drawing attention to any matters which, in his opinion, may be of assistance to the court in considering the application; or
  - make an interim report to the court if a parent or guardian of the child is unwilling to consent to the placing of the child for adoption or to the making of an adoption order or section 84 order.[155] On receipt of any such report, a court officer must inform the applicant that a parent or guardian of the child is unwilling to consent to the placing of the child for adoption or to the making of an adoption order or section 84 order;[156]

- must attend all directions hearings unless the court directs otherwise.[157]

---

[151] ACA 2002, s 84.
[152] FP(A)R 2005, r 71.
[153] Ibid, r 72(1).
[154] Ibid.
[155] Ibid.
[156] Ibid, r 72(2).
[157] Ibid, r 72(4).

17.116 The reporting officer may at any time before the final hearing make an interim report to the court if he considers it necessary and ask the court for directions.[158]

17.117 Any report to the court will be confidential.[159]

DIRECTIONS AND PREPARATION FOR TRIAL

Directions

Initial steps taken by the court

17.118 As soon as practicable after the application has been issued the court will:

- if there are restrictions on making adoption orders under ACA 2002, s 48 (see **17.29**), consider whether it is proper to hear the application;

- set a date for the first directions hearing or give the directions it would be required to give at the first directions appointment.[160] Unless the court directs otherwise, the first directions hearing must be within 4 weeks beginning with the date on which the application is issued;[161]

- appoint a children's guardian (see **17.96**);

- appoint a reporting officer (see **17.112**);

- consider whether a report relating to the welfare of the child is required; and if so:
  - request such a report from a child and family reporter;[162]
  - set a date for the hearing of the application.[163]

17.119 The court or a court officer will also:

- where the child is not placed for adoption by an adoption agency:
  - ask either CAFCASS or, in Wales, the Assembly to file any relevant form of consent to an adoption order or an order giving parental responsibility prior to adoption abroad;[164] and
  - ask the local authority to prepare a report on the suitability of the prospective adopters if one has not already been prepared;

---

[158] FP(A)R 2005, r 72(3).
[159] Ibid, r 72(5).
[160] Ibid, r 24(4).
[161] Ibid, r 25.
[162] See ibid, r 73.
[163] Ibid, r 24(1).
[164] Ibid, r 71.

- where the child is placed for adoption by an adoption agency, ask the agency:
  - to file any relevant form of consent to:
    - the child being placed for adoption;
    - an adoption order;
    - a future adoption order under ACA 2002, s 20; or
    - a section 84 order;
  - confirm whether a statement of wish not to be informed of any application for an adoption order has been made under s 20(4)(a) and if so, to file that statement;
  - file any withdrawal of such a wish made under s 20(4)(b) as soon as it is received by the adoption agency; and
  - prepare a report on the suitability of the prospective adopters if one has not already been prepared.[165]

The first directions hearing

17.120   At the first directions hearing in the proceedings the court will:

- fix a timetable for the filing of:
  - any report relating to the suitability of the applicants to adopt a child;
  - any report from the local authority;
  - any report from a children's guardian, reporting officer or children and family reporter;
  - if a statement of facts has been filed, any amended statement of facts;
  - any other evidence; and
  give directions relating to the reports and other evidence;

- consider whether an alternative dispute resolution procedure is appropriate and, if so, give directions relating to the use of such procedure (see **18.1**);

- consider whether the child or any other person should be a party to the proceedings and, if so, give directions;

- give directions relating to the appointment of a litigation friend for any patient or non-subject child unless a litigation friend has already been appointed (see Part 7 and **131**);

- consider whether the case needs to be transferred to another court (see **17.75**);

- give directions about:

---

[165]   FP(A)R 2005, r 24(2).

- tracing parents or any other person the court considers to be relevant to the proceedings;
- service of documents;
- disclosure as soon as possible of information and evidence to the parties (see **17.129**); and
- the final hearing.[166]

17.121 The parties or their legal representatives must attend the first directions hearing unless the court directs otherwise.[167]

Additional directions

17.122 Directions may also be given at any stage in the proceedings:

- of the court's own initiative; or

- on the application of a party or any children's guardian; or

- where the direction concerns a report by a reporting officer or children and family reporter, on the application of the reporting officer or children and family reporter.[168]

Monitoring directions

17.123 After the first directions hearing the court will monitor compliance with the court's timetable and directions by the parties.[169]

Witness statements

17.124 The general rule is that any fact which needs to be proved by the evidence of witnesses is to be proved at final hearing, by their oral evidence and at any other hearing, by their evidence in writing.[170]

17.125 Directions for filing witness statements will be considered at the first directions hearing.[171]

17.126 If a party has filed a witness statement which has been served on the other parties and he wishes to rely at the final hearing on the evidence of the witness who made the statement, he must call the witness to give oral evidence unless the court directs otherwise or he puts the statement in as hearsay evidence.[172]

---

[166] FP(A)R 2005, r 26(1).
[167] Ibid, r 26(4).
[168] Ibid, r 26(5).
[169] Ibid, r 26(7).
[170] Ibid, r 124(1).
[171] Ibid, r 26(1)(a)(v).
[172] Ibid, r 127(1).

17.127 Detailed provision for evidence is contained in FP(A)R 2005, rr 122–149 and Practice Directions 15 and 16 paras 1–5 (witnesses within the jurisdiction) and rr 150–153 and Practice Direction 16 paras 6–9 (witness in other jurisdictions).

17.128 For a discussion of hearsay evidence, see **18.142**.

Documentary evidence

17.129 Courts are reluctant to direct disclosure of documents in proceedings relating to children (see **18.111**) but they have the power to do so.

17.130 FP(A)R 2005, r 79 permits the High Court or county court[173] to make orders for disclosure against a person who is not a party to the proceedings but only where the documents of which disclosure is sought are likely to support the case of the applicant or adversely affect the case of one of the other parties to the proceedings and disclosure is necessary in order to dispose fairly of the application or to save costs.[174] The application for such disclosure must be supported by evidence.[175]

Assessments

17.131 See Chapter 8.

Reports and expert evidence

17.132 Part 17 of the Rules regulates expert evidence in similar terms as for private law proceedings (see **10.53**).

Trial bundle

17.133 See **18.121**.

17.134 In all family courts except the FPC, the trial bundle should be lodged with the court 2 clear days before the hearing unless an order is made for this to be done earlier.[176]

---

[173] Not the FPC – FP(A)R 2005, r 79(6).
[174] Ibid, r 79(3).
[175] Ibid, r 79(2).
[176] Practice Direction 27 July 2006 Family Proceedings: Court Bundles (Universal Practice to be Applied in All Courts other than the Family Proceedings Court) [2006] 2 FLR 199.

PROCEEDINGS UNDER PART 9 AND 10 OF THE RULES

Part 9

17.135 An applicant may use the Part 9 procedure if the application is made:

- in the course of existing proceedings;

- to commence proceedings other than those to which Part 5 or r 86(3) applies; or

- in connection with proceedings which have been concluded.

17.136 Part 5 applies to:

- adoption proceedings;

- placement proceedings; or

- proceedings for:
  - the making of a contact order under ACA 2002, s 26;
  - the variation or revocation of a contact order under s 27;
  - an order giving permission to change a child's surname or remove a child from the UK under s 28(2) and (3);
  - a section 84 order;
  - a section 88 direction;
  - a section 89 order; or
  - any other order that may be referred to in a practice direction.[177]

17.137 A Part 9 application is made using Form FP2.

17.138 Part 9 contains specific rules relating to the service of the application, the hearing and dismissal of totally without merit applications.

Part 10

17.139 An applicant may use the Part 10 procedure where the procedure set out in Part 9 does not apply and:

- there is no form prescribed by a rule or practice direction in which to make the application;

- he seeks the court's decision on a question which is unlikely to involve a substantial dispute of fact; or

- it relates to a type of proceeding specified by rule or practice direction permitting the use of the Part 10 procedure.

---

[177] FP(A)R 2005, r 22.

17.140   A Part 10 application is made using Form FP1, FP1A or FP1B.

17.141   Part 10 contains specific rules relating to the service of the application, the hearing and dismissal of totally without merit applications.

Failure of a party to attend

17.142   Where the applicant or any respondent fails to attend the hearing of a Part 9 or 10 application, the court may proceed in his absence.[178] Where the applicant or any respondent fails to attend the hearing of an application and the court makes an order at the hearing, the court may, on application or of its own initiative, re-list the application.

OTHER PROVISIONS IN THE RULES

17.143   The FP(A)R 2005 forms a complete code and, unlike FPR 1991 or FPC(CA)R 1991 contains rules, for example relating to interim injunctions, which would require the application of the Supreme Court Rules 1965 or County Court Rules 1981.

17.144   These include:

Disclosure of documents	Part 8
Disputing the Court's jurisdiction	Part 12
Human rights	Part 13
Interim injunctions	Part 14
Admissions and evidence	Part 15
Witnesses	Part 16
Experts	Part 17
Change of solicitor	Part 18

WITHDRAWING THE APPLICATION

17.145   An application may be withdrawn with the permission of the court. A person seeking permission to withdraw an application must file a written request for permission setting out the reasons for the request but the request may be made orally to the court if the parties and any children's guardian, reporting officer or children and family reporter are present.[179]

17.146   If the request is made in writing, a court officer will notify the other parties and any children's guardian, reporting officer or children and family

---

[178]   FP(A)R 2005, r 95.
[179]   Ibid, r 106(1), (2), (3).

reporter. The court may deal with a written request without a hearing if the other parties and any children's guardian, reporting officer or children and family reporter have had an opportunity to make written representations to the court about the request.[180]

CONFIDENTIALITY AND PROTECTING PRIVATE INFORMATION

Serial numbers

17.147 If the applicant for an adoption order wishes his identity to be kept confidential in the proceedings, he may, before the proceedings start, request a court officer to assign a serial number to him to identify him in connection with the proceedings, and a number will be assigned to him. The court may at any time direct that the serial number must be removed.[181]

17.148 Where a serial number has been assigned the court officer will ensure that any application form or application notice sent in accordance with the Rules does not contain information which discloses, or is likely to disclose, the identity of the applicant to any other party to that application who is not already aware of that person's identity. The proceedings on the application will be conducted with a view to securing that the applicant is not seen by or made known to any party who is not already aware of his identity, except with his consent.[182]

17.149 In *Re X (Adoption: Confidential Procedure)*[183] the mother's solicitor became aware of the identity of the prospective adopters who had looked after the children for 4 years. The prospective adopters insisted that they remain anonymous. The Court of Appeal upheld a refusal to allow the mother's solicitor to disclose the identity to the mother. The decision of the judge at first instance that there was a real possibility of harm to the children from both the birth family intervening in the life of the adoptive family and the anxiety of the prospective adopters was not plainly wrong.

Personal information

17.150 Unless the court directs otherwise, a party is not required to reveal:

- the address or telephone number of their private residence;

- the address of the child;

---

[180] FP(A)R 2005, r 106(4), (5).
[181] Ibid, r 20(2), (3).
[182] Ibid, r 20(4).
[183] [2002] EWCA Civ 828, [2002] 2 FLR 476.

• the name of a person with whom the child is living, if that person is not the applicant.

17.151 Where a party does not wish to reveal any of these particulars he must give notice of those particulars to the court and the particulars will not be revealed to any person unless the court directs otherwise.

Confidential reports

17.152 The reports of the child's guardian,[184] any report by the reporting officer,[185] reports by the agency or local authority[186] and health reports on the child and applicants for an adoption order[187] are confidential and the court may direct that the report will not be disclosed to a party.[188]

Disclosing confidential information

17.153 An entitlement to a fair trial under Art 6 of the European Convention for the Protection of Human Rights and Fundamental Freedoms 1950 does not confer on a party an unqualified right to see all the evidence. The court can, if the situation demands it, limit the disclosure of parts of the evidence to a party. Exceptionally, the court can withhold part of the evidence from a party, but before doing so it must apply the threefold test set out by the House of Lords in *Re D (Adoption Reports: Confidentiality)*:[189]

> 'The court should first consider whether the disclosure of the [whole or part of the evidence] would involve a real possibility of significant harm to the child.

> If it would, the court should next consider whether the overall interests of the child would benefit from non-disclosure, weighing on the one hand the interest of the child in having the material properly tested, the magnitude of the risk that harm will occur and the gravity of the harm if it does occur. If the court is satisfied that the interests of the child point towards non-disclosure, the final step is for the court to weigh that consideration ... against the interest of the parent or other party in having an opportunity to see and respond to the material. In the latter regard the court should take into account the importance of the material to the issues in the case.

> Non-disclosure should be the exception and not the rule. The court should be rigorous in its examination of the risk and gravity of the feared harm to the child, and should order non-disclosure only when the case for doing so is compelling. [Non-disclosure must be limited to what the situation imperatively demands. The

---

[184] FP(A)R 2005, r 65(5).
[185] Ibid, r 72(5).
[186] Ibid, r 29(6).
[187] Ibid, r 30(3).
[188] Ibid, r 77(3).
[189] [1995] 2 FLR 687 per Lord Mustill at 700.

court has to be rigorous in its examination of the feared harm and any difficulty caused to the party counterbalanced by other features which may ensure a fair trial.]'[190]

17.154 This test was developed by the Court of Appeal in *Re X (Adoption: Confidential Procedure)*,[191] When contemplating non-disclosure the issue was striking a fair balance between the various interests involved including:

- the interests of all parties but in particular the birth parents and the children in a fair trial of the issues in which the evidence on both sides could be properly tested and the relevant arguments advanced;

- the interests of the children, and the birth and the adoptive families in protecting their family and private lives from unjustified interference; and

- the interests of the children in being protected from harm and damage to their welfare whether in the short or medium term.

17.155 Although the cases discussed above emphasise that judges have to consider the need to disclose information, when doing so the court should remember the 'sobering experience' of practitioners and judges that the court cannot be sure of anything, including the relevance of information, until all the evidence has been heard.[192] Any non-disclosure therefore needs to be kept under review throughout the case.

17.156 Before ordering disclosure the court will consider whether any information should be deleted including information which discloses, or is likely to disclose, the identity of a person who has been assigned a serial number or discloses the personal particulars (see **17.147**).[193] As a matter of practice, the reports of guardians in placement proceedings, which seldom contain identifying details of any prospective adopters, are commonly disclosed to the parties.

17.157 When considering whether to authorise disclosure of material, the court should bear in mind the risk that confidential material may inadvertently be compromised.[194]

17.158 Where information is disclosed but certain information, for example, identifying information, is to be redacted, great care must be taken.

---

[190] *Re B (Disclosure to Other Parties)* [2001] 2 FLR 1017.
[191] [2002] EWCA Civ 828, [2002] 2 FLR 476 per Hale LJ at [15].
[192] See, in a different context, *Secretary of State v AF (No 3)* [2008] EWCA Civ 1148, [2009] 2 All ER 602 per Sedley LJ at [113]–[116].
[193] FP(A)R 2005, r 77(1), (2).
[194] *Re R (Secure Editing of Documents)* [2007] 2 FLR 759.

- A clear statement must be made that information of a clearly specified kind should not be contained in any document filed, gathered or circulated.

- The documents should be gathered by one party and only be released once they have been carefully checked.

- Responsibility for the process of editing should be given to one or more named individuals who knew the details of the case and the importance of the task. The guardian's solicitor may be an obvious choice.

- It may be appropriate to give the solicitor for the party who wished to withhold the information the opportunity of checking the redaction before the document is disclosed to the other parties.

- There should always be a second editor where there is a significant volume of material to be edited.[195]

Examples

Re D (Adoption Reports: Confidentiality)[196]

17.159 The House of Lords overturned the decision of the Court of Appeal[197] which had upheld the refusal of the trial judge to permit the disclosure to the parents of that part of the guardian's report which dealt with the children's wishes and feelings and remitted the matter for the application to be reconsidered.

Re K (Adoption: Disclosure of Information)[198]

17.160 The case concerned the proposed adoption of a boy and girl. The court applied the threefold test in *Re D (Adoption Reports: Confidentiality)* but refused to direct that information about a conviction of the proposed male adopter 22 years earlier for unlawful sexual intercourse with a 12-year-old girl should be disclosed to the birth mother who was unrepresented. There was a real possibility that the mother would disclose the information to members of the prospective adopter's wider family with the effect that he would be ostracised. The prospective adopter had been fully assessed by a forensic psychologist and had attended treatment courses. The professionals concerned had assessed the risk posed by him as being so low as to be negligible and there was a high probability that any expert instructed by the mother would reach the same conclusion. Disclosing that risk to the birth mother was greatly outweighed by the harm likely to occur if the information were released.

---

[195] *Re R (Secure Editing of Documents)* [2007] 2 FLR 759. The guidance has been approved by the President of the Family Division (see [18]).
[196] [1995] 2 FLR 687.
[197] [1995] 1 FLR 631.
[198] [1997] 2 FLR 74.

Re S (A Minor) (Adoption)[199]

17.161 The Court of Appeal allowed an appeal against a direction that information about a physical disability of one of the proposed adopters should be disclosed to the child's mother. The information about the disability was not so startling and significant that it had to be disclosed 'come what may' and there was a real risk that it would enable the mother to identify the applicant.

THE FINAL HEARING

Concurrent proceedings

17.162 Where there are a number of different proceedings, for example for a care order and a placement order or for an adoption order and for contact, those proceedings should be tried together so that all relevant matters can be considered together before the necessary balancing exercise is carried out.[200] As regards concurrent applications or a care order and placement order, the family justice council has a 'clear view that in the overwhelming majority of cases, the court should strive to determine the placement order application at the same hearing as the care case without any undue delay'.[201]

Notice of hearing

17.163 The court will give notice of the date and place where the application will be heard to:

- the parties;

- any children's guardian, reporting officer or children and family reporter; and

- to any other person that may be referred to in a practice direction.[202]

17.164 The notice will also state that, unless the person wishes or the court requires, the person need not attend.[203]

---

[199] [1993] 2 FLR 204.

[200] *Re G (A Minor) (Adoption and Access Applications)* (1980) 1 FLR 109; *Re G (A Minor) (Adoption and Access Applications)* [1992] 1 FLR 642; *G v G (Children: Concurrent Applications)* [1993] 2 FLR 306; *Re D (Simultaneous Applications for Care Order and Freeing Order)* [1992] 2 FLR 49 and *Re M (Care Order: Freeing Application)* [2003] EWCA Civ 1874, [2004] 1 FLR 826.

[201] *Linked Care and Placement Order Applications: Updated Guidance* 7 July 2008 http://www.family-justice-council.org.uk/docs/ 080707_Linked_Care_and_Placement_Order_Proceedings.pdf

[202] As yet, none.

[203] FP(A)R 2005, r 31.

17.165   However, where a freeing order is in force, there is no requirement under the FP(A)R 2005 or in the Act that notice is given to the birth parents.[204]

Attending the hearing

17.166   Any person who has been given notice may attend the final hearing. The court may direct that any person must attend a final hearing.[205]

17.167   The court cannot make an adoption order or an order giving parental responsibility prior to adoption abroad[206] or an order annulling an overseas or Hague Convention adoption order[207] unless the applicant and the child personally attend the final hearing or the court directs that the applicant or the child need not attend the final hearing.[208] In a case of adoption by a couple, the court may make an adoption order after personal attendance of one only of the applicants if there are special circumstances.[209]

17.168   The court cannot make a placement order unless a legal representative of the applicant attends the final hearing.[210]

17.169   This provision means that parents, whether able or unable to oppose the making of an adoption order, are able to attend proceedings. There is no discretion to dispense with such notice.[211] This has potential for threatening the anonymity or sense of security of the proposed adopters. Lowe and Murch[212] comment that in such cases practitioners need to be alive to the essential need to keep the parties apart and there need to be facilities in court proceedings to accommodate this. 'On the other hand, it seems clear that the parties do not always need to be separated although that will require deft as well as sensitive handling'.

17.170   Each Adoption Centre and each FPC which hears family proceedings must have arrangements in place to provide information to the relevant parties about any special arrangements made for their attendance at and the conduct of the final hearing.[213]

---

[204]   *Re F (Adoption: Natural Parents)* [2006] EWCA Civ 1345.

[205]   FP(A)R 2005, r 32(4).

[206]   Under ACA 2002, s 84.

[207]   Under ibid, s 89.

[208]   FP(A)R 2005, r 32(6), (7).

[209]   Ibid, r 32(8).

[210]   Ibid, r 32(9).

[211]   Practice Direction (Family Proceedings) (Listing Final Hearings in Adoption Cases) 3 October 2008. The Practice Direction does not apply to any case where the child has been freed for adoption under the provisions of the Adoption Act 1976 or where the parent or guardian of the child cannot be found (para 2).

[212]   *Supporting Adoption: Reframing the Approach* (BAAF, 1999) at pp 253–254.

[213]   Practice Direction (Family Proceedings) (Listing Final Hearings in Adoption Cases) op cit para 11.

17.171 When giving directions for the conduct of the final hearing of an adoption application, the court should consider in particular:

- whether to give a direction under FPR 1991, r 32(7) that the applicant or the child need not attend the hearing;

- whether to give a direction under r 32(4) that any person must attend the hearing;

- whether arrangements need to be made to ensure that the birth parent(s) and the applicant or the child do not meet at or in the vicinity of the court;

- the arrangements for ensuring that the ascertainable wishes and feelings of the child regarding the adoption decision are placed before the court;

- the facilities at the place where the final hearing is to take place, including – the availability of suitable accommodation – the use of any electronic information exchange and video or telephone – conferencing links.[214]

17.172 In proceedings in which a serial number has been assigned it will generally be appropriate to excuse the attendance of the child at the final hearing. It may also be appropriate to excuse the attendance of the applicant, if necessary to ensure that confidentiality is preserved. Where in such a case the attendance of the applicant is required, arrangements must be made to ensure that the applicant is not seen by or made known to any party who is not already aware of his identity.[215] In any case in which a direction is given that the applicant or the child need not attend the final hearing, the order and any notice of hearing issued by the court must state clearly that the applicant or the child, as the case may be, should not attend.[216]

17.173 The situation may also require consideration of how and when the final order should be made (see **17.184**).

Making representations

17.174 Any person who has been given notice may be heard on the question of whether an order should be made.[217] Any member or employee of a party which is a local authority, adoption agency or other body may address the court at the final hearing if he is authorised to do so.[218]

---

[214] Practice Direction (Family Proceedings) (Listing Final Hearings in Adoption Cases) op cit para 8.
[215] Ibid, para 9.
[216] Ibid, para 10.
[217] FP(A)R 2005, r 32(1).
[218] Ibid, r 32(3).

17.175   A person whose application for the permission of the court to oppose the making of an adoption order has been refused (see **3.141**) is not entitled to be heard on the question of whether an order should be made.[219] A parent or guardian who has given advance consent to adoption under ACA 2002, s 20 or whose child has been placed for adoption under s 19 or under a placement order may oppose the making of an adoption order only if the court has given leave.[220]

Hearings in public or private?

17.176   The issue of whether the public or the media should be allowed access to cases involving children is discussed in detail at **18.134**.

17.177   In summary, the traditional approach was that both the public and the media should be excluded. In *Re PB (Hearings in Open Court)*[221] the Court of Appeal held that in the absence of unusual circumstances, the normal practice of conducting first instance hearings in private would continue.

> 'The exercise of discretion [to allow the hearing to be conducted in public] remains in the hands of the trial judge and it is a matter for the judge in each case to exercise that discretion if called upon to do so.'

The fathers issued proceedings in the European Court of Human Rights[222] arguing that hearing their case in private infringed their right under Art 6(1) of the European Convention for the Protection of Human Rights which provides for the public hearing and the public pronouncement of judgment of cases but with the proviso that the press and public may be excluded 'in the interest of morals, public order or national security in a democratic society, where the interest of juveniles or the protection of the private life of the parties so requires'.

17.178   The Court found that there had been no violation of the applicants' rights to a fair trial.

17.179   Although the position as regards the presence of the media has changed for proceedings brought under the CA 1989,[223] (see **18.134**) the FPR 1991 and FFPC(CA)R 1991 do not apply to proceedings governed by the FP(A)R 2005 and so the accredited representatives of the media currently have no right to be present even when an application for a placement order is being heard at the same time as an application for a care order for which there is a right to be present. However, in a Guidance note issued by the President of the

---

[219]   FP(A)R 2005, r 32(2).
[220]   ACA 2002, s 47(7).
[221]   [1996] 2 FLR 765.
[222]   *B v United Kingdom; P v United Kingdom* Cases 36337/97 and 35974/97, [2001] 2 FLR 261.
[223]   FPR 1991, r 10.28A, Family Proceedings Courts (Children Act) Rules 1991 r 16A.

Family Division,[224] judges in the High Court and the county courts were reminded that they had a discretion to allow representatives to be present.

'The personal and confidential nature of proceedings for an adoption order means that it would not generally be appropriate for the court to permit media representatives to be present at an adoption hearing. However the same considerations do not usually apply in proceedings for a placement order and in such proceedings … the court may consider it appropriate to allow media representatives to be present. In particular, where an application for a placement order is heard together with care proceedings, the court should … take into account their general right to attend care proceedings. In such a case it would normally be appropriate for the court to allow media representatives to be present unless a direction under FPR 1991 r 10.28(4) is necessary … or there is some feature of the placement application which means that media representatives should not be present (for example, where there is a need to preserve the confidentiality of a proposed placement or where the interests of a prospective adopter or other person who is not before the court may be adversely affected …). The existence of a placement application should not, by itself, be treated as a reason for making a direction under FPR 1991 r 10.28(4) excluding the attendance of media representatives …'

Unrepresented litigants and *McKenzie* friends

17.180   See **18.138**.

17.181   A party may disclose any information relating to the proceedings to a lay adviser or *McKenzie* friend for the purpose of enabling the party to obtain advice or assistance in relation to the proceedings.[225]

Standard of proof

17.182   The standard of proof is the civil standard or the balance of probabilities. See **18.142**.

JUDGMENT

17.183   See **18.146**.

MAKING AN ADOPTION ORDER

17.184   In many cases parents do not attend the final hearing which is soon over. However, the importance to the child, the adopters and the wider adoptive family of the act of granting the order cannot be overestimated. Lowe

---

[224]   President's Guidance Note: Care Proceedings Involving Placement Order Applications – Attendance of the Media 30 April 2009, paras 6 and 7.
[225]   PD 8, para 1.3.

and Murch[226] comment that the need for a ceremony seems important and all those involved in the process need to be aware of this.

> 'What may well be regarded by many court officials and lawyers as a mere formality is clearly regarded by many adopters and their children as a major milestone in the adoption process. Much of our evidence in this respect underlines the symbolic significance of the final court hearing as the culminating rite of passage for the adoptive family.'

17.185 The practice has developed in many courts of the extended adoptive family and the child attending a ceremony when they will meet the judge (robed and wigged for the occasion). Photographs are taken of the child with many of those involved – the adopters, family, social worker, guardian, judge and sometimes the judge's adoption clerk.[227]

17.186 Where birth parents attend the hearing an adoption order may have to be made in the absence of the applicant or the child. In these circumstances the court should consider making facilities available for a celebratory event at a later date. The event should not normally be held before the expiry of the appeal period (generally 14 days). Except in exceptional circumstances, the judge or, in the magistrates' court at least one of the magistrates, who made the adoption order should host the celebratory event. Arrangements for the celebratory event should be made with the applicants by the court.[228]

---

[226]   op cit at p 254.

[227]   For a former High Court judge's experiences of such occasions ('the most enjoyable aspect of the work of the family judge at trial level'), see Sir Nicholas Wilson 'The Ears of the Child in Family Proceedings' [2007] Fam Law 808 at 818–819.

[228]   Practice Direction (Family Proceedings) (Listing Final Hearings in Adoption Cases) op cit at para 13.

Chapter 18

PROCEDURE: SPECIAL GUARDIANSHIP

COMMENCING PROCEEDINGS

Before the issue of proceedings

Alternative dispute resolution

18.1 There is a growing recognition that litigation should be the last and not the first recourse where adults cannot agree issues concerning children. There are twin beliefs that agreements freely reached between adults are more likely to be effective than orders imposed by the courts and that litigation places unnecessary stress both on the parties and on the children. A secondary reason for supporting alternative dispute resolution (ADR) is a desire to reduce the expense of litigation whether funded by the parties themselves, or, more commonly, funded by the Legal Services Commission. Mediation (assisted negotiation outside the court process) and conciliation (assisted negotiation within the process) are both seen as essential tools for promoting settlement.

18.2 Special Guardianship orders can be granted only by the courts and therefore at some stage proceedings will need to be commenced. This does not, however, diminish the desirability of both potential applicants consulting the potential respondents prior to commencing proceedings and of the parties trying to resolve matters without the need for a contested hearing.

Mediation

18.3 The strong support given to ADR in most cases is illustrated by *Al-Khatib v Masry*[1] in which a father had removed his five children from the UK to Saudi Arabia following the collapse of his marriage. The parties attempted mediation which failed but after further encouragement from the Court of Appeal it was reattempted with the parties eventually agreeing to a settlement. Thorpe LJ commented:

> '[This case] supports our conviction that there is no case, however conflicted, which is not potentially open to successful mediation, even if mediation has not been attempted or has failed during the trial process. It also demonstrates how vital it is for there to be judicial supervision of the process of mediation. It is not enough, in a difficult case such as this, for [the judge] directing mediation simply to make the order and thereafter that there will be a smooth passage to the initial

---

[1]   [2004] EWCA Civ 1353, [2005] 1 FLR 381 at [17].

meeting. The selection of the appropriate mediator in a difficult case is crucial and the availability of the supervising judge to deal with crisis is equally important.'

Mediation will not be appropriate in every case. In particular, the risk of domestic abuse to a parent or child needs to be considered.

18.4 Mediation may be desirable in a particular case but may not be effective at the particular stage the dispute has reached. In the jargon of mediators, is the time 'ripe'? Four models of 'ripeness' have been proposed.[2]

- *The hurting stalemate model.* No party can envisage a successful outcome or an end to unbearable costs.

- *The imminent mutual catastrophe model* where both parties face an undeniable disaster, for example a huge increase in costs or public funding is withdrawn.

- *The entrapment model* where parties are reluctant to withdraw because of the financial or emotional investments made in winning.

- *The enticing opportunity model* which envisages the parties being rewarded by adopting alternatives to their present course.

18.5 Wilson argues that there may be many 'ripe' moments when mediation can profitably be attempted and clients who initially reject mediation out of hand often change their minds once they have met the mediator.

18.6 Mediation meetings are privileged and anything which is said will be reported to the court only if both parties agree. An exception to this could apply where a statement is made clearly indicating that there was a risk of serious harm to the well-being of the child. If a CAFCASS report is ordered, another officer must be assigned to the case and should not be given access to any information or statements made in the course of the mediation process.

Family conferences

18.7 A Family Group Conference (FGC) is 'a decision-making meeting in which the child's wider family network makes a plan about the future arrangements for the child, which will ensure that s/he is safe and his/her well-being promoted'.[3] FGCs started in New Zealand in 1989, primarily in relation to restorative justice[4] but became recognised as a key decision-making process by which families make decisions about children and young people in

---

2   See Wilson 'Dispute "Ripeness" Timing and Mediation' [2005] Fam Law 162 citing Mitchell 'The Right Moment: Notes on Four Models of "Ripeness"' [1995] 9(2) *Paradigms* 38.
3   *Using Family Group Conferences for children who are or may become subject to public law proceedings* (Family Rights Group, 2008).
4   Gelsthorpe and Skinns 'Repairing Harm through Kith and Kin' in Ebtehaj, Lindley and Richards (eds) *Kinship Matters* (Hart Publishing, 2006) at p 157.

need of care or protection ('child welfare FGCs'). They were first introduced into this country nearly 16 years ago since when a number of local authorities and agencies (for example, the Family Rights Group) have encouraged and facilitated their use.

18.8 The aim of FGCs is to achieve the best possible decisions and outcomes for children through a collaborative approach.

'Family group conferences promote the involvement of the wider family in the decision-making process to achieve a resolution of difficulties and permanence for their children. There are different approaches to their use, and when they are used. It is clear that they can have a beneficial effect on the decision making process, and often empower the family to develop the supports that are required. Children and young people have also said that they would like them to be used as much as possible, as they see them as promoting family and friends care, which they clearly prefer.'[5]

18.9 The *Prime Minister's Review on Adoption*[6] recommended their use as a way of addressing all the options for achieving a permanent home for the child if rehabilitation with the birth family cannot be achieved.

'Social workers should address options for placement of children with extended family members early in the process but especially before initiating Care Proceedings or accommodating a child, possibly through family group conferences.'

18.10 However, although there appears to be a high level of participation by family members, particularly mothers and a higher attendance of fathers than other meetings, for example child protection case conferences, and very high participant satisfaction[7] there appears to be little research, nationally or internationally which examines placements within the family made as a result of FGCs. However, what research there is seems to suggest that FGCs are effective in involving family members and are more likely to result in kinship placement than other methods of decision making.[8] They produce plans which local authorities feel able to support in over 90% of cases. They have, and children feel they have, increased contact with the wider family. However, they have been under-used for families from the black and minority ethnic communities and there is evidence that families do not always receive the support and resources needed to implement their plan.

18.11 FGCs would seem to have an important ADR role for special guardianship applications, not only in trying to reach an agreement about

[5] *Friends and Family Care (Kinship Care) Current Policy Framework, Issues and Options*: Discussion paper (DCSF, 2002) paras 26 and 27.
[6] (PIU, 2000) at paras 3.25 and 6.8.
[7] Gelsthorpe op cit at 165–166.
[8] Hunt *Family and Friends Carers* Scoping Paper (Department of Health, 2001) at p 77 and *Using Family Group Conferences for children who are or may become subject to public law proceedings* (Family Rights Group, 2008) available for download at www.frg.org.uk.

placement and contact but also in how the special guardian intends to consult the parents before exercising parental responsibility.

18.12 The Family Rights Group has developed a Guide on the use of FGCs in public law proceedings, which has been endorsed by CAFCASS and the Family Justice Council.[9]

Giving notice

18.13 No individual may apply for an order without giving the local authority who is looking after the child or, if the child is not being looked after, the local authority in whose area the applicant is ordinarily resident (for which see **18.20**), written notice of his intention to apply and without 3 months having expired from the date the notice was given.[10]

Obtaining leave

18.14 A person who requires leave to make the application (for which see **5.21**) cannot make the application for a special guardianship order (SGO) or give notice to their local authority under the Children Act 1989 (CA 1989), s 14A(7) of their intention to do so until he has obtained the court's permission.[11]

WHAT APPLICATIONS ARE MADE?

18.15 In 2006, the first year in which SGOs could be made, an estimated 474 orders were made of which 16% were made by the Family Proceedings Court, 83% in the county court and 1% in the High Court.[12] As Hall has commented, these numbers are very low compared with the 4,352 care orders, 2,746 adoption orders and 24,532 residence orders made in the same year.

> 'It remains to be seen in future years whether, with increased awareness and familiarity, the numbers of special guardianship orders will increase and whether their introduction might lead to a reduction in the number of other orders made.'[13]

Hall examined all the cases and found that nearly three-quarters were made in public law rather than private law proceedings.

---

[9] *Using Family Group Conferences for children who are or may become subject to public law proceedings* op cit.

[10] CA 1989, s 14A(7).

[11] *Birmingham City Council v R* [2006] EWCA Civ 1748, [2007] 1 FLR 564 at [93].

[12] Judicial and Court Statistics (Ministry of Justice, 2006).

[13] Hall 'Special Guardianship: A Missed Opportunity – Findings from Research' [2008] Fam Law 148 at p 149.

DO THE COURTS HAVE JURISDICTION?

Residence in England and Wales

18.16   A court in England and Wales has jurisdiction to grant an SGO with respect to a child if the child is habitually resident in England and Wales or is present in England and Wales and is not habitually resident in any other part of the UK or a specified dependent territory.[14]

18.17   This general rule is subject to exceptions if on the date the order is made, matrimonial or civil partnership proceedings are continuing in Scotland, Northern Ireland or a specified dependent territory between the parents of the child.[15]

18.18   'Habitual residence' is not defined by the Family Law Act 1986 or by the Child Abduction and Custody Act 1985. However, there are many cases, particularly under the latter statute, in which the phrase has been analysed.

18.19   Whether or not a person is habitually resident in a particular case is a question of fact to be decided by reference to all the circumstances of the case.[16] A child will normally have the same habitual residence as the parent who has its day-to-day care[17] but not necessarily if the parent does not have day-to-day care.[18] 'Habitual residence' means a person's abode in that place which he has adopted voluntarily and for a settled period of time, however limited.[19] So, a stay for a holiday is not the same as habitual residence.[20] The person must be present in the place before it can be said that he is habitually resident there.[21] While 'habitual residence' can be lost in a day, it cannot be acquired so quickly. If a person has two homes between which he divides his time, habitual residence in both places is possible.[22] The fact that a person is illegally present in a country does not prevent him being habitually resident.[23] In *M v H*[24] it was held that a child who was subject to a shared residence order, one parent living in England and the other in Germany, could be habitually resident in both countries.[25]

Residence in the area of a local authority

18.20   If the child is not being looked after by an authority, the applicant for an SGO has to give notice of the intended application to the local authority 'in

---

14   Family Law Act 1986, ss 2(2A), 3(1).
15   Ibid, s 3(2) and (3).
16   *C v S (Minor: Abduction: Illegitimate Child)* [1990] 2 AC 562, [1990] 2 FLR 442.
17   Ibid.
18   *Re A (Wardship: Habitual Residence)* [2006] EWHC 3338 (Fam), [2007] 1 FLR 1589.
19   *Shah v Barnet LBC* [1983] 2 AC 309.
20   See, for example, *Re D (Abduction: Habitual Residence)* [2005] EWHC 518, [2005] 2 FLR 403.
21   *Re A (Wardship: Habitual Residence)* [2006] EWHC 3338 (Fam), [2007] 1 FLR 1589.
22   *Ikini v Ikini* [2001] 2 FLR 1288.
23   *Mark v Mark* [2005] UKHL 42, [2005] 2 FLR 1193.
24   [2005] EWHC 1186 (Fam).
25   See also *Greenwich LDC v S* [2007] EWHC 820 (Fam).

whose area the individual [making the application] is ordinarily resident'.[26] This seems to impose a precondition that the individual must be 'ordinarily resident' in the area of a local authority.

18.21   In determining 'ordinary residence' any period when the child is in a school or institution or living in a place in accordance with a supervision order made under the CA 1989 or required by virtue of an order made under s 63(1) of the Powers of Criminal Courts (Sentencing) Act 2000 is to be disregarded.[27]

18.22   But what if a child is living with someone with no ordinary residence? A parallel can be drawn with s 22(1) of the Adoption Act 1976 (now repealed) which required notice of an intended adoption application to be given to the local authority 'in whose area [the child] has his home'. In *Re Y (Minors) (Adoption: Jurisdiction)*[28] and *Re SL (Adoption: Home in Jurisdiction)*[29] the courts held that the child must have a home in England and Wales and, if he did not, an adoption order could not be granted. The requirement for adoption has since been changed but this does not affect special guardianship.

18.23   In practice, provided ample opportunity has been given to an authority to prepare the section 14A(8) report, courts are likely to strain to find the condition satisfied in most cases. The phrase 'ordinarily resident' although used in a variety of statutes, does not have a fixed meaning. Whilst it may in certain circumstances have the same meaning as 'habitual residence', the two phrases may not always be synonymous. Each may take a shade of meaning from the context and the object and purpose of the legislation. However they share a 'common core of meaning' of being an abode in a particular place which has been adopted voluntarily and for settled purposes.[30] In s 14A(7) the object of the requirement is to ensure that a local authority has 3 months in which to carry out the s 14A(8) assessment. The applicant is not required to live in the area of the local authority for 3 months. The phrase 'in whose area the individual making the application is ordinarily resident' merely serves to identify the authority on whom the responsibility of preparing the report is placed. Any residence which is more than merely transitory is likely to be enough.

WHICH COURT?

18.24   The allocation of proceedings between courts is governed by the Allocation and Transfer of Proceedings Order 2008 (ATPO 2008),[31] supplemented by the Practice Direction – Allocation and Transfer of

---

26   CA 1989, s 14A(7).
27   Ibid, s 105(6).
28   [1986] 1 FLR 152.
29   [2004] EWHC 1283 (Fam), [2005] 1 FLR 118.
30   *Nessa v Chief Adjudication Officer* [1999] 2 FLR 1116 per Lord Slynn of Hadley at 1120.
31   SI 2008/2836.

Proceedings.[32] The rules are designed to make sure that cases are heard at the appropriate level of judicial expertise, that all issues concerning the child are heard together and that the general principle that any delay is likely to prejudice the child is observed. The objective of the Practice Direction 'is to ensure that the criteria for the transfer of proceedings are applied in such way that proceedings are heard at the appropriate level of court, that the capacity of the magistrates' courts is properly utilised and that proceedings are only dealt with in the High Court if the relevant criteria are met'.[33] These recently introduced Rules and Practice Direction are far more prescriptive than the rules they replace. Three important factors in whether they succeed in achieving one of the desired objectives namely an increase in the use of Family Proceedings Court (FPC) are whether the FPC will have sufficient time available, whether judicial continuity can be secured and whether the remuneration of advocates when parties are publicly funded will be sufficient to secure proper representation.

18.25   The following summary relates only to proceedings under ss 4 (parental responsibility), 4A (step-parent parental responsibility) and 8 and 14A (special guardianship). Other applications have been omitted.

18.26   Subject to exceptions the following applications must be commenced in the FPC:[34]

- s 4 of the 1989 Act (acquisition of parental responsibility by father);

- s 4A of the 1989 Act (acquisition of parental responsibility by step-parent).

18.27   The exceptions are that the proceedings:

- concern a child who is the subject of proceedings which are pending in a county court or the High Court; and

- arise out of the same circumstances as gave rise to those proceedings in which case they may be started in the court in which those proceedings are pending;[35] or

- are proceedings for parental responsibility under CA 1989, s 4 or 4A which are started at the same time as proceedings in a county court or the High Court for an order under s 8 of the 1989 Act (residence, contact and other applications in relation to children) in relation to the same child, in which case they must be started in the court in which proceedings under s 8 are started.[36]

---

[32]   3 November 2008.
[33]   Practice Direction (PD) para1.2.
[34]   ATPO 2008, art 5(2).
[35]   Ibid, art 5(3).
[36]   ATPO 2008, art 5(4).

18.28   Subject to ATPO 2008, art 7 (applications which may be brought in the High Court), applications for leave brought by an applicant who is under the age of 18 under ss 10(2)(b), 11J(6) or 110(7) of, or para 9(6) of Sch A1 to, the CA 1989 must be brought in the county court.[37]

18.29   Other than under ATPO 2008, art 5(4) there is no rule that proceedings must be commenced in the High Court. There is a converse rule, however, that proceedings may not be commenced in the High Court unless:

- arts 5(3), 5(4) or 8 apply; or

- the proceedings are exceptionally complex; or

- the outcome of the proceedings is important to the public in general; or

- there is another substantial reason for the proceedings to be started in the High Court.[38]

18.30   A substantial reason for starting proceedings in the High Court will only exist where the nature of the proceedings or the issues raised are such that they ought to be heard in the High Court.[39]

18.31   See also **18.47**.

18.32   Where adoption proceedings are pending which concern the same child, the following proceedings must be started in the court in which the adoption proceedings are pending:[40]

- leave to apply for a residence order under s 29(4)(b) of the ACA 2002;

- leave to apply for a special guardianship order under s 29(5)(b) of the ACA 2002;

- applications under s 8 of the CA 1989 Act where s 28(1)(a) or s 29(4)(b) of ACA 2002 (leave obtained to make application for a residence order) applies;

- applications under s 14A of the CA 1989 where s 28(1)(b) or s 29(5)(b) of the ACA 2002 applies (leave obtained to make application for a special guardianship order).

---

[37]   Ibid, art 6.
[38]   Ibid, art 7.
[39]   PD para 5.4.
[40]   ATPO 2008, art 8.

TRANSFERRING APPLICATIONS BETWEEN COURTS

18.33   Proceedings may be transferred to another court at any stage of the proceedings, whether or not the proceedings have already been transferred.[41] The question of which court is the most appropriate hearing venue must be addressed by the court speedily as soon as there is sufficient information to determine whether the case meets the criteria for hearing in that court. It must then be kept under effective review at all times. It should not be assumed that proceedings will necessarily remain in the court in which they were started or to which they have been transferred. For example proceedings that have been transferred to a county court because one or more of the criteria in ATPO 2008, art 15 applies should be transferred back to the magistrates' court if the reason for transfer falls away. Conversely, an unforeseen late complication may require a transfer from a magistrates' court to a county court.[42]

18.34   When making any decision about the transfer of proceedings the court must have regard to the need to avoid delay in the proceedings and arts 16 and 19 do not apply if the transfer of proceedings would cause the determination of the proceedings to be delayed.[43] Therefore the listing availability of the court in which the proceedings have been started and in neighbouring FPCs and county courts must always be ascertained before deciding where proceedings should be heard. If an FPC is considering transferring proceedings to a county court or a county court is considering transferring proceedings to the High Court but that decision is finely balanced, the proceedings should not be transferred if the transfer would lead to delay. Conversely, if the High Court is considering transferring proceedings to a county court or a county court is considering transferring proceedings to an FPC but that decision is finely balanced, the proceedings should be transferred if retaining them would lead to delay. Transferring proceedings may mean that there will be a short delay in the proceedings being heard since the papers may need to be sent to the court to which they are being transferred. The court will determine whether the delay is significant, taking into account the circumstances of the case and with reference to the interests of the child.[44]

Transfer of proceedings from one FPC to another

18.35   An FPC (the 'transferring court') may transfer proceedings to another FPC (the 'receiving court') only if the transferring court considers that:

- the transfer will significantly accelerate the determination of the proceedings;

---

[41]   ATPO 2008, art 13.
[42]   PD para 3.1.
[43]   ATPO 2008, art 13.
[44]   PD paras 4.1–4.3.

- it is more convenient for the parties or for the child who is the subject of the proceedings for the proceedings to be dealt with by the receiving court; or

- there is another good reason for the proceedings to be transferred.[45]

18.36 Where an FPC is considering transferring proceedings to another FPC or a county court is considering transferring proceedings to another county court, the court will take into account the following factors (which are not exhaustive) when considering whether it would be more convenient for the parties for the proceedings to be dealt with by the other court:

- the fact that a party is ill or suffers a disability which could make it inconvenient to attend at a particular court;

- the fact that the child lives in the area of the other court;

- the need to avoid delay.[46]

Transfer of proceedings from FPC to county court

18.37 Under ATPO 2008, art 15(1) an FPC may transfer the whole or any part of proceedings to a county court only if the FPC considers that:

'(a) the transfer will significantly accelerate the determination of the proceedings;

(b) there is a real possibility of difficulty in resolving conflicts in the evidence of witnesses;

(c) there is a real possibility of a conflict in the evidence of two or more experts;

(d) there is a novel or difficult point of law;

(e) there are proceedings concerning the child in another jurisdiction or there are international law issues;

(f) there is a real possibility that enforcement proceedings may be necessary and the method of enforcement or the likely penalty is beyond the powers of a magistrates' court;

(g) there is a real possibility that a guardian ad litem will be appointed under rule 9.5 of the Family Proceedings Rules 1991;

(h) there is a real possibility that a party to proceedings is a person lacking capacity within the meaning of the Mental Capacity Act 2005 to conduct the proceedings; or

(i) there is another good reason for the proceedings to be transferred.'

18.38 Certain proceedings (which are not of relevance to proceedings covered in this Handbook) may not be transferred.

18.39 Where an FPC is considering whether one or more of the criteria in ATPO 2008, art 15(1) (except art 15(1)(g) (Rule 9.5 guardian) and (h) (issue of

---

45   ATPO 2008, art 14.
46   PD para 7.

capacity)) apply such that the proceedings ought to be heard in the county court, the FPC must first consider whether another FPC would have suitable experience to deal with the issues which have given rise to consideration of art 15. If so, the FPC will then consider whether the proceedings could be dealt with more quickly or within the same time if they were transferred to the other FPC rather than a county court. If so, the FPC will transfer the proceedings to the other FPC rather than a county court.[47]

18.40 An FPC may only transfer proceedings to a county court under ATPO 2008, art 15(1)(a) if it considers that the transfer will significantly accelerate the determination of the proceedings. Before considering a transfer on this ground, FPC must obtain information about the hearing dates available in other FPCs and in the relevant county court. The fact that a hearing could be arranged in a county court at an earlier date than in any appropriate FPC does not by itself justify the transfer of proceedings under art 15(1)(a); the question of whether the determination of the proceedings would be significantly accelerated must be considered in the light of all the circumstances.[48]

Transfer of proceedings from county court to FPC

18.41 A county court must transfer proceedings to an FPC which were transferred under ATPO 2008, art 15(1) if the county court considers that none of the criteria in the article applies.[49]

18.42 Subject to ATPO 2008, arts 5(3) and (4), 6 and 8, a county court must transfer to an FPC proceedings which were started in the county court if the county court considers that none of the criteria in art 15(1)(b)–(i) applies.[50]

18.43 A county court must transfer to an FPC under ATPO 2008, art 16(1) proceedings that have previously been transferred where the county court considers that none of the criteria in art 15(1) apply. In particular, proceedings transferred to a county court by a magistrates' court for resolution of a single issue, for example, use of the inherent powers of the High Court in respect of medical testing of a child or disclosure of information by HM Revenue and Customs, should be transferred back to the magistrates' court once the issue has been resolved.[51]

18.44 Subject to ATPO 2008, arts 5(3), 6, 8 and 13 and para 4 of the Practice Direction (delay) straightforward proceedings for:

- a residence order;

- a contact order;

---

[47] PD para 8.1.
[48] PD para 8.2.
[49] ATPO 2008, art 16(1).
[50] Ibid, art 16(2).
[51] PD para 9.1.

- a prohibited steps order;

- a specific issue order;

- a special guardianship order; or

- an order under Part 4 of the Family Law Act 1996

which are started in a county court should be transferred to a magistrates' court if the county court considers that none of the criteria in art 15(1)(b)–(i) apply to those proceedings.[52]

Transfer of proceedings from one county court to another

18.45   Subject to ATPO 2008, art 16 (see **18.41**), a county court may transfer proceedings to another county court (the 'receiving court') only if the transferring court considers that:

- the transfer will significantly accelerate the determination of the proceedings;

- it is more convenient for the parties or for the child who is the subject of the proceedings for the proceedings to be dealt with by the receiving court; or

- there is another good reason for the proceedings to be transferred.[53]

18.46   See also **18.34**.

Transfer of proceedings from county court to High Court

18.47   Under ATPO 2008, art 18 a county court may transfer proceedings to the High Court only if the county court considers that:

- the proceedings are exceptionally complex;

- the outcome of the proceedings is important to the public in general; or

- there is another substantial reason for the proceedings to be transferred.

18.48   A court will take into account the following factors (which are not exhaustive) when considering whether the criteria in ATPO 2008, art 7 (see **18.29**) or 18 apply, such that the proceedings ought to be heard in the High Court:

---

[52]   PD para 9.2
[53]   ATPO 2008, art 17.

'(1)   there is alleged to be a risk that a child concerned in the proceedings will suffer serious physical or emotional harm in the light of –

   (a)   the death of another child in the family, a parent or any other material person; or

   (b)   the fact that a parent or other material person may have committed a grave crime, for example, murder, manslaughter or rape, in particular where the essential factual framework is in dispute or there are issues over the causation of injuries or a material conflict of expert evidence; or

(2)   the application concerns medical treatment for a child which involves a risk to the child's physical or emotional health which goes beyond the normal risks of routine medical treatment; or

   [(3) and (4) relate to adoption – see **17.06**)]; or

(5)   it is likely that the proceedings will set a significant new precedent or alter existing principles of common law.'[54]

18.49   The following proceedings are likely to fall within the criteria for hearing in the High Court unless the nature of the issues of fact or law raised in the proceedings may make them more suitable to be dealt with in a county court:

'(1)   proceedings involving a contested issue of domicile;

   …

(4)   proceedings in which an application is opposed on the grounds of want of jurisdiction;

(5)   proceedings in which there is a complex foreign element or where the court has invited submissions to be made under Article 11 (7) of Council Regulation (EC) No 2201/2003 of 27 November 2003 concerning jurisdiction and the recognition and enforcement of judgments in matrimonial matters and the matters of parental responsibility;

(6)   proceedings in which there is an application to remove a child permanently or temporarily from the jurisdiction to a non-Hague Convention country.

(7)   interlocutory applications involving –

   (a) search orders; or

   (b) …'[55]

18.50   Proceedings will not normally be suitable to be dealt with in the High Court merely because of any of the following:

'•   intractable problems with regard to contact;
- sexual abuse;
- injury to a child which is neither life-threatening nor permanently disabling;
- routine neglect, even if it spans many years and there is copious documentation;
- temporary or permanent removal to a Hague Convention country;
- standard human rights issues;
- uncertainty as to immigration status;
- the celebrity of the parties;
- the anticipated length of the hearing;

---

[54]   PD para 5.1.
[55]   PD para 5.2.

- the quantity of evidence;
- the number of experts;
- the possible availability of a speedier hearing.'[56]

Transfer of proceedings from High Court

18.51   The High Court must transfer to a county court or an FPC, proceedings which were started in, or transferred to, the High Court if the High Court considers that none of the criteria in ATPO 2008, art 18 applies.

18.52   Where proceedings have been started in the High Court under ATPO 2008, art 7(c) or para 11.2(4) of the Practice Direction and the High Court considers that there is no substantial reason for them to have been started there, the High Court will transfer the proceedings to a county court or a magistrates' court and may make any orders about costs which it considers appropriate.[57]

WHICH COUNTY COURT?

18.53   County courts with jurisdiction to hear family proceedings are divided into three classes:[58]

- *divorce county courts*, which have to transfer opposed applications under CA 1989, s 14A unless they are also family hearing centres;

- *family hearing centres* designated in Sch 1 to the Order;

- *care centres* designated in Sch 1 to the Order.

Courts may belong to one or more class.

18.54   The Principal Registry of the Family Division is treated as if it were a divorce county court, a family hearing centre and a care centre.[59]

18.55   Free standing applications for SGOs must be commenced in or transferred to a family hearing centre.[60]

THE APPLICATION

18.56   The mode of commencing proceedings is set out in Family Proceedings Rules 1991, r 4.4 in the High Court and county courts and Family Proceedings Court (Children Act 1989) Rules 1991, r 4 in the family proceedings court.

---

[56]   PD para 5.3.
[57]   PD para 5.4.
[58]   ATPO 2008, art 2.
[59]   Ibid, art 3.
[60]   Ibid, arts 9, 14.

18.57 The applicant must file whichever of the following forms are appropriate:

- Form C1 – application for a section 14A order;

- Form C1A – if allegations of domestic violence are made;

- Form C2 – application for an order in existing proceedings or for leave to commence proceedings.

18.58 Form C1 should contain all the relevant information, including a brief outline of the case (but not a detailed statement by the applicant).

18.59 When the court office receives the application, it will fix a date for the hearing or a directions appointment and serve the application with Form C6 (notice of hearing or directions appointment). The applicant must serve[61] the respondents with a copy of the application and Form C6 at least 14 days before the hearing or appointment. Within 14 days of service of a s 14A application, each respondent has to file and serve an acknowledgement of service. Following service of any other application, the respondent may file and serve a written answer no less than 2 days before the hearing.

Ex parte applications

18.60 An application for a section 14A order may not be made without notice.[62]

THE PARTIES

18.61 The rules as to who should be made parties are set out in the Family Proceedings Rules 1991 (FPR 1991), Appendix 3 for the High Court and county courts and in the Family Proceedings Court (Children Act 1989) Rules 1991, Sch 2 for the family proceedings court.

Who must be joined?

18.62 The respondents must include:

- every person whom the applicant considers has parental responsibility for the child;

- where the child is subject to a care order,

---

[61] For service see Family Proceedings Rules 1991 r 4.8 and Family Proceedings Court (Children Act 1989) Rules 1991 r 9.

[62] FPR 1991, r 4.4.

– every person whom the applicant believes to have had parental responsibility immediately prior to the making of a care order; and
– the child;

• in the case of an application to extend, vary or discharge an order, the parties to the proceedings leading to that order.

18.63 In addition, notice of the proceedings must also be given to:

• any local authority providing accommodation for the child;

• any person caring for the child at the time the proceedings are commenced;

• where the child is alleged to be staying in a refuge certified under CA 1989, s 51(1) or (2) (a voluntary home or registered children's home or with a foster parent used to provide refuge for children who appear to be at risk of harm), the person providing the refuge;

• every person whom the applicant believes to be:
  – named in a court order with respect to the child which has not ceased to have effect;
  – a party to pending proceedings in respect of the same child;
  unless in each case the applicant believes that the order or pending proceedings is not relevant to the application; and
  – every person whom the applicant believes to be a person with whom the child has lived for at least 3 years prior to the application;
  – if the child is not accommodated by a local authority, the local authority in whose area the applicant is ordinarily resident;
  – in the case of an application to vary or discharge a special guardianship order, the local authority who prepared the report under CA 1989, s 14A(8) or (9) if different from any other authority who would be notified.

Applications to be joined

Procedure

18.64 A person who wishes to be joined as a party or who wishes to cease being a party must file a request in Form C2. The court may grant the request that a person cease to be a party without a hearing but otherwise a date for hearing the request will be fixed with notice to all parties or all parties will be invited to make written representations within a specified period, after which the court may consider the request without a hearing. However, a request to be joined made by a person with parental responsibility must be granted.[63]

---

[63]   FPR 1991, r 4.7.

Exercise of the court's discretion

18.65   Joining parties inappropriately may have implications for the trial by increasing the length of the hearing. Where any of the parties is publicly funded, it will have cost implications, both directly in relation to the party's own costs and indirectly by increasing the fee payable to counsel acting for any publicly funded party. Effective case management is the key to ensuring that wider family members are joined as parties only where this is necessary. The welfare test of s 1 does not apply to the issue of whether someone should be joined as a party.[64]

18.66   An application by a father without parental responsibility to be joined should normally be allowed. However, any application should be made promptly and delay which would cause the hearing to be postponed may mean the application being refused.[65]

18.67   Where the person wishing to be joined wishes to apply for a section 14A order, the court has to consider the factors set out in CA 1989, s 10(9) before granting permission.

18.68   Where the person wishing to be joined does not wish to apply for a section 14A order, permission should not usually be granted unless he has a separate point of view which needs to be put forward. Where the proposed party's role is essentially to support another party, the appropriate way of proceeding is for him to give evidence on behalf of that party rather than being joined.[66]

18.69   Where a local authority has been directed to file a report under CA 1989, s 37 but has declined to commence care proceedings, it should not be allowed to be joined as a party to private law proceedings.[67]

The child as a party

18.70   If it appears to the court that it is in the best interests of a child to be made a party to the proceedings, the court may appoint a CAFCASS officer, the Official Solicitor (if he consents) or (if he consents) some other proper person[68] to represent the child.[69] It would not normally be appropriate to use a solicitor as guardian with an independent social worker for a child as young as 7.[70]

---

[64]   *North Yorkshire County Council v G* [1993] 2 FLR 732.
[65]   *Re P (Care Proceedings: Father's Application to be Joined as Party)* [2001] 1 FLR 781.
[66]   *Re M (Minors) (Sexual Abuse: Evidence)* [1993] 1 FLR 822 per Butler-Sloss LJ at 825.
[67]   *F v Cambridgeshire County Council* [1995] 1 FLR 516.
[68]   For example, the National Youth Advocacy Service (NYAS). See *Protocol of December 2005* [2006] Fam Law 243. See also Fowler 'Maintaining Independent Socio-Legal Services: NYAS' [2009] Fam Law 612. For the appointment of NYAS to replace CAFCASS, see *Re B (A Child) (Contact: Appointment of Guardian)* [2009] EWCA Civ 435.
[69]   FPR 1991, r 9.5(1).
[70]   *Re W (Contact: Joining Child As Party)* [2001] EWCA Civ 1830, [2003] 1 FLR 681.

18.71   The procedure for inviting CAFCASS to act is set out in the CAFCASS *Practice Note* of 2004.[71] CAFCASS and the National Youth Advocacy Service (NYAS) have protocol which discusses whether CAFCASS or NYAS should be appointed.[72] CAFCASS should be approached first.

18.72   The general view of the courts is that children should not be joined as parties in private law cases, but there is a greater willingness to consider the question than hitherto, although the court has to be aware of the growing demands placed on the limited resources of CAFCASS.[73]

18.73   Guidance has been issued by the President of the Family Division on when children might be joined as parties.[74]

- The proper conduct and disposal of proceedings concerning a child may require the child to be made a party.

- Making the child a party to the proceedings is a step that will be taken only in cases involving an issue of significant difficulty and consequently will occur in only a minority of cases. Before taking the decision to make the child a party, consideration should be given to whether an alternative route might be preferable, such as asking an officer of CAFCASS to carry out further work or by making a referral to social services or possibly, by obtaining expert evidence.

- The decision to make the child a party will always be exclusively that of the judge, made in the light of the facts and circumstances of the particular case. The following are offered, solely by way of guidance, as circumstances which may justify the making of an order.

- Where a CAFCASS officer has notified the court that in his opinion the child should be made a party (see FPR 1991, r 4.11B(6)).

- Where the child has a standpoint or interests which are inconsistent with or incapable of being represented by any of the adult parties.

- Where there is an intractable dispute over residence or contact, including where all contact has ceased, or where there is irrational but implacable hostility to contact or where the child may be suffering harm associated with the contact dispute.

- Where the views and wishes of the child cannot be adequately met by a report to the court.

---

71   *CAFCASS Practice Note (Representation of Children in Family Proceedings Pursuant to Family Proceedings Rules 1991 Rule 9.5)* [2004] 1 FLR 1190.

72   *Protocol of December 2005* [2006] Fam Law 243.

73   See 'CAFCASS, Guardians and Delay' [2009] Fam Law 560.

74   *President's Direction (Representation of Children in Family Proceedings Pursuant to Family Proceedings Rules 1991 Rule 9.5)* [2004] 1 FLR 1188.

- Where an older child is opposing a proposed course of action.

- Where there are complex medical or mental health issues to be determined or there are other unusually complex issues that necessitate separate representation of the child.

- Where there are international complications outside child abduction, in particular where it may be necessary for there to be discussions with overseas authorities or a foreign court.

- Where there are serious allegations of physical, sexual or other abuse in relation to the child or there are allegations of domestic violence not capable of being resolved with the help of a CAFCASS officer.

- Where the proceedings concern more than one child and the welfare of the children is in conflict or one child is in a particularly disadvantaged position.

- Where there is a contested issue about blood testing.

18.74 The Practice Direction pointed out that separate representation of the child may result in a delay in the resolution of the proceedings. 'When deciding whether to direct that a child be made a party, the court will take into account the risk of delay or other facts adverse to the welfare of the child. The court's primary consideration will be the best interests of the child.'

18.75 In order to avoid unnecessary delay, a decision about joining a child should be made as soon as possible.

18.76 In public law (care) cases the child will be separately represented as a matter of course. Cases where a Rule 9.5 guardian might be appropriate in private law SG applications might include an older child where the application is contested. However before a guardian is appointed, the necessity of the appointment in the circumstances of the particular case should be identified rather than merely considering whether the case fits a particular category.

DIRECTIONS APPOINTMENTS AND PREPARATIONS FOR TRIAL

Which judge?

18.77 The jurisdiction of magistrates and judges to hear applications under the CA 1989 is strictly controlled. In relation to judges, the control is exercised by the Family Proceedings (Allocation to Judiciary) Directions 2009.[75]

---

[75] [2009] 2 FLR 51.

18.78   For circuit judges, recorders and district and deputy district judges, the key is whether or not they are authorised to hear public law or private law matters.

18.79   The following outline is not exhaustive but is confined only to those matters which are the subject of this Handbook.

Family proceedings courts

District judges (magistrates' court)

18.80   For the purpose of the Family Proceedings (Allocation to Judiciary) Directions 2009 a district judge (magistrates' court) who is nominated to sit in a FPC is treated the same as a county court district judge.[76]

Lay justices

18.81   A lay justice must be a member of a family panel, that is, a panel of lay justices especially appointed to deal with family proceedings.[77]

18.82   Family proceedings courts have to be composed of two or three lay justices or a district judge as chairman and one or two lay justices or, if it is not practicable for such a court to be composed, a district judge (magistrates' court) sitting alone. Save in the case of a district judge (magistrates' court) sitting alone, the court should, so far as is practicable, include both a man and a woman.[78]

High Court and county courts

High Court judges and deputy High Court judges

18.83   All High Court judges of the Family Division or a deputy ('section 9'[79]) High Court judge (with certain exceptions) have jurisdiction to hear all Children Act applications.[80]

Circuit judge or recorder

18.84   A circuit judge, deputy circuit judge or recorder nominated for public law family proceedings has jurisdiction to hear all private law Children Act applications.[81]

---

[76]   Magistrates' Courts Act 1980 s 67 and Family Proceedings (Allocation to Judiciary) Directions 2009 [2009] 2 FLR 51, para 7.

[77]   Magistrates' Courts Act 1980, s 67(2) and Family Proceedings Court (Constitution) Rules 1991, SI 1991/1405, r 10.

[78]   Magistrates' Courts Act 1980, s 66.

[79]   Of the Supreme Court Act 1981.

[80]   Family Proceedings (Allocation to Judiciary) Directions 2009 [2009] 2 FLR 51, para 7.

[81]   Ibid, para 6.

18.85 A circuit judge, deputy circuit judge or recorder nominated for private law family proceedings has jurisdiction to hear the matters set out in categories A and B of the Schedule to the Regulations. These include applications for parental responsibility under CA 1989, s 4 and 4A. They also include applications for residence orders and SGOs unless the child is placed for adoption or is subject to a placement order.

18.86 A district judge not so nominated has jurisdiction to hear proceedings for section 8 orders (which do not include applications for parental responsibility or special guardianship) sought at a without notice hearing where no nominated judge is available and the order is limited until a hearing before a nominated judge.[82]

District judge

18.87 A district or deputy district judge of the Principal Registry and a district judge who is nominated for public family law proceedings or who is nominated for public law family proceedings has jurisdiction to hear all Children Act applications.[83]

18.88 A district judge who is nominated for private family law proceedings has jurisdiction to hear the matters set out in category B of the Schedule. This includes applications for parental responsibility under CA 1989, ss 4 and 4A. They also include applications for residence orders and SGOs unless the child is placed for adoption or is subject to a placement order.

18.89 A district judge not so nominated has jurisdiction to hear proceedings for section 8 orders (which do not include applications for parental responsibility or special guardianship) sought at a without notice hearing where no nominated judge is available and the order is limited until a hearing before a nominated judge.[84]

Judicial continuity

18.90 The continuity provided by the same judge hearing proceedings concerning the same child is important. Inevitably, a judge will have formed a view of the family situation and the parties will know that the judge has formed a particular view about one or both of them. Unless there are grounds (excluding findings and conclusions properly reached in earlier proceedings) for saying that a litigant can reasonably take the view that the judge is biased against him, those findings and conclusions, far from disqualifying him, make it more desirable that he should hear the subsequent proceedings.[85] Where there

---

[82] Ibid.
[83] Ibid.
[84] Ibid.
[85] *Re M (Minors) (Judicial Continuity)* [1993] 1 FLR 903.

is a split hearing, for example a fact finding hearing followed by a final hearing, there must be judicial continuity. 'Split hearings are one thing; split judging is quite another.'[86]

DIRECTIONS APPOINTMENTS

18.91   Where an application for a special guardianship order is issued within public law proceedings, the new Public Law Outline[87] will be followed and any further directions which are necessary will be given in those proceedings.

18.92   When the court office receives an application for an order which is free standing, it will fix a date for the hearing or a directions appointment 'the First Hearing Dispute Resolution Appointment' (FHDRA).[88]

18.93   The task of the court at the first appointment is to:

• investigate the issues;

• inquire into the possibility of a settlement; and

• give directions in any case which has to proceed.

This will include adjourning the case to enable mediation to take place and considering whether to make substantive orders, whether interim or final.

18.94   The court will be guided in this task by the overriding objective namely to enable the court to deal with every (children) case:

'(a)   justly, expeditiously, fairly and with the minimum of delay;
(b)   in ways which ensure, so far as is practicable, that
　　　a.   the parties are on an equal footing;
　　　b.   the welfare of the children involved is safeguarded; and
　　　c.   distress to all parties is minimised
(c)   so far as is practicable, in ways which are proportionate
　　　a.   to the gravity and complexity of the issues and
　　　b.   to the nature and extent of the intervention proposed in the private and family life of the children and adults involved.'[89]

18.95   Whilst practitioners will most commonly encounter *The Private Law Programme* in section 8 cases, it applies to special guardianship applications and applications for parental responsibility orders as well and is likely to be of

---

86   *Re B (Children)* [2008] UKHL 35, [2008] 2 FLR 141 per Baroness Hale of Richmond at [61].
87   Implemented by *Practice Direction (Guide to Case Management in Public Law Proceedings)* 1 April 2008.
88   FPR 1991, r 4.4(2); Family Proceedings Court (Children Act 1989) Rules 1991 r 4(2).
89   *The Private Law Programme, Guidance Issued by the President of the Family Division* (2004).

assistance in many applications, initially opposed. The *Programme* states that in every case there is to be an early FHDRA:

- that identifies immediate safety issues;

- that exercises effective court control so as to identify the aim of the proceedings;

- that identifies immediate safety issues;

- that exercises effective court control so as to identify the aim of the proceedings, the timescale within which the aim can be achieved, the issues between the parties, the opportunities for the resolution of those issues by appropriate referrals for support and assistance and any subsequent steps that may be permitted or required;

- that, wherever possible, a CAFCASS practitioner shall be available to the court and to the family whose purpose and priority is to facilitate early dispute resolution rather than the provision of a formal report;

- that, save in exceptional circumstances (eg safety) or where immediate agreement is possible so that the principle of early dispute resolution can be facilitated, directs that the family shall be referred for support and assistance to:
  - a Family Resolutions Pilot Project (where available);
  - locally available resolution services (eg ADR, including mediation and conciliation, and/or other service, support, facilitation, treatment and therapy options) that are to be listed and publicised by the Family Justice Council/Family Court Business Committee for each Care Centre (eg provided by CAFCASS, service partnerships – Councils with Social Services Responsibilities and the NHS and/or by voluntary service providers – NACC (National Association of Child Contact Centres) resources and outreach voluntary workers).

18.96   The FHDRA is to be listed within a target window from the issue of the application of 4 to 6 working weeks. It must be attended by the parents and in court centres where the local scheme provides for it and where resources exist may be attended by any child aged 9 or over.

18.97   In court centres where resources exist to provide 'in-court conciliation':

- the FHDRA shall be listed so that a duty CAFCASS practitioner is available to the parties and to the court to facilitate agreements, the identification of issues and any appropriate referrals for assistance;

- where the local scheme provides for it, the detailed content of the conciliation discussions may remain confidential;

- the court may adjourn a FHDRA for further in-court conciliation or a report upon the availability or success of any proposal.

18.98   In court centres where a duty CAFCASS practitioner is not available:

- the court will identify the issues between the parties and use its best endeavours to facilitate agreements and referrals for assistance;

- in appropriate cases where advice is necessary, the court may adjourn the FHDRA for a CAFCASS practitioner to provide oral or short written advice to the parties and the court limited to the facilitation of matters that are agreed and referrals for further assistance.

18.99   In all cases at the conclusion of the FHDRA and generally at the end of any subsequent hearing that may be required the court shall identify on the face of the order:

- the issues that are determined, agreed or disagreed;

- the aim of the order, agreement, referral or hearing that is set out in the order;

- any other basis for the order or directions that are made or the agreement that is recorded;

- in respect of issues that are not agreed and that need to be determined so as to safeguard the welfare of the child:
  - the level of court (and where appropriate the allocated judge(s)) before whom all future non-conciliation hearings and applications are to be heard;
  - the timetable and the sequence of the steps that are required to lead to an early hearing;
  - the filing and service of evidence limited to such of the issues as the court may identify;
  - whether a CAFCASS practitioner's report is necessary and if so, the issues to which the report is to be directed;

- in respect of all orders, agreements and referrals directions for:
  - the facilitation of the same (in particular by a CAFCASS practitioner);
  - the monitoring of the outcome, including by urgent reserved re-listing before the same court within 10 working days of a request by CAFCASS;
  - enforcement.

18.100 Additional matters specified by the Model Scheme include:

- Private Law applications are issued on the day of receipt and a copy of the application is sent or e-mailed to CAFCASS on the day of issue.

- Information sheets about the FHDRA, the role of the CAFCASS practitioner and the court are sent to the parties with the Notice of Hearing. An example is at Annex B. Information about leaflets for children is at Annex C, and there is an approved amended county court Notice of Hearing at Annex E.

- A copy of the acknowledgement form is sent or e-mailed to CAFCASS on day of receipt.

- Prior to the application being listed for the appointment, CAFCASS will undertake their own paper risk assessment in particular as to safety issues. CAFCASS may advise the court that a particular case has risk or safety issues that would best be explored before the judge or magistrates/legal advisor at the FHDRA rather than in discussions between the parties and the CAFCASS practitioner.

- Cases that are very urgent or that involve safety issues or issues that are complex may need to be listed or determined separately and should be referred to a resident judge or magistrates' legal advisor for guidance.

- Subject to any direction to the contrary, in particular as to safety issues, the appointment is listed before a judge or magistrates' legal advisor with a CAFCASS practitioner available to facilitate early dispute resolution in accordance with the local scheme.

- Both parents are expected to attend with their representatives (if they have them). The parties' child or children should only attend where a local scheme provides for it and where the participation can occur in an appropriate child friendly environment.

- Further risk assessment may be undertaken by the CAFCASS practitioner with the child (if appropriate) and each party separately prior to any joint meeting between the practitioner and the parties (it is not expected that any joint meeting between the CAFCASS practitioner and the parties will involve a child unless the CAFCASS practitioner advises that it is in the child's interests and both parties').

Attendance of the parties

18.101 Each party has to attend all directions appointments unless the court otherwise directs, but the court may proceed in the absence of a party. However, it may not begin to hear an application in the absence of a respondent unless it is satisfied that he received reasonable notice of the hearing or it is satisfied that the circumstances of the case justify proceeding. The court may proceed in the absence of the applicant if it is satisfied that sufficient evidence has previously been received or it may refuse the application or it may adjourn the appointment.[90]

18.102 The parties' legal representatives should have both sufficient knowledge and authority to take any necessary decisions.[91]

DIRECTIONS

18.103 Parties need to prepare carefully for the first appointment, even if it is expected that the court will not be in a position to make a substantive order or even an interim one.[92] They should focus on the issues, including the question of how crucial facts are to be proved, the legal framework and the evidence needed to support the case.

18.104 The first appointment should be used imaginatively, anticipating problems and addressing them in advance.

18.105 In pursuing these aims, the court may give, vary or revoke directions for the conduct of the proceedings, including but not limited to:

- the timetable for the proceedings; it will take time for reports to be prepared and for a trial to be listed and directions should be tailored to reduce delay as much as possible;

- varying the time by which an act is required to be carried out; no time-limit, whether contained in the Rules or in an order, may be varied by the parties without the permission of the court;

- the attendance of the child; courts are reluctant to allow children to attend hearings, even if these are care proceedings or involve their liberty. The arguments put forward in support of this reluctance will vary according to the age of the child. It is said that a child who is old enough to understand something of what is taking place ought not to be exposed to arguments and evidence concerning their future. Younger children may become bored and disrupt the proceedings. This said, the presence of young children at short directions hearings because of childcare difficulties is not uncommon;

- the appointment of a guardian (see **18.70**);

- the service of documents;

---

90   FPR 1991, r 4.16; Family Proceedings Court (Children Act 1989) Rules 1991 r 16.
91   *The Children Act Advisory Committee: The Handbook of Best Practice* (Lord Chancellor's Department 1997) para 48.
92   Ibid, Section 4.

- the submission of evidence including experts' reports;

- the transfer of proceedings to another court;

- consolidation with other proceedings.

WITNESS STATEMENTS

18.106 In order to avoid acrimony at an early stage in the proceedings and before the live issues are identified, the rules provide that in CA 1989, s 14A proceedings no party shall file a statement until such time as the court directs.[93] Indeed, if the application is resolved before a final hearing it may be that no statements are filed.

18.107 The rules also impose requirements on the statement. It must be dated, signed by the person making them and contain a declaration that the maker believes it to be true and understands that it will be placed before the court.

18.108 The court should be reluctant to allow the parties to file statements without the relevant issues being identified and without considering whether the number of statements is limited to those which are relevant to disposing of the issues in a proportionate way. Whether this is done or not, solicitors should ensure that statements are as non-inflammatory as possible and discourage clients from a proliferation of witnesses who add nothing to the case. Statements from the child who is the subject of the proceedings should not be filed. The court is unlikely to view favourably the introduction of evidence from other children in the family, even if over the age of 18.

18.109 When giving permission for the filing of statements or later, the court will give directions for the attendance of witnesses at the hearing in order to be cross-examined. A party who has not complied with an order for filing statements may not adduce evidence at a directions appointment or a hearing without the permission of the court.

DOCUMENTS

18.110 The permission of the court is needed before a party can produce a relevant document.

18.111 The procedure of 'disclosure' has never formed part of litigation involving children. However, if the documents are likely to be relevant, the court can order a party to produce them. Documents in the possession of non-parties, for example, social service records, require special consideration. If the non-party will not voluntarily provide a copy of the document, a witness

---

[93] FPR 1991, r 4.17(3); Family Proceedings Court (Children Act 1989) Rules 1991 r 17(3).

summons requiring the document to be produced can be sought under RSC Ord 38, r 13 in the High Court or CCR Ord 20, r 12 in the county court or s 97 of the Magistrates' Court Act 1980. A party who has not complied with an order for disclosure may not produce a document at a directions appointment or a hearing without the permission of the court.

Assessments

18.112   In private law proceedings the court has no jurisdiction to order a residential assessment of the child with one parent against the wishes of the other parent.[94]

Reports and expert evidence

18.113   For a discussion of reports (including reports ordered under s 7 of the Children Act 1989) and expert evidence, see **10.53**.

Section 14A(8) and (9) reports

18.114   The court has to direct a time by which the local authority has to file its report. It must also consider whether the report should be disclosed to all or only some of the parties and whether any information including addresses should be deleted.[95]

LIMITING DISCLOSURE OF EVIDENCE, REPORTS AND DOCUMENTS

18.115   An entitlement to a fair trial under Art 6 of the European Convention for the Protection of Human Rights and Fundamental Freedoms 1950 does not confer an unqualified right to see all the evidence. The court can, if the situation demands it, limit the disclosure of parts of the evidence to a party. Exceptionally, the court can withhold part of the evidence from a party, but before doing so it must apply the threefold test set out by the House of Lords in *Re D (Adoption Reports: Confidentiality)*:[96]

'The court should first consider whether the disclosure of the [whole or part of the evidence] would involve a real possibility of significant harm to the child.

If it would, the court should next consider whether the overall interests of the child would benefit from non-disclosure, weighing on the one hand the interest of the child in having the material properly tested, the magnitude of the risk that harm will occur and the gravity of the harm if it does occur. If the court is satisfied that the interests of the child point towards non-disclosure, the final step is for the court to weigh that consideration ... against the interest of the parent or

---

[94]   *R v R (Private Law Proceedings: Residential Assessment)* [2002] 2 FLR 953.
[95]   FPR 1991, r 4.17A.
[96]   [1995] 2 FLR 687 per Lord Mustill at 700.

other party in having an opportunity to see and respond to the material. In the latter regard the court should take into account the importance of the material to the issues in the case.

Non-disclosure should be the exception and not the rule. The court should be rigorous in its examination of the risk and gravity of the feared harm to the child, and should order non-disclosure only when the case for doing so is compelling. [Non-disclosure must be limited to what the situation imperatively demands. The court has to be rigorous in its examination of the feared harm and any difficulty caused to the party counterbalanced by other features which may ensure a fair trial.]'[97]

FINAL DIRECTIONS APPOINTMENT

18.116 The final directions appointment or pre-trial review should be timetabled to take place after any welfare report and all evidence have been filed. The counsel or solicitor who will be the advocate at the final hearing should attend. If this is not possible, the person attending must be thoroughly conversant with the case and competent to make any necessary concessions or admissions and to advise the client in respect of settlement. The court will expect the parties' advisers to have addressed the question of what evidence can be agreed and what is in dispute.[98] The court will also consider what directions should be given for the attendance of witnesses and the author of any reports, including the children and family reporter.

18.117 The applicant's solicitor must prepare and file an agreed and paginated bundle of documents containing an index and chronology not less than 24 hours before the directions appointment.[99]

WITHDRAWING THE APPLICATION

18.118 An application may be withdrawn only with the permission of the court. A request to withdraw may be made orally if the parties and any welfare officer or child and family reporter (if involved) are present. Otherwise, a written request has to be filed and served which sets out the reasons for wishing to withdraw.

18.119 The judge may decline to grant leave to withdraw, for example if there are still issues of alleged domestic violence which require to be heard or if he considers that an order restraining the making of further applications may be needed under s 91(14) of the Act.[100]

---

[97] *Re B (Disclosure to Other Parties)* [2001] 2 FLR 1017.
[98] *Handbook of Best Practice* op cit section 4.
[99] Ibid.
[100] *Re F (Restrictions on Applications)* [2005] EWCA Civ 499, [2005] 2 FLR 950.

DISMISSAL OF APPLICATIONS WITHOUT A FULL HEARING

18.120 Courts hearing applications under the Children Act have a wide discretion to deal with cases in a way which is both in the best interests of the child and the interests of natural justice. There is no 'right' to a full hearing. In appropriate circumstances, such as an application which is doomed to failure or which seeks to revisit an earlier decision which was not appealed or was unsuccessfully appealed and where there has been no relevant change in circumstances, the court may dismiss the application without a full hearing.[101] However, if there is a demonstrably arguable issue, the judge should hear evidence and argument.[102] The judge should consider:

'(a) whether there was already sufficient evidence to make the decision;
(b) whether the proposed further evidence was likely to affect the outcome of the proceedings;
(c) whether the opportunity to cross-examine witnesses was likely to affect the outcome;
(d) whether a full investigation, including any consequential delay, would be injurious to the welfare of the child;
(e) whether the applicant for a full trial had real prospects of success; and
(f) whether the justice of the case required a full investigation.'[103]

TRIAL

Trial bundle

18.121 A detailed Practice Direction[104] deals with the preparation of a trial bundle for hearings in the High Court and the county courts with a time estimate of more than one hour. It includes the following provisions.

18.122 A bundle should be prepared by the applicant, containing all documents relevant to the hearing in chronological order, paginated, indexed and divided into separate sections as follows:

• preliminary documents and any other case management documents;

• applications and orders;

• statements and affidavits;

• care plans (where appropriate);

---

[101] *Re B (Minors) (Contact)* [1994] 2 FLR 1 per Butler-Sloss LJ at 5 and *Re C (Contact: Conduct of Hearing)* [2006] EWCA Civ 144 [2006] 2 FLR 289 per Wilson LJ at [33].
[102] *Re C (Contact: Conduct of Hearing)* [2006] 2 FLR 289.
[103] *Re B (Minors) (Contact)* [1994] 2 FLR 1 per Butler-Sloss LJ at 5.
[104] *Practice Direction 27 July 2006 Family Proceedings: Court Bundles (Universal Practice to be Applied in All Courts other than the Family Proceedings Court)* [2006] 2 FLR 199.

- experts' reports and other reports including those of the guardian (if any);

- other documents divided into further sections as necessary.

18.123 At the front of the bundle there should be:

- a summary of the background to the hearing limited, if practicable, to one A4 page;

- a statement of the issue or issues to be decided at the hearing and the final hearing;

- a position statement including a summary of the order or directions sought by each party at the hearing and the final hearing;

- an up-to-date chronology if there is a final hearing or if the summary is insufficient (although the practice directions does not require it, if possible the chronology should be cross-referenced to the bundle);

- skeleton arguments may be appropriate together with copies of all authorities relied on;

- a list of essential reading for the hearing.

18.124 If possible, the bundle should be agreed. An index should be provided to all parties no less than 4 working days before the hearing. The bundle should be supplied to counsel no less than 3 working days before the hearing and should be lodged with the court 2 clear days before the hearing unless an order for earlier lodgment is made.

18.125 The party preparing it should ensure that there is a copy at court for use by the witnesses.

18.126 A failure to comply with the Practice Direction may result in sanctions, such as wasted costs orders, being applied to practitioners.[105]

HEARINGS IN PUBLIC OR PRIVATE?

18.127 Currently the default position in the High Court and county court is that the public are excluded from first instance hearings of private law children's cases[106] although they are admitted to appeals heard in the Court of Appeal. In the Family Proceedings Court, the public are excluded but the media may be present.

---

[105] *Re X and Y (Court Bundles)* [2008] EWHC 2058 (Fam), [2008] 2 FLR 2053.
[106] FPR 1991, r 4.16(7).

18.128 In recent years, however, there has been increasing pressure for hearings to be held in public. This current position is under review and accredited members of the media are now admitted as of right to some proceedings (see **18.34**).

Article 6(1)

18.129 Article 6(1) of the European Convention for the Protection of Human Rights provides for the public hearing and the public pronouncement of judgment of cases but with the proviso that the press and public may be excluded 'in the interest of morals, public order or national security in a democratic society, where the interest of juveniles or the protection of the private life of the parties so requires'.[107]

18.130 The European Court of Human Rights examined the implications of Art 6 for England and Wales in *B v United Kingdom; P v United Kingdom*,[108] cases brought by fathers who had been refused permission to have their applications for residence orders held in open court. The Court found that there had been no violation of the applicants' rights to a fair trial. The Court observed that the public character of judicial proceedings protected litigants against the administration of justice in secret with no public scrutiny and was one of the means whereby confidence in the court could be maintained. It contributed to the achievement of the aim of Art 6(1), namely a fair hearing which was one of the foundations of a democratic society. However, the requirement to hold a hearing in public was subject to certain exceptions. It might on occasion be necessary to limit the open and public nature of the proceedings, for example, to protect the safety or privacy of witnesses or to promote the free exchange of information and opinion in the pursuit of justice.

> 'The proceedings which the present applicants wished to take place in public concerned the residence of each man's son following the parents' divorce or separation. The court considers that such proceedings are prime examples of cases where the exclusion of the press and public may be justified to protect the privacy of the child and parties and to avoid prejudicing the interests of justice. To enable the deciding judge to gain as full and accurate picture as possible of the advantages and disadvantages of the various residence and contact options open to the child, it is essential that the parents and other witnesses feel able to express themselves candidly on highly personal issues without fear of public curiosity or comment.'[109]

The English procedural law relating to hearings in private could therefore be seen as a specific reflection of the general exceptions provided for by Art 6(1).

---

[107] Magistrates Court Act 1980, s 69(2).
[108] Cases 36337/97 and 35974/97, [2001] 2 FLR 261.
[109] Cases 36337/97 and 35974/97, [2001] 2 FLR 261 at para 38.

The current legal position

18.131 In *Re PB (Hearings in Open Court)*[110] (which gave rise to *B v United Kingdom; P v United Kingdom*) the Court of Appeal had held that in the absence of unusual circumstances, the normal practice of conducting first instance hearings in private would continue. 'The exercise of discretion [to allow the hearing to be conducted in public] remains in the hands of the trial judge and it is a matter for the judge in each case to exercise that discretion if called upon to do so.' Following *B v United Kingdom; P v United Kingdom*, one of the applicants returned to the Court of Appeal to argue that r 4.16(7) of the Family Proceedings Rules was incompatible with Arts 6 and 8.[111] Not surprisingly the Court rejected his appeal on the grounds that his arguments had already been rejected in his earlier appeal and by the European Court of Human Rights. However, while it remained justifiable to hold hearings in private, greater justification was required for refusing to pronounce judgment in public given the almost universal practice of anonymising public judgments in Children Act cases.

> 'It is not so evident that either the inherent or the statutory jurisdiction justifies the imposition of an automatic restriction without the exercise of a specific discretion in the individual case.'

18.132 So rarely are applications made that the exercise of the discretion might be prejudiced by the tradition of privacy or an unconscious preference for the atmosphere created in chambers. 'Judges need to be aware of this and be prepared to consider another course where appropriate.'

18.133 Following *Pelling v Bruce-Williams*, the House of Lords in *Re S (Identification: Restrictions on Publication)*[112] held, in a case concerning restricting the identity of a child in a criminal trial, that the coming into force of the Human Rights Act 1998 made it unnecessary to consider the preceding case law about the existence and scope of the High Court's inherent jurisdiction to restrain publicity. The foundation of the jurisdiction now derived from rights under the Convention. The importance of the freedom of both the national and local press and the Art 10 right to freedom of expression needs to be addressed.

18.134 Since 27 April 2009, accredited[113] members of the media are permitted to attend at hearings of most family proceedings subject to the Family

---

[110] [1996] 2 FLR 765.
[111] *Pelling v Bruce-Williams (Secretary of State for Constitutional Affairs Intervening)* [2004] EWCA Civ 845, [2004] 2 FLR 823.
[112] [2004] UKHL 47, [2005] 1 FLR 591.
[113] Media representatives are expected to carry with them identification sufficient to enable court staff, or if necessary the court itself, to verify that they are 'accredited' representatives of news gathering or reporting organisations within the meaning of the rule. The Lord Chancellor has decided that a card issued under the scheme operated by the UK Press Card Authority will be the expected form of identification, and production of the Card will be both necessary and

Proceedings Rules 1991 which take place in private, except in relation to hearings conducted for the purpose of judicially assisted conciliation or negotiation.[114] The court is able to exclude such representatives from the whole or part of any hearing if it is satisfied that this is necessary:

- in the interests of any child concerned in, or connected with, the proceedings; or

- for the safety or protection of a party, a witness in the proceedings, or a person connected with such a party or witness; or

- for the orderly conduct of the proceedings; or

- justice will otherwise be impeded or prejudiced.[115]

18.135 For the position in relation to proceedings relating to adoption or placement orders see **17.181**.

18.136 The result of the rule change was described by the President in *Re X (A Child) (Residence and Contact)*.[116]

> 'The net result of all this is that, while the press are entitled to report on the nature of the dispute in the proceedings, and to identify the issues in the case and the identity of the participating witnesses (save those whose published identity would reveal the identity of the child in the case), they are not entitled to set out the content of the evidence or the details of matters investigated by the Court. Thus the position has been created that, whereas the media are now enabled to exercise a role of "watchdog" on the part of the public at large and to observe family justice at work for the purpose of informed comment upon its workings and the behaviour of its judges, they are unable to report in their newspapers or programmes.'

18.137 The President made a number of points about applications to exclude the media under r 10.28.[117]

- Private law family cases concerning the children of celebrities are no different in principle from those involving the children of anyone else.[118] However, in considering whether or not to exclude the press under

---

sufficient to demonstrate accreditation: Practice Direction: Attendance of Media Representatives at Hearings in Family Proceedings, 20 April 2009, para 4.

[114] These do not include Issues Resolution Hearings: Practice Direction ibid para 2.2. See FPR 1991, r 10.28(3). See also Practice Direction: Attendance of Media Representatives at Hearings in Family Proceedings, 20 April 2009 and 'President's Guidance in relation to Applications Consequent upon the Attendance of the Media in Family Proceedings' [2009] Fam Law 535. See also Adams 'Transparency: Now You See Through It And Now You Don't' [2009] Fam Law 598.

[115] FPR 1991, r 10.28(4).

[116] [2009] EWHC 1728 (Fam) at [38].

[117] [2009] EWHC 1728 (Fam) at [51]–[58].

[118] *Crawford v CPS* [2008] EWHC 854 (Admin) per Thomas LJ at [34].

r 10.28(4)(a)(i), the focus is upon the interests of the child and not the parents. It is almost axiomatic that the press interest in and surrounding the case will be more intense in the case of children of celebrities; and the need for protection of the child from intrusion or publicity, and the danger of leakage of information to the public will similarly be the more intense.

- In order to exclude the press on any of the grounds stated, the court must be satisfied that it is necessary[119] to do so.

- Because the ECHR has already held FDR, r 4.16(7) to be Convention-compliant in a form which effectively excluded the press from admission, the introduction of a provision which gives the media the clear prima facie right to be present during the proceedings, subject only to exclusion on limited grounds is plainly Convention compliant from the point of view of the media's Art 10 rights.

- The Practice Direction (see above) is not strictly accurate when it refers to the exercise of the court's discretion to exclude media representatives from all or part of the proceedings. Where the court has a duty to apply a test of necessity in relation to a series of questions as to legitimacy and proportionality its duty is to proceed though the balancing exercise making a value judgment as to the conflicts which arise rather than to regard the matter simply as an exercise of discretion as between two equally legitimate courses.

- The burden of satisfying the court of the grounds set out in r 10.28(4) is upon the party or parties who seek exclusion, or the court itself in a case where it takes steps of its own motion, to exclude the press. This will be an easier burden to satisfy in the case of temporary exclusion in the course of the proceedings, in order to meet concerns arising from the evidence of the particular witness or witnesses.

- In deciding whether or not the grounds advanced for exclusion are sufficient to override the presumptive right of the press to be present and in particular whether or not an order for total exclusion is proportionate, it will be relevant to have regard to the nature and sensitivities of the evidence and the degree to which the watchdog function of the media may be engaged, or whether its apparent interests lie in observing, and reporting on matters relating to the child which may well be the object of interest, in the sense of curiosity, on the part of the public but which are confidential and private and do not themselves involve matters of public interest properly so called. However, while this may be a relevant consideration, it in no sense creates or places any burden of proof or justification upon the media. The burden lies upon the applicant to

---

[119] For a discussion of the meaning of 'necessary', see *R v Shayler* [2003] 1 AC 247 per Lord Bingham at [23].

demonstrate that the matter cannot be appropriately dealt with by allowing the press to attend, subject as they are to the statutory safeguards in respect of identity and under the provisions of s 12 of the 1960 Act.

UNREPRESENTED LITIGANTS AND *MCKENZIE* FRIENDS

18.138 Many litigants, especially fathers, will not qualify for public funding and cannot afford to be represented. As noted by Thorpe LJ in *Re G (Litigants in Person)*:[120]

> 'There has been a significant increase in the percentage of family cases in which one or other of the parties is unrepresented for all or part of the proceedings. There are no statistics to substantiate that assertion but it is universally recognised as the reality by all specialists in this field. The provision of legal aid in family proceedings is a shrinking rather than an expanding welfare service.'

18.139 From 31 October 2005, the Family Proceedings Rules r 10A(3) has permitted a party to disclose any information relating to the proceedings to a lay adviser or *McKenzie* friend for the purpose of obtaining advice or assistance in relation to the proceedings.

18.140 The *President's Guidance: McKenzie Friends*[121] summarises the existing case law and especially the decision of the Court of Appeal in *In the Matter of the Children of Mr O'Connell, Mr Whelan and Mr Watson*.[122]

- A litigant who is not legally represented has the right to have reasonable assistance from a layperson, sometimes called a McKenzie friend (MF).
- A litigant in person wishing to have the help of a MF should be allowed such help unless the judge is satisfied that fairness and the interests of justice do not so require. The presumption in favour of permitting a MF is a strong one. In the event of objection, it is for the objecting party to rebut the presumption in favour of allowing the MF to attend.
- A litigant in person intending to make a request for the assistance of a MF should be encouraged to make the application as soon as possible indicating who the MF will be.
- It will be most helpful to the litigant in person and to the court if the particular MF is in a position to advise the litigant in person throughout the proceedings.
- A favourable decision by the court, allowing the assistance of a MF, should be regarded as final and not as something which another party can ask the court to revisit later, save on the ground of misconduct by the MF or on the ground that the MF's continuing presence will impede the efficient administration of justice.

---

[120]   [2003] EWCA Civ 1055, [2003] 2 FLR 963.
[121]   [2008] 2 FLR 110.
[122]   [2005] EWCA Civ 759, [2005] 2 FLR 967.

- Factors which should not outweigh the presumption in favour of allowing the assistance of a MF include:
  - the fact that proceedings are confidential and that the court papers contain sensitive information relating to the family's affairs
  - the fact that the litigant in person appears to be capable of conducting the case without the assistance of a MF
  - the fact that the litigant in person is unrepresented through choice
  - the fact that the objecting party is not represented
  - the fact that the hearing is a directions hearing or case management hearing
  - the fact that a proposed MF belongs to an organisation that promotes a particular cause
- The proposed MF should not be excluded from the courtroom or chambers while the application for assistance is made, and the MF should ordinarily be allowed to assist the litigant in person to make the application.
- The proposed MF should produce a short curriculum vitae or other statement setting out relevant experience and confirming that he/she has no interest in the case and understands the role of a MF and the duty of confidentiality.
- If a court decides in the exercise of its discretion to refuse to allow a MF to assist the litigant in person, the reasons for the decision should be explained carefully and fully to both the litigant in person and the would-be MF.
- The litigant may appeal that refusal, but the MF has no standing to do so.
- The court may refuse to allow a MF to act or continue to act in that capacity where the judge forms the view that the assistance the MF has given, or may give, impedes the efficient administration of justice. However, the court should also consider whether a firm and unequivocal warning to the litigant and/or MF might suffice in the first instance.
- Where permission has been given for a litigant in person to receive assistance from a MF in care proceedings, the court should consider the attendance of the MF at any Advocates' Meetings directed by the court, and, with regard to cases commenced after 1.4.08, consider directions in accordance with para 13.2 of the Practice Direction, Guide to Case Management in Public Law Proceedings.
- The litigant in person is permitted to communicate any information, including filed evidence, relating to the proceedings to the MF for the purpose of obtaining advice or assistance in relation to the proceedings.
- Legal representatives should ensure that documents are served on the litigant in person in good time to seek assistance regarding their content from the MF in advance of any hearing or advocates' meeting.

What a McKenzie Friend may do

- Provide moral support for the litigant
- Take notes
- Help with case papers
- Quietly give advice on:
  - points of law or procedure;
  - issues that the litigant may wish to raise in court;
  - questions the litigant may wish to ask witnesses.

What a McKenzie Friend may *not* do

- A MF has no right to act on behalf of a litigant in person. It is the right of the litigant who wishes to do so to have the assistance of a MF.
- A MF is not entitled to address the court, nor examine any witnesses. A MF who does so becomes an advocate and requires the grant of a right of audience.
- A MF may not act as the agent of the litigant in relation to the proceedings nor manage the litigant's case outside court, for example, by signing court documents.

Rights of audience

- Sections 27 and 28 of the Courts and Legal Services Act 1990 as amended by the Legal Services Act 2007 govern exhaustively rights of audience and the right to conduct litigation. They provide the court with a discretionary power to grant lay individuals such rights.
- A court may grant an unqualified person a right of audience in exceptional circumstances and after careful consideration. If the litigant in person wishes the MF to be granted a right of audience or the right to conduct the litigation, an application must be made at the start of the hearing.

Personal Support Unit & Citizens' Advice Bureau

- Litigants in person should also be aware of the services provided by local Personal Support Units and Citizens' Advice Bureaux.'

WITNESSES

18.141 The court may give directions as to the order of speeches and evidence at a hearing or directions appointment. Subject to this, the parties will adduce their evidence in the following order:

- the applicant;

- any party with parental responsibility for the child;

- other respondents;

- the guardian ad litem (if any).

STANDARD OF PROOF

18.142 The standard of proof in Children Act proceedings is the same as in other civil proceedings, namely the balance of probability. In *Re B (Children)*[123] Lord Hoffman said that:

'There is only one rule of law, namely that the occurrence of the fact in issue must be proved to have been more probable than not. Common sense, not law, requires that in deciding this question, regard should be had, to whatever extent appropriate, to inherent probabilities. If a child alleges sexual abuse by a parent, it is common sense to start with the assumption that most parents do not abuse their children. But this assumption may be swiftly dispelled by other compelling evidence of the relationship between parent and child or parent and other children. It would be absurd to suggest that the tribunal must in all cases assume that serious conduct is unlikely to have occurred. In many cases, the other evidence will show that it was all too likely. If, for example, it is clear that a child was assaulted by one or other of two people, it would make no sense to start one's reasoning by saying that assaulting children is a serious matter and therefore neither of them is likely to have done so. The fact is that one of them did and the question for the tribunal is simply whether it is more probable that one rather than the other was the perpetrator.'[124]

18.143 In the same case, Baroness Hale of Richmond stated:

'My Lords ... I would go ... announce loud and clear that the standard of proof in finding the facts necessary to establish the threshold under section 31(2) or the welfare considerations in section 1 of the 1989 Act is the simple balance of probabilities, neither more nor less. Neither the seriousness of the allegation nor the seriousness of the consequences should make any difference to the standard of proof to be applied in determining the facts. The inherent probabilities are simply something to be taken into account, where relevant, in deciding where the truth lies.

As to the seriousness of the consequences, they are serious either way. A child may find her relationship with her family seriously disrupted; or she may find herself still at risk of suffering serious harm. A parent may find his relationship with his child seriously disrupted; or he may find himself still at liberty to maltreat this or other children in the future.

As to the seriousness of the allegation, there is no logical or necessary connection between seriousness and probability. Some seriously harmful behaviour, such as murder, is sufficiently rare to be inherently improbable in most circumstances. Even then there are circumstances, such as a body with its throat cut and no weapon to hand, where it is not at all improbable. Other seriously harmful behaviour, such as alcohol or drug abuse, is regrettably all too common and not at all improbable. Nor are serious allegations made in a vacuum. Consider the famous example of the animal seen in Regent's Park. If it is seen outside the zoo on a stretch of greensward regularly used for walking dogs, then of course it is

---

[123] [2008] UKHL 35, [2008] 2 FLR 141 at [11]. See also *Re Doherty* [2008] UKHL 33.
[124] Ibid at [5].

more likely to be a dog than a lion. If it is seen in the zoo next to the lions' enclosure when the door is open, then it may well be more likely to be a lion than a dog.'[125]

HEARSAY EVIDENCE

18.144 By virtue of the Children (Admissibility of Hearsay Evidence) Order 1993 in civil proceedings before the High Court, county court and in family proceedings in a magistrates' court, evidence given in connection with the upbringing, maintenance or welfare of a child is admissible notwithstanding any rule of law relating to hearsay.

18.145 The weight to be given to hearsay evidence must be assessed with care and the rules of natural justice and the right to a fair trial under Art 6 observed. As a matter of practice, it is prudent for courts to have regard to the matters set out in s 4 of the Civil Evidence Act 1995. Regard should be had to any circumstances from which any inference can reasonably be drawn as to the reliability or otherwise of the evidence. Regard may be had in particular to the following:

- whether it would have been reasonable and practicable for the party by whom the evidence was adduced to have produced the maker of the original statement as a witness;

- whether the original statement was made contemporaneously with the occurrence or existence of the matters alleged;

- whether the evidence involves multiple hearsay;

- whether any person involved had any motive to conceal or misrepresent matters;

- whether the original statement was an edited account or was made in collaboration with another or for a particular person;

- whether the circumstances in which the evidence is adduced as hearsay are such as to suggest an attempt to prevent a proper evaluation of its weight.

JUDGMENT

18.146 After the final hearing, the court has to deliver its judgment as soon as is practicable. If judgment is reserved, judges should deliver them no later than 1 month after the hearing, unless the circuit presider gives permission for a later delivery. The extent to which reasons must be given is discussed at **19.47**.

---

[125]   [2008] UKHL 35, [2008] 2 FLR 141 at [70]–[72].

Chapter 19

APPEALS

FORUM AND PROCEDURE

Which rules?

19.1 Appeals in family proceedings are governed by three sets of rules. Appeals under the Children Act 1989 (CA 1989) in cases from the family proceedings court to the county court and from district judges to a circuit judge (in a county court) or a High Court judge (in the Principal Registry of the Family Division) are governed by the Family Proceedings Rules 1991 (FPR 1991). Appeals from a circuit judge or High Court judge to the Court of Appeal are governed by CPR 1998, Part 52 and PD 52.[1] Appeals in adoption matters, whether from family proceedings courts or the county court or High Court are governed by the Family Procedure (Adoption) Rules 2005 (FP(A)R 2005) Part 19 and Practice Direction 19.

Family proceedings court

19.2 Appeals in relation to family proceedings in the magistrates' court lie to the county court.[2] Appeals should be issued at a county court (which includes the Principal Registry of the Family Division)[3] where a circuit judge with the appropriate 'ticket' sits. However, appeals under the Adoption and Children Act 2002 must be filed in an adoption centre or intercountry adoption centre.[4]

19.3 Appeals in the following proceedings have to be heard by a circuit judge nominated for public law proceedings:

- proceedings under s 25 of CA 1989;

- proceedings under CA 1989, Parts IV and V;

- proceedings under CA 1989, Schs 2 and 3;

---

[1] The Civil Procedure Rules 1998 do not apply to family proceedings in the county court and the High Court unless specifically adopted – CPR, r 2.1 and the Matrimonial and Family Proceedings Act 1984, s 40.

[2] Magistrates Courts Act 1980, s 111A as amended by the Access to Justice Act 1999 (Destination of Appeals) (Family Proceedings) Order 2009, SI 2009/871.

[3] Access to Justice Act 1999 (Destination of Appeals) (Family Proceedings) Order 2009, art 11.

[4] Family Procedure (Adoption) Rules 2005 Practice Direction 19 as amended by President's Practice Direction 6 April 2009, para 8.2.

- applications for leave under CA 1989, s 91(14), (15) or (17);

- proceedings under CA 1989, s 102 or the Childcare Act 2006, s 79;

- proceedings for a residence order under CA 1989, s 8 or for a special guardianship order under CA 1989, s 14A with respect to a child who is the subject of a care order;

- proceedings under the Adoption and Children Act 2002 (ACA 2002);

- proceedings for a residence order under CA 1989, s 8 where either ACA 2002, s 28(1) (child placed for adoption) or s 29(4) (placement order in force) applies;

- proceedings for a special guardianship order under CA 1989, s 14A where either ACA 2002, s 28(1) (child placed for adoption) or s 29(5) (placement order in force) applies.[5]

However a circuit judge or district judge nominated for private family law proceedings who is sitting at an adoption centre may, with the agreement of the Family Division Liaison Judge for the relevant region, hear an appeal from an order or decision in proceedings under ACA 2002, limited in the case of a district judge to any powers which may, by any rule or practice direction, be exercised by a district judge.[6] All other appeals are to be heard by a circuit judge nominated for public family law proceedings or private family law proceedings.[7]

19.4 In addition any proceedings may be heard by:

- a judge of the Family Division of the High Court;

- a person acting as a judge of the Family Division of the High Court pursuant to s 9(1) of the Supreme Court Act 1981 (with certain exceptions) but in relation to matters specified in the Schedule, only if the judge has been nominated for public law family proceedings;

- a person sitting as a recorder who has been authorised to act as a judge of the Family Division of the High Court pursuant to s 9(4) of the Supreme Court Act 1981.[8]

19.5 For appeals in proceedings brought under ACA 2002, the procedure is as set out in the Family Procedure (Adoption) Rules 2005 Practice Direction 19 (as amended). For other appeals the procedure is set out in the Family

---

5   Family Proceedings (Allocation to Judiciary) (Appeals) Directions 2009, art 6 and Schedule.
6   Ibid, art 9.
7   Ibid, art 6.
8   Ibid, art 8.

Proceedings Rules 1981, rr 8.A1 and 8.2–8.2H.[9] A President's Practice Direction[10] gives guidance as to the provision of approved transcripts, written reasons and notes of judgment.

To whom does the appeal lie?

19.6 In the county court appeals from a district judge are to a circuit judge with the relevant ticket (see **17.38** and **18.84**).[11] Appeals from a circuit judge are to the Court of Appeal.

19.7 In the High Court appeals from a district judge are to a High Court judge. Appeals from a High Court judge are to the Court of Appeal.

Assignment of appeals to the Court of Appeal

19.8 In adoption proceedings, where the court from which or to whom an appeal or application for permission to appeal is made considers that:

- the appeal would raise an important matter of principle or practice; or

- there is some other compelling reason for the Court of Appeal to hear it,

the relevant court may order the appeal to be transferred to the Court of Appeal.[12]

Rehearing or setting-aside order

19.9 There is an alternative to appealing. The trial judge may direct rehearing where no error of the court is alleged.[13] The judge can set aside the order, make any other order, remit the matter for rehearing or direct a new trial. Thus, the judge can consider the evidence which was originally before him, together with fresh evidence. This remedy applies only where no error of the court (eg as to the law) is alleged. If the aggrieved party is relying on an error, the remedy is an appeal.

Procedure

From a district judge to a judge in the same court

19.10 The procedure is set out in CPR, Part 52, Practice Direction 52, FP(A)R 2005, r 19:

---

[9]   Inserted by the Family Proceedings (Amendment) Rules 2009, SI 2009/636.
[10] 6 April 2009.
[11] FPR 1991, r 8.1, FP(A)R 2005, PD 19, para 2.1.
[12] FP(A)R 2005, r 182.
[13] CCR Ord 37 for the County Court, inherent jurisdiction for the High Court but see also Supreme Court Act 1981, s 17 and *B-T v B-T (Divorce: Procedure)* [1990] 2 FLR 1.

- the notice of appeal has to be filed in the court in which the order was made and served within 21 days (non-adoption appeals) or 14 days (adoption appeals) of the determination;

- a respondent's notice may be filed and served within 14 days of receipt of the notice of appeal;

- as soon as practicable after filing and serving the notice of appeal, the applicant must file and serve:
  - a paginated and indexed bundle;
  - a summary of the hearing;
  - a statement of issues;
  - a chronology; and
  - skeleton arguments.

  The bundle should contain:
  - a certified copy of the application and order;
  - a copy of the notes of evidence; and
  - a copy of the district judge's reasons;[14]

- it should also include the reports and witness statements which were before the court.

The judge hearing the appeal may make such orders as are necessary for the determination of the appeal and such incidental orders as are just.[15]

Any other appeal

19.11   The procedure is set out in CPR, Part 52, Practice Direction 52, FP(A)R 1991, r 19 and the PD Appeals. The appellant must file the appellant's notice at the Court of Appeal within:

- such period as directed by the lower court; or

- where there is no such direction, 21 days (non-adoption appeals) or 14 days (adoption appeals) after the decision which he wishes to appeal. If the appellant requires leave to appeal, this must be requested in the notice. The notice must be served as soon as is practicable and in any event no later than 7 days after it is filed. The grounds of appeal should set out clearly why CPR, r 52(11)(3)(a) or (b) (see below) is said to apply.[16]

19.12   A respondent who seeks permission to appeal or who wishes to ask the Court of Appeal to uphold the decision of the lower court for reasons different from or additional to those given by the lower court, must file a respondent's notice within:

---

[14]   *Practice Direction (Family Proceedings: Court Bundles) (10 March 2000)* [2000] 1 FLR 536.
[15]   CA 1989, s 94.
[16]   CPR, PD 52, para 3.2.

- such period as directed by the lower court; or

- where there is no such direction, 14 days after the date when:
  - he is served with the appellant's notice (if he did not require permission to appeal or the lower court gave permission); or
  - the date when he was notified the Court of Appeal had given permission.

It must be served as soon as is practicable and in any event no later than 7 days after it is filed.

19.13   The appellant must lodge with his documents:

- one additional copy of his notice for the court;

- one copy for each of the respondents;

- one copy of his skeleton argument or, if that is impracticable, it must be lodged and served within 14 days of filing the notice;

- a sealed copy of the order being appealed;

- an order giving or refusing permission to appeal together with a copy of the reasons;

- any witness statements in support of any application to be made;

- a bundle of documents PD 52, para 5.6 containing a detailed list of the documents to be included. If the documents exceed 150 pages excluding transcripts, the bundle should include only those documents which the court may reasonably be expected to pre-read. A full set of the documents should then be brought to the hearing;

- where the judgment has been officially recorded, an approved transcript should be filed with the notice. If it has not, there should be filed:
  - if a written decision was given, a copy of it;
  - if no written decision was given, a note of judgment agreed between the advocates which has been approved by the trial judge should be filed.[17]

Transcripts at public expense

19.14   The lower court or the appeal court may direct that the cost of obtaining a transcript of the judgment should be borne at public expense if:

- the appellant is unrepresented; and

---

[17]   CPR, PD 52, para 5.12, PD Appeals para 5.8, 5.23–5.26, 5.28.

- is in such poor financial circumstances that the cost of a transcript would be an excessive burden; and

- it is satisfied that there are reasonable grounds of appeal.[18]

Wherever possible, the request for a transcript should be made to the lower court when asking for permission to appeal.

19.15   Where a litigant was unrepresented in the lower court, the other party's advocate is under a duty to provide him promptly with a copy of his note of judgment free of charge where there is no officially recorded judgment or the court so directs. The cost of doing this is included in the brief fee.[19]

PERMISSION TO APPEAL

19.16   In Children Act cases, permission to appeal is required.[20] In adoption proceedings, permission is not required unless the matter being appealed relates to a decision made in costs assessment proceedings by a district judge or costs judge.[21]

19.17   The procedure is covered by CPR 1998, r 52.3 and PD 52, para 4. A distinction is drawn between first appeals (ie appeals from the tribunal which decided the case on its merits) and second appeals (ie appeals from a decision which was itself made on appeal).

19.18   In the case of first appeals:

- permission can be granted either by the court below, in which case permission should be made at the hearing when the order was made, or by the Court of Appeal;

- permission to appeal will be granted only where the court considers that:
  - the appeal would have a real prospect of success; or
  - there is some other compelling reason why it should be heard.

19.19   In the case of second appeals:

- permission can be granted only by the Court of Appeal;

- permission will not be granted unless the Court of Appeal considers that:
  - the appeal raises an important point of principle or practice; or
  - there is some other compelling reason for the Court of Appeal to hear the case.

---

18   CPR, PD 52, para 5.17. PD Appeals para 5.23.
19   CPR, PD 52, paras 5.12 and 5.14.
20   CPR, r 52.3. FP(A)R 2005, r 173.
21   FP(A)R 2005, r 173(1).

19.20   In both first and second appeals, permission can be granted subject to conditions[22] and the court can order security for costs.[23]

19.21   Where the appellate court, without a hearing, refuses permission to appeal, a request can be made for the decision to be reconsidered at a hearing. In this case, notice of the hearing need not be given to the respondent unless the court so directs.

WHO CAN APPEAL?

19.22   Any party may seek permission to appeal. In addition, in appropriate circumstances, the court may join a non-party for the purpose of allowing them to make an application for permission to appeal.[24]

FRESH EVIDENCE

19.23   In civil and non-children family appeals, the appellate court has a discretion to admit fresh evidence but this discretion will be exercised according to the rule in *Ladd v Marshall*[25] which have survived the Woolf reforms:[26]

- it must be shown that the evidence could not have been obtained with reasonable diligence for use at the trial;

- the evidence must be such that, if given, it would probably have an important influence on the result of the case, although need not be decisive; and

- the evidence must be such as is presumably to be believed or, in other words, it must be apparently credible although it need not be incontrovertible.

19.24   A judge, hearing an appeal in a child's case has the discretion to admit oral or further evidence as he considers relevant and on such terms as he considers appropriate. He is not strictly bound by the rules in *Ladd v Marshall*.[27]

---

[22]   CPR, r 3.1(3).
[23]   Ibid, r 25.15.
[24]   *Webster v Norfolk County Council* [2009] EWCA Civ 59, [2009] 1 FLR 1378 at [142] in which birth parents who were not parties to an adoption order were joined for this purpose. See **2.127**.
[25]   [1954] 1 WLR 1489 per Denning LJ at 1491.
[26]   *Banks v Cox* (unreported) 17 July 2000, CA.
[27]   *Marsh v Marsh* [1993] 1 FLR 467. See also *Webster v Norfolk County Council* [2009] EWCA Civ 59, [2009] 1 FLR 1378 at [135].

19.25   However, because the appellate judge has a discretion as to how the appeal will be heard, additional evidence will not ordinarily be admitted unless there is good reason to do so.[28] In appeals involving children, fresh evidence relating to matters arising since the decision will be admitted. However, the court will be vigilant to see that the material is genuinely fresh and not a further manifestation of what was before the judge. There is a real difference between a child reacting adversely and dramatically to an order, for example refusing hysterically to go on contact, and one merely repeating what was said earlier to the Children and Family Reporter. The same applies to other evidence. Does it constitute something new or is it another example of material before the trial judge?[29]

19.26   Any attempt to adduce evidence from the child by way of a witness statement will be seriously deprecated.[30]

19.27   When considering the admission of fresh evidence, the appellate court will first consider what view to take of the decision of the court below on the material before the judge, ignoring any fresh information. Only if it considers it would dismiss the appeal on that basis will it then consider whether to admit the fresh evidence. If it does, it will then examine the evidence to see to what extent it invalidates the reasons given by the judge for the decision.[31]

REOPENING APPEALS

19.28   The Court of Appeal has a residual jurisdiction to hear second appeals if:

(a)   it is necessary to do so in order to avoid real injustice;

(b)   the circumstances are exceptional and make it appropriate to reopen the appeal; and

(c)   there is no alternative effective remedy.[32]

19.29   In adoption cases the same considerations apply to the High Court when hearing appeals.[33]

19.30   It appears that a circuit judge does not have these powers when hearing an appeal.

---

[28]   *Marsh v Marsh* [1993] 1 FLR 467, applying *Walters v Walters* [1992] 2 FLR 337. See also *Re W* [2009] EWCA Civ 59 at [135]–[139], [180]–[181].

[29]   See, for example, *Re P (Custody of Children) (Split Custody Order)* [1991] 1 FLR 337.

[30]   *Re M (Family Proceedings: Affidavits)* [1995] 2 FLR 100.

[31]   *M v M (Transfer of Custody: Appeal)* [1987] 2 FLR 146; *Hadmor Productions Ltd v Hamilton* [1983] AC 191.

[32]   CPR, r 52.17 (1).

[33]   FP(A)R 2005, r 183.

19.31 Permission is required from the appellate court – applied for in writing – whether or not the original appeal required permission[34] and the prospective appellant needs to show that a significant injustice has probably occurred and there is no alternative effective remedy. The effect of reopening the appeal on others and the extent to which the effective appellant is the author of his own misfortune will also be important considerations. Where the alternative remedy is an appeal to the House of Lords, the Court of Appeal will only give permission to reopen the appeal if it is satisfied that the House of Lords would not give leave to appeal.[35] The jurisdiction can only be properly revoked where it is shown that the integrity of the earlier litigation process has been critically undermined.[36]

19.32 In *Re U (Re-opening of Appeal)*,[37] for example, permission to reopen an appeal on the ground that there was fresh medical evidence relating to a child's injuries was refused. If the discovery of fresh evidence is to justify the reopening of an appeal, not only must the *Ladd v Marshall* test be satisfied, there must also be shown a 'powerful probability' that an error has resulted and the injustice was so grave as to 'overbear the pressing claims of finality in litigation'.[38] That was not the case in the instant appeal.

THE IMPORTANCE OF SPEED

19.33 Regardless of the time limits for appealing, it is important that appeals involving children, and especially where an adoption order has been made,[39] should be pursued with expedition. Emergency facilities in the Court of Appeal are always available to deal with urgent child cases and can be accessed by telephone where necessary.[40] The trial judge should immediately be asked for permission to appeal and to stay the order pending appeal or at least for such period as would allow the appellant to seek directions from the Court of Appeal.[41] If this is refused the appellant should contact the Court of Appeal (in cases out of hours by contacting the duty officer through the security offices of the Royal Courts of Justice (0207 947 6260)). If the Court is satisfied either that permission to appeal should be granted or that an application for permission should be listed at short notice, it will give such a direction.[42]

---

[34] CPR, r 52.17(4).
[35] *Taylor v Lawrence* [2002] EWCA Civ 90, [2003] QB 528.
[36] *Re U (Re-opening of Appeal)* [2005] EWCA Civ 52, [2005] 2 FLR 444.
[37] Ibid.
[38] Per Butler-Sloss P at paras [21]–[22].
[39] *Re PJ (Adoption: Practice on Appeal)* [1998] 2 FLR 252.
[40] *Re S (Child Proceedings: Urgent Appeals)* [2007] EWCA Civ 958, [2007] 2 FLR 1044.
[41] *Re PJ (Adoption: Practice on Appeal)* op cit at 263, *Re S (Child Proceedings: Urgent Appeals)* ibid at [9].
[42] *Re S (Child Proceedings: Urgent Appeals)* ibid at [10]. In *Re P (Residence: Appeal)* [2007] EWCA Civ 1053, [2008] 1 FLR 198 an appeal in a residence case was heard within 15 days of judgment in the court below, the trial judge staying the order but reducing the time for appealing to 3 days.

WHICH TEST?

19.34 In s 94 appeals, although the appellate judge has an unfettered discretion, the evidence before the court below will normally be adopted as the trial judge's conclusions in relation to the evidence unless there are good reasons for reopening the investigation.[43]

19.35 The positions under CPR, r 52.11 and FP(A)R 1991, r 181 are, in theory, different:

> 'Every appeal will be limited to a review of the decision of the lower court unless ... the court considers that in the circumstances of the individual appeal it would be in the interests of justice to hold a rehearing.'

19.36 The court will allow the appeal where the decision of the lower court was:

- wrong; or

- unjust because of a serious procedural or other irregularity in the proceedings before the lower court.[44]

19.37 The test propounded by the House of Lords in *G v G (Minors: Custody Appeal)*[45] applies to all appeals in which a discretion was exercised at first instance.

> 'The reason for the limited role of the Court of Appeal in custody cases is not that appeals in such cases are subject to any special rules, but that there are often two or more possible decisions, any one of which might reasonably be thought to be the best, and any one of which therefore a judge may make without being held to be wrong.
>
> ... In cases dealing with the custody of children, the desirability of putting an end to litigation, which applies to all classes of case, is particularly strong because the longer legal proceedings last, the more are children, whose welfare is at stake, likely to be disturbed by the uncertainty.
>
> Nevertheless there will be some cases in which the Court of Appeal decides that the judge at first instance has come to a wrong conclusion. In such cases it is the duty of the Court of Appeal to substitute its own decision for that of the judge ... the appellate court should only interfere if they consider that the judge of first instance has not merely preferred an imperfect solution which the Court of Appeal might or would have adopted but has exceeded the generous ambit within which a reasonable disagreement is possible.'[46]

---

[43]   *Marsh v Marsh* [1993] 1 FLR 467.
[44]   CPR, r 52.11.
[45]   [1985] FLR 894.
[46]   [1985] FLR 894, per Lord Fraser of Tullybelton at 898–899.

19.38   The discretion applies equally to findings of fact and of credibility, the evaluation of factors and apportioning weight to those factors. In *Re J (Child Returned Abroad: Convention Rights)*[47] Baroness Hale emphasised in the House of Lords:

'If there is indeed a discretion in which various factors are relevant, the valuation and balancing of those factors is also a matter for the trial judge. Only if his decision is so plainly wrong that he must have given far too much weight to a particular factor is the appellate court entitled to interfere: see *G v G* [reference given]. Too ready an interference by the appellate court, particularly if it always seems to be in the direction of one result rather than the other, risks robbing the trial judge of the discretion entrusted to him by the law. In short, if trial judges are led to believe that, even if they direct themselves impeccably on the law, make findings of fact which are open to them on the evidence, and are careful, as this judge undoubtedly was, in the evaluation and weighing of the relevant factors, their decisions are liable to be overturned unless they reach a particular conclusion, they will come to believe that they do not in fact have any choice or discretion in the matter.'[48]

19.39   Until recently, courts adopted the approach that, where an appeal lay from a district judge to a circuit judge, the circuit judge had to exercise his own discretion, giving such weight to the factors found by the district judge as he thought fit – the '*Marsh v Marsh*' approach. In 1998, however, the Family Appeals Review Group, chaired by Thorpe LJ recommended that appeals under s 94 should be decided by applying *G v G* principles. In 1999, the President held in *Re W, Re A, Re B (Change of Name)*[49] that *G v G* principles should govern all Children Act appeals where all levels of judiciary (including magistrates) have the same jurisdiction and no fresh evidence is adduced:

'The trial judge sees and hears the oral evidence and has the inestimable feel of the case, denied as much to the circuit judge on appeal as to the Court of Appeal.'

This approach has now been adopted for all family appeals.[50]

THE SPECIAL POSITION OF ADOPTION ORDERS

19.40   Because of the finality of adoption orders and the public policy considerations which apply, appellate courts will set aside adoption orders once they have been lawfully and properly made only in high exceptional and very particular circumstances.[51] This is discussed at **2.121**.

---

[47]   [2005] UKHL 40, [2005] 2 FLR 802.
[48]   Ibid, at para 12.
[49]   [1999] 2 FLR 930.
[50]   *Cordle v Cordle* [2002] 1 FLR 207.
[51]   *Re W* [2009] EWCA Civ 59 per Wall LJ at [149].

GROUNDS OF APPEAL[52]

19.41 It is notoriously difficult to prophesy which appeals will engage the Court of Appeal to such an extent that the appellate judges will interfere with the discretion of the trial judge. Some issues occur regularly.

Reasons

19.42 Courts must give proper reasons for their decisions and a failure to do so will vitiate the decision.[53] This was so before the advent of the Human Rights Act 1998 and now, a failure to give reasons will breach the Art 6 right to a fair trial.

19.43 The reasons should include:

• a statement of the issues;

• the court's findings of fact on those issues;

• its reasons for preferring the evidence of a witness on those issues to that of another witness, for disagreeing with the recommendation of a Children and Family Reporter, guardian ad litem or expert witness and its reasons for reaching its decision.

19.44 It is always desirable that a judgment should be comprehensible to the first time reader but that is not the test of adequacy. Adequacy should be tested in the context of the knowledge and understanding of those who had been present at the trial and after reading the pleadings and submissions.[54]

19.45 The appellate court (and the parties) must be able to be satisfied that the trial court took into account all the relevant matters and did not take into account irrelevant ones. Justices' reasons should not be approached in the same way as a judgment but the appellate court might be less ready to assume that magistrates had taken relevant factors into account if they had not referred to them than it might in the case of an experienced judge.[55] Justices cannot supplement their original reasons later.[56] There is a distinction between a court giving no reasons or inadequate reasons and one which fails expressly to mention everything. If the judgment as a whole explains the reasons for the decision, the precise format and phraseology are a matter for the judge.[57]

---

[52]   See also *English v Emery Reimbold & Strick Ltd; DJ & C Withers (Farms) Ltd v Ambic Equipment Ltd; Verrachia (trading as Freightmaster Commercials) v Commissioner of Police for the Metropolis* [2002] EWCA Civ 605, [2002] 1 WLR 2409.

[53]   *W v Hertfordshire CC* [1993] 1 FLR 118; *T v W (Contact: Reasons for Refusing Leave)* [1996] 2 FLR 473, an appeal from a family proceedings court.

[54]   *Harris v CDMR Purfleet Ltd* Court of Appeal 20 Nov 2008, [2008] All ER (D)206 (Nov).

[55]   *Re M (Section 94 Appeals)* [1995] 1 FLR 546.

[56]   *Hillingdon London Borough Council v H* [1992] 2 FLR 372.

[57]   *Re V (Residence: Review)* [1995] 2 FLR 1010; *English v Emery Reimbold & Strick Ltd; DJ &*

19.46 The more experienced the judge the more likely it is that he will display 'the virtue of brevity'.[58]

19.47 When a judgment is given, an advocate ought immediately as a matter of courtesy to draw the judge's attention to any material omission which he believes exists. It is open for the judge then to amend his judgment at any time prior to the order being drawn up.[59] If an application for permission to appeal on the ground of lack of reasons is made to the trial judge, the judge should consider adjourning in order to remedy any defect by the provision of additional reasons before refusing permission to appeal.

> 'It is high time that the Family Bar woke up to *English v Emery Reimbold & Strick Ltd* ... I wish to make it as clear as possible that after a judge has given judgment, counsel have a positive duty to raise with the judge not just any alleged deficiency in the judge's reasoning process but any genuine query or ambiguity which arises on the judgment. Judges should welcome this process.[60]'[61]

If an application for permission to appeal is made to the appellate court and it appears that the application is well founded, the court should consider adjourning the application and remitting the case to the trial judge with an invitation to provide additional reasons.[62]

Children and Family Reporter/Guardian

19.48 Provided the judge takes into account the views of the Children and Family Reporter or guardian, he is not bound to follow his/her recommendations. The judge should, however, indicate in his judgment or reasons, preferably expressly, the reasons for not following the recommendations. The recommendations should be carefully explored in cross-examination.[63] It has been said that even the most experienced judge is not entitled to overrule 'the measured and careful assessments of the attitude of a party merely by observing their conduct during the course of the hearing',

---

Withers (Farms) Ltd v Ambic Equipment Ltd; Verrechia (trading as Freightmaster Commercials) v Commissioner of Police for the Metropolis [2002] EWCA Civ 605, [2002] 1 WLR 2409.

[58] *Re B (Appeal: Lack of Reasons)* [2003] EWCA Civ 881, [2003] 2 FLR 1035 per Thorpe LJ at para [11].

[59] *Re T (Contact: Alienation: Permission to Appeal)* [2002] EWCA Civ 1736, [2003] 1 FLR 531 per Arden LJ at para [41]. Approved in *Re B (Appeal: Lack of Reasons)* [2003] EWCA Civ 881, [2003] 2 FLR 1035.

[60] Judges are less likely to welcome attempts to ask them to reconsider their conclusions save in the most exceptional circumstances – a growing practice in some courts which has been deprecated: *Egan v Motor Services (Bath) Ltd* [2007] EWCA Civ 1002, [2008] 1 FLR 1346 per Smith LJ at [49]–[51] and *Re N (Payments for Benefit of Child)* [2009] EWHC 11 (Fam), [2009] 1 FLR 1442 per Munby J at [106].

[61] *Re M (Fact-finding Hearing: Burden of Proof)* [2008] EWCA Civ 1261, [2009] 1 FLR 1177 per Wall LJ at [36], [38].

[62] *English v Emery Reimbold & Strick Ltd* [2002] EWCA Civ 605, [2002] 1 WLR 2409; *Hicks v Russell Jones & Walker (a firm)* [2007] EWCA Civ 844, [2008] 2 All ER 1089.

[63] *Re P (Custody of Children: Split Custody Order)* [1991] 1 FLR 337. See also *Re M (Residence)* [2004] EWCA Civ 1574, [2005] 1 FLR 656.

but this may depend on the relative opportunities to observe the parties. Where there are clear-cut recommendations and warnings of risk in reports, the judge should not depart from them without first hearing evidence from the Children and Family Reporter.[64] This is not to say that the court should never depart from the recommendations without hearing from the Children and Family Reporter especially where neither party has requested the Children and Family Reporter's attendance.[65]

Experts

19.49 Similar considerations apply to recommendations from expert witnesses.

Interim orders

19.50 The Court of Appeal is reluctant to hear appeals on interim matters. If there has been a change in circumstances, the proper course is to apply for further directions to the court below. However, it will hear appeals in respect of issues determined as a preliminary part of the case without waiting for the second part of a split trial.[66]

Change in circumstances

19.51 A significant change in circumstances, supported by fresh evidence, may result in the court setting aside the order and directing a retrial. For adoption appeals under this category, see **2.121**.

'Misapplication' of the welfare test and the checklist

19.52 There are no presumptions when the welfare checklist is applied. Every case must be decided on its own facts:

> 'The only direction that can be given to the trial judge is to apply the welfare principle and the welfare checklist ... to the facts of the specific case.'[67]

Therefore, an appeal which relies, for example, on the mere assertion that a judge was 'wrong' to separate siblings contrary to some perceived principle or norm is unlikely to succeed.

19.53 The more difficult the decision and finely balanced the conclusion, the less prospect there is of the decision being successfully appealed.

> 'The exercise of discretion by the judge in a family case is often made against extremely difficult circumstances where he is faced with the least satisfactory

---

[64] *Re CB (Access: Attendance of Court Welfare Officer)* [1995] 1 FLR 622.
[65] *Re L (Residence: Justices' Reasons)* [1995] 2 FLR 445.
[66] *Re B (Split Hearings: Jurisdiction)* [2000] 1 FLR 334.
[67] *S v M (Access Order)* [1997] 1 FLR 980, per Thorpe LJ at 370.

solution for children who are suffering from the breakdown of the [relationship] of their parents and where there are factors that mean that no solution ... is a satisfactory one. No decision can be seen to be the right one. One cannot tell in family courts whether decisions are right or wrong. The judge has the unenviable task of using a crystal ball and, based on the past facts, doing the best he can, with the welfare of the children as the paramount consideration and praying that he or she gets it right. The more difficult the decision that has to be made, then the more finely balanced the conclusion and the more difficult it is for the loser in the court below to succeed in the Court of Appeal. It is unlikely the judge can be shown to be plainly wrong because he might have gone, as any member of this court might have gone, either way in this case, as in so many others. It means that those who seek to appeal against the decision of, in particular, a High Court judge but also a circuit judge, dealing with difficult problems and finely balanced decisions, ought to consider very carefully the wisdom of attempting to appeal and what the prospects of success are in the Court of Appeal, limited as the Court of Appeal always is in setting aside findings of fact or assessments of the credibility of witnesses.'[68]

'If, as I suspect, [this hopeless appeal] has been brought on public funds, then it is another of the all-too-frequent examples of public money being spent to no good effect and, indeed, in an adverse way, because it continues to raise the temperature, to exacerbate the unhappy feelings between the parents and to have an adverse effect upon the children who are the subject of the proceedings ... these are appeals brought in, perhaps, the height of emotion and understandable upset by a parent, where it requires a particular degree of detachment and common sense from the legal advisers not to be carried away by the enthusiasm, frustration and hurt of their lay clients.'[69]

19.54 In relation to adoption and special guardianship orders, the Court of Appeal in *Re S (Adoption Order or Special Guardianship Order)*[70] said that:

'Provided the judge has carefully examined the facts, made appropriate findings in relation to them and applied the welfare checklists contained in s 1(3) of the 1989 Act and s 1 of the 2002 Act, it is unlikely that this court will be able properly to interfere with the exercise of judicial discretion, particularly in a finely balanced case.'[71]

Legal advisers who bring hopeless appeals are vulnerable to a wasted costs order.[72]

---

[68] *Re N (Residence: Hopeless Appeals)* [1995] 2 FLR 230, per Butler-Sloss LJ at 231. See also Ward LJ at 236.
[69] Ibid, per Butler-Sloss LJ at 231.
[70] [2007] EWCA Civ 54, [2007] 1 FLR 819.
[71] Ibid, per Wall J at [48].
[72] *B v B (Wasted Costs: Abuse of Process)* [2001] 1 FLR 843. See Chapter 20.

ORDERS WHICH CAN BE MADE

19.55 The appellate court can exercise all the powers of the court below. When allowing an appeal, it can:

- make a substantive order;

- remit the case for a rehearing either to the original tribunal or another tribunal;

- remit the case for a rehearing, transferring it to a higher court, either a county court or the High Court. However, the Court of Appeal in children's cases is very reluctant to order a rehearing:

> 'The desirability of putting an end to litigation is particularly strong because the longer the legal proceedings last, the more are the children, whose welfare is at stake, likely to be disturbed by the uncertainty.'[73]

19.56 Attempting to resolve disputes by mediation is just as appropriate in appeals as for cases at first instance and the Court of Appeal has its own Alternative Dispute Resolution scheme operated by the Centre of Effective Dispute Resolution (CEDR).[74] In *Al-Khatib v Masry*[75] Thorpe LJ said:

> '[This case] supports our conviction that there is no case, however conflicted, which is not potentially open to successful mediation, even if mediation has not been attempted or has failed during the trial process. It also demonstrates how vital it is for there to be judicial supervision of the process of mediation. It is not enough, in a difficult family case such as this, for the supervising Lord Justice or the Lord Justice directing mediation simply to make the order and thereafter assume that there will be a smooth passage to an initial meeting. The selection of the appropriate mediator is crucial and the availability of the supervising judge to deal with crisis is equally important.'[76]

It may be difficult but not impossible to conceive of cases concerning adoption where mediation may be appropriate but less so in special guardianship cases. Where the child is going to be looked after by a kinship carer, a family conference (see **18.7**) may be of help.

---

[73] *G v G (Minors: Custody Appeal)* [1985] FLR 894, per Lord Fraser of Tullybelton at 898.
[74] The Scheme has a relatively low take up but an 'encouragingly high' success rate. *Rothwell v Rothwell* [2008] EWCA Civ 1600, [2009] 2 FLR 96 per Thorpe LJ at [8].
[75] [2004] EWCA Civ 1353, [2005] 1 FLR 381.
[76] Ibid, at para 17.

Chapter 20

COSTS

INTRODUCTION

20.1   Cost orders are seldom made between parties in proceedings involving children. However, there are occasions when this could be justified.

COSTS IN THE FAMILY PROCEEDINGS COURT

20.2   At any time during the proceedings, the court may make an order that a party pay the whole or any part of the costs of any other party.[1] Any party against whom the court is considering making an order must have the opportunity to make representations.

20.3   In the family proceedings court, the discretion to make an order is unfettered by legislation other than that which applies to a Legal Services Commission-funded litigant. However, it is not usual for a costs order to be made in children's cases.[2] The approach to the exercise of the discretion is discussed below.

20.4   There are three possible courses that the court can take to quantify the costs, none of them being wholly satisfactory because justices are inexperienced in assessing large amounts of costs:

- it can assess the amount payable there and then;

- it can adjourn until a bill has been prepared or, in the case of a LSC-funded receiving party, an assessment of the LSC costs has taken place; or

- In the case of a LSC-funded receiving party, it can order the paying party to pay a proportion of the assessed LSC costs.[3] This later course has the disadvantage that the paying party has no opportunity of making representations as to the amount and should be the least preferred option. However, this difficulty can be overcome to some extent by the court imposing a maximum amount payable.

---

[1]   Family Proceedings Court (Children Act 1989) Rules 1991, SI 1991/1395, r 22.
[2]   *Gojkovic v Gojkovic (No 2)* [1991] 2 FLR 233.
[3]   *London Borough of Sutton v Davis (Costs) (No 2)* [1994] 2 FLR 569.

COSTS IN THE COUNTY COURT AND THE HIGH COURT

20.5   Both the award of costs and their assessment are covered by Parts 43, 44 (except rr 44.9–44.12), 47 and 48 of Civil Procedure Rules 1998 (CPR) and the accompanying Practice Directions.[4]

20.6   The orders which a court can make include an order that a party pay:

- a proportion of another party's costs;

- a stated amount in respect of another party's costs;

- costs from or until a certain date;

- costs incurred before proceedings have begun;

- costs relating to particular steps taken in the proceedings;

- costs relating only to a distinct part of the proceedings; and

- interest on costs from or until a certain date including a date before judgment (CPR, r 44.3(6)).

20.7   One of the aims of the CPR is to simplify the regime for the assessment of costs and so, when a court is considering making a costs order relating to a distinct part of the proceedings, it must instead, if practicable, order that the party pay a proportion of the overall costs or a stated amount.[5]

20.8   In family proceedings, the need to avoid the expense, delay and aggravation involved in protracted assessment proceedings, especially in complex cases, may make it desirable for courts to continue the practice set out in the pre-CPR cases of *Leary v Leary*[6] and *Newton v Newton*[7] and order a fixed sum to be paid rather than a sum ascertained by summary or detailed assessment.[8]

Discretion

20.9   The court has a discretion to order costs. The 'general' rule applicable in civil proceedings, that the unsuccessful party will be ordered to pay the costs of the successful party but it may make a different order,[9] does not apply to family

---

4   Applied to family proceedings by Family Proceedings (Miscellaneous Amendments) Rules 1999, SI 1999/1012, r 4.
5   CPR, r 44.3(7).
6   [1987] 1 FLR 384.
7   [1990] 1 FLR 33.
8   *Q v Q (Costs: Summary Assessment)* [2002] 2 FLR 668.
9   CPR, r 44.3(2).

proceedings.[10] However, the rest of CPR, r 44.3 applies and so the court must have regard to all the circumstances, including:

- the conduct of all the parties which includes:
  - conduct before as well as during the proceedings and in particular the extent to which the parties followed any particular protocol;
  - whether it was reasonable for a party to raise, pursue or contest a particular allegation or issue;
  - the manner in which a party has pursued or defended his case or a particular allegation or issue; and
  - whether a party who has succeeded in his case, in whole or in part, exaggerated his case;

- whether a party has succeeded on part of his case even if he has not been wholly successful;

- any admissible offer to settle made by a party which is drawn to the court's attention (CPR, r 44.3(4) and (5)).

20.10   At the present time, there is no Pre-action Protocol relating to children cases, but the court might take into account the extent to which the parties have attempted to negotiate with all cards on the table before commencing proceedings and the extent to which the Family Law Protocol issued by The Law Society has been followed.

20.11   Before the introduction of CPR, Part 44, it was unusual for a court to order one party to pay another party's costs in children cases but it was recognised that the power existed. It is unlikely that CPR, Part 44 has brought about any change in the approach of the courts. Bearing in mind that 'it is unnecessary and undesirable to try to limit or place into rigid categories the cases which a court might regard as suitable' for an order for costs,[11] guidance as to the factors special to family proceedings which impact on the consideration of a costs order can be obtained from pre-CPR cases as well as more recent ones:

- Reprehensible conduct. For example, in *Re A (Family Proceedings: Expert Witnesses)*,[12] a father who made unwarranted personal attacks on the integrity of a family centre was ordered to pay its costs of intervening.

- Commencing or continuing the proceedings when it was no longer reasonable to do so. For example, in *Re B (Costs)*,[13] a father who persisted with an application for a residence order on the grounds that the mother posed a risk to the children after two psychiatrists advised to the

---

[10]   Family Proceedings (Miscellaneous Amendments) Rules 1993, SI 1993/1183, r 4.
[11]   *London Borough of Sutton v Davis (Costs) (No 2)* [1994] 2 FLR 569, per Neill LJ at 268.
[12]   [2001] 1 FLR 723.
[13]   [1999] 2 FLR 221.

contrary, was ordered to pay 80% of the mother's costs from the date when the psychiatrists filed their joint accord.

> 'It is, of course, right in principle that in Children Act proceedings orders for costs against a parent are exceptionally rare, but that is as against a parent acting responsibly and it seems to me that Circuit Judges should have recourse to [order costs] in cases in which they conclude that a parent has acted irresponsibly both in relation to [the other parent] and in relation to the child and in relation to public funds.'[14]

However, a distinction has to be drawn between unreasonableness in relation to the child and unreasonableness in relation to the litigation:

> 'Of course, the parties should not be deterred, by the prospect of having to pay costs, from putting before the court that which they think to be in the best interests of the child, but there have to be limits. Children should not be put through the strain of being subject to claims which have little real prospect of success ...'[15]

The court should ask whether there was conduct in relation to the litigation which went way beyond the usual sort of attitude which a concerned parent shows in relation to the future of his children.

- The extent to which a party has brought the proceedings upon themselves by unwise or inappropriate conduct.

- A marked disparity in the respective wealth of the parties such that 'the wife's costs would bear harshly on her economy but could be discharged by the husband without significant impact on his economy might give rise to an order against him'.[16]

- The court should bear in mind that the parties will have to continue to work together and an inappropriate order for costs may have an adverse impact on the relationship to the detriment of the child.[17]

20.12   In most cases, the proper consideration of all the factors will lead to there being no order for costs. Where, however, an order is made, it ought to be made clear in the judgment or, preferably, on the face of the order itself why the order was made.

20.13   An order for costs on the indemnity basis is a wholly exceptional order in family proceedings and has to be very carefully thought through and justified.[18]

---

14   *Khatun v Fayez* Court of Appeal, 2 March 1998, unreported per Thorpe LJ.
15   *R v R (Costs: Child Case)* [1997] 2 FLR 95, per Hale J at 98.
16   *Keller v Keller and Legal Aid Board* [1995] 1 FLR 259, per Wilson J at 265.
17   *Re M (Local Authority's Costs)* [1995] 1 FLR 533, per Cazalet J at 541.
18   *Re B (Indemnity Costs)* [2007] EWCA Civ 921 [2008] 1 FLR 205.

Examples

M v H (Costs: Residence Proceedings)[19]

20.14 A father seeking orders for a shared residence and defined contact orders who had unreasonably rejected a proposal to resolve the matter by mediation unless the mother agreed to a shared residence order, who 'took every possible basis for criticising the mother and blowing it into an issue of her parental fitness', who continued with his application for a shared residence order despite the recommendations of the Children and Family Reporter until 4 days before the start of a hearing listed for 3 days and who had taken advantage of his financial superiority over the mother, was ordered to pay 75% of her costs.

Q v Q (Costs: Summary Assessment)[20]

20.15 A father who should never have applied for a residence order and who had failed to undergo medical tests designed to establish whether he was abusing alcohol and drugs and who had failed to attend interviews with a clinical psychologist who had been instructed to interview both parents and the child was ordered to pay 'a significant' part of the mother's costs.

T v T (A Child: Costs Order)[21]

20.16 The mother's opposition to the father taking their son abroad on holiday related only to an issue of whether it was a prelude to three possible future visits. When this was made clear at the hearing, the father offered an undertaking which the mother accepted. Sumner J held that the mother's failure to clarify matters earlier was unreasonable and irresponsible and ordered her to pay half of his costs.

Re T (Order for Costs)[22]

20.17 An intractable contact dispute in which there were three hearings when the judge found that the mother's concerns were unfounded, rejected later allegations of sexual abuse and finally made a residence order in favour of the father. The Court of Appeal dismissed the mother's appeal against an order that she pay the father's costs of all three hearings on the grounds that she had behaved unreasonably both in regard to the welfare of the child and to the conduct of the litigation. The trial judge had been justified in feeling that despite aspects of the mother's personality which allowed suspicions to take hold, 'it would be an affront to justice to expect the father to pay the costs of defending himself against these most serious allegations'. Wall LJ added:[23]

---

[19] [2000] 1 FLR 394.
[20] [2002] 2 FLR 668.
[21] [2004] EWHC 1067 (Fam) Sumner J.
[22] [2005] EWCA Civ 1029, [2005] 2 FLR 681.
[23] Ibid, at para [56].

'We do not think that the orders for costs which we have upheld are either likely to or should deter a resident parent from advancing a reasonable opposition to contact which is genuinely based on a proper perception of the child's interests. But those who unreasonably frustrate contact need to be aware that the court has power to make cost orders in appropriate cases and that the consequences of such unreasonable behaviour may well be an order for costs against the resident parent who has behaved unreasonably.'

WASTED COSTS ORDERS

20.18 The court may disallow costs (eg on a solicitor/client assessment or public funded costs assessment) or order the legal or other representative to pay them.[24] Where costs are incurred by a party as a result of:

* any improper, unreasonable or negligent act or omission on the part of a legal or other representative; or

* which, in the light of any such act or omission after they have been incurred, the court considers it unreasonable to expect that party to pay.

20.19 'Improper' covers, but is not restricted to, conduct which might lead to a serious professional penalty or offends professional consensus as to what is professional conduct. 'Unreasonable' includes conduct which is vexatious or harasses other parties, designed to harass the other side rather than advance the resolution of the case. It does not include an approach which merely leads to an unsuccessful result or which a more cautious representative might not have adopted. The acid test is whether the conduct permits of a reasonable explanation. 'Negligent' should be approached in a non-technical way. It may include failing to act with the competence reasonably to be expected of a member of the legal profession.[25] It is not limited to the representative's conduct when exercising a right of audience. Negligence in advising or in drafting documents is also included.[26] However, any impropriety must be serious and something more than mere negligence is required to justify a wasted costs order.[27]

20.20 Lawyers should not however be penalised merely for pursuing a hopeless case:

'Parents [in care proceedings] are at risk of losing their children; no decision could be more important ... and all parents at such risk are entitled to proper representation and to have their cases put.'[28]

---

[24]   Supreme Court Act 1981, s 51(6).
[25]   *Ridehalgh v Horsefield; Watson v Watson (Wasted Costs Orders)* [1994] 2 FLR 194.
[26]   *Medcalf v Mardell* [2002] 3 All ER 721.
[27]   *Persaud (Luke) v Persaud (Mohan)* [2003] EWCA Civ 394, [2003] PNLR 26.
[28]   *Re G, S and M (Wasted Costs)* [2000] 1 FLR 52, per Wall J at 60.

20.21 The procedure is governed by CPR, r 48.7 and Practice Direction Part 48 Costs.[29] In *Ridehalgh v Horsefield; Watson v Watson (Wasted Costs Orders)*,[30] the Court of Appeal gave guidance on how the issue should be approached:

- Has the legal representative acted improperly, unreasonably or negligently?

- If so, did the conduct cause the party to incur unnecessary costs?

- If so, is it in all the circumstances just to order the legal representative to compensate the party for the whole or any part of the costs?

- The representative should be given the opportunity of making representations either at the time or on a subsequent occasion in which case the notice of the hearing should state the reasons why the court is considering making the order;

- The order should state:
    - the reasons why it is made; and
    - the amount to be paid or disallowed.

20.22 The issue of client confidentiality may give rise to difficulties in the representative defending himself and, save in the clearest case, the application should be decided at a separate hearing.[31] Often, the circumstances of the litigation may make it necessary to reserve the issue until after the conclusion of the case but this may not be necessary, for example, when the client has ceased to instruct the representative, or the case does not involve issues of client confidentiality or the matter is simple and straightforward:[32]

> 'When a wasted costs order is sought against a practitioner precluded by legal professional privilege from giving his full answer to the application, the court should not make a wasted costs order unless, proceeding with extreme care, it is satisfied (a) that there is nothing the practitioner could say, if unconstrained, to resist the order and (b) that it is in all the circumstances fair to make the order.'[33]

Examples

Re G, S and M (Wasted Costs)[34]

20.23 An order was made against counsel because of its failure to ensure that expert witnesses had seen all the relevant information before giving oral evidence.

---

29 Section 53.
30 [1994] 2 FLR 194.
31 *Medcalf v Mardell* [2002] 3 All ER 721.
32 See, for example, *B v B (Wasted Costs: Abuse of Process)* [2001] 1 FLR 843.
33 *Medcalf v Mardell* [2002] 3 All ER 721, per Lord Bingham of Cornhill at 734.
34 [2000] 1 FLR 52.

B v B (Wasted Costs: Abuse of Process)[35]

20.24   An order was made against counsel (75%) and solicitor (25%) because they were pursuing a hopeless appeal in a publicly funded case without reporting to the Legal Services Commission.

Harrison v Harrison[36]

20.25   The court refused to make an order for wasted costs in an application to set aside an order for ancillary relief. The jurisdiction to make the order was not a punitive or regulatory one but a compensatory one.[37] Furthermore, as the House of Lords had said in *Medcalf v Mardell*,[38] 'it is [a remedy of] last resort. The party seeking relief had to show that the conduct complained of had caused them loss.' This the applicant had failed to do. Moreover, even if the conduct was improper (in relation to which the court made no finding), the court had a discretion; lack of proportionality of the remedy might disentitle the applicant to relief. In the instant case even if a five figure claim could be justified, the applicant's costs in seeking the remedy were in excess of £57,000 and were disproportionate.

COSTS AGAINST NON-PARTIES

20.26   In principle a costs order can be made against someone who is not a party to the proceedings. In *Phillips v Symes*[39] Peter Smith J held that costs could be ordered against an expert witness who by his evidence caused significant expense to be incurred in flagrant disregard of his duties to the court. Orders against expert witnesses have rarely, if ever, been made.

ASSESSMENT OF COSTS

20.27   When the court orders a party to pay costs, it may either assess costs summarily or make an order for detailed assessment.[40] However, the court cannot summarily assess costs to be paid to (as opposed to by) an LSC-funded litigant.[41] A summary assessment of costs to be paid by an LSC-funded party is not by itself a determination of that person's liability to pay (for which see CPR, r 44.17 and Costs PD Sections 21–23).

---

[35]   [2001] 1 FLR 843.
[36]   [2009] EWHC 428 (QB), [2009] 1 FLR 1434.
[37]   But see *D v H (costs)* [2008] EWHC 559 (Fam), [2008] 2 FLR 824 per Sumner J at [29]: 'A wasted costs application is a punitive remedy…'.
[38]   [2002] UKHL 27, [2003] 1 AC 120 per Lord Hobhouse at [56].
[39]   [2004] EWHC 2330 (Ch), [2005] 4 All ER 519.
[40]   CPR, r 44.7.
[41]   PD 44, para 13.9.

20.28 The general rule is that there should be summary assessment at the conclusion of any hearing which has lasted for no more than 1 day unless there is good reason not to do so (eg where the paying party shows substantial grounds for disputing the amount claimed that cannot be dealt with summarily or there is insufficient time to carry out a summary assessment). There is a move towards summary assessment, even for the costs of longer hearings. Summary assessment is appropriate in family proceedings because it avoids delay and expense.[42]

20.29 If that hearing disposes of the case, the court may deal with the costs of the whole of the case. Otherwise, it will deal with only the costs of the particular hearing. When the court has ordered a party to pay costs, but does not proceed to assess them immediately, it can order the paying party to pay an amount on account.

20.30 The procedure for summary assessment is set out in CPR Part 44 and Practice Direction 44 Section 13.

20.31 A written statement of costs should be filed and served no less than 24 hours before the hearing. A failure to serve the statement does not prevent the court dealing summarily with the assessment.[43] The court can:

- deal with the assessment without a statement;

- adjourn for a few minutes to enable a statement to be prepared;

- adjourn the summary assessment to a short appointment. If it does this, it must be before the same judge[44] and the failure to serve the statement will be taken into account in deciding what order to make about the costs of the application and the further hearing;[45]

- order a detailed assessment.

Payment of costs

20.32 Unless the court orders otherwise, the costs must be paid within 14 days of the assessment.[46]

---

[42] *Q v Q (Costs: Summary Assessment)* [2002] 2 FLR 668. Strictly speaking, this was not a case where costs were assessed summarily but one where the paying party was ordered to pay a stated amount towards the receiving party's costs (estimated at £336,000).

[43] *Macdonald v Taree Holdings Ltd* (2000) *The Times*, 28 December.

[44] PD Costs, Section 13.

[45] PD Costs, para 13.6.

[46] CPR, r 44.8.

Appendix 1

STATUTORY MATERIAL

ADOPTION AND CHILDREN ACT 2002

PART 1
ADOPTION

Chapter 1
Introductory

1 Considerations applying to the exercise of powers

(1) This section applies whenever a court or adoption agency is coming to a decision relating to the adoption of a child.

(2) The paramount consideration of the court or adoption agency must be the child's welfare, throughout his life.

(3) The court or adoption agency must at all times bear in mind that, in general, any delay in coming to the decision is likely to prejudice the child's welfare.

(4) The court or adoption agency must have regard to the following matters (among others) –

    (a)   the child's ascertainable wishes and feelings regarding the decision (considered in the light of the child's age and understanding),

    (b)   the child's particular needs,

    (c)   the likely effect on the child (throughout his life) of having ceased to be a member of the original family and become an adopted person,

    (d)   the child's age, sex, background and any of the child's characteristics which the court or agency considers relevant,

    (e)   any harm (within the meaning of the Children Act 1989) which the child has suffered or is at risk of suffering,

    (f)   the relationship which the child has with relatives, and with any other person in relation to whom the court or agency considers the relationship to be relevant, including –

        (i)   the likelihood of any such relationship continuing and the value to the child of its doing so,

        (ii)   the ability and willingness of any of the child's relatives, or of any such person, to provide the child with a secure environment in which the child can develop, and otherwise to meet the child's needs,

        (iii)   the wishes and feelings of any of the child's relatives, or of any such person, regarding the child.

(5) In placing the child for adoption, the adoption agency must give due consideration to the child's religious persuasion, racial origin and cultural and linguistic background.

(6) The court or adoption agency must always consider the whole range of powers available to it in the child's case (whether under this Act or the Children Act 1989); and the court must not make any order under this Act unless it considers that making the order would be better for the child than not doing so.

(7) In this section, 'coming to a decision relating to the adoption of a child', in relation to a court, includes –

    (a)   coming to a decision in any proceedings where the orders that might be made by the court include an adoption order (or the revocation of such an order), a placement order (or the revocation of such an order) or an order under section 26 (or the revocation or variation of such an order),

    (b)   coming to a decision about granting leave in respect of any action (other than the initiation of proceedings in any court) which may be taken by an adoption agency or individual under this Act,

but does not include coming to a decision about granting leave in any other circumstances.

(8) For the purposes of this section –

    (a)   references to relationships are not confined to legal relationships,

    (b)   references to a relative, in relation to a child, include the child's mother and father.

****

Chapter 3
Placement for Adoption and Adoption Orders

Placement of children by adoption agency for adoption

18 Placement for adoption by agencies

(1) An adoption agency may –

    (a)   place a child for adoption with prospective adopters, or

    (b)   where it has placed a child with any persons (whether under this Part or not), leave the child with them as prospective adopters,

but, except in the case of a child who is less than six weeks old, may only do so under section 19 or a placement order.

(2) An adoption agency may only place a child for adoption with prospective adopters if the agency is satisfied that the child ought to be placed for adoption.

(3) A child who is placed or authorised to be placed for adoption with prospective adopters by a local authority is looked after by the authority.

(4) If an application for an adoption order has been made by any persons in respect of a child and has not been disposed of –

    (a)   an adoption agency which placed the child with those persons may leave the child with them until the application is disposed of, but

    (b)   apart from that, the child may not be placed for adoption with any prospective adopters.

'Adoption order' includes a Scottish or Northern Irish adoption order.

(5) References in this Act (apart from this section) to an adoption agency placing a child for adoption –

    (a)   are to its placing a child for adoption with prospective adopters, and

    (b)   include, where it has placed a child with any persons (whether under this Act or not), leaving the child with them as prospective adopters;

and references in this Act (apart from this section) to a child who is placed for adoption by an adoption agency are to be interpreted accordingly.

(6) References in this Chapter to an adoption agency being, or not being, authorised to place a child for adoption are to the agency being or (as the case may be) not being authorised to do so under section 19 or a placement order.

(7) This section is subject to sections 30 to 35 (removal of children placed by adoption agencies).

19 Placing children with parental consent

(1) Where an adoption agency is satisfied that each parent or guardian of a child has consented to the child –

(a) being placed for adoption with prospective adopters identified in the consent, or

(b) being placed for adoption with any prospective adopters who may be chosen by the agency,

and has not withdrawn the consent, the agency is authorised to place the child for adoption accordingly.

(2) Consent to a child being placed for adoption with prospective adopters identified in the consent may be combined with consent to the child subsequently being placed for adoption with any prospective adopters who may be chosen by the agency in circumstances where the child is removed from or returned by the identified prospective adopters.

(3) Subsection (1) does not apply where –

(a) an application has been made on which a care order might be made and the application has not been disposed of, or

(b) a care order or placement order has been made after the consent was given.

(4) References in this Act to a child placed for adoption under this section include a child who was placed under this section with prospective adopters and continues to be placed with them, whether or not consent to the placement has been withdrawn.

(5) This section is subject to section 52 (parental etc consent).

20 Advance consent to adoption

(1) A parent or guardian of a child who consents to the child being placed for adoption by an adoption agency under section 19 may, at the same or any subsequent time, consent to the making of a future adoption order.

(2) Consent under this section –

(a) where the parent or guardian has consented to the child being placed for adoption with prospective adopters identified in the consent, may be consent to adoption by them, or

(b) may be consent to adoption by any prospective adopters who may be chosen by the agency.

(3) A person may withdraw any consent given under this section.

(4) A person who gives consent under this section may, at the same or any subsequent time, by notice given to the adoption agency –

(a) state that he does not wish to be informed of any application for an adoption order, or

(b) withdraw such a statement.

(5) A notice under subsection (4) has effect from the time when it is received by the adoption agency but has no effect if the person concerned has withdrawn his consent.

(6) This section is subject to section 52 (parental etc consent).

21 Placement orders

(1) A placement order is an order made by the court authorising a local authority to place a child for adoption with any prospective adopters who may be chosen by the authority.

(2) The court may not make a placement order in respect of a child unless –

(a) the child is subject to a care order,

(b) the court is satisfied that the conditions in section 31(2) of the 1989 Act (conditions for making a care order) are met, or

(c)   the child has no parent or guardian.

(3) The court may only make a placement order if, in the case of each parent or guardian of the child, the court is satisfied –

(a)   that the parent or guardian has consented to the child being placed for adoption with any prospective adopters who may be chosen by the local authority and has not withdrawn the consent, or

(b)   that the parent's or guardian's consent should be dispensed with.

This subsection is subject to section 52 (parental etc consent).

(4) A placement order continues in force until –

(a)   it is revoked under section 24,

(b)   an adoption order is made in respect of the child, or

(c)   the child marries, forms a civil partnership or attains the age of 18 years.

'Adoption order' includes a Scottish or Northern Irish adoption order.

Amendments—Civil Partnership Act 2004, s 79(1), (2).

22 Applications for placement orders

(1) A local authority must apply to the court for a placement order in respect of a child if –

(a)   the child is placed for adoption by them or is being provided with accommodation by them,

(b)   no adoption agency is authorised to place the child for adoption,

(c)   the child has no parent or guardian or the authority consider that the conditions in section 31(2) of the 1989 Act are met, and

(d)   the authority are satisfied that the child ought to be placed for adoption.

(2) If –

(a)   an application has been made (and has not been disposed of) on which a care order might be made in respect of a child, or

(b)   a child is subject to a care order and the appropriate local authority are not authorised to place the child for adoption,

the appropriate local authority must apply to the court for a placement order if they are satisfied that the child ought to be placed for adoption.

(3) If –

(a)   a child is subject to a care order, and

(b)   the appropriate local authority are authorised to place the child for adoption under section 19,

the authority may apply to the court for a placement order.

(4) If a local authority –

(a)   are under a duty to apply to the court for a placement order in respect of a child, or

(b)   have applied for a placement order in respect of a child and the application has not been disposed of,

the child is looked after by the authority.

(5) Subsections (1) to (3) do not apply in respect of a child –

(a)   if any persons have given notice of intention to adopt, unless the period of four months beginning with the giving of the notice has expired without them applying for an adoption order or their application for such an order has been withdrawn or refused, or

(b)   if an application for an adoption order has been made and has not been disposed of.

'Adoption order' includes a Scottish or Northern Irish adoption order.

(6) Where –

    (a)   an application for a placement order in respect of a child has been made and has not been disposed of, and

    (b)   no interim care order is in force,

the court may give any directions it considers appropriate for the medical or psychiatric examination or other assessment of the child; but a child who is of sufficient understanding to make an informed decision may refuse to submit to the examination or other assessment.

(7) The appropriate local authority –

    (a)   in relation to a care order, is the local authority in whose care the child is placed by the order, and

    (b)   in relation to an application on which a care order might be made, is the local authority which makes the application.

23 Varying placement orders

(1) The court may vary a placement order so as to substitute another local authority for the local authority authorised by the order to place the child for adoption.

(2) The variation may only be made on the joint application of both authorities.

24 Revoking placement orders

(1) The court may revoke a placement order on the application of any person.

(2) But an application may not be made by a person other than the child or the local authority authorised by the order to place the child for adoption unless –

    (a)   the court has given leave to apply, and

    (b)   the child is not placed for adoption by the authority.

(3) The court cannot give leave under subsection (2)(a) unless satisfied that there has been a change in circumstances since the order was made.

(4) If the court determines, on an application for an adoption order, not to make the order, it may revoke any placement order in respect of the child.

(5) Where –

    (a)   an application for the revocation of a placement order has been made and has not been disposed of, and

    (b)   the child is not placed for adoption by the authority,

the child may not without the court's leave be placed for adoption under the order.

25 Parental responsibility

(1) This section applies while –

    (a)   a child is placed for adoption under section 19 or an adoption agency is authorised to place a child for adoption under that section, or

    (b)   a placement order is in force in respect of a child.

(2) Parental responsibility for the child is given to the agency concerned.

(3) While the child is placed with prospective adopters, parental responsibility is given to them.

(4) The agency may determine that the parental responsibility of any parent or guardian, or of prospective adopters, is to be restricted to the extent specified in the determination.

26 Contact

(1) On an adoption agency being authorised to place a child for adoption, or placing a child for adoption who is less than six weeks old, any provision for contact under the 1989 Act ceases to have effect and any contact activity direction relating to contact with the child is discharged.

(2) While an adoption agency is so authorised or a child is placed for adoption –

    (a)   no application may be made for any provision for contact under that Act, but

    (b)   the court may make an order under this section requiring the person with whom the child lives, or is to live, to allow the child to visit or stay with the person named in the order, or for the person named in the order and the child otherwise to have contact with each other.

(3) An application for an order under this section may be made by –

    (a)   the child or the agency,

    (b)   any parent, guardian or relative,

    (c)   any person in whose favour there was provision for contact under the 1989 Act which ceased to have effect by virtue of subsection (1),

    (d)   if a residence order was in force immediately before the adoption agency was authorised to place the child for adoption or (as the case may be) placed the child for adoption at a time when he was less than six weeks old, the person in whose favour the order was made,

    (e)   if a person had care of the child immediately before that time by virtue of an order made in the exercise of the High Court's inherent jurisdiction with respect to children, that person,

    (f)   any person who has obtained the court's leave to make the application.

(4) When making a placement order, the court may on its own initiative make an order under this section.

(5) This section does not prevent an application for a contact order under section 8 of the 1989 Act being made where the application is to be heard together with an application for an adoption order in respect of the child.

(6) In this section, 'contact activity direction' has the meaning given by section 11A of the 1989 Act and 'provision for contact under the 1989 Act' means a contact order under section 8 of that Act or an order under section 34 of that Act (parental contact with children in care).

Amendments—Children and Adoption Act 2006, s 15(1), Sch 2, paras 13, 14.

27 Contact: supplementary

(1) An order under section 26 –

    (a)   has effect while the adoption agency is authorised to place the child for adoption or the child is placed for adoption, but

    (b)   may be varied or revoked by the court on an application by the child, the agency or a person named in the order.

(2) The agency may refuse to allow the contact that would otherwise be required by virtue of an order under that section if –

    (a)   it is satisfied that it is necessary to do so in order to safeguard or promote the child's welfare, and

    (b)   the refusal is decided upon as a matter of urgency and does not last for more than seven days.

(3) Regulations may make provision as to –

    (a)   the steps to be taken by an agency which has exercised its power under subsection (2),

(b)   the circumstances in which, and conditions subject to which, the terms of any order under section 26 may be departed from by agreement between the agency and any person for whose contact with the child the order provides,

(c)   notification by an agency of any variation or suspension of arrangements made (otherwise than under an order under that section) with a view to allowing any person contact with the child.

(4) Before making a placement order the court must –

(a)   consider the arrangements which the adoption agency has made, or proposes to make, for allowing any person contact with the child, and

(b)   invite the parties to the proceedings to comment on those arrangements.

(5) An order under section 26 may provide for contact on any conditions the court considers appropriate.

28 Further consequences of placement

(1) Where a child is placed for adoption under section 19 or an adoption agency is authorised to place a child for adoption under that section –

(a)   a parent or guardian of the child may not apply for a residence order unless an application for an adoption order has been made and the parent or guardian has obtained the court's leave under subsection (3) or (5) of section 47,

(b)   if an application has been made for an adoption order, a guardian of the child may not apply for a special guardianship order unless he has obtained the court's leave under subsection (3) or (5) of that section.

(2) Where –

(a)   a child is placed for adoption under section 19 or an adoption agency is authorised to place a child for adoption under that section, or

(b)   a placement order is in force in respect of a child,

then (whether or not the child is in England and Wales) a person may not do either of the following things, unless the court gives leave or each parent or guardian of the child gives written consent.

(3) Those things are –

(a)   causing the child to be known by a new surname, or

(b)   removing the child from the United Kingdom.

(4) Subsection (3) does not prevent the removal of a child from the United Kingdom for a period of less than one month by a person who provides the child's home.

29 Further consequences of placement orders

(1) Where a placement order is made in respect of a child and either –

(a)   the child is subject to a care order, or

(b)   the court at the same time makes a care order in respect of the child,

the care order does not have effect at any time when the placement order is in force.

(2) On the making of a placement order in respect of a child, any order mentioned in section 8(1) of the 1989 Act, and any supervision order in respect of the child, ceases to have effect.

(3) Where a placement order is in force –

(a)   no prohibited steps order, residence order or specific issue order, and

(b)   no supervision order or child assessment order,

may be made in respect of the child.

(4) Subsection (3)(a) does not apply in respect of a residence order if –

(a)   an application for an adoption order has been made in respect of the child, and

(b)   the residence order is applied for by a parent or guardian who has obtained the court's leave under subsection (3) or (5) of section 47 or by any other person who has obtained the court's leave under this subsection.

(5) Where a placement order is in force, no special guardianship order may be made in respect of the child unless –

(a)   an application has been made for an adoption order, and

(b)   the person applying for the special guardianship order has obtained the court's leave under this subsection or, if he is a guardian of the child, has obtained the court's leave under section 47(5).

(6) Section 14A(7) of the 1989 Act applies in respect of an application for a special guardianship order for which leave has been given as mentioned in subsection (5)(b) with the omission of the words 'the beginning of the period of three months ending with'.

(7) Where a placement order is in force –

(a)   section 14C(1)(b) of the 1989 Act (special guardianship: parental responsibility) has effect subject to any determination under section 25(4) of this Act,

(b)   section 14C(3) and (4) of the 1989 Act (special guardianship: removal of child from UK etc) does not apply.

****

Preliminaries to adoption

42 Child to live with adopters before application

(1) An application for an adoption order may not be made unless –

(a)   if subsection (2) applies, the condition in that subsection is met,

(b)   if that subsection does not apply, the condition in whichever is applicable of subsections (3) to (5) applies.

(2) If –

(a)   the child was placed for adoption with the applicant or applicants by an adoption agency or in pursuance of an order of the High Court, or

(b)   the applicant is a parent of the child,

the condition is that the child must have had his home with the applicant or, in the case of an application by a couple, with one or both of them at all times during the period of ten weeks preceding the application.

(3) If the applicant or one of the applicants is the partner of a parent of the child, the condition is that the child must have had his home with the applicant or, as the case may be, applicants at all times during the period of six months preceding the application.

(4) If the applicants are local authority foster parents, the condition is that the child must have had his home with the applicants at all times during the period of one year preceding the application.

(5) In any other case, the condition is that the child must have had his home with the applicant or, in the case of an application by a couple, with one or both of them for not less than three years (whether continuous or not) during the period of five years preceding the application.

(6) But subsections (4) and (5) do not prevent an application being made if the court gives leave to make it.

(7) An adoption order may not be made unless the court is satisfied that sufficient opportunities to see the child with the applicant or, in the case of an application by a couple, both of them together in the home environment have been given –

(a)   where the child was placed for adoption with the applicant or applicants by an adoption agency, to that agency,

(b)   in any other case, to the local authority within whose area the home is.

(8) In this section and sections 43 and 44(1) –

(a)   references to an adoption agency include a Scottish or Northern Irish adoption agency,

(b)   references to a child placed for adoption by an adoption agency are to be read accordingly.

43 Reports where child placed by agency

Where an application for an adoption order relates to a child placed for adoption by an adoption agency, the agency must –

(a)   submit to the court a report on the suitability of the applicants and on any other matters relevant to the operation of section 1, and

(b)   assist the court in any manner the court directs.

44 Notice of intention to adopt

(1) This section applies where persons (referred to in this section as 'proposed adopters') wish to adopt a child who is not placed for adoption with them by an adoption agency.

(2) An adoption order may not be made in respect of the child unless the proposed adopters have given notice to the appropriate local authority of their intention to apply for the adoption order (referred to in this Act as a 'notice of intention to adopt').

(3) The notice must be given not more than two years, or less than three months, before the date on which the application for the adoption order is made.

(4) Where –

(a)   if a person were seeking to apply for an adoption order, subsection (4) or (5) of section 42 would apply, but

(b)   the condition in the subsection in question is not met,

the person may not give notice of intention to adopt unless he has the court's leave to apply for an adoption order.

(5) On receipt of a notice of intention to adopt, the local authority must arrange for the investigation of the matter and submit to the court a report of the investigation.

(6) In particular, the investigation must, so far as practicable, include the suitability of the proposed adopters and any other matters relevant to the operation of section 1 in relation to the application.

(7) If a local authority receive a notice of intention to adopt in respect of a child whom they know was (immediately before the notice was given) looked after by another local authority, they must, not more than seven days after the receipt of the notice, inform the other local authority in writing that they have received the notice.

(8) Where –

(a)   a local authority have placed a child with any persons otherwise than as prospective adopters, and

(b)   the persons give notice of intention to adopt,

the authority are not to be treated as leaving the child with them as prospective adopters for the purposes of section 18(1)(b).

(9) In this section, references to the appropriate local authority, in relation to any proposed adopters, are –

(a)   in prescribed cases, references to the prescribed local authority,

(b)   in any other case, references to the local authority for the area in which, at the time of giving the notice of intention to adopt, they have their home,

and 'prescribed' means prescribed by regulations.

****

The making of adoption orders

46 Adoption orders

(1) An adoption order is an order made by the court on an application under section 50 or 51 giving parental responsibility for a child to the adopters or adopter.

(2) The making of an adoption order operates to extinguish –

(a)   the parental responsibility which any person other than the adopters or adopter has for the adopted child immediately before the making of the order,

(b)   any order under the 1989 Act or the Children (Northern Ireland) Order 1995 (SI 1995/755 (NI 2)),

(c)   any order under the Children (Scotland) Act 1995 other than an excepted order, and

(d)   any duty arising by virtue of an agreement or an order of a court to make payments, so far as the payments are in respect of the adopted child's maintenance or upbringing for any period after the making of the adoption order.

'Excepted order' means an order under section 9, 11(1)(d) or 13 of the Children (Scotland) Act 1995 or an exclusion order within the meaning of section 76(1) of that Act.

(3) An adoption order –

(a)   does not affect parental responsibility so far as it relates to any period before the making of the order, and

(b)   in the case of an order made on an application under section 51(2) by the partner of a parent of the adopted child, does not affect the parental responsibility of that parent or any duties of that parent within subsection (2)(d).

(4) Subsection (2)(d) does not apply to a duty arising by virtue of an agreement –

(a)   which constitutes a trust, or

(b)   which expressly provides that the duty is not to be extinguished by the making of an adoption order.

(5) An adoption order may be made even if the child to be adopted is already an adopted child.

(6) Before making an adoption order, the court must consider whether there should be arrangements for allowing any person contact with the child; and for that purpose the court must consider any existing or proposed arrangements and obtain any views of the parties to the proceedings.

47 Conditions for making adoption orders

(1) An adoption order may not be made if the child has a parent or guardian unless one of the following three conditions is met; but this section is subject to section 52 (parental etc consent).

(2) The first condition is that, in the case of each parent or guardian of the child, the court is satisfied –

(a)   that the parent or guardian consents to the making of the adoption order,

(b)   that the parent or guardian has consented under section 20 (and has not withdrawn the consent) and does not oppose the making of the adoption order, or

(c)   that the parent's or guardian's consent should be dispensed with.

(3) A parent or guardian may not oppose the making of an adoption order under subsection (2)(b) without the court's leave.

(4) The second condition is that –

    (a)   the child has been placed for adoption by an adoption agency with the prospective adopters in whose favour the order is proposed to be made,

    (b)   either –

        (i)   the child was placed for adoption with the consent of each parent or guardian and the consent of the mother was given when the child was at least six weeks old, or

        (ii)   the child was placed for adoption under a placement order, and

    (c)   no parent or guardian opposes the making of the adoption order.

(5) A parent or guardian may not oppose the making of an adoption order under the second condition without the court's leave.

(6) The third condition is that the child is free for adoption by virtue of an order made –

    (a)   in Scotland, under section 18 of the Adoption (Scotland) Act 1978, or

    (b)   in Northern Ireland, under Article 17(1) or 18(1) of the Adoption (Northern Ireland) Order 1987 (SI 1987/2203 (NI 22)).

(7) The court cannot give leave under subsection (3) or (5) unless satisfied that there has been a change in circumstances since the consent of the parent or guardian was given or, as the case may be, the placement order was made.

(8) An adoption order may not be made in relation to a person who is or has been married.

(8A) An adoption order may not be made in relation to a person who is or has been a civil partner.

(9) An adoption order may not be made in relation to a person who has attained the age of 19 years.

Amendments—Civil Partnership Act 2004, s 79(1), (3).

48 Restrictions on making adoption orders

(1) The court may not hear an application for an adoption order in relation to a child, where a previous application to which subsection (2) applies made in relation to the child by the same persons was refused by any court, unless it appears to the court that, because of a change in circumstances or for any other reason, it is proper to hear the application.

(2) This subsection applies to any application –

    (a)   for an adoption order or a Scottish or Northern Irish adoption order, or

    (b)   for an order for adoption made in the Isle of Man or any of the Channel Islands.

49 Applications for adoption

(1) An application for an adoption order may be made by –

    (a)   a couple, or

    (b)   one person,

but only if it is made under section 50 or 51 and one of the following conditions is met.

(2) The first condition is that at least one of the couple (in the case of an application under section 50) or the applicant (in the case of an application under section 51) is domiciled in a part of the British Islands.

(3) The second condition is that both of the couple (in the case of an application under section 50) or the applicant (in the case of an application under section 51) have been habitually resident in a part of the British Islands for a period of not less than one year ending with the date of the application.

(4) An application for an adoption order may only be made if the person to be adopted has not attained the age of 18 years on the date of the application.

(5) References in this Act to a child, in connection with any proceedings (whether or not concluded) for adoption, (such as 'child to be adopted' or 'adopted child') include a person who has attained the age of 18 years before the proceedings are concluded.

50 Adoption by couple

(1) An adoption order may be made on the application of a couple where both of them have attained the age of 21 years.

(2) An adoption order may be made on the application of a couple where –

(a)   one of the couple is the mother or the father of the person to be adopted and has attained the age of 18 years, and

(b)   the other has attained the age of 21 years.

51 Adoption by one person

(1) An adoption order may be made on the application of one person who has attained the age of 21 years and is not married or a civil partner.

(2) An adoption order may be made on the application of one person who has attained the age of 21 years if the court is satisfied that the person is the partner of a parent of the person to be adopted.

(3) An adoption order may be made on the application of one person who has attained the age of 21 years and is married if the court is satisfied that –

(a)   the person's spouse cannot be found,

(b)   the spouses have separated and are living apart, and the separation is likely to be permanent, or

(c)   the person's spouse is by reason of ill-health, whether physical or mental, incapable of making an application for an adoption order.

(3A) An adoption order may be made on the application of one person who has attained the age of 21 years and is a civil partner if the court is satisfied that –

(a)   the person's civil partner cannot be found,

(b)   the civil partners have separated and are living apart, and the separation is likely to be permanent, or

(c)   the person's civil partner is by reason of ill-health, whether physical or mental, incapable of making an application for an adoption order.

(4) An adoption order may not be made on an application under this section by the mother or the father of the person to be adopted unless the court is satisfied that –

(a)   the other natural parent is dead or cannot be found,

(b)   by virtue of section 28 of the Human Fertilisation and Embryology Act 1990 (disregarding subsections (5A) to (5I) of that section), there is no other parent, or

(c)   there is some other reason justifying the child's being adopted by the applicant alone,

and, where the court makes an adoption order on such an application, the court must record that it is satisfied as to the fact mentioned in paragraph (a) or (b) or, in the case of paragraph (c), record the reason.

Amendments—Human Fertilisation and Embryology (Deceased Fathers) Act 2003, s 2(1), Schedule, para 18; Civil Partnership Act 2004, s 79(1)–(5).

Placement and adoption: general

52 Parental etc consent

(1) The court cannot dispense with the consent of any parent or guardian of a child to the child being placed for adoption or to the making of an adoption order in respect of the child unless the court is satisfied that –

    (a)   the parent or guardian cannot be found or lacks capacity (within the meaning of the Mental Capacity Act 2005) to give consent, or

    (b)   the welfare of the child requires the consent to be dispensed with.

(2) The following provisions apply to references in this Chapter to any parent or guardian of a child giving or withdrawing –

    (a)   consent to the placement of a child for adoption, or

    (b)   consent to the making of an adoption order (including a future adoption order).

(3) Any consent given by the mother to the making of an adoption order is ineffective if it is given less than six weeks after the child's birth.

(4) The withdrawal of any consent to the placement of a child for adoption, or of any consent given under section 20, is ineffective if it is given after an application for an adoption order is made.

(5) 'Consent' means consent given unconditionally and with full understanding of what is involved; but a person may consent to adoption without knowing the identity of the persons in whose favour the order will be made.

(6) 'Parent' (except in subsections (9) and (10) below) means a parent having parental responsibility.

(7) Consent under section 19 or 20 must be given in the form prescribed by rules, and the rules may prescribe forms in which a person giving consent under any other provision of this Part may do so (if he wishes).

(8) Consent given under section 19 or 20 must be withdrawn –

    (a)   in the form prescribed by rules, or

    (b)   by notice given to the agency.

(9) Subsection (10) applies if –

    (a)   an agency has placed a child for adoption under section 19 in pursuance of consent given by a parent of the child, and

    (b)   at a later time, the other parent of the child acquires parental responsibility for the child.

(10) The other parent is to be treated as having at that time given consent in accordance with this section in the same terms as those in which the first parent gave consent.

Amendments—Mental Capacity Act 2005, s 67(1), Sch 6, para 45.

****

67 Status conferred by adoption

(1) An adopted person is to be treated in law as if born as the child of the adopters or adopter.

(2) An adopted person is the legitimate child of the adopters or adopter and, if adopted by –

    (a)   a couple, or

    (b)   one of a couple under section 51(2),

is to be treated as the child of the relationship of the couple in question.

(3) An adopted person –

(a)   if adopted by one of a couple under section 51(2), is to be treated in law as not being the child of any person other than the adopter and the other one of the couple, and

(b)   in any other case, is to be treated in law, subject to subsection (4), as not being the child of any person other than the adopters or adopter;

but this subsection does not affect any reference in this Act to a person's natural parent or to any other natural relationship.

(4) In the case of a person adopted by one of the person's natural parents as sole adoptive parent, subsection (3)(b) has no effect as respects entitlement to property depending on relationship to that parent, or as respects anything else depending on that relationship.

(5) This section has effect from the date of the adoption.

(6) Subject to the provisions of this Chapter and Schedule 4, this section –

(a)   applies for the interpretation of enactments or instruments passed or made before as well as after the adoption, and so applies subject to any contrary indication, and

(b)   has effect as respects things done, or events occurring, on or after the adoption.

68 Adoptive relatives

(1) A relationship existing by virtue of section 67 may be referred to as an adoptive relationship, and –

(a)   an adopter may be referred to as an adoptive parent or (as the case may be) as an adoptive father or adoptive mother,

(b)   any other relative of any degree under an adoptive relationship may be referred to as an adoptive relative of that degree.

(2) Subsection (1) does not affect the interpretation of any reference, not qualified by the word 'adoptive', to a relationship.

(3) A reference (however expressed) to the adoptive mother and father of a child adopted by –

(a)   a couple of the same sex, or

(b)   a partner of the child's parent, where the couple are of the same sex,

is to be read as a reference to the child's adoptive parents.

****

84 Giving parental responsibility prior to adoption abroad

(1) The High Court may, on an application by persons who the court is satisfied intend to adopt a child under the law of a country or territory outside the British Islands, make an order giving parental responsibility for the child to them.

(2) An order under this section may not give parental responsibility to persons who the court is satisfied meet those requirements as to domicile, or habitual residence, in England and Wales which have to be met if an adoption order is to be made in favour of those persons.

(3) An order under this section may not be made unless any requirements prescribed by regulations are satisfied.

(4) An application for an order under this section may not be made unless at all times during the preceding ten weeks the child's home was with the applicant or, in the case of an application by two people, both of them.

(5) Section 46(2) to (4) has effect in relation to an order under this section as it has effect in relation to adoption orders.

(6) Regulations may provide for any provision of this Act which refers to adoption orders to apply, with or without modifications, to orders under this section.

(7) In this section, 'regulations' means regulations made by the Secretary of State, after consultation with the Assembly.

****

Overseas adoptions

87 Overseas adoptions

(1) In this Act, 'overseas adoption' –

(a) means an adoption of a description specified in an order made by the Secretary of State, being a description of adoptions effected under the law of any country or territory outside the British Islands, but

(b) does not include a Convention adoption.

(2) Regulations may prescribe the requirements that ought to be met by an adoption of any description effected after the commencement of the regulations for it to be an overseas adoption for the purposes of this Act.

(3) At any time when such regulations have effect, the Secretary of State must exercise his powers under this section so as to secure that subsequently effected adoptions of any description are not overseas adoptions for the purposes of this Act if he considers that they are not likely within a reasonable time to meet the prescribed requirements.

(4) In this section references to this Act include the Adoption Act 1976.

(5) An order under this section may contain provision as to the manner in which evidence of any overseas adoption may be given.

(6) In this section –

'adoption' means an adoption of a child or of a person who was a child at the time the adoption was applied for,

'regulations' means regulations made by the Secretary of State after consultation with the Assembly.

Miscellaneous

88 Modification of section 67 for Hague Convention adoptions

(1) If the High Court is satisfied, on an application under this section, that each of the following conditions is met in the case of a Convention adoption, it may direct that section 67(3) does not apply, or does not apply to any extent specified in the direction.

(2) The conditions are –

(a) that under the law of the country in which the adoption was effected, the adoption is not a full adoption,

(b) that the consents referred to in Article 4(c) and (d) of the Convention have not been given for a full adoption or that the United Kingdom is not the receiving State (within the meaning of Article 2 of the Convention),

(c) that it would be more favourable to the adopted child for a direction to be given under subsection (1).

(3) A full adoption is an adoption by virtue of which the child is to be treated in law as not being the child of any person other than the adopters or adopter.

(4) In relation to a direction under this section and an application for it, sections 59 and 60 of the Family Law Act 1986 (declarations under Part 3 of that Act as to marital status) apply as they apply in relation to a direction under that Part and an application for such a direction.

89 Annulment etc of overseas or Hague Convention adoptions

(1) The High Court may, on an application under this subsection, by order annul a Convention adoption or Convention adoption order on the ground that the adoption is contrary to public policy.

(2) The High Court may, on an application under this subsection –

    (a)   by order provide for an overseas adoption or a determination under section 91 to cease to be valid on the ground that the adoption or determination is contrary to public policy or that the authority which purported to authorise the adoption or make the determination was not competent to entertain the case, or

    (b)   decide the extent, if any, to which a determination under section 91 has been affected by a subsequent determination under that section.

(3) The High Court may, in any proceedings in that court, decide that an overseas adoption or a determination under section 91 is to be treated, for the purposes of those proceedings, as invalid on either of the grounds mentioned in subsection (2)(a).

(4) Subject to the preceding provisions, the validity of a Convention adoption, Convention adoption order or overseas adoption or a determination under section 91 cannot be called in question in proceedings in any court in England and Wales.

****

CHILDREN ACT 1989

PART I
INTRODUCTORY

1 Welfare of the child

(1) When a court determines any question with respect to –

    (a)   the upbringing of a child; or
    (b)   the administration of a child's property or the application of any income arising from it,

the child's welfare shall be the court's paramount consideration.

(2) In any proceedings in which any question with respect to the upbringing of a child arises, the court shall have regard to the general principle that any delay in determining the question is likely to prejudice the welfare of the child.

(3) In the circumstances mentioned in subsection (4), a court shall have regard in particular to –

    (a)   the ascertainable wishes and feelings of the child concerned (considered in the light of his age and understanding);
    (b)   his physical, emotional and educational needs;
    (c)   the likely effect on him of any change in his circumstances;
    (d)   his age, sex, background and any characteristics of his which the court considers relevant;
    (e)   any harm which he has suffered or is at risk of suffering;
    (f)   how capable each of his parents, and any other person in relation to whom the court considers the question to be relevant, is of meeting his needs;
    (g)   the range of powers available to the court under this Act in the proceedings in question.

(4) The circumstances are that –

    (a)   the court is considering whether to make, vary or discharge a special guardianship order or a section 8 order, and the making, variation or discharge of the order is opposed by any party to the proceedings; or
    (b)   the court is considering whether to make, vary or discharge an order under Part IV.

(5) Where a court is considering whether or not to make one or more orders under this Act with respect to a child, it shall not make the order or any of the orders unless it considers that doing so would be better for the child than making no order at all.

Amendments—Adoption and Children Act 2002, s 115(2), (3).

2 Parental responsibility for children

(1) Where a child's father and mother were married to each other at the time of his birth, they shall each have parental responsibility for the child.

(2) Where a child's father and mother were not married to each other at the time of his birth –

    (a)   the mother shall have parental responsibility for the child;

    (b)   the father shall have parental responsibility for the child if he has acquired it (and has not ceased to have it) in accordance with the provisions of this Act.

(3) References in this Act to a child whose father and mother were, or (as the case may be) were not, married to each other at the time of his birth must be read with section 1 of the Family Law Reform Act 1987 (which extends their meaning).

(4) The rule of law that a father is the natural guardian of his legitimate child is abolished.

(5) More than one person may have parental responsibility for the same child at the same time.

(6) A person who has parental responsibility for a child at any time shall not cease to have that responsibility solely because some other person subsequently acquires parental responsibility for the child.

(7) Where more than one person has parental responsibility for a child, each of them may act alone and without the other (or others) in meeting that responsibility; but nothing in this Part shall be taken to affect the operation of any enactment which requires the consent of more than one person in a matter affecting the child.

(8) The fact that a person has parental responsibility for a child shall not entitle him to act in any way which would be incompatible with any order made with respect to the child under this Act.

(9) A person who has parental responsibility for a child may not surrender or transfer any part of that responsibility to another but may arrange for some or all of it to be met by one or more persons acting on his behalf.

(10) The person with whom any such arrangement is made may himself be a person who already has parental responsibility for the child concerned.

(11) The making of any such arrangement shall not affect any liability of the person making it which may arise from any failure to meet any part of his parental responsibility for the child concerned.

Amendments—Adoption and Children Act 2002, s 111(5).

3 Meaning of 'parental responsibility'

(1) In this Act 'parental responsibility' means all the rights, duties, powers, responsibilities and authority which by law a parent of a child has in relation to the child and his property.

(2) It also includes the rights, powers and duties which a guardian of the child's estate (appointed, before the commencement of section 5, to act generally) would have had in relation to the child and his property.

(3) The rights referred to in subsection (2) include, in particular, the right of the guardian to receive or recover in his own name, for the benefit of the child, property of whatever description and wherever situated which the child is entitled to receive or recover.

(4) The fact that a person has, or does not have, parental responsibility for a child shall not affect –

(a) any obligation which he may have in relation to the child (such as a statutory duty to maintain the child); or

(b) any rights which, in the event of the child's death, he (or any other person) may have in relation to the child's property.

(5) A person who –

(a) does not have parental responsibility for a particular child; but

(b) has care of the child,

may (subject to the provisions of this Act) do what is reasonable in all the circumstances of the case for the purpose of safeguarding or promoting the child's welfare.

4 Acquisition of parental responsibility by father

(1) Where a child's father and mother were not married to each other at the time of his birth, the father shall acquire parental responsibility for the child if –

(a) he becomes registered as the child's father under any of the enactments specified in subsection (1A);

(b) he and the child's mother make an agreement (a 'parental responsibility agreement') providing for him to have parental responsibility for the child; or

(c) the court, on his application, orders that he shall have parental responsibility for the child.

(1A) The enactments referred to in subsection (1)(a) are –

(a) paragraphs (a), (b) and (c) of section 10(1) and of section 10A(1) of the Births and Deaths Registration Act 1953;

(b) paragraphs (a), (b)(i) and (c) of section 18(1), and sections 18(2)(b) and 20(1)(a) of the Registration of Births, Deaths and Marriages (Scotland) Act 1965; and

(c) sub-paragraphs (a), (b) and (c) of Article 14(3) of the Births and Deaths Registration (Northern Ireland) Order 1976.

(1B) The Secretary of State may by order amend subsection (1A) so as to add further enactments to the list in that subsection.

(2) No parental responsibility agreement shall have effect for the purposes of this Act unless –

(a) it is made in the form prescribed by regulations made by the Lord Chancellor; and

(b) where regulations are made by the Lord Chancellor prescribing the manner in which such agreements must be recorded, it is recorded in the prescribed manner.

(2A) A person who has acquired parental responsibility under subsection (1) shall cease to have that responsibility only if the court so orders.

(3) The court may make an order under subsection (2A) on the application –

(a) of any person who has parental responsibility for the child; or

(b) with the leave of the court, of the child himself,

subject, in the case of parental responsibility acquired under subsection (1)(c), to section 12(4).

(4) The court may only grant leave under subsection (3)(b) if it is satisfied that the child has sufficient understanding to make the proposed application.

Amendments—Adoption and Children Act 2002, s 111(1), (2), (3), (4), (7); SI 2003/3191.

4A Acquisition of parental responsibility by step-parent

(1) Where a child's parent ('parent A') who has parental responsibility for the child is married to, or a civil partner of, a person who is not the child's parent ('the step-parent') –

(a)   parent A or, if the other parent of the child also has parental responsibility for the child, both parents may by agreement with the step-parent provide for the step-parent to have parental responsibility for the child; or

(b)   the court may, on the application of the step-parent, order that the step-parent shall have parental responsibility for the child.

(2) An agreement under subsection (1)(a) is also a 'parental responsibility agreement', and section 4(2) applies in relation to such agreements as it applies in relation to parental responsibility agreements under section 4.

(3) A parental responsibility agreement under subsection (1)(a), or an order under subsection (1)(b), may only be brought to an end by an order of the court made on the application –

(a)   of any person who has parental responsibility for the child; or

(b)   with the leave of the court, of the child himself.

(4) The court may only grant leave under subsection (3)(b) if it is satisfied that the child has sufficient understanding to make the proposed application.

****

PART II
ORDERS WITH RESPECT TO CHILDREN IN FAMILY PROCEEDINGS

General

8 Residence, contact and other orders with respect to children

(1) In this Act –

'a contact order' means an order requiring the person with whom a child lives, or is to live, to allow the child to visit or stay with the person named in the order, or for that person and the child otherwise to have contact with each other;

'a prohibited steps order' means an order that no step which could be taken by a parent in meeting his parental responsibility for a child, and which is of a kind specified in the order, shall be taken by any person without the consent of the court;

'a residence order' means an order settling the arrangements to be made as to the person with whom a child is to live; and

'a specific issue order' means an order giving directions for the purpose of determining a specific question which has arisen, or which may arise, in connection with any aspect of parental responsibility for a child.

(2) In this Act 'a section 8 order' means any of the orders mentioned in subsection (1) and any order varying or discharging such an order.

(3) For the purposes of this Act 'family proceedings' means any proceedings –

(a)   under the inherent jurisdiction of the High Court in relation to children; and

(b)   under the enactments mentioned in subsection (4),

but does not include proceedings on an application for leave under section 100(3).

(4) The enactments are –

(a)   Parts I, II and IV of this Act;

(b)   the Matrimonial Causes Act 1973;

(ba)   Schedule 5 to the Civil Partnership Act 2004;

(c)   ...

(d)   the Adoption and Children Act 2002;

(e)   the Domestic Proceedings and Magistrates' Courts Act 1978;

(ea)   Schedule 6 to the Civil Partnership Act 2004;

(f)   ...

(g)   Part III of the Matrimonial and Family Proceedings Act 1984;

(h)   the Family Law Act 1996;

(i)   sections 11 and 12 of the Crime and Disorder Act 1998.

Amendments—Family Law Act 1996, s 66(1), Sch 8, Pt III, para 60; Crime and Disorder Act 1998, s 119, Sch 8, para 68; Adoption and Children Act 2002, s 139(1), Sch 3, paras 54, 55; Civil Partnership Act 2004, s 261(1), Sch 27, para 129(1), (2), (3). Prospectively amended by Family Law Act 1996, s 66(1), Sch 8, para 41(3).

9 Restrictions on making section 8 orders

(1) No court shall make any section 8 order, other than a residence order, with respect to a child who is in the care of a local authority.

(2) No application may be made by a local authority for a residence order or contact order and no court shall make such an order in favour of a local authority.

(3) A person who is, or was at any time within the last six months, a local authority foster parent of a child may not apply for leave to apply for a section 8 order with respect to the child unless –

(a)   he has the consent of the authority;

(b)   he is relative of the child; or

(c)   the child has lived with him for at least one year preceding the application.

(4) ...

(5) No court shall exercise its powers to make a specific issue order or prohibited steps order –

(a)   with a view to achieving a result which could be achieved by making a residence or contact order; or

(b)   in any way which is denied to the High Court (by section 100(2)) in the exercise of its inherent jurisdiction with respect to children.

(6) Subject to section 12(5) no court shall make any section 8 order which is to have effect for a period which will end after the child has reached the age of sixteen unless it is satisfied that the circumstances of the case are exceptional.

(7) No court shall make any section 8 order, other than one varying or discharging such an order, with respect to a child who has reached the age of sixteen unless it is satisfied that the circumstances of the case are exceptional.

Amendments—Adoption and Children Act 2002, ss 113(a), (b), 114(2), 139(3), Sch 5.

10 Power of court to make section 8 orders

(1) In any family proceedings in which a question arises with respect to the welfare of any child, the court may make a section 8 order with respect to the child if –

(a)   an application for the order has been made by a person who –
(i)   is entitled to apply for a section 8 order with respect to the child; or
(ii)   has obtained the leave of the court to make the application; or

(b)   the court considers that the order should be made even though no such application has been made.

(2) The court may also make a section 8 order with respect to any child on the application of a person who –

(a)   is entitled to apply for a section 8 order with respect to the child; or

(b)   has obtained the leave of the court to make the application.

(3) This section is subject to the restrictions imposed by section 9.

(4) The following persons are entitled to apply to the court for any section 8 order with respect to a child –

(a)   any parent, guardian or special guardian of the child;

(aa)   any person who by virtue of section 4A has parental responsibility for the child;

(b)   any person in whose favour a residence order is in force with respect to the child.

(5) The following persons are entitled to apply for a residence or contact order with respect to a child –

(a) any party to a marriage (whether or not subsisting) in relation to whom the child is a child of the family;

(aa) any civil partner in a civil partnership (whether or not subsisting) in relation to whom the child is a child of the family;

(b) any person with whom the child has lived for a period of at least three years;

(c) any person who –

(i) in any case where a residence order is in force with respect to the child, has the consent of each of the persons in whose favour the order was made;

(ii) in any case where the child is in the care of a local authority, has the consent of that authority; or

(iii) in any other case, has the consent of each of those (if any) who have parental responsibility for the child.

(5A) A local authority foster parent is entitled to apply for a residence order with respect to a child if the child has lived with him for a period of at least one year immediately preceding the application.

(6) A person who would not otherwise be entitled (under the previous provisions of this section) to apply for the variation or discharge of a section 8 order shall be entitled to do so if –

(a) the order was made on his application; or

(b) in the case of a contact order, he is named in the order.

(7) Any person who falls within a category of person prescribed by rules of court is entitled to apply for any such section 8 order as may be prescribed in relation to that category of person.

(7A) If a special guardianship order is in force with respect to a child, an application for a residence order may only be made with respect to him, if apart from this subsection the leave of the court is not required, with such leave.

(8) Where the person applying for leave to make an application for a section 8 order is the child concerned, the court may only grant leave if it is satisfied that he has sufficient understanding to make the proposed application for the section 8 order.

(9) Where the person applying for leave to make an application for a section 8 order is not the child concerned, the court shall, in deciding whether or not to grant leave, have particular regard to –

(a) the nature of the proposed application for the section 8 order;

(b) the applicant's connection with the child;

(c) any risk there might be of that proposed application disrupting the child's life to such an extent that he would be harmed by it; and

(d) where the child is being looked after by a local authority –

(i) the authority's plans for the child's future; and

(ii) the wishes and feelings of the child's parents.

(10) The period of three years mentioned in subsection (5)(b) need not be continuous but must not have begun more than five years before, or ended more than three months before, the making of the application.

Amendments—Adoption and Children Act 2002, s 139(1), Sch 3, paras 54, 56; Civil Partnership Act 2004, s 77.

11 General principles and supplementary provisions

(1) In proceedings in which any question of making a section 8 order, or any other question with respect to such an order, arises, the court shall (in the light of any rules made by virtue of subsection (2)) –

(a) draw up a timetable with a view to determining the question without delay; and

(b) give such directions as it considers appropriate for the purpose of ensuring, so far as is reasonably practicable, that that timetable is adhered to.

(2) Rules of court may –

(a) specify periods within which specified steps must be taken in relation to proceedings in which such questions arise; and

(b) make other provision with respect to such proceedings for the purpose of ensuring, so far as is reasonably practicable, that such questions are determined without delay.

(3) Where a court has power to make a section 8 order, it may do so at any time during the course of the proceedings in question even though it is not in a position to dispose finally of those proceedings.

(4) Where a residence order is made in favour of two or more persons who do not themselves all live together, the order may specify the periods during which the child is to live in the different households concerned.

(5) Where –

(a) a residence order has been made with respect to a child; and

(b) as a result of the order the child lives, or is to live, with one of two parents who each have parental responsibility for him,

the residence order shall cease to have effect if the parents live together for a continuous period of more than six months.

(6) A contact order which requires the parent with whom a child lives to allow the child to visit, or otherwise have contact with, his other parent shall cease to have effect if the parents live together for a continuous period of more than six months.

(7) A section 8 order may –

(a) contain directions about how it is to be carried into effect;

(b) impose conditions which must be complied with by any person –

(i) in whose favour the order is made;

(ii) who is a parent of the child concerned;

(iii) who is not a parent of his but who has parental responsibility for him; or

(iv) with whom the child is living,

and to whom the conditions are expressed to apply;

(c) be made to have effect for a specified period, or contain provisions which are to have effect for a specified period;

(d) make such incidental, supplemental or consequential provision as the court thinks fit.

****

12 Residence orders and parental responsibility

(1) Where the court makes a residence order in favour of the father of a child it shall, if the father would not otherwise have parental responsibility for the child, also make an order under section 4 giving him that responsibility.

(2) Where the court makes a residence order in favour of any person who is not the parent or guardian of the child concerned that person shall have parental responsibility for the child while the residence order remains in force.

(3) Where a person has parental responsibility for a child as a result of subsection (2), he shall not have the right –

(a) ...

(b) to agree, or refuse to agree, to the making of an adoption order, or an order under section 84 of the Adoption and Children Act 2002, with respect to the child; or

(c) to appoint a guardian for the child.

(4) Where subsection (1) requires the court to make an order under section 4 in respect of the father of a child, the court shall not bring that order to an end at any time while the residence order concerned remains in force.

(5) The power of a court to make a residence order in favour of any person who is not the parent or guardian of the child concerned includes power to direct, at the request of that person, that the order continue in force until the child reaches the age of eighteen (unless the order is brought to an end earlier); and any power to vary a residence order is exercisable accordingly.

(6) Where a residence order includes such a direction, an application to vary or discharge the order may only be made, if apart from this subsection the leave of the court is not required, with such leave.

Amendments—Adoption and Children Act 2002, ss 114(1), 139(1), (3), Sch 3, paras 54, 57(a), (b), Sch 5.

****

Special guardianship

14A Special guardianship orders

(1) A 'special guardianship order' is an order appointing one or more individuals to be a child's 'special guardian' (or special guardians).

(2) A special guardian –

(a)   must be aged eighteen or over; and
(b)   must not be a parent of the child in question,

and subsections (3) to (6) are to be read in that light.

(3) The court may make a special guardianship order with respect to any child on the application of an individual who –

(a)   is entitled to make such an application with respect to the child; or
(b)   has obtained the leave of the court to make the application,

or on the joint application of more than one such individual.

(4) Section 9(3) applies in relation to an application for leave to apply for a special guardianship order as it applies in relation to an application for leave to apply for a section 8 order.

(5) The individuals who are entitled to apply for a special guardianship order with respect to a child are –

(a)   any guardian of the child;
(b)   any individual in whose favour a residence order is in force with respect to the child;
(c)   any individual listed in subsection (5)(b) or (c) of section 10 (as read with subsection (10) of that section);
(d)   a local authority foster parent with whom the child has lived for a period of at least one year immediately preceding the application.

(6) The court may also make a special guardianship order with respect to a child in any family proceedings in which a question arises with respect to the welfare of the child if –

(a)   an application for the order has been made by an individual who falls within subsection (3)(a) or (b) (or more than one such individual jointly); or
(b)   the court considers that a special guardianship order should be made even though no such application has been made.

(7) No individual may make an application under subsection (3) or (6)(a) unless, before the beginning of the period of three months ending with the date of the application, he has given written notice of his intention to make the application –

(a)   if the child in question is being looked after by a local authority, to that local authority, or
(b)   otherwise, to the local authority in whose area the individual is ordinarily resident.

(8) On receipt of such a notice, the local authority must investigate the matter and prepare a report for the court dealing with –

   (a)   the suitability of the applicant to be a special guardian;

   (b)   such matters (if any) as may be prescribed by the Secretary of State; and

   (c)   any other matter which the local authority consider to be relevant.

(9) The court may itself ask a local authority to conduct such an investigation and prepare such a report, and the local authority must do so.

(10) The local authority may make such arrangements as they see fit for any person to act on their behalf in connection with conducting an investigation or preparing a report referred to in subsection (8) or (9).

(11) The court may not make a special guardianship order unless it has received a report dealing with the matters referred to in subsection (8).

(12) Subsections (8) and (9) of section 10 apply in relation to special guardianship orders as they apply in relation to section 8 orders.

(13) This section is subject to section 29(5) and (6) of the Adoption and Children Act 2002.

Amendments—Inserted by Adoption and Children Act 2002, s 115(1).

14B Special guardianship orders: making

(1) Before making a special guardianship order, the court must consider whether, if the order were made –

   (a)   a contact order should also be made with respect to the child, ...

   (b)   any section 8 order in force with respect to the child should be varied or discharged.

   (c)   where a contact order made with respect to the child is not discharged, any enforcement order relating to that contact order should be revoked, and

   (d)   where a contact activity direction has been made as regards contact with the child and is in force, that contact activity direction should be discharged.

(2) On making a special guardianship order, the court may also –

   (a)   give leave for the child to be known by a new surname;

   (b)   grant the leave required by section 14C(3)(b), either generally or for specified purposes.

Amendments—Inserted by Adoption and Children Act 2002, s 115(1). Amended by Children and Adoption Act 2006, s 15, Sch 2, paras 7, 8(a), Sch 3.

14C Special guardianship orders: effect

(1) The effect of a special guardianship order is that while the order remains in force –

   (a)   a special guardian appointed by the order has parental responsibility for the child in respect of whom it is made; and

   (b)   subject to any other order in force with respect to the child under this Act, a special guardian is entitled to exercise parental responsibility to the exclusion of any other person with parental responsibility for the child (apart from another special guardian).

(2) Subsection (1) does not affect –

   (a)   the operation of any enactment or rule of law which requires the consent of more than one person with parental responsibility in a matter affecting the child; or

   (b)   any rights which a parent of the child has in relation to the child's adoption or placement for adoption.

(3) While a special guardianship order is in force with respect to a child, no person may –

   (a)   cause the child to be known by a new surname; or

   (b)   remove him from the United Kingdom,

without either the written consent of every person who has parental responsibility for the child or the leave of the court.

(4) Subsection (3)(b) does not prevent the removal of a child, for a period of less than three months, by a special guardian of his.

(5) If the child with respect to whom a special guardianship order is in force dies, his special guardian must take reasonable steps to give notice of that fact to –

(a) each parent of the child with parental responsibility; and
(b) each guardian of the child,

but if the child has more than one special guardian, and one of them has taken such steps in relation to a particular parent or guardian, any other special guardian need not do so as respects that parent or guardian.

(6) This section is subject to section 29(7) of the Adoption and Children Act 2002.

Amendments—Inserted by Adoption and Children Act 2002, s 115(1).

14D Special guardianship orders: variation and discharge

(1) The court may vary or discharge a special guardianship order on the application of –

(a) the special guardian (or any of them, if there are more than one);
(b) any parent or guardian of the child concerned;
(c) any individual in whose favour a residence order is in force with respect to the child;
(d) any individual not falling within any of paragraphs (a) to (c) who has, or immediately before the making of the special guardianship order had, parental responsibility for the child;
(e) the child himself; or
(f) a local authority designated in a care order with respect to the child.

(2) In any family proceedings in which a question arises with respect to the welfare of a child with respect to whom a special guardianship order is in force, the court may also vary or discharge the special guardianship order if it considers that the order should be varied or discharged, even though no application has been made under subsection (1).

(3) The following must obtain the leave of the court before making an application under subsection (1) –

(a) the child;
(b) any parent or guardian of his;
(c) any step-parent of his who has acquired, and has not lost, parental responsibility for him by virtue of section 4A;
(d) any individual falling within subsection (1)(d) who immediately before the making of the special guardianship order had, but no longer has, parental responsibility for him.

(4) Where the person applying for leave to make an application under subsection (1) is the child, the court may only grant leave if it is satisfied that he has sufficient understanding to make the proposed application under subsection (1).

(5) The court may not grant leave to a person falling within subsection (3)(b)(c) or (d) unless it is satisfied that there has been a significant change in circumstances since the making of the special guardianship order.

Amendments—Inserted by Adoption and Children Act 2002, s 115(1).

14E Special guardianship orders: supplementary

(1) In proceedings in which any question of making, varying or discharging a special guardianship order arises, the court shall (in the light of any rules made by virtue of subsection (3)) –

(a) draw up a timetable with a view to determining the question without delay; and

(b)   give such directions as it considers appropriate for the purpose of ensuring, so far as is reasonably practicable, that the timetable is adhered to.

(2) Subsection (1) applies also in relation to proceedings in which any other question with respect to a special guardianship order arises.

(3) The power to make rules in subsection (2) of section 11 applies for the purposes of this section as it applies for the purposes of that.

(4) A special guardianship order, or an order varying one, may contain provisions which are to have effect for a specified period.

(5) Section 11(7) (apart from paragraph (c)) applies in relation to special guardianship orders and orders varying them as it applies in relation to section 8 orders.

Amendments—Inserted by Adoption and Children Act 2002, s 115(1).

14F Special guardianship support services

(1) Each local authority must make arrangements for the provision within their area of special guardianship support services, which means –

(a)   counselling, advice and information; and
(b)   such other services as are prescribed,

in relation to special guardianship.

(2) The power to make regulations under subsection (1)(b) is to be exercised so as to secure that local authorities provide financial support.

(3) At the request of any of the following persons –

(a)   a child with respect to whom a special guardianship order is in force;
(b)   a special guardian;
(c)   a parent;
(d)   any other person who falls within a prescribed description,

a local authority may carry out an assessment of that person's needs for special guardianship support services (but, if the Secretary of State so provides in regulations, they must do so if he is a person of a prescribed description, or if his case falls within a prescribed description, or if both he and his case fall within prescribed descriptions).

(4) A local authority may, at the request of any other person, carry out an assessment of that person's needs for special guardianship support services.

(5) Where, as a result of an assessment, a local authority decide that a person has needs for special guardianship support services, they must then decide whether to provide any such services to that person.

(6) If –

(a)   a local authority decide to provide any special guardianship support services to a person, and
(b)   the circumstances fall within a prescribed description,

the local authority must prepare a plan in accordance with which special guardianship support services are to be provided to him, and keep the plan under review.

(7) The Secretary of State may by regulations make provision about assessments, preparing and reviewing plans, the provision of special guardianship support services in accordance with plans and reviewing the provision of special guardianship support services.

(8) The regulations may in particular make provision –

(a)   about the type of assessment which is to be carried out, or the way in which an assessment is to be carried out;

(b)   about the way in which a plan is to be prepared;

(c)   about the way in which, and the time at which, a plan or the provision of special guardianship support services is to be reviewed;

(d)   about the considerations to which a local authority are to have regard in carrying out an assessment or review or preparing a plan;

(e)   as to the circumstances in which a local authority may provide special guardianship support services subject to conditions (including conditions as to payment for the support or the repayment of financial support);

(f)   as to the consequences of conditions imposed by virtue of paragraph (e) not being met (including the recovery of any financial support provided);

(g)   as to the circumstances in which this section may apply to a local authority in respect of persons who are outside that local authority's area;

(h)   as to the circumstances in which a local authority may recover from another local authority the expenses of providing special guardianship support services to any person.

(9) A local authority may provide special guardianship support services (or any part of them) by securing their provision by –

(a)   another local authority; or

(b)   a person within a description prescribed in regulations of persons who may provide special guardianship support services,

and may also arrange with any such authority or person for that other authority or that person to carry out the local authority's functions in relation to assessments under this section.

(10) A local authority may carry out an assessment of the needs of any person for the purposes of this section at the same time as an assessment of his needs is made under any other provision of this Act or under any other enactment.

(11) Section 27 (co-operation between authorities) applies in relation to the exercise of functions of a local authority under this section as it applies in relation to the exercise of functions of a local authority under Part 3.

Amendments—Inserted by Adoption and Children Act 2002, s 115(1).

Family assistance orders

16 Family assistance orders

(1) Where, in any family proceedings, the court has power to make an order under this Part with respect to any child, it may (whether or not it makes such an order) make an order requiring –

(a)   an officer of the Service or a Welsh family proceedings officer to be made available; or

(b)   a local authority to make an officer of the authority available,

to advise, assist and (where appropriate) befriend any person named in the order.

(2) The persons who may be named in an order under this section ('a family assistance order') are –

(a)   any parent, guardian or special guardian of the child;

(b)   any person with whom the child is living or in whose favour a contact order is in force with respect to the child;

(c)   the child himself.

(3) No court may make a family assistance order unless –

(a)   ....

(b)   it has obtained the consent of every person to be named in the order other than the child.

(4) A family assistance order may direct –

(a)   the person named in the order; or

(b)   such of the persons named in the order as may be specified in the order, to take such steps as may be so specified with a view to enabling the officer concerned to be kept informed of the address of any person named in the order and to be allowed to visit any such person.

(4A) If the court makes a family assistance order with respect to a child and the order is to be in force at the same time as a contact order made with respect to the child, the family assistance order may direct the officer concerned to give advice and assistance as regards establishing, improving and maintaining contact to such of the persons named in the order as may be specified in the order.

(5) Unless it specifies a shorter period, a family assistance order shall have effect for a period of twelve months beginning with the day on which it is made.

(6) If the court makes a family assistance order with respect to a child and the order is to be in force at the same time as a section 8 order made with respect to the child, the family assistance order may direct the officer concerned to report to the court on such matters relating to the section 8 order as the court may require (including the question whether the section 8 order ought to be varied or discharged).

(7) A family assistance order shall not be made so as to require a local authority to make an officer of theirs available unless –

    (a)   the authority agree; or
    (b)   the child concerned lives or will live within their area.

(8), (9) ...

Amendments—Criminal Justice and Court Services Act 2000, s 74, Sch 7, paras 87, 89, Sch 8; Adoption and Children Act 2002, s 139(1), Sch 3, paras 54, 58; Children Act 2004, s 40, Sch 3, paras 5, 7; Children and Adoption Act 2006, ss 6, 15(2), Sch 3.

****

Duties of local authorities in relation to children looked after by them

22 General duty of local authority in relation to children looked after by them

(1) In this Act, any reference to a child who is looked after by a local authority is a reference to a child who is –

    (a)   in their care; or
    (b)   provided with accommodation by the authority in the exercise of any functions (in particular those under this Act) which are social services functions within the meaning of the Local Authority Social Services Act 1970 , apart from functions under sections 17 23B and 24B.

(2) In subsection (1) 'accommodation' means accommodation which is provided for a continuous period of more than 24 hours.

(3) It shall be the duty of a local authority looking after any child –

    (a)   to safeguard and promote his welfare; and
    (b)   to make such use of services available for children cared for by their own parents as appears to the authority reasonable in his case.

(3A) The duty of a local authority under subsection (3)(a) to safeguard and promote the welfare of a child looked after by them includes in particular a duty to promote the child's educational achievement.

(4) Before making any decision with respect to a child whom they are looking after, or proposing to look after, a local authority shall, so far as is reasonably practicable, ascertain the wishes and feelings of –

    (a)   the child;
    (b)   his parents;
    (c)   any person who is not a parent of his but who has parental responsibility for him; and
    (d)   any other person whose wishes and feelings the authority consider to be relevant,

regarding the matter to be decided.

(5) In making any such decision a local authority shall give due consideration –

(a) having regard to his age and understanding, to such wishes and feelings of the child as they have been able to ascertain;

(b) to such wishes and feelings of any person mentioned in subsection (4)(b) to (d) as they have been able to ascertain; and

(c) to the child's religious persuasion, racial origin and cultural and linguistic background.

(6) If it appears to a local authority that it is necessary, for the purposes of protecting members of the public from serious injury, to exercise their powers with respect to a child whom they are looking after in a manner which may not be consistent with their duties under this section, they may do so.

(7) If the appropriate national authority considers it necessary, for the purpose of protecting members of the public from serious injury, to give directions to a local authority with respect to the exercise of their powers with respect to a child whom they are looking after, the appropriate national authority may give such directions to the local authority.

(8) Where any such directions are given to an authority they shall comply with them even though doing so is inconsistent with their duties under this section.

Amendments—Children (Leaving Care) Act 2000, s 2(1), (2); Local Government Act 2000, s 107, Sch 5, para 19; Adoption and Children Act 2002, s 116(2); Children Act 2004, s 52; Children and Young Persons Act 2008, s 39, Sch 3, paras 1, 6.

[22A Provision of accommodation for children in care

When a child is in the care of a local authority, it is their duty to provide the child with accommodation.

22B Maintenance of looked after children

It is the duty of a local authority to maintain a child they are looking after in other respects apart from the provision of accommodation.

22C Ways in which looked after children are to be accommodated and maintained

(1) This section applies where a local authority are looking after a child ("C").

(2) The local authority must make arrangements for C to live with a person who falls within subsection (3) (but subject to subsection (4)).

(3) A person ("P") falls within this subsection if –

(a) P is a parent of C;

(b) P is not a parent of C but has parental responsibility for C; or

(c) in a case where C is in the care of the local authority and there was a residence order in force with respect to C immediately before the care order was made, P was a person in whose favour the residence order was made.

(4) Subsection (2) does not require the local authority to make arrangements of the kind mentioned in that subsection if doing so –

(a) would not be consistent with C's welfare; or

(b) would not be reasonably practicable.

(5) If the local authority are unable to make arrangements under subsection (2), they must place C in the placement which is, in their opinion, the most appropriate placement available.

(6) In subsection (5) "placement" means –

(a) placement with an individual who is a relative, friend or other person connected with C and who is also a local authority foster parent;

(b)   placement with a local authority foster parent who does not fall within paragraph (a);

(c)   placement in a children's home in respect of which a person is registered under Part 2 of the Care Standards Act 2000; or

(d)   subject to section 22D, placement in accordance with other arrangements which comply with any regulations made for the purposes of this section.

(7) In determining the most appropriate placement for C, the local authority must, subject to the other provisions of this Part (in particular, to their duties under section 22) –

(a)   give preference to a placement falling within paragraph (a) of subsection (6) over placements falling within the other paragraphs of that subsection;

(b)   comply, so far as is reasonably practicable in all the circumstances of C's case, with the requirements of subsection (8); and

(c)   comply with subsection (9) unless that is not reasonably practicable.

(8) The local authority must ensure that the placement is such that—

(a)   it allows C to live near C's home;

(b)   it does not disrupt C's education or training;

(c)   if C has a sibling for whom the local authority are also providing accommodation, it enables C and the sibling to live together;

(d)   if C is disabled, the accommodation provided is suitable to C's particular needs.

(9) The placement must be such that C is provided with accommodation within the local authority's area.

(10) The local authority may determine –

(a)   the terms of any arrangements they make under subsection (2) in relation to C (including terms as to payment); and

(b)   the terms on which they place C with a local authority foster parent (including terms as to payment but subject to any order made under section 49 of the Children Act 2004).

(11) The appropriate national authority may make regulations for, and in connection with, the purposes of this section.

(12) In this Act "local authority foster parent" means a person who is approved as a local authority foster parent in accordance with regulations made by virtue of paragraph 12F of Schedule 2.

22D Review of child's case before making alternative arrangements for accommodation

(1) Where a local authority are providing accommodation for a child ("C") other than by arrangements under section 22C(6)(d), they must not make such arrangements for C unless they have decided to do so in consequence of a review of C's case carried out in accordance with regulations made under section 26.

(2) But subsection (1) does not prevent a local authority making arrangements for C under section 22C(6)(d) if they are satisfied that in order to safeguard C's welfare it is necessary –

(a)   to make such arrangements; and

(b)   to do so as a matter of urgency.]

Amendments—Children and Young Persons Act 2008, s 8. Sections 22A–22D come into effect from a date to be appointed.

23 Provision of accommodation and maintenance by local authority for children whom they are looking after

(1) It shall be the duty of any local authority looking after a child –

(a)   when he is in their care, to provide accommodation for him; and

(b)   to maintain him in other respects apart from providing accommodation for him.

(2) A local authority shall provide accommodation and maintenance for any child whom they are looking after by –

(a) placing him (subject to subsection (5) and any regulations made by the Secretary of State) with –
  (i) a family;
  (ii) a relative of his; or
  (iii) any other suitable person,
  on such terms as to payment by the authority and otherwise as the authority may determine (subject to section 49 of the Children Act 2004);
(aa) maintaining him in an appropriate children's home;
(f) making such other arrangements as –
  (i) seem appropriate to them; and
  (ii) comply with any regulations made by the appropriate national authority.

(2A) Where under subsection (2)(aa) a local authority maintains a child in a home provided, equipped and maintained by an appropriate national authority under section 82(5), it shall do so on such terms as that national authority may from time to time determine.

(3) Any person with whom a child has been placed under subsection (2)(a) is referred to in this Act as a local authority foster parent unless he falls within subsection (4).

(4) A person falls within this subsection if he is –

(a) a parent of the child;
(b) a person who is not a parent of the child but who has parental responsibility for him; or
(c) where the child is in care and there was a residence order in force with respect to him immediately before the care order was made, a person in whose favour the residence order was made.

(5) Where a child is in the care of a local authority, the authority may only allow him to live with a person who falls within subsection (4) in accordance with regulations made by the appropriate national authority.

(5A) For the purposes of subsection (5) a child shall be regarded as living with a person if he stays with that person for a continuous period of more than 24 hours.

(6) Subject to any regulations made by the appropriate national authority for the purposes of this subsection, any local authority looking after a child shall make arrangements to enable him to live with –

(a) a person falling within subsection (4); or
(b) a relative, friend or other person connected with him,

unless that would not be reasonably practicable or consistent with his welfare.

(7) Where a local authority provide accommodation for a child whom they are looking after, they shall, subject to the provisions of this Part and so far as is reasonably practicable and consistent with his welfare, secure that –

(a) the accommodation is near his home; and
(b) where the authority are also providing accommodation for a sibling of his, they are accommodated together.

(8) Where a local authority provide accommodation for a child whom they are looking after and who is disabled, they shall, so far as is reasonably practicable, secure that the accommodation is not unsuitable to his particular needs.

(9) Part II of Schedule 2 shall have effect for the purposes of making further provision as to children looked after by local authorities and in particular as to the regulations that may be made under subsections (2)(a) and (f) and (5).

(10) In this Act –

'appropriate children's home' means a children's home in respect of which a person is registered under Part II of the Care Standards Act 2000; and
'children's home' has the same meaning as in that Act.

Amendments—Courts and Legal Services Act 1990, s 116, Sch 16, para 12(2); Care Standards Act 2000, s 116, Sch 4, para 14(1), (3)(a), (b), (c); Children Act 2004, s 49(3); Children and Young Persons Act 2008, s 39, Sch 3, paras 1, 7.

****

34 Parental contact etc with children in care

(1) Where a child is in the care of a local authority, the authority shall (subject to the provisions of this section) allow the child reasonable contact with –

   (a)   his parents;
   (b)   any guardian or special guardian of his;
   (ba) any person who by virtue of section 4A has parental responsibility for him;
   (c)   where there was a residence order in force with respect to the child immediately before the care order was made, the person in whose favour the order was made; and
   (d)   where, immediately before the care order was made, a person had care of the child by virtue of an order made in the exercise of the High Court's inherent jurisdiction with respect to children, that person.

(2) On an application made by the authority or the child, the court may make such order as it considers appropriate with respect to the contact which is to be allowed between the child and any named person.

(3) On an application made by –

   (a)   any person mentioned in paragraphs (a) to (d) of subsection (1); or
   (b)   any person who has obtained the leave of the court to make the application,

the court may make such order as it considers appropriate with respect to the contact which is to be allowed between the child and that person.

(4) On an application made by the authority or the child, the court may make an order authorising the authority to refuse to allow contact between the child and any person who is mentioned in paragraphs (a) to (d) of subsection (1) and named in the order.

(5) When making a care order with respect to a child, or in any family proceedings in connection with a child who is in the care of a local authority, the court may make an order under this section, even though no application for such an order has been made with respect to the child, if it considers that the order should be made.

(6) An authority may refuse to allow the contact that would otherwise be required by virtue of subsection (1) or an order under this section if –

   (a)   they are satisfied that it is necessary to do so in order to safeguard or promote the child's welfare; and
   (b)   the refusal –
         (i)   is decided upon as a matter of urgency; and
         (ii)   does not last for more than seven days.

(7) An order under this section may impose such conditions as the court considers appropriate.

(8) The Secretary of State may by regulations make provision as to –

   (a)   the steps to be taken by a local authority who have exercised their powers under subsection (6);
   (b)   the circumstances in which, and conditions subject to which, the terms of any order under this section may be departed from by agreement between the local authority and the person in relation to whom the order is made;

(c)   notification by a local authority of any variation or suspension of arrangements made (otherwise than under an order under this section) with a view to affording any person contact with a child to whom this section applies.

(9) The court may vary or discharge any order made under this section on the application of the authority, the child concerned or the person named in the order.

(10) An order under this section may be made either at the same time as the care order itself or later.

(11) Before making a care order with respect to any child the court shall –

(a)   consider the arrangements which the authority have made, or propose to make, for affording any person contact with a child to whom this section applies; and

(b)   invite the parties to the proceedings to comment on those arrangements.

Amendments—Adoption and Children Act 2002, s 139(1), Sch 3, paras 54, 64(b).

Appendix 2

PROCEDURAL RULES

FAMILY PROCEDURE (ADOPTION) RULES 2005

SI 2005/2795

PART 1
OVERRIDING OBJECTIVE

1 The overriding objective

(1) These Rules are a new procedural code with the overriding objective of enabling the court to deal with cases justly, having regard to the welfare issues involved.

(2) Dealing with a case justly includes, so far as is practicable –

(a) ensuring that it is dealt with expeditiously and fairly;

(b) dealing with the case in ways which are proportionate to the nature, importance and complexity of the issues;

(c) ensuring that the parties are on an equal footing;

(d) saving expense; and

(e) allotting to it an appropriate share of the court's resources, while taking into account the need to allot resources to other cases.

2 Application by the court of the overriding objective

The court must seek to give effect to the overriding objective when it –

(a) exercises any power given to it by these Rules; or

(b) interprets any rule.

3 Duty of the parties

The parties are required to help the court to further the overriding objective.

4 Court's duty to manage cases

(1) The court must further the overriding objective by actively managing cases.

(2) Active case management includes –

(a) encouraging the parties to co-operate with each other in the conduct of the proceedings;

(b) identifying at an early stage –

(i) the issues; and

(ii) who should be a party to the proceedings;

(c) deciding promptly –

(i) which issues need full investigation and hearing and which do not; and

(ii) the procedure to be followed in the case;

(d) deciding the order in which issues are to be resolved;

(e)   encouraging the parties to use an alternative dispute resolution procedure if the court considers that appropriate and facilitating the use of such procedure;

(f)   helping the parties to settle the whole or part of the case;

(g)   fixing timetables or otherwise controlling the progress of the case;

(h)   considering whether the likely benefits of taking a particular step justify the cost of taking it;

(i)   dealing with as many aspects of the case as it can on the same occasion;

(j)   dealing with the case without the parties needing to attend at court;

(k)   making use of technology; and

(l)   giving directions to ensure that the case proceeds quickly and efficiently.

PART 3
GENERAL CASE MANAGEMENT POWERS

12 The court's general powers of management

(1) The list of powers in this rule is in addition to any powers given to the court by any other rule or practice direction or by any other enactment or any powers it may otherwise have.

(2) Except where these Rules provide otherwise, the court may –

(a)   extend or shorten the time for compliance with any rule, practice direction or court direction (even if an application for extension is made after the time for compliance has expired);

(b)   adjourn or bring forward a hearing;

(c)   require a party or a party's legal representative to attend the court;

(d)   hold a hearing and receive evidence by telephone or by using any other method of direct oral communication;

(e)   direct that part of any proceedings be dealt with as separate proceedings;

(f)   stay the whole or part of any proceedings or judgment either generally or until a specified date or event;

(g)   consolidate proceedings;

(h)   hear two or more applications on the same occasion;

(i)   direct a separate hearing of any issue;

(j)   decide the order in which issues are to be heard;

(k)   exclude an issue from consideration;

(l)   dismiss or give judgment on an application after a decision on a preliminary issue;

(m)   direct any party to file and serve an estimate of costs; and

(n)   take any other step or give any other direction for the purpose of managing the case and furthering the overriding objective.

(3) The court may not extend the period within which a section 89 order must be made.

(4) Paragraph (2)(f) does not apply to proceedings in a magistrates' court.

13 Exercise of powers of court's own initiative

(1) Except where an enactment provides otherwise, the court may exercise the powers in rule 12 on an application or of its own initiative.

(Part 9 sets out the procedure for making an application.)

(2) Where the court proposes to exercise its powers of its own initiative –

(a)   it may give any person likely to be affected an opportunity to make representations; and

(b)   where it does so it must specify the time by and the manner in which the representations must be made.

(3) Where the court proposes to hold a hearing to decide whether to exercise its powers of its own initiative it must give each party likely to be affected at least 3 days' notice of the hearing.

(4) The court may exercise its powers of its own initiative, without hearing the parties or giving them an opportunity to make representations.

(5) Where the court has exercised its powers under paragraph (4) –

    (a)   a party affected by the direction may apply to have it set aside or varied; and

    (b)   the direction must contain a statement of the right to make such an application.

(6) An application under paragraph (5)(a) must be made –

    (a)   within such period as may be specified by the court; or

    (b)   if the court does not specify a period, within 7 days beginning with the date on which the order was served on the party making the application.

(7) If the High Court or a county court of its own initiative dismisses an application (including an application for permission to appeal) and it considers that the application is totally without merit –

    (a)   the court's order must record that fact; and

    (b)   the court must at the same time consider whether it is appropriate to make a civil restraint order.

14 Court officer's power to refer to the court

Where these Rules require a step to be taken by a court officer –

    (a)   the court officer may consult the court before taking that step;

    (b)   the step may be taken by the court instead of the court officer.

****

PART 4
HOW TO START PROCEEDINGS

****

20 Application for a serial number

(1) This rule applies to any application in proceedings by a person who intends to adopt the child.

(2) If the applicant wishes his identity to be kept confidential in the proceedings, he may, before those proceedings have started, request a court officer to assign a serial number to him to identify him in connection with the proceedings, and a number will be assigned to him.

(3) The court may at any time direct that a serial number identifying the applicant in the proceedings referred to in paragraph (2) must be removed.

(4) If a serial number has been assigned to a person under paragraph (2) –

    (a)   the court officer will ensure that any application form or application notice sent in accordance with these Rules does not contain information which discloses, or is likely to disclose, the identity of that person to any other party to that application who is not already aware of that person's identity; and

    (b)   the proceedings on the application will be conducted with a view to securing that the applicant is not seen by or made known to any party who is not already aware of his identity except with his consent.

21 Personal details

(1) Unless the court directs otherwise, a party is not required to reveal –

    (a)   the address or telephone number of their private residence;

    (b)   the address of the child;

    (c)   the name of a person with whom the child is living, if that person is not the applicant; or

(d)   in relation to an application under section 28(2) (application for permission to change the child's surname), the proposed new surname of the child.

(2) Where a party does not wish to reveal any of the particulars in paragraph (1), he must give notice of those particulars to the court and the particulars will not be revealed to any person unless the court directs otherwise.

(3) Where a party changes his home address during the course of proceedings, he must give notice of the change to the court.

PART 5
PROCEDURE FOR APPLICATIONS IN ADOPTION, PLACEMENT AND RELATED PROCEEDINGS

22 Application of this Part

The rules in this Part apply to the following proceedings –

(a)   adoption proceedings;
(b)   placement proceedings; or
(c)   proceedings for –
  (i)   the making of a contact order under section 26;
  (ii)   the variation or revocation of a contact order under section 27;
  (iii)   an order giving permission to change a child's surname or remove a child from the United Kingdom under section 28(2) and (3);
  (iv)   a section 84 order;
  (v)   a section 88 direction;
  (vi)   a section 89 order; or
  (vii)   any other order that may be referred to in a practice direction.

(Parts 9 and 10 set out the procedure for making an application in proceedings not dealt with in this Part.)

23 Who the parties are

(1) In relation to the proceedings set out in column 1 of each of the following tables, column 2 of Table 1 sets out who the application may be made by and column 2 of Table 2 sets out who the respondents to those proceedings will be.

Table 1

Proceedings for	Applicants
An adoption order (section 46)	The prospective adopters (section 50 and 51).
A section 84 order	The prospective adopters asking for parental responsibility prior to adoption abroad.
A placement order (section 21)	A local authority (section 22).
An order varying a placement order (section 23)	The joint application of the local authority authorised by the placement order to place the child for adoption and the local authority which is to be substituted for that authority (section 23).
An order revoking a placement order (section 24)	The child;

Proceedings for	Applicants
	the local authority authorised to place the child for adoption; or where the child is not placed for adoption by the authority, any other person who has the permission of the court to apply (section 24).
A contact order (section 26)	The child; the adoption agency; any parent, guardian or relative; any person in whose favour there was provision for contact under the 1989 Act which ceased to have effect on an adoption agency being authorised to place a child for adoption, or placing a child for adoption who is less than six weeks old (section 26(1)); a person in whose favour there was a residence order in force immediately before the adoption agency was authorised to place the child for adoption or placed the child for adoption at a time when he was less than six weeks old; a person who by virtue of an order made in the exercise of the High Court's inherent jurisdiction with respect to children had care of the child immediately before that time; or any person who has the permission of the court to make the application (section 26).
An order varying or revoking a contact order (section 27)	The child; the adoption agency; or any person named in the contact order (section 27(1)).
An order permitting the child's name to be changed or the removal of the child from the United Kingdom (section 28(2) and (3))	Any person including the adoption agency or the local authority authorised to place, or which has placed, the child for adoption (section 28(2)).
A section 88 direction	The adopted child; the adopters; any parent; or any other person.
A section 89 order	The adopters; the adopted person; any parent; the relevant Central Authority;

Proceedings for	Applicants
	the adoption agency; the local authority to whom notice under section 44 (notice of intention to adopt or apply for a section 84 order) has been given; the Secretary of State for the Home Department; or any other person.

Table 2

Proceedings for	Respondents
An adoption order (section 46) or a section 84 order	Each parent who has parental responsibility for the child or guardian of the child unless he has given notice under section 20(4)(a) (statement of wish not to be informed of any application for an adoption order) which has effect; any person in whose favour there is provision for contact; any adoption agency having parental responsibility for the child under section 25; any adoption agency which has taken part at any stage in the arrangements for adoption of the child; any local authority to whom notice under section 44 (notice of intention to adopt or apply for a section 84 order) has been given; any local authority or voluntary organisation which has parental responsibility for, is looking after, or is caring for, the child; and the child where – permission has been granted to a parent or guardian to oppose the making of the adoption order (section 47(3) or 47(5)); he opposes the making of an adoption order; a children and family reporter recommends that it is in the best interests of the child to be a party to the proceedings and that recommendation is accepted by the court; he is already an adopted child; any party to the proceedings or the child is opposed to the arrangements for allowing any person contact with the child, or a person not being allowed contact with the child after the making of the adoption order;

Proceedings for	Respondents
	the application is for a Convention adoption order or a section 84 order;
	he has been brought into the United Kingdom in the circumstances where section 83(1) applies (restriction on bringing children in);
	the application is for an adoption order other than a Convention adoption order and the prospective adopters intend the child to live in a country or territory outside the British Islands after the making of the adoption order; or –
	the prospective adopters are relatives of the child.
A placement order (section 21)	Each parent who has parental responsibility for the child or guardian of the child;
	any person in whose favour an order under the 1989 Act is in force in relation to the child;
	any adoption agency or voluntary organisation which has parental responsibility for, is looking after, or is caring for, the child;
	the child; and
	the parties or any persons who are or have been parties to proceedings for a care order in respect of the child where those proceedings have led to the application for the placement order.
An order varying a placement order (section 23)	The parties to the proceedings leading to the placement order which it is sought to have varied except the child who was the subject of those proceedings; and
	any person in whose favour there is provision for contact.
An order revoking a placement order (section 24)	The parties to the proceedings leading to the placement order which it is sought to have revoked; and
	any person in whose favour there is provision for contact.
A contact order (section 26)	The adoption agency authorised to place the child for adoption or which has placed the child for adoption;
	the person with whom the child lives or is to live;
	each parent with parental responsibility for the child or guardian of the child; and
	the child where –

Proceedings for	Respondents
	the adoption agency authorised to place the child for adoption or which has placed the child for adoption or a parent with parental responsibility for the child opposes the making of the contact order under section 26; he opposes the making of the contact order under section 26; existing provision for contact is to be revoked; relatives of the child do not agree to the arrangements for allowing any person contact with the child, or a person not being allowed contact with the child; or he is suffering or is at risk of suffering harm within the meaning of the 1989 Act.
An order varying or revoking a contact order (section 27)	The parties to the proceedings leading to the contact order which it is sought to have varied or revoked; and any person named in the contact order.
An order permitting the child's name to be changed or the removal of the child from the United Kingdom (section 28(2) and (3))	The parties to proceedings leading to any placement order; the adoption agency authorised to place the child for adoption or which has placed the child for adoption; any prospective adopters with whom the child is living; and each parent with parental responsibility for the child or guardian of the child.
A section 88 direction	The adopters; the parents; the adoption agency; the local authority to whom notice under section 44 (notice of intention to apply for a section 84 order) has been given; and the Attorney-General.
A section 89 order	The adopters; the parents; the adoption agency; and the local authority to whom notice under section 44 (notice of intention to adopt or apply for a section 84 order) has been given.

(2) The court may at any time direct that a child, who is not already a respondent to proceedings, be made a respondent to proceedings where –

(a)   the child –
    (i)   wishes to make an application; or
    (ii)   has evidence to give to the court or a legal submission to make which has not been given or made by any other party; or
(b)   there are other special circumstances.

(3) The court may at any time direct that –

(a)   any other person or body be made a respondent to proceedings; or
(b)   a respondent be removed.

(4) If the court makes a direction for the addition or removal of a party, it may give consequential directions about –

(a)   serving a copy of the application form on any new respondent;
(b)   serving relevant documents on the new party; and
(c)   the management of the proceedings.

24 What the court or a court officer will do when the application has been issued

(1) As soon as practicable after the application has been issued in proceedings –

(a)   the court will –
    (i)   if section 48(1) (restrictions on making adoption orders) applies, consider whether it is proper to hear the application;
    (ii)   subject to paragraph (4), set a date for the first directions hearing;
    (iii)   appoint a children's guardian in accordance with rule 59;
    (iv)   appoint a reporting officer in accordance with rule 69;
    (v)   consider whether a report relating to the welfare of the child is required, and if so, request such a report in accordance with rule 73;
    (vi)   set a date for the hearing of the application; and
    (vii)   do anything else that may be set out in a practice direction; and
(b)   a court officer will –
    (i)   subject to receiving confirmation in accordance with paragraph (2)(b)(ii), give notice of any directions hearing set by the court to the parties and to any children's guardian, reporting officer or children and family reporter;
    (ii)   serve a copy of the application form (but, subject to sub-paragraphs (iii) and (iv), not the documents attached to it) on the persons referred to in the relevant practice direction;
    (iii)   send a copy of the certified copy of the entry in the register of live-births or Adopted Children Register and any health report attached to an application for an adoption order to –
        (aa)   any children's guardian, reporting officer or children and family reporter; and
        (bb)   the local authority to whom notice under section 44 (notice of intention to adopt or apply for a section 84 order) has been given;
    (iv)   if notice under rule 27 has been given (request to dispense with consent of parent or guardian), in accordance with that rule inform the parent or guardian of the request and send a copy of the statement of facts to –
        (aa)   the parent or guardian;
        (bb)   any children's guardian, reporting officer or children and family reporter;
        (cc)   any local authority to whom notice under section 44 (notice of intention to adopt or apply for a section 84 order) has been given; and
        (dd)   any adoption agency which has placed the child for adoption; and
    (v)   do anything else that may be set out in a practice direction.

(2) In addition to the matters referred to in paragraph (1), as soon as practicable after an application for an adoption order or a section 84 order has been issued the court or the court officer will –

    (a)   where the child is not placed for adoption by an adoption agency –

        (i)   ask either the Service or the Assembly to file any relevant form of consent to an adoption order or a section 84 order; and

        (ii)   ask the local authority to prepare a report on the suitability of the prospective adopters if one has not already been prepared; and

    (b)   where the child is placed for adoption by an adoption agency, ask the adoption agency to –

        (i)   file any relevant form of consent to –

            (aa)   the child being placed for adoption;

            (bb)   an adoption order;

            (cc)   a future adoption order under section 20; or

            (dd)   a section 84 order;

        (ii)   confirm whether a statement has been made under section 20(4)(a) (statement of wish not to be informed of any application for an adoption order) and if so, to file that statement;

        (iii)   file any statement made under section 20(4)(b) (withdrawal of wish not to be informed of any application for an adoption order) as soon as it is received by the adoption agency; and

        (iv)   prepare a report on the suitability of the prospective adopters if one has not already been prepared.

(3) In addition to the matters referred to in paragraph (1), as soon as practicable after an application for a placement order has been issued –

    (a)   the court will consider whether a report giving the local authority's reasons for placing the child for adoption is required, and if so, will direct the local authority to prepare such a report; and

    (b)   the court or the court officer will ask either the Service or the Assembly to file any form of consent to the child being placed for adoption.

(4) Where it considers it appropriate the court may, instead of setting a date for a first directions hearing, give the directions provided for by rule 26.

25 Date for first directions hearing

Unless the court directs otherwise, the first directions hearing must be within 4 weeks beginning with the date on which the application is issued.

26 The first directions hearing

(1) At the first directions hearing in the proceedings the court will –

    (a)   fix a timetable for the filing of –

        (i)   any report relating to the suitability of the applicants to adopt a child;

        (ii)   any report from the local authority;

        (iii)   any report from a children's guardian, reporting officer or children and family reporter;

        (iv)   if a statement of facts has been filed, any amended statement of facts;

        (v)   any other evidence, and

        give directions relating to the reports and other evidence;

    (b)   consider whether an alternative dispute resolution procedure is appropriate and, if so, give directions relating to the use of such procedure;

    (c)   consider whether the child or any other person should be a party to the proceedings and, if so, give directions in accordance with rule 23(2) or (3) joining that child or person as a party;

(d) give directions relating to the appointment of a litigation friend for any protected party or non-subject child unless a litigation friend has already been appointed;

(e) consider whether the case needs to be transferred to another court and, if so, give directions to transfer the proceedings to another court in accordance with any order made by the Lord Chancellor under Part I of Schedule 11 to the 1989 Act;

(f) give directions about –

    (i) tracing parents or any other person the court considers to be relevant to the proceedings;

    (ii) service of documents;

    (iii) subject to paragraph (2), disclosure as soon as possible of information and evidence to the parties; and

    (iv) the final hearing; and

(2) Rule 77(2) applies to any direction given under paragraph (1)(f)(iii) as it applies to a direction given under rule 77(1).

(3) In addition to the matters referred to in paragraph (1), the court will give any of the directions listed in the relevant practice direction in proceedings for –

(a) a Convention adoption order;

(b) a section 84 order;

(c) a section 88 direction;

(d) a section 89 order; or

(e) an adoption order where section 83(1) applies (restriction on bringing children in).

(4) The parties or their legal representatives must attend the first directions hearing unless the court directs otherwise.

(5) Directions may also be given at any stage in the proceedings –

(a) of the court's own initiative; or

(b) on the application of a party or any children's guardian or, where the direction concerns a report by a reporting officer or children and family reporter, the reporting officer or children and family reporter.

(6) For the purposes of giving directions or for such purposes as the court directs –

(a) the court may set a date for a further directions hearing or other hearing; and

(b) the court officer will give notice of any date so fixed to the parties and to any children's guardian, reporting officer or children and family reporter.

(7) After the first directions hearing the court will monitor compliance with the court's timetable and directions by the parties.

Amendment—SI 2007/2189.

27 Requesting the court to dispense with the consent of any parent or guardian

(1) The following paragraphs apply where the applicant wants to ask the court to dispense with the consent of any parent or guardian of a child to –

(a) the child being placed for adoption;

(b) the making of an adoption order except a Convention adoption order; or

(c) the making of a section 84 order.

(2) The applicant requesting the court to dispense with the consent must –

(a) give notice of the request in the application form or at any later stage by filing a written request setting out the reasons for the request; and

(b) file a statement of facts setting out a summary of the history of the case and any other facts to satisfy the court that –

    (i) the parent or guardian cannot be found or is incapable of giving consent; or

    (ii) the welfare of the child requires the consent to be dispensed with.

(3) If a serial number has been assigned to the applicant under rule 20, the statement of facts supplied under paragraph (2)(b) must be framed so that it does not disclose the identity of the applicant.

(4) On receipt of the notice of the request –

    (a)   a court officer will –
        (i)   inform the parent or guardian of the request; and
        (ii)   send a copy of the statement of facts filed in accordance with paragraph (2)(b) to –
            (aa)   the parent or guardian;
            (bb)   any children's guardian, reporting officer or children and family reporter;
            (cc)   any local authority to whom notice under section 44 (notice of intention to adopt or apply for a section 84 order) has been given; and
            (dd)   any adoption agency which has placed the child for adoption; and

    (b)   if the applicant considers that the parent or guardian is incapable of giving consent, the court will consider whether to –
        (i)   appoint a litigation friend for the parent or guardian under rule 55(1); or
        (ii)   give directions for an application to be made under rule 55(3),
        unless a litigation friend is already appointed for that parent or guardian.

28 Consent

(1) Consent of any parent or guardian of a child –

    (a)   under section 19, to the child being placed for adoption; and
    (b)   under section 20, to the making of a future adoption order

must be given in the form required by the relevant practice direction or a form to the like effect.

(2) Subject to paragraph (3), consent –

    (a)   to the making of an adoption order; or
    (b)   to the making of a section 84 order,

may be given in the form required by the relevant practice direction or a form to the like effect.

(3) Any consent to a Convention adoption order must be in a form which complies with the internal law relating to adoption of the Convention country of which the child is habitually resident.

(4) Any form of consent executed in Scotland must be witnessed by a Justice of the Peace or a Sheriff.

(5) Any form of consent executed in Northern Ireland must be witnessed by a Justice of the Peace.

(6) Any form of consent executed outside the United Kingdom must be witnessed by –

    (a)   any person for the time being authorised by law in the place where the document is executed to administer an oath for any judicial or other legal purpose;
    (b)   a British Consular officer;
    (c)   a notary public; or
    (d)   if the person executing the document is serving in any of the regular armed forces of the Crown, an officer holding a commission in any of those forces.

29 Reports by the adoption agency or local authority

(1) The adoption agency or local authority must file the report on the suitability of the applicant to adopt a child within the timetable fixed by the court.

(2) A local authority that is directed to prepare a report on the placement of the child for adoption must file that report within the timetable fixed by the court.

(3) The reports must cover the matters specified in the relevant practice direction.

(4) The court may at any stage request a further report or ask the adoption agency or local authority to assist the court in any other manner.

(5) A court officer will send a copy of any report referred to in this rule to any children's guardian, reporting officer or children and family reporter.

(6) Any report to the court under this rule will be confidential.

30 Health reports

(1) Reports by a registered medical practitioner ('health reports') made not more than three months earlier on the health of the child and of each applicant must be attached to an application for an adoption order or a section 84 order except where –

  (a)   the child was placed for adoption with the applicant by an adoption agency;
  (b)   the applicant or one of the applicants is a parent of the child; or
  (c)   the applicant is the partner of a parent of the child.

(2) Health reports must contain the matters set out in the relevant practice direction.

(3) Any health report will be confidential.

31 Notice of final hearing

A court officer will give notice to the parties, any children's guardian, reporting officer or children and family reporter and to any other person that may be referred to in a practice direction –

  (a)   of the date and place where the application will be heard; and
  (b)   of the fact that, unless the person wishes or the court requires, the person need not attend.

32 The final hearing

(1) Any person who has been given notice in accordance with rule 31 may attend the final hearing and, subject to paragraph (2), be heard on the question of whether an order should be made.

(2) A person whose application for the permission of the court to oppose the making of an adoption order under section 47(3) or (5) has been refused is not entitled to be heard on the question of whether an order should be made.

(3) Any member or employee of a party which is a local authority, adoption agency or other body may address the court at the final hearing if he is authorised to do so.

(4) The court may direct that any person must attend a final hearing.

(5) Paragraphs (6) and (7) apply to –

  (a)   an adoption order;
  (b)   a section 84 order; or
  (c)   a section 89 order.

(6) Subject to paragraphs (7) and (8), the court cannot make an order unless the applicant and the child personally attend the final hearing.

(7) The court may direct that the applicant or the child need not attend the final hearing.

(8) In a case of adoption by a couple under section 50 the court may make an adoption order after personal attendance of one only of the applicants if there are special circumstances.

(9) The court cannot make a placement order unless a legal representative of the applicant attends the final hearing.

33 Proof of identity of the child

(1) Unless the contrary is shown, the child referred to in the application will be deemed to be the child referred to in the form of consent –

   (a)   to the child being placed for adoption;

   (b)   to the making of an adoption order; or

   (c)   to the making of a section 84 order

where the conditions in paragraph (2) apply.

(2) The conditions are –

   (a)   the application identifies the child by reference to a full certified copy of an entry in the registers of live-births;

   (b)   the form of consent identifies the child by reference to a full certified copy of an entry in the registers of live-births attached to the form; and

   (c)   the copy of the entry in the registers of live-births referred to in sub-paragraph (a) is the same or relates to the same entry in the registers of live-births as the copy of the entry in the registers of live-births attached to the form of consent.

(3) Where the child is already an adopted child paragraph (2) will have effect as if for the references to the registers of live-births there were substituted references to the Adopted Children Register.

(4) Subject to paragraph (7), where the precise date of the child's birth is not proved to the satisfaction of the court, the court will determine the probable date of birth.

(5) The probable date of the child's birth may be specified in the placement order, adoption order or section 84 order as the date of his birth.

(6) Subject to paragraph (7), where the child's place of birth cannot be proved to the satisfaction of the court –

   (a)   he may be treated as having been born in the registration district of the court where it is probable that the child may have been born in –

       (i)   the United Kingdom;

       (ii)   the Channel Islands; or

       (iii) the Isle of Man; or

   (b)   in any other case, the particulars of the country of birth may be omitted from the placement order, adoption order or section 84 order.

(7) A placement order identifying the probable date and place of birth of the child will be sufficient proof of the date and place of birth of the child in adoption proceedings and proceedings for a section 84 order.

****

PART 7

LITIGATION FRIEND, CHILDREN'S GUARDIAN, REPORTING OFFICER AND CHILDREN AND FAMILY REPORTER

Section 1 – Litigation Friend

49 Application of this Section

(1) This Section –

   (a)   contains special provisions which apply in proceedings involving non-subject children and protected parties; and

   (b)   sets out how a person becomes a litigation friend.

(2) The provisions of this Section also apply to a child who does not have a children's guardian, in which case, any reference to a 'non-subject child' in these Rules is to be taken as including a child.

50 Requirement for litigation friend in proceedings

(1) Subject to rule 51, a non-subject child must have a litigation friend to conduct proceedings on his behalf.

(2) A protected party must have a litigation friend to conduct proceedings on his behalf.

Amendment—SI 2007/2189.

51 Circumstances in which the non-subject child does not need a litigation friend

(1) A non-subject child may conduct proceedings without a litigation friend –

    (a)   where he has obtained the court's permission to do so; or
    (b)   where a solicitor –
        (i)   considers that the non-subject child is able, having regard to his understanding, to give instructions in relation to the proceedings; and
        (ii)   has accepted instructions from that child to act for him in the proceedings and, if the proceedings have begun, he is already acting.

(2) An application for permission under paragraph (1)(a) may be made by the non-subject child without notice.

(3) Where a non-subject child has a litigation friend in proceedings and he wishes to conduct the remaining stages of the proceedings without a litigation friend, the non-subject child may apply to the court, on notice to the litigation friend, for permission for that purpose and for the removal of the litigation friend.

(4) Where the court is considering whether to –

    (a)   grant permission under paragraph (1)(a); or
    (b)   grant permission under paragraph (3) and remove a litigation friend

it will grant the permission sought and, as the case may be, remove the litigation friend if it considers that the non-subject child concerned has sufficient understanding to conduct the proceedings concerned or proposed without a litigation friend.

(5) In exercising its powers under paragraph (4) the court may require the litigation friend to take such part in the proceedings as the court directs.

(6) The court may revoke any permission granted under paragraph (1)(a) where it considers that the non-subject child does not have sufficient understanding to participate as a party in the proceedings concerned without a litigation friend.

(7) Where a solicitor is acting for a non-subject child in proceedings without a litigation friend by virtue of paragraph (1)(b) and either of the conditions specified in paragraph (1)(b)(i) or (ii) cease to be fulfilled, he must inform the court immediately.

(8) Where –

    (a)   the court revokes any permission under paragraph (6); or
    (b)   either of the conditions specified in paragraph (1)(b)(i) or (ii) is no longer fulfilled

the court may, if it considers it necessary in order to protect the interests of the non-subject child concerned, appoint a person to be that child's litigation friend.

52 Stage of proceedings at which a litigation friend becomes necessary

(1) This rule does not apply where a non-subject child is conducting proceedings without a litigation friend in accordance with rule 51.

(2) A person may not without the permission of the court take any step in proceedings except –

    (a)   filing an application form; or
    (b)   applying for the appointment of a litigation friend under rule 55

until the non-subject child or protected party has a litigation friend.

(3) If during proceedings a party lacks capacity (within the meaning of the 2005 Act) to continue to conduct the proceedings, no party may take any step in proceedings without the permission of the court until the protected party has a litigation friend.

Amendments—SI 2007/2189.

53 Who may be a litigation friend for a protected party without a court order

(1) This rule does not apply if the court has appointed a person to be a litigation friend.

(2) A person with authority as a deputy to conduct the proceedings in the name of a protected party or on his behalf is entitled to be the litigation friend of the protected party in any proceedings to which his authority extends.

(3) If nobody has been appointed by the court or, in the case of a protected party, with authority as a deputy to conduct the proceedings in the name of a protected party or on his behalf, a person may act as a litigation friend if he –

   (a)   can fairly and competently conduct proceedings on behalf of the non-subject child or protected party;

   (b)   has no interest adverse to that of the non-subject child or protected party; and

   (c)   subject to paragraph (4), undertakes to pay any costs which the non-subject child or protected party may be ordered to pay in relation to the proceedings, subject to any right he may have to be repaid from the assets of the non-subject child or protected party.

(4) Paragraph (3)(c) does not apply to the Official Solicitor, an officer of the Service or a Welsh family proceedings officer.

Amendments—SI 2007/2189.

54 How a person becomes a litigation friend without a court order

(1) If the court has not appointed a litigation friend, a person who wishes to act as a litigation friend must follow the procedure set out in this rule.

(2) A person with authority as a deputy to conduct the proceedings in the name of a protected party or on his behalf must file an official copy of the order, declaration or other document which confers his authority to act.

(3) Any other person must file a certificate of suitability stating that he satisfies the conditions specified in rule 53(3).

(4) A person who is to act as a litigation friend must file –

   (a)   the document conferring his authority to act; or

   (b)   the certificate of suitability

at the time when he first takes a step in the proceedings on behalf of the non-subject child or protected party.

(5) A court officer will send the certificate of suitability to every person on whom, in accordance with rule 37(1) (service on parent, guardian etc), the application form should be served.

(6) This rule does not apply to the Official Solicitor, an officer of the Service or a Welsh family proceedings officer.

Amendments—SI 2007/2189.

55 How a person becomes a litigation friend by court order

(1) The court may make an order appointing –

   (a)   the Official Solicitor if he consents;

(b)   in the case of a non-subject child, an officer of the Service or a Welsh family proceedings officer (if he consents); or

(c)   some other person (if he consents)

as a litigation friend.

(2) An order appointing a litigation friend may be made by the court of its own initiative or on the application of –

(a)   a person who wishes to be a litigation friend; or

(b)   a party to the proceedings.

(3) The court may at any time direct that a party make an application for an order under paragraph (2).

(4) An application for an order appointing a litigation friend must be supported by evidence.

(5) Unless the court directs otherwise, a person appointed under this rule to be a litigation friend for a non-subject child or protected party will be treated as a party for the purpose of any provision in these Rules requiring a document to be served on, or sent to, or notice to be given to, a party to the proceedings.

(6) Subject to rule 53(4), the court may not appoint a litigation friend under this rule unless it is satisfied that the person to be appointed complies with the conditions specified in rule 53(3).

Amendment—SI 2007/2189; SI 2008/2447.

56 Court's power to change litigation friend and to prevent person acting as litigation friend

(1) The court may –

(a)   direct that a person may not act as a litigation friend;

(b)   terminate a litigation friend's appointment; or

(c)   appoint a new litigation friend in substitution for an existing one.

(2) An application for an order under paragraph (1) must be supported by evidence.

(3) Subject to rule 53(4), the court may not appoint a litigation friend under this rule unless it is satisfied that the person to be appointed complies with the conditions specified in rule 53(3).

57 Appointment of litigation friend by court order–supplementary

(1) A copy of the application for an order under rule 55 or 56 must be sent by a court officer to every person on whom, in accordance with rule 37(1) (service on parent, guardian etc), the application form should be served.

(2) Where an application for an order under rule 55 is in respect of a protected party, the court officer must also send a copy of the application to the protected party unless the court directs otherwise.

(3) A copy of an application for an order under rule 56 must also be sent to –

(a)   the person who is the litigation friend, or who is purporting to act as the litigation friend, when the application is made; and

(b)   the person who it is proposed should be the litigation friend, if he is not the applicant.

Amendments—SI 2007/2189.

58 Procedure where appointment of litigation friend comes to an end

(1) When a non-subject child who is not a protected party reaches the age of 18, a litigation friend's appointment comes to an end.

(2) When a party ceases to be a protected party, the litigation friend's appointment continues until it is brought to an end by a court order.

(3) An application for an order under paragraph (2) may be made by –

(a)   the former protected party;
(b)   the litigation friend; or
(c)   a party.

(4) A court officer will send a notice to the other parties stating that the appointment of the non-subject child or protected party's litigation friend to act has ended.

Amendments—SI 2007/2189.

Section 2 – Children's Guardian

59 Appointment of children's guardian

(1) In proceedings to which Part 5 applies, the court will appoint a children's guardian where the child is a party to the proceedings unless it is satisfied that it is not necessary to do so to safeguard the interests of the child.

(2) At any stage in proceedings where the child is a party to the proceedings –

(a)   a party may apply, without notice to the other parties unless the court directs otherwise, for the appointment of a children's guardian; or
(b)   the court may of its own initiative appoint a children's guardian.

(3) The court will grant an application under paragraph (2)(a) unless it considers that such an appointment is not necessary to safeguard the interests of the child.

(4) When appointing a children's guardian the court will consider the appointment of anyone who has previously acted as a children's guardian of the same child.

60 What the court or a court officer will do once the court has made a decision about appointing a children's guardian

(1) Where the court refuses an application under rule 59(2)(a) it will give reasons for the refusal and the court or a court officer will –

(a)   record the refusal and the reasons for it; and
(b)   as soon as practicable, notify the parties and either the Service or the Assembly of a decision not to appoint a children's guardian.

(2) Where the court appoints a children's guardian under rule 59 a court officer will record the appointment and, as soon as practicable, will –

(a)   inform the parties and either the Service or the Assembly; and
(b)   unless it has already been sent, send the children's guardian a copy of the application and copies of any document filed with the court in the proceedings.

(3) A court officer also has a continuing duty to send the children's guardian a copy of any other document filed with the court during the course of the proceedings.

61 Termination of the appointment of the children's guardian

(1) The appointment of a children's guardian under rule 59 continues for such time as is specified in the appointment or until terminated by the court.

(2) When terminating an appointment in accordance with paragraph (1), the court will give reasons for doing so, a note of which will be taken by the court or a court officer.

62 Powers and duties of the children's guardian

(1) The children's guardian is to act on behalf of the child upon the hearing of any application in proceedings to which Part 5 applies with the duty of safeguarding the interests of the child.

(2) The children's guardian must also provide the court with such other assistance as it may require.

63 How the children's guardian exercises his duties –investigations and appointment of solicitor

(1) The children's guardian must make such investigations as are necessary for him to carry out his duties and must, in particular –

    (a)   contact or seek to interview such persons as he thinks appropriate or as the court directs; and

    (b)   obtain such professional assistance as is available to him which he thinks appropriate or which the court directs him to obtain.

(2) The children's guardian must –

    (a)   appoint a solicitor for the child unless a solicitor has already been appointed;

    (b)   give such advice to the child as is appropriate having regard to his understanding; and

    (c)   where appropriate instruct the solicitor representing the child on all matters relevant to the interests of the child, including possibilities for appeal, arising in the course of proceedings.

(3) Where the children's guardian is authorised in the terms mentioned by and in accordance with section 15(1) of the Criminal Justice and Court Services Act 2000 or section 37(1) of the Children Act 2004 (right of officer of the Service or Welsh family proceedings officer to conduct litigation or exercise a right of audience), paragraph (2)(a) will not apply if he intends to have conduct of the proceedings on behalf of the child unless –

    (a)   the child wishes to instruct a solicitor direct; and

    (b)   the children's guardian or the court considers that he is of sufficient understanding to do so.

64 Where the child instructs a solicitor or conducts proceedings on his own behalf

(1) Where it appears to the children's guardian that the child –

    (a)   is instructing his solicitor direct; or

    (b)   intends to conduct and is capable of conducting the proceedings on his own behalf

he must inform the court of that fact.

(2) Where paragraph (1) applies, the children's guardian –

    (a)   must perform the duties set out in rules 62, 63, 65 to 67 and this rule, other than those duties in rule 63(2)(a) and (c), and such other duties as the court may direct;

    (b)   must take such part in the proceedings as the court may direct; and

    (c)   may, with the permission of the court, have legal representation in the conduct of those duties.

65 How the children's guardian exercises his duties–attendance at court, advice to the court and reports

(1) The children's guardian or the solicitor appointed under section 41(3) of the 1989 Act or in accordance with rule 63(2)(a) must attend all directions hearings unless the court directs otherwise.

(2) The children's guardian must advise the court on the following matters –

    (a)   whether the child is of sufficient understanding for any purpose including the child's refusal to submit to a medical or psychiatric examination or other assessment that the court has the power to require, direct or order;

    (b)   the wishes of the child in respect of any matter relevant to the proceedings including his attendance at court;

    (c)   the appropriate forum for the proceedings;

    (d)   the appropriate timing of the proceedings or any part of them;

(e)   the options available to it in respect of the child and the suitability of each such option including what order should be made in determining the application; and

(f)   any other matter on which the court seeks his advice or on which he considers that the court should be informed.

(3) The advice given under paragraph (2) may, subject to any direction of the court, be given orally or in writing.

(4) The children's guardian must –

(a)   unless the court directs otherwise, file a written report advising on the interests of the child in accordance with the timetable set by the court; and

(b)   where practicable, notify any person the joining of whom as a party to those proceedings would be likely, in his opinion, to safeguard the interests of the child, of the court's power to join that person as a party under rule 23 and must inform the court –

(i)   of any notification;

(ii)   of anyone whom he attempted to notify under this paragraph but was unable to contact; and

(iii)   of anyone whom he believes may wish to be joined to the proceedings.

(5) Any report to the court under this rule will be confidential.

(Part 9 sets out the procedure for making an application to be joined as a party in proceedings.)

66 How the children's guardian exercises his duties – service of documents and inspection of records

(1) The children's guardian must –

(a)   serve documents on behalf of the child in accordance with rule 37(2)(b); and

(b)   accept service of documents on behalf of the child in accordance with the table in rule 37(1),

and, where the child has not himself been served and has sufficient understanding, advise the child of the contents of any document so served.

(2) Where the children's guardian inspects records of the kinds referred to in –

(a)   section 42 of the 1989 Act (right to have access to local authority records); or

(b)   section 103 (right to have access to adoption agency records)

he must bring all records and documents which may, in his opinion, assist in the proper determination of the proceedings to the attention of –

(i)   the court; and

(ii)   unless the court directs otherwise, the other parties to the proceedings.

67 How the children's guardian exercises his duties – communication of a court's decision to the child

The children's guardian must ensure that, in relation to a decision made by the court in the proceedings –

(a)   if he considers it appropriate to the age and understanding of the child, the child is notified of that decision; and

(b)   if the child is notified of the decision, it is explained to the child in a manner appropriate to his age and understanding.

68 Solicitor for child

(1) A solicitor appointed under section 41(3) of the 1989 Act or in accordance with rule 63(2)(a) must represent the child –

(a) in accordance with instructions received from the children's guardian unless the solicitor considers, having taken into account the views of the children's guardian and any direction of the court under rule 64(2) –

    (i) that the child wishes to give instructions which conflict with those of the children's guardian; and

    (ii) that he is able, having regard to his understanding, to give such instructions on his own behalf,

    in which case the solicitor must conduct the proceedings in accordance with instructions received from the child;

(b) where no children's guardian has been appointed and the condition in section 41(4)(b) of the 1989 Act is satisfied, in accordance with instructions received from the child; or

(c) in default of instructions under sub-paragraph (a) or (b), in furtherance of the best interests of the child.

(2) A solicitor appointed under section 41(3) of the 1989 Act or in accordance with rule 63(2)(a) must –

(a) serve documents on behalf of the child in accordance with rule 37(2)(a); and

(b) accept service of documents on behalf of the child in accordance with the table in rule 37(1),

and, where the child has not himself been served and has sufficient understanding, advise the child of the contents of any document so served.

(3) Where the child wishes an appointment of a solicitor under section 41(3) of the 1989 Act or in accordance with rule 63(2)(a) to be terminated –

(a) he may apply to the court for an order terminating the appointment; and

(b) the solicitor and the children's guardian will be given an opportunity to make representations.

(4) Where the children's guardian wishes an appointment of a solicitor under section 41(3) of the 1989 Act or in accordance with rule 63(2)(a) to be terminated –

(a) he may apply to the court for an order terminating the appointment; and

(b) the solicitor and, if he is of sufficient understanding, the child, will be given an opportunity to make representations.

(5) When terminating an appointment in accordance with paragraph (3) or (4), the court will give its reasons for so doing, a note of which will be taken by the court or a court officer.

(6) The court or a court officer will record the appointment under section 41(3) of the 1989 Act or in accordance with rule 63(2)(a) or the refusal to make the appointment.

Section 3 – Reporting Officer

69 When the court appoints a reporting officer

In proceedings to which Part 5 applies, the court will appoint a reporting officer where –

(a) it appears that a parent or guardian of the child is willing to consent to the placing of the child for adoption, to the making of an adoption order or to a section 84 order; and

(b) that parent or guardian is in England or Wales.

70 Appointment of the same reporting officer in respect of two or more parents or guardians

The same person may be appointed as the reporting officer for two or more parents or guardians of the child.

71 The duties of the reporting officer

The reporting officer must witness the signature by a parent or guardian on the document in which consent is given to –

(a)   the placing of the child for adoption;
(b)   the making of an adoption order; or
(c)   the making of a section 84 order.

72 How the reporting officer exercises his duties

(1) The reporting officer must –

(a)   ensure so far as reasonably practicable that the parent or guardian is –
  (i)   giving consent unconditionally; and
  (ii)   with full understanding of what is involved;
(b)   investigate all the circumstances relevant to a parent's or guardian's consent to the placing of the child for adoption or to the making of an adoption order or a section 84 order; and
(c)   on completing his investigations the reporting officer must –
  (i)   make a report in writing to the court in accordance with the timetable set by the court, drawing attention to any matters which, in his opinion, may be of assistance to the court in considering the application; or
  (ii)   make an interim report to the court if a parent or guardian of the child is unwilling to consent to the placing of the child for adoption or to the making of an adoption order or section 84 order.

(2) On receipt of an interim report under paragraph (1)(c)(ii) a court officer must inform the applicant that a parent or guardian of the child is unwilling to consent to the placing of the child for adoption or to the making of an adoption order or section 84 order.

(3) The reporting officer may at any time before the final hearing make an interim report to the court if he considers necessary and ask the court for directions.

(4) The reporting officer must attend all directions hearings unless the court directs otherwise.

(5) Any report to the court under this rule will be confidential.

Section 4 – Children and Family Reporter

73 Request by court for a welfare report in respect of the child

(1) In proceedings to which Part 5 applies, where the court is considering an application for an order in proceedings the court may ask a children and family reporter to prepare a report on matters relating to the welfare of the child.

(2) It is the duty of a children and family reporter to –

(a)   comply with any request for a report under this rule; and
(b)   provide the court with such other assistance as it may require.

(3) Any report to the court under this rule will be confidential.

74 How the children and family reporter exercises his powers and duties

(1) The children and family reporter must make such investigations as may be necessary for him to perform his powers and duties and must, in particular –

(a)   contact or seek to interview such persons as he thinks appropriate or as the court directs; and
(b)   obtain such professional assistance as is available to him which he thinks appropriate or which the court directs him to obtain.

(2) The children and family reporter must –

(a)   notify the child of such contents of his report (if any) as he considers appropriate to the age and understanding of the child, including any reference to the child's own views on the application and his recommendation; and

(b)   if he does notify the child of any contents of his report, explain them to the child in a manner appropriate to his age and understanding.

(3) The children and family reporter must –

(a)   attend all directions hearings unless the court directs otherwise;
(b)   advise the court of the child's wishes and feelings;
(c)   advise the court if he considers that the joining of a person as a party to the proceedings would be likely to safeguard the interests of the child;
(d)   consider whether it is in the best interests of the child for the child to be made a party to the proceedings, and if so, notify the court of his opinion together with the reasons for that opinion; and
(e)   where the court has directed that a written report be made, file the report in accordance with the timetable set by the court.

****

PART 8
DOCUMENTS AND DISCLOSURE OF DOCUMENTS AND INFORMATION

77 Confidential reports to the court and disclosure to the parties

(1) The court will consider whether to give a direction that a confidential report be disclosed to each party to the proceedings.

(2) Before giving such a direction the court will consider whether any information should be deleted including information which –

(a)   discloses, or is likely to disclose, the identity of a person who has been assigned a serial number under rule 20(2); or
(b)   discloses the particulars referred to in rule 21(1) where a party has given notice under rule 21(2) (disclosure of personal details).

(3) The court may direct that the report will not be disclosed to a party.

78 Communication of information relating to proceedings

(1) For the purposes of the law relating to contempt of court, information (whether or not it is recorded in any form) relating to proceedings held in private may be communicated –

(a)   where the court gives permission;
(b)   unless the court directs otherwise, in accordance with the relevant practice direction; or
(c)   where the communication is to –
    (i)   a party;
    (ii)   the legal representative of a party;
    (iii)   a professional legal adviser;
    (iv)   an officer of the Service or a Welsh family proceedings officer;
    (v)   a welfare officer;
    (vi)   the Legal Services Commission;
    (vii)   an expert whose instruction by a party has been authorised by the court; or
    (viii) a professional acting in furtherance of the protection of children.

(2) In this rule –

'professional acting in furtherance of the protection of children' includes –
    (a)   an officer of a local authority exercising child protection functions;
    (b)   a police officer who is –
        (i)   exercising powers under section 46 of the 1989 Act; or
        (ii)   serving in a child protection unit or a paedophile unit of a police force;
    (c)   any professional person attending a child protection conference or review in relation to a child who is the subject of the proceedings to which the information relates; or

(d)   an officer of the National Society for the Prevention of Cruelty to Children;

'professional legal adviser' means a barrister or a solicitor, solicitor's employee or other authorised litigator (as defined in section 119 of the Courts and Legal Services Act 1990) who is providing advice to a party but is not instructed to represent that party in the proceedings;

'welfare officer' means a person who has been asked to prepare a report under section 7(1)(b) of the 1989 Act.

79 Orders for disclosure against a person not a party

(1) This rule applies where an application is made to the court under any Act for disclosure by a person who is not a party to the proceedings.

(2) The application must be supported by evidence.

(3) The court may make an order under this rule only where –

(a)   the documents of which disclosure is sought are likely to support the case of the applicant or adversely affect the case of one of the other parties to the proceedings; and

(b)   disclosure is necessary in order to dispose fairly of the application or to save costs.

(4) An order under this rule must –

(a)   specify the documents or the classes of documents which the respondent must disclose; and

(b)   require the respondent, when making disclosure, to specify any of those documents –
(i)   which are no longer in his control; or
(ii)   in respect of which he claims a right or duty to withhold inspection.

(5) Such an order may –

(a)   require the respondent to indicate what has happened to any documents which are no longer in his control; and

(b)   specify the time and place for disclosure and inspection.

(6) This rule does not apply to proceedings in a magistrates' court.

80 Rules not to limit other powers of the court to order disclosure

(1) Rule 79 does not limit any other power which the court may have to order –

(a)   disclosure before proceedings have started; and
(b)   disclosure against a person who is not a party to proceedings.

(2) This rule does not apply to proceedings in a magistrates' court.

81 Claim to withhold inspection or disclosure of a document

(1) A person may apply, without notice, for an order permitting him to withhold disclosure of a document on the ground that disclosure would damage the public interest.

(2) Unless the court orders otherwise, an order of the court under paragraph (1) –

(a)   must not be served on any other person; and
(b)   must not be open to inspection by any person.

(3) A person who wishes to claim that he has a right or a duty to withhold inspection of a document, or part of a document, must state in writing –

(a)   that he has such a right or duty; and
(b)   the grounds on which he claims that right or duty.

(4) The statement referred to in paragraph (3) must be made to the person wishing to inspect the document.

(5) A party may apply to the court to decide whether a claim made under paragraph (3) should be upheld.

(6) For the purpose of deciding an application under paragraph (1) (application to withhold disclosure) or paragraph (3) (claim to withhold inspection) the court may –

(a) require the person seeking to withhold disclosure or inspection of a document to produce that document to the court; and

(b) invite any person, whether or not a party, to make representations.

(7) An application under paragraph (1) or (5) must be supported by evidence.

(8) This rule does not affect any rule of law which permits or requires a document to be withheld from disclosure or inspection on the ground that its disclosure or inspection would damage the public interest.

(9) This rule does not apply to proceedings in a magistrates' court.

****

PART 9
PROCEDURE FOR OTHER APPLICATIONS IN PROCEEDINGS

86 Types of application for which Part 9 procedure may be followed

(1) The Part 9 procedure is the procedure set out in this Part.

(2) An applicant may use the Part 9 procedure if the application is made –

(a) in the course of existing proceedings;

(b) to commence proceedings other than those to which Part 5 applies; or

(c) in connection with proceedings which have been concluded.

(Rule 22 lists the proceedings to which Part 5 applies.)

(3) Paragraph (2) does not apply –

(a) to applications made in accordance with –

(i) section 60(3) (order to prevent disclosure of information to an adopted person);

(ii) section 79(4) (order for Registrar General to give any information referred to in section 79(3));

(iii) rule 27 (request to dispense with consent);

(iv) rule 59(2) (appointment of children's guardian);

(v) rule 84 (disclosure of information to adopted adult);

(vi) rule 106 (withdrawal of application); or

(vii) rule 107 (recovery orders); or

(b) if a practice direction provides that the Part 9 procedure may not be used in relation to the type of application in question.

(4) The following persons are to be respondents to an application under this Part –

(a) where there are existing proceedings or the proceedings have concluded, the parties to those proceedings;

(b) where there are no existing proceedings –

(i) if notice has been given under section 44 (notice of intention to adopt or apply for a section 84 order), the local authority to whom notice has been given; and

(ii) if an application is made in accordance with –

(aa) section 26(3)(f) (permission to apply for contact order); or

(bb) section 42(6) (permission to apply for adoption order),

any person who, in accordance with rule 23, will be a party to the proceedings brought if permission is granted; and

(c) any other person as the court may direct.

87 Application notice to be filed

(1) Subject to paragraph (2), the applicant must file an application notice.

(2) An applicant may make an application without filing an application notice if –

    (a)   this is permitted by a rule or practice direction; or

    (b)   the court dispenses with the requirement for an application notice.

88 Notice of an application

(1) Subject to paragraph (2), a copy of the application notice will be served on each respondent.

(2) An application may be made without serving a copy of the application notice if this is permitted by –

    (a)   a rule;

    (b)   a practice direction; or

    (c)   the court.

(Rule 91 deals with service of a copy of the application notice.)

89 Time when an application is made

Where an application must be made within a specified time, it is so made if the court receives the application notice within that time.

90 What an application notice must include

(1) An application notice must state –

    (a)   what order the applicant is seeking; and

    (b)   briefly, why the applicant is seeking the order.

(2) The applicant may rely on the matters set out in his application notice as evidence if the application is verified by a statement of truth.

91 Service of a copy of an application notice

(1) A court officer will serve a copy of the application notice –

    (a)   as soon as practicable after it is filed; and

    (b)   in any event at least 7 days before the court is to deal with the application.

(2) The applicant must, when he files the application notice, file a copy of any written evidence in support.

(3) When a copy of an application notice is served by a court officer it will be accompanied by –

    (a)   a notice of the date and place where the application will be heard;

    (b)   a copy of any witness statement in support; and

    (c)   a copy of any draft order which the applicant has attached to his application.

(4) If –

    (a)   an application notice is served; but

    (b)   the period of notice is shorter than the period required by these Rules or a practice direction,

the court may direct that, in the circumstances of the case, sufficient notice has been given and hear the application.

(5) This rule does not require written evidence –

    (a)   to be filed if it has already been filed; or

    (b)   to be served on a party on whom it has already been served.

92 Applications which may be dealt with without a hearing

The court may deal with an application without a hearing if –

(a)   the parties agree as to the terms of the order sought;
(b)   the parties agree that the court should dispose of the application without a hearing; or
(c)   the court does not consider that a hearing would be appropriate.

93 Service of application where application made without notice

(1) This rule applies where the court has disposed of an application which it permitted to be made without service of a copy of the application notice.

(2) Where the court makes an order, whether granting or dismissing the application, a copy of the application notice and any evidence in support will, unless the court directs otherwise, be served with the order on all the parties in the proceedings.

(3) The order must contain a statement of the right to make an application to set aside or vary the order under rule 94.

94 Application to set aside or vary order made without notice

(1) A person who was not served with a copy of the application notice before an order was made under rule 93 may apply to have the order set aside or varied.

(2) An application under this rule must be made within 7 days beginning with the date on which the order was served on the person making the application.

95 Power of the court to proceed in the absence of a party

(1) Where the applicant or any respondent fails to attend the hearing of an application, the court may proceed in his absence.

(2) Where –

(a)   the applicant or any respondent fails to attend the hearing of an application; and
(b)   the court makes an order at the hearing,

the court may, on application or of its own initiative, re-list the application.

(3) Paragraph (2) of this rule does not apply to magistrates' courts.

Amendment—SI 2008/2447; SI 2009/638.

96 Dismissal of totally without merit applications

If the High Court or a county court dismisses an application (including an application for permission to appeal) and it considers that the application is totally without merit –

(a)   the court's order must record that fact; and
(b)   the court must at the same time consider whether it is appropriate to make a civil restraint order.

PART 10
ALTERNATIVE PROCEDURE FOR APPLICATIONS

97 Types of application for which Part 10 procedure may be followed

(1) The Part 10 procedure is the procedure set out in this Part.

(2) An applicant may use the Part 10 procedure where the procedure set out in Part 9 does not apply and –

(a)   there is no form prescribed by a rule or practice direction in which to make the application;

(b)   he seeks the court's decision on a question which is unlikely to involve a substantial dispute of fact; or

(c)   paragraph (5) applies.

(3) The court may at any stage direct that the application is to continue as if the applicant had not used the Part 10 procedure and, if it does so, the court may give any directions it considers appropriate.

(4) Paragraph (2) does not apply –

(a)   to applications made in accordance with –
    (i)   rule 27 (request to dispense with consent);
    (ii)   rule 59(2) (appointment of children's guardian);
    (iii)   rule 84 (disclosure of information to adopted adult);
    (iv)   rule 106 (withdrawal of application); or
    (v)   rule 107 (recovery orders); or

(b)   if a practice direction provides that the Part 10 procedure may not be used in relation to the type of application in question.

(5) A rule or practice direction may, in relation to a specified type of proceedings –

(a)   require or permit the use of the Part 10 procedure; and

(b)   disapply or modify any of the rules set out in this Part as they apply to those proceedings.

98 Contents of the application

(1) In this Part 'application' means an application made under this Part.

(2) Where the applicant uses the Part 10 procedure the application must state –

(a)   that this Part applies;

(b) –
    (i)   the question which the applicant wants the court to decide; or
    (ii)   the order which the applicant is seeking and the legal basis of the application for that order;

(c)   if the application is being made under an enactment, what that enactment is;

(d)   if the applicant is applying in a representative capacity, what that capacity is; and

(e)   if the respondent appears or is to appear in a representative capacity, what that capacity is.

(3) A court officer will serve a copy of the application on the respondent.

99 Issue of application without naming respondents

(1) A practice direction may set out circumstances in which an application may be issued under this Part without naming a respondent.

(2) The practice direction may set out those cases in which an application for permission must be made before the application is issued.

(3) The application for permission –

(a)   need not be served on any other person; and

(b)   must be accompanied by a copy of the application that the applicant proposes to issue.

(4) Where the court gives permission it will give directions about the future management of the application.

100 Acknowledgement of service

(1) Subject to paragraph (2), each respondent must file an acknowledgement of service within 14 days beginning with the date on which the application is served.

(2) If the application is to be served out of the jurisdiction the respondent must file an acknowledgement of service within the period set out in the practice direction supplementing Part 6, section 2.

(3) A court officer will serve the acknowledgement of service on the applicant and any other party.

(4) The acknowledgement of service must –

    (a)   state whether the respondent contests the application;

    (b)   state, if the respondent seeks a different order from that set out in the application, what that order is; and

    (c)   be signed by the respondent or his legal representative.

101 Consequence of not filing an acknowledgement of service

(1) This rule applies where –

    (a)   the respondent has failed to file an acknowledgement of service; and

    (b)   the time period for doing so has expired.

(2) The respondent must attend the hearing of the application but may not take part in the hearing unless the court gives permission.

102 Filing and serving written evidence

(1) The applicant must file written evidence on which he intends to rely when he files his application.

(2) A court officer will serve the applicant's evidence on the respondent with the application.

(3) A respondent who wishes to rely on written evidence must file it when he files his acknowledgement of service.

(4) A court officer will serve the respondent's evidence, if any, on the other parties with the acknowledgement of service.

(5) The applicant may, within 14 days beginning with the date on which a respondent's evidence was served on him, file further written evidence in reply.

(6) If he does so, a court officer will serve a copy of that evidence on the other parties.

(7) The applicant may rely on the matters set out in his application as evidence under this rule if the application is verified by a statement of truth.

103 Evidence – general

(1) No written evidence may be relied on at the hearing of the application unless –

    (a)   it has been served in accordance with rule 102; or

    (b)   the court gives permission.

(2) The court may require or permit a party to give oral evidence at the hearing.

(3) The court may give directions requiring the attendance for cross-examination of a witness who has given written evidence.

104 Procedure where respondent objects to use of the Part 10 procedure

(1) Where a respondent contends that the Part 10 procedure should not be used because –

(a)   there is a substantial dispute of fact; and
(b)   the use of the Part 10 procedure is not required or permitted by a rule or practice direction,

he must state his reasons when he files his acknowledgement of service.

(2) When the court receives the acknowledgement of service and any written evidence it will give directions as to the future management of the case.

105 Applications under section 60(3) and 79(4) or rule 108

(1) The Part 10 procedure must be used in an application made in accordance with –

(a)   section 60(3) (order to prevent disclosure of information to an adopted person);
(b)   section 79(4) (order for Registrar General to give any information referred to in section 79(3)); and
(c)   rule 108 (directions of High Court regarding fathers without parental responsibility).

(2) The respondent to an application made in accordance with paragraph (1)(b) is the Registrar General.

PART 11
MISCELLANEOUS

106 Withdrawal of application

(1) An application may be withdrawn with the permission of the court.

(2) Subject to paragraph (3), a person seeking permission to withdraw an application must file a written request for permission setting out the reasons for the request.

(3) The request under paragraph (2) may be made orally to the court if the parties and any children's guardian, reporting officer or children and family reporter are present.

(4) A court officer will notify the other parties and any children's guardian, reporting officer or children and family reporter of a written request.

(5) The court may deal with a written request under paragraph (2) without a hearing if the other parties and any children's guardian, reporting officer or children and family reporter have had an opportunity to make written representations to the court about the request.

*****

PART 13
HUMAN RIGHTS

116 Human Rights Act 1998

(1) A party who seeks to rely on any provision of or right arising under the Human Rights Act 1998 or seeks a remedy available under that Act must inform the court in his application or otherwise in writing specifying –

(a)   the Convention right which it is alleged has been infringed and details of the alleged infringement; and
(b)   the relief sought and whether this includes a declaration of incompatibility.

(2) The High Court may not make a declaration of incompatibility unless 21 days' notice, or such other period of notice as the court directs, has been given to the Crown.

(3) Where notice has been given to the Crown, a Minister, or other person permitted by that Act, will be joined as a party on giving notice to the court.

(4) Where a claim is made under section 7(1) of the Human Rights Act 1998 (claim that public authority acted unlawfully) in respect of a judicial act –

(a) that claim must be set out in the application form or the appeal notice; and
(b) notice must be given to the Crown.

(5) Where paragraph (4) applies and the appropriate person (as defined in section 9(5) of the Human Rights Act 1998) has not applied within 21 days, or such other period as the court directs, beginning with the date on which the notice to be joined as a party was served, the court may join the appropriate person as a party.

(6) On any application concerning a committal order, if the court ordering the release of the person concludes that his Convention rights have been infringed by the making of the order to which the application or appeal relates, the judgment or order should so state, but if the court does not do so, that failure will not prevent another court from deciding the matter.

(7) Where by reason of a rule, practice direction or court order the Crown is permitted or required –

(a) to make a witness statement;
(b) to swear an affidavit;
(c) to verify a document by a statement of truth; or
(d) to discharge any other procedural obligation,

that function will be performed by an appropriate officer acting on behalf of the Crown, and the court may if necessary nominate an appropriate officer.

(8) In this rule –

'Convention right' has the same meaning as in the Human Rights Act 1998; and
'declaration of incompatibility' means a declaration of incompatibility under section 4 of the Human Rights Act 1998.

(A practice direction makes provision for the notices mentioned in this rule.)
****

PART 15
ADMISSIONS AND EVIDENCE

122 Making an admission

(1) A party may admit the truth of the whole or any part of another party's case by giving notice in writing.

(2) The court may allow a party to amend or withdraw an admission.

123 Power of court to control evidence

(1) The court may control the evidence by giving directions as to –

(a) the issues on which it requires evidence;
(b) the nature of the evidence which it requires to decide those issues; and
(c) the way in which the evidence is to be placed before the court.

(2) The court may use its power under this rule to exclude evidence that would otherwise be admissible.

(3) The court may limit cross-examination.

124 Evidence of witnesses – general rule

(1) The general rule is that any fact which needs to be proved by the evidence of witnesses is to be proved –

(a)   at final hearing, by their oral evidence; and
(b)   at any other hearing, by their evidence in writing.

(2) This is subject –

(a)   to any provision to the contrary contained in these Rules or elsewhere; or
(b)   to any order of the court.

125 Evidence by video link or other means

The court may allow a witness to give evidence through a video link or by other means.

126 Service of witness statements for use at final hearing

(1) A witness statement is a written statement signed by a person which contains the evidence which that person would be allowed to give orally.

(2) The court will give directions about the service of any witness statement of the oral evidence which a party intends to rely on in relation to any issues of fact to be decided at the final hearing on the other parties.

(3) The court may give directions as to –

(a)   the order in which witness statements are to be served; and
(b)   whether or not the witness statements are to be filed.

127 Use at final hearing of witness statements which have been served

(1) If –

(a)   a party has filed a witness statement which has been served on the other parties; and
(b)   he wishes to rely at the final hearing on the evidence of the witness who made the statement,

he must call the witness to give oral evidence unless the court directs otherwise or he puts the statement in as hearsay evidence.

(2) Where a witness is called to give oral evidence under paragraph (1), his witness statement shall stand as his evidence in chief unless the court directs otherwise.

(3) A witness giving oral evidence at final hearing may with the permission of the court –

(a)   amplify his witness statement; and
(b)   give evidence in relation to new matters which have arisen since the witness statement was served on the other parties.

(4) The court will give permission under paragraph (3) only if it considers that there is good reason not to confine the evidence of the witness to the contents of his witness statement.

(5) If a party who has filed a witness statement which has been served on the other parties does not –

(a)   call the witness to give evidence at final hearing; or
(b)   put the witness statement in as hearsay evidence, any other party may put the witness statement in as hearsay evidence.

128 Evidence in proceedings other than at final hearing

(1) Subject to paragraph (2), the general rule is that evidence at hearings other than the final hearing is to be by witness statement unless the court, a practice direction or any other enactment requires otherwise.

(2) At hearings other than the final hearing, a party may, rely on the matters set out in –

(a)   his application form; or

(b)   his application notice, if it is verified by a statement of truth.

129 Order for cross-examination

(1) Where, at a hearing other than the final hearing, evidence is given in writing, any party may apply to the court for permission to cross-examine the person giving the evidence.

(2) If the court gives permission under paragraph (1) but the person in question does not attend as required by the order, his evidence may not be used unless the court gives permission.

130 Form of witness statement

A witness statement must comply with the requirements set out in the relevant practice direction.

131 Witness summaries

(1) A party who –

(a)   is required to file a witness statement for use at final hearing; but
(b)   is unable to obtain one, may apply, without notice, for permission to file a witness summary instead.

(2) A witness summary is a summary of –

(a)   the evidence, if known, which would otherwise be included in a witness statement; or
(b)   if the evidence is not known, the matters about which the party filing the witness summary proposes to question the witness.

(3) Unless the court directs otherwise, a witness summary must include the name and address of the intended witness.

(4) Unless the court directs otherwise, a witness summary must be filed within the period in which a witness statement would have had to be filed.

(5) Where a party files a witness summary, so far as practicable, rules 126 (service of witness statements for use at final hearing), 127(3) (amplifying witness statements), and 130 (form of witness statement) shall apply to the summary.

132 Cross-examination on a witness statement

Where a witness is called to give evidence at final hearing, he may be cross-examined on his witness statement whether or not the statement or any part of it was referred to during the witness's evidence in chief.

133 False statements

(1) Proceedings for contempt of court may be brought against a person if he makes, or causes to be made, a false statement in a document verified by a statement of truth without an honest belief in its truth.

(2) Proceedings under this rule may be brought only –

(a)   by the Attorney General; or
(b)   with the permission of the court.

(3) This rule does not apply to proceedings in a magistrates' court.

****

PART 17
EXPERTS

154 Duty to restrict expert evidence

Expert evidence shall be restricted to that which is reasonably required to resolve the proceedings.

155 Interpretation

A reference to an 'expert' in this Part –

(a)   is a reference to an expert who has been instructed to give or prepare evidence for the purpose of court proceedings; and

(b)   does not include –

  (i)   a person who is within a prescribed description for the purposes of section 94(1) of the Act (persons who may prepare a report for any person about the suitability of a child for adoption or of a person to adopt a child or about the adoption, or placement for adoption, of a child); or

  (ii)   an officer of the Service or a Welsh family proceedings officer when acting in that capacity.

(Regulation 3 of the Restriction on the Preparation of Adoption Reports Regulations 2005 (SI 2005/1711) sets out which persons are within a prescribed description for the purposes of section 94(1) of the Act.)

156 Experts – overriding duty to the court

(1) It is the duty of an expert to help the court on the matters within his expertise.

(2) This duty overrides any obligation to the person from whom he has received instructions or by whom he is paid.

157 Court's power to restrict expert evidence

(1) No party may call an expert or put in evidence an expert's report without the court's permission.

(2) When a party applies for permission under this rule he must identify –

(a)   the field in which he wishes to rely on expert evidence; and

(b)   where practicable the expert in that field on whose evidence he wishes to rely.

(3) If permission is granted under this rule it shall be in relation only to the expert named or the field identified under paragraph (2).

(4) The court may limit the amount of the expert's fees and expenses that the party who wishes to rely on the expert may recover from any other party.

158 General requirement for expert evidence to be given in a written report

Expert evidence is to be given in a written report unless the court directs otherwise.

159 Written questions to experts

(1) A party may put to –

(a)   an expert instructed by another party; or

(b)   a single joint expert appointed under rule 160,

written questions about his report.

(2) Written questions under paragraph (1) –

(a)   may be put once only;

(b)   must be put within 5 days beginning with the date on which the expert's report was served; and

(c)   must be for the purpose only of clarification of the report,

unless in any case –

    (i)   the court gives permission;

    (ii)   the other party agrees; or

    (iii)   any practice direction provides otherwise.

(3) An expert's answers to questions put in accordance with paragraph (1) shall be treated as part of the expert's report.

(4) Where –

(a)   a party has put a written question to an expert instructed by another party in accordance with this rule; and

(b)   the expert does not answer that question,

the court may make one or both of the following orders in relation to the party who instructed the expert –

    (i)   that the party may not rely on the evidence of that expert; or

    (ii)   that the party may not recover the fees and expenses of that expert from any other party.

160 Court's power to direct that evidence is to be given by a single joint expert

(1) Where two or more parties wish to submit expert evidence on a particular issue, the court may direct that the evidence on that issue is to given by one expert only.

(2) The parties wishing to submit the expert evidence are called 'the instructing parties'.

(3) Where the instructing parties cannot agree who should be the expert, the court may –

(a)   select the expert from a list prepared or identified by the instructing parties; or

(b)   direct that the expert be selected in such other manner as the court may direct.

161 Instructions to a single joint expert

(1) Where the court gives a direction under rule 160 for a single joint expert to be used, each instructing party may give instructions to the expert.

(2) When an instructing party gives instructions to the expert he must, at the same time, send a copy of the instructions to the other instructing parties.

(3) The court may give directions about –

(a)   the payment of the expert's fees and expenses; and

(b)   any inspection, examination or experiments which the expert wishes to carry out.

(4) The court may, before an expert is instructed, limit the amount that can be paid by way of fees and expenses to the expert.

(5) Unless the court otherwise directs, the instructing parties are jointly and severally liable for the payment of the expert's fees and expenses.

162 Power of court to direct a party to provide information

(1) Where a party has access to information which is not reasonably available to the other party, the court may direct the party who has access to the information to prepare and file a document recording the information.

(2) A court officer will send a copy of that document to the other party.

163 Contents of report

(1) An expert's report must comply with the requirements set out in the relevant practice direction.

(2) At the end of an expert's report there must be a statement that –

    (a)   the expert understands his duty to the court; and

    (b)   he has complied with that duty.

(3) The expert's report must state the substance of all material instructions, whether written or oral, on the basis of which the report was written.

(4) The instructions referred to in paragraph (3) shall not be privileged against disclosure.

164 Use by one party of expert's report disclosed by another

Where a party has disclosed an expert's report, any party may use that expert's report as evidence at the final hearing.

165 Discussions between experts

(1) The court may, at any stage, direct a discussion between experts for the purpose of requiring the experts to –

    (a)   identify and discuss the expert issues in the proceedings; and

    (b)   where possible, reach an agreed opinion on those issues.

(2) The court may specify the issues which the experts must discuss.

(3) The court may direct that following a discussion between the experts they must prepare a statement for the court showing –

    (a)   those issues on which they agree; and

    (b)   those issues on which they disagree and a summary of their reasons for disagreeing.

166 Consequence of failure to disclose expert's report

A party who fails to disclose an expert's report may not use the report at the final hearing or call the expert to give evidence orally unless the court gives permission.

167 Expert's right to ask court for directions

(1) An expert may file a written request for directions to assist him in carrying out his function as an expert.

(2) An expert must, unless the court directs otherwise, provide a copy of any proposed request for directions under paragraph (1) –

    (a)   to the party instructing him, at least 7 days before he files the request; and

    (b)   to all other parties, at least 4 days before he files it.

(3) The court, when it gives directions, may also direct that a party be served with a copy of the directions.

****

PART 19
APPEALS

171 Scope and interpretation

(1) The rules in this Part apply to appeals to –

    (a)   the High Court; and

(b)   a county court.

(2) This Part does not apply to an appeal in detailed assessment proceedings against a decision of an authorised court officer

(Rules 47.20 to 47.23 of the CPR deal with appeals against a decision of an authorised court officer in detailed assessment proceedings.)

(3) In this Part –

'appeal' includes an appeal by way of case stated;
'appeal court' means the court to which an appeal is made;
'appeal notice' means an appellant's or respondent's notice;
'appellant' means a person who brings or seeks to bring an appeal;
'lower court' means the court from whose decision an appeal is brought;
'respondent' means –

(a)   a person other than the appellant who was a party to the proceedings in the lower court and who is affected by the appeal; and

(b)   a person who is permitted by the appeal court to be a party to the appeal.

(4) This Part is subject to any rule, enactment or practice direction which sets out special provisions with regard to any particular category of appeal.

172 Parties to comply with the practice direction

All parties to an appeal must comply with the relevant practice direction.

173 Permission

(1) An appellant or respondent requires permission to appeal –

(a)   against a decision in assessment proceedings relating to costs in proceedings where the decision appealed against was made by a district judge or a costs judge; or

(b)   as provided by the relevant practice direction.

(2) An application for permission to appeal may be made –

(a)   to the lower court, if that court is a county court or the High Court, at the hearing at which the decision to be appealed was made; or

(b)   to the appeal court in an appeal notice.

(Rule 174 sets out the time limits for filing an appellant's notice at the appeal court. Rule 175 sets out the time limits for filing a respondent's notice at the appeal court. Any application for permission to appeal to the appeal court must be made in the appeal notice (see rules 174(1) and 175(3).)

(3) Where the lower court refuses an application for permission to appeal, a further application for permission to appeal may be made to the appeal court.

(4) Where the appeal court, without a hearing, refuses permission to appeal, the person seeking permission may request the decision to be reconsidered at a hearing.

(5) A request under paragraph (4) must be filed within 7 days beginning with the date on which the notice that permission has been refused was served.

(6) Permission to appeal will only be given where –

(a)   the court considers that the appeal would have a real prospect of success; or

(b)   there is some other compelling reason why the appeal should be heard.

(7) An order giving permission may –

(a)   limit the issues to be heard; and

(b)   be made subject to conditions.

(8) In this rule 'costs judge' means a taxing master of the Supreme Court.

174 Appellant's notice

(1) Where the appellant seeks permission from the appeal court it must be requested in the appellant's notice.

(2) The appellant must file the appellant's notice at the appeal court within –

    (a)   such period as may be directed by the lower court, if that court is a county court or the High Court; or

    (b) –

        (i)   where the lower court makes no such direction; or

        (ii)   the lower court is a magistrates' court,

        14 days beginning with the date on which the decision of the lower court that the appellant wishes to appeal was made.

(3) Unless the appeal court directs otherwise, an appeal notice must be served on the persons referred to in paragraph (4) –

    (a)   as soon as practicable; and

    (b)   in any event not later than 7 days,

after it is filed.

(4) The persons referred to in paragraph (3) are –

    (a)   each respondent;

    (b)   any children's guardian, reporting officer or children and family reporter; and

    (c)   where the appeal is from a magistrates' court, the court officer.

(5) Unless the appeal court directs otherwise, a court officer will serve the appeal notice.

175 Respondent's notice

(1) A respondent may file a respondent's notice.

(2) A respondent who –

    (a)   is seeking permission to appeal from the appeal court; or

    (b)   wishes to ask the appeal court to uphold the order of the lower court for reasons different from or additional to those given by the lower court,

must file a respondent's notice.

(3) Where the respondent seeks permission from the appeal court it must be requested in the respondent's notice.

(4) A respondent's notice must be filed within –

    (a)   such period as may be directed by the lower court, if that court is a county court or the High Court; or

    (b) –

        (i)   where the lower court makes no such direction; or

        (ii)   the lower court is a magistrates' court,

        14 days beginning with the date referred to in paragraph (5).

(5) The date referred to in paragraph (4) is –

    (a)   the date on which the respondent is served with the appellant's notice where –

        (i)   permission to appeal was given by the lower court; or

        (ii)   permission to appeal is not required;

    (b)   the date on which the respondent is served with notification that the appeal court has given the appellant permission to appeal; or

(c)   the date on which the respondent is served with notification that the application for permission to appeal and the appeal itself are to be heard together.

(6) Unless the appeal court directs otherwise, a respondent's notice must be served on the appellant and any other respondent –

(a)   as soon as practicable; and
(b)   in any event not later than 7 days,

after it is filed.

(7) Unless the appeal court directs otherwise, a court officer will serve a respondent's notice.

176 Variation of time

(1) An application to vary the time limit for filing an appeal notice must be made to the appeal court.

(2) The parties may not agree to extend any date or time limit set by –

(a)   these Rules;
(b)   the relevant practice direction; or
(c)   an order of the appeal court or the lower court.

(Rule 12(2)(a) provides that the court may extend or shorten the time for compliance with any rule, practice direction or court order (even if an application for extension is made after the time for compliance has expired).)

(Rule 12(2)(b) provides that the court may adjourn or bring forward a hearing.)

177 Stay

Unless the appeal court or the lower court, other than a magistrates' court, orders otherwise an appeal shall not operate as a stay of any order or decision of the lower court.

178 Amendment of appeal notice

An appeal notice may not be amended without the permission of the appeal court.

179 Striking out appeal notices and setting aside or imposing conditions on permission to appeal

(1) The appeal court may –

(a)   strike out the whole or part of an appeal notice;
(b)   set aside permission to appeal in whole or in part; or
(c)   impose or vary conditions upon which an appeal may be brought.

(2) The court will only exercise its powers under paragraph (1) where there is a compelling reason for doing so.

(3) Where a party was present at the hearing at which permission was given he may not subsequently apply for an order that the court exercise its powers under paragraphs (1)(b) or (c).

180 Appeal court's powers

(1) In relation to an appeal the appeal court has all the powers of the lower court.

(Rule 171(4) provides that this Part is subject to any enactment that sets out special provisions with regard to any particular category of appeal.)

(2) The appeal court has power to –

(a)   affirm, set aside or vary any order or judgment made or given by the lower court;
(b)   refer any application or issue for determination by the lower court;

(c)   order a new hearing;

(d)   make orders for the payment of interest; and

(e)   make a costs order.

(3) The appeal court may exercise its powers in relation to the whole or part of an order of the lower court.

(Rule 12 contains general rules about the court's case management powers.)

(4) If the appeal court –

(a)   refuses an application for permission to appeal;

(b)   strikes out an appellant's notice; or

(c)   dismisses an appeal,

and it considers that the application, the appellant's notice or the appeal is totally without merit, the provisions of paragraph (5) must be complied with.

(5) Where paragraph (4) applies –

(a)   the court's order must record the fact that it considers the application, the appellant's notice or the appeal to be totally without merit; and

(b)   the court must at the same time consider whether it is appropriate to make a civil restraint order.

181 Hearing of appeals

(1) Every appeal will be limited to a review of the decision of the lower court unless –

(a)   a practice direction makes different provision for a particular category of appeal; or

(b)   the court considers that in the circumstances of an individual appeal it would be in the interests of justice to hold a re-hearing.

(2) Unless it orders otherwise, the appeal court will not receive –

(a)   oral evidence; or

(b)   evidence which was not before the lower court.

(3) The appeal court will allow an appeal where the decision of the lower court was –

(a)   wrong; or

(b)   unjust because of a serious procedural or other irregularity in the proceedings in the lower court.

(4) The appeal court may draw any inference of fact which it considers justified on the evidence.

(5) At the hearing of the appeal a party may not rely on a matter not contained in his appeal notice unless the appeal court gives permission.

182 Assignment of appeals to the Court of Appeal

(1) Where the court from or to which an appeal is made or from which permission to appeal is sought ('the relevant court') considers that –

(a)   an appeal which is to be heard by a county court or the High Court would raise an important point of principle or practice; or

(b)   there is some other compelling reason for the Court of Appeal to hear it,

the relevant court may order the appeal to be transferred to the Court of Appeal.

(2) This rule does not apply to proceedings in a magistrates' court.

183 Reopening of final appeals

(1) The High Court will not reopen a final determination of any appeal unless –

(a)   it is necessary to do so in order to avoid real injustice;
(b)   the circumstances are exceptional and make it appropriate to reopen the appeal; and
(c)   there is no alternative effective remedy.

(2) In paragraphs (1), (3), (4) and (6), 'appeal' includes an application for permission to appeal.

(3) This rule does not apply to appeals to a county court.

(4) Permission is needed to make an application under this rule to reopen a final determination of an appeal.

(5) There is no right to an oral hearing of an application for permission unless, exceptionally, the judge so directs.

(6) The judge will not grant permission without directing the application to be served on the other party to the original appeal and giving him an opportunity to make representations.

(7) There is no right of appeal or review from the decision of the judge on the application for permission, which is final.

(8) The procedure for making an application for permission is set out in the practice direction.
****

FAMILY PROCEDURE RULES 1991

SI 1991/1247

****

PART IV
PROCEEDINGS UNDER THE CHILDREN ACT 1989, ETC

Amendment—SI 2009/636.

4.1 Interpretation and application

(1) In this Part of these rules, unless a contrary intention appears –

a section or schedule referred to means the section or schedule so numbered in the Act of 1989;

'a section 8 order' has the meaning assigned to it by section 8(2);
'application' means an application made under or by virtue of the Act of 1989 or under these rules, and 'applicant' shall be construed accordingly;
'child', in relation to proceedings to which this Part applies –
   (a)   means, subject to sub-paragraph (b), a person under the age of 18 with respect to whom the proceedings are brought, and
   (b)   where the proceedings are under Schedule 1, also includes a person who has reached the age of 18;
'children and family reporter' means an officer of the service or a Welsh family proceedings officer who has been asked to prepare a welfare report under section 7(1)(a);
'children's guardian' –
   (a)   means an officer of the service or a Welsh family proceedings officer appointed under section 41 for the child with respect to whom the proceedings are brought; but
   (b)   does not include such an officer appointed in relation to proceedings specified by Part IVA;

'contact activity condition' has the meaning assigned to it by section 11C(2);
'contact activity direction' has the meaning assigned to it by section 11A(3);
'contact order' has the meaning assigned to it by section 8(1);

'directions appointment' means a hearing for directions under rule 4.14(2);

'emergency protection order' means an order under section 44;

'enforcement order' has the meaning assigned to it by section 11J(2);

'family assistance order report' means a report to the court pursuant to a direction in a family assistance order under section 16(6);

'financial compensation order' means an order made under section 11O(2);

'leave' includes permission and approval;

'note' includes a record made by mechanical means;

'parental responsibility' has the meaning assigned to it by section 3;

'recovery order' means an order under section 50;

'risk assessment' has the meaning assigned to it by section 16A(3);

'special guardianship order' has the meaning assigned to it by section 14A;

'specified proceedings' has the meaning assigned to it by section 41(6) and rule 4.2(2);

'warning notice' means a notice attached to a contact order pursuant to section 8(2) of the Act of 2006; and

'welfare officer' means a person who has been asked to prepare a welfare report under section 7(1)(b).

(2) Except where the contrary intention appears, the provisions of this Part apply to proceedings in the High Court and the county courts –

(a)   on an application for a section 8 order;

(b)   on an application for a care order or a supervision order;

(c)   on an application under section 4(1)(c), 4(3), 4A(1)(b), 4A(3), 5(1), 6(7), 11J(5), 11O(5), 13(1), 14A, 14C(3), 14D, 33(7), 34(2), 34(3), 34(4), 34(9), 36(1), 38(8)(b), 39(1), 39(2), 39(3), 39(4), 43(1), 43(12), 44, 45, 46(7), 48(9), 50(1) or 102(1);

(d)   under Schedule 1, except where financial relief is also sought by or on behalf of an adult;

(da)   on an application under paragraph 4(3), 5(3), 6(4), 7(3) or 9(5) of Schedule A1;

(e)   on an application under paragraph 19(1) of Schedule 2;

(f)   on an application under paragraph 6(3), 15(2) or 17(1) of Schedule 3;

(g)   on an application under paragraph 11(3) or 16(5) of Schedule 14;

(h)   under section 25;

(i)   on an application for a warning notice; or

(j)   on an application for a warrant under section 79 of the Childcare Act 2006.

Amendments—SI 1991/2113; SI 2001/821; SI 2003/2839; SI 2005/559; SI 2005/2922; SI 2007/2187; SI 2008/2861; SI 2009/636.

4.2 Matters prescribed for the purposes of the Act of 1989

(1) The parties to proceedings in which directions are given under section 38(6), and any person named in such a direction, form the prescribed class for the purposes of section 38(8) (application to vary directions made with interim care or interim supervision order).

(2) The following proceedings are specified for the purposes of section 41 in accordance with subsection (6)(i) thereof –

(a)   proceedings under section 25;

(b)   applications under section 33(7);

(c)   proceedings under paragraph 19(1) of Schedule 2;

(d)   applications under paragraph 6(3) of Schedule 3;

(e)   appeals against the determination of proceedings of a kind set out in sub-paragraphs (a) to (d).

(3) The applicant for an order that has been made under section 43(1) and the persons referred to in section 43(11) may, in any circumstances, apply under section 43(12) for a child assessment order to be varied or discharged.

(4) The following persons form the prescribed class for the purposes of section 44(9) (application to vary directions) –

(a)   the parties to the application for the order in respect of which it is sought to vary the directions;

(b)   the children's guardian;

(c)   the local authority in whose area the child concerned is ordinarily resident;

(d)   any person who is named in the directions.

Amendments—SI 1991/2113; SI 2001/821.

4.3 Application for leave to commence proceedings

(1) Where the leave of the court is required to bring any proceedings to which this Part applies, the person seeking leave shall file –

(a)   a written request for leave in Form C2 setting out the reasons for the application; and

(b)   a draft of the application (being the documents referred to in rule 4.4 (1A)) for the making of which leave is sought together with sufficient copies for one to be served on each respondent.

(2) On considering a request for leave filed under paragraph (1), the court shall –

(a)   grant the request, whereupon the proper officer shall inform the person making the request and any local authority that is preparing, or has prepared, a report under section 14A(8) or (9) of the decision, or

(b)   direct that a date be fixed for the hearing of the request, whereupon the proper officer shall fix such a date and give such notice as the court directs to the person making the request and any local authority that is preparing, or has prepared, a report under section 14A(8) or (9) and to such other persons as the court requires to be notified, of the date so fixed.

(3) Where leave is granted to bring proceedings to which this Part applies the application shall proceed in accordance with rule 4.4; but paragraph (1)(a) of that rule shall not apply.

(4) In the case of a request for leave to bring proceedings under Schedule 1, the draft application under paragraph (1) shall be accompanied by a statement setting out the financial details which the person seeking leave believes to be relevant to the request and containing a declaration that it is true to the maker's best knowledge and belief, together with sufficient copies for one to be served on each respondent.

Amendments—SI 1994/3155; SI 2005/2922.

4.4 Application

(1) Subject to paragraph (4) and rule 4.4A, an applicant shall –

(a)   file the documents referred to in paragraph (1A) below (which documents shall together be called the 'application') together with sufficient copies for one to be served on each respondent, and

(b)   serve a copy of the application together with Form C6 and such (if any) of Forms C1A, C7 and C10A as are given to him by the proper officer under paragraph (2)(b) on each respondent such number of days prior to the date fixed under paragraph (2)(a) as is specified for that application in column (ii) of Appendix 3 to these rules.

(1A) the documents to be filed under paragraph (1)(a) above are –

(a) –

    (i)   whichever is appropriate of C1, C100, C2, C3, C4, C51 or C79, and

    (ii)   such of the supplemental Forms C10 or C11 to C20 as may be appropriate, and

    (iii)   in the case of an application for a section 8 order or an order under section 4(1)(c) where question 7 on Form C1, or (as the case may be) question 5 on Form C100, or question 4 on Form C2, is answered in the affirmative, supplemental Form C1A, or

(b)   where there is no appropriate form a statement in writing of the order sought, and where the application is made in respect of more than one child, all the children shall be included in one application.

(2) On receipt of the documents filed under paragraph (1)(a) the proper officer shall –

(a)   fix the date for a hearing or a directions appointment, allowing sufficient time for the applicant to comply with paragraph (1)(b),

(b)   endorse the date so fixed upon Form C6 and, where appropriate, Form C6A, and

(c)   return forthwith to the applicant the copies of the application and Form C10A if filed with it, together with Form C6 and such of Forms C6A and C7 as are appropriate, and, in the case of an application for a section 8 order or an order under section 4(1)(c), Form C1A.

(3) The applicant shall, at the same time as complying with paragraph (1)(b), serve Form C6A on the persons set out for the relevant class of proceedings in column (iv) of Appendix 3 to these rules.

(3A) In the case of an application under –

(a)   section 11J; or

(b)   section 11O,

in addition to complying with paragraph (3), the applicant shall serve a copy of the application on the person who was the children's guardian, guardian ad litem, next friend or legal representative as referred to in the relevant entry in column (iv) of Appendix 3 to these rules.

(4) An application for –

(a)   a section 8 order,

(b)   an emergency protection order,

(c)   a warrant under section 48(9),

(d)   a recovery order,

(e)   a warrant under section 102(1); or

(f)   a warrant under section 79 of the Childcare Act 2006,

may be made ex parte in which case the applicant shall –

    (i)   file the application in the appropriate form in Appendix 1 to these rules –

        (a)   where the application is made by telephone, within 24 hours after the making of the application, or

        (b)   in any other case, at the time when the application is made, and

    (ii)   in the case of an application for a section 8 order or an emergency protection order, serve a copy of the application on each respondent within 48 hours after the making of the order.

(5) Where the court refuses to make an order on an ex parte application it may direct that the application be made inter partes.

(6) In the case of proceedings under Schedule 1, the application under paragraph (1) shall be accompanied by a statement in Form C10A setting out the financial details which the applicant believes to be relevant to the application, together with sufficient copies for one to be served on each respondent.

Amendments—SI 1991/2113; SI 1992/2067; SI 1994/3155; SI 2004/3375; SI 2008/2861; SI 2009/636.

4.4A Application for a warning notice or application to amend enforcement order by reason of change of residence

(1) This rule applies in relation to an application for a warning notice or for an order under paragraph 5 of Schedule A1 (to amend an enforcement order by reason of change of residence).

(2) The application shall be made –

(a)   in the case of an application for a warning notice, ex parte on Form C78; or

(b   in the case of an application for an order under paragraph 5 of Schedule A1, ex parte on Form C79.

(3) The court may deal with the application without a hearing.

(4) Where the court determines that the application shall be dealt with at a hearing –

(a) rule 4.4(1)(b) and (3) shall apply; and
(b) rule 4.4(2) shall apply as if for the words before 'the proper officer' there were substituted 'On the court determining that the application shall be dealt with at a hearing'.

Amendments—SI 2008/2861.

4.5 Withdrawal of application

(1) An application may be withdrawn only with leave of the court.

(2) Subject to paragraph (3), a person seeking leave to withdraw an application shall file and serve on the parties a written request for leave setting out the reasons for the request.

(3) The request under paragraph (2) may be made orally to the court if the parties and the children's guardian, the welfare officer, children and family reporter, or the officer of the service or the Welsh family proceedings officer who is acting or has acted under a duty referred to in rule 4.11AA(1)(a) to (g) are present.

(4) Upon receipt of a written request under paragraph (2) the court shall –

(a) if –
   (i)   the parties consent in writing,
   (ii) the children's guardian has had an opportunity to make representations, and
   (iii) the court thinks fit,
   grant the request, in which case the proper officer shall notify the parties, any local authority that is preparing, or has prepared, a report under section 14A(8) or (9), the children's guardian and the welfare officer, the children and family reporter or the officer of the service or the Welsh family proceedings officer who is preparing or has prepared a family assistance order report or a risk assessment of the granting of the request, or
(b) direct that a date be fixed for the hearing of the request in which case the proper officer shall give at least 7 days' notice to the parties, any local authority that is preparing, or has prepared, a report under section 14A(8) or (9), the children's guardian, the welfare officer, children and family reporter and the officer of the service or the Welsh family proceedings officer who is preparing or has prepared a family assistance order report or a risk assessment, of the date fixed.

Amendments—SI 2001/821; SI 2005/2922; SI 2007/2187; SI 2008/2861.

…

4.7 Parties

(1) The respondents to proceedings to which this Part applies shall be those persons set out in the relevant entry in column (iii) of Appendix 3 to these rules.

(2) In proceedings to which this Part applies, a person may file a request in Form C2 that he or another person –

(a) be joined as a party, or
(b) cease to be a party.

(3) On considering a request under paragraph (2) the court shall, subject to paragraph (4) –

(a) grant it without a hearing or representations, save that this shall be done only in the case of a request under paragraph (2)(a), whereupon the proper officer shall inform the parties and any local authority that is preparing, or has prepared, a report under section 14A(8) or (9) and the person making the request of that decision, or

(b) order that a date be fixed for the consideration of the request, whereupon the proper officer shall give notice of the date so fixed, together with a copy of the request –

    (i) in the case of a request under paragraph (2)(a), to the applicant and any local authority that is preparing, or has prepared, a report under section 14A(8) or (9), and

    (ii) in the case of a request under paragraph (2)(b), to the parties and any local authority that is preparing, or has prepared, a report under section 14A(8) or (9), or

(c) invite the parties or any of them to make written representations, within a specified period, as to whether the request should be granted; and upon the expiry of the period the court shall act in accordance with sub-paragraph (a) or (b).

(4) Where a person with parental responsibility requests that he be joined under paragraph (2)(a), the court shall grant his request.

(5) In proceedings to which this Part applies the court may direct –

(a) that a person who would not otherwise be a respondent under these rules be joined as a party to the proceedings, or

(b) that a party to the proceedings cease to be a party.

Amendments—SI 1992/2067; SI 1994/3155; SI 2005/2922.

...

4.9 Answer to application

(1) Within 14 days of service of an application for –

(a) an order under section 4(1)(c);

(b) a section 8 order;

...

each respondent shall file, and serve on the parties, an acknowledgement of the application in Form C7 and, if both parts of question 6 or question 7 (or both) on Form C7 are answered in the affirmative, Form C1A.

(2) (*revoked*)

(3) Following service of an application to which this Part applies, other than –

(a) an application under rule 4.3; and

(b) an application referred to in paragraph (1)(a), (b), (e) or (h),

a respondent may, subject to paragraph (4), file a written answer, which shall be served on the other parties.

(4) An answer under paragraph (3) shall, except in the case of an application under section 25, 31, 34, 38, 43, 44, 45, 46, 48 or 50, be filed, and served, not less than 2 days before the date fixed for the hearing of the application.

Amendments—SI 1994/3155; SI 2004/3375; SI 2005/2922; SI 2008/2861.

4.10 Appointment of children's guardian

(1) As soon as practicable after the commencement of specified proceedings, or the transfer of such proceedings to the court, the court shall appoint a children's guardian, unless –

(a) such an appointment has already been made by the court which made the transfer and is subsisting, or

(b) the court considers that such an appointment is not necessary to safeguard the interests of the child.

(2) At any stage in specified proceedings a party may apply, without notice to the other parties unless the court directs otherwise, for the appointment of a children's guardian.

(3) The court shall grant an application under paragraph (2) unless it considers such an appointment not to be necessary to safeguard the interests of the child, in which case it shall give its reasons; and a note of such reasons shall be taken by the proper officer.

(4) At any stage in specified proceedings the court may, of its own motion, appoint a children's guardian.

(4A) The court may, in specified proceedings, appoint more than one children's guardian in respect of the same child

(5) The proper officer shall, as soon as practicable, notify the parties and any welfare officer or children and family reporter of an appointment under this rule or, as the case may be, of a decision not to make such an appointment.

(6) Upon the appointment of a children's guardian the proper officer shall, as soon as practicable, notify him of the appointment and serve on him copies of the application and of documents filed under rule 4.17(1).

(7) A children's guardian appointed by the court under this rule shall not –

(a) be a member, officer or servant of a local authority which, or an authorised person (within the meaning of section 31(9)) who, is a party to the proceedings;

(b) be, or have been, a member, officer or servant of a local authority or voluntary organisation (within the meaning of section 105(1)) who has been directly concerned in that capacity in arrangements relating to the care, accommodation or welfare of the child during the five years prior to the commencement of the proceedings; or

(c) be a serving probation officer who has, in that capacity, been previously concerned with the child or his family.

(8) When appointing a children's guardian the court shall consider the appointment of anyone who has previously acted as children's guardian of the same child.

(9) The appointment of a children's guardian under this rule shall continue for such time as is specified in the appointment or until terminated by the court.

(10) When terminating an appointment in accordance with paragraph (9), the court shall give its reasons in writing for so doing.

(11) Where the court appoints a children's guardian in accordance with this rule or refuses to make such an appointment, the court or the proper officer shall record the appointment or refusal in Form C47.

Amendments—SI 1994/3155; SI 2001/821.

4.11 Powers and duties of officers of the service and Welsh family proceedings officers

(1) In carrying out his duty under section 7(1)(a), or section 41(2) or in acting under a duty referred to in rule 4.11AA(1), the officer of the service or the Welsh family proceedings officer shall have regard to the principle set out in section 1(2) and the matters set out in section 1(3)(a) to (f) as if for the word 'court' in that section there were substituted the words 'officer of the service or Welsh family proceedings officer'.

(2) The officer of the service or the Welsh family proceedings officer shall make such investigations as may be necessary for him to carry out his duties and shall, in particular –

(a) contact or seek to interview such persons as he thinks appropriate or as the court directs;

(b) obtain such professional assistance as is available to him which he thinks appropriate or which the court directs him to obtain.

(3) In addition to his duties, under other paragraphs of this rule, or rules 4.11A, 4.11AA and 4.11B, the officer of the service or the Welsh family proceedings officer shall provide to the court such other assistance as it may require.

(4) A party may question the officer of the service or the Welsh family proceedings officer about oral or written advice tendered by him to the court.

Amendments—SI 2001/821; SI 2005/559; SI 2007/2187; SI 2008/2861.

4.11A Additional powers and duties of children's guardian

(1) The children's guardian shall –

(a)   appoint a solicitor to represent the child unless such a solicitor has already been appointed; and

(b)   give such advice to the child as is appropriate having regard to his understanding and, subject to rule 4.12(1)(a), instruct the solicitor representing the child on all matters relevant to the interests of the child including possibilities for appeal, arising in the course of proceedings.

(2) Where the children's guardian is an officer of the service authorised by the Service in the terms mentioned by and in accordance with section 15(1) of the Criminal Justice and Court Services Act 2000, paragraph (1)(a) shall not require him to appoint a solicitor for the child if he intends to have conduct of the proceedings on behalf of the child unless –

(a)   the child wishes to instruct a solicitor direct; and

(b)   the children's guardian or the court considers that he is of sufficient understanding to do so.

(2A) Where the children's guardian is a Welsh family proceedings officer authorised by the National Assembly for Wales in the terms mentioned by and in accordance with section 37(1) of the Children Act 2004, paragraph (1)(a) shall not require him to appoint a solicitor for the child if he intends to have conduct of the proceedings on behalf of the child unless –

(a)   the child wishes to instruct a solicitor direct; and

(b)   the children's guardian or the court considers that he is of sufficient understanding to do so.

(3) Where it appears to the children's guardian that the child –

(a)   is instructing his solicitor direct; or

(b)   intends to conduct and is capable of conducting the proceedings on his own behalf,

he shall inform the court and from then he –

(i)   shall perform all of his duties set out in rule 4.11 and this rule, other than those duties under paragraph (1)(a) of this rule, and such other duties as the court may direct;

(ii)   shall take such part in the proceedings as the court may direct; and

(iii)   may, with the leave of the court, have legal representation in the conduct of those duties.

(4) Unless excused by the court, the children's guardian shall attend all directions appointments in and hearings of the proceedings and shall advise the court on the following matters –

(a)   whether the child is of sufficient understanding for any purpose including the child's refusal to submit to a medical or psychiatric examination or other assessment that the court has the power to require, direct or order.

(b)   the wishes of the child in respect of any matter relevant to the proceedings including his attendance at court;

(c)   the appropriate forum for the proceedings;

(d)   the appropriate timing of the proceedings or any part of them;

(e)   the options available to it in respect of the child and the suitability of each such option including what order should be made in determining the application; and

(f)   any other matter concerning which the court seeks his advice or concerning which he considers that the court should be informed.

(5) The advice given under paragraph (4) may, subject to any order of the court, by given orally or in writing; and if the advice be given orally, a note of it shall be taken by the court or the proper officer.

(6) The children's guardian shall, where practicable, notify any person whose joinder as a party to those proceedings would be likely, in the opinion of the children's guardian, to safeguard the interests of the child of that person's right to apply to be joined under rule 4.7(2) and shall inform the court –

(a)   of any such notification given;
(b)   of anyone whom he attempted to notify under this paragraph but was unable to contact; and
(c)   of anyone whom he believes may wish to be joined to the proceedings.

(7) The children's guardian shall, unless the court otherwise directs, not less than 14 days before the date fixed for the final hearing of the proceedings –

(a)   file a written report advising on the interests of the child; and
(b)   serve a copy of the filed report on the other parties and any local authority that is preparing, or has prepared, a report under section 14A(8) or (9).

(8) The children's guardian shall serve and accept service of documents on behalf of the child in accordance with rule 4.8(3)(b) and (4)(b) and, where the child has not himself been served, and has sufficient understanding, advise the child of the contents of any document so served.

(9) If the children's guardian inspects records of the kinds referred to in section 42, he shall bring to the attention of –

(a)   the court; and
(b)   unless the court otherwise directs, the other parties to the proceedings,

all records and documents which may, in his opinion, assist in the proper determination of the proceedings.

(10) The children's guardian shall ensure that, in relation to a decision made by the court in the proceedings –

(a)   if he considers it appropriate to the age and understanding of the child, the child is notified of that decision; and
(b)   if the child is notified of the decision, it is explained to the child in a manner appropriate to his age and understanding.

Amendments—SI 2001/821; SI 2005/559; SI 2005/2922.

4.11AA Additional powers and duties of officers of the service and Welsh family proceedings officers: reports and risk assessments

(1) This rule applies where an officer of the service or a Welsh family proceedings officer is acting under a duty in accordance with –

(a)   section 11E(7) (providing the court with information as to the making of a contact activity direction or a contact activity condition);
(b)   section 11G(2) (monitoring compliance with a contact activity direction or a contact activity condition);
(c)   section 11H(2) (monitoring compliance with a contact order);
(d)   section 11L(5) (providing the court with information as to the making of an enforcement order);
(e)   section 11M(1) (monitoring compliance with an enforcement order);
(f)   section 16(6) (providing a family assistance order report to the court); and
(g)   section 16A (making a risk assessment).

(2) When an officer of the service or a Welsh family proceedings officer is acting under a duty referred to in paragraph (1)(a) to (g) he must consider whether –

    (a)   to notify the child of such of the contents of any report or risk assessment he makes as he considers appropriate to the age and understanding of the child;

    (b)   to recommend in any report or risk assessment he makes that the court lists a hearing for the purposes of considering the report or assessment;

    (c)   it is in the best interests of the child for the child to be made a party to the proceedings.

(3) If the officer of the service or the Welsh family proceedings officer decides to notify the child of any of the contents of any report or risk assessment he makes, he must explain those contents to the child in a manner appropriate to the child's age and understanding.

(4) If the officer of the service or the Welsh family proceedings officer considers that the child should be made a party to the proceedings he must notify the court of his opinion together with the reasons for that opinion.

(5) If the officer of the service or the Welsh family proceedings officer considers that the court should exercise its discretion under rule 4.17AA(2) in relation to service of a risk assessment, he must state in the risk assessment –

    (a)   the way in which he considers the court should exercise its discretion (including his view on the length of any suggested delay in service); and

    (b)   his reasons for reaching his view.

(6) The officer of the service or the Welsh family proceedings officer must file any report or risk assessment he makes with the court –

    (a)   at or by the time directed by the court;

    (b)   in the absence of any such direction, at least 14 days before a relevant hearing; or

    (c)   where there has been no direction from the court and no relevant hearing is listed, as soon as possible following completion of any report or risk assessment he makes.

(7) In paragraph (6), a hearing is a relevant hearing if the proper officer has given the officer of the service or the Welsh family proceedings officer notice that the report or assessment is to be considered at it.

(8) When an officer of the service or a Welsh family proceedings officer prepares a report as a result of acting under a duty referred to in paragraph (1)(a) to (f), he shall, as soon as practicable, serve copies of that report on –

    (a)   each party; and

    (b)   any local authority that is preparing or has prepared a report under section 14A(8) or (9).

(9) At any hearing where a report prepared as a result of acting under a duty referred to in paragraph (1)(a) to (f) or a risk assessment is considered, any party may question the officer of the service or the Welsh family proceedings officer about the report or assessment.

Amendments—SI 2007/2187; SI 2008/2861.

4.11B Additional powers and duties of a children and family reporter

(1) The children and family reporter shall –

    (a)   notify the child of such contents of his report (if any) as he considers appropriate to the age and understanding of the child, including any reference to the child's own views on the application and the recommendation of the children and family reporter; and

    (b)   if he does notify the child of any contents of his report, explain them to the child in a manner appropriate to his age and understanding.

(2) Where the court has –

    (a)   directed that a written report be made by a children and family reporter;

and

(b)   notified the children and family reporter that his report is to be considered at a hearing, the children and family reporter shall –

      (i)   file the report; and

      (ii)   serve a copy on the other parties, any local authority that is preparing, or has prepared, a report under section 14A(8) or (9) and on the children's guardian (if any),

      by such time as the court may direct, and if no direction is given, not less than 14 days before that hearing.

(3) The court may direct that the children and family reporter attend any hearing at which his report is to be considered.

(4) The children and family reporter shall advise the court if he considers that the joinder of a person as a party to the proceedings would be likely to safeguard the interests of the child.

(5) The children and family reporter shall consider whether it is in the best interests of the child for the child to be made a party to the proceedings.

(6) If the children and family reporter considers the child should be made a party to the proceedings he shall notify the court of his opinion together with the reasons for that opinion.

Amendments—SI 2001/821; SI 2005/2922.

4.12 Solicitor for child

(1) A solicitor appointed under section 41(3) or in accordance with rule 4.11A(1)(a) shall represent the child –

    (a)   in accordance with instructions received from the children's guardian (unless the solicitor considers, having taken into account the views of the children's guardian and any direction of the court under rule 4.11A(3), that the child wishes to give instructions which conflict with those of the children's guardian and that he is able, having regard to his understanding, to give such instructions on his own behalf in which case he shall conduct the proceedings in accordance with instructions received from the child), or

    (b)   where no children's guardian has been appointed for the child and the condition in section 41(4)(b) is satisfied, in accordance with instructions received from the child, or

    (c)   in default of instructions under (a) or (b), in furtherance of the best interests of the child.

(2) A solicitor appointed under section 41(3) or in accordance with rule 4.11A(1)(a) shall serve and accept service of documents on behalf of the child in accordance with rule 4.8(3)(a) and (4)(a) and, where the child has not himself been served and has sufficient understanding, advise the child of the contents of any document so served.

(3) Where the child wishes an appointment of a solicitor under section 41(3) or in accordance with rule 4.11A(1)(a) to be terminated, he may apply to the court for an order terminating the appointment; and the solicitor and the children's guardian shall be given an opportunity to make representations.

(4) Where the children's guardian wishes an appointment of a solicitor under section 41(3) to be terminated, he may apply to the court for an order terminating the appointment; and the solicitor and, if he is of sufficient understanding, the child, shall be given an opportunity to make representations.

(5) When terminating an appointment in accordance with paragraph (3) or (4), the court shall give its reasons for so doing, a note of which shall be taken by the court or the proper officer.

(6) Where the court appoints a solicitor under section 41(3) or refuses to make such an appointment, the court or the proper officer shall record the appointment or refusal in Form C48.

Amendments—SI 1994/3155; SI 2001/821.

4.13 Welfare officer

(1) Where the court has directed that a written report be made by a welfare officer in accordance with section 7(1)(b), the report shall be filed at or by such time as the court directs or, in the absence of such a direction, at least 14 days before a relevant hearing; and the proper officer shall, as soon as practicable, serve a copy of the report on the parties, any local authority that is preparing, or has prepared, a report under section 14A(8) or (9) and any children's guardian.

(2) In paragraph (1), a hearing is relevant if the proper officer has given the welfare officer notice that his report is to be considered at it.

(3) After the filing of a report by a welfare officer, the court may direct that the welfare officer attend any hearing at which the report is to be considered; and –

(a)   except where such a direction is given at a hearing attended by the welfare officer, the proper officer shall inform the welfare officer of the direction; and

(b)   at the hearing at which the report is considered any party may question the welfare officer about his report.

(3A) The welfare officer shall consider whether it is in the best interests of the child for the child to be made a party to the proceedings.

(3B) If the welfare officer considers the child should be made a party to the proceedings he shall notify the court of his opinion together with the reasons for that opinion.

(4) This rule is without prejudice to any power to give directions under rule 4.14.

Amendments—SI 1992/2067; SI 2001/821; SI 2005/2922.

4.13A Local authority officers preparing family assistance order reports

Where a family assistance order directs a local authority officer to prepare a family assistance order report, rules 4.5, 4.13, 4.14(1)(a)(i) and (2), 4.15(2) and 4.17(1) shall apply to, or in respect of, the local authority officer preparing a family assistance order report as they would apply to, or in respect of, a welfare officer preparing a report in accordance with section 7(1)(b).

Amendments—SI 2007/2187.

4.13B Section 11J or 11O: duties of person notified

Where there has been a notification of an application in accordance with rule 4.4(3A), the person notified shall –

(a)   consider whether it is in the best interests of the child for the child to be a party to the proceedings to which that application relates; and

(b)   before the date fixed for the first hearing or directions appointment, notify the court, orally or in writing, of his opinion on this question, together with the reasons for this opinion.

Amendments—SI 2008/2861.

4.14 Directions

(1) In this rule, 'party' includes the children's guardian and, where a request or direction is or concerned with –

(a)   a report under
       (i)   section 7, the welfare officer or children and family reporter;
       (ii)   section 14A(8) or (9), the local authority preparing that report.

(b)   a duty referred to in rule 4.11AA(1)(a) to (f), the officer of the service of the Welsh family proceedings officer who is acting under the duty in question;

(c)   a risk assessment, the officer of the service or the Welsh family proceedings officer who is preparing the assessment.

(2) In proceedings to which this Part applies the court may, subject to paragraph (3), give, vary or revoke directions for the conduct of the proceedings, including –

(a) the timetable for the proceedings;
(b) varying the time within which or by which an act is required, by these rules or by other rules of court, to be done;
(c) the attendance of the child;
(d) the appointment of a children's guardian, a guardian ad litem, or a solicitor under section 41(3);
(e) the service of documents;
(f) the submission of evidence including experts' reports;
(g) the preparation of welfare reports under section 7;
(h) the transfer of the proceedings to another court;
(i) consolidation with other proceedings;
(j) the preparation of reports under section 14A(8) or (9);
(k) the attendance of the person who prepared the report under section 14A(8) or (9) at any hearing at which the report is to be considered;
(l) the preparation of family assistance order reports;
(m) listing a hearing for the purposes of considering the contents of a risk assessment;
(n) the exercise by an officer of the service or a Welsh family proceedings officer of any duty referred to in rule 4.11AA(1)(a) to (e).

(3) Directions under paragraph (2) may be given, varied or revoked either –

(a) of the court's own motion having given the parties notice of its intention to do so, and an opportunity to attend and be heard or to make written representations,
(b) on the written request in Form C2 of a party specifying the direction which is sought, filed and served on the other parties, or
(c) on the written request in Form C2 of a party specifying the direction which is sought, to which the other parties consent and which they or their representatives have signed.

(4) In an urgent case the request under paragraph (3)(b) may, with the leave of the court, be made –

(a) orally, or
(b) without notice to the parties, or
(c) both as in sub-paragraph (a) and as in sub-paragraph (b).

(5) On receipt of a written request under paragraph (3)(b) the proper officer shall fix a date for the hearing of the request and give not less than 2 days' notice in Form C6 to the parties of the date so fixed.

(6) On considering a request under paragraph (3)(c) the court shall either –

(a) grant the request, whereupon the proper officer shall inform the parties of the decision, or
(b) direct that a date be fixed for the hearing of the request, whereupon the proper officer shall fix such a date and give not less than 2 days' notice to the parties of the date so fixed.

(7) A party may apply for an order to be made under section 11(3) or, if he is entitled to apply for such an order, under section 38(1) in accordance with paragraph (3)(b) or (c).

(8) Where a court is considering making, of its own motion, a section 8 order, or an order under section 14A, 14D, 31, 34 or 38 or under paragraph 4, 5, 6 or 7 of Schedule A1, the power to give directions under paragraph (2) shall apply.

(9) Directions of a court which are still in force immediately prior to the transfer of proceedings to which this Part applies to another court shall continue to apply following the transfer, subject to any changes of terminology which are required to apply those directions to the court to which the proceedings are transferred, unless varied or discharged by directions under paragraph (2).

(9A) After the filing of a report prepared as a result of acting under a duty referred to in rule 4.11AA(1)(a) to (f) or a risk assessment, the court may direct that the officer of the service or the Welsh family proceedings officer attend any hearing at which the report or assessment is to be considered.

(10) The court or the proper officer shall take a note of the giving, variation or revocation of a direction under this rule and serve, as soon as practicable, a copy of the note on any party who was not present at the giving, variation or revocation.

Amendments—SI 1994/3155; SI 2001/821; SI 2005/2922; SI 2007/2187; SI 2008/2861.

4.16 Attendance at directions appointment and hearing

(1) Subject to paragraph (2), a party shall attend a directions appointment of which he has been given notice in accordance with rule 4.14(5) unless the court otherwise directs.

(1A) Paragraphs (2) to (4) do not apply where –

    (a)   the hearing relates to –
        (i)   a decision about whether to make a contact activity direction or to attach a contact activity condition to a contact order; or
        (ii)   an application for a financial compensation order, an enforcement order or an order under paragraph 9(2) of Schedule A1; and
    (b)   the court has yet to obtain sufficient evidence from, or in relation to, the person who may be the subject of the direction, condition or order to enable it to determine the matter.

(2) Proceedings or any part of them shall take place in the absence of any party, including the child, if –

    (a)   the court considers it in the interests of the child, having regard to the matters to be discussed or the evidence likely to be given, and
    (b)   the party is represented by a children's guardian or solicitor;

and when considering the interests of the child under sub-paragraph (a) the court shall give the children's guardian, the solicitor for the child and, if he is of sufficient understanding, the child an opportunity to make representations.

(3) Subject to paragraph (4), where at the time and place appointed for a hearing or directions appointment the applicant appears but one or more of the respondents do not, the court may proceed with the hearing or appointment.

(4) The court shall not begin to hear an application in the absence of a respondent unless –

    (a)   it is proved to the satisfaction of the court that he received reasonable notice of the date of the hearing; or
    (b)   the court is satisfied that the circumstances of the case justify proceeding with the hearing.

(5) Where, at the time and place appointed for a hearing or directions appointment one or more of the respondents appear but the applicant does not, the court may refuse the application or, if sufficient evidence has previously been received, proceed in the absence of the applicant.

(6) Where at the time and place appointed for a hearing or directions appointment neither the applicant nor any respondent appears, the court may refuse the application.

(7) Unless the court otherwise directs, a hearing of, or directions appointment in, proceedings to which this Part applies shall be in chambers.

Amendments—SI 2001/821; SI 2008/2861.

4.17 Documentary evidence

(1) Subject to paragraphs (4) and (5), in proceedings to which this Part applies a party shall file and serve on the parties, any local authority that is preparing, or has prepared, a report under section 14A(8) or (9), any welfare officer, any children and family reporter, any officer of the service or any Welsh family proceedings officer who is acting or has acted under a duty referred to in rule 4.11AA(1)(a) to (g) and any children's guardian of whose appointment he has been given notice under rule 4.10(5) –

(a) written statements of the substance of the oral evidence which the party intends to adduce at a hearing of, or a directions appointment in, those proceedings, which shall –
    (i) be dated,
    (ii) be signed by the person making the statement,
    (iii) contain a declaration that the maker of the statement believes it to be true and understands that it may be placed before the court; and
    (iv) show in the top right hand corner of the first page –
        (a) the initials and surname of the person making the statement,
        (b) the number of the statement in relation to the maker,
        (c) the date on which the statement was made, and
        (d) the party on whose behalf it is filed; and

(b) copies of any documents, including experts' reports, upon which the party intends to rely at a hearing of, or a directions appointment in, those proceedings,

at or by such time as the court directs or, in the absence of a direction, before the hearing or appointment.

(2) A party may, subject to any direction of the court about the timing of statements under this rule, file and serve on the parties a statement which is supplementary to a statement served under paragraph (1).

(3) At a hearing or a directions appointment a party may not, without the leave of the court –

(a) adduce evidence, or
(b) seek to rely on a document,

in respect of which he has failed to comply with the requirements of paragraph (1).

(4) In proceedings for a section 8 order or a special guardianship order a party shall –

(a) neither file nor serve any document other than as required or authorised by these rules, and
(b) in completing a form prescribed by these rules, neither give information, nor make a statement, which is not required or authorised by that form,

without the leave of the court.

(5) In proceedings for a section 8 order or a special guardianship order no statement or copy may be filed under paragraph (1) until such time as the court directs.

Amendments—SI 1992/2067; SI 2001/821; SI 2005/2922; SI 2007/2187; SI 2008/2861.

4.17A Disclosure of report under section 14A(8) or (9)

(1) In proceedings for a special guardianship order, the local authority shall file the report under section 14A(8) or (9) within the timetable fixed by the court.

(2) The court shall consider whether to give a direction that the report under section 14A(8) or (9) be disclosed to each party to the proceedings.

(3) Before giving such a direction the court shall consider whether any information should be deleted including information which reveals the party's address in a case where he has declined to reveal it in accordance with rule 10.21 (disclosure of addresses).

(4) The court may direct that the report will not be disclosed to a party.

(5) The proper officer shall serve a copy of the report filed under paragraph (1) –

(i)   in accordance with any direction given under paragraph (2); and

(ii)   on any children's guardian, welfare officer or children and family reporter.

Amendments—SI 2005/2922.

4.17AA Service of risk assessments

(1) Where an officer of the service or a Welsh family proceedings officer has filed a risk assessment with the court, subject to paragraph (2), the proper officer shall as soon as practicable serve copies of the risk assessment on –

(a)   each party; and

(b)   any local authority that is preparing or has prepared a report under section 14A(8) or (9).

(2) Before serving the risk assessment, the court must consider whether, in order to prevent a risk of harm to the child, it is necessary for –

(a)   information to be deleted from a copy of the risk assessment before that copy is served on a party; or

(b)   service of a copy of the risk assessment (whether with information deleted from it or not) on a party to be delayed for a specified period,

and may direct accordingly.

Amendment—SI 2007/2187.

4.18 Expert evidence – examination of child

(1) No person may, without the leave of the court, cause the child to be medically or psychiatrically examined, or otherwise assessed, for the purpose of the preparation of expert evidence for use in the proceedings.

(2) An application for leave under paragraph (1) shall, unless the court otherwise directs, be served on all parties to the proceedings and on the children's guardian.

(3) Where the leave of the court has not been given under paragraph (1), no evidence arising out of an examination or assessment to which that paragraph applies may be adduced without the leave of the court.

Amendments—SI 2001/821.

4.19 Amendment

(1) Subject to rule 4.17(2), a document which has been filed or served in proceedings to which this Part applies, may not be amended without the leave of the court which shall, unless the court otherwise directs, be requested in writing.

(2) On considering a request for leave to amend a document the court shall either –

(a)   grant the request, whereupon the proper officer shall inform the person making the request of that decision, or

(b)   invite the parties or any of them to make representations, within a specified period, as to whether such an order should be made.

(3) A person amending a document shall file it and serve it on those persons on whom it was served prior to amendment; and the amendments shall be identified.

4.20 Oral evidence

The court or the proper officer shall keep a note of the substance of the oral evidence given at a hearing of, or directions appointment in, proceedings to which this Part applies.

4.21 Hearing

(1) The court may give directions as to the order of speeches and evidence at a hearing, or directions appointment, in the course of proceedings to which this Part applies.

(2) Subject to directions under paragraph (1), at a hearing of, or directions appointment in, proceedings to which this Part applies, the parties and the children's guardian shall adduce their evidence in the following order –

    (a)   the applicant,
    (b)   any party with parental responsibility for the child,
    (c)   other respondents,
    (d)   the children's guardian,
    (e)   the child, if he is a party to the proceedings and there is no children's guardian.

(2A) At the hearing at which the report under section 14A(8) or (9) is considered a party to whom the report, or part of it, has been disclosed may question the person who prepared the report about it.

(3) After the final hearing of proceedings to which this Part applies, the court shall deliver its judgment as soon as is practicable.

(4) When making an order or when refusing an application, the court shall –

    (a)   where it makes a finding of fact state such finding and complete Form C22; and
    (b)   state the reasons for the court's decision.

(5) An order made in proceedings to which this Part applies shall be recorded, by the court or the proper officer, either in the appropriate form in Appendix 1 to these rules or, where there is no such form, in writing.

(6) Subject to paragraph (7) and rule 4.21AA, a copy of an order made in accordance with paragraph (5) shall, as soon as practicable after it has been made, be served by the proper officer on the parties to the proceedings in which it was made and on any person with whom the child is living, and where applicable, on the local authority that prepared the report under section 14A(8) or (9).

(7) Within 48 hours after the making ex parte of –

    (a)   a section 8 order, or
    (b)   an order under section 44, 48(4), 48(9) or 50,
the applicant shall serve a copy of the order in the appropriate form in Appendix 1 to these Rules on –

    (i)   each party,
    (ii)   any person who has actual care of the child or who had such care immediately prior to the making of the order, and
    (iii)   in the case of an order referred to in sub-paragraph (b), the local authority in whose area the child lives or is found.

(8) At a hearing of, or directions appointment in, an application which takes place outside the hours during which the court office is normally open, the court or the proper officer shall take a note of the substance of the proceedings.

Amendments—SI 1992/456; SI 1992/2067; SI 1994/3155; SI 2001/821; SI 2005/2922; SI 2008/2861.

****

CIVIL PROCEDURE RULES 1998

SI 1998/3132

****

Part 52

Appeals

Section I – General Rules about Appeals

52.1 Scope and interpretation

(1) The rules in this Part apply to appeals to –

(a)   the civil division of the Court of Appeal;
(b)   the High Court; and
(c)   a county court.

(2) This Part does not apply to an appeal in detailed assessment proceedings against a decision of an authorised court officer.

(Rules 47.20 to 47.23 deal with appeals against a decision of an authorised court officer in detailed assessment proceedings)

(3) In this Part –

(a)   'appeal' includes an appeal by way of case stated;
(b)   'appeal court' means the court to which an appeal is made;
(c)   'lower court' means the court, tribunal or other person or body from whose decision an appeal is brought;
(d)   'appellant' means a person who brings or seeks to bring an appeal;
(e)   'respondent' means –
     (i)   a person other than the appellant who was a party to the proceedings in the lower court and who is affected by the appeal; and
     (ii)   a person who is permitted by the appeal court to be a party to the appeal; and
(f)   'appeal notice' means an appellant's or respondent's notice.

(4) This Part is subject to any rule, enactment or practice direction which sets out special provisions with regard to any particular category of appeal.

Amendments—Inserted by SI 2000/221; amended by SI 2000/2092; SI 2005/3515.

52.2 Parties to comply with the practice direction

All parties to an appeal must comply with the relevant practice direction.

Amendments—Inserted by SI 2000/221.

52.3 Permission

(1) An appellant or respondent requires permission to appeal –

(a)   where the appeal is from a decision of a judge in a county court or the High Court, except where the appeal is against –
     (i)   a committal order;
     (ii)   a refusal to grant habeas corpus; or
     (iii)   a secure accommodation order made under section 25 of the Children Act 1989; or

(b)   as provided by the relevant practice direction.

(other enactments may provide that permission is required for particular appeals)

(2) An application for permission to appeal may be made –

(a)   to the lower court at the hearing at which the decision to be appealed was made; or
(b)   to the appeal court in an appeal notice.

(Rule 52.4 sets out the time limits for filing an appellant's notice at the appeal court. Rule 52.5 sets out the time limits for filing a respondent's notice at the appeal court. Any application for permission to appeal to the appeal court must be made in the appeal notice (see rules 52.4(1) and 52.5(3))

(Rule 52.13(1) provides that permission is required from the Court of Appeal for all appeals to that court from a decision of a county court or the High Court which was itself made on appeal)

(3) Where the lower court refuses an application for permission to appeal, a further application for permission to appeal may be made to the appeal court.

(4) Subject to paragraph (4A), where the appeal court, without a hearing, refuses permission to appeal, the person seeking permission may request the decision to be reconsidered at a hearing.

(4A) Where the Court of Appeal refuses permission to appeal without a hearing, it may, if it considers that the application is totally without merit, make an order that the person seeking permission may not request the decision to be reconsidered at a hearing.

(4B) Rule 3.3(5) will not apply to an order that the person seeking permission may not request the decision to be reconsidered at a hearing made under paragraph (4A).

(5) A request under paragraph (4) must be filed within seven days after service of the notice that permission has been refused.

(6) Permission to appeal may be given only where –

(a)   the court considers that the appeal would have a real prospect of success; or
(b)   there is some other compelling reason why the appeal should be heard.

(7) An order giving permission may –

(a)   limit the issues to be heard; and
(b)   be made subject to conditions.

(Rule 3.1(3) also provides that the court may make an order subject to conditions)

(Rule 25.15 provides for the court to order security for costs of an appeal)

Amendments—Inserted by SI 2000/221; amended by SI 2005/3515; SI 2006/1689, SI 2008/2178.

52.4 Appellant's notice

(1) Where the appellant seeks permission from the appeal court it must be requested in the appellant's notice.

(2) The appellant must file the appellant's notice at the appeal court within –

(a)   such period as may be directed by the lower court (which may be longer or shorter than the period referred to in sub-paragraph (b)); or
(b)   where the court makes no such direction, 21 days after the date of the decision of the lower court that the appellant wishes to appeal.

(3) Unless the appeal court orders otherwise, an appellant's notice must be served on each respondent –

(a)   as soon as practicable; and
(b)   in any event not later than 7 days,

after it is filed.

Amendments—Inserted by SI 2000/221; amended by SI 2005/3515.

52.5 Respondent's notice

(1) A respondent may file and serve a respondent's notice.

(2) A respondent who –

    (a)   is seeking permission to appeal from the appeal court; or

    (b)   wishes to ask the appeal court to uphold the order of the lower court for reasons different from or additional to those given by the lower court,

must file a respondent's notice.

(3) Where the respondent seeks permission from the appeal court it must be requested in the respondent's notice.

(4) A respondent's notice must be filed within –

    (a)   such period as may be directed by the lower court; or

    (b)   where the court makes no such direction, 14 days, after the date in paragraph (5).

(5) The date referred to in paragraph (4) is –

    (a)   the date the respondent is served with the appellant's notice where –

        (i)   permission to appeal was given by the lower court; or

        (ii)   permission to appeal is not required;

    (b)   the date the respondent is served with notification that the appeal court has given the appellant permission to appeal; or

    (c)   the date the respondent is served with notification that the application for permission to appeal and the appeal itself are to be heard together.

(6) Unless the appeal court orders otherwise a respondent's notice must be served on the appellant and any other respondent –

    (a)   as soon as practicable; and

    (b)   in any event not later than 7 days,

after it is filed.

Amendments—Inserted by SI 2000/221.

52.6 Variation of time

(1) An application to vary the time limit for filing an appeal notice must be made to the appeal court.

(2) The parties may not agree to extend any date or time limit set by –

    (a)   these Rules;

    (b)   the relevant practice direction; or

    (c)   an order of the appeal court or the lower court.

    (Rule 3.1(2)(*a*) provides that the court may extend or shorten the time for compliance with any rule, practice direction or court order (even if an application for extension is made after the time for compliance has expired))

    (Rule 3.1(2)(*b*) provides that the court may adjourn or bring forward a hearing)

Amendments—Inserted by SI 2000/221.

52.7 Stay

Unless –

    (a)   the appeal court or the lower court orders otherwise; or

(b)   the appeal is from the Asylum and Immigration Tribunal,

an appeal shall not operate as a stay of any order or decision of the lower court.

Amendments—Inserted by SI 2000/221; amended by SI 2006/1689.

52.8 Amendment of appeal notice

An appeal notice may not be amended without the permission of the appeal court.

Amendments—Inserted by SI 2000/221.

52.9 Striking out appeal notices and setting aside or imposing conditions on permission to appeal

(1) The appeal court may –

    (a)   strike out the whole or part of an appeal notice;
    (b)   set aside permission to appeal in whole or in part;
    (c)   impose or vary conditions upon which an appeal may be brought.

(2) The court will only exercise its powers under paragraph (1) where there is a compelling reason for doing so.

(3) Where a party was present at the hearing at which permission was given he may not subsequently apply for an order that the court exercise its powers under sub-paragraphs (1)(b) or (1)(c).

Amendments—Inserted by SI 2000/221.

52.10 Appeal court's powers

(1) In relation to an appeal the appeal court has all the powers of the lower court.

> (Rule 52.1(4) provides that this Part is subject to any enactment that sets out special provisions with regard to any particular category of appeal – where such an enactment gives a statutory power to a tribunal, person or other body it may be the case that the appeal court may not exercise that power on an appeal)

(2) The appeal court has power to –

    (a)   affirm, set aside or vary any order or judgment made or given by the lower court;
    (b)   refer any claim or issue for determination by the lower court;
    (c)   order a new trial or hearing;
    (d)   make orders for the payment of interest;
    (e)   make a costs order.

(3) In an appeal from a claim tried with a jury the Court of Appeal may, instead of ordering a new trial –

    (a)   make an order for damages; or
    (b)   vary an award of damages made by the jury.

(4) The appeal court may exercise its powers in relation to the whole or part of an order of the lower court.

(5) If the appeal court –

    (a)   refuses an application for permission to appeal;
    (b)   strikes out an appellant's notice; or
    (c)   dismisses an appeal,

and it considers that the application, the appellant's notice or the appeal is totally without merit, the provisions of paragraph (6) must be complied with.

(6) Where paragraph (5) applies –

(a)   the court's order must record the fact that it considers the application, the appellant's notice or the appeal to be totally without merit; and

(b)   the court must at the same time consider whether it is appropriate to make a civil restraint order.

(Part 3 contains general rules about the court's case management powers)

Amendments—Inserted by SI 2000/221; amended by SI 2004/2072.

52.11 Hearing of appeals

(1) Every appeal will be limited to a review of the decision of the lower court unless –

(a)   a practice direction makes different provision for a particular category of appeal; or

(b)   the court considers that in the circumstances of an individual appeal it would be in the interests of justice to hold a re-hearing.

(2) Unless it orders otherwise, the appeal court will not receive –

(a)   oral evidence; or

(b)   evidence which was not before the lower court.

(3) The appeal court will allow an appeal where the decision of the lower court was –

(a)   wrong; or

(b)   unjust because of a serious procedural or other irregularity in the proceedings in the lower court.

(4) The appeal court may draw any inference of fact which it considers justified on the evidence.

(5) At the hearing of the appeal a party may not rely on a matter not contained in his appeal notice unless the appeal court gives permission.

Amendments—Inserted by SI 2000/221.

Section III – Provisions About Reopening Appeals

52.17 Reopening of final appeals

(1) The Court of Appeal or the High Court will not reopen a final determination of any appeal unless –

(a)   it is necessary to do so in order to avoid real injustice;

(b)   the circumstances are exceptional and make it appropriate to reopen the appeal; and

(c)   there is no alternative effective remedy.

(2) In paragraphs (1), (3), (4) and (6), 'appeal' includes an application for permission to appeal.

(3) This rule does not apply to appeals to a county court.

(4) Permission is needed to make an application under this rule to reopen a final determination of an appeal even in cases where under rule 52.3(1) permission was not needed for the original appeal.

(5) There is no right to an oral hearing of an application for permission unless, exceptionally, the judge so directs.

(6) The judge will not grant permission without directing the application to be served on the other party to the original appeal and giving him an opportunity to make representations.

(7) There is no right of appeal or review from the decision of the judge on the application for permission, which is final.

(8) The procedure for making an application for permission is set out in the practice direction.

Amendments—Inserted by SI 2003/2113.

****

Appendix 3

ADOPTION CIRCULAR LAC(98)20

(28 August 1998; amended on 25 June 1999)

ADOPTION – ACHIEVING THE RIGHT BALANCE

Introduction

1. This circular raises a number of issues for the overall improvement of the adoption service provided by local authority social services departments, approved adoption agencies and other organisations. It focuses attention on adoption as an important and beneficial option in the care of children and is intended to bring adoption back into the mainstream of children's services. The circular emphasises the importance of strategic planning, the responsibilities expected of senior managers, avoidance of delay and drift in the care system, race and culture, health, the recruitment of prospective adopters and intercountry adoption; it also builds on existing adoption guidance.

The Adoption Service

2. The Adoption Act 1976 and its regulations place duties and responsibilities on local authorities to provide, or arrange to provide an adoption service. Many local authorities achieve high standards in the provision of children's services and provide models of good practice in some or all of their work. However, recent Social Services Inspectorate reports involving a number of local authorities demonstrate a lack of consistency and co-ordination in England in the overall quality of their adoption services. Although variations in the delivery of services are not always a bad sign they should be minor and limited to local circumstances and need. This circular addresses some of the main causes of inconsistency associated with adoption and some of the problems uncovered by inspections. It also takes account of the House of Commons Second Report on 'Children Looked After by Local Authorities', published on 16 July 1998.

Benefits of adoption

3. The importance of family life to a child cannot be overstated. It is the fundamental right of every child to belong to a family; this principle underpins the 1989 United Nations Convention on the Rights of the Child which the United Kingdom ratified in 1991. Where children cannot live with their families, for whatever reason, society has a duty to provide them with a fresh start and where appropriate a permanent alternative home. Adoption is the means of giving children an opportunity to start again; for many children, adoption may be their only chance of experiencing family life.

4. Adoption has become firmly entrenched in the social fabric since enactment of the first adoption legislation; many thousands of children have benefited from the generosity and commitment of adoptive families. Adoption is not an option of last resort; to regard it as such is a failure to understand the nature of adoption and its advantages for a child unable to live with his own family.

5. Adoption continues to provide an important service for children, offering a positive and beneficial outcome. Research shows that generally adopted children make very good progress through their childhood and into adulthood compared with children brought up by their own

parents and do considerably better than children who have remained in the care system throughout most of their childhood. Adoption provides children with a unique opportunity for a fresh start as permanent members of new families, enjoying a sense of security and well-being so far denied them in their young lives.

6. It is important that those responsible for the adoption service, its policies and procedures – elected members, directors, managers, practitioners and adoption panel members – should understand the benefits of adoption and not see it as an acknowledgement that other possibilities have failed.

Getting the balance right

7. Where a child is in the care of a local authority, the Children Act 1989 places a duty on them to make all reasonable efforts to rehabilitate the child with his or her family whenever possible, unless it is clear that the child can no longer live with his family or that the authority has sufficient evidence to suggest that further attempts at rehabilitation are unlikely to succeed. In this context, there is a common perception among too many in the field that efforts to rehabilitate a child should be constrained by no timetable: that every effort should be made and all possibilities exhausted to try to secure the return of the child to his family – no matter how long it might take.

8. Such a perception lacks proper balance. Time is not on the side of the child. Efforts to return a child to his or her family should of course be reasonable and will require intensive work; time spent in such work with families and children should be constructive and should be recorded in detail. A stage is reached in many cases, however, when it is apparent that rehabilitation is unlikely to be successful. Experienced practitioners are aware that knowing when the time is right to plan for alternative forms of care is one of the many skills expected of social services staff; that it includes an awareness of the importance of time in the rehabilitation process and of the damage which might be done to children where time is allowed to pass without any visible signs of their future being secured. Where it is clear that they can no longer live with their birth family, decisions about placing children with permanent families should be made as a matter of priority. Managers should therefore include effective measures to monitor progress of these cases, ensuring that they are formally reviewed at regular intervals to prevent a child drifting in the care system.

Changing nature of adoption

9. The nature of adoption has changed in recent decades. Fewer children are being adopted. Older children rather than babies constitute the main group of children needing new families. They tend to have more complex needs; many have traumatic histories of neglect or mental, sexual and physical abuse; some have complex physical or learning difficulties. The impact of these changes on adoption practices should not be ignored; they have important implications for an agency's policy, management, staffing and other resources. Some agencies have adapted well to these changes. Finding suitable and committed carers for older children in particular presents considerable challenges to adoption agencies; the time and effort invested to recruit, prepare and support carers for them therefore will be that much the greater.

Keeping Members informed

10. In recognition of their responsibilities and as a matter of good practice, Directors of Social Services should provide reports to Elected Members at regular intervals during the year about children who are in the care of their local authority and who wait to be placed with new families. As a minimum. these reports should include the number, type, age and length of time children have been waiting for placement; progress in the recruitment of suitable adoptive families; the number of children placed for adoption since the last report.

Race, culture, religion and language

Understanding the needs of children from black and minority ethnic communities

11. In recent years there has been significant progress by agencies in learning about the particular needs of children from minority ethnic backgrounds and the need to take account of their heritage when making decisions about their future. However, more work needs to be done. The structure of minority ethnic groups is often complex and their heritage diverse, where the race, religion, language and culture of each community has varying degrees of importance in the daily lives of their members. Families from these communities should have confidence that their local social services understands, appreciates and is respectful of their particular racial, cultural, and religious values.

12. A principal tenet in the care of children is the importance of a child's family background. A child's ethnic origin, culture, language and religion are significant factors to be taken into account when adoption agencies are considering the most appropriate placement for a child; however, such consideration has to take account of all the child's needs. Simply identifying a child's ethnic background is not sufficient in itself. Adoption agencies need to go further and be aware of the implications for a child of these cultural elements – how the culture of a family, community or society can influence the way a child sees the world; the significance of religion in a child's daily life and the importance of maintaining a knowledge of his history, culture and language.

13. Choice of placement should also take account of a child's previous family experience and his or her wishes and feelings while recognising that their wishes and feelings may be restrictive or unrealistic. Placement with a family of similar ethnic origin and religion is very often most likely to meet the child's needs as fully as possible, safeguarding his welfare most effectively and preparing him for life as a member of a multi-racial society. These are, however, only some among a number of other significant factors and should not of themselves be regarded as the decisive ones.

14. Where no family can be identified which matches significantly closely the child's ethnic origin and cultural heritage, the adoption agency's efforts to find an alternative suitable family should be proactive and diligent; this work should also include setting agreed and realistic time limits to avoid a child having to wait indefinitely for a new family. A child's concept of time differs considerably from that of an adult. The Government has made it clear that it is unacceptable for a child to be denied loving adoptive parents solely on the grounds that the child and adopters do not share the same racial or cultural background.

15. All families should assist children placed with them to understand and appreciate their background and culture and to this end enlist the help and support of others; this can include providing opportunities for children to meet others from similar backgrounds, to practice their religion – both in a formal place of worship and in the home. Maintaining continuity of the heritage of their birth family in their day-to-day life is important to most children; it is a means of retaining knowledge of their identity and feeling that although they have left their birth family they have not abandoned important cultural, religious or linguistic values of their community. This will be of particular significance as they reach adulthood.

16. Racism can take many forms and is a destructive force, especially in the life of a child. Children from minority ethnic groups are particularly vulnerable to racism and its effects. The issue of racism will inevitably arise at some stage in the life of a child at school, work and leisure; the adoptive family will need to prepare the child for when it occurs and how to deal with it so that the child can maintain a positive attitude about himself and continue to be proud of his heritage. This is true for all children from minority ethnic communities and therefore the responsibility to prepare children to deal with racism rests with all families caring for them. These families may need help in understanding and preparing their children for the times when they and their children encounter racism.

17. As society becomes increasingly complex with children often having diverse ethnicity and cultures in their background, it is even more important that social workers should avoid 'labelling' a child and ignoring some elements of his background. Children of mixed origin should be helped to understand and take pride in all elements in their racial heritage and feel comfortable about their origins.

18. The increase in the number of couples who are not of the same ethnic origin or who are of mixed origin should provide adoption agencies with an opportunity to address more effectively the needs of a range of children who are themselves from different backgrounds including mixed and minority ethnic backgrounds. The availability of such couples should not therefore be an obstacle to the placement of these children. Any practice which classifies such couples in a way that effectively rules out the adoption of a child whose origins differ from either or both prospective adopters is unacceptable. The issue is, as in every case, that the prospective adopter is sympathetic to and understands the issues to be confronted by a child of minority ethnic or mixed race origins who, growing up, will face discrimination and racism. This applies equally whether a child is placed with a black or minority ethnic family, a white family or a family which includes members of differing ethnic origins.

Wishes of birth parents

19. Where a birth parent decides to place his or her child for adoption, the adoption agency works closely with them in making plans to secure the child's future. Part of this preparation includes finding out the parent's wishes about the qualities and skills they wish to see in the adoptive parents for their child. Birth parents differ in their priorities and wishes; some place cultural ties or religious preferences above all other considerations while others express a preference for their child to be placed with adopters of the same age or from a similar background to themselves. Where birth parents say that they want their child to be brought up in their own religion, this wish should normally be respected unless, because of a shortage of adoptive parents in that religion, the child's prospects of having a permanent family would be threatened.

20. Adoption agencies are obliged to take the wishes of birth parents into account and should do their best to place the child with a family which comes as close as possible to that envisaged by the parents. However, it may not always possible to do this; their wishes may be too restrictive, looking to their own needs rather than the child's, or may be unrealistic or even misguided. Adoption is a service essentially focused on meeting the needs of children as the first consideration. It may also be the case that the particular needs of a child are so complex or diverse as to limit the availability of choice.

Avoiding delay

Children who wait

21. The Government is concerned about the length of time some children have to wait before being able to join an adoptive family. The social and emotional development of children is strongly influenced by their early childhood experiences, especially the quality and security of their attachment relationships with their birth family, relatives and carers. Allowing children to 'drift' is never in their best interests and is likely to make successful placements all the more difficult to achieve. It has to be recognised that certainty is rarely possible: professional judgement has to work with the balance of probabilities. The longer a child spends in temporary care before being placed with permanent carers, the more difficult it is likely to be for that child to make the necessary social and emotional adjustments within the new family. Delay deprives children of the opportunity to form long-term relationships and many, especially those who have spent some years in care, find it difficult to do so as they become older, often an underlying cause of subsequent disruptions.

Responsibility of senior managers

22. The Department expects senior managers to implement and maintain effective measures for improving both the efficiency and the quality of management and administration in the adoption service. They should ensure that their strategic plans for children's services place adoption firmly at the centre of options available for the long-term care of children. It is a function of senior management to ensure that their strategic plans provide for sufficient numbers and range of adopters to be recruited to allow choice in the placement of children.

23. Senior managers must also take more direct responsibility for monitoring the time children spend in care, both where there are attempts at rehabilitation and also the interval between coming into care and being placed with adoptive families. They will be expected to pay particular attention to the time children from minority ethnic backgrounds wait for a substitute family; managers will also be expected to look critically at the causes of delay in placing all children with new families. Senior managers should introduce effective systems for monitoring progress in implementing plans for their future – particularly that a plan's objectives are met and within the agreed timescales – and ensure that the necessary work of their legal advisers maintain the same rate of progress. Senior managers should also ensure that responsibility for making important decisions involving the placement of children is given to members of staff with the appropriate level of skill, experience and seniority.

Children's services plans

24. Preparation and publication of children's services plans provided for by The Children Act 1989 (Amendment) (Children's Services Planning) Order 1996 relate to services for children in need. Some of these children are eventually placed for adoption. Local authorities therefore should consider including adoption services within their service plans for children, where appropriate. These plans may include arrangements for the provision of services in consultation with other agencies, such as local education and medical services, up to and beyond the making of an adoption order to ensure the continuation of these services to meet the needs of particular children.

Effective planning

25. A common cause of delay is the time taken before adoption agencies make clear plans for adoption, or revised plans where adoption has become the preferred option. There are sometimes good or unavoidable reasons for delaying the placement of a child; for example, many adoption cases have been preceded by a series of legal challenges by a birth parent or relative who oppose the plan for adoption, or delay is due to a series of meetings with families to explore the possibility of a suitable relative caring for the child. But this is not invariably the case. Too many children 'drift' in the care system where few or no plans are being made to secure their future; this will do little for the child's wellbeing and therefore cannot be in a child's best interests. Drift has much to do with the lack of effective planning and diligent management within some social services departments. Local authorities have other responsibilities to children, particularly child protection; however, senior managers should ensure that these responsibilities are not carried out at the expense of children waiting for placement.

26. An adoption plan should give clear indications how it is to be achieved and the timescales envisaged. The statutory review process for looked after children provides an ideal opportunity for senior managers to consider adoption as a possible option for children; if appropriate, such reviews should be brought forward to facilitate early discussion and decision making.

27. There should be few inherent difficulties in adoption agencies preparing provisional contingency plans for a child in the event of attempts to rehabilitate the child with his family proving unsuccessful. However, these plans need sensitive handling and are only likely to operate successfully with selected families. To avoid any sense of duplicity or bad faith, the child's family should be fully informed of the proposals and give their consent to any contingency arrangements.

Contingency planning should be applied in such a way as to avoid prejudicing the original aim of rehabilitating the child with his birth family. Such contingency planning can save valuable resources and reduce the time some children spend in temporary care before joining new and permanent families. To avoid the risk of unnecessary delay in another context, agencies should give priority to dealing with issues needing lengthy consideration such as finding a suitable placement for siblings and the possibility of children remaining with foster carers who wish to adopt them.

Care proceedings and adoption

28. In a minority of applications for a care order, it becomes apparent during the proceedings that adoption will be the preferred option set out in the care plan, should a care order be made at the final hearing. Some courts are presented at the final care application hearing with evidence about the preliminary steps that the local authority has taken to effect an adoption placement should a care order be made. Elsewhere, courts are informed that no or only minimal preparatory work has been undertaken. This poses the likelihood of serious delay before placement and, as such, may well be detrimental to the child's welfare. Because each child and family situation is different, guidance setting out the preferred approach has to be flexible. Where adoption is the probable option, the courts will need to be advised of the likely steps and time-scales to implement the plan. The following paragraphs offer a framework where adoption is envisaged which is intended to achieve greater consistency within both the care proceedings and the preparation of the care plan.

29. Where the facts of the case remain in dispute up to the final hearing, the choice of placement may significantly depend on findings of fact and, indeed, in some cases no care order is made at all. It is these cases where it is likely to be most difficult to effect much, if any, detailed preparatory work prior to the final hearing concerning possible adoptive placement. But even here, it should normally be possible to explain within the care plan, the principal steps which would need to be taken before an adoptive placement could be made and give estimated time-scales for each of the key steps. This would include those cases where it is necessary to time-table therapeutic work with the child before preparing the child for placement.

30. Even where the facts in certain cases of the care application are not disputed and the preferred option in the care plan is adoption, it is important that local authorities have satisfied themselves that sufficient assessment has taken place to rule out rehabilitation or placement with relatives, for example, under a section 8 residence order. In these cases, local authority procedures should facilitate the process of finding an adoptive placement. How much progress can be made before the final hearing will depend on a range of factors, including the overall time-scale of the care proceedings. In addition, sensitivity is needed to ensure that the child's parent(s) understands that the care hearing under the Children Act is not the same as any later hearing under adoption legislation which would need to address questions of parental consent, unless a freeing application is being considered at the same time (see paragraph 32 below).

31. In respect of the cases described in paragraph 30 where the local authority has ruled out rehabilitation or placement with relatives and has confirmed adoption as the preferred option, the following should always be addressed:

a.   that appropriate steps been taken within the local authority to co-ordinate information between the team responsible for the care proceedings application and those responsible for family finding and to allocate responsibilities for carrying out the necessary work;

b.   the BAAF Form E (details about the child) should be completed as far as possible, including obtaining from the parent(s) relevant medical and other details, although there may be difficulty in obtaining the necessary medical and other information from the parents;

c.   the adoption panel should consider the case, with a view to making a recommendation on whether adoption is in the child's best interests;

d.   the local authority should have identified the key steps and timetable, including family finding and any necessary therapy, and issues of contact (for inclusion in the care plan) which would lead to an adoptive placement, if the court made a care order;

e.   the care plan should include a contingency plan for use in specified circumstances if the preferred option for adoption cannot be achieved;

f.   consideration should be given as to whether a freeing application is appropriate (see paragraph 32 below).

32. There are also some (but not many) care cases with a view to adoption which may also require the child to be freed for adoption as soon as possible. It is important that there is full discussion with the local authority's legal advisors to ensure that such cases are identified as early as possible so that evidence and time-tabling of the court hearings can be co-ordinated. It is expensive for the local authority, stressful for the parent and possible unnecessary further delay for the child to have a care application followed months later by a freeing application, both of which may be contested.

33. However, it is not appropriate before the final care hearing for there to have been introductions between the child and the prospective adopters or for the agency to have confirmed the panel's recommendations

Collaborative working

34. Directors of social services are reminded of the potential benefits in engaging in collaborative ventures with other local authorities and approved adoption agencies in the provision of an adoption service to meet local needs. Advantages include the avoidance of unnecessary duplication, promoting good practice more widely, retaining expertise and making best use of scarce resources such as recruitment of prospective adopters, finding families for older children or children with special needs and certain post adoption work. Combining services in this way can help to provide a co-ordinated and comprehensive service. Also, people who enquire about the possibility of becoming adoptive parents should be re-directed to other agencies if the first agency is unable to take them on, particularly in response to enquiries from black or minority ethnic families.

Training

35. Placing children for adoption makes a variety of demands on the skills and experience of social workers. Sufficient training opportunities should be made available to them to carry out these demanding and sensitive functions more effectively. Adoption agencies are therefore expected to make training a high priority. Senior managers should identify training needs and satisfy themselves that social workers specialising in adoption or who work with children and families take advantage of opportunities to improve their skills in working with families and children.

36. Staff cannot be expected to provide good quality counselling and otherwise work productively with children, birth families and adoptive families if they have little or no opportunity to develop the necessary skills to do so. Gaining a child's confidence and learning about the traumatic experiences and their effects in their young lives requires skill and patience. Managers should ensure that the workload of social workers allows sufficient time for them to devote to the children, getting to know them and their history, assessing their needs, preparing them for adoption and identifying the most suitable family for them.

37. Training and preparation of carers is a major task of adoption agencies in planning for the placement of children. The Children Act 1989 Guidance and Regulations, Volume 3: 'Family Placement' issued by the Department in 1991 included helpful advice to local authorities on this subject. Participation of experienced adopters is particularly important in the preparation and delivery of training programmes, making the content of these events appropriate both in meeting the needs of children and the parenting experience of prospective adopters. Two national voluntary

organisations, British Agencies for Adoption and Fostering (BAAF) and National Foster Care Association (NFCA) provide training courses and materials to assist local authorities and voluntary agencies in this task.

Prospective adopters

Recruitment

38. Adoptive parents are a valuable resource to all adoption agencies. The work of recruiting suitable parents to care for older children, many of whom have challenging patterns of behaviour, is an on-going task of adoption agencies. Social services depend on the response of families to come forward as adoptive parents. Agencies have to take a positive attitude to recruitment. Preparation of prospective adopters should be designed to draw out their strengths – to discover the qualities they have to offer a child and build on those strengths in working with them and assessing their suitability to become adoptive parents. Reasons for an adoption agency deciding not to accept an applicant as an adoptive parent must be sound and defensible. In this context attention is drawn to Regulation 2(10) of The Adoption Agencies and Children (Arrangements for Placement and Reviews) (Miscellaneous Amendments) Regulations 1997 about informing adoptive applicants of the reasons why the adoption agency decision maker is minded not to accept their application.

39. Programmes specifically aimed at developing and sustaining recruitment of prospective adopters from minority ethnic backgrounds must form part of the planning strategy for the adoption service prepared by each social services department. More work may need to be done to encourage families from within those communities who do not have a tradition of adopting children unrelated to them to consider becoming adoptive parents. It is also important that adoption agencies maintain active and regular links with their approved prospective adopters about the type of children needing new families. Where an agency has approved a particular family but, after a year or two considers that they are unlikely to be able to place a child with them, they should discuss the situation with the family and, with their agreement, be prepared to make that family available to other agencies. This can be carried out, for example, by reference to the national resource linking programme operated by BAAF or the scheme operated by Parent to Parent Information on Adoption Services (PPIAS).

40. Where a local authority is aware that the needs of a child can best be met by a particular adoptive parent recruited and approved by another adoption agency, they should give serious consideration to negotiating with that agency about the possible placement of the child with that family. Unwillingness to pay an inter-agency fee should not be made the sole determinant for not placing the child.

41. Caring for unrelated children – whether care is provided for the short or long-term, or permanently through adoption – requires careful preparation if the quality of care is to be beneficial to the child. The importance of preparation and training for prospective carers is recognised by agencies. Many children needing alternative families have already experienced difficulties and trauma in their lives which can be manifest in many ways, particularly in extreme forms of behaviour. Agencies should prepare their training programmes on the basis of knowledge and experience in placing older children with prospective adopters and their outcomes.

Sharing information

42. It is essential that adoption agencies make available to adoptive parents all material facts about children to be placed in their care. It is unacceptable for adoption agencies to withhold information about a child to the extent that the picture of a child provided to prospective adopters is so lacking in substance as to bear little relation to reality. Supplying information to adoptive parents is a legal requirement. It should include details about a child's background, history in care, including number and duration of placements, educational progress and special medical conditions. Such information is a vital tool for prospective adopters if they are to be able to understand and deal effectively with

the particular needs of a child. One source of helpful information for this purpose is the material collected by local authorities as part of the 'looked after' review of the child.

Assessment criteria

Age

43. Many women are choosing to have their children later in life and it is less unusual now for mothers to have their first child in their late thirties or even forties. This should be reflected in the approach of adoption agencies to this issue. The acceptability of an adopter's age must be considered in the context of the children who need to be adopted. Fewer babies have been placed for adoption in the last two decades; the focus has shifted to the adoption of older children. In this respect, older and more experienced people could take on the care of these children, provided that they enjoy sufficient health and vigour to meet their varied demands. The more mature person has a greater experience of life; some may be established in their careers and others may have already brought up children of their own and have developed good parenting skills.

44. There is no upper age restriction to people applying to become adoptive parents. Age is one consideration among many taken into account in assessing the suitability of prospective adopters. Age is also necessarily linked to general health, fitness and emotional wellbeing. Some older people may score higher in this regard than some younger ones. Adoption agencies are therefore expected to recruit adoptive parents who will have the health and vigour to meet the many and varied demands of children in their growing years and be there for them into adulthood.

45. The age of a prospective adopter must also be considered in the light of the gap in age between them and the child to be placed with them. Too large a gap may have an adverse effect upon the child and possibly upon his relationship with the adoptive parent. Where a child has already suffered change, deprivation and loss in their early years, demands on adoptive parents, both physical and emotional, are likely to be considerable, particularly as the child grows older.

Health

46. Agencies have a duty to satisfy themselves that adopters who are about to have a child placed with them have a reasonable expectation of continuing to enjoy good health. The opinion of the adopter's general practitioner and the agency's medical adviser about the health status of prospective adopters needs to be given sufficient weight by adoption panels and agency decision makers. Mild chronic conditions are unlikely to preclude people from adopting provided that the condition does not place the child at risk through an inability to protect the child from commonplace hazards or limit them in providing children with a range of beneficial experiences and opportunities. More severe conditions must raise a question about the suitability of an applicant; in such cases the agency will need to give such factors very careful consideration in its decision to accept an application.

Smoking

47. Following reports in the early 1990s from the Royal College of Physicians and the Chief Medical Officer's Expert Group on Cot Deaths, there was sufficient evidence for the Department to be concerned about the effects of passive smoking where babies and very young children were being placed for adoption with families who smoke. A local authority may have to restrict smokers in the age and type of child who may be placed with them, especially a baby or very young child or a child who has a heart or chest complaint or a history of asthma.

48. An adoption agency has a duty to consider the effects of smoking on children in their care; therefore agencies should discuss with prospective adopters the issues and implications of smoking

such as expecting them to ensure that a child does not spend its time in smoke-filled rooms. However, the use of criteria whose application is in reality to ban people who smoke from adopting is not appropriate.

49. In all these areas – age, health and smoking, including health risks and life-style – the agency should expect its medical adviser to investigate and obtain relevant information about an applicant in order to be satisfied that the applicant is able to take on the task of adopting a child and has the expectation of caring for the child through childhood and into adulthood.

Intercountry adoption

Children in need

50. Many children living abroad, for whatever reason, have been abandoned or relinquished for adoption by their birth parents. Their chances of being adopted or otherwise cared for by substitute families in their own country are often remote. Both the 1989 United Nations Convention on the Rights of the Child and the 1993 Hague Convention on Protection of Children and Co-operation in Respect of Intercountry Adoption acknowledge the right of a child to belong to a family and recognises that intercountry adoption may offer the advantage of a permanent family to a child for whom a suitable family cannot be found in his or her state of origin. The realistic alternative for the vast majority of these children is a childhood spent in institutional care.

The nature of intercountry adoption

51. The primary purpose of intercountry adoption is to provide a child with a family where this cannot be provided in the child's own country; it is not about improving the material quality of life of children from overseas, although this is likely to be one of its effects. Intercountry adoption is now a major feature of adoption in the United Kingdom. Most intercountry adoption applications involve a child leaving his or her own country to live permanently with families in the United Kingdom. This necessarily brings radical changes to the life of a child in many ways. Intercountry adoption also brings profound changes to the lives of the adopters and affects not only their immediate families but their relatives and friends. Adoption agencies need to be satisfied that prospective adopters are not only equal to the task of adopting a child from overseas but that they fully appreciate the implications of bringing an unrelated child from abroad into their own family. Prospective adopters also need to understand the implications for a child to be taken from his or her own country, family, friends, familiar environment etc. and begin life afresh in a totally unfamiliar setting.

Assisting prospective adopters

52. The Government recognises and understands the humanitarian and altruistic response of some people who wish to adopt children living overseas, particularly those described as orphaned or abandoned. Adoption agencies should be aware of both the nature and effects of intercountry adoption in their assessment of applicants. However, it is not acceptable for an applicant to be denied the opportunity to be assessed by an agency on the grounds that the agency does not agree with the notion of intercountry adoption or that the applicant does not share the same ethnic or cultural background as children from their country of choice. Local authority policies therefore must reflect the positive view of adoption referred to in legislation and in Government guidance and not support policies and attitudes of their own. Thus, people seeking to adopt children from overseas should have the opportunity to be assessed as prospective intercountry adopters. Senior managers should satisfy themselves that arrangements are in place to meet requests for assessment or for them to be carried out on their behalf.

Applying the same principles

53. Assessments and checks are necessarily thorough to ensure that prospective adopters are equal to the task in the very serious commitment they wish to undertake and, so far as possible, avoid future disruption of a placement. Such assessments and checks are also important to the countries from which the children originate; countries seek the assurance of the United Kingdom that prospective adopters have been assessed as suitable by agencies authorised to do so. The standards and criteria applied in domestic adoption concerning the assessment of prospective adopters are to be applied to families seeking to adopt a child from overseas. To do less would leave the United Kingdom open to accusations of applying double standards in their assessment process. These standards and associated criteria allow agencies to apply sufficient measures of flexibility and discretion to reflect conditions of children commonly encountered in intercountry adoption.

Post adoption support

Duties of adoption agencies

54. Post-adoption support for families and children affected by adoption is a requirement of the Adoption Act 1976. Post-adoption support can be difficult in many cases, particularly for example where the child is placed outside the local authority area or when, after some years, the placement is under threat as a result of a child's challenging behaviour. Adopted children and their families are entitled to the same range of social services and other support as other families in having access to special educational and medical services as well as advice and counselling. Most parents who adopt children who are not babies will almost certainly require on-going support from these services. Support may also be sought by adopters whose children have become older, particularly when they reach their adolescent years. Adoptive parents should not be left with the feeling of being isolated once the adoption order is made. There should be a continuing 'partnership' between the agency and adoptive parents to ease the parents' task, particularly in the first few years following adoption, to ensure the best possible start for the child and his new family. With this in mind, agencies should have clear policies and procedures in writing, setting out their range of services for post adoption support which should be made available to all prospective adopters.

Adoption allowances

55. The Children Act 1989 provided for regulations to be prepared which would permit adoption agencies to make assessments about the payment of adoption allowances in certain circumstances; these were introduced under the Adoption Allowance Regulations 1991. Agencies are reminded that under section 57A of the 1976 Act, they have a duty to make available information on adoption allowances to prospective adopters. Guidance on the operation of these regulations is set out in The Children Act 1989 Guidance and Regulations, Volume 9: 'Adoption Issues'. One of the main purposes of the 1991 Regulations is to provide adoption agencies with sufficient flexibility to be able to respond to the individual needs of an child and his circumstances in order to secure an adoption placement. Support for adoptive families in the form of adoption allowances should be considered in every case whether the circumstances require consideration of the payment of an adoption allowance. Payment of an adoption allowance continues the concept of partnership.

Contact arrangements

56. In any consideration of a child retaining some form of contact with their birth relatives and others, both before and after the adoption order is made, adoption agencies need to bear in mind that the purpose of contact is primarily for the benefit of the child. In some cases contact will not be in the best interests of the child. Contact should never be used as a bargaining tool to obtain parental consent to adoption.

57. The majority of children who are having to live with new families have clear memories of their birth families and relatives. For many children, relationships with members of their family, previous

carers and others are valued. Consequently, for some children, contact may provide a positive aid to a successful placement with their new family. Making contact arrangements is a skilful task, balancing the needs and wishes of the child with the importance of preserving the stability of the adoptive family. Arrangements which tend to have the best chance of success are those which are mutually agreed between the birth family, relatives and others and the adopters and have the details set out and confirmed in writing. The practicalities of arranging for indirect contact such as 'post box' requires careful planning.

58. In the exceptional case where siblings cannot be placed together with the same family, it is important for agencies to ensure that contact arrangements with other siblings are given very careful attention and plans for maintaining contact are robust.

59. Adoption agencies may find it helpful to refer to the judgement given in the Court of Appeal in April 1993 – (*Re E. A Minor*) (*Care Order: Contact*) – by Simon Brown LJ who held the view that:

> '... contact may well be of singular importance to the long-term welfare of the child: first, in giving the child the security of knowing that his parents love him and are interested in his welfare; secondly, by avoiding any damaging sense of loss to the child in seeing himself abandoned by his parents; thirdly, by enabling the child to commit himself to the substitute family with the seal of approval of the natural parents; and, fourthly, by giving the child the necessary sense of family and personal identity. Contact, if maintained, is capable of reinforcing and increasing the chances of success of a permanent placement, whether on a long-term fostering basis or by adoption.' [1994] 1 FLR 146-155 (pp 154H–155B).

Action

60. Directors:

a. arrange to inform Elected Members at regular intervals about the current position of children awaiting placement with adoptive parents;

b. investigate the possibilities of collaborative working;

c. bring this guidance to the attention of all staff working in children's services.

Senior managers:

a. satisfy themselves that adoption services are included in children's services plans;

b. identify who is responsible for managing the adoption service;

c. ensure that adoption services are reviewed every three years;

d. identify staff to be responsible for linking with other agencies, particularly education and health, as part of the arrangements for meeting a child's needs;

e. introduce systems for the effective monitoring of children to be placed for adoption which prevent them drifting in the care system;

f. ensure that important decisions about the placement of children are taken by experienced and senior members of staff;

g. monitor the progress of recruitment of adoptive families, particularly from black and minority ethnic families;

h. ensure that responsibilities for child protection are not carried out at the expense of children awaiting new families;

i.   ensure that adoption is given its proper place in the development of strategic plans for children services;

j.   make adequate arrangements for staff to attend training opportunities in child care and adoption practice;

k.   satisfy themselves that people wishing to adopt children from overseas are provided with relevant information and given the opportunity to be assessed as an adoptive parent without undue delay;

l.   review adoption policies and practice in the light of this latest guidance;

m.   introduce measures to satisfy themselves that this guidance is understood and implemented without delay.

Enquiries

Enquiries about this Circular should be addressed to:

Michael Brennan
Social Care Group 3B
Department of Health
Room 121 Wellington House
133-155 Waterloo Road
LONDON SE1 8UG

Further copies of this Circular may be obtained from Department of Health, PO Box 410, Wetherby, LS23 7LN. Fax 01937 845381. Please quote the code and serial number appearing on the top righthand corner. Current Circulars are now listed on the Department of Health web site on the Internet at: http://www.open.gov.uk/doh/dhhome.htm. Full text of recent circulars is also accessible at this site.

© Crown copyright 1998.

This circular may be freely reproduced by all to whom it is addressed.

Appendix 4

THE ADOPTION ACT 1976

THE TEST

'In reaching any decision relating to the adoption of a child a court or adoption agency shall have regard to all the circumstances, first consideration being given to the need to safeguard and promote the welfare of the child throughout his childhood; and shall so far as practicable ascertain the wishes and feelings of the child regarding the decision and give due consideration to them, having regard to his age and understanding.'[1]

CONSENT

An adoption order could not be made unless:

- the child was free for adoption by virtue of an order made in England and Wales, under s 18, in Scotland, under s 18 of the Adoption (Scotland) Act 1978 or in Northern Ireland, under Art 17(1) or 18(1) of the Adoption (Northern Ireland) Order 1987; or

- in the case of each parent or guardian of the child the court was satisfied that:
  - he freely, and with full understanding of what is involved, agreed unconditionally to the making of an adoption order (whether or not he knew the identity of the applicants) and, in the case of the mother, the consent was given when the child was at least 6 weeks old; or
  - his agreement to the making of the adoption order should be dispensed with on the grounds that:
    - he could not be found or was incapable of giving agreement;
    - was withholding his agreement unreasonably;
    - had persistently failed without reasonable cause to discharge his parental responsibility for the child;
    - had abandoned or neglected the child;
    - had persistently ill-treated the child;
    - had seriously ill-treated the child and, because of the ill-treatment or for other reasons, the rehabilitation of the child within the household of the parent or guardian was unlikely.[2]

The classic exposition of the test for dispensing with consent on the ground that it was being unreasonably withheld was given by Lord Hailsham in *Re W (An Infant)*:[3]

> 'The test is reasonableness and not anything else. It is not culpability. It is not indifference. It is not failure to discharge parental duties. It is reasonableness and reasonableness in the context of the totality of the circumstances ... Two reasonable parents can perfectly reasonably come to the opposite conclusions on the same set of facts without forfeiting their title to be regarded as reasonable. The question in any given case is whether a parental veto comes within the band of possible reasonable decisions and not whether it

[1] Section 6.
[2] Section 16.
[3] [1971] AC 682 at 698–699.

is right or wrong. Not every reasonable exercise of judgment is right and not every mistaken exercise of judgment is unreasonable. There is a band of decisions within which no court should seek to replace the individual's judgment with his own.'

FREEING ORDER

Where, on an application by an adoption agency, a court was satisfied in the case of each parent or guardian of the child that:

- he freely, and with full understanding of what is involved, agreed generally and unconditionally to the making of an adoption order; or

- his agreement to the making of an adoption order should be dispensed with on one of the grounds stated above

the court had to make an order declaring the child free for adoption.[4]

No application could be made unless:

- it was made with the consent of a parent or guardian of a child; or

- the adoption agency was applying for dispensation under subs (1)(b) of the agreement of each parent or guardian of the child, and the child is in the care of the adoption agency. In this case, no agreement could be dispensed with on the ground that it was being unreasonably withheld unless the child was already placed for adoption or the court was satisfied that it is likely that the child will be placed for adoption.[5]

On the making of an order, parental responsibility for the child was given to the adoption agency; s 12(2)–(4) applied as if the order were an adoption order and the agency were the adopters.[6]

Before making a freeing order, the court had to be satisfied:

- in relation to each parent or guardian of the child who can be found, that he had been given an opportunity of making, if he so wished, a declaration that he preferred not to be involved in future questions concerning the adoption of the child;

- in relation to any person claiming to be the father that:
  - he had no intention of applying for:
    - an order for parental responsibility; or
    - a residence order under CA 1989, s 10; or
  - if he did make any such application, it would be likely to be refused.[7]

TRANSITIONAL PROVISIONS

Nothing in the Adoption and Children Act 2002 affects any freeing order and ss 19 (progress reports), 20 (revocation) and 21 (variation to substitute one agency for another) of the 1976 Act continue to have effect.[8]

---

4   Section 18(1).
5   Section 18(4).
6   Section 18(5).
7   Section 18(6), (7).
8   Adoption and Children Act 2002, Sch 4, para 7.

Where a child is free for adoption by virtue of an order made under s 18 of that Act, the third condition in s 47(6) (see **2.80**) is to be treated as satisfied.

Appendix 5

USEFUL ADDRESSES

Royal Courts of Justice
Strand, London WC2A 2CC
Tel: 020 7947 6000 (This is also the out-of-hours emergency number.)

The Ministry of Justice
102 Petty France, London SW1H 9AH
Tel: 020 7334 3555
www.justice.gov.uk

Family Justice Council
E201 East Block, Royal Courts of Justice, Strand, London WC2A 2GL
Tel: 020 7947 7333
Fax: 020 7947 7875
www.family-justice-council.org.uk

Children and Family Court Advisory and Support Services (CAFCASS)
6th Floor, Sanctuary Buildings, Great Smith Street, London SW1P 3BT
Tel: 0844 353 3350 Fax: 0844 3543 3351
www.cafcass.gov.uk

CAFCASS Legal Services
Details as above.

European Court of Human Rights Database (Hudoc)
www.echr.coe.int/Hudoc.htm

British Association for Adoption & Fostering (BAAF)
Saffron House, 6-10 Kirby Street, London EC1N 8TS
Tel: 020 7421 2600
Fax: 020 7421 2601
email: mail@baaf.org.uk
www.baaf.org.uk

Family Rights Group
The Print House, 18 Ashwin Street, London E8 3DL
Tel: 0208 7923 2628
Fax: 020 7923 2683
email: office@frg.org.uk
www.frg.org.uk

The National Youth Advocacy Service (NYAS)
Egerton House, Tower Road, Birkenhead, Wirral, Merseyside, CH4 1FN
Tel: 0151 649 8700
Fax: 0151 649 8701
www.nyas.net

Joseph Rowntree Foundation
The Homestead, 40 Water End, York, North Yorkshire YO30 6WP
Tel: 01904 629241
Fax: 01904 620072
www.jrf.org.uk
The website provides access to Findings, the summary of research commissioned by the JRF.

INDEX

References are to paragraph numbers.